Pieter Muysken, Norval Smith (Eds.)
Surviving the Middle Passage

Trends in Linguistics
Studies and Monographs 275

Editor
Volker Gast

Editorial Board
Walter Bisang
Jan Terje Faarlund
Hans Henrich Hock
Natalia Levshina
Heiko Narrog
Matthias Schlesewsky
Amir Zeldes
Niina Ning Zhang

Editor responsible for this volume
Volker Gast

De Gruyter Mouton

Surviving the Middle Passage

The West Africa-Surinam Sprachbund

Edited by
Pieter Muysken
Norval Smith

With the assistance of
Robert Borges

De Gruyter Mouton

ISBN 978-3-11-055542-4
e-ISBN (PDF) 978-3-11-034397-7
e-ISBN (EPUB) 978-3-11-039499-3
ISSN 1861-4302

Library of Congress Cataloging-in-Publication Data
A CIP catalog record for this book has been applied for at the Library of Congress.

Bibliographic information published by the Deutsche Nationalbibliothek
The Deutsche Nationalbibliothek lists this publication in the Deutsche Nationalbibliografie; detailed bibliographic data are available on the Internet at http://dnb.dnb.de.

© 2017 Walter de Gruyter GmbH, Berlin/Boston
This volume is text- and page-identical with the hardback published in 2015.

Printing and binding: CPI books GmbH, Leck
♾ Printed on acid-free paper
Printed in Germany

www.degruyter.com

Acknowledgements

The research for this book was carried out at the Universities of Amsterdam, Leiden, and Nijmegen, and made possible with Programme Project grant nr. 360-70-020 from the Netherlands Foundation for Research (NWO). It was also funded in part by the NWO Spinoza Prize and ensuing project 'Lexicon and Syntax' awarded to Pieter Muysken. The title of the project was "A Trans-Atlantic Sprachbund? The structural relationships between the Gbe-languages of West Africa and the Surinamese Creole languages." We are grateful for helpful discussion and comments from Felix Ameka and Maarten Mous. The late Jacques Arends and Hans den Besten were also frequently present at our project meetings, and we owe a lot to their expert comments as well. Bob Borges helped edit the material for this book.

CVs of editors and authors

Enoch Aboh is professor of linguistics at the University of Amsterdam and a specialist on theoretical syntax, comparative syntax (e.g., Kwa vs. Germanic/Romance, Kwa vs. Sinitic, Kwa vs. Caribbean Creoles), the discourse-syntax interface, and language creation and language change. His recently completed research project TOPIC AND FOCUS had as its aim of this research project to investigate the nature of the interface between discourse pragmatics and syntax. It proposed to study how focus and topic interact with clause structure and how syntactic rules driving clause structure and discourse/pragmatic properties interact.

Margot van den Berg was working as a postdoc at Radboud University Nijmegen, working on Caribbean Creoles, and is currently assistant professor in the linguistics department of Utrecht University. In January of 2009, Margot van den Berg started her project 'Creoles at birth? The role of nativization in language formation', investigating Sranan and Neger-hollands, as well as contemporary L2 English and Dutch by native Twi and Gbe speaking Ghanaians. She is further the coordinator of the Suriname section within the LinC group, and of the Suriname Creole Archive (SUCA).

Robert Borges obtained his PhD in 2014 from Radboud University Nijmegen working on various aspects of language contact in Suriname. His publications include *The life of Language: dynamics of language contact in Suriname* (dissertation), *Linguistic archaeology, Kinship terms and language contact in Suriname* (Anthropological Linguistics), *The role of extralinguistic factors in linguistic variation and contact-induced language change among Suriname's Coppename Kwinti and Ndyuka Maroons* (Acta Linguistica Hafniensia, and *Particle verbs in Suriname's creole languages* (Journal of Germanic Linguistics).

Adrienne Bruyn worked as a postdoc at the Universities of Amsterdam and Leiden at Radboud University Nijmegen. Her special interests include philology and historical linguistics (in particular language contact and grammaticalization), noun phrase syntax and semantics, and the history of Sranan. She is currently employed at the Institute for Dutch Lexicology (INL) in Leiden.

James Essegbey is currently associate professor in the Department of African and Asian languages and literature at the University of Florida. His research interests and areas of specialization include Descriptive, documentary and theoretical linguistics, the Syntax-semantics interface, the Semantics-Pragmatics interface, Contact linguistics, African languages, especially Gbe, Akan, and Ghana-Togo Mountain languages, and Creole studies. A recent project of his is the Nyangbo Documentation Project

Pieter Muysken is professor of linguistics at Radboud University Nijmegen, after previously working at the Universities of Amsterdam and Leiden. He is a specialist on language contact and has worked on the languages of the Caribbean, the Andes, as well as immigrant languages in the Netherlands. Recent publications of his include P. Muysken (2000) *Bilingual speech: a typology of code-mixing* (Cambridge), W. Adelaar in collaboration with P. Muysken (2004) *The languages of the Andes* (Cambridge), P. Muysken Functional Categories (Cambridge). Muysken has authored and edited books published with Foris, Kluwer, Edward Arnold, Benjamins, Brill, and Plural Editores (La Paz, Bolivia).

Norval Smith until recently was associate professor of linguistics at the University of Amsterdam. His work is focused on phonology, Creole studies, and descriptive linguistics, areas in which he has contributed numerous books and articles. He is a specialist on the phonological history of the Surinam Creoles, phonological theory, and the phonological reconstruction of the extinct varieties of Yokuts. He has authored and edited books with North-Holland/Elsevier, Routledge, Foris, Benjamins, and Mouton.

Tonjes Veenstra is researcher at the Berlin Centre for General Linguistics (ZAS), and a specialist on formal approaches to syntax, Creole studies (particularly focusing on Saramaccan and Mauritian), language contact, language acquisition and evolutionary linguistics, and colonial varieties of English. He did his PhD at the University of Amsterdam with a thesis of Saramaccan serial verbs.

Kofi Yakpo was working as a postdoc at Radboud University Nijmegen, and is currently lecturer in the linguistics department of Hongkong University. He received a Magister Artium in linguistics, social anthropology and political science from the University of Cologne and earned a Masters degree in Business Administration from the University of Geneva. He was awarded a PhD in linguistics by the University of Nijmegen for his grammatical description of Pichi, also known as Fernando Po Creole English. He is currently investigating contact phenomena in the languages of Suriname and The Netherlands, with particular focus on the languages of the contract labourers in Surinam. Other activities include research on the English-lexicon Creoles and Pidgins of West Africa and language promotion and advocacy.

Contents

Acknowledgements v

Introduction: Creole studies and Contact Linguistics 1
Margot van den Berg, Pieter Muysken, and Norval Smith

Part 1. Setting the Scene

The early history of Surinam: Why is Surinam different? 17
Norval Smith

Migrations, ethno-dynamics and geolinguistics in the Eastern
Aja-Tado cultural Area 43
Enoch Aboh and Norval Smith

Ingredient X: The shared African lexical element in the English-
lexifier Atlantic Creoles, and the theory of rapid creolization 67
Norval Smith

Relexification, and other language contact scenarios for explaining
substrate effects 107
Pieter Muysken

Part II. Language structures: a Sprachbund?

Trans-Atlantic patterns: the relexification of locative constructions
in Sranan 135
Kofi Yakpo and Adrienne Bruyn

Verb Semantics and Argument Structure in the Gbe and Sranan 175
James Essegbey

Morphology, cross-linguistic effects, and Creole formation 207
Margot van den Berg

Non-iconic reduplications in Eastern Gbe and Surinam 241
Enoch Aboh and Noval Smith

Substrate phonology, superstrate phonology and adstrate
phonology in creole languages 261
Norval Smith

The left periphery in the Surinamese creoles and Gbe:
on the modularity of substrate transfer 323
Enoch Aboh

Relexification and clause-embedding predicates 369
Tonjes Veenstra

Part III. Wrapping up

Conclusion: feature distribution in the West Africa-Surinam
Trans-Atlantic Sprachbund 393
Pieter Muysken

Bibliography of work resulting from the Trans-Atlantic
Sprachbund project 409
Pieter Muysken

A preliminary list of probable Kikongo lexical items in
the Surinam Creole languages 417
Norval Smith

A preliminary list of probable Gbe lexical items in
the Surinam Creole languages 463
Norval Smith

References 477

Indices 517

Introduction: Creole Studies and Contact Linguistics

Margot van den Berg, Pieter Muysken, and Norval Smith

1. Language contact in Creole Studies

The study of pidgins, creoles, intertwined languages, and other outcomes of language contact has seen many lively debates regarding their origin over the years. While it is generally undisputed that these new languages emerge in a situation where two or more languages are in contact, the degree in which the languages in contact contribute to the emergence of the new language, and the way in which this happens, is a particularly controversial matter.

Some scholars have argued that the specific grammatical properties of creole languages directly reflect universal aspects of the human language capacity, thus reducing the role of the individual languages in the creole formation process to a minimum. Others have argued that creole languages reflect patterns of the native languages of the main agents of creole formation, which are the substrate groups of the enslaved in a typical colonial setting. Yet others have stressed the role of the European lexifiers. The Surinam Creoles feature prominently in this debate, resulting in a wealth of studies on Sranan, Ndyuka, Pamaka (also referred to as Paramaccan in the literature), and Saamaka (also referred to as Saramaccan), often with conflicting outcomes.[1]

For example, McWhorter (1999) maintains that the Surinam Creole Tense Mood Aspect (TMA) system developed largely according to its own

---

1. Here we will mention only Rens (1953), Simons (1941), Voorhoeve (1957), Charry, Koefoed, and Muysken. (1983), Seuren (1981, 1983), Alleyne (1987), Byrne (1987), Sebba (1987), Wendelaar and Koefoed (1988), Huttar & Huttar (1994), Veenstra (1995), Arends and Perl (1995), McWhorter (1999), Carlin and Arends (2002), Essegbey (2005), Aboh (2006c), Lefebvre and Loranger (2006), Damonte (2002), Migge (2003a, 2006), Narrog (2005), Winford (2000), van den Berg (2007), Bally (1932), Goury (2003), but this is not an exhaustive list. Note that the Surinam Creoles of the Kwinti and Matawai are understudied.

dictates. From his point of view, it only dimly reflects patterns of the West African substrate languages that contributed to the Surinam Creoles. Migge (2006), Winford and Migge (2007) and Migge and Winford (2009), on the other hand, find that the TMA systems of the Surinam Creoles display many features that parallel those of the Gbe languages, a major substrate or adstrate group present in early eighteenth century Surinam. This raises the question: What constitutes evidence of substrate influence in creole formation, and how is this demonstrated? Since the 1980s, most scholars within the Creole subfield combine historical socio-demographic data with linguistic data to demonstrate substrate influence: The socio-demographic data must show that speakers of the substrate languages were in the right place at the right time (Bickerton 1981), while the linguistic data bring out the similarities and differences between the creole, the substrate languages and the superstrate/lexifier-languages. Muysken and Smith (1986) argue that the linguistic data that feed into the comparison of creole, substrate and superstrate/lexifier need to be selected in a principled manner. General parallels with substrate or superstrate/lexifier languages are not sufficient to demonstrate substrate influence. Rather, features must be selected on the basis of markedness; the linguistic data should represent typologically marked (as opposed to unmarked) features in order to prove substrate influence, as creole – substrate parallels "cannot prove the substratist case if the same phenomena are also claimed by universalists to represent the unmarked settings of various parameters" (Muysken & Smith 1986: 2).

2. Transfer and sub-disciplines of linguistics

The role of language transfer due to language contact is not just posited in Pidgin and Creole studies, but is also utilized in historical linguistics, sociolinguistics and second language acquisition research. A brief overview of some examples of what counts as proof of transfer in the various sub-disciplines of linguistics follows below, showing that transfer can be demonstrated in multiple ways, ranging from qualitative to quantitative research methods, on the basis of very different types of data.

In historical linguistics, the emergence of a certain feature is commonly ascribed to language contact on the basis of the consideration of 'all' the changes that have occurred in the language, and not just a particular feature. If this feature is an isolated instance of claimed language change in the direction of the language from which it is apparently transferred, it is generally not regarded as a promising candidate for an explanation in terms of contact in the field of historical linguistics. However, if there are also other phenomena that suggest change towards the language from which the features are transferred, this is usually taken as a convincing demonstration of contact induced change. Transferred forms of morphemes are, of course, the most compelling evidence of transfer. Strong evidence of transfer can be provided on the basis of a number of marked features that can be shown to have changed in the direction of the source language in different subsystems of the recipient language (Thomason 2003: 710).

In sociolinguistics, language contact is acknowledged as a possible cause of language change, but most sociolinguistic studies of language change are primarily concerned with changes that emerge within a linguistic system. Language-internal changes expose the problem of the causation of language change in its sharpest form (Labov 2001: 20). However, the effects of contact among sublinguistic systems such as regional dialects and sociolects on language change feature prominently in the sociolinguistic subfield of dialect contact and dialect mixture (e.g. Auer, Hinskens, and Kerswill. 2006 on dialect contact in Europe; Otheguy, Zentella, and Livert. 2007 on the New York Spanish speech community). The latter study shows that both dialect and language contact contribute to the emergence of a variety of Spanish that may be regarded as typical of the city of New York, i.e. 'New York Spanish'. It is based on a quantitative corpus-based, variationist approach to rates of overt pronoun usage, variable and constraint hierarchies, involving speakers from different regions and different generations. Using statistical methods, Otheguy et al. argue that hierarchies of independent linguistic variables and constraint hierarchies are both needed in particular to bring "issues of dialect contact and speech community ... into sharp relief" (Otheguy, Zentella, and Livert 2007: 773).

Cross-linguistic influence is also demonstrated in another manner in language acquisition studies. Jarvis (2000, 2010) distinguishes between comparison-based and detection-based approaches. The latter, relatively new approach relies on automated, computerized detection of background characteristics of language samples in order to bring out learner's source-language backgrounds on the basis of their target-language performance. The former includes different types of comparisons, ranging from 1) within-group comparisons of people from the same language backgrounds using the same target languages, to 2) between-group comparisons of people from different source-language backgrounds using the same target language, to 3) cross-language comparisons of people using both the source and target languages (Jarvis 2010: 170). Each comparison brings about a different type of evidence to argue for or against the transfer of forms, features, functions, meanings or distributional properties from one language to another. These types of evidence are referred to as intra-group homogeneity (within-group similarities), inter-group heterogeneity (between-group differences) and cross-language congruity (between-language similarities and intra-lingual contrasts). Jarvis (2000, 2010) stresses that these types can manifest both qualitatively and quantitatively. However, within-group similarities and between-group differences are most frequently demonstrated by means of quantitative studies, for example, how common a particular pattern of target-language use is among a group of learners from a particular source-language background (within-group homogeneity). The third type of evidence is often of a qualitative nature, focusing on qualitative similarities in speaker performances in their source and target languages. All three types are always relevant, but at least two should be presented to make a case for transfer. It sometimes suffices to draw one or two types of evidence from "other sources, such as the results of prior studies, published grammars and language histories, and personal experiences" (Jarvis 2010: 173).

3. Creole formation

Creole formation is regarded as a complex process operating on two connected levels, namely at the individual and the community levels. At the level of the individual, creole formation is understood as a mental process. The creole language emerges as the linguistic outcome of developments in individual speakers' minds – an instance of individual grammar construction. At the community level, the locus of creole formation is not the individual's mind, but the social interaction between individuals, out of which a newly formed and shared linguistic code emerges. DeGraff (1999) proposes the terms I-Creole and E-Creole along the lines of Chomsky's (1986) distinction between I-language and E-language: the term I-Creole refers to the relatively stable grammar in the mind of an individual speaker who grew up with this emerging language, whereas the term E-Creole refers to the new community language. The relationship between I-Creole and E-Creole is represented by DeGraff (1999: 9) as follows:

> E-creoles are epiphenomenal upon I-creoles insofar as the former are by-products of the 'spreading' of parameter settings associated with the latter; such spreading takes place via further instances of acquisition as (speakers endowed with) I-Creoles become more numerous, thus more influential in

the makeup of the linguistic environment for the emerging Creole community and its language acquirers.

Thus, the emergence of the E-Creole depends on an increase of I-Creole forms, due to locally-born children who grow up with the emerging creole as one of their mother tongues; more I-Creoles will result in a higher incidence of creole features. DeGraff and others thus link the emergence of the community creole to native speakers of the emerging language. Native speakers are the main agents in creole formation. Others focus on non-native speakers as the main agents in creole formation. Lefebvre (1998), for example, sees speakers of Fongbe as the main agents in the formation of Haitian Creole. In the initial stages of creole formation, when these speakers were targeting the superstrate language, they would "use the properties of the native lexicons, the parametric values and semantic interpretation rules of their native grammar in creating the creole" (Lefebvre 1998: 9). When they stopped targeting the lexifier language and started targeting the emerging creole, their relexified creole lexicons fed into the processes of reanalysis and dialect levelling, after which a more stabilized or focussed creole would emerge. Thus, creole formation would involve a target shift from lexifier to emerging creole, an instance of targeted second language acquisition. This, however, has been questioned.

Scholars such as Baker (1990) and Siegel (2008) object that speakers of the emerging creole did not aspire to learn a language, be it the lexifier or the emerging creole. Their goal was not grammatical acquisition, but rather successful communication and mutual comprehension in a multilingual and multicultural context (bilingual or multilingual language use). Speakers employ different strategies and types of knowledge in the case of grammatical acquisition or successful communication. For example, functional transfer is found to occur more frequently in the case of the latter (Siegel 2008).

A slightly different set of motives is imputed to new language creators, whether it be mixed language speakers like those of Media Lengua (Musyken 1980, 1981, 1997, 2013), or expanded pidgins like Pijin (Jourdain 2008), or the creoles developed among slave populations in plantation colonies (Smith 2006, 2009, this volume on Ingredient X). Muysken suggested that a new in-between group (in this case between rural Quechua and urban Spanish-speakers) developed a new in-between ethnicity, and therefore language. For a similar example consider the mixed French-Cree language of the Michif (Bakker 1997). Smith basically follows Jourdain in seeing the new language as a vehicle of resistance. The advantages of a neutral language vis-à-vis the various African languages of the slaves, but incomprehensible (initially at least) to the European colonizers seems obvious.

In order to gain a deeper understanding of the process of creole formation we need to include insights on multilingual language use as well as second language acquisition. The linguistic innovations that constitute the emerging creole result from mental processes in an individual speaker's mind just as much as from social interaction, accommodation and negotiation between speakers. Hence, creole formation should not be limited to processes that operate in the individual speaker's mind. Furthermore, as Pennycook (2010) reminds us, language use is part of a multifaceted interplay between humans and the world. What people do with language in a particular place at a given time results from their interpretation of the situation. In addition there are the mental processes in individual speakers' minds, social interactions, accommodation and negotiation among speakers. As the language practices these people engage in reinforce that interpretation of the situation, we need to account for history as well as location, if we want to understand creole formation.

Creole formation happens over time. The question is how much time is, or how many generations are, involved. DeGraff (1999) and Lefebvre (1998) both view creole formation as a two stage process: a highly variable, irregular, unsystematic diffuse initial stage is followed by a less variable, more regular, systematic, focussed stage. Reanalysis and dialect levelling give rise to the latter stage in Lefebvre's view, while it is nativization in that of DeGraff. They seem to agree, however, that cross-linguistic effects are mostly likely to occur in the initial stage:

> Substratist accounts predict, correctly I think, the existence, in the pre-homogenization period, of a complex array of proto-Creole nonnative interlanguages influenced by a variety of substrate languages – Fongbe, Ewe, Akan, Gã, Gur, Efik, Ibibio, Igbo, Yoruba, Bamana/Malinke, Fula, Kikongo, etc. In this pre-levelling stage, there could *not* exist one single Creole variety, or a small set of Creole varieties, *with relatively homogeneous morphosyntactic profile(s)* (DeGraff 2009: 941-942).

A particularly convincing case of the impact of nativization on creole formation is presented by Roberts (2000). She shows, on the basis of sociohistorical and linguistic evidence, that nativization plays an important role in the structural elaboration that distinguishes the creole from the pidgin of foreign-born adults in Hawaii. While Bickerton assumes a two-generational model, Roberts posits a three-generational account for the emergence of Hawaiian Creole. In the classic view of Bickerton (1981), Hawaiian Creole was formed relatively abruptly by children of immigrants (G(eneration)2) who acquire their parent's pidgin (G1) as their mother tongue. Roberts shows that a three-generational model is more appropriate to account for the emergence of Hawaiian Creole: it is not the locally-born children (G2), but the locally-born grandchildren (G3) of the immigrants who are responsible for the linguistic innovations that are now recognized as Hawaiian Creole. The three-generational model relates not only to language birth but also to language death, as the rise of the creole coincides with the falling out of use of the ancestral or first language(s) of the immigrants. As pointed out by Roberts (2000: 295), this is not unique to Hawaiian Creole. It is found frequently in other immigrant societies, such as America (Fishman 1985), New Caledonia (Corne 1994), and the South Pacific region (Siegel 2008). These cases further show that when the ancestral or first language(s) of the immigrants continue(s) to be used by their locally born children, who are typically bilingual in the ancestral and the superstrate languages, substratal influence on the developing creole becomes possible: G2 speakers and subsequent generations may introduce substratal patterns from the ancestral languages in the creole as long as they remain bilingual. These cross-linguistic effects are even more likely to occur when the ancestral language and the superstrate converge (Corne 1994). Thus, cross-linguistic effects are expected to occur not only in the foreign-born G1, as suggested by DeGraff, Lefebvre and others, but also in the locally-born G2 as long as bilingualism is maintained.

The circum-Caribbean English-lexifier creoles possess shared morphosyntactic features (McWhorter 1995; Smith, this volume on Ingredient X), as well as significant phonological parallels among those creoles lacking an extended superstrate influence from English (Smith, this volume on creole phonology). Smith terms this the Proto-Atlantic Slave Community Language (PASCL) and concludes that its creation took place in the Caribbean. When this was brought to Surinam with slaves (probably) from Barbados, it would be rapidly nativized. A total period of about 30 years might be sufficient.

4. The present volume: Substrate in Surinam

In order to contribute to this longstanding debate about cross-linguistic effects in creole genesis, this book is about the close historical and linguistic relationship between the languages of Surinam in the Caribbean and, in particular, Benin in West-Africa. This relationship can be viewed, we argue, in terms of a Trans-Atlantic linguistic area or Sprachbund. It consists of a detailed analysis of various possible substrate and adstrate influences in a number of components of the grammars of the Surinam Creole languages, primarily from the Gbe languages of Benin, but also from Kikongo, a Bantu language from further south in West Central Africa.

The Surinam Creoles constitute one of the richest and best-documented sources for the study of creole genesis. There are early sources available, and detailed descriptions of many aspects of their structure and development. Furthermore, there is abundant and indisputable historical, demographic, and lexical linguistic evidence that the Gbe languages, in particular the varieties spoken in Benin, as well as Kikongo, were of crucial importance in shaping the Surinam Creoles. This book deals with a number of aspects of linguistic structure, ranging from phonology to semantics, as well as with socio-historical considerations.

It reflects the detailed work carried out on the nature and history of the Surinam Creoles by members of the research group, including the late Jacques Arends of the University of Amsterdam (1952–2005). The group, and also many others, has worked on the languages of Surinam in considerable detail, notably the coastal language Sranan, and the maroon languages Saramaccan and Ndyuka. These are currently among the best-documented creole languages of the world.

The book is intended to bring new evidence to the discussion about Africanisms in language varieties of the New World. Two of the post-doctoral researchers in the project, James Essegbey and Enoch Aboh, are native speakers of relevant West-African languages: Akan and Gungbe, respectively, and trained experts in the comparative grammar of West African languages. Furthermore, the search for potentially significant contributing languages can be limited, for socio-historical reasons, to just a few languages, which have all been fairly well studied.

The book contributes to the discussion about and definition of linguistic areas by postulating a linguistic area, not so much characterized by geographical contiguity as by the historical evidence of massive population movement due to the capture and forced transportation of slaves. In Section 5, and in Muysken (2007b), this perspective is further explored.

Finally, it explores new dimensions of the process of linguistic interference or transfer. As Herskovits and Herskovits (1936: 131) put it "... the peculiarities of Negro speech are primarily due to the fact that the Negroes have been using words from European languages to render literally the underlying morphological patterns of West African tongues." This leads us directly to the issue of relexification, extensively discussed in Muysken's contribution (see Chapter 5), and which provided a starting point for the research undertaken here. New in this book is that the various alternatives to the classical relexification scenario are considered and discussed in detail.

Our main conclusions are that creole formation was a fairly rapid process, but that there was a subsequent period of prolonged bilingualism in at least Gbe (languages) and Kikongo. The crowded timetable of events in the early history of Surinam does not allow for a gradual process of creolization. However, it is clear that the Surinam creoles display more African features than most circum-Caribbean creole languages. This argues for a longer period of adstratal, rather than substratal, influence, which can be explained by several generations of bilingualism.

The idea that structural (in this case substrate) links exist between West African languages and creole languages, including those spoken in Surinam, is not at all new. This idea was proposed by Schuchardt (1914), for example, and has enjoyed a degree of popularity at various periods during the 20th century, in particular in the 30's (e.g. Sylvain 1936 on the relationship between Haitian Creole and Ewe(Gbe). And for anthropological parallels between Surinam and Benin (Dahomey), see Herskovits & Herskovits (1936). In the 70's, the idea made its reappearance, in particular in respect of English-lexifier creoles, in works such as Voorhoeve (1975), Huttar (1975), and Alleyne (1981). In the 80's and 90's, the emphasis moved back to the French-lexifier Haitian Creole again, with the work of a research team under Claire Lefebvre in Montréal (cf. Lefebvre 1998). In hindsight, it is striking that the Surinam Creoles and Haitian should continue to feature most strongly in this connection – Surinam in Schuchardt (1914), Herskovits & Herskovits (1936), and Voorhoeve (1973), and Haitian in Sylvain (1936), and in the work of Lefebvre's team. Now in the 21st century, in work by the present NWO programme project team, and also by an NSF-supported team (Winford & Migge) working complementarily with ours, the focus has returned once again to the Surinam Creoles.

This should not create the impression that the substrate theory has ever been "the theory" of choice for the creolist community. Its greatest popularity was in the 70's but even then it had to compete with other approaches.

The two other basic approaches are the universalist model (of which the main champion has been Derek Bickerton (1981)) and the superstrate model (whose main proponent is Chaudenson (1992)). Typical of the last two approaches, at least as formulated by the authors quoted, is a generally denigrating attitude towards proposals imputing an important role to influence from substrate languages. This opinion was certainly stimulated by the wilder and more poorly informed substratist proposals of the 1970's – *substratomania(c)*, in the words of Bickerton.

With respect to these three main types of linguistic explanations for creole genesis, workers in the field of creole languages have come to realise that linguistic arguments have to be backed up by socio-historical ones. Why did groups of slaves, or others collected together on plantations, develop new languages? What was the function of these new languages? Were they trying to learn the colonial languages or not? How long did they maintain their original languages? How many speakers of the various languages were really present at the different historical periods?[2] What was the social and demographic structure of plantations? It is still also true however that socio-historical arguments must be backed-up by linguistic arguments. How directly can these questions be answered by an examination of the records of the Atlantic slave trade?

In addition, new types of linguistic approaches have been applied to the problems of Creole genesis. Are there aspects to be found in creole language structures that are reminiscent of what we are now learning about the early stages of language acquisition? This question is relevant for both first and second language acquisition. In particular the latter appears relevant for creole genesis, along with the growing realization that the interlanguage stages seen by some in naturalistic second language acquisition, may well be susceptible to explanation in terms of first language (i.e. substrate) influence (Sprouse 2006), and that there can be cross-linguistic (adstrate) influence through prolonged bilingual usage.

Where previous attempts to study substrate influence have missed the mark is because there was a presumption in Creole studies that one of the three above-mentioned approaches was necessarily the best one, the one that basically told the whole story. Either the substrate approach was the

---

2. See Smith (2009: 313–314) for relative numbers of English, Portuguese and Dutch in the first 40 years of the colony, including the transition from English to Dutch rule. See also Smith (this volume on the early history of Surinam) for a detailed summing-up of the sources of slaves imported into Surinam from various parts of Africa during the first 60 years of the colony's existence.

touchstone, or the superstrate approach, or the universalist approach. This has been proved by experience not to be the case. In reality, things are much more complex, and different creole languages also differ from each other in this respect.

In proposing this project, we felt that the substrate approach in particular had received an unnecessarily bad press. The most attractive solutions tend to be the simplest ones, or even the most simplistic ones. Various individuals in the field have made their name and fame by pushing each of the three alternatives to the limit. Not that this is necessarily bad in methodological terms. However, the substrate hypothesis as it had hitherto been employed had not been convincing. The reason for the criticisms of the substratist approach was not so much, we thought, because of its inherent wrongness, but that it had not been tested on the right languages, or in reality tested properly at all.

Smith, Robertson & Williamson (1987) had shown that if the right substrate language was selected – in the case of Berbice Dutch, the Eastern Ịjọ language of the Niger Delta – a number of features of the creole could be satisfactorily explained in terms of substrate mechanisms. One reaction was that Berbice Dutch was a special case – a kind of mixed creole – and that therefore the result was not generalizable. It was felt that this was in some way more like the Mixed Language type first identified by Muysken (1981), where one effect of substrate influence, relexification, plays an overwhelming role.

However, Smith had also identified the Gbe language group as being of importance for the Surinam Creoles in terms of lexicon, and to some extent function words. Smith (1996), for example, demonstrates the near-identity of the syntax of contrastive focus in Fon/Gungbe and Saramaccan, down to the use of the same low-toned marker *wɛ* in post-focus position, which reinforced the work on aspects of morphosyntax by Bruyn (1995). Hence we felt confident that in these two groups of languages we had very good candidates for a valid test of the substrate hypothesis in what were widely accepted as canonical creole languages, if such exist. Aboh, in fieldwork in Surinam, has since established that the morphosyntax of contrastive focus is virtually identical in Fon/Gungbe and Saramaccan (Aboh 2006c).

All the more reason to again test the substrate hypothesis for Surinam, in our view the most solid historical case, next to Berbice Dutch, that the Caribbean creoles have to offer.

5. The notion of Sprachbund or linguistic area

In the title of our book, we suggest that the issue of West African substrate in the creole languages can be profitably pursued from the perspective of the notion of Sprachbund. Since Creole studies are not generally linked to this notion, it is useful to look at it a bit closer. Thomason (2001: 99) defines a linguistic area or Sprachbund (Trubetzkoy 1930) as "... a geographical region containing a group of three or more languages that share some structural features as a result of contact rather than as a result of accident or inheritance from a common ancestor." This definition contains a number of key elements that call for independent justification for our perspective.

Geographical region. Of course, Surinam and Benin do not form a geographical region in the strict sense. However, historically, they form a contact network, *in casu* through the slave trade.

Three or more languages. In the case of Surinam, there are about five major contributing languages or language complexes: Gbe, Kikongo, English, Portuguese, Dutch, and a handful of resulting creole languages.

Shared structural features. The number of shared structural features is of course a matter of investigation and debate, but Surinam certainly conforms to this criterion, it will turn out.

Contact. The issue of contact was covered above, under geographical region.

Not an accident. The features are of the creoles certainly do not resemble those of the contributing languages by accident, but there is a debate in Creole typology on the issue of the origin of the creole structural features. Following Bickerton (1981), they could be due to universal properties of the process of creole genesis.

Not inheritance from a common ancestor. There are two different families involved in the emergence of the creoles: Niger-Congo and Indo-European, as well as individual languages descending from different branches of these families.

6. The contents of the book

The various chapters that are contained here, illustrating various types of substrate effect, all provide evidence of one sort or another bearing on various aspects of the process of creole genesis. In addition to this introduction, a chapter with the full bibliography of the Wesr Africa-Surinam

Sprachbund project, a new inventory of all words in Surinam Creoles with etyma in the Gbe language family and Kikongo, and a combined list of references, there are twelve other chapters.

Migge (2003a: 25) conveniently lists five key components in any account of creole formation:

1. a historical scenario for creole formation
2. a characterization of the nature of the linguistic inputs
3. processes and mechanisms of contact
4. the factors that constrained them
5. the nature of the outcome

The remainder of the book is divided into three parts. In Part I *Setting the scene,* establishes the relevant background information for the linguistic studies in Part II. The first two chapters in Part I deal with the **early history of Surinam** (by Smith) [component 1] and **Benin** (by Smith and Aboh), and the specific varieties of Gbe relevant to Surinam [component 2]. In the next chapter, Smith then presents the evidence for an **antecedent extended Atlantic pidgin** feeding into the Surinam Creoles. Muysken then analyzes the history of the study of **substrate** effects, and provides an analytic overview of language contact mechanisms, particularly **relexification, second language learning,** and **bilingual convergence** [components 3 and 4].

The chapters in Part II *Language structures: a sprachbund?* focus mostly on the nature of the outcome of creole genesis [component 5]. Four chapters focus on the lexicon, taking into account both morphological, semantic, and categorical aspects. Building on the discussion in Muysken's chapter, Yakpo and Bruyn, explore **locative constructions** in Sranan: are we dealing with relexification of items or of patterns? Essegbey surveys verb semantics and argument structure in Gbe and in the Surinam Creoles. Then, van den Berg explores the role of cross-linguistic influence in **nominal morphology** in Sranan and on **property concepts** (often realized as stative predicates), also citing recent work on multilingual language use in West Africa [component 3]. Aboh & Smith, study non-iconic **reduplications** in Eastern Gbe and Surinam Creoles. Finally, Smith discusses key aspects of substrate, superstrate, and adstrate **phonology** in creole languages. The two subsequent chapters proceed with formal syntax. Aboh focuses on the **left periphery** in the Surinam Creoles and Gbe, arguing for the modularity of substrate transfer. Then Veenstra explores the role of relexification in the genesis of **clause-embedding predicates**.

Part III *Wrapping up*, begins with the concluding chapter, based on work of all the authors, and compiled by Muysken, contains the conclusions from the papers in the volume and develops new perspectives from the perspective of **structural phylogenetics**. We conclude that the Surinam Creole languages share structural features both with the Gbe languages and Kikongo and with their European lexifiers. The process of adoption of West-African features however, was adstratal, i.e. selective, creative, and gradual, rather than instantaneous and automatic, as the relexification hypothesis would suggest.

We then provide a list of additional publications resulting from the project and the combined list of references cited. Included are also two appending lists of probable **Kikongo** and **Gbe lexical items** in the Surinam Creole languages, prepared by Smith. These chapters show the extraordinary role that just two (minor) African language groups played in the languages of Surinam in contributing the large majority of African-derived words, contrasting with the general impressions that Caribbean creoles have had significant input from a wide variety of African languages[3]. Further work will be needed to study the degree of regularity in the sound changes through which these words were adopted in the Surinam Creole languages, and identify possible additional items.

---

3. Left out of consideration here is a lesser body of African words from Akan/Twi (Ghana/Gold Coast). These are much less numerous than the Gbe and Kikongo words, reflecting presumably the largely eighteenth century importations of slaves from this area.

Part I:
Setting the scene

The early history of Surinam: Why is Surinam different?

Norval Smith

1. Introduction

In the view of the editors, Surinam formed an ideal test bed for hypotheses involving substrate influence. Two important factors were:

- The concrete linguistic evidence for this kind of influence (there are many words of African origin, many of which are listed in the appended chapters on Kikongo and Gbe).
- The demographic evidence on the origins of the slave population of Surinam, based until recently on Arends (1995a). Arends had extracted the relevant data from Postma (1990). Recently new data has become available, in the form of the slave trade Voyages Database (2009). An extract from this database made by Robert Borges concerning the slave trade to the Dutch Guianas was made available to me. From that I have extracted the data for shipments to Surinam. Some differences between Arends/Postma and the Voyages Database are given in Borges (2013: 27–32). This new data has caused me to rethink some of my conclusions.

A combination of this new slave trade data and the crowded timetable of events in Surinam, which only allows a short time for the formation of the creole languages spoken there, have led to a reassessment of the uses of the terms *substrate* and *superstrate* in discussing creolization. For the moment, I will talk about "substrates", and deal with the topic in Section 4.

The most important "substrate" influence observed in the creole languages of Surinam is clearly that of Fongbe spoken on the former Slave Coast of West Africa, now represented largely in the coastal areas of Benin. Influence from Kikongo, spoken in West Central Africa, the only other African language to demonstrate more than vestigial lexical influence on the Surinam Creoles, is much more superficial. It seems only to manifest itself with regard to certain differential aspects of phonotactic word construction in Fongbe and Kikongo (cf. Smith, this volume on creole phonology).

The influence of these two African sources seemed to be paralleled nicely by the demographic facts of known slave imports contained in the Voyages Database (2009). As in Smith (1999a) this data is presented in the form of half-decade figures, in order to show the more detailed variations in a slightly clearer form than in Arends' and Borges' presentations in terms of decades. In this way, it is hoped to capture significant patterns of importations, whilst still avoiding the randomness of using year-by-year figures, which sometimes fluctuate wildly. These last variations are to be explained by the vagaries of supply.

The new (2009) figure for the total number of Slave Coast slaves imported in the period 1675–1719 is 18,462, as compared with 14,647 slaves of West Central African origin. These figures are not that dramatically different from each other. The reason for the apparent dominance of slaves speaking Fongbe (and related varieties) is however less obvious. From the available figures it is now apparent that slaves from West Central Africa outnumbered those from the Slave Coast, taken cumulatively, from the mid-1680s for about 20 years. Only towards the end of the first decade of the 18th century did the notional cumulative numbers of slaves from the Gbe country begin to surpass those from West Central Africa. Notional, because I have not taken account of the period of high marronnage in the period from 1690 to 1710 – the period in which the Saramaccan tribe was created, according to Price (1983 and other works). The disparity in numbers is however partly due to an astonishing 3961 slaves from West Central Africa in the years 1685–9. In particular according to the figures[1], a much higher number of slaves were imported than usual, 7131[2] from 1685–1689. This must have placed unusual strains on the infrastructure. Slaves had to be fed and housed.

As I have noted in Smith (2009a), we have poll-tax figures for the years of 1684 and 1695. The numbers of slaves declared in these years were 3332 (1684) and 4618 (1695). I adjusted these to 3,650 and 5,100 respectively to take account of under-reporting to evade taxation. In Smith (2009a) I suggested that there were about 6250[3] slaves missing from the statistics if a loss from deaths of 4% per year and a natural increase of 2% per year are taken into account. These percentages would seem reasonable if Lamur (1987) is taken as typical of Surinam plantations in general.

---

1. The figures in the Voyages Database (2009) do not show major differences with those in Postma (1990) in the period 1680–1704.
2. From the shipments recorded in the Voyages Database.
3. In fact, this number stays virtually the same in the new database.

Table 1. Slave imports to Surinam (based on data in slave trade Voyages Database (2009)). "Westward" refers to slaves imported from Senegambia and the Windward Coast.

	Westward	Gold C	Slave Coast	Bight of Biafra	W C Africa	Unknown	Total	Decade total
1660–1664				130 (100%)			130	130
1665–1669				996 (37.2%)	980 (36.6%)	705 (26.3%)	2681	2811
1670–1674				753 (39.1%)	1173 (60.9%)		1926	4607
1675–1679	422 (12.4%)	758 (22.3%)	816 (24.0%)	281 (7.6%)	1027 (30.2%)	391 (11.2%)	3695	5621
1680–1684	255 (8.5%)		1322 (44.2%)	281 (9.4%)	1134 (37.9%)		2992	6687
1685–1689		175 (2.5%)	1734 (24.3%)	844 (11.8%)	3961 (55.5%)	417 (5.8%)	7131	10123
1690–1694			1467 (68.8%)		665 (31.2%)		2132	9263
1695–1699			2269 (46.6%)		2384 (48.9%)	220 (4.5%)	4873	7005
1700–1704			2855 (86.0%)		465 (14.0%)		3320	8193
1705–1709	387 (5.9%)	421 (7.4%)	2964 (52.1%)		1078 (19.0%)	834 (14.7%)	5684	9004
1710–1714			1375 (66.1%)		705 (33.9%)		2080	7764
1715–1719		174 (3.0%)	3660 (63.7%)		1075 (18.7%)	837 (14.6%)	5746	7826 7977

A new perspective is offered by the addition of additional slave voyages at the beginning of the known slave-trade to Surinam, especially for the period 1665–1680. We now know that the recorded trade from the Slave Coast only begins in 1677. Previously, the slaves came from West Central Africa, and a new area, the Bight of Biafra. Ten voyages are recorded from West Central Africa from 1669 till 1675, and eleven from the Bight of Biafra from 1664 till 1671. After this the traffic from the Bight of Biafra tails off rapidly. In addition, for a short while in the late 1670s the Gold Coast plays a fair-sized role in Surinam too. This is revealed by the new data.

Also, for what it is worth, Warren (1667) reports, regarding the English period in Surinam, that the slaves ".... are most brought out of Guiny in Africa to these parts, ...", where "Guinea" refers to West Africa and not to Central Africa. The first arrival of a slave-ship in Surinam recorded in the Voyages Database (2009) was in 1664, and of the voyages or which the source in Africa has been recorded, the first six are from the Bight of Biafra (in "Guinea"). However, only the first three or four ships date from the English period. From 1651 to 1663 we have no records in the Voyages Database. In Lack (2007b) we hear of two slave-ships from Guinea, which arrived in 1661 under a Captain Nicholas Sulke. So we still have a major gap in our knowledge in the critical years at the beginning of the English colony. It is reasonable to assume, that the very first slaves were brought from other English colonies, in particular Barbados, but we have no record of this.

An important new factor is the addition of an early new source in West Africa, the Bight of Biafra. This makes the Surinam trade resemble that of Jamaica to a greater degree. It is true that this source appears to lose its importance earlier for Surinam than for Jamaica, but this difference is probably to be explained by the general replacement of English slavers by Dutch ones.

However, the concrete linguistic evidence and the demographic evidence are not sufficient in themselves to explain the African "substrate" phenomena found in the Surinam Creole languages. And not least when we take the new information into account. Note that the Bight of Biafra includes a diverse group of languages which we may expect to have been spoken by the slaves imported from that region principally various Ijo, Cross River, Igboid and possibly Edo languages. This is confirmed by the ports named in the Voyages Database: Calabar (on the Cross River), New Calabar (on the New Calabar River in the Niger Delta) and Cape Lopez. Cape Lopez is an outlier in that it forms the geographical boundary between the Gulf of Guinea (of which the Bight of Biafra is a part) and the South Atlantic Ocean. Linguistically it belongs to Central Africa – most of the population speak one of a great variety of Bantu languages. We may conclude that no one language would have dominated among the slaves imported from the Bight of Biafra.

The difference between the Surinam creoles and other English-based creoles of the Atlantic region can no longer be claimed to lie in the unique quality of the demographic data available for Surinam alone. Other plantation colonies now have comparable qualities of data available. Consider the case of Jamaica, where the demographic detail available (Kouwenberg 2008) now possesses a greater similarity to that for Surinam. Yet the "substrate" effects on Jamaican Creole are still less apparent. One can no longer argue that this has to do with the fact that four different major catchment areas contribute in significant proportions to the Jamaican slave population, while only two are involved in the formative years in Surinam. Surinam now has a very similar proportion of sources to Jamaica. However, if we examine the half-decade figures provided by Kouwenberg more closely, this is seen not to be true of the whole early period.

From 1655 – the start of English colonization on Jamaica – until 1680, the largest number of slaves hailed from the Bight of Biafra area (Nigeria). In this area, the most important coastal language is Igbo, although there are numerous other languages spoken in the coastal area, as mentioned above. I will look at Kouwenberg's figures in terms of cumulative totals from each catchment area, and ignore slaves whose provenance is unknown. While the percentage of Bight of Biafra slaves calculated this way declines from 67% in 1665 to 41% in 1680, this area remains twice as significant as any other. However, by 1685, the Bight of Benin (formerly known as the Slave Coast), the area where Fongbe and related Eastern Gbe languages are spoken, has overtaken the Bight of Biafra. Together they contribute more than 60% of slaves imported in that period. Only in 1690 does a third player make its presence felt – West Central Africa, moving into second place behind the Bight of Benin. By 1695 the Bight of Biafra has dropped to below 20% of the slaves. Now the Bight of Benin and West Central Africa together provide more than 60% of the slaves. Considering the relative periods the various catchment areas supplied varying amounts of slaves, one would expect the relative influence of the three main areas to be: 1. Bight of Biafra; 2. Bight of Benin; 3. West Central Africa.

Summarizing the catchment areas together supplying more than 60% of slaves in total in each period, the following picture emerges (catchment areas listed in order of importance by period), which can no longer be understood to be any more complex than the Surinamese context. The substantial difference in the degree of obvious "substrate" influence observed in the two areas must be due to another factor.

1655–1675	**Bight of Biafra**
1675–1680	**Bight of Biafra**, Gold Coast[4], Bight of Benin
1680–1685	**Bight of Benin**, Bight of Biafra
1685–1690	**Bight of Benin**, West Central Africa, Bight of Biafra
1690–1695	**Bight of Benin**, West Central Africa, Bight of Biafra
1695–1700	**Bight of Benin**, West Central Africa, Bight of Biafra

2. Why Surinam is different

Why Surinam is so different is therefore not the presence of one or two major African languages, which then function as "substrate" languages for the developing creole. In Section 4, I will discuss the question of substrate in more detail. After all, as we have now seen, the Jamaican situation hardly differs from the Surinam situation.

I believe the most important factor is that the original superstrate language was removed, to all intents and purposes, within 30 years or so of the foundation of the colony (Smith 2009a). Whereas English, the superstrate language, both of Jamaican Creole and the Surinam Creoles, is still present in Jamaica 350 years after its colonization by the English. In Surinam the superstrate was only significant for less than a tenth of this time. After the effective removal of English from Surinam, it could be argued of course that a new superstrate, or rather adstrate, language Dutch was introduced (I will deal briefly with the political change-over below). However, in terms of numbers of speakers, the Dutch language was very weak at first, and the Portuguese of the Jewish population was a significant linguistic rival for quite some time. Clearly Dutch has had increasing influence on the coastal creole, Sranan, but this influence has not been significant on the maroon Creoles until modern times, and is still fairly minor in scope.

So the reason why it seems that the Surinam Creoles provide an ideal testing-ground for substrate influence ies in the early colonial change of power. There are other similar "deviant" English-lexifier Creoles in the

---

4. In the period 1675–1679, the Gold Coast briefly surfaces as an equal supplier to West Central Africa and the Bight of Benin (Slave Coast) in Surinam as well.

Atlantic region, to wit, Krio, and what is now best known under the name of the Jamaican Maroon Spirit Language (Bilby 1983, 1992), but also as the Eastern Maroon Creole (of Jamaica), but these are less obvious objects of study at first sight for various reasons. The history of Krio is, at the very least, the subject of controversy due to the fact that possible speakers of predecessor varieties were moved around by the British. Before they were taken to Sierra Leone, two candidate groups had been in Nova Scotia. I will claim that the main linguistic input to Krio comes from the Western Maroons of Jamaica.

The Maroon Spirit Language of the Eastern Maroons of Jamaica is to some extent disqualified by its very obsolescence and lack of complete documentation. It is possible, however, that *both* these creoles have their origins in creole languages spoken by Jamaican maroon groups. If this were true, as I am inclined to believe, then they would also have been exposed to much less influence from Standard English. The Maroon connection will be discussed in Smith (this volume on Ingredient X).

The Surinam Creoles are made more suitable as a test-bed by the large amount of data available from the 18th century for both Sranan and Saramaccan. While Sranan may have undergone 300 years of contact with Dutch, the form of plantation Sranan that became maroon Ndyuka has not. Ndyuka, although the data available is not comparable to that from Sranan or Saramaccan in its temporal depth, does give us a window on the past in that it gives us much additional evidence for reconstructing early 18th century Plantation Sranan. Although it has to be said that I have come to see the nature of this test-bed as demonstrating more clearly what the results of the creolization of English were, rather than providing evidence for the effects of substrate languages.

3. A clearer picture

The clarity of the picture we observe in Surinam is also enhanced by the nature of the demographic developments. According to Arends (2002), Surinam was not a typical colony in one crucial way. It did not pass through the stage that Chaudenson (1992) has termed the *société d'habitation* (settlement society). Warren (1667) states that there were already forty to fifty sugar plantations in the mid 1660's, only 15 years after the foundation of the colony. The rapidity of the creation of a sugar-based economy is explained by the fact that Surinam was a secondary colony, principally colonized from Barbados, which had been colonized by the English a generation beforehand in 1627.

Arends utilizes the early introduction of a sugar-based economy in Surinam to explain why perhaps "the restructuring of English began relatively early but also that it was perhaps more drastic than in other colonies, which went through longer establishment phases". The more drastic restructuring of English is explained by other causes in Smith (2006), but the apparent earliness of the "restructuring" seems indisputable. In fact, as I have already suggested, it is not so much a case of a more drastic restructuring but the very lack of long-standing adstratal influence from Standard English that is responsible for the great differences between the Surinam Creoles and Jamaican Creole.

A cautionary note that probably needs to be sounded here vis-à-vis the question of Chaudenson's *société d'habitation* concerns the frequently small-scale nature of the Surinam plantation economy during the English period. Whatever small-scale actually means in plantation terms.

3.1. The English in Surinam

Accounts of events relevant to the possible linguistic scenarios for creolization during the English period are fairly sparse. Warren (1667) is in general not very informative on anything of this nature. See below, however, for some snippets of information. There is of course ample information regarding the main characters involved in the colonization of Surinam, Francis Willoughby, Earl of Parham, who was the financier of the initial colony, and Lieutenant General William Byam, Governor of Surinam from 1654 till 1667. Two articles in Lack (2007a, 2007b) collect some of the relevant English sources together. In the following two sections devoted to Willoughby and Byam a number of interesting facts will emerge.

In order to better understand the geographical relationships among the various English colonies I provide a map of the Caribbean area (based on Smith 1999a).

The early history of Surinam   25

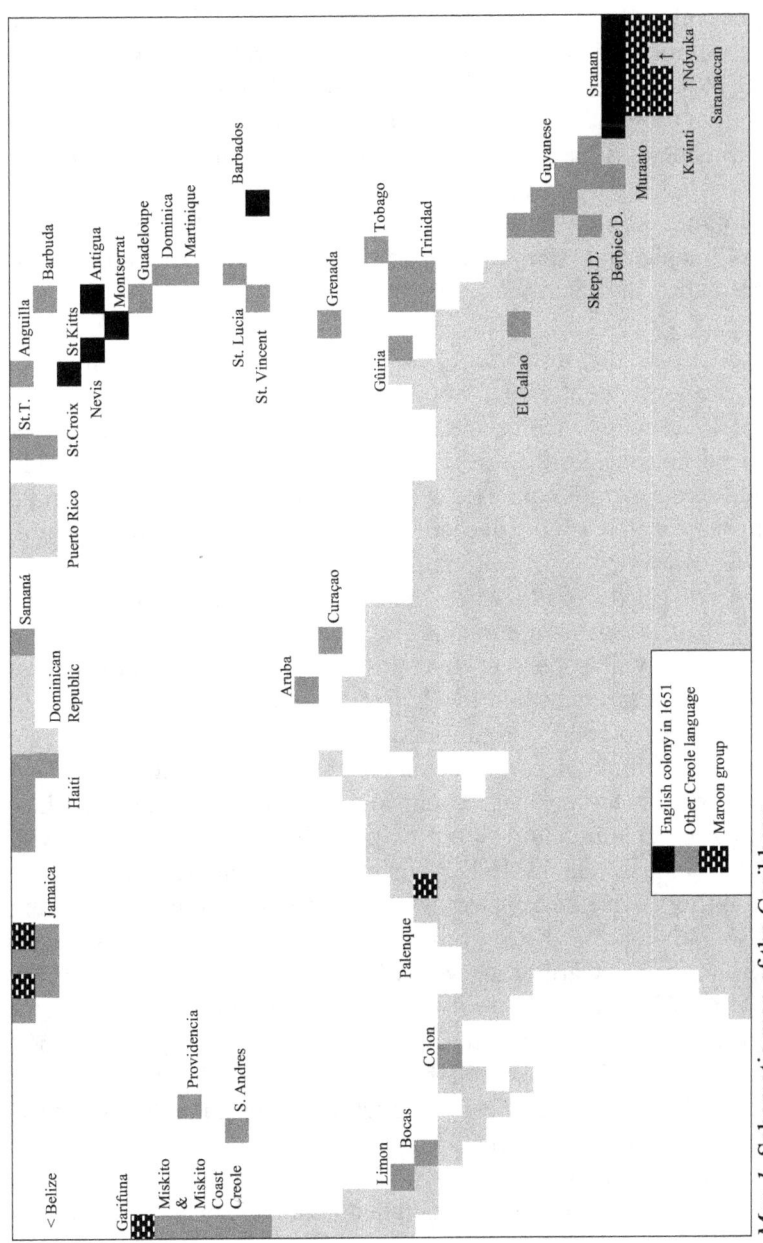

Map 1. Schematic map of the Caribbean

3.2. The external history: Willoughby, the colonizer of Surinam

The earliest history of English Surinam, or *Willoughby Land*, named from its founder, requires to be seen in the context of the general religious and political upheaval in England, and other parts of the British Isles. As the result of the Catholic(izing) tendencies of King Charles I, a civil war had broken out (1642–1645), followed by another a few years later (1648–1649). In both of these he was defeated, the second leading to his execution in 1649. The general situation of conflict and dissension was extremely complex and is not really relevant for our topic here, so that I will only provide a summary account of the happenings. What is relevant is the fact that England's upheaval was directly reflected in England's colonies, including Barbados and Surinam, although with a certain delay in each case.

The Royalists, as the supporters of King Charles were known, were opposed by the Parliamentarians, who believed in the supremacy of the parliament. The leader of the Parliamentary party at this period was Oliver Cromwell, who became Lord Protector of England, Scotland, and Ireland (at this time three separate countries with a single leadership but separate parliaments) from 1653–1660, succeeded very briefly by his son Richard. Barbados was controlled by the Royalists until 1652 (a more than three-year delay in respect of 1649), when the Parliamentarians gained control after a naval battle. Surinam remained a (pretty insignificant) Royalist outpost. But as we will soon see, there was also a parliamentary faction there too. England was controlled by Parliamentarians from 1642 to 1660, Barbados from 1652 to 1660, and Surinam not at all.

Willoughby, the founder of the colony of Surinam, initially chose the side of the Parliamentarians, and even commanded a regiment in their military forces in England in 1643. However, he speedily fell out with them, and was imprisoned in 1647. When he was released after a few months he fled to the Netherlands to join the Royalist camp (led by King Charles I's son Charles II). After Parliament had confiscated his estates in England, he went to the Caribbean, where Charles II created him Governor of Barbados in 1650. In 1650 he also sent an expeditionary force under Anthony Rowse to Surinam (as noted in the backdated royal grant of 1662 (Hartsinck 1770: 521–558)). Willoughby invested heavily in the colony that arose from this expedition. Fort Willoughby (or Willoughby Fort, now Fort Zeelandia) was established in his honor.

The colonists came mainly from Barbados (as might be expected from Willoughby's involvement), but also included people from St. Kitts, Nevis and Montserrat. Willoughby himself invested £26,000 in Surinam on two plantations, one on the Surinam River, called Parham Hill, and another on the Commewijne River.

Barbados in 1650 was also divided into Royalist and Parliamentarian camps. Between October and December 1651 a Parliamentarian fleet first blockaded and then assaulted Barbados. In January 1652, Willoughby surrendered, and was replaced as Governor.

Willoughby paid a short visit to Surinam in March, and in August returned to England, where his properties had in the meantime been returned. However, in the period up to 1656 he was imprisoned twice for involvement in Royalist plots. In that year, he was promised his freedom, with a bail of £10,000, provided that he left within 6 months for Surinam. He did not go to Surinam, but did remain free.

After the restoration of the crown in 1660, Willoughby was appointed Governor of the Lesser Antillean islands of St. Kitts, Nevis, Montserrat and Antigua. As referred to above, he received a (backdated) royal grant in 1662 of:

> ... all the mayne Tract of Land Region and continent of Land and Territorie and the Soyle and Grounde and the Coasts thereof beinge part of the continent of Guiana in America called Serrinam also Surrinam lying in breadth East and West one English Mile next beyond the Westerly Banks of the River of Copenam and Easterly one Mile from or beyond the River Marawyne conteyninge from East to West Forty Leagues or thereabouts ...

to be held jointly with Lawrence Hyde/Hide, the son of Lord Clarendon. He was also reappointed governor of Barbados.

The general chaos engendered by the civil wars had gradually filtered down to the various colonies, making them more vulnerable to the Dutch and the French, a fact that both of these powers exploited. Consequently, the development and maintenance of the English colony of Surinam was severely disrupted, which led ultimately to the linguistic removal of English from Surinam, which I think plays a very important role in our study of the process of creolization, in the sense that a clearer picture of what it meant to be an English-lexifier creole is probably to be had from a study of the Surinam creole languages, than from any other English-lexifier creole. The Surinam creoles are unique among the Atlantic English Creole languages in the combination of the early removal of English linguistic influence and the availability of rich sources of linguistic data from the 18th century on.

3.3. The government and governors of Surinam

The first governor of Surinam was the same Anthony Rowse who Willoughby had put in charge of his expeditionary force, a single ship with a complement of 40 men. This expedition spent five months in Surinam. Willoughby wrote to his wife the next year (Lack 2007a), saying that Surinam was reported to be "the sweetest place that ever was seen". He was going to send "a hundred men to take possession", and presumably did so that year (1651). This is referred to in the 1662 grant as the *second expedition* involving three ships. By 1652, as described in the grant, several other ships had been dispatched to Surinam at Willoughby's expense, and in that year he sailed there himself, as indicated above. Apparently he arranged for the construction of (the wooden) Fort Willoughby during this visit.

Rowse was apparently succeeded in 1654 by Lieutenant General Byam after a successful period as governor. The royalist Byam had been imprisoned in 1645, following the disastrous defeat of the Royalist forces by the Parliamentary army at the battle of Bridgewater, in South-Western England. After a few months in the Tower of London, he was exiled to Barbados, where he speedily obtained the post of Treasurer, as well as grants of land (Lack 2007a), under Willoughby. On the surrender of the Royalist forces in Barbados in January 1652, Byam was exiled to Surinam.

Byam was apparently a pragmatist. While Surinam seems to have been a Royalist stronghold, in the absence of direct royal rule, democratic elections were held for the governorship, apparently in 1658, 1659, and 1660, which Byam won. After the restoration of Royal rule in 1660, no more elections were held, and Byam continued as governor.

There was also a Parliamentary faction, though, in Surinam. Apparently, this group desired the continuation of the more democratic and less autocratic form of government under which Surinam had been ruled during, and as a partial reflection of, the Parliamentarian period in England. One focus of resentment was the fact that the governor had abolished the yearly elections for the governorship. English Surinam was ruled by a Council and a General Assembly elected by the (English) inhabitants of the various divisions at divisional meetings. There was also a General Convention of the Freeholders called at least once by Byam. The elections for the governor were described by Byam in the proclamation abolishing them as follows (Lack 2007b):

> The Governor of Surinam hath been for these three years past, annually elected by delegates chosen by the freeholders thereof: a power which necessity enforced them to assume during the distractions of our nation, but always with submission to the Supreme Authority of England.... [8th May 1661]

With the restoration, Byam indicated, this was no longer necessary. This was not to the liking of the Parliamentary minority of the population, who found him too authoritarian.

In November 1661 worries about the native Amerindian inhabitants of Surinam arose, which Lieutenant Colonel R. Sanford, a member of the "Parliamentary" camp, was sent by Byam to deal with. It had been reported that the Indians were angry with the English for punishments they had received for detaining runaway slaves. This turned out to be only a rumour, but one which was not unexpected in a region where whole colonies had been wiped out by hostile Indians. This unease on the part of the colonists is then also reminiscent of the later unease engendered by the lop-sided demographic relationship with the slave population.

In the course of the interactions described in Lack (2007b) between Byam and his democratic opponents, a number of interesting facts come to light, which I summarize here.

- As mentioned above, two slave-ships arrived from Guinea under Captain Nicholas Sulke in November 1661. These two ships are not included in the Voyages Database.
- A number of Byams's enemies, including Sanford's brother, seized a boat by force of arms. This was a shallop, or light river boat, belonging to a Dutchman who had been fishing. Byam's enemies wanted to seize the boat as a prize for the King, in order to force Byam to reveal under which power he was continuing to function as governor. He had not as yet been able to produce any written royal authority to support his abolition of the gubernatorial elections.
- This Dutchman, Cryn Jacobson, had been in Surinam since *before the English*, and was a partner in the ownership of the boat, and also in a plantation, with an Englishman. This is a unique reference to a non-English European presence in Surinam which overlapped with the beginnings of the English colony.
- Ultimately, as a result of this, several of Byam's opponents were exiled to England in 1661. Once again, divisions within the colony contributed to its weakening, and ultimate downfall.

Byam reports in his diary (Lack 2007a) on various tribulations the colony went through in 1665. Willoughby Land had its zenith in May of that year, he stated. From then on, until the end, it went into a decline that was to prove terminal. At or shortly after the time of Willoughby's last visit (January to May 1665), 200 settlers left out of discontent, according to Byam. At the same time an epidemic struck first the English capital Torarica (described by Warren (1667) as containing about a hundred houses), and then spread to the plantations. Many people apparently died. Around this time the English attempted to extend their control over a larger chunk of the Guiana coast. Ultimately these attempts failed in what is now Guyana, where the Dutch soon recaptured their colonies of Essequibo and Nieuw Zeeland (Pomeroon-Morocco). They had more success with the Dutch colony of Aprowaco (Aprouak), to the east of Cayenne. An attack commissioned by Byam brought back arms, slaves and sugar-manufacturing machinery to Surinam in March 1666. Later on they had a similar success at Cayenne, capturing the French governor and 50 prisoners.

In 1666, Byam addressed an urgent request to Willoughby for arms and ammunition in May, but this was not acted upon. In June, Willoughby instructed him to erect a stone fort at Paramaribo (Willoughby Fort) to replace the original wooden one. In August the (same?) sickness spread through the whole colony, killing "200 men, and very many women and children." In a letter quoted by Byam mention is made of "one forth part of our ablest men". At one point there were apparently only a hundred able men capable of resisting an attack. "Most of all our masons and many negroes which were at work on the fort were most sadly visited [by the sickness]." Finally, in August the ammunition requested from Barbados arrived. At the end of December the news of Willoughby's death was learned. Meanwhile Byam had put the colony on an emergency footing as far as was possible.

On the 15th of February 1667 the Dutch fleet under Crijnssen arrived, leading to the speedy surrender of the half-completed stone fort the next day. Byam then went to Torarica, where he found the English very divided about the course to follow. In the end, he surrendered the whole colony to the Dutch. Byam was subsequently court-martialed in England for his part in the loss of Surinam. He was however acquitted. And the large majority of the colonists appear to have had no problems with his rule.

When the political problems and dissension within the colony were compounded by sickness and an epidemic, the colony ceased to have the ability to defend itself against the Dutch.

3.4. Plantations, population, and slaves

According to the Calendar of State Papers (Sainsbury 1880) the population of Surinam was about 4000 in 1663, divided between the capital Torarica, and about 175 plantations. In a similar vein, a memorandum by Under-Secretary Williamson refers to a total of 1200 (European) men in Surinam. This is not incompatible with the preceding figure. This allows us to make some kind of estimate of the distribution of the population at a significant period, just before the loss of the colony to the Dutch. Over the next 10 or 15 years, the majority of the European population of Surinam would be replaced, while many slaves were removed as well, the largest number in 1675.

In May 1665, Byam states the colony had "near 1500 men, but only half armed". Arends (1995a) quotes an estimate by Voorhoeve & Lichtveld (1975), based on historical documents giving the total white population as 1500. It would appear that Byam's statement regarding the number of adult males has been wrongly interpreted, even if Byam might have been overstating the facts. Even if there were an unusually high proportion of single men among the Surinamese English population, this would presumably apply to a much greater extent to the plantations than to the capital, Voorhoeve & Lichtveld's figures cannot be correct. If we assumed that the ratio of 1:2 was correct, then we would have roughly 1300 English and 2600 slaves. If we take 500 to be the population of Torarica, splitting it 80%:20%, with 400 whites and 100 blacks. That would give us 900 English and 2500 slaves on the plantations. If we take 178 as the number of plantations (this is the number shown on a 1667 map of Surinam, surveyed at the time of the English surrender to the Dutch), then that would give us 5 Englishmen (on average), and about 14 or 15 slaves per plantation. On the whole these would not be surprising figures, but the whole question requires more attention than I have time for in this brief introduction.

In August 1665, the members of the "Hebrew" nation in Surinam were granted English nationality. Most Jews in Surinam can be assumed to have come from Cayenne following the capture of the Dutch colony there by the French in 1664. Smith (1999a) and others refer to their arrival in 1665, but this should possibly be corrected to 1664.

The remnant of the Jewish population of Cayenne now came to Surinam. The circumstances are rather obscure (these may have been the 50 "prisoners" referred to above), but it seems that the English very much wanted their skills, particularly those involved in sugar production. The Cayenne Jews speedily moved to the area around their later settlement (as it were, their capital) of Jews Savannah. The first dated burial in the Jewish cemetery at Cassipora is dated 1666 (Ben-Ur & Frankel 2009). When the Dutch took over, they recognized the great value of the Portuguese Jews' skills in running plantations. They were quickly granted Dutch nationality in 1667, and not allowed to leave despite their status as English citizens, which the Dutch denied.

As I noted above Warren describes Torarica as consisting of about 100 houses. The study of the demographics of Surinam indicates that, as far as the figures are known the ratio of Europeans to Africans in the colony during the English period remained fairly constant at about 1:2 (Arends 1995a). On the assumption that the hundred houses in the capital represent about a hundred families, we could calculate the approximate population of Torarica if we knew what the average family size was. Luckily Rens (1953) contains information that we can use to calculate this. In 1671, 102 families leave, totalling 517 people. It has up till now usually been assumed that this exodus included slaves, leading to estimates of around 250 whites and 250 blacks involved. This assumption appears to be based on the fact that departures in 1668 and 1675 both involved specific numbers of both slaves and Europeans. In fact, it is nowhere stated that slaves were removed in 1671. The very use of the word family might suggest that the people involved were largely Europeans, as no family relationships were recognized for slaves. These 102 families amounted to 517 people. This, if correct, allows us to estimate the population of Torarica as amounting to approximately 400 Europeans, together with a number, say 100, of house-slaves. I assume that the Europeans would largely be English at this time, and would include some indentured servants. Byam had to compel the plantation-owners to contribute 10% of their slave labour to help strengthen Willoughby Fort in 1666, suggesting that there was not much local labour available.

The 1671 exodus had been arranged between the Dutch and English authorities so that the English who so desired could leave Surinam (Sainsbury 1886). However, the Dutch Governor of Surinam, Philip Julius Lichtenberghe, put every possible obstacle in the path of those English who wanted to leave at this time. The English negotiator and former English Governor, Major James Banister, who himself owned a plantation on the Suriname River, came ashore in Surinam on the 12th of January following his arrival on the 9th. The Governor then read a proclamation stating among other things that English citizens who wanted to leave should give notice to him during the ten days following 16th January (Julian calendar – England)/26th January (Gregorian calendar – Netherlands). The two available ships, the America and the Johanna, were only allowed to stay in Surinam for a total of six weeks.

All the people of the Paramaribo division (except one) handed in their names. The English could leave with their possessions and old slaves (bought under English rule). In the other divisions of Surinam, the Governor indicated that people could not apply to leave until they had paid all their debts in cash, sugar, or specklewood. New slaves would have to be sold, and disagreements as to price resolved in a special court in Paramaribo on 31st January/10th February. Banister wanted the "removers" to be paid the debts owed to them first so that they could in turn pay their creditors. The Governor, however, obstructed the smooth transaction of the financial affairs as much as possible. Banister was allowed to go to his own plantation, but was prevented from communicating with anyone until after the ten day period had past. Banister says:

> "He .... would have brought all his Majesty's subjects from Surinam had things been carried as they ought and he had had shipping ; but by the perverseness of the Governor was forced to leave above half and they who had the best estates ..." (Sainsbury, p. 191)

It is fairly clear that with such a short period to settle one's affairs there was a strong disincentive for most plantation owners to leave. In Van Alphen (1962/3), Jan Reeps (writing in 1693) states that in general much sugar was planted as the rainy season was getting under way around the turn of the year, which would likely complicate matters further.

3.5. Early marronnage

Precisely because the Dutch hold on Surinam was not much more secure in the beginning than that of the English had been, there was a significant problem with runaway slaves. Already, under the English, several groups of maroons had existed. In particular, a group under their leader Jermes had built a fort in the Para region, from which they raided the plantations in that area, as Hartsinck (1770) reports. Du Plessis et al. (1752) identifiy Jermes and his group as Cormantyn Negroes, from the Gold Coast. Later this group moved west to the Coppename. Shortly afterwards the Dutch governor Van Sommelsdijk agreed peace treaties in 1684 with the Caribs, Waraus, and Arawaks, granting them freedom from enslavement, and also reportedly concluded a treaty with the Coppename Maroons.[5] This group later merged with the Western Caribs. These are now referred to in the Carib language as *Muraato* (i.e. Mulatto) referring to their mixed origin. In Dutch they were referred to as *Karboegers*,[6] a term of Brazilian Portuguese provenance. It is derived from the Brazilian term *caboclo* "a person of mixed Brazilian Amerindian and European descent', the common factor in the semantics being the reference to a person of mixed Amerindian origin.

Table 2. Time table (based on Smith 2002) of the early historical development of the Surinam colony

Date	Historical events	Hypothesized linguistic events
1651	Willoughby's settlement of Surinam	
1652	Earliest recorded slave shipment from Slave Coast by the English	
c.1660	Marronnage of Jermes' group in the Para region	
1664	The main group of Jewish settlers arrives from Cayenne	... conceivably with **Portuguese Creole**-speaking slaves (a hypothesis discussed in Smith (1999a))
c.1665		**Sranan** creolized from Caribbean Plantation Pidgin (a hypothesis defended in Smith (1999a))
1665	200 English leave (Lack 2007a).	
1667	The treaty of Breda, by which Surinam was surrendered to the Dutch.	
1668	67 English leave with 412 slaves (Arends 1995a)	
1671	512 English leave	
1675	250 English leave with 981 slaves	
1679	European population hits a low of ca. 460 (Arends 2002)	
c.1680	ca. 50 English leave with ca. 50 slaves (Arends 1995a)	*Sranan* partly relexified to *Portuguese* (*Creole*), and named ***Dju-tongo*** ('Jew-language') on the Middle Suriname River plantations (defended in Smith 1999a)

---

5. It is in fact possible that this treaty included the Karboegers because of their symbiosis with the Western Caribs.
6. Earlier *Carboekel* (Sranan: *Carboekloe*) (Nepveu 1770).

c.1684	Treaty with Jermes' maroons on the Coppename	[The mixed Afro-Amerindian descendants of these speak a Carib (Amerindian)dialect]
1690	Mass escape of slaves who founded the Matjáu clan of the Saramaccan tribe	The Matjáu spoke ***Dju-tongo***, i.e. Saramaccan (in addition to African languages, including Fongbe)
1712	Supposed mass escape of slaves who founded the Ndyuka tribe	[The Ndyuka spoke *Plantation Sranan*.]
1715	Departure of Matjáu from the general area of Providence plantation. Other clans remain longer (Price 1983).	
1749–1762	All Saramaccan clans in general area of Bákakuúun (Price 1983)	
1760s	Treaties with Ndyuka, Matawai, Saramaccan maroons	

Notably, this group did not end up speaking a Creole language, or an African one, but an Amerindian one, possibly suggesting that when this group was formed (around 1660) no *creole* first language as such existed, although, as we will see later (Smith, this volume on Ingredient X), there is reason to assume that an extended English-lexifier pidgin had been brought from Barbados.

Price (1983) has described the beginnings of the Saramaccan tribe of maroons in the period from around 1690 to 1710. The origin of many clans is bound up with the history of the Portuguese Jews, from whose language they have taken many Portuguese words (cf. Smith & Cardoso 2004), and whose names are preserved in a number of clan names.

Striking in general is the very tight timetable involved in the formation of the various creole languages in Surinam. The rapid sequence of historical and linguistic events has much to tell us about the formation of the creole languages in Surinam. In Table 2, I provide a revised version of the timetable of these events given in Smith (2002). Some events are hypothesized; others are historical.

4. Substrate or adstrate?

During the revision of this chapter, my co-editor, Pieter Muysken, drew my attention to the fact that as well as post-creolization linguistic influence from colonial languages (Dutch with regard to Surinam, and English with regard to Jamaican Creole) being regarded as *adstrates* instead of *superstrates* (cf. Smith 2009a), that also Kikongo and Gbe influences in the Surinam Creole languages might be regarded as *adstratal* rather than *substratal*. The idea of very rapid creolization (Smith 2006) would tend to support this idea (cf. also van den Berg, Muysken, and Smith, this volume). Two considerations encourage me to believe that this is correct.

One is a striking difference in the form and syntax of the (often contrastive) focus marker/highlighter in Saramaccan as against that in Sranan and Ndyuka.

(1) Focus-marking in the Surinam Creoles
Sranan (1765): **da da** ply ...   'that's the place that ...'
                FOCDEF.SG place   (van den Berg 2007: 292)
Sranan: **na** yu ...   'it's you that ...'
                FOC 2SG.EMPH
Ndyuka: **na** yu ...   'it's you that ...'
                FOC 2SG.EMPH
Saramaccan: dí   mujée **wε** ... 'it's the woman that ...'
                DEF.ART woman FOC   (Veenstra p.c.)

We find *da* (*a/na*, which are developments of older *da*) as a highlighter used in Sranan and Ndyuka preceding the focussed element, but we find *wε* in Saramaccan following the focussed element. In Smith (1996), I identified *wε* as being virtually identical in function and syntax to the focus-marker in Fongbe. Note that it is not only identical segmentally, but also tonewise. It bears an explicit low tone in Saramaccan, and in those Eastern Gbe languages in which it occurs.

(2) Focus marking in Saramaccan and certain Eastern Gbe languages
Saramaccan: dí   mujée **wε** ... 'it's the woman that ...'
             DEF.ART woman FOC   (Veenstra p.c.)
Fongbe: wémà lé **wè** ...   'it's the books that ...'
             book DEF.PL FOC   (Höftmann 2003: 30)
Gungbe: wémà **wè** ...   'A BOOK ...'
             book FOC   (Aboh 2004a: 240)

With our knowledge that Gbe (and Kikongo) were the principal African languages represented by the slaves that were around in large numbers in the date (1690) assigned by Price (1983) to the formation of the Saramaccan tribe, we can suspect that this periodization had something to do with the adoption of a Fongbe highlighter in Saramaccan. Above I showed that this coincides with a major disappearance of slaves from the poll-tax statistics between 1684 and 1695. Why should a Fongbe structure replace the already existing Sranan one? Why, the reader may ask, do I assume a pre-existing Sranan basis on which Saramaccan was constructed (see also Table 2)? The short answer is that the similarities in phonology and syntax are so great between the two languages that this must be assumed. Note that I assume a date of around 1680 for the creation of "Djutongo" ('Jew language') on the Portuguese Jewish plantations on the Middle Suriname River. The mixed English-Portuguese creole that Saramaccan is must have been formed on plantations where Portuguese was spoken. In what follows, I will devote some space to a consideration of the work of Richard Price on the earliest Saramaccan escapees and the major clans they formed. I concentrate on the linguistic background where such evidence is mentioned.

Price (1983: 51–52) ascribes the formation of the senior clan of the Saramaccan tribe, the Matjáu, to a raid in 1690, which he terms "The Great Raid", on a plantation on the Cassewinica Creek mentioned in Nassy (1788: 76) belonging to a Portuguese Jew called Imanuël Machado.[7]

Another important early clan, the Abaísa (formerly *Labadissa*), was called after the owners of La Providence plantation, the Labadisten (a pietist Christian sect), whose members had acquired a reputation in Surinam for treating their slaves with unusual cruelty (Price 1983: 70–71). The slaves here rebelled in 1693. Price (1983: 72) supplies the following commentary:

The documentary evidence ... reveals the Abaísas from the first to have possessed unusually large villages (known to outsiders as the Papa Dorpen ['Papa Villages', NS] ... as well as fierce warriors, and they seem to have constituted a major force within the nascent Saramaka nation.

---

7. This surname is derived from the Portuguese word *machado* 'axe'. The name of the Matjáu clan is identical to the Saramaccan word *matjáu* 'axe' which is clearly derived from the Portuguese word. Price (1983) relates the clan name to the name of the owner, who was killed in the raid.

At least two other important clans came into being in the 1690s, the Nasí and the Lángu. The Nasí, who get their name from the most important Jewish family in Surinam, do not appear to have any regional connections, although a study of their personal names might provide some clues.

The Lángu derived their name from Loango, a former kingdom near the mouth of the Congo (Zaire) River. In the 18th century, they were known as Loango.[8] They consist of two sub-clans, the Kaapátu and the Kadósu. The leader of Kaapátu was Káasi (Kaásipúmbu[9]). He led an escape of a work-gang working on a creek to the south of Paramaribo (Price 1983: 77). The name Kaapátu is homophonous with the Saramaccan word *kaapátu* 'tick'.[10] The Kadósu sub-clan only fled around twenty years later according to Price, and I will not discuss them.

Price discusses Matjáu-Abaísa rivalry:

> Saramakas express the rivalry between Matjáus and Abaísas in various ways. One of its neatest formulations – in the ritual language known as Papá – recalls a famous singing contest. *Papá* performances take place as the climactic event of funerals. ... Each song has a leader and a chorus. This famous contest involved two leaders – one Matáu and one Abaísa – who agreed to sing as it were, "to the death." (1983: 148)

> The choice of *papá*-playing as the idiom for expressing Matjáu-Abaísa rivalry is not gratuitous. Abaísas since the time of their collective escape nearly three hundred years ago [in 1983, NS], have referred to themselves by variants of this name (Alabaisa, Labadissa), ... Outsiders (non-Saramakas) during the eighteenth century, however, generally called them instead "Papa negers," and their village "Papa Dorp." (1983: 149)

> Today, Abaísas and Matjáus are considered the best Saramaka *papá* players, with everyone agreeing (including Matjáus) agreeing that the Abaísas are the true Masters. (1983: 149)

> Its speakers/players refer to *papá* as *aladá*, confirming its specific African roots. (1983: 149, footnote)

---

8. Price (1983: 92, footnote) refers to the large village of Tuído (Toledo) being called Loangodorp in 1747.
9. Káasi (a Saramaccan rendition of the Dutch name *Claas*) is from Púmbu (Price 1983: 77). Púmbu is from Kikongo Mpúmbu, and refers to Stanley Pool, 300 km. upstream from the Atlantic. Púmbu is also the name of a Kikongo-based ritual language used by the Saramaccans.
10. Conceivably in reference to the *bites* they were inflicting on the Dutch colonists.

The early history of Surinam   39

These quotations from Price (1983) suggest strongly that the Matjáu and Abaísa clans were strongly subject to Gbe linguistic influence. This offers us a way of accounting for the Saramaccan focus marker *wɛ* in contrast to the *da/na* of Sranan and Ndyuka. It could be hypothesized that this particular usage, as also that of Fongbe question words for "who" and "what" (see Smith, this volume on the Gbe lexical contribution to the Surinam Creoles) was an adstratal feature present in early Saramaccan, rather than some kind of substrate feature, which latter position would actually make a simple explanation much more difficult. The mention of Papá – Offra/Xwla/(Grande) Popo on the Benin Coast – and Aladá – the name of the inland capital of the Kingdom of Aladá/Allada/Ardra captured by the Fon in 1724 (see Aboh & Smith, this volume on the Eastern Aja-Tado culture area for an account of Gbe wars and migrations) – reveals the linguistic and cultural importance of Gbe ethnicity in Surinam, but this is more easily explained as an adstratal linguistic feature than a substratal one.

Table 3. The disparate origins of the earliest recorded slaves in the Voyages Database (2009)

	Senegambia	Gold Coast	Slave Coast	Bight of Biafra	W C Africa	Unknown	**Total**
1660–1664				130 (100%)			**130**
1665–1669				996 (37.2%)	980 (36.6%)	705 (26.3%)	**2681**
1670–1674				753 (39.1%)	1173 (60.9%)		**1926**
1675–1679	422 (12.4%)	758 (22.3%)	816 (24.0%)	281 (7.6%)	1027 (30.2%)	391 (11.2%)	**3695**

This would be in agreement with what is known about the various sources of the slave population and the conclusions regarding ethnicity which can probably be drawn from them. The first recorded shipment of slaves from the Bight of Benin (Slave Coast) arrives in 1677, followed by another in 1678. The third one only arrives in 1682, and others rapidly followed. In Table 2, I estimate the creolization/nativization of Sranan at about 1665. This would obviously be incompatible with the Gbe languages forming a substrate for the Surinam Creole languages, as there would have been no Gbe speakers in Surinam at the time as far as we know. Putting the formation of Sranan so early is necessary if we are to assume that Sranan formed one of the inputs to the formation of Dju-tongo around 1680. I regard Dju-tongo as the precursor of Saramaccan (see Smith 1999a).

Several chapters in this volume deal with or include discussion of parallels between the Surinam Creoles and the Gbe languages. Yakpo & Bruyn discuss parallels in locative structures between Sranan and Ewe(Gbe). Essegbey deals with likely influence on verb semantics. Van den Berg includes discussion of derivational morphology and property items. Aboh and Smith (on non-iconic reduplications) deal with the syntax of reduplication as an inheritance from the Gbe languages. Smith (on creole phonology) includes discussion of phonological influence from Gbe and Kikongo. And Smith (on the Gbe lexical contribution to the Surinam Creoles) deals with the lexical contribution from the Gbe languages. Many features appear to reflect Gbe influence, but this must be adstratal.

The Lángu, by their name (Loango) have a Kikongo heritage. Is their lexical contribution to the Surinam creoles indicative of a Kikongo substrate? Between 1669 and 1675 we have 10 shipments from West Central Africa. Three ports of departure are specified, Loango, Malembo and Mpinda. Loango was the capital of the Kingdom of Loango north of the former Kingdom of Kakongo; Malembo was the capital of the former Kingdom of Kakongo, later incorporated into the Kingdom of Kongo (now in the Angolan exclave of Cabinda); Mpinda was the port of the province of So(n)yo in the Kingdom of Kongo near the mouth of the Congo River.

As the contribution of Kikongo appears at present to be restricted to two things – the lexicon (Smith, this volume on the Kikongo lexical contribution to the Surinam Creoles) and the phonological patterning of nasality (Smith, this volume on creole phonology) – it would seem that Kikongo also is not a substrate but an adstrate of the Surinam creoles. The timing, although more favourable, is not sufficient justification for considering Kikongo as a substrate language. In Smith (this volume on creole phonology), I will argue that the influence of Kikongo should be regarded as coterminous with that of Gbe.

Another reason for not regarding either the Kikongo or the Gbe-speakers to be substratal, though vaguer, can be found in an early metalinguistic remark on African language usage in Surinam in Warren (1667).

> They [the slaves, NS] are there a mixture of several nations, which are always clashing with one another, so that no conspiracy can be hatching, but it is presently detected by some party amongst themselves disaffected to the plot, because their enemies have a share in it ... (1667: 19)

Although the earliest years of the slave trade are missing from the records, this remark of Warren's seems to ring true in the light of what we do know.

5. Ritual languages

Three ritual languages continued (and continue) to be spoken in Surinam by Winti adepts: The *Papá, Fodu* or *Aladá* with a nucleus of Gbe lexical items; The *Púmbu* or *A(m)púku* with a nucleus of Kikongo lexical items; and the *K(r)omanti* with a nucleus of Twi/Akan lexical items. They are used to communicate with the various gods of the syncretized Winti religion, which is shared by all the creole-speaking groups in Surinam. Although they are ritual languages, much reduced and fairly formulaic, their existence does indicate that these three African languages remained in use for some time as regular spoken languages. How many generations this situation lasted is completely unclear, although it seems credible that, in settlements called *Papa Dorpen*[11] or *Loangodorp*, the *Papá* or *Loango* languages would have been spoken.

6. Summary

We can conclude that the situation of Surinam is special, amongst the Caribbean colonies, and that its creole languages offer us a unique linguistic test-bed for a number of reasons:

- The historical demographic evidence suggests that several African regions were involved as slave-catchment areas in the formative period, which did not result in any particular "substrate" language being involved in the creolization of Sranan or Saramaccan.
- What seems to have been the case is that from about 1675 till about 1720 the imported slaves tended more and more to belong to two language-groups, the closely related Eastern Gbe languages, and Kikongo. The influence of these two languages looks likely for various reasons to have been adstratal. In particular the many identified words of African origin in the Surinam Creoles are predominantly of Gbe and Kikongo origin (see Smith, this volume on the Gbe and Kikongo lexical contribution to the Surinam Creoles).

---

11. *Dorp* is Dutch for 'village'.

- After 1720 or so, the Gold Coast became the principal supplier of slaves. Although the Twi/Akan language shared the fate of becoming the nucleus of a ritual language, the number of lexical items entering the ordinary languages appears to have been much fewer in number than in the case of the Gbe and Kikongo which were present earlier .
- Due to its peculiar history, first as an English, and then a Dutch, colony the original superstrate or lexifier-language, English, disappeared to all extents and purposes after about thirty years or so. This meant that its influence on the creole languages that developed in Surinam was constrained.
- The new superstrate/adstrate language, Dutch, was in strong competition in the relevant early period with Portuguese, and not well established. It has left a heritage of numerous words in Sranan, with much fewer in the Maroon Creoles.
- The Dutch colonial power had insufficient control over the plantations, leading to very substantial early marronage. The hived-off Maroon Creoles provide us with a unique window on the early stages of Creole language formation in Surinam.
- There has been very substantial historical, ethnohistorical, and anthropological work on Surinam. It was recognized early on that Surinam could provide an important source of insights into creole language and culture formation.
- Due to the presence, primarily, of the Hernnhut missionaries starting in the 18th century, there is abundant documentation of early forms of the creole languages of Surinam.

For all these reasons, the Surinam Creoles provide a unique opportunity for studying the role of the African languages in creole genesis.

Migrations, ethnodynamics, and geolinguistics in the Eastern Aja-Tado cultural area

Enoch Aboh and Norval Smith

1. Introduction

In this chapter, we will attempt to identify the type of Gbe-language responsible for the substantial Gbe linguistic influence on the creole languages of Surinam. To be able to do this, we have to carry out two main exercises. Firstly, we have to get a sufficiently clear picture of the complex political and ethnic interactions among the main ethnic groups[1] (hence EGs) in the eastern Gbe territory, and in the 17th century in particular. We have decided to restrict things to the eastern part of the Gbe world for a simple reason. All the ports, from which slaves were exported and markets at which slaves were traded during this period, were located there.

With regard to the Surinamese Creoles, work by Smith (this volume on the Gbe lexical contribution to the Surinam Creoles) makes clear that the phonological developments in the identifiable Gbe words in Saramaccan are those typical of eastern forms of Gbe, in terms of Capo's groundbreaking work on Gbe historical phonology (Capo 1991).

The Gbe elements in the Surinam creole languages give us some clues as to which elements to look for. Unfortunately the Gbe varieties spoken by the different EGs, which we refer to in the rest of this chapter as Gbe lects,[2] and in particular the eastern Gbe lects, often share the same phonological developments, and have many lexical items in common. Across the whole spectrum of Gbe, there is however a rather striking difference in the forms of grammatical words and affixes. For this reason the actual Gbe lexical

---

1. We will use the term ethnic group to refer to the various identifiable Gbe communities regardless of their present or former political status.
2. Many Gbe speech-forms do not differ sufficiently from each other to be regarded as different languages. In order not to get involved in futile discussions as to the number of languages involved we prefer to use the term *lect*. So each ethnic group has its own lect (and even sublects in the case of EGs that are spoken over a larger area, or in two separate areas). The vaguer term *variety* will range over lects and sublects.

items in Saramaccan and other Surinam Creoles are not always terribly useful for the identification of their source Gbe lects. In addition, there is no extensive lexical material available for most eastern Gbe lects. For this reason, we will restrict our attention to Gbe functional elements. Our examination of these will take place in the second section.

We do have at our disposal three Gbe function words that have rather unusually made it into Saramaccan, apparently uniquely among Surinam Creoles. These are known from the literature (Smith 1987, 1996), and do provide valuable information for our purposes. We will return to this at the end of our contribution. The main part of the second part of this chapter will however be concerned with something that is at first sight utterly trivial. However, it is a triviality which is the source of a great deal of differentiation among the eastern Gbe lects, and which can be used as a diagnostic feature providing clues as to which Gbe variety was dominant among the Gbe-speaking slaves taken to Surinam. The Gbe languages have retained as a vestige of the Volta-Congo noun-class prefix system a number of prefixes (invariant for number) of apparent zero-functionality. These prefixes differ in number and shape among the various lects, and provide us then with a tool we can use for comparison with the Gbe words in the Surinam Creoles.

We will attempt to understand the extent to which the realization of such functional elements among the Gbe varieties can be related to the population movements described in Sections 2–4 of this chapter during the period in question. While this study will help us understand the grouping of the Gbe languages as they are spoken today (Capo 1991; Kluge 2000), it may also shed some light on earlier forms of these languages and the places where they were spoken. This, of course, is relevant to the genesis of the Surinamese Creoles because it sheds a clearer light on the languages spoken by Gbe slaves that have contributed to the development of these Creoles.

2. Introduction to Gbe ethnodynamics

This section of the paper discusses the migrations of the Gbe-speaking EGs in the Aja-Tado area[3] during the 17th and early 18th centuries. It focuses on possible interactions of such population movements with the slave trade

---

3. The Aja-Tado is an area straddling the border of present-day Togo and Benin (formerly Dahomey).

with Surinam, and the role of the slaves imported from this area in the development of the Surinam Creoles. During the 17th century, all the major ports on the Slave Coast (e.g. Jeken, Whydah) were in the east of the Gbe-speaking area. Since these ports played a crucial role in the geo-politics of this area and were often at the source of political conflicts that resulted in various migrations, while at the same time affecting the slave-trade, we will only concern ourselves with those Gbe-speaking EGs that migrated to the east side of the river Mono, as we have already mentioned. In other words, we will treat the various migrations involving the kingdom of Allada and its surrounding satellites (Jeken, Offra, Whydah), and the later migrations involving the kingdoms of Agbomey, and Xogbonu.

2.1. Migrations in the Aja-Tado area

Not much is known[4] about the migrations of the Gbe-speaking communities before their settlement in what became the kingdom of Tado[5] on the Mono River, though oral traditions suggest that they came from southern Nigeria (i.e. the former Oyo empire) via the former kingdom of Ketu (in present-day Benin) probably before the 14th century. For the purposes of this chapter, we take Tado to be the source of expansion of the Gbe speaking community eastwards. As Map 1 shows, we focus on the area delimited to the west by the river Mono (i.e. Tado and environs, on the north west, and Grand Popo on the south west) to the north by Agbomey, to the east by the river Wo/Weme/Oueme (i.e. Xogbonu and environs), and to the south by the sea. This area roughly corresponds to what was to become the kingdom of Allada (Law 1997: 15).

We distinguish two migration periods: before and after 1600. These migrations also coincide with the rise and fall of Allada, and are therefore of particular interest to our study of the diffusion of noun-class prefixes in a south-eastern direction, and ultimately across the Atlantic as a consequence of the slave trade.

---

4. In what say about the history of the Aja-Tado peoples in Sections 2-4 we base ourselves primarily on the work of Pazzi (1979), Akindélé and Aquessy (1953), and Law (1997).
5. This is now represented by the village of Tado near the Benin border.

46 Enoch Aboh and Norval Smith

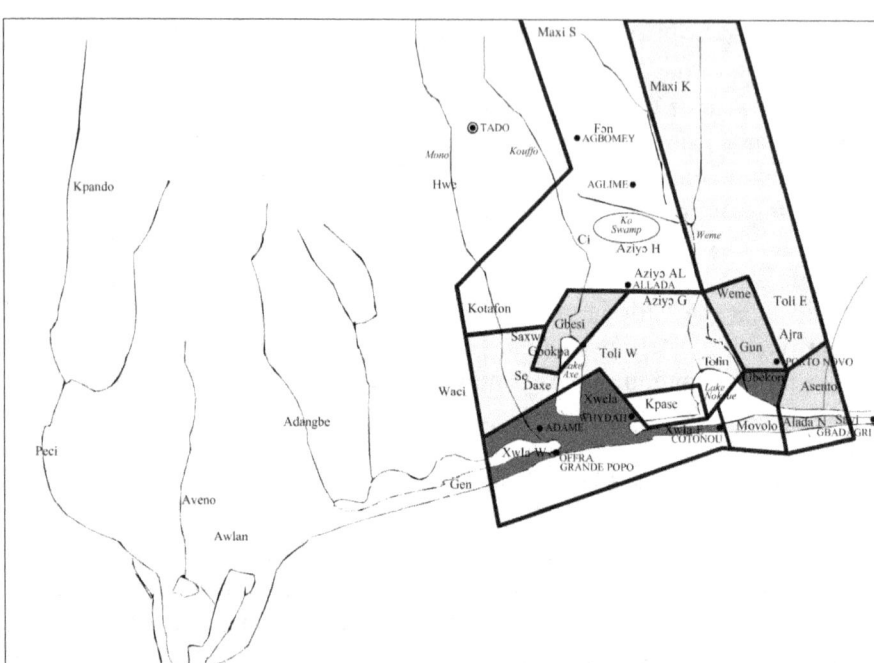

Map 1. The Eastern Gbe speaking area. Gbe Groups are indicated by their 20th century distribution.

The shading on the map will be explained later.

2.2. Migrations before 1600

According to Pazzi (1979), the first major migrations out of Tado (see Map 1) towards the east led different Aja groups to settle to the East of the river Mono in roughly the 14th and 15th centuries. This period corresponds to the migration of the Hwe people in the direction of the Kouffo River (see Map 1) under Adja-Fofolili. Similarly, the Ayizo (under the rule of Adja-Dosu) crossed the marshes of Ko, then Tofa and founded Davye (the future Allada). The Ayizo expansion then continued south-east where different groups emerged such as the Toli, the Ajala (Ajla or Ajra), and the Kada. These groups settled between the River Weme and the River Kouffo, as well as on the shores of Lake Nokoue. It is also during this period that the Xwla founded Adame on the shore of Lake Axe where they produced salt.

With regard to areal politics, it is worth noting that the Hwe people and the Ayizo people remained under the authority of Tado even after their migrations. The Xwla, however, became virtually politically independent, presumably as a result of their economic independence.

2.3. The settlement of the Agasuvi

The migrations after 1600 were subsequent to the settlement of the Agasuvi clan in Allada. According to the tradition, this clan left Tado following a falling-out within the royal family.[6] They went eastward and crossed the Ko marsh in the direction of Lake Axe, which they crossed and settled in Dekame. They later joined the Ayizo people in Davye (the future Allada (see Map 1)). The Ayizo people were then under the authority of the Xwla chief in Adame, which was probably at that time a satellite of Tado.

2.4. The Independence of Allada

Under the influence of the Agasuvi clan Allada quickly developed into a powerful and prosperous kingdom in the West African coastal area. For instance, the village Dauma (situated on the east side of the Mono) has been known to travellers since at least 1513. Similarly, the oldest document referring to Allada is a letter dating from 1539 that reported the behaviour of the king of Benin (Nigeria) with regard to ambassadors including those coming from Allada. That the king of Allada could send ambassadors to neighbouring kingdoms suggests that this was a well-established kingdom.

The political stability of Allada, as well as its flourishing economy, is indicated by several documents dating from the 16th century. For example, a document dating from 1570 mentioned trading relations between Allada and São Tomé. Similarly a Portuguese trader reported in 1574 that the king of Allada was trading in slaves, palm oil, cloth, yams, etc. In the same period, there was also mention of slave trade from the port of Allada, which at that time is thought to have been Gbagri (Gbadagri). The importance of Allada, and its cooperation with Western kingdoms, is suggested by the fact that European traders as well as missionaries settled there or nearby (e.g. in

---

6. Agasu married a princess from Aja-Tado. His descendants (first generation), the Agasuvi, wanted to succeed the dead king but this was impossible because only the princes or their sons could become King (i.e. the children of a princess could not become King). There was a dispute as a result of which Agasu and his people had to leave Aja-Tado.

Whydah/Ouidah) in the first half of the 17th century. Note, for instance, that Spanish missionaries published "La Doctrina Christina", a catechism in Spanish text and its translation into a Gbe language in 1658 (Labouret & Rivet 1929). Similarly, it was reported that the Allada king sent an ambassador to Philip IV, king of Spain, in 1658/1660, and to France in 1670. This clearly indicates that Allada was a powerful and stable kingdom with international allies, and controlling various (slave) trading ports.

2.5. Migrations from Allada to Jeken and Dame 1600–1620/migrations after 1600

In the early 17th century (i.e.1600–1620), the Agasuvi clan split into three groups. Some members of the royal family (following Agbokoli Kokpon) settled in Allada, now the central nucleus of the kingdom. Other members of the royal family (following Avesu Dangbasa) migrated southwards to settle in Jeken. As a first approximation, we assume that this clan includes the ancestors of the founder of Xogbonu (Porto Novo) after the fall of Allada in 1724. A third group (following Degbagli Do Aklin) migrated northwards in the direction of Danme. This is basically the same location as Danxome (= Dahomey), the nucleus of the future Fon kingdom.

After this division, the Allada kingdom can be said to consist of a central nucleus, Allada, under the rule of the 'King of the Kings' (*àxɔ́sú àxɔ́sú lé tɔ̀n*), and two satellite regions Agbomey and Jeken, which were ruled by simple chiefs (*tò gán*) or subordinated state kings (*àxɔ́sú*) (see Law 1997: 20). This suggests that the Kingdom of Allada was relatively decentralized. However, the competition between these three poles of power and the growth of slave trade quickly led to a period of conquest and defeat that would shape the geopolitics of the southeastern Gbe country for the following centuries.

3. Migrations and the trans-Atlantic slave trade

The development of Allada was primarily based on both trans-Saharan trade and trans-Atlantic trade. The latter implied control over the ports involved in the slave trade. As this reached its peak, the competition between the regional political entities for the control over these ports led to a period of instability that would change the political organisation of the region and adversely affect the slave trade.

For instance, the development of Jeken and its port led the local power-base to rebel against the central authority of Allada. As a consequence of this Allada imposed embargos on Jeken, favouring the rival port of Glexwe (Whydah). Within 20 years or so, Glexwe became one of the most important ports involved in the trans-Atlantic trade: missionaries visited Glexwe in 1667, and Father Celestin (from Brussels) opened a school there in 1682, indicating its importance for the outside world. This rapid development led to a succession of conflicts between Allada and the Xwla of Jeken, between Allada and the Oyo of Ekpe, between the Xwla (of Jeken) and the Xweda (Xwela) in Glexwe (Whydah), between the Xwla and the Gen who had shortly before migrated from Accra on the Gold Coast, and so on.

This period of instability and successive migrations is also characterised by the expansion of the Kingdom of Dahomey and its search for an outlet to the coast. This of course brought further conflict and thus reinforced the migration process.

With regard to the slave trade, it seems reasonable to say that given this period of great instability, the victims of slavery are likely also to have been the victims of conflicts. This working hypothesis is supported by the fact that it was common practice to install blockades on trade roads in order to damage the economy of the enemy state. In this case, since Agbomey, the capital of Dahomey was located to the north of Allada, it is conceivable that most slaves would not have been imported from further north than the northern frontiers of Dahomey. Put differently, we consider Agbomey and environs to be the northern limit of most slave imports in this area.

The following section presents some key dates with regard to the expansion of Dahomey and its consequence on migration.

4. The expansion of Dahomey and its consequences for southward migrations

By 1640, the kingdom of Dahomey started a policy of expansion (probably motivated by the desire to take control of Allada and extend its authority to the coast). This policy led to a number of conflicts that culminated in the fall of Allada in 1724. In 1727 Glexwe, the capital of the Xweda kingdom was defeated. The Xweda people were then dispersed and new populations (i.e. Fon, or communities favourable to them) settled in Glexwe.[7] This would mean that by the mid of the 18th century, Dahomey had colonised the entire area between the Couffo river and the Oueme (Weme) river. In addition, the Dahomey power had developed a linguistic policy that involved imposing its language (i.e. Fongbe) on the defeated peoples.

During the expansion period, in 1707, the Ayizo people living north to the Ko were defeated and migrated to the South-East in direction to the Wo (Oueme/Weme) river where they founded Dangbo. The Xwla people were force to leave Jeken. Similarly, the Toli (a group affiliated to the Ayizo) migrated eastwards towards Avrankou (near Xogbonu). The Maxi people were also defeated and fell under the authority of Dahomey. This period is also characterised by a series of conflicts between Dahomey and Xogbonu that only ended during the era of colonisation.

4.1. Tensions, conflicts, and slave trade

Even though one would expect that such a period of instability would have favoured the slave trade by increasing the number of slaves, Table 1 suggests the contrary. Observe, for instance that while slave trade was flourishing under the rule of Allada, it slows down, in proportional terms, during the period of the expansion of Dahomey, and finally comes to a virtual stop. Many fewer slaves were exported from the Slave Coast after 1740.

With regard to the number of slaves embarked at ports located on the Slave Coast and transported to Surinam, it is interesting to notice that the relevant period for Gbe influence on the Surinam Creoles coincides with the rule of Allada. Note that slave imports from the ports of Jeken and Whydah are significantly reduced after the fall of Allada in 1724. When exports do resume in 1729, slaves are exported initially from Jeken, and later from Gbadagri after the destruction of Jeken by the Fon in 1732.

Taken alone, this table does not tell us much about the exact origins of the slaves deported to Surinam.

---

7. There are no recorded slave exports from the Slave Coast in the years 1726–1728, presumably reflecting the years of instability in Glexwe (Whydah).

Table 1. Slave imports from Africa to Surinam (Voyages Database 2009)[8]

5 year period	westward areas	Gold Coast	Slave Coast	Bight of Biafra	W C Africa	Unknown	Total
1665–1669				996 (37.2%)	980 (36.6%)	705 (26.3%)	2681
1670–1674				753 939.1%	1173 (60.9%)		1926
1675–1679	422 (12.4%)	758 (22.3%)	816 (24.0%)	281 (7.6%)	1027 (30.2%)	391 (11.2%)	3695
1680–1684	255 (8.5%)		1322 (44.2%)	281 (9.4%)	1134 (37.9%)		2992
1685–1689		175 (2.5%)	1734 (24.3%)	844 (11.8%)	3961 (55.5%)	417 (5.8%)	7131
1690–1694			1467 (68.8%)		665 (31.2%)		2132
1695–1699			2269 (46.6%)		2384 (48.9%)	220 (4.5%)	4873
1700–1704			2855 (86.0%)		465 (14.0%)		3320
1705–1709	387 (5.9%)	421 (7.4%)	2964 (52.1%)		1078 (19.0%)	834 (14.7%)	5684
1710–1714			1375 (66.1%)		705 (33.9%)		2080
1715–1719		174 (3.0%)	3660 (63.7%)		1075 (18.7%)	837 (14.6%)	5746
1720–1724		277 (12.4%)	1954 (86.6%)				2231
1725–1729		4731 (59.1%)	2229 (27.8%)		632 (7.9%)	417 (5.2%)	8009
1730–1734		4190 (48.6%)	3879 (45.0%)		544 (6.3%)		8613
1735–1739		5383 (67.5%)	2321 (29.1%)			276 (3.5%)	7980
1740–1749	5941 (25.0%)	1839 (7.8%)	478 (2.0%)		7193 (30.3%)	8281 (34.9%)	23732

8. Grey cells indicate sources supplying more than 40% of the imported in a given half-decade. The figures for the *decade* 1740–1749 are directly taken from Borges (2013). The *half-decade* figures are recalculated from the same source.

But when put in context, that is, the constant pressure from Dahomey on the coastal region, which generated many captives (Law 1997), but often had the effect of blocking the slave trade routes and affecting Allada economically, the need for Allada to control slave trade in the area and keep contact with Europeans, the competition between Jeken and Whydah, and their claims for independence that often led Allada to embargo the slave trade from these two ports, this table suggests that the slaves deported to Surinam between 1651 and 1749 could not have originated further north than Agbomey (Dahomey) as we have suggested above.

More to the point, we may speculate that the slave sources were located between Dahomey and Allada to the north and between Allada and Whydah and Jeken to the south. Taking into consideration the facts mentioned concerning migrations in this area, we may further speculate that the people who suffered most from this were the earliest migrants, that is, the Ayizo.

5. Eastern Gbe Noun-Prefix Systems

The second part of the chapter switches to patterns of migration and domination revealed by the occurrences of the various noun-class prefix systems. We attempt to relate the various developments in these in the Eastern Gbe area, and their possible relationship to the prefix-system seen in Saramaccan and the other Surinam Creoles.

Our purpose in examining class prefixes in the various Eastern Gbe varieties is to trace patterns of influence among the various lects. In particular, we hope to be able to observe the linguistic effects of the increasing domination of the Eastern Gbe region by the Agasuvi, and in particular the Fon. This domination reveals itself in two fashions: firstly, the physical movement of populations, and secondly, the spread of influence from one lect to another in the class-prefix system.

So, in in the southern half of the Eastern Gbe country we will see that there are Gbe groups who can be basically classified as Fon-type or Gun-type. In addition, other Gbe groups' noun-class systems reveal the influence of one or other of these two. In this way, the routes of influence southwards can be traced.

In addition, the central town of Alada and the southern town of Whydah early on became Fon-speaking as the result of conquest.

5.1. The present day Gbe ethnic groups and their prefix classes

The communities associated with the various Gbe lects were provisionally grouped in terms of a combination of historical and linguistic factors into three main groups. We repeat Map 1 here for convenience.

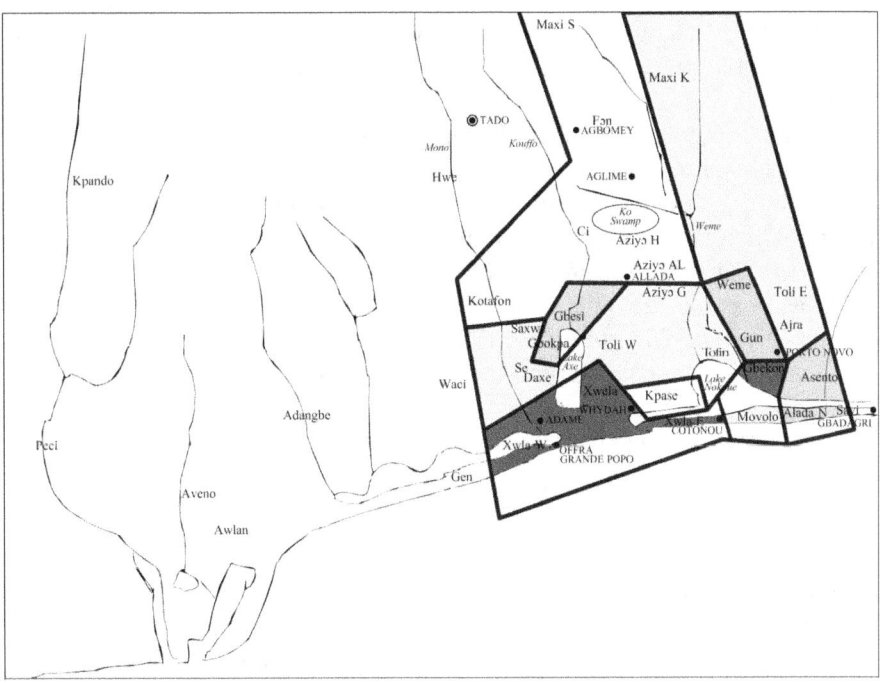

Map 1. The Eastern Gbe speaking area. Gbe Groups are indicated by their 20th century distribution.

The Xwla-Xwela on the coast are marked in dark grey), the Emigrant Ayizo in a band behind the coast, in light grey, and the Agasuvi in two groups – the Fon-type to the north, in white, and the Gun-type, intermediate grey, penetrating the Ayizo. It was unclear to us which group the Maxi belong to, but this is irrelevant for our present purposes as they are the northernmost Eastern Gbe people.

We have examined the distribution of five noun-class prefixes in the Eastern Gbe varieties. The relevance of a classification based on such a restricted domain may of course be questioned, but some considerations lead us to believe that this may well be an advantage. Firstly, consider the low functional load of these prefixes. Some class prefixes have disappeared in some lects, apparently without impairing comprehension. Because of the open syllable nature of Gbe phonological structure, and the existence in Gbe of the same apocope-under-hiatus processes that we find in many West African languages, class prefixes are frequently deleted sentence-internally and always compound-internally, anyway, leading to a situation where prefixes are more frequently not realised than realised. It is precisely because of the non-critical nature of these prefixes then, their lack of functionality, that we think that the present largely "decorative" systems may in fact represent the situation of several hundred years ago fairly faithfully.

We have numbered the prefix classes arbitrarily from 1–5. The larger combinations resulting from merging prefix classes we will term prefix sets. Class 5 nouns take the prefix /a-/ uniformly across all Gbe lects, so we will not devote too much attention to it. In the tables below the columns are not ordered in terms of the various classes. This is in order to reflect as much as possible the collapsing of prefix-marking that has occurred in all groups. Distinguishing prefixes are indicated with boldface.

Our sources for data on prefixes are taken from the following sources:

- Atlas et etudes sociolinguistiques des états du conseil de l'entente (1983)
- Capo (1991)
- Houssou (1990)
- Kluge (2000)
- Kossouho (1999)
- Koudenoukpo (1991)
- Soremikun (1986)
- Historical data: in Labat (1730), and Labouret and Rivet (1929)
- Fieldwork by Enoch Aboh

In what follows we try to summarizes the main features of the groups that we have distinguished. Diagnostic prefixes are put in bold.

5.2. The class prefixes of the Agasuvi ethnic groups (Fon/Gun)

These EGs are very easily identified (see Table 2). They uniformly group nouns into two prefix-sets: a) a set consisting of Classes 1, 3, and 5 which take the prefix /a-/; and b) a set consisting of Classes 2 and 4 which take no prefix (Fon-type), or a prefix /o-/ (Gun-type). For Gun itself this prefix is optional, and this may be the case for other Gun-type lects as well.

Table 2. Class prefixes of the Agasuvi ethnic groups.

Agasuvi Group	Class 4	Class 2	Class 3	Class 1	Class 5	No.
Fon	zero-	zero-	**a-**	a-	a-	2
Gun	o-/zero-	o-/zero-	**a-**	a-	a-	2

The locus of the split between two subgroups, typified by the Fon and Gun lects which we illustrate here, appears to be the town of Allada. The Fon kingdom of Dahomey was founded around Agbomey, while the Gun kingdom was founded later around Hugbono (Porto Novo). The third Agasuvi group remained in Allada, where it was later to be threatened by the expanding Fon kingdom.

5.3. The class prefixes of the emigrant Ayizo ethnic groups

Most of these EGs group nouns into four prefix-sets: a) a set consisting of Classes 1 and 4 which take the prefix /o-/; b) a set consisting solely of Class 2, which takes the prefix /ɛ-/; c) a set solely consisting of Class 3, which takes the prefix /ɔ-/[9]; and d) of course Class 5 (/a-/) (see Table 3).

In the Appendix of class prefixes we illustrate the fact that several lects we have assigned to this group display (diferentially) the penetration of Agasuvi forms into Classes 1, 2, and 3, the three Classes that distinguish the two groups. The eastern varieties in this group appear to be less affected by Fon influence.

Table 3. Noun class markers in the Emigrant Aziyo groups.

Emigrant Ayizo	Class 4	Class 2	Class 3	Class 1	Class 5	No.
Ajra	o-	ɛ-	ɔ-	o-	a-	4

The Ajra/Ajla system would appear to be typical of this group. Note that Classes 4 and 1 have the same prefix /o-/. The position of Maxi appears to be somewhat problematic with the dialect of Covè appearing to possess a system possibly intermediate between the Emigrant Ayizo group proper and Gun (Table 4). Typical of most EGs in this group is a state of complementary distribution between Classes 2 and 3, whereby Class 3 with

---

9. Since, in every case of the occurrence of this prefix, the following stem vowel is also /ɔ/, or the initial consonant of the stem /w/, the suspicion arises that what we have here is we actually assimilation of the original Class 5 prefix vowel /a-/ to the vowel of the stem.

a rounded low mid vowel only occurs before stems whose first vowel is /ɔ/ or whose first consonant is /w. This effect is clearly due to assimilation

Table 4. Noun class markers of Maxi (Cove).

	Class 4	Class 2	Class 3	Class 1	Class 5	No.
Maxi (Covè)	*o-*	*e-*	*o-*	*a-*	*a-*	4

The other Maxi source, representing the far northern variety of Savalou (strictly speaking right off the map), appears to be virtually identical to Fon.

5.4. The influence of Whydah?

The Fon influence observable in the western Emigrant Ayizo varieties, as also the presence of the Gun-like Gbesi and Gbokpa, and the Fon-like Kpase, would appear to be due to the presence of the Fon-speaking town of Whydah, located to the south of the Xwela area (the Xwela are the original inhabitants of Whydah).

5.5. The class prefixes of the Xwla-Xwela ethnic groups

The prefix systems of these are a mixed bunch. Some eastern lects display some influence from Gun with Class 4 marked with /o-/, and Class 1 with /a-/, while some western lects appear to have some influence from Waci (Ewe dialect), or Gen (a mixed Ewe-eastern lect with an Ewe prefix system). These lects have Class 4 marked by a front vowel prefix. This is unique in the Eastern Gbe area, but neighbouring Western Gbe lects also have front vowels here, e.g. Gen /e-/, and Waci (Ewe) /e, ɛ-/.

The Xwla-Xwela groups are divided by their noun-class prefixes into two subgroups: the Eastern Xwla and the Western Xwla (see Table 5).

Table 5. Noun class markers of the Xwla groups

Eastern Xwla Group	Class 4	Class 2	Class 3	Class 1	Class 5	No.
Xwla (East)	o-	ɛ-	ɔ-	a-	a-	4
Gbekon	o-/zero-	e- (o-)	o-	a-	a-	4
Western Xwla Group						
Xwela	i-	e-	o-	o-	a-	4
Xwla (West)	e-	ɛ-	ɔ-	ɔ-	a-	4

Both subgroups distinguish 4 prefixes among these 5 Classes, but they are differently distributed. Once again, both subgroups exhibit a complementary distribution between Classes 2 and 3, whereby Class 3 with a rounded mid vowel only occurs before stems whose first vowel is /ɔ/ or whose first consonant is /w/, as in the case of the Emigrant Ayizo groups. The eastern varieties have /a-/ in Class 1, and the western varieties have a front vowel in Class 4, presumably due to contact with lects spoken further west. We discuss this again when we look at the distribution of the individual class-prefixes in map-form. This makes it easier to observe these effects.

This group is so much influenced by neighbouring EGs that it is unclear what the original prefix was for some classes. The only distinctive feature present in the Western lects is the identity between the prefixes of Class 3 and Class 4.

6. The geographic distribution of class prefixes

In this section, we will turn to an examination of the geographical distribution of the various realizations of the individual class-prefixes. Although our numbering of the prefix-classes was arbitrary we will follow the same order here for the sake of consistency.

The general idea is to trace both the migration paths of the Agasuvi group, and patterns of lect contact phenomena in other groups such as the Emigrant Ayizo Group and the Xwla group.

6.1. The behavior of Class 1 words

In these words, we can observe a double effect proceeding from the Agasuvi area in the north – a main effect of spread towards the southeast due to migration, and a subsidiary effect towards the southwest due to language-contact.

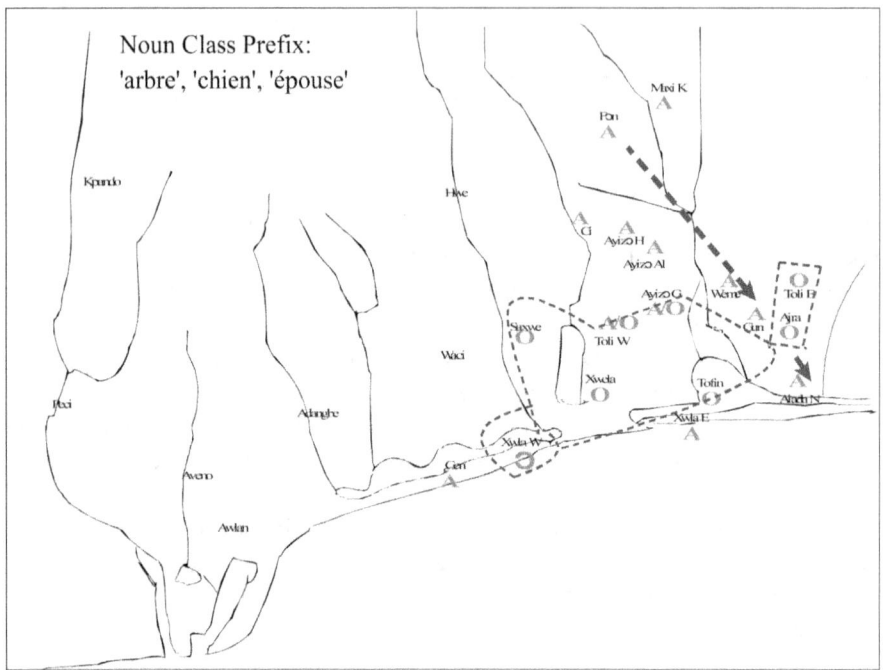

Map 2. Class 1 words.

The first effect manifests itself in the fact that a Gun-type lect has reached the coast in the form of one so-called Allada dialect whose speakers have migrated from Porto Novo to Gbadagri.

The second effect is seen in the western variety of Toli, and in the Ayizo lect spoken in Glo, which like Toli is also an Emigrant Ayizo dialect. In both cases, it manifests iteself as variation between the original /ɔ-/ and the Agasuvi /a-/. Additionally Eastern Xwla has also taken over the /a-/ prefix.

6.2. The behavior of Class 2 words

The map of Class 2 prefixes again illustrates the movement of Agasuvi dialects towards the coast. Gun itself represents an intrusion between Emigrant Ayizo dialects to the east and west. for the second time the so-called Allada dialect illustrates that Gun-type reflexes have reached the coast.

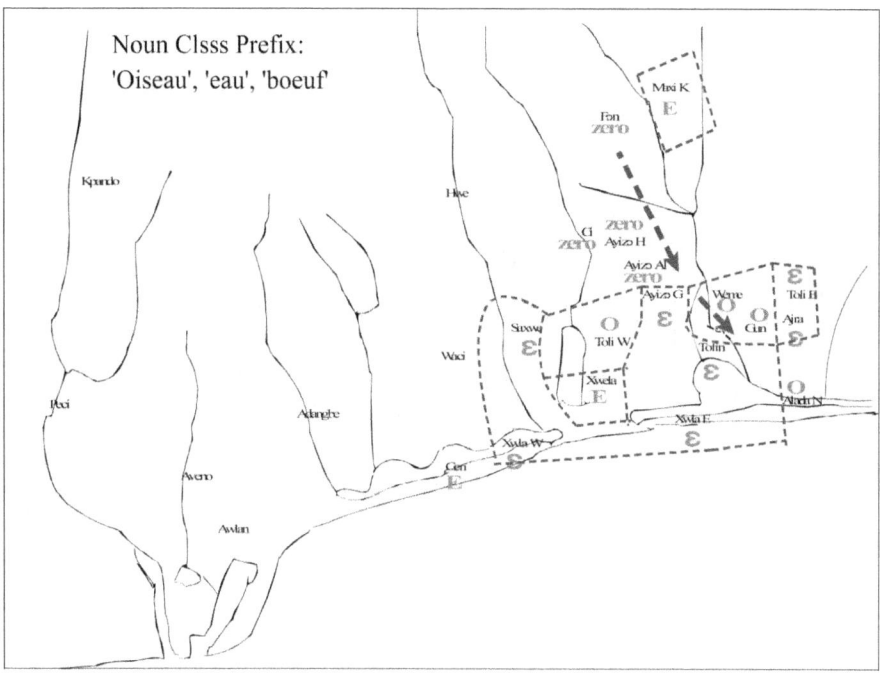

Map 3. Class 2 words.

The Agasuvi influence on Emigrant Ayizo dialects appears on the map in the Western Toli dialect (Toli W on the map), which has optionally replaced its /ɛ-/ class-marker with /o-/.

6.3. The behavior of Class 3 words

Similarly to the previous diagram, this map demonstrates the spread of Agasuvi influence to the south. The main effect is visible in the physical migrations in a southeasterly direction. The southeasternmost dialect of Allada illustrates the end-point of this migration.

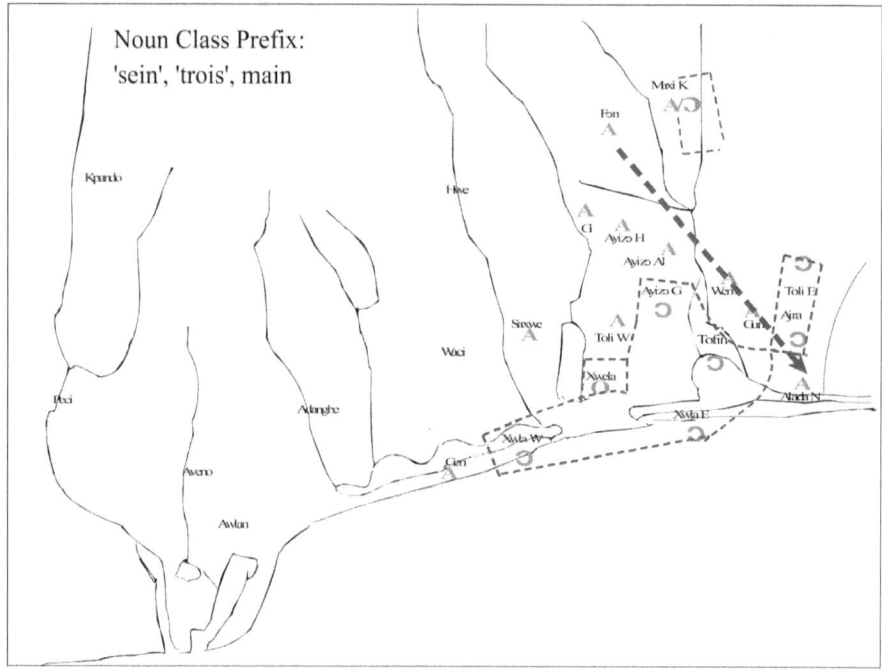

Map 4. Class 3 words.

There is also a subsidiary effect to the southwestwards. This manifests itself by the appearance of the Agasuvi /a-/ form of the prefix in Western Toli and Saxwe, where it appears to have replaced the inherited reflex of this prefix..

6.4. The behavior of Class 4 words

This map of the realizations of Class 4 prefixes is not terribly informative. The basic thing it shows is the spread from the north of the zero-realization for this class. Or at least of the option between zero and /o-/. However, it is unclear whether some of the lects described as having /o-/ do not also have the zero-option.

A zero-realization as the only possibility for Class 4 is not illustrated on the map as having proceeded any further than Allada (in the so-called Ayizo spoken in that Fon-speaking town). There is, however, a further southern extension in the Kpase lect spoken to the south-east of the location given for Xwela on Map 5.

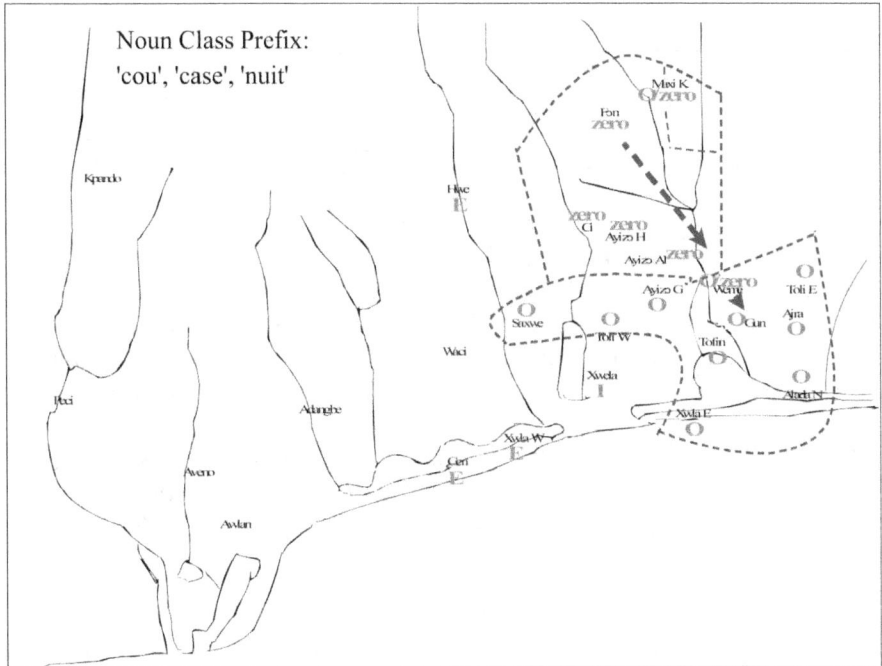

Map 5. Class 4 words.

The only other thing displayed on this map is the possible influence on the western coastal lects of Eastern Gbe from neighbouring Western Gbe lects such as Gen and Waci, manifested in the realization of the class-prefix as a front-vowel.

7. Early linguistic records from Allada and Whydah

We are fortunate in possessing early linguistic records from both Allada (1658) (Labouret and Rivet 1929) and Whydah (1730) (Labat 1730). The information on noun-class systems is not really complete, but what we do have is of some interest. Both towns are now Fon-speaking, so any change in class-prefix systems is of interest. In both cases, we can see what seems to be a fair amount of Fon influence. But both places also appear to retain traces of southern-type systems, visible particularly in Classes 2 and 3. What we see in these earlier materials, appear to be remnants of the respective earlier (southern) Ayizo and Xwela varieties spoken in these places.

Table 6. Noun class markers of Allada (1658) and Whydah (1730). [10]

Old sources	Class 4	Class 2	Class 3	Class 1	Class 5	No.
Allada 1658	zero-	e-[11]	a-	a-	(a-)[12]	[3]
Whydah 1730	zero-/o-	e-/zero-	a-/o-[13]		a-	?

8. The picture in Saramaccan

What can we conclude from the Gbe noun-class system material preserved in Saramaccan. Note that this also represents an early source insofar as Price (1983) is correct in his characterization of the formative period of the Saramaccan clans as being in the twenty year period between 1690 and 1710. In other words, the evidence from Gbe prefix-classes must refer back to the period around 1700. Unfortunately we do not have evidence from all five classes in the Saramaccan materials. The picture is as in Table 3.7.

Table 7. Remnants of noun class markers in Saramaccan, as compared to older African sources:

"Old" sources	Class 4	Class 2	Class 3	Class 1	Class 5	No.
Saramaccan	zero-		a-		a-	?
Allada 1658	zero-	e-[14]	a-	a-	(a-)[15]	[3]
Whydah 1730	zero-/o-	e-/zero-	a-/o-[16]		a-	?

The occurrence of Class 4 words with a zero-prefix indicates at least strong Fon influence. The /a-/ prefix found in Class 3 items is also indicative of Agasuvi influence. Class 5 has /a-/ in all systems, so tells us nothing. Finally, it is also of interest that the Saramaccan system is at least non-distinct from the 1658 Allada material, so that the possibility exists that if

---

10. Only a small number of cases are evidenced in some classes.
11. Note that orthographic e- in both cases might actually mean /ɛ-/.
12. This is not evidenced but as all Eastern Gbe systems have /a-/, we can be confident that this was realised the same way.
13. Note that orthographic o- might actually mean /ɔ-/.
14. Note that orthographic e- in both cases might actually mean /ɛ-/.
15. This is not evidenced but as all Eastern Gbe systems have /a-/, we can be confident that this was realised the same way.
16. Note that orthographic o- might actually mean /ɔ-/.

Saramaccan had evidenced Gbe items belonging to Class 2 these might have had /ɛ-/. This is purely speculative, of course.

9. Gbe function words in Saramaccan

Three function words of Gbe origin occur in Saramaccan.

(1)   ambɛ́   'who?'
(2)   andí   'what?'
(3)   wè   Contrastive Focus Marker (low-toned).

9.1. ambɛ́

It is difficult to associate this question-word with any particular modern Gbe lect. It clearly derives from a predecessor form /*amɛ/ but this does not actually occur at present in any Gbe lect. In fact, forms with a prefix /a-/ are now restricted in their occurrence to Ewe (Western Gbe), and appear in the form /amɛ-ka/. Eastern Gbe lects frequently have /mɛ/, but this does not tell us much.

9.2. andí

Kluge's study (2007) reveals that the form ancestral to /andí/ only occurs in a subset of Fongbe lects. Ci and Kpase both have /ani/ 'what?' These localities are both in the western part of the Fongbe-speaking area. It also occurs in Gbekon, which we have assigned to Eastern Xwla on the basis of its class prefixes. The majority of Fongbe lects have /etɛ/ rather than /ani/.

9.3. wè

The low-toned form /wɛ/ occurs in Eastern Gbe, according to Kluge (2000) in two of three areas demarcated by her: the Fon and Western Phla-Phera areas. It does not appear in what she terms the Eastern Phla-Phera area. In our terms it does not occur in the Eastern Emigrant Ayizo group. In the Xwla groups, the distribution is inconsistent. It does not occur in Xwela and Eastern Xwla, but does occur in Western Xwla and Gbekon. Obviously the couple of features we have examined cannot provide a definitive classification of these lects.

9.4. Summing up on function words

We conclude that the most informative are the facts discussed in Section 9.2. and 9.3. /ani/ occurs, today, in a very restricted portion of the Eastern Gbe area. It must be emphasized that the area in which /ani/ was used was not necessarily as restricted in the 17th century.

/wɛ/ is restricted to Eastern Gbe. Western Gbe lects have /(y)e/ as their marker of contrastive focus. In the Eastern Emigrant Ayizo group, /nɛ/ occurs, as also in Xwela and Eastern Xwla.

10. Conclusion

Taking both the known population movements into consideration and the information available for Saramaccan (no information on Classes 2 or 1), a source to the south of Agbomey, including the regions of Allada or Whydah would seem likely. In other words, the slaves that were sold in Surinam probably derive from the local wars fought by the Fon in these areas. We suspect that Fon was already widely known among these groups.

Appendix. Noun Class prefixes in Gbe and Saramaccan

Lect	Class 4	Class 2	Class 3	Class 1	Class 5	No.
Agasuvi Group						
Fon subgroup						
Maxi (Savalou)	zero-	zero-	zero-/*a*-	*a*-	*a*-	2
Fon	zero-	zero-	*a*-	*a*-	*a*-	2
Ci	zero-	zero-	*a*-	*a*-	*a*-	2
Ayizo (H.)	zero-	zero-	*a*-	*a*-	*a*-	2
Ayizo (Allada)	zero-	zero-	*a*-	*a*-	*a*-	2
Kotafon	zero-	zero-	*a*-	*a*-	*a*-	2
- Kpase	zero-	zero-	*a*-	*a*-	*a*-	2
Gun subgroup						
Weme	*o*-/zero-	*o*-/zero-	*a*-	*a*-	*a*-	2
Gun	*o*-/zero-	*o*-/zero-	*a*-	*a*-	*a*-	2
Allada	*o*-	*o*-	*a*-	*a*-	*a*-	2

Seto	o-	o-	a-	a-	a-	2
- Gbokpa	o-	o-	a-	a-	a-	2
- Gbesi	o-	o-	a-	a-	a-	2
Emigrant Ayizo Group						
eastern group						
Maxi (Covè)	o-	e-	ɔ-	a-	a-	3
Ajra	o-	ɛ-	ɔ-	o-	a-	4
Toli (East)	o-	ɛ -	ɔ-	o-	a-	4
Movolo	o-	ɛ -	ɔ-	o-	a-	4
Tofin	o-	ɛ -	ɔ-	o-	a-	4
Ayizo (Glo)	o-	ɛ -	ɔ-	o-/a-	a-	4
western group						
Se	o-	o-/ɛ-	ɔ-	o-	a-	4
Daxe	o-	o-/ɛ-	ɔ-	o-	a-	4
Toli (West)	o-	o- (ɛ-)	a-	o-/a-	a-	3
Saxwe	o-	ɛ -	a-	o-	a-	3
Eastern Xwla Group						
Xwla (East)	o-	ɛ-	ɔ-	a-	a-	4
Gbekon	o-/zero-	e- (o-)	o-	a-	a-	4
Western Xwla Group						
Xwela	i-	e-	o-	o-	a-	4
Xwla (West)	e-	ɛ-	ɔ-	ɔ-	a-	4
Old sources						
Allada 1658	zero-	e-	a-	a-		3
Whydah 1730	zero	e-/zero-	a-/o-		a-	?
Saramaccan	zero-		a-		a-	?

Meaning of shading: 35% a-prefix in Classes 3, 1, 5
25% o/ɔ-prefix in Class 1
15% ɛ/(e)-prefix in Class 2
15% ɔ/(o)-prefix in Class1
5% front vowel prefix in Class 4
0% zero/o-prefix in Class 4

Ingredient X: the shared African lexical element in the English-lexifier Atlantic Creoles, and the theory of rapid creolization

Norval Smith

1. Introduction

A striking feature of many Atlantic Creoles, which has not received any satisfactory explanation so far, even in terms of the various *Out of Africa* theories, concerns the existence of a small body of shared lexical items of African origin, which I will label Ingredient X. These items appear to come from a fairly diverse set of African languages, which is a problem in itself, in that, in the best-studied individual Atlantic Creole languages, the large majority of African-derived words can be traced to a very few African languages. Furthermore, a number of the languages in this small but diverse set have only donated one or two words. However, the only solution that has been suggested so far is one of the *Out of Africa* theories, that is, that somewhere on the West African coast a pidgin form of English had developed, which was taken across the Atlantic with slaves. If we only have one single proto-pidgin-language the problem of resemblances among circum-Caribbean Creoles becomes tractable. While a single African language could easily have gifted a single word to a single proto-pidgin language, that this same single African language could have gifted the same single word *independently* to a whole series of Atlantic Creole languages certainly stretches the bounds of credibility.

In this chapter, I first address this problem. It will turn out that trying to explain this problem touches on various other related problems, which taken together, provide us with a possible new scenario on the history of the development of the English-lexifier Creole languages of the Atlantic area.

McWhorter (1995) represents a solid demonstration that all the English-lexifier Creole languages must have some kind of common origin, on the

---

I would like to acknowledge my gratitude to John Singler and Ken Bilby for assistance with various points.

basis of their common possession of a locative copula *de*, an equative copula *da/na¹/a*, a modal *fi/fo/fu*, a second person plural pronoun *unu*, an anterior marker *bin*, and an adverb derived from English *self*. He places the origin of this on the Gold Coast at the fort of Cormantin, from whence an expanded pidgin English was taken to Barbados, and thence on to Surinam and Jamaica and other circum-Caribbean colonies. He assumes that this pidgin was best preserved where sharp discrepancies in black-white population ratios developed, while cases of less discrepancy resulted in decreolisation (although he does not use the term in this context). This was not the first but the most comprehensive demonstration that the parent expanded pidgin had its origins in Africa. Hancock (1969) derived all the Atlantic Creole languages from a pidgin spoken in Upper Guinea (the area centring on Sierra Leone), while Smith (1987) saw their origin in Lower Guinea (in particular the Slave Coast), for instance.

While I (still) share his basic thesis of a single ancestor for this group of languages, I will propose a different, Caribbean, source for the relationship among the Atlantic Creoles (see Smith (1997, 1999c, 2001a; van de Vate (2003) for similar views). I will proceed, as I said, from Ingredient X, the shared body of diverse lexical items (including the above-mentioned *unu*) (Smith 1987), as well as the so-called *make*-imperatives (Smith 1997), vowel-system typology (Smith 1999c), and a further look at the two copulas, *da and *de.

Further topics play an important role in the development of my Caribbean thesis. The distinction of two types of Atlantic Creoles, depending on the degree of colonial control that was present (Smith & van de Vate 2006), the sociological context for the formation of a group language (Smith 2006), and the concept of very rapid creolization (Smith 2006).

Finally Krio of Sierra Leone bears an unusual resemblance to the Surinam Creoles, as does the so-called Maroon Spirit Language of Jamaica. I will claim that these three languages/groups of languages exemplify best what an English-lexifier Creole looked like in the absence of colonial political control, and thereby the absence of an English adstrate, and so provide us with a better picture of the original result of creolization in the English Atlantic.

---

1. I will have something to say on the topic of *na* below.

2. Ingredient X

The first Creolist to do large-scale comparisons of Atlantic Creole language lexicons was Ian Hancock (1969). As his list covered 570 lexical items, he unavoidably refers to various items of African origin. He covers Krio, Sranan, Saramaccan, Ndyuka, Cameroon Pidgin English, Guyanese Creole, Jamaican Creole, and Gullah.

In Smith (1997), the term "Ingredient X" was introduced, on the model of a term found in typical British TV soap powder advertisements. The implication was that an unexplained element involving African words of disparate origin was present in many English-lexifier Creoles in the Atlantic area. The African words in the present list number 29. Quite a few of these words appeared in Hancock's list.

The basis for present list list was formed in Smith (1987: 103–110), where 12 items from the larger list were given. The list is given in Table 1. I proceed from Jamaican, one of the languages with the most representatives of Ingredient X. Table 1 contains many empty cells. On the left-hand side, the creole side, the reason is partly that not all creoles are equally well-equipped with dictionaries and wordlists. The best-covered are the Surinam Creoles, Krio and Jamaican. The right-hand side, with possible African sources, is no doubt incomplete as well.

70   Norval Smith

Table 1.[2] Ingredient X words

Approx. gloss	Jamaican	Sranan	Sara-maccan	Krio	Guyanese	Miskito Coast Cr.	Baha-mian	African source 1	African source 2	African source 3
1. beancake	ákra	akará 1855	akala	akara			akárá/ akrá	Igbo: àkàrà	Yor.: àkàrà	Fongbe: àklà
2. akee[3]	áki	aki		akí	akee 1916		ákiy	Kru: aki		
3. spider	(a)nansí	anansí	anasi	nansi-	anánsi	anánsi	(a)nánsi	Twi: ananse	Ewe: ananse	
4. white man	bákra	bákra	bakáa		bákra	bákra	bʌ́kra	Efik: mbakara		
5. boa		(a)bóma	(a)bóma	bomán				Kik.: mboma		
6. vulva	bómbo	bómbo	boómba	bombó			booboo	Kik.: bumbu		
7. monster	bubu	bubú	bubú 'jaguar'		booboo-man	buubuu		Kik.: mbuubu		
8. untidy	jágajága	dyaga-dyaga		ʤaga-ʤágá	ʤúga-ʤúga			Ewe: jagajaga		
9. ghost	jómbi/ júmbi	dyumbi		ʤombí	ʤʌ́mbi	ʤombi	ʤʌ́mbi	Kim.: nzumbi		
10. dumpling	dókunu	dokún	dokúnu	dɔkunũ				Twi: ɔ-dɔkono	Yor.: ɔdɔkũ	

2. The words written in Italics are obsolete words, known only from written sources. Saramaccan words with underlined *b* are items the nature of whose voicing, plain or implosive is unclear. Sources are Schumann (1778, 1783), Focke (1855), Westermann (1905-6), Schuchardt (1914), Christaller (1933), Turner (1949), Donicie & Voorhoeve (1963), Berry (1966), Cassidy & LePage (1967), Hancock (1969, 1987), Holm & Shilling (1982), Huttar (1972, 1985, 1986), Wilner (2003).
3. A tree.

Ingredient X 71

Approx. gloss	Jamaican	Sranan	Sara-maccan	Krio	Guyanese	Miskito Coast Cr.	Baha-mian	African source 1	African source 2	African source 3
11. evil ghost	dópi	adúpi			adopi 1916	dópi	duppy	Gã: adúpὲ		
12. strike (v)	fom	fon	fón					E. Ijo: fóm		
13. lungs		fokofóko 1783	fukɔfukɔ					Yor.: fukufúku		
14. fufu [4]	fufú	afufu	fufú	fufú	fufú	fufu	fufú	Twi: fufúú	Ewe: fufu	Yor.: fúufúu fiufú
15. peanut	gubgúb	gobo-góbo	gobo-góbo akata		gúba			Kim.: ngúba		
16. headpad	kóta			katá	kata	káta		Kik.: nkáta		
17. leprosy	kokobie	kokobé	kokobé	kakabé	kʌkʌbé	kuokobé	kóokóobe	Twi: kokobé		
18. gossip	konkonsá	gongosá	gongosá	kongosá	kɔngɔsá		conjessy	Twi: nko-nkonsá		
19. deaf, dumb	mumú	mumu		mumú	mumú	mumu		Twi: múmu	Ewe: múmu	Mende: múmú
20. yam	nyaams	yámsi	nyámisi	nyâms				Mende: njamisi		
21. eat (v)	nyam	nyan	nyán	nyâm	nyam	nyam	nyam	Wolof: njam		
22. magic	óbia	obia	óbia		óbia		ówbiya	Efik: ubio		

4. A staple food.

72 Norval Smith

Approx. gloss	Jamaican	Sranan	Sara-maccan	Krio	Guyanese	Miskito Coast Cr.	Baha-mian	African source 1	African source 2	African source 3
23. okra	ókro	okro		ɔ́krɔ	okró	uókra	okra	Igbo: ókwùlù	E. Ijo: ók(u)rụ	
24. peanut	pínda	pindá	pindá			pinda		Kik.: mpínda		
25. mud	potopóto/ potopotá	potopóto	pɔtɔpɔ́tɔ	pɔtɔpɔ́tɔ	pʎtapʎta			Twi: pàtàpɔtɔ Efik: nsak	Igbo: pòtòpotò	Kik.: potopoto
26. rattle	shaká	saká 1855	sakasaka 1883	shaká	shakshák					
27. only	súoso	sóso	sɔ́sɔ	sósó	sóso	so-so	soso	Igbo: sọ̀ọsọ̀	Yor.: sọọsọ	
28. you (pl)	únu	unu	únu	únu/úna		unu	ona	Igbo: unu		
29. game type	wári	awári		wari			worry	Twi: wàre		

2.1. Baker (1999)

In Baker (1999), a list of 138 features is given, including 20 of the African-derived lexical items given in Table 1. I have given these items in Table 2, indicating by *x* where these items occur in Creole languages additional to those mentioned in Table 1. Note that there are only three items out of the twenty where a row in the table remains blank.

Table 2. Ingredient X words in Baker's list of shared features in the Atlantic English Creoles

Approximate gloss	Jamaican	Baker (1999)	Bajan	St. Kitts	Antiguan	St. Vincent	Gullah
1. beancake	*akra*	F115					
3. spider	*(a)nansí*	F6	x	x	x	x	x
4. white man	*bákra*	F24	x	x	x	x	x
6. vulva	*bómbo*	F90			x		x
9. ghost	*júmbi*	F32	x	x	x	x	
11. evil ghost	*dópi*	F101	x				
12. strike (v)	*fom*	F103	x			x	
13. lungs		F102					x
14. fufu	*fufú*	F82					x
16. headpad	*kóta*	F63		x	x		
18. gossip	*konkonsá*	F84			x		
20. yam	*nyaams*	F114	x				
21. eat (v)	*nyam*	F20	x	x	x	x	x
22. magic	*óbia*	F48	x	x	x	x	
24. peanut	*pínda*	F122					x
25. mud	*potopóto*	F90					x
27. only	*súoso*	F72		x			x
28. you (pl)	*únu*	F95	x				x
29. type of game	*wári*	F74	x	x	x		

Among the problems Baker's list of features involves is the lack of comparability in the mixture of African-derived words, Portuguese items, English words with dialect phonology, phrases, question words, complementizers, TMA markers, copula forms, prepositions, pronominal forms, etc. It is extremely unlikely that all these features should receive an equal weighting. Yet they are treated as if they have this, while other features involving, for instance, the presence or absence of derivational morphology, are ignored.

3. Discussion of Ingredient X forms.

Rows in Table 1 shaded grey are also listed in the Kikongo list (see Smith, this volume on the Kikongo lexical contribution to the Surinam Creoles). Two of the seven items concerned are clearly Kimbundu rather Kikongo, and are in fact the only such items included in the Kikongo list[5].

The main point made on the African (right) side of Table 1 is that the potential sources, which are certainly not exhaustive, display considerable variation in terms of geographical location. One striking case is that of form nr. 12, which is *fom* or forms derived from that. The precise form of this Eastern Ijo word is apparently (now) restricted to the Ibani dialect, spoken in the former notorious slave-exporting town of Bonny, now in Nigeria.

The etymologies given here suggest that the languages represented stretch all the way from Sierra Leone (Mende, Wolof) to Angola (Kimbundu).

If we consider the languages represented in both Table 1 and Table 2, and the twenty words of Table 2 this gives us the result illustrated in Table 3. Rearranging Table 3 in terms of frequency from left to right, and top to bottom gives the picture in Table 4.

This is by no means a perfect (implicational) Guttman Scale, as there are 21 empty cells on the left side and 11 filled cells on the right side. This comes to 32 wrongly situated cells out of 240, which is 13.3%. The table does still suggest that there are hierarchical implications present, meaning that we likely have to do with an original single body of words.

One hedge that requires to be made here is that the study of the various English-lexifier Creole varieties' lexica is very uneven. The creoles represented in the first five columns in Table 4 have all undergone extensive lexical study. The result is then partially, at least, no accident.

---

5. The Kikongo list includes a few words from neighbouring Bantu languages. It is not completely clear where the boundary of what one might call Kikongo should be drawn.

Ingredient X   75

Table 3. Ingredient X words in Baker (1999)[6]

Approx. gloss	(Baker)	**Jam**	**Sran**	Sara	**Krio**	Guya	MCC	Baha	**Barb**	**Kitt**	Ant	Vinc	Gull	12
1. beancake	F115	x	x	x	x									5
3. spider	F6	x	x	x	x	x	x	x	x	x	x	x	x	12
4. white man	F24	x	x	x	x	x	x	x	x	x	x	x		11
6. vulva	F90	x	x	x				x			x		x	6
9. ghost	F32	x	x		x	x	x	x	x	x	x	x		10
11. evil ghost	F101	x	x			x	x	x	x					6
12. strike (v)	F103	x	x	x				x	x			x		5
13. lungs	F102		x	x									x	3
14. fufu	F82	x	x		x	x	x	x					x	7
16. headpad	F63	x	x		x	x					x	x		7
18. gossip	F84	x	x	x	x	x		x			x			7
20. yam	F114	x	x	x	x					x				5
21. eat (v)	F20	x	x	x	x	x	x	x	x	x	x	x	x	12
22. magic	F48	x	x	x		x		x	x	x	x	x		9
24. peanut	F122	x	x	x		x	x							5
25. mud	F90	x	x	x	x	x							x	5
27. only	F72	x	x	x	x		x	x		x			x	8
28. you (pl)	F95	x	x	x	x		x	x	x				x	8
29. type game	F74	x	x	x	x			x	x	x	x			7
	20	19	19	17	14	11	10	13	9	8	9	7	10	

6. The language names given in bold type can be supposed to be of greater importance, in the sense that most of the others can be regarded as "derived" by colonization from one or other of them.

76 Norval Smith

Table 4. Rearranged table of Ingredient X words in Baker (1999).

Approx. gloss	(Baker)	Jam	Sran	Sara	Krio	Baha	Guya	Ant	Gull	MCC	Barb	Kitt	Vinc	12	-	+
3. spider	F6	x	x	x	x	x	x	x	x	x	x	x	x	12		
21. eat (v)	F20	x	x	x	x	x	x	x	x	x	x	x	x	12		
4. white man	F24	x	x	x		x	x	x	x	x	x	x	x	11	1	
9. ghost	F32	x	x		x	x	x	x	x	x	x	x	x	10	2	
22. magic	F48	x	x	x		x	x	x		x	x	x	x	9	3	
27. only	F72	x	x	x	x	x	x	x	x	x		x		9	2	
29. type game	F74	x	x	x		x		x	x	x	x	x		7	3	
28. you (pl)	F95	x	x	x	x	x	x	x	x	x	x			8	2	
14. fufu	F82	x	x	x	x		x	x	x	x	x			8	1	
6. vulva	F90	x	x	x	x	x	x	x						7	1	
18. gossip	F84	x	x	x	x	x		x						7		
16. headpad	F63	x	x	x	x	x	x			x			x	7	2	2
25. mud	F90	x	x	x	x		x		x					6	1	1
11. evil ghost	F101	x	x			x	x			x	x			6	2	2
1. beancake	F115	x	x	x	x	x								5		
20. yam	F114	x	x	x								x		5	1	
24. peanut	F122	x	x	x					x	x				5	2	
12. strike (v)	F103	x	x	x							x		x	5	2	
13. lungs	F102		x	x					x					3	1	1
		20	19	19	17	14	13	11	9	10	10	9	8	7		

4. Locating Ingredient X in time and space

In this and following sections, I will examine, not just the question of when and where the words making up (the core of) Ingredient X were first used together, but also whether there are other common features of the Atlantic English-lexifier Creoles that can be related to the presence of Ingredient X. By this, I will not refer here to features of a purely typological syntactic nature, as these, by their very nature, are less precise for historical investigations. This is not to deny the valuable work that has been done recently in terms of the notion of "feature pool" (Mufwene, 2001, 2005; Aboh & Ansaldo 2006; Aboh 2009b). I will restrict myself rather to features of a lexical, morpholexical and phonological nature, which by their very nature can be related more easily to historical antecedents.

Let us first consider the Ingredient X vocabulary itself. While it is not completely clear what the total make-up of this list should be, I would suggest that it is indisputable that there is a common group of African words appearing in many English-lexifier Creole languages in the Atlantic area. Note that the Ingredient X words differ considerably from the African-derived vocabulary noted in the Gbe and Kikongo[7] studies (Smith, this volume). These are both fairly large lists – respectively 138 and 185 words long. Together with a smaller body of Twi vocabulary not treated in this volume, they represent solid bodies of words from single groups of closely related dialects or languages. They are not shared as a group with other Atlantic Creole languages, which is not to deny that some words in the lists may occur in other Atlantic English-lexifier Creoles, or even in French-lexifier or Portuguese-lexifier Creoles.

What do these Ingredient X words prove? I would suggest that the fact that the Atlantic Creoles share a lexical component of some kind means that they share part of their history. In view of the fact that some languages, such as the Surinamese creoles, have been long isolated from contact with other Creole languages, it would seem most likely that the Ingredient X items go back to a very early period in the history of the English plantation economies. The default assumption would be to assume that the diffusion of these words follows the spread of these same English colonies. These had their start on St. Kitts in 1623, and Barbados in 1627 (the island was claimed by the English in 1625). However, Barbados had a much larger population than St. Kitts, and was dominant in the settlement of other colonies far and wide.

---

7. With the exception of the small overlap with Kikongo noted above.

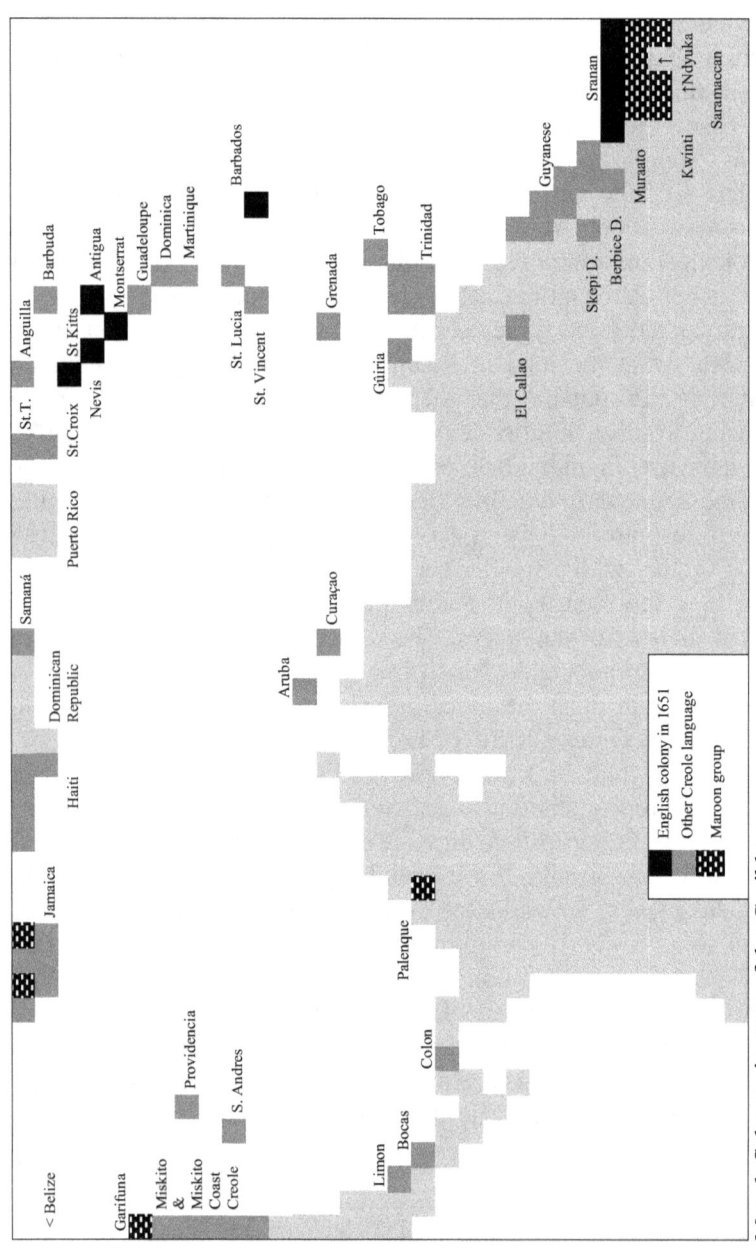

Map 1. Schematic map of the Caribbean

The list includes Surinam, Jamaica, Carolina, Demerara, and later the rest of Guyana. The political influence of St. Kitts was largely restricted to the neighbouring islands of Nevis, Montserrat and Antigua. The resemblances among the Creole languages spoken in the various English Caribbean colonies, and the settlement relationships among them suggest that the initial differences can not have been great. Baker (1999) sees the linguistic influences as emanating from St. Kitts, while Smith (1997) & Van de Vate (2003) prefer Barbados. In hindsight, I consider that more or less identical forms of Creole speech must have developed on, and spread from, both.

It has often been claimed that Barbadian (Bajan) has always resembled Standard English, rather than creole languages like those spoken at present on other Caribbean islands. Such a view was taken by Hancock (1980). However, there has been a lot of evidence offered for the opposing view, i.e. that Barbadian had a basilectal end to its claimed continuum. This was summed up in Rickford & Handler (1994), including the claim that it is still a Creole. I am however not so concerned with its present, without at all wishing to suggest that I disagree, as I am with the fact that it clearly had a creole past.

5. Timetable of events relevant to Surinam

The following timetable of events and hypothesized events is relevant primarily to the colonization of Surinam by the English, and then the Dutch. It also places events in Surinam in the context of England's other colonizing activities (and, after 1707, those of the British). The events preceding the colonization of Surinam concern the important early acts of colonization, partly leading to the colonization of Surinam itself.

Table 5. Historical and linguistic timetable, with the focus on Surinam[8]

Date	Event
1624	*Colonization of St. Kitts (island claimed 1623)*
1627	*Colonization of Barbados (island claimed 1625)*
1628	*Colonization of Nevis (St. Kitts)*
1629-1631	*Colonization of Providence (Bermuda[9])*
1632	*Colonization of Montserrat (Nevis)*

---

8. The geographical names in brackets represent what I understand to have the main source(s) of the initial colonizing populations. In the case of Surinam and Jamaica the names are in order of importance.
9. See Bernhard (1999).

1632	*Colonization of Antigua (St. Kitts)*
1651	*Colonization of Surinam (Barbados, St. Kitts, Nevis, Montserrat)*
1655	*Conquest of Jamaica from the Spanish (Barbados, St. Kitts)*
c.1660	Marronnage of Jermes' group in the Para region
1664	**Portuguese-speaking Jewish settlers arrive from Cayenne**
1665	**Latest possible date for the creolization of Sranan**
1667	Surrender of Surinam by the English to the Dutch
1668	Effective beginning of Dutch administration in Surinam
1667–1675	80% of English leave with around 1400 slaves for Jamaica (some to Surinam Quarters in St. Elizabeth, now in Westmoreland Parish).
1670	*Colonization of Carolina (Barbados)*
c.1680	**Partial relexification of Sranan to Dju-tongo ('Jews' language') on the Middle Suriname River plantations**
1684	Peace treaty signed with the Para Maroons who had moved to the Coppename River. Now known as the Karboegers (Smith 2000)
1690–1695	**First mass marronnage of slaves to form the Saramaccan tribe in Surinam, in particular from Jewish plantations (Price 1983). They take with them Dju-tongo, which later becomes restricted to this group (dying out on the Jewish-owned plantations on the Middle Suriname River); now known as Saamaka-tongo (Saramaccan).**
1707	**First record of a Sranan sentence (van den Berg 2007)**
1712	**First mass marronnage of slaves to form the Ndyuka tribe. They take with them a plantation variety of Sranan.**
1700s	*Settlement of Miskito Coast (Jamaica)*
before 1724	*Settlement of Belize Coast (Jamaica)*
1746	*Settlement of Demerara (Barbados)*
1760	Peace treaty signed with Ndyuka tribe
1762	Peace treaty signed with Saramaccan tribe
1767	Peace treaty signed with Matawai tribe
1783	*Large scale immigration on Bahamas of Loyalists with Gullah-speaking slaves, from Georgia and South Carolina (Hackert 2004)*
1814	*Colony of British Guiana (Barbados)*

Events, or hypothesized events, relevant for the linguistic history of Surinam, are shown in bold type in Table 5. An attempt to provide the general Caribbean colonization and settlement context is given in italics. Administrative events and a few other items without relevance for creole languages are left in plain type. As can be seen the timetable preceding the colonization of Surinam is brief, and the Surinam timetable itself is very crowded. I will discuss some of the ramifications of this in the next section.

6. Beginnings and speed of creolization

Immediately, we enter the (actually two separate) discussions of when the conditions for the formation of a creole language first became present, and of whether creolization is a rapid or slow process. I personally do not believe in the slightest that creole languages represent failed attempts at second language learning (there is no evidence for this, after all), whether due to an increasing lack of European models for a koiné colonial English or anything else, but rather have to be seen in terms of an in-group need for a community language (Muysken 1981; Smith 1987, 2006). The motivations for such a need must be sought in various sociological factors.

In one sense, one could say that the necessity for a common slave plantation language was forced on the slave community by the brutal circumstances of slavery. Also, for the proposal that creole languages are expressions of resistance, compare Jourdan (2008).

In van den Berg, Muysken, and Smith (this volume), the point is made that processes of "gradual creolization", extending even into the 19th century in some accounts, cannot be reconciled with the very crowded "timetable" required for an explanation of the history of the formation of the creole languages of Surinam. And, if creolization was a rapid process in Surinam, then it should also have been a rapid process under similar sociological conditions elsewhere. I will therefore proceed from the assumption that the creolization of a language need not take longer than a period of, say, five years or so. By creolization I mean the formation of a *new* language. A necessary prerequisite for the creation of a new language largely based on English vocabulary, and adopting at least some syntactic patterns from English, such as the Adjective-Noun order encountered in English-lexifier creoles, as compared with the basic Noun-Adjective order encountered in French-lexifier creoles, is the reasonably successful learning of the colonial koiné variety of Standard English spoken in the 17th century Caribbean. Note the Gbe languages of the former "Slave Coast" (the largest group in Surinam) also have a Noun-Adjective order, like French.

Most whites were also faced with the same or similar issues as the slaves to varying degrees. The majority of English speakers in the early-mid 18th century, outside the very small hereditary Upper Class, and small but growing professional Middle Classes, were first language speakers of a very disparate set of traditional local dialects, in some cases mutually unintelligible. Great Britain was largely a farming-based society, or rather a congeries of societies, at this period, with a significant artisan class also largely based in the countryside or in small market-towns. The majority of people would have no need for Standard English at all. One's passive, and in particular, active competence in some kind of Standard English would vary very much in accordance with one's specific occupation, and the social contacts related to these. A farm-labourer had no need of any other communication system than his own local dialect.

In the early part of the 17th century, the proportion of people with some competence in Standard English in Britain was certainly vastly less. Puttenham (1589) wrote the following a generation before the English colonization of islands in the Caribbean: "ye ſhall therfore take the vſuall speach of the Court, and that of London and the ſhires lying about London within lx. myles, and not much aboue. I ſay not this but that in euery ſhyre of England there be gentlemen and others that ſpeake but ſpecially write as good Southerne as we of Middlesex or Surrey do, *but not the common people of euery ſhire,* to whom the gentlemen, and also their learned clarkes do for the most part condeſcend..." [My emphasis, NS.]

The "common people" referred to here formed the vast majority of "English" speakers, and did not speak "good Southerne". And there were many common people in the colonies. Although the study of the various regional contributions to the Caribbean creole vocabulary is considerably inhibited by the great qualititative and quantitative differences in dialect lexicography in England (see Holm & Shilling 1982; Smith 1983), it is clear that immigrants from all parts of England, and of the British Isles as a whole, were present in the Caribbean. If we are to take the early (and admittedly piecemeal) records of indentured labourers going to the West Indies as a guide, it would seem that the majority, though by no means all, were speakers of Southern or Southwestern English dialects,. Those speakers of other languages such as (Germanic) Scots, Scottish Gaelic, Irish, and Welsh were in a partly comparable situation linguistically to the slave population in the English colonies, in that many of them would also not be speakers of any kind of English.

Ingredient X does not do much more than provide evidence for a bit of shared linguistic history in the second quarter of the 17th century. At this time, the only English colonies other than Barbados were on St. Kitts, Nevis, Antigua, Montserrat, and Providence (now Providencia, Colombia). However, it is a very important bit of shared linguistic history, and there is a lot more besides.

7. Ingredient X is not alone

There are various other shared features among English creole languages of the Atlantic region. I will briefly mention a number here.

7.1. Make-Imperatives

Compelling evidence for an English-lexifier "Proto-Pidgin" with some degree of complexity is provided by various usages referred to traditionally as imperatives, including so-called first and third person "imperatives" (Smith 1997). Yakpo (2009) refers to all these as "directives", distinguishing between true "imperatives" (2nd person directives), and "jussives" (1st and 3rd person directives). In all Atlantic Creoles, jussives involve the use of a form involving the local reflex of the Englsh word *make*, and imperatives seem also to allow this. Compare the following forms:

(1) a. *tjá di wóyo kó,* ***mbéi*** *mi sí*
 carry DEF eye come, MAKE 1SG see
 'let me see your eye' (lit. 'bring your eye, let me see'
 Saramaccan, De Groot 1977)
 b. ***mbó**=u gó*
 MAKE=1PL go
 'let's go'(Saramaccan, Donicie & Voorhoeve 1963)
 c. ***meke*** *u nyan kwakwa*
 MAKE 1PL eat farina
 'let's eat some farina' (Ndyuka, Huttar & Huttar 1994)
 d. ***meke*** *mi gwe komoto ya*
 MAKE 1SG leave come.out here
 'let me go from here'[10] (Ndyuka, Shanks 2000)
 e. ***mek*** *a tel yu sontiŋ*
 MAKE 1SG tell 2SG something
 'let me tell you something' (Belizean, Greene 1999)
 f. ***mek*** *I see*
 MAKE 1SG see
 'let me see!' (Bahamian, Holm & Shilling 1982)

---

10. Translation modified.

g. **mek** à giv=am nyam!
   MAKE 1SG give=3SG yam
   'let me give him some yam' (Nigerian Pidgin, Faraclas 1996)
h. **mek** wuna push moto
   MAKE 2PL push vehicle
   'please push the vehicle' (Kamtok, Ayafor 2008)
i. **mek** jù pe fɔti tausen sidi!
   MAKE 2 pay forty thousand cedi
   'pay forty thousand cedis!' (Ghanaian Pidgin, Huber 1999a)
j. **mek** yù mɛn=àn ò!
   MAKE[11] 2SG care.for=3SG SP
   'make sure to take care of her!' (Pichi,[12] Yakpo 2009)
k. **mek** wi keep yo niem huoly
   MAKE 1PL keep 2SG name holy
   'let us keep your name holy.' = 'hallowed be thy name.'[13]
   (Islander[14], [Matthew 6:9] Islander NT 2010)

That this is not a recent development, although this would be difficult to comprehend anyway given the diversity of the languages involved, can be seen from the following 18th century examples from Surinam.

(2) a. **mekk**-a tan booy
   MAKE-3SG stay, boy'
   'let him stay, boy' (Early Sranan [1747], van den Berg 2000)
b. ...kaba **meki** buka va mi dindra na unu jessi
   ...then MAKE mouth POSS 1SG enter LOC 2PL ear
   '...then let my words enter your ears' (Early Saramaccan [NT Acts 2:14] Br. Wietz 1805, in Schuchardt 1914)

As can be seen from these examples their morpho-syntax is identical to that of the more modern examples. This construction raises a serious problem. Here we are presented with significant evidence of a shared directive construction present in a wide range of Atlantic Creole languages. The logical conclusion we should be led to here would be that what I have

---

11. Yakpo (2009) glosses *mek* as subjunctive.
12. Pichi is a Krio variety spoken on the Gulf of Guinea island of Fernando Po.
13. This is a nice illustration of why Yakpo refers to this usage as subjunctive.
14. The term *Islander* is used to refer to the English-lexifier creole language spoken on San Andrés and Providencia islands, which form part of Colombia.

referred to above as "Proto-Pidgin", and will henceforth call the Proto-Atlantic Slave Community Language (PASCL), had this construction. What does this imply? Certainly that the PASCL was a means of communication involving complex sentence structures.

7.2. Atlantic Creole copulas derived from deictics, and the imperfective markers derived from them

A striking resemblance exists among some aspects of the copula systems of the Atlantic Creole languages. This has already been discussed at some length by McWhorter (1995), but I will treat it in somewhat different terms.

In many Atlantic Creole languages there are two copula forms derived from the English words *there* and *that*. There are also various other words used to express various copular meanings, largely also derived from English sources, such as Islander *gat* with an existential meaning (Bartens to appear). I leave this particular structure out of consideration here, as it clearly has a different syntax involving two NP arguments:

(3) a. NP_1 gat NP_2:
  Dem_1 ... don gat wan joj_2 already
  'There is a $judge_2$ for the one_1 who ...' (Islander, John 12:48)

This as compared with the rarer construction with a single NP argument.

(3) b. NP de:
  (di Sadducee dem seh) no rezorekshon no deh, ...
  '(That Sadducees say that) there is no resurrection, ...'
  (Islander, Acts 23:8)

The latter construction is the one that we are interested in here. It corresponds to the English *there is NP[-def]* construction, using a marker derived from English *there*. In Table 6, I will only mention cases corresponding to the English words *that* and *there*, or their structural equivalents.

I distinguish four copula functions:[15] locative, existential, identificational-equative, and highlighter (*it's*). In all the creoles illustrated in Table 6, the first two functions are carried out by forms identical with, and derived from the equivalent of the English word *there*.[16] In the case of the other two copulative functions one or both of them is/are carried out by abbreviated forms derived from the English word *that*.

The imperfective marker, which I have located in the centre row of the table is indicated by now one, now the other, or even both in the case of Jamaican. The variability in the imperfective marker may well indicate that a fixed imperfective marker did not exist in PASCL. There is some evidence, for instance, from Sranan (cf. van den Berg 2007), that it was only in the early 18th century that a definite choice was made between *tan* 'stay' (derived from English *stand*), and *de* (modern *e*) (see also Smith 2009a). *Tan* became the imperfective marker in Saramaccan (evidenced from the final quarter of the 18th century, and now modern *tá*), but has only been used in recent Sranan either as an auxiliary with the sense of 'keep on V-ing', clearly still related to the imperfective in meaning, or as a full verb with the sense of 'stay'.

Similarly, the variability between *de* and *da* in Table 6 for the form of the imperfective aspect marker might suggest something similar. Even to this day we have dialectal variability in Jamaican. Note that this does not necessarily mean that PASCL did not possess imperfective markers, only that there might have been variability.

What the table also demonstrates, however, is that the expression of the locative-existential copula functions by a *there*-word in the Atlantic Creoles dates back to PASCL times, as does the expression of the identificational-equative copula functions by a *that*-word. We can also assume that the highlighter function was associated with the same *that*-word form from an early time.

---

15. I will not treat the occurrence of copulas with predicative adjectives here, as this impinges on the differential treatment of quality expressions both between and within creole languages.
16. I could not find satisfactory examples for the existential (i.e. the *there-is*) copula in Gullah.

Table 6. Some copular verbs in the Atlantic Creole languages[17]

	Sran.	Sara.	Jam. 1	Jam. 2	Isl.	Guy.	Gull.	Bel.	Pichi
there	*de*	*de*	*de*	*de*	*de*	*de*	*de*	*de*	*de*
locative copula	*de*	*de*	*de*	*de*	*de*	*de*	*dɛ*	*dɛ*	*de*
existential copula	*de*	*de*	*de*	*de*	*de*	*de*	?	*dɛ*	*de*
imperfective marker	*e* < *de*	*ta*	*a/da*	*de*[18]	*de*	*a*	*də*	*de*[19]	*de*[20]
identificational copula	*(n)a* < *da*	*da*	*a*	*a*	*da*	*a*	*də*	*da/a*	*nà*[21]
highlighter	*(n)a* < *da*	_*wɛ̂*[22]	*a/da/iz*	*a/da/iz*	*da*	*a*	*iz/(də)*	*da/a*	*nà*
that	*dati*	*di de*	*da*	*da*	*dat*	*da(t)*	*da(t)*	*da(t)*	*da(t)*

---

17. Sran. = Sranan; Sara. = Saramaccan; Jam. = Jamaican; Isl. = San Andrés (Islander Creole); Guy. = Guyanese; Gull. = Gullah; Bel. = Belizean.
18. In parts of Jamaica including St. Elizabeth parish the imperfective marker is *de* (Bailey 1966, Cassidy & LePage 1967).
19. The higher vowel quality in the imperfective marker is according to Escure (2008).
20. The imperfective (imperfective) marker bears a low tone (Yakpo 2009).
21. Note that there is no evidence that Pichi/Krio *nà* is related to the *da* met with in other creoles. The modern Sraran *na–a* is derived from older *da*. See Section 11 for further discussion.
22. Saramaccan *wɛ̀* is derived from Fongbe *wɛ̀* (see Smith, this volume on the Gbe lexical contribution to the Surinam Creoles).

8. Differences among Atlantic Creoles

A glance at Hancock (1987) reveals many similarities among English-lexifier creoles in the Atlantic area, but also a great deal of variety. I will reflect briefly on one feature here, the nature of the vowel systems found in this area, and their relationship to the vowel system of Early Modern English.

A striking phonological difference among these Creoles is whether they neutralize the English sub-systems of long/tense vowels and short/lax vowels. Some do, but most do not. So we have Surinam-type (Type-A) systems that do not preserve the Early Modern English situation, and Jamaica-type (Type-B) systems that do.

Table 7. Reflexes of the tense and lax vowels of English

Gloss	Early Modern English (Dobson 1957)	Sranan (Smith 1987)	Jamaican Creole (Cassidy & LePage 1967)
meet	m**iː**t	m**i**ti	m**ii**t
big	bɪg	bigi	big
call	k**ɒː**l	k**a**ri	k**aa**l
God	gɒd	gado	gad

I have noted the EME long vowels in bold type, as also their congeners in Sranan (Type-A) and Jamaican (Type-B).[23]

It turns out that by far the majority of Atlantic Creoles belong to Type-B, preserving (in general) the short-long distinctions of EME (as also do the present Standard Englishes of England and the Americas). It is therefore of particular interest to examine the Type-A systems. There are only three groups of these:

(4) a. Surinam: Sranan;
 Eastern Maroon Creole (Ndyuka, Pamaka, Aluku, Kwinti)
 Western Maroon Creole (Saamaka, Matawai)
 b. Jamaica: Eastern Maroon Creole[24] (Maroon Spirit Language (MSL)

---

23. The fact that length is indicated by a length-symbol [ː] in EME, and by doubling the vowel in Jamaican is irrelevant here, being purely a matter of notation and/or interpretation. The point is that there is a contrast between two types of vowels.

c. Krio: Krio (Sierra Leone Krio, Aku (Gambia), Pichi, Kamtok, etc.)

A related type of behaviour can be seen in the treatment of Early Modern English diphthongs followed by a coda consonant. Here the dimoraic diphthong is reduced to a monomoraic monophthong, indicated in bold type.

Table 8. Type A systems compared with Jamaican

English	Jamaican	MSL	Krio	Sranan
white	wait	*wete*	*wεt*	*weti*
fight	fait	*fete*	*fεt*	*feti*
night	nait	*net*	*nεt*	*neti*
knife	naif	*indepe*	*nεf*	*-nefi*
time	taim	*tεm*	*tεm*	*ten*
climb	klaim	*krεm*	*klεm*	*kren*
house	hous	?	*ɔs*	*oso*

9. Coexistence between creole languages and colonial languages

The fact that the word "Maroon" occurs more than once in (4) is not, I think, a mere coincidence, as we will see shortly. Of course, Sranan, the first language in the list, never was a Maroon language, so what is the connection between these languages? To cut a long story short, I believe a case can be made for two types of development in the Atlantic area English-lexifier creoles along the following lines:

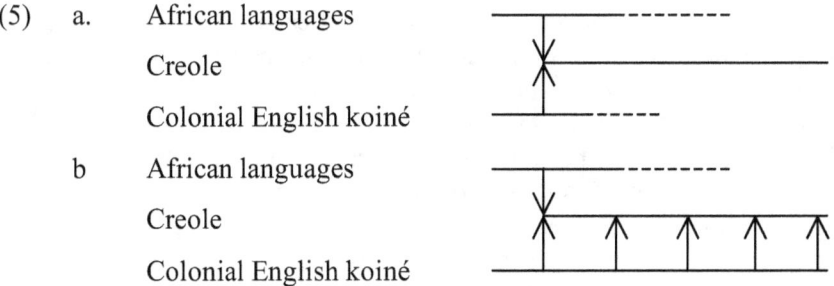

(5) a. African languages

Creole

Colonial English koiné

b. African languages

Creole

Colonial English koiné

---

24. This is no longer functional as a daily language, although it seems still to have been so at the beginning of the 20th century (Bilby 1983; Harris 1994). Present day utterances may be mixed with normal Jamaican Creole.

In the situations of creole creation at issue here, we find African languages and what we have called the Colonial English koiné spoken together in some colony. If the right sociological conditions are present – individuals repressed together, a new sense of community, (Muysken 1981), feelings of resistance (Jourdan 2008), etc. – a new language will be created, *not* because of any wish to approximate the oppressor's language, which they would have learned anyway for reasons of self-preservation, but for two other reasons: To mark the new "pseudo-ethnic" identity created by external forces, and to exclude the oppressor from in-group communication.

It was in fact *necessary* for the creole language's creators to learn the colonial language to a fair degree in the first instance, otherwise the influences from the colonial language in terms of language structure we observe even in the most isolated Maroon Creole would not be present, and could not be explained. Why create a creole at all, and not just continue to use an African language? Because in all cases of slave societies in the English Atlantic colonies we find at least two or three major African languages spoken. There are a number of reasons militating against a single African language (or dialect) from becoming dominant. One's own language was emotionally bound up, for instance, with one's own (African) "country" of origin, and in fact we know that in Jamaica (Cassidy & LePage 1967) using African languages was referred to as "speaking country (language)". Other factors were of course no doubt also relevant.

In the case of Creoles with Type-A vowel systems, the circumstances were such that the influence of Standard English was fairly rapidly removed. There were two sets of circumstances under which this could happen. Firstly, marronnage could occur to such a degree and under such circumstances that it would become a long-lasting state of affairs. In other words, the slaves removed themselves physically from the plantation colony. The second scenario is when the colonial power is removed from the equation by reason of conquest by another colonial power. After the Dutch conquest of Surinam, in accord with the Treaty of Breda, the English and Dutch exchanged the colonies of Surinam and New York. A third possible scenario, the defeat of the colonial power by the slaves, did not occur in the English colonies.[25]

In case (5a), that of marronnage, English became redundant with the lack of communication between slaves and slave-owners. In the second,

---

25. I exclude here victories by maroons over the English/British colonists. These did not permanently affect the status quo.

that of withdrawal by the former colonial power, English would be replaced by Dutch.[26] In the case of Surinam, there was a transition period in which English at first remained dominant (Smith 2009a). This lasted probably for something like twenty years. After that there would be no real function for English any more.

The new functions ascribed to speaking a creole language (Jourdan 2008) are such, I think, as to render fairly pointless the degree of concentration of many creolists on the black-white ratios in the population. It is not so much the lack of opportunity for L2-learning that creates a creole language, but the sociological need for a language of one's own (cf. Muysken 1981, 1994a; Bakker 1997). If the necessary conditions are present for the formation of a creole "society", then a creole language will result. After working hours, in Surinam, for instance, field-slaves were fairly free to associate with others in neighbouring plantations (Arends 1995a). Under such circumstances, two socially parallel societies could co-exist in the same overlapping geographical space. Obviously, the larger the slave group is, as a whole, the more likely a creole language is to have developed. Why a particular percentage should be specified as required for the development of a creole language is the stuff of pure speculation. Compare also Rickford (1977: 193): "Questions of motivation and attitude must also be added to data on numbers and apparent opportunities for black/white contact." I would say that the two first questions are much more important than numerical factors, though of course they cannot be entirely divorced from them.

In Smith (2009a), I work out a scenario in which towards the end of English linguistic dominance in Surinam the majority of English speakers would in fact have been slaves. It would seem odd to assume that because one was black one was unable to learn to speak English functionally. In many African societies, multilingualism is/was the norm. Adding English to the equation would be nothing special.

In case (5b) an extended period of coexistence between a creole language and its colonial lexifier language would presumably result in considerable adstrate influence on the creole. This influence would be different in kind from that involved in the creation of the creole, for which I would reserve the term *substrate influence*. The 300+ years of post-creolization influence from English on Jamaican Creole would just be another case of language contact, or adstrate influence, in other words.

---

26. In the beginning of Dutch rule, the slaves were not "allowed" to learn the colonial language.

I suspect that the typological classification into Type-A and Type-B vowel systems is one of the features that illustrates this. I believe too that a Surinam Creole language like Ndyuka probably gives us the best idea of what an average Atlantic English-lexifier Creole language actually looked like in the early 18th century. If you abstract away from various simple phonological changes, such as the partial loss of liquids, then you have a good idea of its original nature. Sranan itself has undergone a larger degree of adstrate influence from Dutch, but Ndyuka, and its fellow dialects, Aluku, Paramaccan and Kwinti, are all basically descended from Plantation Sranan as it was spoken on 18th century Dutch plantations, although they too are not without Dutch influence.

Before I reach my final conclusion regarding Type-A and Type-B systems, and the family relationship of the Atlantic Creoles, I must state a number of things in regard to the history of Krio, the creole language of Sierra Leone.

10. Where did Krio come from?

Huber (1999a) presents very detailed population data for the Sierra Leone Colony, reproduced here in Table 9. The figures in brackets represent his estimates. Huber believes that the primary linguistic influence on Krio is that of the Nova Scotian settlers. The Nova Scotians were freed slaves from various states of America. Of those who travelled from Birch Town, Nova Scotia, about half the whole group, ca. 20% were from the Carolinas, and ca. 40% from Virginia, according to Huber (1999a). Nearly 30% had been born in Africa but it could be assumed that these had acquired some knowledge of an American slave language, in the intervening period of at least twelve years according to Huber (1999a). I agree, though not about the actual slave language.

Huber (1999a) assumed that the Virginians would speak some form of Virginian Black English, and the Carolinians Gullah. By 2004, however, he was favouring the position that some of the Virginians might have spoken Gullah-like varieties. In footnote 15 in Hackert & Huber (2007), it is stated:

> As Huber (2004: 73) notes, the assumed Gullah-Krio connection is made problematic by the fact that only a quarter of the Nova Scotian Sierra Leone settlers actually came from what is now the Gullah-speaking area; what this indicates, according to Huber (2004: 77), is that, in the eighteenth century, Gullah-like varieties may have been in existence in Virginia, which would

Table 9. Sierra Leone census figures from Huber (1999a)[27]

	4/1792	12/1792	10/1800	3/1802	4/1811	12/1818	7/1820	1/1822	4/1826	12/1844
Poor Blacks	(56)	(55)	(37)							
Europeans	(124)	(69)	~24	27	28	115	120	128	113	175
Nova Scotians	1091	1025	(954)	913	982	691	730	722	578	597
Maroons			525	515	807	610	595	601	636	470
Indigenous Africans			~50	40	100	997	1046	3526	3275	2971
Kru			40-50	60	(750)	746	727	947	947	717
Liberated Africans					~1000	6406	8041	7969	10714	36990
Disbanded soldiers							1216	1103	949	382
West Indians							85	85	141	106
Liberians										82
Total	1329	1207	1635	1555	3702	9565	12509	15081	17354	42490

27. I omit several columns from the late 1840s.

be in agreement with the 'Rainbow Hypothesis' (Kautzsch & Schneider 2000: 251–252), which states the following: 'Historically speaking, the boundaries of Gullah were not as clearly delimited as they appear today, either regionally or structurally. Apparently, during (at least) the 19th century, the African American population of the southernmost third of South Carolina spoke a variety different from the rest of the country, and more closely related to present-day Gullah. In other words Sea Island Creole (Gullah) was not sharply delimited from mainland earlier AAVE, but there was a form of 'South Carolina Lowland Earlier AAVE' which formed a transition zone between Sea Island Creole and inland AAVE.

This is a complex piece of reasoning. I can see why Huber would like Gullah-like varieties to have been present in Virginia, as this would make the proportion of creole language speakers among the Nova Scotia Sierra Leone settlers potentially much higher. But Kautzsch & Schneider's Rainbow Hypothesis was concerned with the southernmost part of South Carolina, and not with Virginia.

To look for evidence for the speech of the Nova Scotia settlers Huber examines a collection of letters emanating from the Nova Scotian settlers in Nova Scotia and Sierra Leone between 1791 and 1800 (Fyfe 1991). His final conclusion is however that "the letters do not in themselves offer firm proof that the language of the NS settlers was Gullah-like."

In the absence of such firm proof, it would seem justified to re-examine the only other reasonable hypothesis, that Krio is basically descended from the Western Maroon language of Trelawny Town in the so-called Cockpit Country in Jamaica. I will do this in Section 11.

11. Krio as a Maroon language

Before going into any detail on the Maroon-origin hypothesis, I will remind the reader of some of the important sequence of events that are relevant for the history of the Jamaican Maroons, and in particular the Western Maroons. Events of *possible* relevance for the Maroon communities are in normal type, contextual information is italicized. Also important are questions of long-tem lack of English colonial control.

After the conquest of Jamaica by the English in 1655, most of the Spanish slaves reputedly became Maroons. They supposedly formed the basis of the Eastern Maroons (Dallas 1803), who became English-lexifier creole-speaking at some unspecified period. At the time of the Maroon treaties, the Eastern Maroons had three settlements, all of which still had some individuals with some knoweledge of MSL at the time of Bilby's Jamaican fieldwork (Bilby 1983).

Table 10. Maroon timetable

Date	Event
1624	*Colonization of St. Kitts (claimed 1623)*
1627	*Colonization of Barbados (claimed 1625)*
1655	Conquest of Jamaica from the Spanish (Barbados, St. Kitts)
1655	Marronnage of Spanish slaves on Jamaica (supposed basis for Eastern Maroons) (Dallas 1803, Vol. 1: 27)
1667–1675	80% of Surinam English leave with around 1400 slaves for Jamaica (some to Surinam Quarters, now in Westmoreland Parish).
1690	Slave insurrection in Parish of Clarendon, Jamaica (this formed the basis of the Western Maroons (Dallas 1803)
1731	Beginning of 1st Maroon War
1738	Treaty with the Western (Leeward) Maroons of Trelawny Town, Jamaica (including those of Accompong)
1739	Treaty with the Eastern (Windward) Maroons of Jamaica
1775–1783	*American War of Independence*
1783–1784	*Black Loyalists (pro-British) ex-slaves transported to Nova Scotia*[28]
1792	*Black Loyalist Nova Scotian ex-slaves transported to Sierra Leone*
1795–1796	2nd Maroon War with the Maroons of Trelawny Town, Jamaica
1796	Trelawny Town Maroons deported to Nova Scotia
1800	Trelawny Town Maroons transported to Sierra Leone, where, on arrival, they put down a revolt by the Nova Scotians.

The Western Maroon settlements, of relevance for Krio as we shall see, apparently owe their existence largely to a large-scale insurrection in Clarendon parish in 1690 (Dallas 1803). After the so-called First Maroon War – about 1731–1738, separate peace treaties were drawn up with the two groups. The war had resulted in a stalemate. The leader of the Western Maroons was Cudjoe, based in what was later called Trelawny Town. His brother Accompong, who was the second signatory to the treaty between the Westen Maroons and the English, was based in the settlement of Accompong (Town), which is named after him (Dallas 1803).

---

28. See http://www.gov.ns.ca/nsarm/virtual/africanns/ "African Nova Scotians: in the Age of Slavery and Abolition".

Fifty-seven years later, in 1795, the so-called Second Maroon War began, provoked by the British colonial leadership, in the person of Lord Balcarres (Bilby 1984). This involved only one of the two Western Maroon towns, Trelawny Town. The Maroons of Accompong did not take part. In short, the Trelawny Town Maroons, the largest Maroon group, were promised that they could remain on Jamaica if they surrendered, but Balcarres reneged on this promise. They were deported to Nova Scotia in 1796, followed in 1800 by a further move across the Atlantic to warmer climes in Sierra Leone, like the Nova Scotia settlers before them.

On their arrival in Sierra Leone, they were immediately employed to help the English garrison put down a rebellion among the Nova Scotia settlers, who were dissatisfied with conditions there. The Maroons also dominated handcrafts and various other small trades for a time (Fortin 2006). These factors may be supposed to have resulted in a higher status for the Maroons vis-à-vis the Nova Scotia settlers.

Huber (1999a: 72) quotes one valuable witness, who compares the language of the Nova Scotians with that of the Maroons. "In 1820, an observer of Freetown said about the Nova Scotians: "They speak English well and it is their mother tongue; ... The Maroons ... speak a language of their own, which is a corrupt English" (quoted from Jones 1971: 67)." Huber (1999a),[29] does not further discuss this observation, but it is the only source he reports which discusses differences between the speech of the Maroons and the Nova Scotians. "... speak English well" does not have to mean anything more than that their speech was comprehensible to English-speakers from Britain. Something similar to Afro-American Vernacular English (AAVE) would fit the bill. "... a language of their own" suggests, however, that a largely incomprehensible form of speech was spoken by the Maroons. I will point out a number of reasons for thinking this language to have been a Maroon Creole brought from Jamaica, and one that was to form the basis of present-day Krio.

To mention right away what might be seen as a drawback to the Maroon-Krio hypothesis, the Accompong Maroons of today do not speak Krio or Western Maroon Creole, and apparently have only spoken ordinary Jamaican Creole within human memory. One reason for this, however, may well have been their very small numbers. In 1801, a census was held among the Maroons, following the departure of the 550 or so Trelawny Maroons (Dallas 1803). The returns were as follows:

---

29. He also mentions this in Huber (1999b), but does not expand on it.

Table 11. 1801 Jamaican Maroon census

Town	Eastern Moore Town	Charles Town	Scotts Hall	Western Accompong Town
Men	53	65	13	38
Officers		7		
Boys	20	30	12	25
Women	83	81	10	47
Girls	12	24	11	11
Children	110	54		15
Invalids		2		
Totals	278	263	46	136
Grand total				723

To provide a preliminary justification for what I claim counts as a lack of English/British colonial control, compare the Surinam situation. The period of English control in Surinam only lasted 17 years, from 1651 to 1667. However, I have argued that the influence of English could have remained strong until at least the 1680's (see Smith 2009a). By this time the majority of "English speakers" would have been slaves, I argue. However, with the departure of most of the English planters by 1675 with their pre-1667 slaves, the function and utility of English – the second language of most slaves after Sranan – would have rapidly come to an end.

This is the basic reason why the Surinam Creoles look so different from the other English-lexifier creole languages of the Atlantic area, the lack of English infuence during a long period of colonial control.[30] However, if we examine Table 12 (an extract from Table 10), we can see that prior to the removal of most Western Maroons from Jamaica to Nova Scotia, and thence to Sierra Leone in 1800, they had enjoyed more than a hundred years of lack of significant influence from Standard English, as compared with 35 years under this influence.

What I need to do now is provide more evidence a) that Krio has its origins in the Caribbean, and b) that the Black Loyalists were not likely to have spoken anything resembling Krio. If the Caribbean connection is likely, then the only possible basic source for Krio must have been the original language of the Trelawny Town Maroons.

---

30. This was already proposed as a possible explanation by Schuchardt (ca. 1892) (translated in Gilbert 1985).

Table 12. The Western (Leeward) Maroon timetable

1655	Conquest of Jamaica from the Spanish (Barbados)
1660s	Development of Clarendon planations by the English
1690	Slave insurrection in Parish of Clarendon, Jamaica (this formed the basis of the Western Maroons)
1731	Beginning of 1st Maroon War
1738	Treaty with the Western Maroons of Trelawny Town, Jamaica (including Maroons of Accompong)
1796	Trelawny Town Maroons deported to Nova Scotia
1800	Trelawny Town Maroons transported to Sierra Leone, where they put down a revolt by the Black Loyalist Nova Scotians.

I have already shown that Krio and the Surinam Creole languages both have Type-A vowel systems, which also involves the demoraicization of diphthongs. I have associated this with the lack of colonial control in both cases. In general, other creoles have dimoraic equivalents for English tense (long) vowels and diphthongs. I have also shown that Type-A vowel systems also occur in the Maroon Spirit Language of the Eastern Maroons, which used to function as a group language up till roughly the end of the period 1870–1900. Before this these maroons had been living in comparative isolation for the better part of 200 years. The only present function of the Maroon Spirit Language (or *deep language*) is to communicate with ancestral spirits born on Jamaica, whereas the the spirits of the earliest ancestors (often born in Africa) are addressed in Kromanti (with a basis of Twi-derived lexicon) (Bilby 1983).

Do the two putative Jamaican Maroon Creole languages have anything else in common apart from their vowel systems, and history of extra-colonial status? The answer to this question is in the affirmative. However, we can ask the following more relevant question: Do the two putative Jamaican Maroon Creole languages have anything uniquely in common? And the answer to this question also seems to be *yes*. Krio (and its descendants) have an identificational copula *na* as does MSL. As we have seen in other (basilectal) creole varieties the highlighter in cleft focus constructions is the same as the identificational copula. This highlighter is frequently used in question word questions in Krio. Question words are also frequently accompanied by contrastive focus markers in other creoles, Saramaccan being a case in point (Smith 1996). In (6), I give examples of these usages of *na*:

(6) *Na* copulas
    i. IDENTIFICATIONAL COPULA
  a.   *da   man de   **na**   mi ongkul*
       DEM man DIST ICOP 1SP uncle
       'That man is my uncle.' (Krio, Peace Corps 1985)
  b.   *mi   **na**   gaad amaiti*
       1SG ICOP God Almighty
       'I am God Almighty.' (MSL, Bilby 1983)
    ii. SPECIFICATIONAL COPULA[31]
  c.   ***na**   mi os*
       ICOP 1SP house
       'It's my house.' (Krio, Peace Corps 1985)
  d.   *teh mi ef   **na** Nyakepong ta'k na   mi*
       tell 1SG COND ICOP God   talk REC 1SG
       'Tell me if it is God who talked to me.' (MSL, Harris n.d.)
    iii. HIGHLIGHTER
  e.   ***na** **na**w yu pikin de   go skul*
       FOC now 2SG child IMPF go school
       'It is now that your child is going to school.' (Krio, Peace Corps 1985)
  f.   ***na**   yu bin[32] na   legonanan*
       FOC 2SG PST   LOC distant.place
       'You were at a distant place.' (MSL, Bilby 1983)
    iv. HIGHLIGHTER + Q-WORD
  g.   ***na** **we-tin** yu de   du*
       FOC Q-thing 2SG IMPF do?
       'What are you doing?' (Krio, Peace Corps 1985)
  h.   ***na** **huma** kuda du mi dat   sonti*
       FOC Q.HU   POT do 1SG DIST thing
       'Who could have done that thing to me?' (MSL, Bilby 1983)
    v. PREDICATE CLEFT
  j.   ***na** **it** i   bin dohn it*
       FOC eat 3SS PST PRF   eat
       'He had eaten.' (Krio, Peace Corps 1985)

---

31. Here I follow Declerck 1988.
32. In Pichi (Yakpo 2009), this would have to be *bìn de nà*, rather than *bin na*. It must also be stated that in this example, there is no indication in the translation that *you* was focussed, although from the context this seems quite likely.

k. **nà waka** wì waka go de
FOC walk 1PL walk go DST.A
'We walked there.' (Pichi, Yakpo 2009)

vi. DESCRIPTIONALLY IDENTIFICATIONAL COPULAS[33]

l. **nà** rop **dat**
FOC rope DIST
'That's a rope.' (Pichi, Yakpo 2009)

m. **na** di wan **dat**
FOC DEF one DIST
'That's the one.' (MSL. Bilby 1983)

The occurrence of *na* has been examined in greater detail as regards the individual categories distinguished. For reasons of space I could not give all the examples for each language examined. However, the overall picture is given in Table 13.

Table 13. The "Jamaican Maroon"-family copulas

	Krio	Pichi	NigP	Kamtok	MSL
there	de	de	dyar/de	de	
locative copula	de	de	de	de	
existential copula	de	de	de	de	
imperfective marker	de	dè	dè	di	(d)e/he
identificational copula	na	nà	bì/nà	na	na
specificational copula	na	nà	nà	na	na
highlighter	na	nà	nà	na	na
highlighter + Q-word	na	nà	nà	na	na
highlighter + predicate cleft	na	nà	nà	na	
descriptionally id. copula		nà	nà	na	na
that	da(t)	da(t)	dat	dat	da(t)

The top four rows of the table are the same as those of Table 6. However, the two rows of *identificational copula* and *highlighter* have been expanded to six, with constructions that seemed to employ the same markers in Krio/Pichi, for which the fullest data was available. The relationship and contribution of Krio to the (originally) pidgin forms of West Africa, such as Nigerian Pidgin and Kamtok (a.k.a. Cameroonian Pidgin), is well-known. I

---

33. Yakpo (2009) refers to these as presentative, rather they appear to form a subtype of what Declerck (1988) has called *descriptionally identificational*. Yakpo further characterizes them as "inverted copula clauses with deictic force".

am of course particularly interested in MSL in the last column, on which I will expand in the next paragraph.

Considering the small amount of published sentence material on MSL, and the fact that it has now downgraded to ritual language status, it is very striking to see how much parallelism can be found in the use of *na* with what we could call the "Jamaican Maroon family". The lack of information at the top of the MSL column is of lesser importance, since the (Basilectal) Atlantic English-lexifier creoles universally have a *there*-derived form here. I regard the dark-grey-shaded part of Table 14, however, as very important in the question of the putative relationship between Krio *cum suis* and MSL (as the likely former creole of the Eastern Maroons of Jamaica). This can, I think, be interpreted as positive linguistic evidence that Krio is basically descended from the Western Maroon Creole of Jamaica.

In Table 14, I compare all the basic [–colonial control] languages in a table with Saramaccan of two periods, 1778–1805 and 20th/21st century; Sranan of three periods, late 18th century, mid-19th century, and 20th century; Ndyuka; Krio; and MSL. The purpose of this is to compare the above-mentioned features, and provide information on some additional ones, where such information was available to me.

Many creolists have compared the copular Krio *na*-usages to Sranan *na*. This is a mistake, however, for all types apart from the locative prepositional usages. I will briefly sum up here what must have happened. A number of function words in Sranan and the closely related Ndyuka have lost their initial consonants (cf. Rickford 1980). For our purposes we are concerned with:

(7) CV-proclitics which tend to lose their initial consonant
 imperfective marker *de > e*
 identificational copula/highlighter *da > a*
 definite article *da > a*
 general locative prep. *na > a*

The identificational copula and the article are the same in origin, but can be regarded as functionally distinct. What apparently happened is that in the 19th century at some point the *da*-words apparently ceased to have an initial *d* in the grammars of speakers, while the preposition *na* retained its *optional* full form.

Table 14. The Surinam Creoles compared with the Jamaican Maroon Creoles[34]

	Sara 1778–1805	Sara	Sran 1783	Sran 1855	Sran	Ndyu	Krio	MSL
there	*de*	*dɛ*	*de*	*dè*	*de*	*de*	*de*	
locative copula	*de*	*dɛ*	*de*	*de*	*de*	*de*	*de*	
existential copula	*de*	*dɛ*	*de*	*de*	*de*		*de*	
imperfective marker	*tann*	*ta*	*de*	*de*	*e*	*e*	*de*	*(d)e*
identificational copula	*da*	*da*	*da*	*(d)a/na*	*(n)a*	*(n)a*	*na*	*na*
specificational copula	*da*		*da*	*(d)a/na*	*na*	*(n)a*	*na*	*na*
highlighter	_*weh*	_*wè*	*da*	*na*	*(n)a*	*(n)a*	*na*	*na*
highlighter + Q-word	_*weh*	_*wè*		*na*	*na*	*na*	*na*	*na*
highlighter + predicate cleft		_*wè*	*da*	*da/na*	*na*	*na*	*na*	
descriptionally id. copula		_*wè*	*da*	*da*		*na*	*na*[35]	*na*
that	*da/dide*	*dí de*	*da(tti)*	*datti*	*dati*	*dati*	*da(t)*	*da(t)*
general locative *at, in, to,...*	*na*	*a*	*na*	*na*	*(n)a*	*(n)a*	*na*	*na*
recipient (talk, give, to)	*na*	*na*		*na*			*na*	*na*
recipient (serial)	*da*	*dá*	*gi*	*gi*	*gi*	*gi*		
negative	*no*	*ná/án no (na)*	*no*		*no*	*(n)á*	*nɔ*	*no*
definite article	*di*	*dí*	*da*	*da*	*(n)a*	*(n)a*	*di*	*di*

All three cases then came to be treated as (*n*)*a* with an optional initial nasal, by a wrong analogy in the first two cases. We can visualize the following stages:

(8) Stages in the development of *da* to *(n)a*
  forms   copula/highlighter   article   preposition
  stage 1:   *da*   *da*   *na*
  stage 2:   *(d)a*   *(d)a*   *(n)a*
  stage 3:   *a*   *a*   *(n)a*
  stage 4:   *(n)a*   *(n)a*   *(n)a*

---

34. I employ various shades of grey with bold and plain type to emphasize the relatedness of various forms.
35. Evidenced from Pichi.

If we did not have early evidence on the Surinam Creoles at our disposal we would not be in position to restrict the *na* cases to Krio and MSL. At this point one might ask whether it is not possible that Krio and MSL did not also go through the same "replacement" process as operated in the Surinam Creoles. However, early forms of Krio *na* do not exhibit any consonant loss (Schuchardt, ca. 1892, in Gilbert 1985; Hutchinson 1861).

Assuming the correctness of the changes in the forms of copula/article/preposition markers as set out schematically in (8), we would end up with the corresponding stage to stage 4 in (9):

(9) Krio and MSL forms

forms	copula/highlighter	article	preposition
Krio	*na*	*di*	*na*
MSL	*na*	*di*	*na*

The definite article has a different vowel in these languages; so it has no role to play. There is also the problem that recorded forms without an initial consonant are lacking. It is true that MSL utterances do display Jamaican-1 *da/a*-reflexes for the imperfective marker. That is, the initial consonant is optional here. I suspect that these are in fact ordinary Jamaican Creole intrusions. Crucially, however, no such form as *na* occurs for the imperfective marker. Furthermore, the only imperfective form restricted to MSL is (*h*)*e* which can be explained as developments of the Jamaican-2 form *de*, with optional consonant deletion. Lastly, in neither the copula/highlighter nor the preposition – the cases we are interested in here – has optionality of the initial consonant been reported.

12. Why the language of the Nova Scotian settlers cannot be considered Proto-Krio

We saw in 10 that the sociohistorical basis for Huber arguing a Gullah-like creole to have been spoken in Virginia (Huber 2004) is doubtful. In addition, if Krio were to be basically descended from a Gullah-like creole, we would expect Krio and Gullah to share the same typology in vowel systems. Krio, as we saw above, has a Type-A vowel system. Gullah has a Type-B system, most easily seen in Turner's (1949) transcription of diphthongs. For monophthongs he uses IPA symbols indicating the quality of the vowels rather the quantity.[36] For Gullah a type-B system is not unexpected, given the long period of Carolina's history as an English/British colony. I give a comparison in Table 15.

Table 15. Gullah's type B-diphthongs

English	Jamaican	MSL	Krio	Sranan	Gullah[37]
white	*wait*	***wete***	*wɛt*	*weti*	*wɐɪt*
fight	*fait*	***fete***	*fɛt*	*feti*	*fɐɪt*
night	*nait*	***nɛt***	*nɛt*	*neti*	*nɐɪt*
knife	*naif*	***indepe***	*nɛf*	*-nefi*	
time	*taim*	***tem***	*tɛm*	*ten*	*tɒɪm*
climb	*klaim*	***krem***	*klɛm*	*kren*	
house	*hous*	***?***	*ɔs*	*oso*	*hɒʊs*

13. Concluding remarks

What can we conclude from the above? Firstly, the very existence of an Ingredient X demonstrates that all the creoles that exhibit a significant part of it must go back to a common origin, in some sense. By itself it does not of course prove that more than a disparate set of African-derived lexical items were inherited. And it does not prove that more than a jargon was involved.

The problem is how it was inherited. The fact of rapid colonization gives us the only possible explanation, as a number of creolists working with the diffusion of creole "features" like Baker (1999), and Hancock (1969), before him, have realized. But there is still the problem of the carrier, the means. What was the linguistic context of transmission?

I pointed out (Smith 1997) the problem of the *make*-imperatives, or as Yakpo (2009) has it, the *make*-directives. This syntactic construction is as widely disseminated as Ingredient X itself. But now we're talking about syntax. This might give us a better idea of the nature of the carrier, a Proto-Atlantic Slave Community Language, of some complexity. For this idea to work, creolization either has to be very rapid, or we have to conceive of an already-existing expanded pidgin imported from Africa. McWhorter's Cormantin hypothesis is not robust enough, however. I accept in general the criticisms of the Cormantin hypothesis made in Huber (1997).

---

36. Weldon (2008) is silent on the aspect of vowel quantity.
37. The phonetic transcriptions used come from Turner's texts (1949).

As McWhorter points out (McWhorter 1995) a scenario whereby each of the circum-Caribbean creole languages independently selected the English distal locative adverb *there* to function as the locative copula would seem positively miraculous. [38]

I have associated the possession of a Type-A vowel system with the lack of colonial control for long periods, and the possession of a Type-B vowel system with the presence of colonial control for long periods. The second case leads to a significant degree of adstrate influence from colonial English. That such a short period of colonial control was sufficient to create a creole language in the 17th century, means that creolization must be a rapid process. The PASCL was only created once, at the very beginnings of creolization.

The first population figures from Barbados are from 1645.

(10) whites 18,300 (males)
      slaves 6400 (Rickford & Handler 1994)

The fact that these slaves only formed 26% of the population, does not preclude their having developed a separate language of their own. The next figures we have are from Jamaica in 1662, a mere seven years after the English conquest.

(11) whites 5176
      slaves 552 (Lalla & D'Costa 1990)

But these slaves came from mostly from Barbados, where the PASCL was already used, I hypothesize.

Ingredient X and the correspondences in markers and structures force the conclusion that all the Atlantic English-based creoles have a common origin. For a long time the only option appeared to be an African origin. A new view on the speed and functions of creolization makes a Caribbean origin possible.

Our three creole language groups with Type-A vowel systems, the Surinam Creoles, the Maroon Spirit Language (originally the language of the Eastern Maroons of Jamaica), and the Krio group (descended ultimately

---

38. However, to disassociate the selection of the locative copula implicitly from any existential usage of the adverbial, as he does in footnote 5 (1995: 296) would seem unwise, as the existential copula (*there's an X*; *an X exists*) is generally identical to the locative copula.

from the language of the Western Maroons of Jamaica, as I hope to have made plausible) represent early versions of the PASCL – the Proto-Atlantic Slave Community Language. These give us a picture of what the original PASCL looked like. All other Atlantic English-lexifier creoles have been modified by the effects of 300 years of contact with colonial Standard English.

Abbreviations

1PL	first person plural	HU	human
1SG	first person singular	ICOP	indentificational copula
1SP	first person singular possessive	IMPF	imperfective
		IN	inanimate
1SS	first person singular subject	LCOP	locative copula
2	second person	LOC	locative preposition
2PL	second person plural	MAKE	make-directive
2SG	second person singular	NP	noun phrase
3SG	third person singular	POT	potential
3SS	hird person singular subject	PRF	perfect
COND	conditional	PROX	proximate deixis
DEF	definite	PRX.A	proximate Adverb.
DEM	demonstrative pronoun	PST	past
DIST	distal deixis	Q	question marker
DST.A	distal adverb	REC	recipient.
FOC	focus		

Relexification and other language contact scenarios for explaining substrate effects

Pieter Muysken

1. Introduction

In the introductory chapter we discussed the issue of West African substrate influence in the Caribbean Creoles. This chapter focuses on possible explanations for this substrate influence with the process of relexification as the starting point. I contrast this process with a number of other language contact scenarios, as a backdrop to the case studies presented in the next chapters and to our joint conclusions.

At least since the publication of Lucien Adam's *Les parlers afroaryen et malayoaryen* (1883), many people, scholars and educated laymen alike, have assumed that the Caribbean Creoles show evidence of surviving African language features (often termed Africanisms). This assumption has been controversial, both for ideological and for scholarly reasons. We will not dwell here on the powerful ideological dimensions, interesting and important as these may be, but briefly turn to the scholarly issues. These may be divided into two clusters:

(a) Issues of fact: which features in the creoles can plausibly be attributed to African inheritance, and which African languages are involved?
(b) Issues of explanation: how did those features survive in the slave communities, and by which mechanisms did they become part of the creole languages?

These two clusters of issues will be discussed in the subsequent sections of this chapter. After surveying the factual claims in the earlier literature in section 2, the emphasis in section 3 will be on methodological problems and conceptual issues in the study of substrates, and on the possible scenarios that we need to take into account. Section 4 will deal with the process of relexification as the explanatory principle originally dominant in our own research project, exploring several different aspects of relexification. Sections 5–9 contrast relexification with five other possible language contact scenarios: second language learning (5), bilingual convergence and pattern replication (6), code-mixing (7), lexical borrowing (8), and language attrition (9). In 10, I will briefly draw some conclusions, and argue that it is more profitable to study the phenomenon of substrate effects from the overall perspective of bilingual speech, which encompasses L2 learning, relexification, as well as convergence and code-mixing.

2. The facts: earlier studies on African substrate in the Caribbean Creoles

Implicitly or explicitly the observation that there were African influences in the Caribbean Creoles has been part of some creolists' thinking since the early developments of the field, e.g. in the work of Lucien Adam (1883), and subsequently Sylvain (1936) and Herskovits and Herskovits (1936). I am putting aside the issue of lexical elements here as that is covered by Norval Smith's chapters in this volume.

Table 1 contains an overview of the structural features in some of the principal concrete proposals for African survivals in the creoles in more recent times, starting with Turner (1949) (cf. also Holm 1988)). Turner (1949) did research on Gullah English Creole and tried to isolate numerous lexical and structural features of African languages contributing to the make-up of Gullah. He started his work on Gullah after he had heard the language spoken in South Carolina in 1929 and made numerous recordings from the 1930's onward. He pioneered the tracing of African etyma for words in Gullah without a clear English origin, and spent many years exploring various possible African substrate languages.

Alleyne (1980) studied the English-lexifier creoles of the Caribbean in a comparative perspective, arguing for their shared West African roots on the basis of a number of structural similarities. He coined the term 'Afro-American' for the Caribbean Creole languages. As the title of his book suggests, he takes these similarities to be sufficient enough to speak of the group of creoles involved as a genealogical unit, rooted in a common West African substrate.

Boretzky (1983) took a much wider perspective, including all Atlantic Creoles, with an excursus on the Indian Ocean and Pacific creoles. His analysis is purely structural, rather than historical or contact-process oriented, although he does make some remarks concerning contact processes.

Table 1. An overview of earlier surveys of structural African substrate features in the Caribbean Creoles

	Turner 1949	Alleyne 1980	Boretzky 1983	Lefebvre 1998	Parkvall 2000	Migge 2003
Creole languages studied	Gullah	English-lexifier creoles	Various	Haitian	Atlantic	Ndjuka
African languages considered	West African	Niger-Congo	Various	Fongbe	Atlantic African coast	Gbe
Lexicon						61–64 lexical semantics
Segmental phonology		co-artic. stops CV pattern vowel harmony laterals	nasal V nasal harmony prenas. stops e/ɛ and o/ɔ distinction		co-artic. stops high nasal V no Z /b/=/v/ prenas. stops	
Supra-segmental phonology		tones	tones			
Pronominal systems	227–228			141–183		
Determiners				79–84		
Plural			plural marking	84–87	3PL=PL	
Postpositional deictics				89–101		
Fronting	213	171–173				
Predicate cleft		172				
Serial verbs	210–213	167–171			+	90–99

		copula 162–166		111–140	PROG = FUT	64–78
TMA-particles and copula						
Compounding				334–348		
Derivational morphology		noun class prefix Sar. *a-* 154–158	limited morphology	303–339		79–84
Predicate syntax	voice, verbal adjectives	deep structures 158–162		250–278		verbal adjectives 84–90
Reflexives					+	
Complementizers of verbs of saying					+	
Reduplication		173			+	
Adpositions						location 99–105

Boretzky stresses several general issues (36–7): (a) It is not always easy on structural grounds to attribute a substrate feature to a particular African source languages. There are e.g. many structural correspondences between the Kwa and the Mande languages. (b) Many English-, Portuguese-, and French-lexifier pidgins developed first at specific locations along the African coast, and hence may have been influenced by quite specific African languages; (c) the potential substrate influence depends also on contrasts in the structural features of the languages involved.

Lefebvre (1998), studying the relation between Fongbe and Haitian Creole, postulated that relexification of Fongbe lexical items with French phonetic shapes was a major factor, perhaps the major factor, in the genesis of Haitian Creole. In her work she tests this hypothesis for a number of domains, keeping the substrate language constant for methodological reasons, and taking recourse to other explanations only when there is a major discrepancy between the Fongbe structures and the Haitian Creole structures.

In contrast, Parkvall (2000) took a very different approach. In his massive and very dense study, Parkvall (4) notes a bias towards the Kwa languages as potential substrates in earlier work, and decides to take "any African language spoken close to the coast between Senegal and Angola" as a potential source of substratum features, on the basis of the observation that "creoles should first be examined without reference to demographical data". This is to avoid the potential pitfall of deciding ahead of time which language to take into consideration. Parkvall considers 168 African languages (5–8), and in his conclusions he notes that important substrate languages were potentially Igbo, Ijo (for Berbice), Bantu as a group, Delto-Benuic, Kwa, Atlantic as a group, Akan, and Fulfulde. He notes a strong Kwa influence, which he is not entirely able to account for. There are several problems with Parkvall's study (besides being difficult to process the information it provides).

Note that there is a contradiction between not taking demographic data into account at first and restricting himself to coastal Atlantic Africa, since the latter choice is indeed based on demography. Otherwise the whole world could have provided potential substrate influence. Second, why not limit oneself by historical and demographical considerations when isolating potential substrate languages that may have contributed linguistic features to the creoles? Third, by casting the net so wide, it is never clear, out of a group of similar languages, which one may have provided the substrate feature.

On the positive side, a strong methodological point made by Parkvall (2000: 24) is to contrast features on four dimensions, as in Table 2.

Table 2. Criteria for establishing the source of a particular feature, based on Parkvall (2000: 24)

Certain case of ...	Lexifier language	Substrate language	Common in languages of the world	Common in other pidgins and creoles
Lexifier retention	+	-	-	-
Substrate transfer	-	+	-	-
Restructuring universal	-	-	-	+
Independent development	-	-	+	-

From the analysis of the distribution of the particular feature in the substrate languages, the lexifier languages, the languages of the world as a group, and other pidgins and creole languages it is possible to determine which features can unequivocally be attributed to a specific source.

Migge (2003), working on the Surinamese creole Ndyuka (Eastern Maroon Creole, or EMC), in contrast, focused on individual languages, notably the Gbe languages. Her analysis, both historical and linguistic, is somewhat similar to Lefebvre's work, but considers the historical situation in more detail. Migge's proposed model for the mechanism of substrate influence will be discussed in section 5 below.

Interestingly, no single feature is mentioned by all of the authors discussed here in Table 1. Many features are mentioned only by one or two authors. In addition to considerable divergence, there are also some features common to some of the lists. Particularly in the verbal system there is considerable correspondence between the listings. Serial verbs are mentioned by four authors, as are the TMA system, the copula, and predicate syntax.

The lack of agreement between the authors may simply be the result of the fact that no systematic or quantitative structural comparative research has taken place so far in this area of the type proposed by Dunn et al. (2008). This will become possible now that the Atlas of Pidgin and Creole Language Structures (APiCS, Michaelis et al. 2013) is completed and information on relevant substrate languages will have been added. In chapter 13, we make a first attempt at systematizing our own data in this respect.

For this same reason, we do not know whether the consensus that the verbal system in particular is the locus of West African substrate influence simply reflects a tendency to study this aspect closer or whether it has to with inherent properties of verbal systems.

3. Methodological and conceptual issues

In the identification and analysis of substrate effects, a number of methodological and conceptual issues play a role, worth discussing briefly. A number of general principles should be kept in mind, also with respect to the question of how the substrate features may have entered into the creole languages, the issue of contact scenarios further discussed in sections 4–9.

The first one is presupposed by the discussion in this section, to wit the *Uniformitarian Principle*, which states that processes postulated to have occurred in the past must be explainable in terms of current developments. Without this principle, all speculation about what happened before is futile. However, 17th century sugar plantations were very different from any current social setting, as far as we know, so we have to be cautious in applying this principle, using whatever historical data about plantation societies are available.

Oft-cited is also the *Cafeteria Principle* (Dillard 1970), which holds that we should avoid loading our trays, looking for a large variety of African languages to find a possible substrate source for a feature in a particular creole language. Only a few languages have been found to be really relevant in a given setting, and in this project we have limited ourselves to Kikongo and Gbe.

The limitation to a few languages is particularly relevant because of the *Founder Principle*, brought into Creole Studies from population genetics, which states that the original population brought into a new setting has disproportional influence because of the features transmitted to its offspring (Mufwene 1990). During the long history of a plantation colony slaves with many different language backgrounds were typically put to work though the languages of the slaves that were there near the beginning are the most influential in the eventual structural make up of the resulting creole. However, the same does not hold for lexical influence. Some languages which arrived relatively late in a plantation colony may have left a large number of lexical borrowings.

A fourth principle that is often invoked is that of *Cultural Predominance* as playing a more important role than demographic predominance. It is assumed that certain African groups present in Caribbean slave societies have played a role disproportionate to their size in shaping the eventual creole because their religion or cultural value systems were adopted by others outside their own language group. Thus Lefebvre (1999) argues that the Fon people were not only important numerically, but also because of their role in organizing African religious cults.

Fifth, it is important to take account the *lingua franca* practices in Africa in the pre-slavery period, as today (see Singler 1988 for a demonstration of the importance of substrate homogeneity). The African slaves may have spoken several African languages, and those languages used as a lingua franca may have had more of a chance to leave their imprint on the eventual creoles than others only used within a single ethnic group.

A further methodological point is that substrate influence may interact with *universal properties* of language systems (cf. the contributions in Muysken and Smith 1986). As argued by Singler (1988), more marked properties will only survive in the creole if there is a homogeneous substrate presence. Otherwise, only unmarked properties, for the origin of which a multi-causal explanation is available, will survive. Therefore substrate influence is subject to *convergence* or *restructuring*, and substrate properties do not always survive intact. Thus an African substrate property in a creole need not be an exact structural copy of that property in an African language. The same also holds for superstrate properties.

A final methodological point to consider is the nature of the exact European target language in processes of second language learning. A simplifying assumption is to take some standard variety as the point of departure, but this assumption has already been criticized for a long time, e.g. by the proponents of *français populaire* as a dominant factor in the genesis of the French-lexifier creoles. Obviously, ordinary spoken forms of European languages are likely to have been the target. However, it is not always the case that these corresponded to regional dialect forms, since the colonization effort often was initiated from the metropolitan centers. Exceptions would be e.g. Berbice Dutch in Guyana and Negerhollands in the Virgin Islands, where the colonial settlers were speakers of Zealandic or West-Flemish dialects rather than of Amsterdam Dutch. However, sometimes, the target may have already been a form of interlanguage, since newly arrived slaves did not learn their version of the emerging pidgin/creole primarily on the basis of input from the colonial settlers, but rather from slaves already present.

Turning next to the question of **how** substrate features may possibly have entered the Caribbean Creoles, we will adopt the uniformitarian position that we should answer this by having recourse to studying processes or scenarios that could occur in present-day contact settings as well. It is true that present-day social settings are very different from the 17th and 18th century slavery plantation settings, but this should mostly mean that the intensity with which these processes have occurred may differ from what we know from contemporary settings. We can divide the scenarios into three groups:

- those particularly relevant to the *earliest* stages of pidgin/creole genesis: relexification and L2 learning
- those particularly relevant to *intermediate* stages: bilingual convergence and code-mixing
- those particularly relevant to *late* stages in the process: borrowing and attrition.

These scenarios should be evaluated on three dimensions: (a) How **well studied** is the process at hand? How well do we comprehend it? (b) How **plausible** is it historically that this process occurred in the plantation setting, as far as we understand it? (c) How **effective** would the scenario be, given what we know of the features and outcomes of the process in general, in bringing about the linguistic result that we observe?

In the project on which this book reports, the results from a number of subprojects were compared and interpreted in the light of theoretical perspectives that emerge from recent work on language contact and bilingual language use, including the domains of code-switching and second language acquisition. The central issue was to which extent the different components – lexical items, function words with lexical content, purely grammatical function words, and phonological and morphological patterns – behave differently in the processes of relexification and retention. I will first turn to a more detailed analysis of the processes involved, taking relexification as the point of departure since this was the process we had initially postulated as responsible for the genesis of the Surinam Creoles.

4. Relexification

The first early stage scenario, *relexification*, is characterized by rather specific features. Given its rarity as a process of language contact world-wide, it has not been very well studied, and generally not as an ongoing process. Its outcomes are not at all the same in different settings where it is supposed to have occurred. It is not implausible, under certain assumptions, that relexification occurred in the plantation setting, and it certainly would be effective in leading to strong African structural survivals in the creoles.

Relexification involves the replacement of the word form of a lexical entry or lemma from language A with a form from language B, while maintaining the further properties of the original lemma. Dutch *zeggen* 'say' takes a bare noun phrase dative complement in some constructions (*zeg hem dat* Y 'tell him that Y') or prepositional phrase with *tegen* 'against' (*ik zei tegen Jan dat* Y 'I said to John that Y'). Now we could relexify *zeggen* with English *say*, and the result would be *say him that* Y ('tell him that Y') or *I say against him that* Y ('I say to him that Y'). An English word form would be introduced, but the use and range of meanings of the verb would remain Dutch.

Relexification occurs occasionally in ordinary forms of language contact, and is often referred to as 'interference' when it concerns individual lexical items. However, on a massive scale it only occurs in very specific settings (e.g. the case of Media Lengua studied by Muysken 1981, 1988, 1997, 2013, where Ecuadorian Quechua has been relexified with Spanish roots). An example from Gómez Rendón (2008: 85; glosses adapted) is:

(1)   ai-**manda**   lexo-**ta**   bi-**kpi-ka**   uno   blanko   asienda
       there-ABL   far-ACC   see-SUB-TOP one   white   hacienda
       kaza-**mi**   asoma-**ri-xu-shka-n-ga**   **wagra**   dueño-ka
       house-AF show.up-RE-PR-NPST-3SG-TOP cow   owner-TOP
       alla-**man-mi**   contento   i-**shka**
       there-AL-AF   happy   go-NPST
       'Then, while he saw it far away, a white hacienda house became visible, and the owner of the cow walked towards it happily.'

Notice here that all affixes are Quechua, and all roots Spanish. The word *shuk* 'numeral one, determiner a' has been relexified as numeral *uno* rather than as the equivalent *un*, which would reflect the grammaticalized indefinite determiner meaning of the Quechua original. The reflexive meaning of *asomarse* 'show up' has been reconstructed by the Quechua reflexive suffix *-ri-*. Spanish verbs have been regularized to a (C)V- form, as in *bi-* 'see' and *i-* 'go'.

A comparative study of these settings has been undertaken by specialists in language contact studies such as Peter Bakker (1996), often in the context of 'intertwined' or 'mixed' languages. Relexification has also been claimed to be a major mechanism in the genesis of creole languages. Notably, Lefebvre (1998) has argued that Haitian Creole emerged through the relexification of Fongbe (one of the Gbe languages) with French lexical items. Thus the precise properties of the relexification process merit closer scrutiny.

How does a (partially) bilingual speaker relexify vocabulary? At some conceptual level a match is found between the meaning of a lemma in the source language A and some aspect of the meaning to a target language item B. On the basis of this correspondence, the word form (sound shape) of target item B is then grafted onto lemma A. There need not be complete meaning correspondence or correspondence in grammatical category. The Spanish noun form *hambre* 'hunger' has been grafted onto a Quechua impersonal verb root *yarka-* 'be hungry' to yield a new Media Lengua verb *ambrina-* or *ambrinaya-* 'be hungry'. Supposedly, there is a somewhat language-independent notion HUNGER available to the speaker to build the bridge between the two languages. For many verbs indeed such as a conceptual level is plausibly present. Verbs often denote actions that can be portrayed in language-independent conceptual terms even if there are considerable differences in how these languages organize concepts.

4.1. Formally defining relexification

The first studies invoking the notion of relexification were mostly historical and philological, and defined it simply as massive replacement of vocabulary (Whinnom 1956, Voorhoeve 1973). This was at the time that monogenesis of pidgins and creoles on the basis of a single West African Portuguese Pidgin was discussed as a serious option (roughly 1960–1975), and relexification was postulated as the mechanism through which lexical diversity among the creoles (English-lexifier versus French-lexifier, etc.) emerged (Whinnom 1956). In fact, Thomason (2001: 74) and Myers-Scotton (2002: 290) also use this definition.

More structurally oriented definitions followed in the wake of Jackendoff's (1975) more articulated view of the lexicon, illustrated in (2). Since these features are seen as to some extent independent, there are ample possibilities for dissociation between them.

In (Muysken 1981), relexification was defined as the systematic replacement of phonetic shapes of lexical items – the top layer in (2) – with retention of lexical structures. This is illustrated here with the example given above involving the notion of HUNGER.

118   Pieter Muysken

(2) /phon/   /gɪv/   phonological representation
     +F   +V   syntactic categorical feature
                                                    (e.g. [+V])
     STEM+x   gɪv/ge:v/gɪvən   morphological composition
                                                    and properties
     stratal   Anglosaxon   possible stratal feature
     +___X   ___NP1 NP2, ___NP2 to NP1   subcategorization feature
     SELECT   NP1 = animate; NP2 =   selectional feature
                      bounded obj.
     MEANING   TRANSFER OBJECT INTO   semantic feature
                      POSSESSION OF PERSON

(3) /phon/   /ambri-na-/   (Quechua   phonological representation
                      original /yarka-/)
     +F   +V   syntactic categorical feature
                                                    (e.g. [+V])
     STEM+x   Root with required suf-   morphological composition
                      fixes   and properties
     x___+   (NP1) NP2+ta [ACC]   subcategorization feature
                      ___+
     SELECT   NP1 = impersonal null   selectional feature
                      subject; NP2 = animate
                      experience
     MEANING   EXPERIENCER HAS A   semantic feature
                      FEELING OF WANTING TO
                      EAT SOMETHING

While often it is hard to find evidence that the original lexical entries have been maintained, specific examples are telling in this respect:

(4)   *Quechua*   *Media Lengua*   *Spanish*
      [*illa-*]   [*nuway*]   *no hay*
      V   →   V
      'NEG-EXIST'   'NEG-EXIST'   'NEG EXIST.3SG'
      [*tiya-*]   [*sinta-*]   *sentarse*
      V   →   V
      'sit, live, exist' 'sit, live, exist' 'sit'

The negative existential verb *illa-* has been relexified with a new verb *nuway*, modeled on the Spanish combination *no hay*. The positive existential verb *tiya-* has been relexified with *sinta*. Notice that in this case as well, the non-grammaticalized meaning of *tiya-* 'sit' shows up in the Spanish form selected for relexification.

Elaborating on the original proposal for relexification in Muysken (1981), Lefebvre (1998: 16–8) provides the schematic representation for relexification in Figure 5.1:

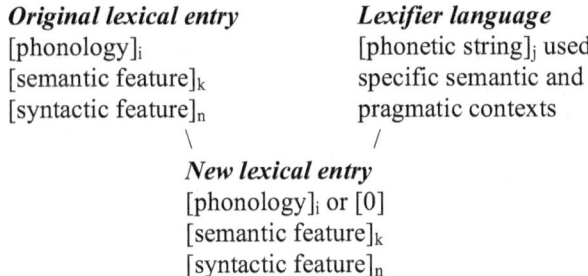

Figure 1. The relexification process, as in Lefebvre (1998)

As noted, Lefebvre (1998) has claimed that relexification was *the* dominant factor operant in the genesis of Haitian Creole. An example of the type of matching between Fongbe and Haitian Creole is given in (4):

(4) Mari te prepare pat   Haitian Creole
     Mari kò ḑà   wɔ̀   Fongbe
     Mary ANT prepare dough
     'Mary prepared dough.'

While in Muysken (1986) relexification was assumed to be only successful for content words, in Lefebvre (1998) all elements are assumed to undergo relexification. There were several other innovations in Lefebvre's model, with respect to the earlier suggestions of Muysken (1981). An important substantial change in Lefebvre's definition is that the new lexical entry can be a null form. A second claim in Lefebvre (1998) is that relexification may involve a change in the word order of the immediate environment of the relexified item. Thus Fongbe functional structures may have been retained independently of the associated word order patterns (Lefebvre 1999). This result appears to conflict with the claim of Myers-Scotton (1993) that function words and word order are closely linked.

The definition given in Mous (1994) for *paralexification* elaborates on Lefebvre's model by suggesting that two phonological representations may become available for a single original lexical entry: the original one and an innovative one used in a special register of the language.

A relexification account commits one, in the strict form of Figure 1, to the transfer of semantic organization features, lexical subcategorization and selection features of individual items. In this sense, the Muysken/Lefebvre definition differs from the earlier definition by Whinnom (1956) and Voorhoeve (1973); whole lexical entries are not taken from the second language, only phonetic shapes.

Furthermore, in the Muysken/Lefebvre definition, any postulated substrate feature should be tied to specific lexical elements rather than to structural properties of classes of items or properties not closely linked to lexical items. Thus the Saramaccan serial verb *poi* (<Eng. spoil) 'subsequent events turn out badly' in the strict relexification logic needs to be derived from a specific West African source. It cannot simply be modeled on a general structural pattern from a West African language. Patterns are not relexified, lexemes are.

Of course it may well be that there are lexical redundancy rules that hold for classes of lexical items, and these rules could be the input to relexification processes. Under such an account, Saramaccan *poi* would not need a specific lexical ancestor in a West African language, but rather could be modeled on other serial verbs, once the serial lexical pattern has been relexified as such. I will return to this possibility below. It is further explored in Yakpo and Bruyn (this vol.) on complex PPs in Sranan. Notice that relexification in this broader sense impinges on the theoretical issue of how to model the differences between languages, and on the lexical learning hypothesis.

The lexical learning hypothesis (Borer and Wexler 1987) was proposed as one way to account for cross-linguistic variation. If cross-linguistic grammatical variation is indeed lexically determined, relexification can lead to structural substrate influence. With the properties of the new lexical items, new grammatical patterns come into a language. If e.g. the postnominal position of an adjective in language X is determined by features of that adjective itself, relexification of that adjective into language Y may lead to the possibility of a post-nominal adjective in that language, even if the language did not have this originally. Thus in Dutch the adjective *generaal* 'general' can occur post-nominally in a few fixed expressions (*Staten Generaal* 'Parliament', *Procureur Generaal* 'State Prosecutor'), based as it is on French post-nominal *général*. However, other Dutch adjectives have to precede their noun, and even *generaal* sometimes occurs pre-nominally, as in *generaal pardon* 'general amnesty', suggesting the prevalence of general patterns over individual lexical representations.

4.2. Relexification and bilingual mixed languages

There are a number of languages that are assumed to have resulted from processes akin to relexification. These are referred to with labels such as 'mixed languages', 'intertwined languages', 'relexified languages', and 'split languages'. However, these bilingual mixed languages are not all similar to one another in the division of labor of the contributing languages, at least in part due to typological properties of the languages involved. A case in point is Media Lengua, the language that led to the original formulation of the relexification process.

Media Lengua owes its particular structure – a radical disjunction between roots, almost exclusively from Spanish, and affixes and enclitics, almost exclusively from Quechua – in large part to the typological features of Quechua, with its highly agglutinative morphology. Quechua is rather exceptional in allowing free borrowing of Spanish verb stems (Muysken 2000), something we only find either among highly isolating languages such as Bazar Malay or Chinese, or among radically agglutinative languages such as Quechua. Even a textbook agglutinative language such as Turkish does not allow direct borrowing of verb roots.

Other reported instances of relexification show different patterns, leading to different types of mixed languages. Much like Media Lengua is Basters Hottentot (den Besten 1987: 23), where also a root (Afrikaans) / affix (Nama / Khoikhoin) distinction is maintained. In contrast, the mixed language Michif, also claimed to have resulted from relexification, shows a noun phrase/verb phrase division between French and Cree (Bakker 1997). Only the material in the noun phrase or determiner phrase is in French; in the verb phrase and at the clausal level Cree is retained. Both Cree and French elements are found among prepositions and adverbs.

Yet a third possible type of relexification is exhibited by languages such as Petjoh (van Rheeden 1994: 226), a mixture of Malay and Dutch. Here both languages contribute functional elements, in different proportions for each category. Very roughly, the verbal and clausal systems show stronger Malay retentions, and in the nominal system, Dutch plays a stronger role.

All these differences imply that whatever happened with Media Lengua is not necessarily illustrative of relexification in general, which is a heterogeneous concept in its different dimensions. Moreover, none of the Caribbean Creoles look like one of these intertwined languages: retention of functional categories from a substrate language is very rare. Berbice Dutch (Smith, Robertson and Williamson 1987; Kouwenberg 1994) shows the largest number of retained elements in this respect.

4.3. Lexical versus functional categories in relexification: different models and predictions

This brings us to the issue of the distinction of content words versus function words. In Muysken (1988) the claim was made that "real" or "pure" relexification, without accompanying semantic change, can only involve content words, since their conceptual equivalents could be established independently of a particular language. Relexification of function words would automatically involve the target language, since function words necessarily depend, for their meaning definition, on L2-internal paradigmatic and syntagmatic relationships.

Consider the case of demonstrative pronouns. In English, we have *this* and *that*, while Spanish has *este* 'this (near speaker)', *ese* 'that (near hearer)' and *aquel* 'that (near neither speaker nor hearer)'. In this case, relexification between English and Spanish becomes tricky. The form *this* can plausibly be relexified as *este*, since in both cases proximity to the speaker (a fairly universal conceptual spatial category) is involved, but for *that* there is a choice, and this choice is difficult to make without involving specific semantic aspects of Spanish.

Consider as a second example the relexification of the English conjunction and preposition *for* in a Dutch context. Here several Dutch candidates are available (*voor, om, want*) and both the access to them and the choice between them involves considerable activation of the Dutch grammatical system in particular.

Verbs, demonstratives and conjunctions can be placed, from a psycholinguistic perspective, on a scale ranging from purely conceptually accessible to purely grammatically accessible. This may have implications for the relexification patterns involved. The following hypothesis can be formulated:

> The more grammatical structure is activated in the access to a lexical item, the more the relexification of this lexical item will involve restructuring due to properties of the target language.

This hypothesis predicts that properties of African lexical items, such as nouns and content verbs, will survive relatively intact in the Surinamese creoles under relexification, while properties of purely grammatical items such as complementizers will undergo extensive restructuring under the influence of the target language, in this case English. Properties of semi-grammatical items such as demonstratives are predicted to form an in-between case.

A further issue, raised by Media Lengua and in Bakker's account of Michif, is whether functional categories receive a phonetic shape from the target language at all, or are retained in their source language shape. In Muysken's (1986) account of Media Lengua, there is a three-fold division between morphological categories.

Table 3. Morphological cartegories in Media Lengua

category	source
affixes and clitics	retained from the L1
function word roots (e.g. deictics and interrogatives)	relexified and restructured
content words	relexified

Lexicalized affixes can either be treated as separate elements or as part of the root, as shown by the example of the verb 'show'. The Quechua form in (5a) can take the various Media Lengua shapes (5b–d). In (5b) the form *bi-* from Sp. *ver* is introduced together with the Quechua causative affix *-chi-*, in (5c) a full Spanish root , and in (5d) both:

(5)   a.   *riku-chi-*
               see-CAU
       b.   *bi-chi-*
               see-CAU
       c.   *mustra-*
               show
       d.   *mustra-chi-*
               show-CAU

As noted above, in Lefebvre (1998) global relexification of all source language elements is proposed. There is no retention of Fongbe lexical shapes in Haitian, even if some Fongbe loans have entered the language. In Myers-Scotton's (2002) account of mixed languages, rather the opposite is predicted based on Muysken's (1986) suggestions about Media Lengua: functional elements are directly relexified, while content words are restructured under relexification. Altogether, as already noted in section 2, there is no unified account at present. Different options are found and predicted.

4.4. Grammaticalization and relexification

I have already mentioned several times that in Media Lengua relexification precedes grammaticalization, since the 'match' is made on the basis of content word correspondences. However, in other cases, the match is made on correspondences that result from grammaticalization. Consider the case of *moro* (in Sranan) or *moo* (in Ndyuka). The latter has been analyzed by Huttar (1981). Consider first the verbal use of *moo*, as in (6) (Huttar 1981: 314):

(6) a. *angii moo mi*
hunger MORE 1SG
'I'm hungry.'
b. *wataa moo mi*
water MORE 1SG
'I'm thirsty.'

The element *moo* can also function as an adverb 'more' and as a comparative marker (7a). In (7b) it appears as both (Huttar 1981: 315):

(7) a. *a langa moo mi*
3SG tall MORE 1SG
'He is taller than I am.'
b. *a moo langa moo mi*
3SG MORE tall MORE 1SG
'He is taller than I am.'

The distribution of *moo* (there are also other uses parallel to the ones listed here) suggest that it is a serial verb with 'exceed, overpower' as its basic meaning and 'more than' as a secondary meaning, which can then be grammaticalized as the adverb 'more'. Huttar (1981: 318–319) points to grammatical parallels in Efik, Twi, and Ewe to the Ndyuka constructions, which could have been the model for the Surinam Creole constructions.

Notice, however, that the relexified form *moo* or *moro* departs from the already grammaticalized form, not from the original lexical form.[1] Thus the type of 'relexification' found in the Surinam Creoles differs from what we

---

1. There is also a verb *pasa* in Ndyuka (Huttar 1981: 317) with a similar but more limited distribution that may have resulted from relexification of the non-gramm-aticalized structure in the West African languages.

find in Media Lengua in that the result of grammaticalization (the end of the chain or the whole chain) may be relexified rather than the starting point (the beginning of the chain). This point has been stressed on numerous occasions by Bruyn (e.g. 2008). Bruyn argues that with Sranan *fesi* the most grammaticalized function is the basis for relexification, while with Sranan *abra* 'to cross' the beginning of the chain is.

5. Transfer in second language acquisition.

The second scenario characteristic of an early stage of creole genesis is that of second language (L2) acquisition with reduced input. If we ask ourselves whether the process is well studied, the immediate answer would be: yes. There has been a flourishing tradition of second language research at least for the last thirty years; there are numerous journals, handbooks, collection of state-of-the-art surveys, etc. However, there are two caveats: much of the research deals with classroom situations, with abundant target input, and with only a limited number of target languages. Second, there is little consensus about the role of the first language, even when only the outcomes of untutored second language acquisition with reduced input are taken into consideration. Of course, it is entirely plausible that second language learning was very important in the plantation setting. Migge (2003: 106) suggests that there are two constraints on substrate influence through second language learning (Andersen 1983; Siegel 1999; Winford 2003): (a) crucial is the availability of a specific target model, phrased by Migge as "enough of a semantic and structural match"; (b) the process of substrate transfer depends on "degree of knowledge of the different source structures". However, it is not clear how effective the L2 learning scenario would be. The model sketched by Migge (2003: 105) to account for the type of L2 acquisition involved in creole genesis is presented in Table 4.

Table 4. Steps in the restructuring of function morphemes from Gbe in the Surinam Creoles (based on Migge 2003: 106)

1	Agents established interlingual identity between a given English input and a semantically equivalent and structurally similar L1 structure
2	Projected the structural principles of their L1 structure onto the English input structure
3	The elements in the English input structure became associated with specific L1 structural slots or elements
4	The English elements were assigned several or all of the semantic, syntactic, and distributional properties of the L1 elment they had been identified with

Regarding the potential relation between relexification and second language acquisition, in second language acquisition research, there has been a considerable divergence of opinions with respect to the role of knowledge of first language lexical items and structural patterns in the process and its outcome. While for many years this role was downplayed, a number of recent proposals have brought it to the forefront again. One of these proposals is to formalize traditional notions about transfer in terms of the Structure Conservation Hypothesis (van de Craats, Corver, and van Hout 2000). The basic idea here is that second language learners will tend to maintain the functional structure of their native language as much as possible when re-creating the second language. This suggests a link between relexification and L2 learning.

In earlier work, Muysken (e.g. 1980) had systematically contrasted relexification and L2 learning, as alternative contact strategies, again drawing an absolute dividing line. There were several reasons for the strict bifurcation between the two strategies. First of all, in my fieldwork around Salcedo in the central Andes of Ecuador, I noted that the type of Spanish interlanguage spoken by incipient Quechua-Spanish bilinguals, migrant *cargadores* (load-bearers) in the urban center differed considerably from the Media Lengua of the originally Quechua-speaking communities near the town. The differences are summarized in Table 5.

Table 5. Schematic contrast between Media Lengua and Quechua-Spanish Interlanguage in central Ecuador

	Media Lengua (relexification)	Interlanguage (L2 learning)
Structure	Complex	highly simplified
Degree of stabilization	rigid	highly variable
Properties	Quechua morpho-syntax and and phonology with slight Spanish influence	Spanish morpho-syntax and phonology with some Quechua influence
Function	in-group language	interethnic communication

Presented in this way, the two contact strategies are completely different. There is no way they can be confused, and consequently relexification and L2 learning were portrayed as alternative routes to pidgin/creole genesis. The question now is whether the Media Lengua/Interlanguage contrast in this extreme form should be generalized to other situations as well, and particularly whether creoles can plausibly be argued to resemble Media Lengua in having resulted from relexification and not more straightforward

L2-learning. The answer is certainly not an unqualified yes, for a number of reasons. First of all, Muysken discovered other contact varieties in Ecuador, which must have resulted from a mixture of relexification and L2-learning, notably Catalangu (e.g. Muysken 1997: 413–414).

A second problem is that at the time the original disjunction between relexification and second language learning was developed, L2 learning was assumed not to be characterized by transfer to any great extent (cf. the work by Dulay and Burt 1974 and much subsequent research). As mentioned above, this has changed in recent years, with the work of researchers such as Van de Craats (van de Craats, Corver, and van Hout. 2000, 2002) and Schwartz (Schwartz and Sprouse 1996). With various caveats and nuances, these researchers claim that the grammatical skeletons erected by the projections from the functional categories of the speakers' native languages, e.g. in the DP (nominal) and CP (clausal) systems, remain intact as the initial hypotheses that L2 learners make about the new target language.

Third, models of L2 vocabulary acquisition present a complex picture, allowing for considerable L1 semantic influence, as found in relexification. When a L2 lexical form is acquired, first, part of its meaning is learned, and only later on, the other dimensions are filled in. As Kroll and Tokowicz phrase it (2001: 49): "During early stages of acquisition, words in the second language, L2, may rely on their counterparts in the first language, L1, to mediate access to meaning." Thus, relexification in its strict sense can be modeled as very initial L2 vocabulary learning without concomitant L2 syntactic learning. Treating relexification as incomplete L2 vocabulary learning has the advantage that it can be viewed as a differentiated process in which the saliency and frequency of the vocabulary items in the L2 input can help determine to what extent they are relexified. Malt and Sloman (2003) show that this even holds for words referring to fairly concrete concepts like 'cup'.

Lexical meaning transfer in L2 vocabulary development thus has been shown to be characteristic of learners in early stages (Kroll and Tokowicz 2001). According to Gass (1996) it is a cognitive strategy in competition with other strategies, while Kellerman (1979) has argued that it is sensitive to L1/L2 distance as well as considerations of markedness. It is particularly prevalent in semantic overextension, according to Odlin (1989).

In any case, processes very much akin to relexification have been assumed both for early L2 acquisition of functional and of lexical categories. However, other types of transfer (e.g. of word order) have been assumed to be much less prevalent, particularly when the output conflicts overtly with target language structures.

6. Bilingual convergence and pattern replication

Bilingual convergence and replication of grammaticalization patterns are operant from the intermediate stage onward. In many communities where languages are spoken next to each other, there is a tendency towards convergence between them. The two languages will start sharing different kinds of patterns: grammatical, lexical, and pragmatic.

The constraints on convergence remain fairly mysterious. Recently some studies have appeared on Spanish-English bilingual convergence, which suggest that there certainly are subtle interference effects between the two languages in speakers who have been bilingual from an early age onward. However, it is not clear how strong these effects are and to what extent they are counter-acted by pressure from monolingual norms in the immediate environment. An influential proposal comes from Silva-Corvalán (1994), who argues that convergence is particularly prevalent when there already similar pre-existing target structures exist. It could be that in the plantation setting, in the absence of strong normative pressure from the colonial standard, interference effects are much stronger.

As noted by Boretzky (1983: 33), Schuchardt, in his article on Saramaccan, already argued that substrate influence is most likely to play a role in the developmental phase of the incipient creole, after initial pidgin formation, but before the creole has been fully nativized.

Thus effects similar to those claimed to have resulted from relexification could emerge after the initial stage, provided that the two languages remain present in the community. Bilingual convergence as a source for Africanisms in the Caribbean Creoles, presupposes, to be sure, the prolonged survival of the African languages on the plantations. This scenario is further elaborated by Margot van de Berg (this vol.) and Tonjes Veenstra (this vol.).

Table 6. Contrasting relexification and pattern replication

	Relexification	Pattern replication
Triggered by	Content word matching	Grammatical pattern matching
Link to grammaticalization	Precedes grammaticalization	May follow grammaticalization
Affects	Lexical entries	Structures
Restructuring	±	+
Local	+	±
Type of bilingualism	Incipient	Balanced

In Table 6, I contrast the results for relexification and pattern replication on several dimensions, summarizing the discussion so far: (a) Is it triggered by corresponding content word meanings or corresponding patterns? (b) Does it precede grammaticalization and may it provide the input for it, or can it follow it? (c) Does it affect lexical items or syntactic patterns? (d) Does it lead to restructuring of the lexical entry involved? (e) Is the process local, affecting just a single point in the clause, or not? (f) Which type of bilingualism is required?

7. Code-mixing

Convergence has often been linked to code-mixing. In an active bilingual community, and hence potentially in an intermediate stage of creole genesis, there often is code-mixing or code-switching. This process is relatively well understood. Code-mixing is frequent in informal in-group conversations in bilingual populations, particularly among younger speakers, as far as we know. It takes various forms, depending both on structural, psychological, and social factors. From what we know of the plantation setting and the languages involved, it is not impossible that there was intimate switching of the congruent lexicalization type (Muysken 2000) between Fongbe or another West African language and L2 English or English pidgin (cf. Muysken, 2008). This may have lead to further convergence between the pidgin and the West African languages. However, the resulting creole is in no way the direct result of code-mixing, since in mixing, considerable amount of lexical material of all contributing languages survives.

In code-switching and code-mixing studies, both the work of Carol Myers-Scotton and associates (1993) on matrix language/embedded language asymmetries, and that of Poplack and associates on nonce borrowings have touched on lexical semantics and the role of functional elements. Of particular relevance is the work by Poplack & Meecham (1995) on the properties of noun phrases in Fongbe / French bilingual speech. These studies can be taken as a point of comparison for the possible bilingual speech behavior of Fongbe speakers in the Surinamese slave setting, as can be seen in van den Berg (this vol.).

If we extend the Fongbe/French code-mixing account to creole genesis, purely insertional code-mixing (Muysken 2000) would lead to the retention of Fongbe grammar, while innovative code-mixing more associated with congruent lexicalization could lead to creole structures not present in the source language.

8. Relexification and lexical borrowing

In my work on Media Lengua (Muysken 1981), a principled dividing line was drawn between relexification and lexical borrowing, a scenario characteristic of the later developmental stages of the creole. Three differences were assumed between the two processes:

Borrowing never involves more than 40% of the vocabulary on the type level, while Media Lengua-style relexification involved all or almost all root vocabulary. Second, in borrowing core lexical elements (e.g. the Swadesh 100 word list) were unaffected, while in Media Lengua these are affected. Third, in relexification, but not in borrowing, the semantic properties of the original lexical entry are retained.

A more comprehensive look at language contact phenomena involving Quechua and Spanish throughout the Andes shows that the sharp division is perhaps not quite warranted, for several reasons. In Bolivian varieties of Quechua, particularly those of Cochabamba, higher percentages of borrowing are found than in Ecuador. There is very extensive Spanish verb borrowing in all Quechua varieties, more than found in other language pairs. There is borrowing of core lexical items in a special register, that of the *waynos* (bilingual mixed songs) in both Peru and Bolivia, although no relexification has been documented there. Finally, for many items, such as Quechua *miku-* 'eat', the semantic distinction between relexification and borrowing cannot be made very readily. The semantics of EAT in the two languages overlaps to a considerable extent.

This does not mean that the processes can be equated. However, within the processes of borrowing between Spanish and Quechua, the potential for relexification is already there even in the varieties where relexification has not been documented: those of Peru and Bolivia.

However, the scenario of lexical borrowing is rather peripheral to creole genesis. Even massive lexical borrowing cannot result in anything like the Caribbean Creoles. Possibly, the surviving African lexical elements can be thought of as borrowings into the emerging creole.

9. Attrition

The final scenario to be discussed here is that of attrition. Since there were relatively few children born in the first half century of the creole societies, intergenerational transmission of the original languages that the captured slaves brought with them was limited. The use of most African languages started declining fairly rapidly, we must assume, and as the slave captures moved southward further along the African coast, slaves of different eras were likely to speak different languages as well.

Attrition, within the individual and across generations, is characterized by a number of processes:

–Loss of infrequent words
–Reduction of morphological and phonological complexity
–Borrowing of more complex grammatical patterns from a dominant language, often with borrowing of the functional elements carrying those patterns
–Loss of stylistic diversity

While attrition of the African languages was undoubtedly an integral part of the sociolinguistic setting in which the creole languages emerged, it is clear that creole languages are not the last traces of the original African languages of the captured slaves, the result of attrition. However, if we add calquing of original African expressions with European lexical items, relexification, some form of attrition may have been involved in creole genesis. Also, the processes of reduction and loss in attrition are also reminiscent of some of the features of creole genesis, as argued by Essegbey (this vol.).

10. Concluding remarks

The overview of the links between relexification and other language contact processes, and the variability of the outcomes that have been claimed as the result of relexification in mixed languages, suggest that there are several options for accounting for the Africanisms in the Caribbean Creoles. Where there is historical evidence, this may be brought in to decide on the most likely scenario. The findings of an overall evaluation can be summarized as in Table 7. Pending the results presented in the following chapters, it looks like bilingual convergence and pattern replication is the most promising scenario to explain the presence of West African features in the Caribbean Creole languages.

This brief survey suggests that closer links between language contact studies, psycholinguistic work on bilingual processing, and creole studies are called for. Even though researchers do not use the same vocabulary, they are often talking about the same thing. In the subsequent chapters we will examine various aspects of the grammar of the Surinam Creoles in the light of their links to the languages of West Africa and to possible scenarios for genesis.

Table 7. An evaluation of possible processes leading to substrate effects in the Caribbean Creole languages

	Well-studied	Plausible	Effective	Rating
EARLY STAGES				
Relexification	no	somewhat	yes	remains open
L2 learning	yes	yes	not really	not really promising
INTERMEDIATE STAGES				
Bilingual convergence and pattern replication	no	yes	yes	promising
Code-mixing	yes	yes	doubtful	suggestive
LATE STAGES				
Borrowing	yes	somewhat	no	wrong track
Arrition	moderate	yes	no	not directly relevant

Abbreviations:

ABL	ablative	NEG	negator
ACC	accusative	NPST	narrative past tense
AF	affirmative	PR	progressive aspect
AL	allative	RE	reflexive
ANT	anterior tense	SUB	adverbial subordinator
CAU	causative	TOP	topic
EXIST	existential	3SG, etc	third person etc singular
MORE	more, exceed, surpass		

**Part II:
Language structures: a sprachbund?**

Trans-Atlantic patterns: the relexification of locative constructions in Sranan

Kofi Yakpo and Adrienne Bruyn

1. Introduction

Sranan and the other creoles of Suriname have long been noted for their use of postpositions in the expression of spatial relations (cf. e.g. Muysken 1987). This characteristic sets these languages apart from the vast majority of Afro-Caribbean English-lexifier Creoles, both in the Americas as well as in West Africa. The use of postpositions, some of which are derived from English words for body-parts, is one of the more conspicuous features pointing towards substrate influence in Sranan. Beyond this particularly visible African presence, the grammar of spatial relations in Sranan contains many more features that suggest a diffusion from Africa, and to be more precise, from the Gbe languages, as well as Western Bantu via Kikongo (for the dominant role of the Gbe substrate of Sranan, as well as the secondary role of the Kikongo substrate cf. e.g. Arends 1995a; Arends, Kouwenberg, and Smith 1995; Huttar 1981, 1986; Migge 1998a, 1998b, 2000, 2003a; Smith 1987; Winford 2000). The affinities of Sranan with these African language(s)/families can be traced in the semantics of individual locative elements. For example, the word *baka*, derived from English 'back' is the regular form employed for the expression of the body part as well as the spatial concept 'behind' in Sranan. The semantics of *baka* overlaps with that of the Gbe (Ewe) item *mègbé* back', which is also employed with both senses. There is good reason to assume that such systematic correspondences in meaning and function represent cases of local relexification, that is, of individual forms. The main purpose of this chapter is, however, to show that the participation of relexified Sranan forms like *baka* in multi-constituent locative constructions constitute cases of *pattern* relexification.

We will show that the concept of pattern relexification can explain the behaviour of Sranan locative elements in instances where an account based on local relexification alone would be stretched to its limits. Pattern relexification makes allowance for differences between Sranan and the substrate languages in the behaviour of individual items. The reason is that the relexification of patterns involves the transfer of lexical properties of individual forms plus their *relational* properties. A central part of the argument for pattern relexification is that Niger-Congo substrate patterns manifest a large degree of homogeneity, and that this probably facilitated the relexification of morphosyntactic blue-prints, or skeletons, in Sranan. At the same time, we will see that Sranan locative constructions also reveal the intricate interplay of substrate patterns, patterns inherited from the lexifier English, influence from Dutch, which has served as a superstrate for more than three hundred years, as well as internal development. In this context, we should justify our use of the terms "lexifier" and "superstrate". Suriname constitutes a case in which the lexifier (the language that provides the bulk of the lexicon, and that of the basic lexicon in particular) and the superstrate (the language that serves as the language of the socially dominant group) of the creoles are not identical (cf. Selbach 2008). The ancestor language of Sranan and the other Surinam Creoles was formed during a relatively brief period of English colonial rule (Smith, this volume on the early history of Surinam), with English serving as the lexifier, and by default, also as the superstrate language. When the Dutch took control of Surinam in 1667, Dutch replaced English as the colonial language, and has thenceforth also served as the superstrate language of Surinam.

One conclusion drawn from the data presented in this chapter is that the presence of substrate patterns in locative constructions is significant, both in a diachronic and a synchronic perspective. The strong parallels in the grammar of spatial relations between Sranan and Gbe in particular provide further support for the existence of a Trans-Atlantic Sprachbund that unites the Surinamese creoles and the Gbe languages with respect to a substantial number of isoglosses.

The Sranan examples in this chapter for which references are not provided stem from a corpus of primary data collected in Suriname and the Netherlands in 2011 by Kofi Yakpo as part of the "Traces of Contact" project of Radboud University Nijmegen. Unless otherwise indicated, examples from the Gbe languages are also from field data, collected by Kofi Yakpo in Ghana and Togo between 2003 and 2011, and/or speaker intuitions of Kofi Yakpo. Tone-marking is provided for the authors' primary data and wherever contained in the sources.

After providing an overview of locative elements in Sranan in Section 2, we describe the expression of three important spatial relations in Sranan and Gbe in Section 3. In Section 4, we attempt to explain the variation encountered in Sranan locative constructions by additionally drawing on

Kikongo data. Section 5 summarizes and systematizes the findings, and Section 6 concludes the chapter.

2. Locative elements in Sranan

This section provides a brief overview of the forms and functions of locative elements in Sranan. The inventory of locative elements (i.e. prepositions and locative nouns) in modern Sranan largely consists of items of English origin, with a minority of Dutch origin. However, these locative elements may appear in constructions that represent substantial departures from the corresponding ones in the English and Dutch. We conclude that the differences between Sranan on the one hand, and the English and the Dutch on the other, are largely due to substrate transfer.

We base our analyses on examples from the Gbe languages Ewe (Ghana, Togo), Gen (Togo), Aja (Togo, Benin), Gun (Benin) and Fon (Benin). We should mention here that the historical evidence suggests that Fon varieties (hence the eastern reaches of the Gbe continuum) constituted the single most important substrates of Sranan, rather than more western varieties like Gen and Ewe. However, we have found it useful to consider corresponding structures from varieties other than Fon because it shows that the templates for expressing spatial relations in all the Gbe languages are virtually identical. This strengthens the argument for a general Gbe origin of the patterns employed to express spatial relations in Sranan, since there is no need to show an exclusive, or even predominant influence of Fon.

The Sranan locative elements employed for expressing the basic spatial relations relevant for the discussion are given in Table 1.

Table 1. Sranan locative elements

Locative element	Meaning	Source language(s)
ini	inner part; in	'in' (Du./Eng.)
na doro	outside	'LOC door' (Eng.)
tapu	top, on	'(on) top (of)'
ondro	bottom, under	'onder/under' (Du./Eng.)
fesi	face; in front	'face'
baka	back, behind	'(at the) back (of)'
fu	general location; Source-oriented	'for' (Eng.)
na	general location	'na' (Igbo/Port. cf. Parkvall 2000: 108)

Some of the forms in the table have corresponding near-homophones in English and Dutch (e.g. Sranan *ondro,* English *under,* Dutch *onder).* Although simultaneous influences from Dutch and English, hence convergence, are in principle possible, the entire system of specific prepositions is derived from the lexifier English. We therefore assume English forms to be the source forms unless the contrary can be proven. The forms *ini* 'inside' and *ondro* 'under' are derived from the corresponding prepositions in English. The elements *baka* 'back, behind' and *tapu* 'top, on' are only found in complex locative structures in English (e.g. *at the back of the car*) and have nominal uses (e.g. *my back*) as well. The element *fesi* is only found with a locative sense in specialized contexts in English but not with a general meaning as in Sranan (e.g. the face of the building). The element *na doro,* literally 'at the door' and with the meaning 'outside' is a Sranan neologism that has no exact correspondence in English or Dutch. Among its spatial senses, the element *fu* functions as a general locative preposition to denote a PLACE, however less prominently so than *na*, which follows below. The preposition *fu* may also be employed to denote a SOURCE and if this is the case, appear without support from other PATH-denoting locative elements, as in (1). One possible explanation for the PLACE and SOURCE senses of this preposition is that the English prepositions *for* and *from* may have converged into *fu* during the formative period of the language.

(1) ala den   wroko disi wi leri **fu** mi papa
     all DEF.PL work this 1PL learn ABL 1SG father
     'All these (types of) works we learned from my father.' (Hart 1996: 17)

At the bottom of the table, we find the only element without a Dutch or English etymology, namely the general locative preposition *na* 'LOC' (with its modern variant *a*). Reflexes of this form are present throughout the family of Afro-Caribbean English-lexifier Creoles, even if *na* is not found in all languages. In Sranan, the preposition *na* 'LOC' functions as a general GROUND marker and may introduce participants with PLACE (2), GOAL (3), SOURCE (4) and PATH (5) roles. In the following sections, we will see how corresponding forms fulfill very similar functions in the substrate languages of Sranan:

(2) mi e   tan **na** boiti   Sranan
     1SG IPFV stay LOC countryside
     'I live in the countryside.' (Hart 1996: 38)

(3) a   waka esesi   go **na** oso   Sranan
    3SG walk quickly go LOC   house
    'She walked to the house quickly.'
(4) mamanten a   komopo   **na** oso   Sranan
    morning   3SG come.out   LOC   house
    'In the morning, he left the house.'
(5) mi   boro   **na** a   **busi** kon   na   oso Sranan
    1SG pierce LOC   DEF.SG   forest   come LOC house
    'I (took a short-)cut through the forest to the house.'

Na 'LOC' is one of the very few items in Sranan that functions unambiguously as a locative *preposition* (rather than alternatively, as a postposition) in a way resembling prepositions in English and other Indo-European languages. However, we will see that beyond a superficial linear equivalence of locative constructions like (3) and (4) above with English prepositional phrases like *at/in/to the house,* the functions of *na* 'LOC' are very different from that of any English locative preposition. Aside from the fact that only the two elements *ini* and *ondro* are derived from forms serving exclusively locative functions in the source languages as well. The remaining forms *tapu, baka* and *fesi* are derived from landmark and body part expressions that are not used as basic locative elements in the source language in the same way as in Sranan.

What characterizes all the European-derived forms in Table 1 is that they may appear in morphosyntactic structures very different from English ones in the corresponding contexts. In the following sentence, the Sranan locative element *ondro* 'under(part)' co-occurs with an additional locative element, the general locative preposition *na* 'LOC'. Unlike its English counterpart *under,* Sranan *ondro* may also appear in a post- rather than a prenominal position.

(6) a   buku de   **na** a   tafra **ondro**   Sranan
    DEF.SG book be.at LOC   DEF.SG   table bottom
    'The book is under the table'

We are thus confronted with a situation in which the system employed for the expression of basic spatial relations in Sranan is characterized by a substantial departure from the corresponding English and Dutch ones. In this system, Sranan locative prepositions are either (a) not derived from English locative prepositions at all (e.g. *na*); or (b) are derived from simple or complex English locative prepositions and employed with locative meanings in

Sranan as well but may appear in wholly different morphosyntactic structures (e.g. *ini, ondro* and *tapu* in postnominal position); (c) are derived from English body part expressions not normally employed as basic locative elements in English and also appear in wholly different morphosyntactic structures (e.g. *baka* and *fesi* in postnominal position). In the following sections, we will show that comparable strategies involving morphosyntactically and semantically similar forms are also employed for the expression of spatial relations in the substrate languages of Sranan.

We also address Sranan cases in which English-derived locative elements are used in genuinely prepositional functions. These uses are the consequence of language contact with Dutch and are not attested in earlier stages of the language. Such a development can be seen as forming part of a larger restructuring process, in which many of the typologically (West) African features of Sranan have entered into competition with Germanic features via contact with Dutch (cf. eg. Essegbey and Bruyn 2002; Essegbey 2005).

3. Locative constructions in Sranan and Gbe

In this section, we will be concerned with two types of spatial descriptions: static location involving a GROUND with a PLACE role and motion events involving GROUNDS with a GOAL and a SOURCE role. We suggest that the overall picture with respect to locative constructions in Sranan and the substrates is one of unity in diversity. This means that we often find non-negligible local differences between Sranan and substrates in the semantic and the morphosyntactic behavior of individual elements. At the same time, striking similarities in the semantic organization and the morphosyntactic realizations of the relevant spatial relations can be observed at a higher, paradigmatic and syntagmatic level. We conclude that this similarity in patterns is due to relexification.

Henceforth, the term "locative construction" is employed for the various structures covered here that instantiate spatial relations – whether they involve static location or motion. The term "locative element" refers to prepositions, postpositions and locative nouns alike. The following terms employed for the constituents of locative constructions are presented by means of the Sranan and Fon spatial descriptions in (7) and (8) and their English equivalent in (9): FIGURE [1] = entity located or moving; GROUND [2] = the entity which acts as a spatial reference point for the location or motion of the FIGURE; PATH [3] = the path of motion of the FIGURE to

(GOAL) or from (SOURCE) the GROUND; REGION [4] = the space anchored to the GROUND; (SPATIAL) RELATION [5] = relationship between the FIGURE and the GROUND, mediated through location-denoting predicates, adpositions and locative nouns (cf. e.g. Talmy 1985, 2000; Levinson 1992).

(7)   mi   teki   moni^1 komoto^3 na^5 a   dosu^2 ini^{45} Sranan
      1SG   take   money   come.out   LOC   DEF.SG   box   inside.
(8)   ń   sɔ́   àkwɛ́^{1} sĭn^3 gbàvĭ^2 ɔ̀   mɛ̀^{45} Fon
      1SG   take   money   come.from   box   DEF   inside. (Höftmann 1993: 140)
(9)   *I took money^1 from^{345} the box^2*

A comparison of the examples above reveals a cline in the semantic transparency of the spatial description in the three languages. Sranan manifests the highest degree of isomorphism in that most participating elements denote only one particular aspect of the spatial description. English is characterized by maximal opacity. English utilizes a single form, the preposition *from* conflates PATH, REGION and SPATIAL RELATION aspects. Fon is situated in the middle, with the element *mè* conflating two aspects of the spatial description. The portmanteau nature of the English preposition *from* contrasts with the Sranan and Gbe constructions in two ways. Firstly, the PATH component of the spatial description is indicated by a PATH-denoting V2 in an SVC in the latter two languages. Secondly, Sranan and Gbe feature an additional locative element, where English only has one, namely a REGION-denoting locative element. These aspects represent two major typological differences in the realization of spatial descriptions between Sranan and Gbe on the one hand, and Germanic (and Standard Average European as a whole) on the other (cf. Creissels 2006; Heine, Claudi, and Hünnemeyer 1991: 140–143).

In the remainder of this paper, we employ the term PLACE when referring to a spatial relation that involves a static, at-rest relation (sometimes referred to as "essive" in the literature). The terms GOAL and SOURCE refer to the two basic motion-oriented spatial relations, namely movement towards a GROUND (also referred to as "allative") and movement away from a GROUND (also referred to as "ablative").

3.1. Place-oriented relations

The first type of construction that we address involves a FIGURE located with respect to a GROUND without any motion involved. Such PLACE relations include "basic locative constructions", which answer where-questions (Ameka and Levinson 2007).These constructions are semantically and structurally less complex than motion descriptions and we will therefore use them in order to discuss some general characteristics of locative constructions in Sranan and Gbe. We will show that the expression of a PLACE relation in Sranan is highly similar to that found in the Gbe languages, both in terms of the semantics of the elements employed as well as with respect to morphosyntax. The differences that can nonetheless be found between Sranan and Gbe can be attributed to competing substrate patterns and contact with Dutch.

In the basic locative construction, both Sranan and the Gbe languages feature a locative-existential copula which is semantically rich enough to express the spatial relation by itself. Hence neither in Sranan nor Fon do named places and other known or expected locations require to be marked by an additional locative element unless a higher degree of specificity is desired. Although the English lexifier and Dutch superstrate may feature reduced definiteness marking in these contexts, prepositions are still necessary besides the copula (e.g. *hij **is op** school / he **is at** school*):

(10)   mè   cè   lɛ́   **ɖò**   Paraku   Fon
      relative   1SG.POSS   PL   be.at   PLACE
      'My relatives are in Paraku.' (Höftmann 1993: 189)

Sranan also employs a separate locative-existential copula in basic locative constructions. However, a difference with Gbe is that in Sranan the GROUND is additionally marked by the general locative preposition *na*:

(11)   a   **de**   **na**   wasi-oso   Sranan
      3SG   be.at   LOC   wash-house
      'She is in the bathroom.'

A higher degree of specificity may be obtained in these constructions through the use of a 'nouny' locative element denoting the REGION in Sranan (cf. (12)) and the Gbe languages (cf. (13)). In both Sranan and Gbe, the locative noun may be seen to function as a possessed/modified noun and syntactic head to the preceding GROUND NP (cf. Aboh 2010) in an "associative construction" (Welmers 1973: 283)

(12) a buku **de** a tafra **tapu** Sranan
 DEF book be.at LOC table top
 'The book is on the table.'

(13) nɔ̀ cè **ɖò** àxǐ **mɛ̀** Fon
 mother 1SG.POSS be.at market inside
 'My mother is at [in] the market.' (Höftmann 1993: 189)

Postpositional locative nouns already occur in historical records of Sranan in such complex locative structures, cf. (14).

(14) sinsi a komm **na** hosso **inni** Sranan
 since 3SG come LOC house inside
 'since she entered the house' (Schumann 1783)

Our corpus, however, only contains a handful of postpositional structures like the ones above. The overwhelming majority of locative constructions in the corpus involve prepositional locative nouns. (cf. Essegbey 2005: 237). Prepositional structures are also already attested in Early Sranan, as shown in the following example. It is however, impossible to assess the relative frequency of pre- and postpositional structures in Early Sranan:

(15) trueh da dotti **na ondro** boom Sranan
 throw that dirt LOC underside tree
 'Throw that soil to the bottom of the tree.'
 (Schumann 1783, cited in Essegbey and Bruyn 2002)

We can conclude that Sranan locative elements have retained a large part of the phonological shape and a considerable part of the lexical information of their English etymons. At the same time, they have undergone a morphosyntactic recategorization from preposition to locative noun (e.g. *ini* 'inside') or common noun to locative noun (e.g. *fesi* 'in front of'). They thereby come to resemble their Gbe counterparts much more than their English etymons. One difference between the Gbe substrate and the Sranan, is that these locative constructions, whether pre- or postpositional, whether involving motion or not, may invariably be introduced by the general locative preposition *na* 'LOC'. This circumstance sets Sranan locative constructions apart from the corresponding Gbe ones and will be addressed in due course.

However, the use of the general locative preposition *na* is far from obligatory – if it was in Early Sranan this is certainly no longer the case in contemporary Sranan. In our corpus, locative structures introduced by *na* (or its variant *a)* are equally common as ones where the locative preposition is absent. Dutch influence may be held responsible for what seems to be a rather fundamental ongoing reorganization of the locative system (cf. Essegbey and Bruyn 2002). In the corpus data, *na*-less structures are attested in the description of static location as well as motion events. They are found with the entire range of English/Dutch-derived locative elements listed in Table 1. Compare *ondro* 'under(side)' in (16), *baka* 'back(side)' in (17), *ini* 'inside' in (18) and *fesi* 'in front of, opposite' in (19):

(16) a   buku de   **ondro** a   tafra   Sranan
     DEF book be.at under DEF.SG table
     'The book is under the table.'

(17) den dringi biri kibrikibri **baka** a   oso   Sranan
     3PL drink beer secretly   behind DEF.SG house
     'They drank beer secretely behind the house.'

(18) a   e   sidon **ini** a   oso   Sranan
     3SG IPFV sit   in   DEF.SG house
     'She is sitting in the house.'

(19) a   sidon **fesi**   a   oso   Sranan
     3SG sit   in.front.of DEF.SG house
     'She sat down in front of the house.'

We assume these Sranan structures to be induced by contact with Dutch because the uses of the locative elements are indistinguishable from the uses of prepositions and Dutch. Hence they conflate Region and Spatial Relation as in the four sentences above and additionally, Path as with *ini* in (20) below.

(20) a   e   poti a   spun **ini** a   preti   Sranan
     3SG   IPFV put DEF.SG spoon in   DEF.SG plate
     'He is putting the the spoon into the plate.'

So Sranan may make use of structures for expressing PLACE relations that are virtually identical to the ones found in the Gbe languages. In both (groups of) languages we find postpositional locative nouns instead of prepositions. One difference in need of an explanation is the obligatory presence of the general locative preposition *na* 'LOC' where Gbe has no corresponding element. This question will be addressed further in due course. Besides that, Sranan also features purely prepositional uses of the same locative elements that function as postpositions in other contexts. Following Essegbey and Bruyn (2002), we assume that these prepositional uses are a fairly recent development induced by contact with Dutch. In the following section, we explore further parallels between Sranan and Gbe in the expression of motion events involving Goal- and Source-oriented locative relations.

3.2. GOAL- and SOURCE-oriented relations

Locative constructions that involve motion events display strong similarities in Gbe and Sranan in their overall make-up. The major Gbe characteristic reflected in Sranan motion descriptions is that verbs or verb-derived prepositions are used in functions occupied by prepositions with no verbal etymologies in English and Dutch.

In Sranan and in the Gbe languages, GOAL-oriented motion events are expressed through the interaction of verb(s) and locative elements. Some Gbe directional verbs may appear in clauses in which the GOAL is expressed as a direct argument of the verb. Hence, the GOAL of the locomotion verb *yì* 'go (to)' is not preceded by a preposition or serial verb and is therefore encoded like any transitive object in the Gbe language Gen:

(21) wò **yì kɔ́jí** à?   Gen
      2SG go hospital Q
      'Did you go to the hospital?'

In caused-motion events involving inanimate transitive objects, the general picture in Gbe is that verbid prepositions – *ɖé* (in Ewe) and *dò* (in Fon/Aja) mark the GOAL. These verbids are derived from a verb meaning 'reach, enter' and are glossed as 'ALL(ative)' in their prepositional function (cf. Ansre 1966; Ameka, Aboh, and Essegbey 2007). Ameka, Aboh, and Essegbey (2007) present a detailed analysis of these forms, which have grammaticalized into prepositions in some Gbe varieties but are characterized by residual verbiness in others (e.g. the inland varieties of Ewe). A relevant characteristic of the prepositional uses of the form *ɖé/dò*, which may also be seen to be indicative of its advanced degree of grammaticalization, is the fact that the allative preposition may be used to mark inanimate and animate GOALS (i.e. RECIPIENTS) alike. Compare example (22), which involves the inanimate GOAL *egli* 'wall' in Aja with example (23), which involve the animate GOAL (RECIPIENT)'friend' in Ewe and Fon respectively.

(22) *Kojó só eba ló xɔ do egli nu* Aja
 NAME take stick DEF hit ALL wall outer.surface
 'Kojo hit the stick against the wall.' (Morley 2008: 95
(23) *n sè wèmá dò xɔ́ntɔ̀n cè* Fon
 1SG throw book ALL friend 1SG.POSS
 'I sent a book to my friend.' (Höftmann 1993: 111)

Gbe GOAL-oriented constructions differ from SOURCE-oriented constructions in an important aspect: GOALS cannot be marked by the general locative preposition (*lè* in Ewe/Aja and *ɖò* in Fon). Given the origins of these prepositions in the locative-existential copula (which instantiates a static concept) it is not too surprising that they may not mark syntactic GOAL objects in Gbe (which represent the endpoints of a motion).

We have already seen in (3) abovethat Sranan GOALS are canonically marked with *na* 'LOC' in GOAL-oriented motion events where Gbe may feature unmarked GOALS, as in (21) above. At the same time, Sranan does not have a Gbe-style general allative (GOAL) preposition derived from a verb meaning 'reach' or 'enter'. In fact, the use of *doro* 'reach', the lexical equivalent in Sranan to the Gbe verb *dò/ɖé*, instead of *na* is judged ungrammatical by my informants, cf. (24).

(24) **mi seni a buku doro mi mati*
 1SG send DEF.SG book reach 1SG friend
 'I sent the book to my friend.'

Seen from a Gbe perspective, the absence of a general allative preposition in Sranan leads to a shift of the GOAL-oriented meaning component of the motion event from verb plus (verby) preposition in Gbe to common SVCs consisting of the string V1+V2 in Sranan. Hence in caused-motion events like (22), Sranan features a variety of specialized/lexicalized SVCs in which there is (an albeit limited) variability of the V2. Hence the V2 may change according to semantic factors such as animacy of the GOAL or type of contact with the GOAL. In this vein, the equivalent of the Gbe sentence in (22) aboveinvolves the verb string *fringi – naki* 'throw – hit' in Sranan.

(25) a   fringi a   tiki **naki** a   skotu   Sranan
     3SG throw   DEF.SG stick hit   DEF.SG wall
     'He threw the stick against the wall.'

Likewise, a corresponding way of rendering the Gbe example (23), which features the allative preposition with an animate GOAL, i.e. RECIPIENT, must involve the verb-derived dative marker *gi* (<'give') in Sranan. Compare (26) with the ungrammatical example in (24) above.

(26) mi   seni a   buku **gi** mi   mati   Sranan
     1SG send DEF.SG book DAT   1SG friend
     'I sent the book to my friend.'

The data presented above therefore suggests that a local relexification of the Gbe verby allative preposition did not take place in Sranan. What we do find in both (groups of) languages however, is the use of verb(id)s rather than dedicated prepositions for marking GOALS. In both Gbe and Sranan, a verby rather than a prepositional strategy is therefore marshalled for the expression of GOAL-oriented motion. In some Gbe varieties, the one-time V2 has progressed far enough along the grammaticalization chain to warrant being called a preposition, while in others, the V2 retains verby characteristics. But in none of the Gbe varieties have the verbal origins of the GOAL-marking element been wholly obscured. This suggests that Sranan speakers could have modelled the realization of GOAL-oriented motion events on an originally verbal Gbe pattern. This tendency would have been reinforced by the existence of numerous lexicalized caused-motion and locomotion SVCs in Gbe that involve the use of full verbs in the pre-GROUND position (e.g. Ewe: *tsɔ́–vá* [take–come] 'bring', *kplɔ́–yĭ* [lead–go]'accompany').

The realization of ablative, i.e. SOURCE-oriented motion events is also characterized by minor differences between Sranan and Gbe. Consider the following example from Fon.

(27) ǹ   sɔ́   àkwɛ́ **ɖò** gbàvî ɔ̀   mɛ̀   Fon
     1SG take money LOC   box   DEF   inside
     'I took money out of the box.' (Höftmann 1993: 140)

In the most common type of SOURCE-oriented motion description in Gbe, the general locative preposition (*ɖò* in the example above) marks the Source and specifies the Relation between FIGURE and GROUND. At the same time, a postpositional locative noun (*mè* 'inside' in the example above) expresses the REGION. What both types of locative elements share in semantic terms is that they do not contribute any directional meanings to the construction. Instead, both merely express PLACE notions. Since *só* is a manner-of-motion verb rather than a directional verb, the PATH component of the motion event described in (27) arises solely by implicature. Contrast this with example (28) from Ewe, which features the directional verb *dò* 'exit' and which contributes a PATH reference to the SOURCE-oriented motion event.

(28) *lè   yèmáyĭ-á,   nyè   hã mè-**dò** lè sùkû xóxó*   Ewe
     LOC that.time-DEF 1SG.EMP too 1SG-exit LOC school already
     'At that time, I too had already left school.'

In the Gbe languages, the general locative preposition found in SOURCE-oriented constructions is formally identical with the locative-existential copula found as a predicator in PLACE-oriented constructions (cf. (10)). Although derived from the copula, this form has been analyzed as a fully grammaticalized preposition in the Gbe languages when it occurs in locative constructions. Firstly, the form *lè/ɖò* is not normally marked for aspect or mood in structures like in (27) and (28). In addition, Ameka, Aboh, and Essegbey (2007) adduce evidence for the prepositional status of this form from the observation that a prepositional phrase introduced by *lè* can be fronted as a topic in a sentence like (29).

(29) ***lè   afé-á***   *mè   lá, mè-kpó   Kòfi*   Ewe
     LOC house-DEF inside TOP 1SG-see NAME
     'IN THE HOUSE, I saw Kofi.' (Ameka, Aboh, and Essegbey 2007: 9)

Fronting would not be possible if *lè* were a V2 in a serial verb construction as is the case with *yĭ* in (30) (Ameka, Aboh, and Essegbey 2007: 9):

(30) **yĭ àfémè* lá,   mè-zɔ̀*   Ewe
     go home TOP 1SG-walk
     'I WALKED home.' (Ameka, Aboh, and Essegbey 2007: 9)

The categorial status of the copula-derived locative preposition in Gbe is relevant with respect to the possibility of a local relexification of this form in Sranan. There is a substantial overlap in the functions of *lè* (Ewe, Gen, Aja) and *ɖò* (Fon) with Sranan *na* 'LOC'. The fully prepositional status of *lè* and *ɖò* might therefore help to explain why the Gbe creators of Sranan did not select the corresponding Sranan locative copula *de* for prepositional functions – although they did select motion verbs whose meanings overlap with corresponding Gbe items in the expression of motion events (cf. (36)–(38) below).

A SOURCE-oriented motion event involving the use of a preposition formally identical with the locative copula is complemented by another strategy in the Gbe languages. Alternatively, the directional ablative (i.e. SOURCE-oriented) verbs *tsó* (Ewe) and *sín* (Fon) 'come from' may be used to mark the SOURCE instead of the general locative preposition.

(31) *e*-**tsɔ**   *dziwui ɖeka* **tso**   *e-fe*
      3SG-take shirt   one   (come)from 3SG-POSS
      mɔzɔɖaka me   nɛ   Ewe
      suitcase   inside   DAT.3SG.OBJ
      'He took a shirt from his suitcase (and) gave it to him.'
      (Nyaku 1982: 47)

(32) *ǹ* *sɔ́* *àkwɛ́* **sín**   *gbàví ɔ̀ mɛ̀*   Fon
      1SG take money (come)from box   DEF inside
      'I took money out of the box.' (Höftmann 1993: 140

There appears to be a subtle difference between the alternatives in (27) and (32) above. When a SOURCE GROUND is introduced by the verbid *tsó/sín* rather than *lè/ɖò*, the motion component of the event is emphasised and the event acquires a higher degree of dynamicity.

The elements *tsó* (Ewe) and *sín* (Fon) are more fluid in their categorial status than the fully grammaticalized preposition *lè/ɖò* 'LOC'. Firstly, the two forms may also be employed as common verbs with the meaning 'come from', as shown for Ewe in (33).

(33) *Evè-dùkɔ́ fɛ́   àkpá ɖé, yé-wó ké* **tsó**
      Ewe-nation POSS part INDF LOG-3PL EMP come.from
      kéké Sudan   Ewe
      EMP PLACE
      'A part of the Ewe nation, they even originate in far-away Sudan.'

Secondly, these elements are characterized by a morphosyntactic behaviour suggestive of reduced verbiness (cf. Ansre 1966, Ameka, Aboh, and Essegbey 2007). For example, Ameka, Aboh, and Essegbey (2007) show that when Ewe *tsó* occurs in a locative construction, it may be optionally marked for the same aspect category as the preceding verb. When marked in this way, *tsó* is indistinguishable from the V2 of a common serial verb construction. When left unmarked, its distribution is similar to that of the fully grammaticalized locative prepositions *lè/ɖò* covered above.

(34) *Kofi zɔ*-**na** *tsó(-**ná**)* *aféme ŋdí sía ŋdí* Ewe
NAME walk-HAB come.from(-HAB) home morning every morning
'Kofi walks from home every morning' (Ameka, Aboh, and Essegbey 2007: 10)

Ablative motion events in Sranan are also instantiated in constructions bearing a strong resemblance to their Gbe counterparts (cf. Essegbey and Bruyn 2002). The SOURCE in Sranan SOURCE-oriented constructions is marked by means of a general locative preposition, just like in Gbe, namely the omnipresent (*n*)*a* 'LOC'.

(35) *mi teki a moni* **na** (***ini***) *a dosu* (**ini**) Sranan
1SG take DEF.SG money LOC inside DEF.SG box inside
'I took the money from the box.'

The only notable difference between the Sranan and Gbe constructions is that the locative noun expressing the REGION (*ini* 'inside' in the example above) may once more be found either in a pre-GROUND or a post-GROUND position in Sranan – the alternatives are in parentheses. In addition, Sranan has the additional option of expressing SOURCE-oriented motion events through employing the directional verbs *puru* 'remove' or *komoto/komopo* 'take out' as V2s in argument-introducing SVCs. Sentences like (36)–(38) below are close Sranan equivalents to the Gbe constructions in (31) and (32). In the following three Sranan sentences, the locative noun *ini* 'inside' is again optional and may appear either in a pre- or a post-GROUND position. The possibility of a lexical choice between the near-synonyms *puru*, *komoto*, and *komopo* shows that the structures below do not involve grammaticalized preposition(-like element)s in the V2 position, and that we are dealing with genuine serial verb constructions. Further, the SOURCE in the Sranan constructions is once more obligatorily marked with the general locative preposition *na* 'LOC'.

(36) mi teki a   moni **puru na** a   dosu (*ini*)   Sranan
     1SG take DEF.SG money remove LOC DEF.SG box inside
     'I took the money out of the box.'
(37) mi teki a   moni **komoto na** (*ini*) a   dosu   Sranan
     1SG take DEF.SG money take.out LOC inside DEF.SG box
     'I took the money out of the box.'
(38) mi teki a   moni **komopo na** (*ini*) a   dosu   Sranan
     1SG take DEF.SG money take.out LOC inside DEF.SG box
     'I took the money out of the box.'

We have established that both Gbe and Sranan make use of complex locative constructions in which motion descriptions are jointly realized by verbs, prepositions, and locative nouns. One reason for the participation of these different word classes in locative constructions lies in the scarcity of dedicated prepositions in Gbe, a typological feature that in fact characterizes the entire Niger-Congo phylum. This scarcity is made up for by the use of locative constructions ranging from more phrasal to more clausal structures. Indo-European, in turn, are typically phrasal.

If we now direct attention towards GROUND-marking strategies in the three spatial relations of PLACE (essive), GOAL (allative) and SOURCE (ablative) we however see a significant difference between Sranan and Gbe. Sranan employs a unitary system, in which GROUNDS in the three relations are marked in the same way via *na* 'LOC', hence characterized by the pattern (PLACE/GOAL/SOURCE). Gbe, in contrast, features two alternatives: one is a bipartite system (PLACE/GOAL, SOURCE) in which PLACE and GOAL GROUNDS are marked in the same way (no pre-GROUND locative element). The other is a tripartite system (ESS, ALL, ABL) in which the GROUND in all three relations is marked by separate pre-GROUND elements (no locative element, *ɖé/dò* 'ALL' or *lè/ɖò* 'LOC'/*(t)só* 'ABL').

We can also establish that in typological terms, and disregarding more recent contact induced changes in Sranan, motion descriptions in Gbe and Sranan represent the serializing type, in which *originally*, PATH (and RELATION) components of the motion event are exclusively expressed by verb(-string)s. In this, Sranan and Gbe differ from English and Dutch where PATH and Relation components are exclusively lexicalized in a preposition if a directional verb is absent. At the same time, it has also been shown that Gbe motion descriptions may be situated along a continuum with respect to the categorial status of the pre-GROUND element. While the elements *ɖé/dò* 'reach; ALL' *(t)só* 'come from; ABL' retain distributional characteristics peculiar to verbs, the element *lè/ɖò* behaves like a proper preposition when it appears in a pre-GROUND position. Disregarding the obligatory use of a REGION element for the moment, the use of the PATH-denoting verbids ɖé/dò and (t)só as prepositions therefore represents a partial shift from the serializing type of locative construction towards the 'prepositional' pole of the continuum in which a preposition rather than a verb expresses PATH.

In comparison to Gbe, parts of the Sranan system represent a tidier form of the serializing type. For in Sranan, there are no half-way or fully grammaticalized locative prepositions with verbal origins. Instead, the V2s of a variety of conventionalized, "asymmetrical" SVCs (Aikhenvald 2006: 21) are recruited to express the locative meanings encoded by verby prepositions in Gbe (cf. ex. (25), (36)–(38). At the same time, we have seen that contact with Dutch is a pull factor in a similar movement towards the prepositional pole of the continuum. However, in Sranan the grammaticalization process is leading to the use of locative nouns in a pre-GROUND position rather than verbs, as in Gbe (cf. Sranan ex. (16)–(19). Despite these tendencies, Sranan and Gbe share a typological pattern in which SVC(-like) structures involving verbs or verbids may fulfil locative functions, while analogous structures in English and Dutch make exclusive use of prepositions.

3.3. From preposition in the lexifier to verb in Sranan

We now turn to a phenomenon that further corroborates the view that Sranan locative expressions are largely the outcome of pattern relexification. In the following, we will look at a set of five elements in Sranan whose etyma function as prepositions and locative particles in Dutch and English respectively. In Sranan, these elements are, however, multicategorial. On the one hand, they occur as prepositions or particles, as in their lexifiers. On the other hand, they are used as full verbs, and therefore appear in functions alien to those of the corresponding items in their lexifiers. We arrive at the conclusion that the presence of multicategorial verby prepositions in Gbe in the same syntactic position as these prepositions/particles in their lexifiers must have been the door-opener for the reanalysis of these elements into verbs in Early Sranan (cf. Bruyn 2008, 2009). As in the other cases treated so far, there is however no exact correspondence between Gbe and Sranan. The influences from Dutch are non-negligible, and at the same time the independent development of some of these forms in Sranan must also be factored in.

The five Sranan items contained in Table 2 are derived from English and Dutch prepositions, verbal particles and adverbs, and hence are non-verbal forms. In Sranan however, these items occur with verbal functions, while prepositional and particle uses are also attested. In what follows, we attempt to provide explanations for their behavior.

Table 2. Multicategorial locative elements in Sranan

Sranan item	Verbal meaning	Non-verbal meaning	Lexifier etymon	Lexifier word class
doro	'pass, arrive'	'through'	*door* 'through' (Du.)	preposition/particle
romboto/ lomboto	'surround'	----	*roundabout* (Eng.), but also Gungbe *lòbòtò* 'round'	adverb/particle
lontu	'surround'	'around'	*rond* '(a)round' (Du.)	preposition/adverb
abra	'cross'	'over, across'	*over* (Eng.)	preposition/adverb
opo	'rise, raise'	'up, above'	*up/op* (Eng./Du.)	preposition/adverb

The individual Sranan forms in can be situated on a cline from top to bottom with respect to the degree of local relexification of Gbe forms. We will see that the two forms at the lower end (*opo* and *abra*) do not correspond to specific substrate forms. The uses of these forms nonetheless show the kind of incorporation into substrate derived structures that we have already observed with some of the locative nouns covered in the preceding sections. The first three forms in Table 2 manifest a close correspondence in terms of their semantic organization and morphosyntactic behaviour with corresponding Gbe forms. A point-by-point comparison between the Sranan and Gbe forms follows in Table 3. We exemplify the parallels between Sranan and Gbe by using the corresponding Ewe forms.

Table 3. Multicategorial locative elements in Ewe/Fon

Ewe element	Fon element	Verbal meaning	Spatial meaning
ɖé	dò	'reach, arrive at'	'towards, to'
fò xlã	lélédó	'surround'	'round about'
tsò	gbò	'sever, separate, cut'	'across'

The Sranan verb *doro* 'pass (through), arrive' in Table 3 is (phonologically) derived from the Dutch form *door* 'through'. Dutch *door* is not used as a verb. It can be employed as a MEDIUM-denoting preposition as in *door het boos lopen* [through the forest walk] 'walk through the forest'. It is also used as verb particle in more or less lexicalized collocations with more or less spatial meanings, e.g. *door-kruisen* [through-cross] 'traverse', *door-leven* [through-live] 'live through (an experience)'. The following sentence shows the focal uses of Sranan *doro* as a telic GOAL-oriented motion verb with the meaning 'arrive'.

(39) fa   mi **doro** na oso, mi sisa lusu kaba   Sranan
     when 1SG arrive LOC house 1SG sister leave PRF
     'When I arrived at home, my sister had already left.'

The case of *doro* in (39) above is a fine example of the reanalysis of an originally non-verbal form in Dutch into a verb in Sranan. We assume that this peculiar process of reanalysis was possible in this case and in the ones that follow below due to the multicategoriality of corresponding substrate items. The preceding section showed that the Gbe languages feature a grammaticalized allative preposition derived from a verb meaning 'reach' that can be employed as a lexical verb in some varieties. At the same time, Sranan was shown to employ lexicalized SVCs instead of the Sranan equivalent *doro*, albeit along a Gbe-type syntactic pattern. Beyond that *doro* has retained (or developed) semantic and syntactic characteristics of its Dutch prepositional source form. It is also used as a preposition and adverb/particle-like element with vague and metaphoric MEDIUM semantics in Dutch-influenced idioms like *go doro* [go through] 'continue' (<Du. *door-gaan*).

A comparable situation holds with the Sranan forms *lomboto/romboto* 'roundabout, around; surround' and the near synonym *lontu* (< Du. 'rond'/Eng. '(a)round'). These forms are presumably derived from English and Dutch etyma respectively and possibly convergence with Gbe forms like *lóbó(e)* 'round(ish)' (Ewe) and *lòbòtò/ròbòtò* 'round' (Gun; Aboh, p.c.) should not be discarded. For one part, both forms are used as predicative nuclei in sentences like the following ones:

(40) a   liba **lomboto** den   oso   Sranan
     DEF.SG river surround DEF.PL house
     'The river flows around the houses.'

(41) den   skowtu **lontu**   a   oso (...)   Sranan
     DEF.PL police surround DEF.SG house
     'The police surrounded the house (...)' (Wilner 2007: 94)

Secondly, *lomboto/romboto*, just like *doro* above, is not normally employed as a PATH-denoting verby preposition/V2 in locative constructions like (42). Only *lontu* is accepted by our informants in a pre-GROUND position in a sentence like (43).

(42) *a   liba e   **lon lomboto** den   oso   Sranan
     DEF.SG river IPFV run surround DEF.PL house
     'The river flows around the houses.'
(43) a   liba e   **lon lontu**   den   oso   Sranan
     DEF.SG river IPFV run (sur)round DEF.PL house.
     'The river flows around the houses.'

One possibility why the use of *lomboto* is rejected by our informants as a V2 in a structure like (42) above may be the contraction of the distributional potential of this item due to obsolescence – the form is classified as archaic by Wilner (2007). The form *lomboto* is already present in Schumann (1783) in examples such as (44) – one of several, in which the form functions as a verb:

(44) meki wi **rombotto** hem   Sranan
     SBJV 1PL surround   3SG.OBJ
     'Let's surround him.' (Schuhmann 1783)

Contrary to *lomboto*, for which we therefore have historical evidence for a verbal use, the categorial status of *lontu* in an example like (41) above is unclear. The form may simply be used as a preposition rather than a V2 in very much the same way as its English and Dutch cognate forms in clauses like *the river flows around the houses/ de rivier stroomt rondom de huizen*. Such multicategoriality is also attested with *doro*, as well as with *abra* further below. An unequivocal example of a nonverbal, in this case adverbial use of *lontu* is given in (45).

(45) a   luku **lontu**   Sranan
     3SG IPFV around
     'He looked around.' (Blanker and Dubbeldam 2005: 127)

Prepositional/ adverbial uses of *lomboto*, as in (43) and (45) respectively, are not attested in our data. This is presumably because the archaic form *lomboto* has retained its earlier uniquely verbal uses while *lontu* has acquired new nonverbal functions through contact with Dutch, probably reinforced by the phonological proximity of *lontu* and Dutch *rond*.

A look at the Gbe substrate once more reveals close parallels with Sranan in the way functionally corresponding forms are used. The Fon form *lélédó* 'surround' appears as a finite verb preceded by a personal pronoun in (46). In (47), *lélédó* is found in a V2 slot in a structure that looks like an SVC, just like the corresponding Sranan form in (43).

(46) ye **lélédó** mĭ   Fon
     3PL surround 1SG.OBJ
     'They have surrounded me.' (Höftmann 2003: 285)

(47) é dó kpá **lélédó** glè tòn   Fon
     3SG put fence surround field 3SG.POSS
     'He put up a fence around his field.' (Höftmann 2003: 285)

In the same vein, the Ewe expression *fò xlã* 'surround' (composed of the verb *fò* 'beat' and the inherent complement *xlã* 'crookedness') appears as a finite verb marked for habitual aspect in (48).

(48) wo-**fo-a**   **xla**   du-a   kplefia la   zi   ḍeka   Ewe
     3PL-beat-HAB crookedness town-DEF and chief DEF time one
     'They at once surround the town and the chief.' (Obianim 1990: 21)

In (49), *fò xlã* appears in a pre-GROUND position similar to *lontu* in (43) above (disregarding the composite nature of the Ewe expression for 'surround'). Hence, irrespective of the categorial status that we may assign to *lontu* in (43) above, the surface structure of these constructions is similar in both languages.

(49) agbledela lá ḍe-**a**   mɔ   **fo-a**   **xla**   e-fe
     farmer   DEF remove-HAB path beat-HAB crookedness 3SG-POSS
     agble yeye   Ewe
     farm new
     'The farmer clears a path around his new farm.'
     (Obianim 1990: 147)

Further, in Ewe, just like in Sranan, the element denoting 'surround' is categorially ambivalent between verb and preposition. It is far less grammaticalized to prepositional status in Ewe than the verb-derived prepositions ɖé 'ALL', tsó 'ABL' and lè 'LOC'. Evidence for this is provided by the optional use of TMA marking with fò xlã when it is found in the V2 position of an SVC, as evidenced by habitual aspect marking on both verbs present in the example above. So where the Sranan expression for 'surround' tends towards a prepositional status – and we suggest that this is through Dutch influence – the equivalent Ewe expression retains its verbal characteristics.

A similarly complex case that once more shows the competition in Sranan between semantic and syntactic specifications likely to have been inherited from the substrates, internal development and Dutch influence is the case of *abra*, derived from English 'over' The item *abra* is employed as a main verb with the meaning '(to) cross' in (50).

(50) wi o **abra** wan liba dyonsro Sranan
 1PL FUT cross one river soon
 'We are going to cross a river soon.'

The item *abra* is also attested in Sranan in the collocation *koti abra* '(cut a)cross', cf. (51). In the absence of further evidence, this could at first glance bean alyzed as a lexicalized SVC in line with the analysis proposed for analogous structures involving *komoto* 'go out, motion outward' and *go* 'go, motion toward' (cf. (36)ff.). Just like example (43) involving *lontu* 'around; sur(round)', the structure may alternatively also be seen to involve a particle/adverbial use of *abra*.

(51) wi o **koti** wan liba **abra** dyonsro Sranan
 1PL FUT cut one river (a)cross soon
 'We are soon going to (cut a)cross a river.'

However, it seems that an adverbial interpretation of *abra* is more convincing because the adjacency of *koti* and *abra* is not accepted by our informants when the GROUND is explicitly mentioned, as shown in (52).

(52) *wi o **koti abra** wan liba dyonsro Sranan
 1PL FUT cut (a)cross one river soon
 'We are soon going to (cut a)cross a river.'

Example (51) shows a linear equivalence of constituents with the corresponding Dutch structure in (53), which involves the complex verb *oversteken*, composed of the particle *over* 'over, across' and the verb *steken* 'jab'. In Dutch too, the adjacency of *steken* and *over* and hence a pre-GROUND position of *over* in these constructions is ungrammatical. Dutch influence on the semantics and the syntax of *kotiabra* appears quite straightforward. We see this as supporting evidence for an adverbial interpretation of *abra* in these sentences.

(53) we **steken** de rivier **over**   Dutch
      1PL jab:PRS:PL DEF river across
      'We are going to cross the river.'

(54) **we **steken over** de rivier*   Dutch
      1PL jab   across DEF river
      'We are going to cross the river.'

We also have adpositional uses of *abra*. We have evidence for historical uses of *abra* in a post-GROUND position in structures no different from the post-GROUND uses of locative nouns like *tapu* and *ini*, cf. (55).

(55) na mi hosso **abra**   Sranan
      LOC 1SG house across
      'across from my house' (Schuhmann 1783)

In modern Sranan however, *abra* seems to appear exclusively in pre-GROUND position with a prepositional function.

(56) a opolangi frei **abra** a foto   Sranan
      DEF.SG plane fly over DEF.SG town
      'The plane flew over the town.'

The relexification and contact scenario becomes even more intricate when we bring the corresponding English and Gbe structures into the picture. The equivalent English expression *cut across* is not only replicated structurally and semantically by the bi-composite structure of *kotiabra*. However, a grammatical Sranan sentence can also be constructed without the adverb and with the "verb of crossing" alone. However, in English, the verb *cut* alone cannot be used for the act of crossing by itself. Compare the Sranan example in (57) and its English translation.

(57) wi   o   **koti**   wan liba dyonsro   Sranan
     1PL   FUT cut/cross   one river soon
     'We are soon going to cross/cut across a river.'

This peculiarity of Sranan can be explained by turning to the Gbe languages. In Gbe, the verb of crossing is equivalent to the verb 'separate, sever, cut'. Hence we find the same Ewe verb *tsò* in (58) with a PATIENT and (59) with a GROUND object. In Fon, the verb *gbò* may be used in the same two contexts (cf. Segurola and Rassinoux 2000: 220–221).

(58) amesi   **tso** lã   la   fe   ve   la   xɔ-a   lã   la
     whoever cut   animal   DEF   POSS   throat TOP get-HAB animal DEF
     fe   kɔ   Ewe
     POSS   neck
     'He who cuts the animal's throat gets the animal's neck.'
     (Obianim 1990: 166)
(59) esi   wo-**tso** tɔsisi-a   vɔ   la,   dzidzi   fo   Yakobo   Ewe
     when   3PL-cut   river-DEF   COMPL   TOP   pleasure hit   NAME
     'When they had crossed the river, pleasure struck Yakobo.'
     (Nyaku 1982: 47)

In contrast to English and Dutch however, Gbe features no lexicalized bi-composite structure equivalent to Sranan *koti abra* 'cut across'in the description of the crossing event. Distributional evidence suggests that *tsò* – like *fò xlã* 'surround' – is not a grammaticalized preposition with the meaning 'across' either. The form retains verbal properties regardless of its syntactic position.

Hence a scenario is plausible in which a Gbe verb for 'cut' was relexified in Sranan to encompass the meaning of 'cross'. At the same time, a carry-over from English and contact with Dutch and would have encouraged the retention of *abra* with an adverbial function. This might have initially been limited to the act of 'crossing' in the collocation *kotiabra*. However, the existence of other multicategorial elements with adpositional and verbal characteristics in Sranan and Gbe would have facilitated the extension of *abra* to verbal functions not found in English and Dutch. This once more shows how competing substrate, lexifier and superstrate forces have produced a versatile, multicategorial item like *abra* with its wide range of verbal, adverbial and adpositional uses.

The final element in Table 2 is *opo*, a form that is attested in earlier stages of Sranan with the verbal meanings of 'rise' and 'raise'.

(60) *effi ju srefi no kann* **hoppo**, *mi sa* **hoppo** *ju*
 if 2SG self NEG can rise 1SG FUT raise 2SG
 'If you yourself cannot get up, I'll get you up' (Schumann 1783)

Such intransitive and transitive uses of *opo* are still commonplace in contemporary Sranan, an example for the latter use is given in (61).

(61) *op gegeven moment wan hei* **opo** *en ede* Sranan
 on given moment one agouti raise 3SG head
 'Suddenly an agouti raised its head.'

The form *opo* has no exact equivalent in Gbe, where separate lexemes and expressions cover the intransitive and transitive notions respectively. In Ewe, for example, we find *fɔ́* 'get up' and the SVC *kɔ́ – yĭ dz* [take – go – upper surface] 'raise'. In this respect, these uses of *opo* in Sranan are innovative vis-à-vis both English and Gbe. Still, the preceding discussion has shown that the reanalysis of the source language preposition *up/op* to a verb in Sranan proceeded along the same path as that of the other four forms. The remarkable aspect of this trajectory is that the forms have retained (or (re-)acquired through contact with Dutch) at least some of the prepositional/particle uses of their source language etymons.

Within the broader scenario of relexification, here too, the Gbe languages seem to have provided the blueprint for the reanalysis of individual forms and of morphosyntactic patterns. In this vein, a local relexification may be seen to have led to the overlap in semantics and morphosyntactic behaviour between a Sranan form like *lontu* 'surround' and Ewe *fòxlã́* in examples like (41) and (49) above. At the same time, the development of the verbal uses of a form like *abra* '(to) cross' can only be seen within a more generous relexification perspective. This view includes the possibility of a carry-over of morphosyntactic specifications and functions, hence patterns, without necessarily involving a one-to-one mapping of an individual phonological shape in the lexifier language with a specific lexical item in the substrate (cf. Bruyn 2008, 2009). The following section explores this possibility further and attempts to find explanations for the large degree of variation encountered in Sranan.

4. Towards an explanation of variation in Sranan

Previous sections have shown that Sranan locative constructions are characterized by quite a high degree of morphosyntactic and functional variation of the participating elements. In this section, we will suggest that besides adstratal influence from Dutch, and transfer from the lexifier English in earlier stages of Sranan, the cause of variation can also be sought in the equally broad variety of constructions found across the substrates of Sranan. In this respect, the situation in the other (group of) substrate(s) is relevant, namely the Kikongo cluster and closely related languages like Kimbundu, which have been shown to constitute the second most important group of substrates next to Gbe (cf. e.g. Arends, Kouwenberg, and Smith 1995; Huttar 1986).

The first characteristic in need of explanationconcerns the variation encountered in the use of pre-GROUND and post-Ground locative nouns in Sranan. Sranan structures in which the locative noun is found in a pre-GROUND position may have been influenced by substrate structures just as much as by the lexifier English and the superstrate Dutch.

In Ewe, some locative nouns may also appear in a pre-GROUND position. When used in this way, the locative noun is linked to the GROUND via the dative marker *ná*, derived from a verb meaning 'give'. In such instances, the dative marker may in fact be likened to a possessive linker. The following examples show both alternatives in Ewe:

(62) àfi lè ŋgɔ́ ná Kòfi   Ewe
    NAME be.at:PRS front DAT NAME
    'Afi is in front of Kofi.'

(63) àfi lè Kòfi ŋgɔ́   Ewe
    NAME be.at:PRS NAME front
    'Afi is in front of Kofi.'

Kikongo locative nouns canonically appear in a pre-GROUND position, a feature common to the Narrow Bantu branch of the Niger-Congo phylum. Beyond that, the language features the typical bipartite structure of locative expressions encountered throughout Niger-Congo, and as an areal feature, far beyond (e.g. in the Chadic language Zina Kotoko, c.f. Aboh 2010). Hence, in (64), there is a general locative element *ku* 'LOC' (generally a noun class prefix in the Bantu languages, but written separately from the noun in some of the sources consulted). There is also a locative noun indicating the region, namely *ntundu* 'top', as well as a possessive element *a* 'POSS' that links these locative elements to the GROUND.

(64) e   mpu ame   iina   **ku ntundu a**   meza   Kikongo
     DEF hat 1SG.POSS be.at LOC top   POSS table
     'My hat is (lying) on the table.' (Tavares 1915: 80)

Kimbundu, an immediate relative of Kikongo spoken in Northern Angola, features analogous locative constructions. Example (65) involves the use of a general locative element (the noun class prefix *bu* 'LOC') and a locative noun (*kanga* 'outside'), which invariably appears in a pre-GROUND position. Just like in the Kikongo and Gbe examples above the locative noun is linked to the GROUND noun via an intervening element, in this case the possessive linker *ria* 'POSS' (which concords with the noun class of the preceding head noun):

(65) o   sanzala ietu a-i-tung-u   **bu   kanga**
     DEF village our 3PL.SBJ-3SG.OBJ-build-PFV LOC outside
     ria   muxitu   Kimbundu
     POSS forest
     'Our village is built outside of the forest.' *Lit.* 'Our village, they built it outside of the forest.'   (Chatelain 1888: 116)

In Kikongo and Kimbundu, we therefore find constructions with a surface structure similar to Sranan locative constructions involving pre-GROUND locative nouns, except that Sranan has no prefixes. The only element "missing" to make Sranan structures like (37) above virtually isomorphic with the Bantu and the Gbe structures covered above is the possessive linker. We will return to this aspect in due course.

A characteristic that sets Sranan apart from Gbe is the categorical use of the general locative preposition *na* 'LOC' before all types of GROUNDS. We saw in (2)–(5) that the preposition appears before GROUNDS with a PLACE, a GOAL and next to the preposition *fu,* a SOURCE role. We have shown that the first and second of these three participant roles are not marked by the corresponding general locative preposition in Gbe (cf.(21) above). How can the more extensive participant marking functions of the Sranan general locative preposition *na* be explained? We do not reject the explanation by Essegbey (2005: 256) that leveling ("generalization" in the author's terms) may have at least contributed to the crystallization of Sranan *na* into an obligatory locative marker. But we will also go on to show that the origins of the obligatory presence of *na* in Sranan locative adjuncts may as well lie in corresponding ones in the substrate. Bantu locative constructions are characterized by the use of general locative elements in a pre-GROUND position. These elements have a similarly broad range of functions as Sranan *na* 'LOC'. Also relevant in this context is that the corresponding Bantu locative prepositions are, just like *na* in Sranan, normally not derived from verbs, at least not in a synchronically transparent way.

Three sentences follow that exemplify the use of the general locative element *ku* with a PLACE (66), a GOAL (67) and a SOURCE (68) in Kikongo.

(66) **ku** Matadi tuamonana (...) Kikongo
 LOC PLACE see:RECP:PST:1PL
 'In Matadi we saw each other (...)'
 (Söderberg and Widman 1966: 57)
(67) **ku** Kisantu kayele Kikongo
 LOC PLACE go:PST.HST:3SG
 'He went to Kisantu.' (Anonymous1964: 37)
(68) ntama yâkatuka **ku** bwâla dyâme Kikongo
 since.long leave:PST:1SG LOC village 1SG.POSS
 'It's a long time since I left my village.' (Dereau 1955: 138)

The Bantu languages in general do not employ the kind of prototypical SVCs that we have seen in Gbe. Nevertheless, it has been observed that structures reminiscent of SVCs are specifically employed to express PATH throughout Niger-Congo, whether a language is serializing or not (Creissels et al. 2008: 146). This allows the conclusion that the relexification of PATH patterns in Sranan involving motion-verbs like *komoto* 'come out', *puru* 'remove' and *go* 'go' may have been modelled not only on Gbe, but also on Bantu. And indeed, we also find a verb-derived element expressing (SOURCE-oriented) PATH in Kikongo, namely the verb *-tuka* 'come from'. The use of a derived verb *katuka* 'leave' as a finite lexical verb can be seen in (68) above. Example (69) shows the use of *-tuka* as a verbid preposition with the meaning 'from', once more in combination with the general locative preposition.

(69) **tuka** ku Matadi nate ye Leopoldville Kikongo
 (come)from LOC PLACE until with PLACE
 'From Matadi to Leopoldville.' (Söderberg and Widman 1966: 61)

What remains to be explained at this point is the absence of a possessive linker in Sranan locative constructions involving pre-GROUND locative nouns that we have seen so far (cf. e.g. (16)–(19) above). An explanation is required because Sranan possessive/modification structures involving full nouns either have the constituent order [Possessor – Possessed] as in *Pieter oso* 'Pieter's house', or they feature the inverse order with an intervening possessive linker, namely the associative preposition *fu* [Possessed – *fu* – Possessor] as in *a oso fu Pieter*. The order [Possessed – Possessor] encountered in locative constructions with a pre-GROUND locative noun like *na ini a dosu* [LOC inside DEF box] is therefore not encountered elsewhere in the language.

The answer may be found in Early Sranan as well as in contemporary Sranan. In contemporary Sranan, we sometimes find locative constructions featuring the possessive linker *fu* between the locative noun and the Ground, as in the following example.

(70)   na   fesi/tapu **fu**   a   skowtu-oso   Sranan
       LOC   front/top POSS   DEF.SG   police-house
       'to an area in front/above the police-station'
       (Norval Smith, p.c., data provided by Lilian Adamson)

The Sranan speakers consulted see a slight semantic difference between structures involving the possessive linker *fu* 'of' as in (70), and those without them (cf. (16)–(19) above). Structures with the possessive linker are seen as more "literal" and "emphatic" in their spatial meaning (Hein Eersel, p.c.), and the translation of (70) provided by Lilian Adamson suggests a more specific meaning of these structures as well.

It seems, however, that structures involving the possessive linker were less specialized in their meaning in Early Sranan, and could have constituted a regular means of forming locative constructions, cf. (71).

(71)   na   inni   **va**   wi   hatti   Sranan
       LOC   inside POSS   1PL   heart
       'in our hearts.' (Schuhmann 1783)

It is from these kinds of overt possessive structures in Sranan, that the pre-GROUND use of locative nouns as in (16)–(19) above without a linking element could have developed and been conventionalized, presumably already reinforced at an early stage by English and Dutch prepositional structures. The optionality and marginal use of the linker in Modern Sranan will have also facilitated the development of purely prepositional functions of locative nouns in recent times.

One conclusion that can be drawn from the discussion so far is that the input into Sranan could have been highly varied from the very beginning. In fact, there is quite a degree of morphosyntactic diversity already present within and between the Gbe languages themselves. What Sranan, Gbe, and Bantu share is the scarcity of Indo-European style prepositions and the corresponding use of bipartite locative structures involving a general locative preposition, locative nouns, and to some extent, verby PATH-denoting locative elements. We therefore concur with other accounts claiming that the underlying typological unity of the African input into Sranan, and the Afro-Caribbean Creoles in general, facilitated the transfer of substrate features (cf. e.g. Alleyne 1980; Faraclas 1987; Singler 1988).

In addition, while Gbe has no exact equivalent of the Sranan general locative preposition, we do find a functionally identical form in Kikongo and a closely related language like Kimbundu. It is therefore not necessary to look at English and Dutch influence as the primary sources of the variation in the pre- and post-GROUND position of locative nouns. Yet, these two languages have of course contributed to the structural and semantic diversification of Sranan locative expressions. The next section will show that Sranan in fact maximizes the possibilities inherited from various sources.

5. Summary of findings and discussion

We can now summarize the features of the entities that we have been referring to as "patterns". A pattern has been shown to consist of a systematic functional-semantic and morphosyntactic relation of at least two forms with each other. A pattern therefore includes specifications of relational features. In the following, we attempt to classify these features according to their possible origins in the input or contact languages of Sranan. We arrive at the conclusion that Gbe and Kikongo provided the patterns for the majority of the semantic and morphosyntactic features of locative constructions in Sranan. That said, locative constructions in *contemporary* Sranan are nevertheless the outcome of a complex interaction of substrate and superstrate (i.e. Dutch) patterns. As a result, Sranan manifests an unusual richness in the expressive possibilities of locative relations. The characteristics of locative constructions in Sranan and their relation vis-à-vis constructions in the other relevant languages are summed up in the following ten points:

1. Many Sranan locative constructions are complex syntactic structures that may be seen to involve two interlocked dependency relations: a general locative preposition introduces a prepositional phrase; within the PP in turn, a locative noun functions as the head and possessed noun in a possessive relation, with the dependent, the GROUND, functioning as a possessor noun.
2. Sranan, Gbe, and Kikongo all have a distinct locative copula and only few fully grammaticalized locative prepositions.
3. Sranan, Gbe, and Kikongo have a general locative preposition which may introduce participants with PLACE and SOURCE roles. In Sranan, the preposition also introduces participants with GOAL and PATH roles. In contrast to Gbe, the Sranan locative preposition is not transparently derived from a verb in the language.
4. Sranan, Gbe, and Kikongo employ locative nouns denoting a REGION. In Gbe, these are mostly found in a post-GROUND position, but a pre-GROUND position is also possible. In Kikongo, only a pre-GROUND position is attested. In Sranan both a pre- and a post-GROUND position is possible.
5. The use of locative nouns is not obligatory in Sranan. While Gbe locative constructions only dispense with locative nouns in the context of referential specificity, corresponding Sranan and Kikongo constructions are grammatical and self-contained through the use of the general locative preposition alone.
6. While Gbe locative nouns differ quite a lot in their degree of nouniness, all Sranan locative nouns covered appear to occupy more or less the same intermediary position between noun and adposition.
7. In Gbe, the GOAL can be realized as a transitive object or be introduced by a verby allative preposition. In Sranan and Kikongo, GOALs in both types of motion events are introduced by the locative preposition. In Sranan, Kikongo, and Gbe, SOURCE is marked overtly and neither the general locative preposition nor locative nouns contribute any directional meanings.
8. However, the picture becomes more complex in both Sranan and Gbe when ongoing grammaticalization is taken into account. In some Gbe varieties, the pre-GROUND locative elements *tsó/sín* and *ɖé/dò* appear to have completed the transition to full prepositions. In such varieties, these grammaticalized prepositions encode PATH information in the same way as the English prepositions *out of/from* and *to(ward)*. However, REGION is still expressed separately in a locative noun.
9. In Sranan, the grammaticalization path towards prepositional status has taken the opposite route. Contact with Dutch has led to the rise of European-style locative structures: locative nouns now overwhelmingly in the pre-GROUND position while the general locative preposition *na* and a locative noun denoting Region are omitted. This development has led to an isomorphism of Sranan and Dutch patterns, but also to the partial overlap of contemporary Sranan/English/Dutch and Gbe patterns.
10. Sranan also features a small set of items derived from lexifier prepositions/adverbials that have acquired verbal uses. These elements retain their

prepositional functions in Sranan and may also be used adverbially, like in Dutch and English.

Table 4 compares the features of locative constructions in Sranan and the African European input languages. The Table also implicitly provides hypotheses about the origins of each of these features in Sranan as a consequence of substrate transfer (also present in Gbe and Kikongo), lexifier transfer (also present in English), superstrate transfer (also present in Dutch) and internal development (not attested in any of the four languages, indicated by N.A. in the table heading). Note that the term "preposition" refers to the kind of verby preposition that we have seen to be characteristic for Gbe, as well as the unicategorial type of preposition that we find in English and Dutch.

Table 4. Functions of elements in Sranan locative constructions

Feature in Sranan	No.	Gbe	Kikongo	English/Dutch	N/A
LOC copula expresses spatial relation	1	+	+		
General LOC preposition expresses spatial relation	2	+	+		
Locative nouns denote REGION	3	+	+		
Prepositions express PATH & SPATIAL RELATION only	4	+	+		
Prepositions express PATH, SPATIAL RELATION & REGION	5			+	
Some prepositions function as verb particles	6			+	
General LOC preposition marks PLACE & GOAL	7		+		
General LOC preposition marks SOURCE	8	+	+		
POSS marker may link locative element & GROUND	9	+	+	+	
Relatively open class of V2s may mark GOAL & PATH	10				+

On the basis of the characteristics enumerated in points 1–10 above, and the summary of functions in Table 4, we can establish the following: seen from the perspective of Gbe, the principal source of relexified patterns in Sranan, we find features in Sranan that represent the workings of centripetal and centrifugal forces. Centripetal forces manifest themselves where the functions of Sranan elements are coterminous with those found in Gbe. Hence we would expect Gbe substrate patterns to have driven the emergence of points 1–4 and 8. Centrifugal forces show themselves in features not found in Gbe, hence points 5–7. Among these, features points 5 and 6 reflect the dominance of adstratal transfer from the superstrate Dutch, and potentially also lexifier transfer from English. Point 7 is particularly interesting because it represents the only instance where the two substrates diverge. Hence with respect to the functions of locative elements there is a near-complete overlap between Gbe and Kikongo. Yet, we also pointed out earlier that internal development may have also contributed to the existence of 7. In between these two poles, 10 seems to represent a case of internal development, albeit closely modelled along the Gbe pattern in which SVCs rather than "pure" prepositions express the PATH component in a caused-motion event.

Finally, 9 may represent a case of substrate, lexifier and superstrate convergence, since all input languages may potentially employ structures involving a possessive linker. One conclusion to be drawn from Table 4 is that all types of locative constructions, save two (the Dutch-influenced RELATION/PATH/REGION conflated prepositional phrase and the use of verbal particles) encountered in Sranan can be accounted for by appealing to corresponding structures within the Gbe and Kikongo substrates alone, either fully or in part (i.e. feature 10).

The constituent order (from left to right) and structure of the Sranan, Gbe and Germanic (English and Dutch) locative constructions covered in this chapter are represented schematically in Table 5. The following abbreviations hold for the headers of the slots: No = construction number; PLoc = general locative or other preposition; NLoc1 = locative noun slot 1; Linker = (possessive or other) linker; Ground = ground; NLoc2 = locative noun slot 2.

Table 5. Structure of locative constructions

Language(s)	No.	PLoc	NLoc1	Linker	Ground	NLoc2
Sranan	1	+	+	(+)	+	
	2	+			+	+
	3	+			+	
Gbe	4	+			+	+
	5	+	+	+	+	
Kikongo	6	+	+	+	+	
English/Dutch	7	=		(+)	+	

Table 5 shows an overlap between Sranan, Gbe, and Bantu patterns 1, 5, and 6, bearing in mind that the use of the (possessive) linker in 1, represents a semantically more specialized type of locative construction, and is rather rare in contemporary Sranan, hence (+). The same notation principle applies for 7, where the use of a linker in English structures like *on top of the mountain* are more specific than *on the mountain* as well, hence (+) in the linker column. An overlap between Sranan and Gbe alone exists with respect to patterns 2 and 4, and between Sranan and Germanic alone with respect to patterns 3 and 7. Contemporary Sranan is therefore characterized by a maximal number of options with respect to the number of available patterns. In fact, Sranan unites all the possibilities found in the substrates, the lexifier and the superstrate. Even if we know little about the relative frequency of each pattern in Sranan, the combined result of substrate retention from Gbe and Bantu, lexifier retention from English, adstratal contact with Dutch, as well as internal development, gives Sranan speakers an unusually large range of options in the expression of locative relations.

A final issue to be addressed is the nature of relexification. In the preceding sections, we have argued that certain types of Sranan locative constructions represent instances of pattern relexification, hence of clusters of items, rather than of individual items alone. In our case, the cluster that constitutes a Sranan locative construction forms a syntactic category, composed of a string of morphemes, which in turn, enter into syntactic relations with each other. In the Gbe-like Sranan structures that we have seen so far, these syntactic combination rules involve nested dependency relations; the adjunct PP is headed by the general locative preposition *na* 'LOC', while the GROUND contained in the PP is a dependent of the locative noun. In accordance with its formal complexity, the entire structure may also be seen to have a more complex meaning than a corresponding single item; it contains information on the SPATIAL RELATION, the GROUND, and the REGION. This contrasts with the meaning of a single relexified item like *tapu*, which, taken by itself, only conveys information on a particular SPATIAL RELATION.

An individual item nevertheless has a special role to play in pattern relexification. In fact, a semantic matching, the creation of a "conceptual link" (cf. e.g. Heine and Kuteva 2010: 89) between an individual English(-derived) and a Gbe item must have constituted the basis for the development of semantically and formally more complex structures modelled on Gbe. The interlingual identification of the English item *top* with a Gbe item like *jí* would have occurred on the basis of shared meaning. In this particular case, the match is quite close. Both forms not only designate a superior location, their meaning also includes contact with the GROUND. At the same time, the nouniness of *top* in English must have provided further matching opportunities for Gbe speakers. Therefore individual items must have functioned as "pivots" (Matras 2009: 240-42) during the calquing process of Gbe locative structures. Such pivots entail the occurrence of other forms plus their combinatoric possibilities, hence *relational* structures. This includes morphosyntactic specifications when individual lexical items belong to a paradigmatic class. Thus a superior location designated by *tapu* 'top' requires an inferior location, expressed by *ondro* 'bottom' and so forth. Much of the available evidence suggests that speakers want to emulate underlying semantic relations in the recipient language and that this need drives the recruitment of the corresponding phonological material and morphosyntactic structures in the recipient language (cf. Heine and Kuteva 2010). In the case of *tapu* 'top', the semantic relation is a SUPERIOR PLACE RELATION INVOLVING CONTACT. Further, it is one that requires the presence of elements expressing a FIGURE, a SPATIAL RELATION, a GROUND, and a REGION. This process of matching and extension can be represented schematically, as in Figure 1.

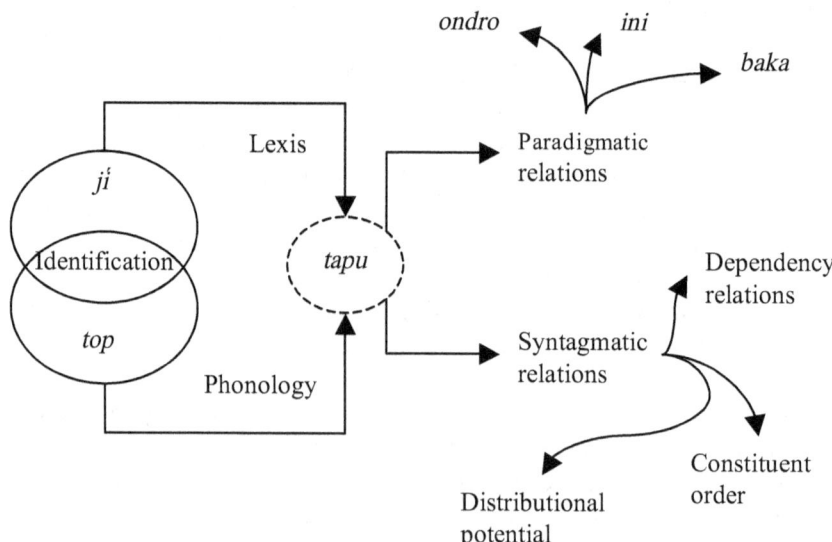

Figure 1. Pattern relexification

In the scenario presented in Figure 1, the relexification of the individual item as a point of departure to pattern relexification is not only crucial because of interlingual identification. Local relexification may also transfer "embryonic" syntactic information along with lexical one. Hence the specification of the syntactic category of an item like *tapu* as (a type of) a noun could be seen to be part of the lexical entry. But this already provides some distributional information about *tapu*, for example, its potential to cooccur with another noun within the same NP. Meanwhile, pattern relexification could be seen to carry over specifications that are more syntactic in nature along the lexicon-syntax cline: constituent structure and order, e.g. the pre- or post-GROUND position of *tapu* or its direct adjacency vs. the presence of an intervening linker or the dependency relation holding between the head noun *tapu* and the GROUND noun. Pattern relexification also allows for minor morphosyntactic differences between Sranan and its main substrate Gbe, e.g. the rather balanced use of pre- and post-GROUND structures, and the obligatory presence of the locative preposition. These changes in constituent order do not affect the nature of the dependency relation between the locative noun *tapu* and the GROUND, nor the REGION function of *tapu*. Likewise, the generalized use of the locative preposition in Sranan, in contexts where Gbe makes no use of it, is not as contradictory as it may seem. This is because an overarching feature of the general locative prepositions in Sranan, Kikongo, and Gbe is their potential to mark GROUNDS in motion events, rather than in static events alone. The respective Sranan and Kikongo locative prepositions apply this function indiscriminately to SOURCE and GOAL GROUNDS. In contrast, Gbe limits the use of the preposition to SOURCE GROUNDS. In that, Gbe displays a typologically common pattern, in which PLACE and GOAL are marked in a unitary fashion, while Source is marked in a different way (cf. Creissels 2006).

6. Concluding remarks

We have seen that spatial relations in contemporary Sranan are expressed through a broad range of constructions. Some of these quite clearly reflect the historically more recent influence of the Dutch superstrate. The original system however clearly reflects the influence of the substrate languages of Sranan. These "Niger-Congo" structures are markedly different from equivalent "Indo-European" ones. They are bipartite, hence feature two functionally distinct locative elements, namely a general locative preposition and a locative noun. In semantic terms, these structures overtly encode two spatial notions separately. While the locative preposition places FIGURE and GROUND in a SPATIAL RELATION to each other in a general manner, the REGION element provides specific information about the space attached to the GROUND. In the Indo-European type of locative construction, we may find conceptually similar spatial descriptions in locative constructions like *at the top of the building* and *at the back of the car*. These constructions also feature a fairly general preposition (*at*) and a REGION element (*back*). But we have noted a profound typological rift between Sranan, Gbe, and Kikongo on the one hand, and English and Dutch on the other, in the way these bipartite structures are employed in the description of motion events. In English and Dutch, prepositions whose meanings include a PATH component are employed when motion events are described. Hence an English clause like **he removed it at the back of the car* cannot be interpreted to involve a SOURCE-oriented motion. In contrast, Sranan and its substrates have the option of describing certain types of motion events in exactly this way because these languages offer the possibility of expressing the motion component through verbs alone. At the same time, the bipartite structure featuring the general locative preposition with its static semantics is maintained. Although a deeper analysis of these structures in Gbe and Kikongo revealed subtle differences between the two, the general constellation was found to be characteristic of languages from other branches of Niger-Congo as well. The rather isomorphic nature of locative constructions in Niger-Congo contrasts with the portmanteau prepositions characteristic of Indo-European, which conflate RELATION, PATH, and REGION (Talmy 1985, 2000). The large number and manifold origins of locative prepositions in Indo-European languages tallies with the heavy functional load of this word class. In English, for example, we find denominal forms like (*in*) *front* (*of*) and *down*, adverb-noun combinations like *inside*, *outside* and (*a*)*midst*, and deverbal elements like *past*.

With respect to the expression of spatial relations, Sranan is typologically unusual. The language appears to allow the use of the entire range of locative structures encountered in the substrate languages, the lexifier and the superstrate. At the same time, the existence of locative constructions with "Niger-Congo" semantics and a Gbe constituent order in particular, quite clearly points to relexification. We identified pattern relexification as the cause of the wholesale carry-over of substrate semantics plus morphosyntactic specifications into Sranan. This approach also makes allowance for minor differences in the functions and behavior of Gbe and Sranan items. The distinction between the transfer of lexical material per se on the one hand, and the transfer of lexical and morphosyntactic properties on the other, is of course not new in the study of language contact. The latter phenomenon has been referred to in the literature (with varying degrees of overlap in meaning) by terms like "calquing" (Haugen 1950), "metatypy" (Ross 1996, 2001), "pattern transfer" (Heath 1984), "grammatical replication" (Heine and Kuteva 2003, 2005, 2010), "pattern replication" (Matras 2009), "rule borrowing" (Boretzky 1993), "apparent grammaticalization" (Bruyn 1996), and last but not least "relexification (of patterns)" (e.g. Lefebvre 1993, 1998; Lumsden 1999; Migge 2003a; Muysken 1981, 1997; Voorhoeve 1973).

Beyond providing more evidence for the reality of the process of pattern relexification, we hope to have additionally shown that the concept of pattern transfer can be used as an analytical tool to describe contact effects that have involved language creation, rather than mere convergence between existing systems. Secondly, a careful areal-typological analysis of the corresponding substrate structures can strengthen the case for substrate transfer and relexification in a "new" language like Sranan. In the absence of such an analysis, certain features (e.g. the general GROUND-marking function of *na* 'LOC' in Sranan) may otherwise be prematurely attributed to internal development. Thirdly, we may well encounter a diversity in Sranan locative constructions that appears bewildering at first sight. But we have seen that much of this apparent diversity is superficial in nature, for it chiefly concerns constituent order. In contrast, morphosyntactic relations like the nature of dependency, as well as the semantic structure of spatial descriptions remain highly similar in Sranan and the substrates. We hope to have shown that these contact-induced similarities are so systematic and profound that they may be seen as yet another manifestation of the Trans-Atlantic Sprachbund that unites the West African coastal belt with the Caribbean.

Abbreviations

ó	high tone	COMPL	completive aspect marker
ò	low tone	COP	locative-existential copula
ō	mid tone	DEF	definite article
ABL	ablative	DP	discourse particle
ADV	adverbial	Du.	Dutch
AFF	affix	Eng.	English
ASS	general associative preposition	HAB	habitual aspect marker
		HST	hesternal
CL	noun class prefix	INDF	indefinite article
COM	comitative preposition	INF	infinitive
COMP	complementizer	INT	intensifier

IPFV	imperfective aspect	PRS	present tense
ITI	itive particle	PST	past tense marker
LOC	general locative preposition	Q	question particle
LOG	logophoric pronoun	SBJV	subjunctive complementizer
NLOC	'nouny' locative element		
m	masculine	SD	sudden discovery and narrative tense
NEG	negator		
NOM	nominalizer	SVC	serial verb construction
P	postposition	TOP	topic
PASS	passive	3SG	third person singular
Ploc	locative preposition	VEN	ventive particle
POSS	possessive	Vloc	'verby' locative element
POT	potential mood marker	V1	initial verb in an SVC
PRF	perfect marker	V2	second verb in an SVC

Verb Semantics and Argument Structure in the Gbe and Sranan

James Essegbey

1. Introduction

Lefebvre (1998: 9) argues that "the creators of a creole language, adult native speakers of the substratum languages, use the properties of their native lexicon, the parametric values and semantic interpretation rules of their native grammars in creating creoles". I tested this hypothesis by comparing the semantics of verbs from three semantic domains in the Gbe languages and Sranan, as well as the argument structure of verbs in general. In this chapter, I summarize the results of my findings. More detailed discussions of the findings can be found in Essegbey (2004), Ameka and Essegbey (2007), Essegbey and Ameka (2007), Essegbey (2007), and Huttar, Essegbey, and Ameka (2007). The verbs that I discuss here are CUT and BREAK verbs, COME and GO verbs and the EAT verb. I show that while the first two are very close to their equivalents in English, the EAT-verb is closer to its equivalent in the Gbe languages. I also show that the argument structure of verbs in Sranan is different from that of the Gbe languages. This is mainly because of the phenomenon of obligatory object verbs in the Gbe languages. I conclude that the creators of Sranan did attempt to acquire the English that was available to them at the time.

2. CUT and BREAK verbs

CUT and BREAK verbs describe "separation in the material integrity of objects" (cf. Hale and Keyser 1987). The semantics of the two classes of verbs have been widely discussed in the literature (cf. Guerssel et al 1985, Pye 1996, Levin and Pinker 1991, etc.). It has been established that in addition to describing a change in the material integrity of an object, CUT-verbs also lexicalize properties like the type of action that brings about the change (e.g. *to slash*), the type of instrument (e.g. *to hammer*), and the manner in which the change occurs (e.g. *to crush*). BREAK-verbs, on the other hand, lexicalize the type of object that undergoes a change (e.g. *vuvu* 'to tear' in Ewegbe, see below) and the type of change that an object undergoes (e.g. *to split*). The widespread interest in the CUT and BREAK verbs has also given rise to sophisticated tools for eliciting them and determining their meaning differences. The verbs discussed in this section were elicited with one such tool developed by Bohnemeyer, Bowermann, and Brown (2001). It consists of 61 short video clips depicting various kinds of spontaneous and caused cutting and breaking scenes. One finding from working with this tool is that the Gbe languages make three different important distinctions that are not made in Sranan. These involve the breaking of things, the cutting of hair, and the peeling of crops and fruits. The following discussion shows that in both their concrete and non-concrete uses, the Sranan equivalents of the verbs are more English-like than Gbe-like in their meanings.

2.1. Break verbs

Let us begin by comparing the semantics of BREAK-verbs in the Gbe languages with those of Sranan. The Gbe languages distinguish two types of breaking events but Sranan does not. Furthermore, there are several uses of the BREAK-verbs in the Gbe languages that do not exist in Sranan. I show that the verb in Sranan is influenced by its English etymon although there is a trace or two of substrate influence.

Not only the Gbe languages but Kwa and, indeed, most West African languages distinguish between a breaking event that separates objects into pieces and another kind that we have referred to as "breaking at a fulcrum" (cf. Ameka and Essegbey, 2007). The first type of breaking event is described in the Gbe languages as *gba*; *gba* describes the breaking of objects like (earthenware) pots and glasses. For instance a video clip in which someone hits a pot with a hammer and smashes it elicited the following sentences:

(1) a. *é-gba   ze-a*   Ewegbe
     b. *é-gba   ze ɔ*   Fongbe/Ayizogbe
         3SG-break pot-DEF
         'She broke the pot.'

I stated at the beginning of this section that in addition to encoding that an object undergoes a change of state BREAK verbs also encode (lexicalize) additional information such as the type of object that undergoes a change or the type of change that an object undergoes. The characterization of *gba* suggests that the additional property that it lexicalizes is the type of change that an object undergoes. As such, it does not matter whether an instrument is used to bring about the change or not. Furthermore, the nature of the object that undergoes the change does not appear to matter much, although it must be admitted that as far as the concrete use of the verb is concerned, it appears to select only hard brittle objects. This is not surprising since those are the kinds of objects that undergo separation into several parts.[1] Thus a video clip that shows a twig being smashed to pieces with a hammer is also described with the verb. Although I have said that the broken object is separated into several parts, the parts do not need to fall apart for *gba* to be used. For instance, the result of a pair of glasses falling to the ground and cracking in several places without the parts necessarily coming off the frame is also described as *gba*.

Contrasted with this kind of break is the "fulcrum-break" that involves an object snapping at what could be considered to be a fulcrum point. This type of breaking event is usually, though not necessarily, due to some sort of pressure. A classic situation is the breaking of a stick across the knee. Fractures of the bone in the body are also conceived as fulcrum-break. Unlike the first type of breaking-event, which all the Gbe languages describe with the same word, this event is described differently in the Gbe languages under discussion. Furthermore the verbs have different selectional restrictions: Ewegbe uses *ŋé*, which refers to the fulcrum-break of hard brittle things. By contrast, Fongbe and Ayizogbe use *wέn*, which can also be used to describe the separation of soft pliable objects like ropes and twines: when the two ends of a rope are pulled so tight that the rope breaks, *wέn* is used. It is possible that such taut ropes are perceived as hard brittle objects. Thus, in a way, they are not conceptually different from sticks, which are broken at a fulcrum point. Ewegbe uses a different verb (i.e. *lã́*) to describe the separation of pliable objects like ropes and twines. Although *lã́* also describes the separation of hard objects, this is only when the latter are cut, not when they are broken. Therefore, *lã́* is not the same as *wέn*.

To sum up the discussion so far, the Gbe languages distinguish between two types of breaking events: one involves the breaking of objects into several parts while the other involves breaking objects at a fulcrum point. The word that describes the breaking of objects into several parts is the same in form and has broadly the same meaning across the Gbe variants.

---

1. It should be noted that I am referring to a change that takes place at once, and not separations that are carried out bit by bit.

By contrast the verbs that describe fulcrum-break are different in form and meaning in Ewegbe, on the one hand, and Fongbe and Ayizogbe, on the other.

Unlike the Gbe languages Sranan does not make any distinction between the two types of breaking events. Instead, it uses *broko*, derived from *break* in English, to describe both the breaking of things like pots and sticks. Although the Sranan strategy is similar to that of English, this does not mean that *broko* is exactly the same as *break*. This is because, unlike *break*, *broko* cannot be used to describe the snapping of pliable objects like ropes. In this sense, it is similar to *ŋé* in Ewegbe, which only describes the snapping of hard objects, and different from *wɛ́n* in Fongbe and Ayizogbe. Note however that *broko* is not the same as *ŋé* because *ŋé* cannot describe the breaking process that involves the separation of things into several parts. In order to describe the separation of pliable objects like ropes, Sranan uses *koti,* derived from *cut* in English. This may appear at first sight to be similar to the verb *lã́* that is used in Ewegbe to describe the separation of pliable as well as hard objects. However, we have shown in Essegbey and Ameka (2007) that *koti* is different from *lã́* because unlike *lã́*, it can be used to describe practically any kind of cutting event. By contrast, specific types of cutting events (e.g. slicing and slashing) cannot be represented with *lã́*.

In sum, the Gbe languages distinguish between the breaking of things like pots and the breaking of things like sticks, while Sranan does not. For Fongbe and Ayizogbe, the word for describing the breaking of stick-like objects is also used to describe the separation of pliable things like ropes that are taut. Such events are described with different verbs in Ewegbe and Sranan. Table 1 represents the distinction summarized in Ameka and Essegbey (2003):

Table 1. Break type verbs

Language	fulcrum-break (hard)	fulcrum-break (pliable)	Shatter-break
Ewegbe	ŋé	lã́	gba
Fongbe and Ayizogbe	wɛ́n	wɛ́n	gba
Sranan	broko	koti	broko
English	break	break/cut	break (*smash*)

Table 1 shows that *broko* is not relexified from Ewegbe or Fongbe /Ayizogbe: had it been relexified from Ewegbe, there would be different verbs for *ɲé* and *gba*. On the other hand, if the Fongbe/Ayizogbe verbs had been relexified, then the verb that describes fulcrum-break in Sranan would be the same for soft and hard objects as occurs in those languages. What we observe from the table rather is a parallel between Sranan and English: where Sranan uses *broko*, *break* is acceptable in English, and where it uses *koti*, *cut* is. I noted above that *broko* differs somewhat from *break* because it cannot be used to describe the separation of pliable objects while *break* can. This is the only similarity between *broko* and a BREAK-verb (i.e. *ɲé*) in Ewegbe. A detailed look at both the concrete and non-concrete uses of the verbs rather suggests a semantic influence from English rather than the Gbe languages.

Across the Gbe languages, *gba* has basically the same concrete and non-concrete uses. For example a person who becomes blind is said to have broken the eye (*gba ŋkú* in Ewegbe) while in Sranan, this is described as *breni*, derived from *blind* in English. Furthermore *gba* is used to describe physical damage to vehicles, most likely brought about by an accident; Westermann (1973) notes for Ewegbe that when *gba* is used to describe a ship it means that the ship is wrecked, and Segurola and Rassinoux (2000) report the same for Fongbe. This shows that *gba* has a concrete-BREAK interpretation when it is predicated of vehicles. This is not the case in Sranan; when *broko* is used to describe cars, it often means that they have broken down, i.e. they have problems with their engines. Clearly, this use derives from English. Other differences include the use of *gba* to describe a smuggling activity in the Gbe languages: people who smuggle things across the border are said to have broken the border (*gba de*) because the border is conceived as a concrete structure that is broken down. Furthermore, in the Gbe languages, a woman who gives birth is said to have broken a gourd (*gba go*). These two uses of the BREAK-verb do not exist in Sranan.

There are expressions that seem to suggest parallels between the Gbe languages and Sranan. However, such expressions tend to exist in English as well, leading one to assume that they rather derive from English. This assumption is supported by the fact that in the cases where the English meaning of the expression differs slightly from that of the Gbe languages, it is the former that occurs in Sranan. For example, the Gbe languages use *gba* to describe the destruction of homes, society and countries. Consider the Ewegbe sentence below adapted from a poem:

(2) *Núvɔwɔlá· gba-a du*
    evildoer   break-HAB town
    'An evildoer/sinner destroys a town/community'

This sentence refers to the physical break up (i.e. dispersal) of the community, and not just financial ruin. Thus when a group is predicated of *gbà*, it means the group does not exist anymore. By contrast, when *broko* is used to describe a community in Sranan, the interpretation is usually one of financial ruin, as the following example from Wilner (1994) indicates:

(3) *Fu di den bigiman gridi, den broko a kondre*
'Because the leaders were greedy, they destroyed [bankrupted] the country.'

Note that in English too, a country that is said to be broke is one that has financial problems. Such a community can still exist, in contrast to one described with *gba*. One can therefore not attribute sentence (3) to the Gbe languages. At best, one can only claim that the Gbe languages reinforced the Sranan use.

A more interesting parallel involves the use of *gba* and *broko* to indicate worry in the Gbe languages and Sranan respectively. For example, Segurola and Rassinoux (2000:200), and Wilner (1994:16) have (4a) and (4b), respectively:

(4) a. *Xó ɔ́ gba tame n'ì*
word DEF break head for 3SG
'Cette affaire lui a causé beaucoup de souci'
'This matter caused him a lot of worries.' (JE)
b. *I no mu broko yu ede gi tamara. Ala dei abi en eigi krasi-ede*
2SG NEG must break 2SG head give tomorrow. All day has 3SG own scrach-head
'Don't worry about tomorrow. Everyday has its worries.'

While one is tempted to jump on this kind of parallel, the existence of expressions like *don't break your head over the problem* in English cannot be ignored.

It is not all uses of *gba* that are the same across the Gbe variants. For instance, Ewegbe has the expression *gba ga*, literally 'break money', which means 'to change money'. In Fongbe, this expression rather means 'to flee'. This interpretation is due to a metonymic shift from the literal meaning, which in Fongbe means 'to break metal/chain'. The same expression is used euphemistically to mean 'to die' (presumably because the one who dies is considered to have done away with life's shackles). *Gba ga* therefore has completely different meanings in Ewegbe and Fongbe. Interestingly Sranan, like Ewegbe, has the expression *broko moni*, which means 'to change money'. However, in this instance, one cannot say that the Sranan expression derives from Ewegbe because a similar expression occurs in English too. Like the previous expressions encountered, one can only say that the Ewegbe expression may have reinforced the use in Sranan. Finally, Fongbe uses *gba ze*, literally 'break pot', to indicate that a girl has gotten pregnant at a young age, and *wén kan*, literally 'break rope', to mean that a girl has lost her virginity. A similar, though not exactly the same, expression in Sranan is the use of *broko* to describe having sexual relations for the first time. Hence *a meisje broko* means 'the girl has lost her virginity' (Wilner 1994: 18). Since there is no reference to a rope in the Sranan expression, it is not likely that this use derives from Fongbe.

There are some non-concrete uses of *broko* in Sranan that are not in any way related to any of the BREAK-verbs in the Gbe languages but rather come from English. One is *brokodey*, which clearly derives from *day-break* in English. Wilner (1994) notes that the word is now used as an adjective to describe activities that go on all night (i.e. till day break). The example he gives is *brokodey fesa* 'all night party'. Such an expression does not occur in any of the Gbe languages.

In sum, the Gbe languages distinguish between two types of breaking events but Sranan does not. This alone would not have posed a serious problem for relexification theory, since one could suggest that the two concepts in the Gbe languages have been relexified with a single verb in Sranan. Such a claim would be understandable, considering that creolization involves a lot of simplification in all areas, including the lexicon. The more serious problem for the strict-relexification hypothesis is that in addition to the fact that important distinctions made in the Gbe languages are non-existent in Sranan, most of the expressions containing *broko* in Sranan can be traced to English. The only clear case where one could say confidently that (a variant of) the Gbe languages alone influenced the meaning of the word is in its inability to occur with soft pliable entities. Where the other parallels discussed are concerned, one can only argue, at best, that the Gbe languages might have reinforced the interpretation in Sranan.

2.2. Barbering

Like the breaking-events, there is a domain of cutting – i.e. barbering – where the Gbe languages make distinctions that are not present in Sranan.

What we see here is a simplification of the Sranan lexicon such that it is neither like English nor the Gbe languages. All the Gbe languages distinguish between three types of barbering events: these are barbering in which long hair is held and cut, one in which the hair is trimmed carefully and, finally, one in which all the hair is shaved off. In the first instance, the hair is seen as any other soft and pliable object that is cut. Ewegbe uses either *lã́* or *sẽ́* to describe this event. *Lã́*, which was discussed in the last section, does not include any information about the type of instrument or manner of cutting. By contrast, *sẽ́* focuses on the fact that a bladed instrument is involved in the cutting process. Fongbe and Ayizogbe also use *sẽ́* to describe this type of cutting-event but, in addition, they also use *gbo*. *Gbo* is translated in Segurola and Rassinoux (2000: 407) as 'couper, trancher, abattre; tailler, retrancher une partie de quelque chose, amputer; séparer, traverser'. It is used to describe cuts that are done in a specific manner for a specific goal. Examples are the cutting up of a piece of cloth for the purpose of making a dress out of it, and the felling of a tree. The use of *gbo* to describe the process of cutting hair is not surprising since the end result is to get the whole hair in proper shape.

Where the barbering process involves the trimming of the hair, a different verb is used. During the elicitation of the CUT-verbs, all the Gbe consultants took pains to point out that there is a barbering process (different from an elicitation clip they were shown which merely involved cutting off of the long hair of a lady, and was completed in seconds) which involves a lengthy process of trimming the hair gradually until it gets to the required length and shape. In the Anlogbe variant of Ewegbe, this process is described with the verb *kó* and the complement *ta* 'head' instead of *ɖa* 'hair'. The inland dialects rather describe the process as *fiá· ɖa/ta*, literally 'burn hair/head'. In Fongbe and Ayizogbe, this form of barbering is known as *kpa ɖa* literally 'carve hair'.

The final type of barbering which involves shaving off the whole hair is described as *lũ ɖa/ta* in Ewegbe, and *xwlɛ ɖa* in Fongbe and Ayizogbe.

The three distinctions noted above do not exist in Sranan. Instead, the same CUT-word *koti* is used to describe the three processes. In sum, the Gbe languages distinguish between simply holding strands of long hair and cutting them off, trimming the hair, and shaving the whole hair. By constrast, Sranan uses the same verb to describe the three types of processes. The differences are shown in Table 2. Thus, unlike with BREAK-verb, Sranan is not heavily influenced by English in its expression of various forms of barbering. This is because whereas the process of cutting off long hair and trimming can both be described as *cut*, that of getting rid of all the hair cannot. The appropriate word in that case is *shave*. What Sranan does in this case is rather simplify the lexicon such that it is neither like English nor the Gbe languages.

Table 2. Barbering verbs

English	Ewegbe	Fongbe	Ayizogbe	Sranan
Cut-off long hair	lã́ / sẽ́	sɛn / gbó	sɛn / gbó	koti
Trim hair	kó ta / fíá ɖa / ta	kpa ɖa	kpa ɖa	koti
Shave-off hair	lũ ɖa / ta	xwlɛ	xwlɛ	koti

2.3. Peeling

The Gbe languages also distinguish between two ways in which the skin of fruits and crops are removed. Where most fruits such as bananas and oranges, and crops like groundnuts and beans are concerned, the process can be done with the hands. For other crops like plantain and cassava, a bladed instrument is needed to cut into the skin before it is rolled or pulled off. The process of rolling/pulling the skin off, whether done with the hand or bladed instrument, is described as *klẽ́* in the Anlogbe variant of Ewegbe. Westermann (1973) translates *klẽ́* as 'to open, be open, burst open', although he also notes that in combination with fruits like banana, it is translated as 'peel'. This means that the verb is, strictly speaking, not a CUT-verb but an OPEN-verb: the process involves the "opening" of the outer layer of the crop to reveal the food that is inside. The inland Ewegbe dialects also describe the process as *fó* while Fongbe and Ayizogbe use *flé*. In addition, Ayizogbe also has *kɔn*.

The second type of peeling involves the use of a bladed object to peel the rind of citrus fruits or the skin of root crops like yams and potatoes. The difference between this type of peeling and the one described above is that in this case the bladed instrument is crucial for the peeling event: it is the blade that really gets the whole skin/rind off the fruit/crop. As noted in the previous type of peeling event, even when bladed objects are used the blade only serves to make an opening in the skin so that it can be peeled off. All the Gbe languages describe the type of peeling event that requires a bladed instrument as *kpa*, which literally means 'to carve'. Sranan describes the two processes as *piri*. This is summed up in Table 3.

Table 3. Peeling verbs

English	Ewegbe	Fongbe	Ayizogbe	Sranan
Peel 1	klẽ / fó	flé	flé / kɔn	piri
Peel 2	kpa	kpa	kpa	piri

Table 3 shows that the Gbe languages distinguish between two types of peeling events. Like English, Sranan uses *piri*, which is derived from 'to peel' in English to describe the two events.

2.4. Summary

This section dealt with verbs that describe caused and spontaneous changes in the material integrity of objects, and are all grouped together under the broad term CUT and BREAK verbs. I have shown that the Gbe languages make important distinctions in breaking, barbering and peeling events that are not made in Sranan. It is tempting to dismiss the lack of distinctions in Sranan as due to the process of simplification that is symptomatic of creolization. However, I have gone on to show that the issue is not only a case of the creole having fewer lexical items to express the distinctions in the Gbe languages. Instead, there are distinctions in Sranan that are clearly influenced by English rather than the Gbe languages. This is especially so in the case of the BREAK-verbs, where I have shown that even where there appear to be parallels between the Gbe and Sranan uses, minute differences between them can usually be traced to differences in English (e.g. the use of *broko* to describe engine problems, in contrast to the Gbe languages where it describes physical damage of the vehicles). In the next section, I discuss COME and GO verbs. Just like the CUT and BREAK verbs, I show that the Gbe languages also make distinctions in this domain that are not present in Sranan and, secondly, that their meanings are not the same. Instead, those of Sranan are rather like their English etymons.

3. COME and GO

COME and GO verbs are considered in the literature to be fairly basic. For instance, Wilkins and Hill (1995) refer to Heine, Claudi, and Hünnemeyer's (1991) claim that they are among the most basic human activities, and Miller and Johnson-Laird's (1976) finding that they are the most common and earliest acquired verbs of motion. An important point made by Wilkins

Verb Semantics and Argument Structure   185

and Hill relevant here is that the two verbs differ in meaning cross-linguistically. In Essegbey (2004), I show that the semantics of the verbs in the Gbe languages differ from those in Sranan, which are rather like those of English. The discussion is summarized in this section.

Wilkins and Hill argue that contrary to general assumptions, COME and GO do not constitute lexical universals which manifest a universal deictic opposition. Among other things they claim that:

- Verbs that describe COME and GO scenes cross-linguistically vary in their base semantics to such an extent that that they cannot be considered linguistic universals
- All languages have a way of indicating the deictic sense of motion towards speaker, although they will vary in morphology and *linguistic entailment* (emphasis mine).

Wilkins and Hill set up a questionnaire with 20 different scenes for testing the semantics of these verbs. The three most important ones for my purposes are reproduced in Figures 1(a–c).

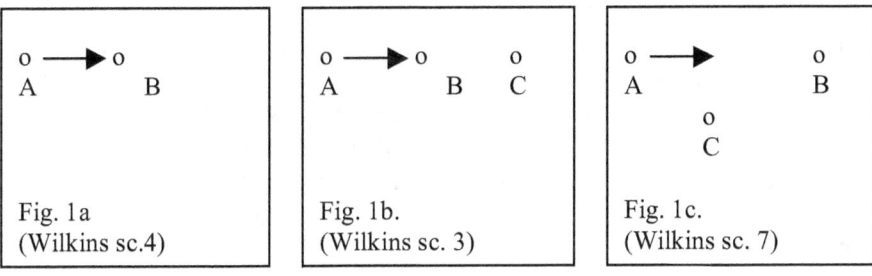

Fig. 1a
(Wilkins sc.4)

Fig. 1b.
(Wilkins sc. 3)

Fig. 1c.
(Wilkins sc. 7)

Figure (1a) represents a situation where someone moves from place A to place B where the speaker or hearer is (i.e. deictic center). In Figure (1b), someone moves from place A to place B which is close to, but not the same as place C, the deictic center. An example of this is when someone living in the outskirts of a city reports the event of another person moving from, say, the train station in the center of the city to a grocery store that is mid-way between the station and his/her house. Figure (1c) involves motion that is neither away from nor towards the deictic center.

The kinds of motion involved in Figures (1a) and (1b) are described with *va* in Ewegbe and *wa* in Fongbe and Ayizogbe. This means that in addition to describing motion to the deictic center (Figure 1a), the COME-verb in the Gbe languages also describe motion to a place that is near or in the direction of the deictic center (Figure 1b). Interestingly, none of the three Gbe variants uses *va/wa* in the progressive to describe progressive motion to(wards) the deictic center. Instead Ewegbe uses *gbɔna*, while Fongbe and Ayizogbe use *jawɛ*. *Gbɔ* is translated as 'to come back, return' by Westermann (1973:92) while Segurola and Rassinoux (2000) also translate *ja* in Fongbe as 'arrive' suggesting that in the Gbe languages, ongoing motion towards the deictic center is expressed as arriving at or returning to the location. One can therefore say that the Gbe languages have two different verbs each for expressing motion to(wards) the deictic center, with one verb expressing completed motion and the other expressing motion that is still in progress. Unlike the first two scenes where they use different verbs, all the Gbe languages describe the type of motion in Figure (1c) with *yi* 'go'. Since this motion is neither towards nor away from the deictic center, it shows that the GO-verb is not inherently deictic in the Gbe languages (cf. Wilkins and Hill 1995).

In contrast to the Gbe languages, Sranan uses only *kon* to express motion to the deictic center and *go* for motion in any other direction. Progressive motion to the deictic center is simply expressed with the progressive morpheme *e* (i.e. *e kon* 'is coming'). This means that like the CUT and BREAK verbs discussed in the previous section, Sranan makes fewer distinctions with the deictic verbs than the Gbe languages make. In addition to this, the semantics of the verbs differ from their counterparts in the Gbe languages. There is some variation in the use of *kon*: for some speakers, only the type of motion in Figure (1a) can be described with *kon*. This means that motion to a place that is near, but not at the deictic center (cf. Figure 1b) is only expressed by such speakers as *go*. Recall that the latter type of motion can only be expressed with the COME-verb in the Gbe languages. There are some Sranan speakers for whom Figure (1b) can also be described with *kon*. However, for these speakers too, *go* is the default choice; *kon* is used when there is a shift in perspective, as reported for English by Fillmore (1983) and Goddard (1997). Thus even for this group of speakers, the semantics of *kon* and *go* are not the same as *va/wa* and *yi*. This is because *va/wa* is obligatory for describing types of directional motion for which *kon* is optional (cf. Figure 1b) while *go*, unlike *yi*, can describe motion to a place that is near the deictic center. The differences are summed up in Table 4. Apart from making fewer distinctions with COME and GO verbs than the Gbe languages do, the Sranan equivalents have meanings that are close to those of English which are their etymons.

Despite the differences in meanings shown above, Sranan uses its COME and GO verbs to express directional manner of motion in a way that is similar to the Gbe languages and different from English.

Table 4. COME and GO verbs

	Ewegbe	Fongbe	Ayizogbe	Sranan	English
Motion to deictic center	*va*	*wa*	*wa*	*kon*	*come*
Ongoing motion to a deictic center	*gbɔna*	*ja-wɛ*	*ja-wɛ*	*e kon*	*is coming*
Motion to place near deictic center	*va*	*wa*	*wa*	*go [kon]*	*go [come]*
Motion to another-direction	*yi*	*yi*	*yi*	*go*	*go*

As extensively discussed by Talmy (1985, 2000), English is a satellite-framed language, meaning that it expresses the directional component of a manner of motion with a non-verbal element, referred to as a satellite. By contrast, Sranan and the Gbe languages use a verb to express this component. The result is shown in the sentences below (see Essegbey and Ameka (2001) for a more extensive discussion):

(5) a. *Kofi crawled into the room.*
 b. *Kofi ta yi xɔ-a me.*
    Kofi crawl go building-DEF containing.region
    'Kofi crawled into the room.'
 c. *Kofi kroipi go na ini a kamra.*
    Kofi crawl go PREP containing.region DEF room
    'Kofi crawled into the room.'

In English, the preposition *in(to)* is what shows that Kofi's crawl takes him into the confines of a room. In the Ewegbe sentence (5b), which is chosen to represent the Gbe strategy, and the Sranan equivalent (5c), it is rather a combination of the verb and the element that I have glossed as 'containing region' (see Essegbey and Bruyn (to appear) for an extensive discussion of *me* and *ini*) that conveys this meaning. For our purposes, it is worth noting that the Gbe and Sranan strategy forces the speaker to state whether he or she was inside or outside the room when Kofi crawled in.

In sum, I have shown that the Gbe languages make distinctions between their COME-verb that are not made in Sranan. More importantly, I have shown that the semantics of the COME and GO verbs in Sranan differ from those of the Gbe languages; they are rather similar to their etymons from English. However, Sranan employs a strategy for coding directional manner of motion similar to that of the Gbe languages and unlike English.

4. The EAT verb

Consider now the meaning of a verb in the Gbe languages and Sranan that that I refer to as the EAT-verb because it is translated as 'eat'. Contrary to the verbs discussed in the previous sections, the EAT-verb in Sranan, *nyan*, does not have an English or Indo-European etymon. Although Smith (1987: 105) reports that it derives from Wolof, it actually derived from *nyam* 'eat' in Pulaar (the EAT-verb in Wolof is *lek*). Furthermore, unlike the verbs discussed earlier whose semantics are largely derived from English, there are several parallels between Sranan and the Gbe languages with regard to this verb, suggesting some influence from the Gbe languages. Even more interesting is that fact that although the word derives from Pulaar, the parallels that I discuss in this section do not exist in that language. As such, one cannot talk of any influence from Pulaar. Instead, many of the expressions exist in other Kwa languages such as Akan, and some other African languages like Hausa (Kemp 1991) and Swahili (Sheikh and Wolff 1981).

Although translated as 'eat', there is evidence that *nyan* and its Gbe counterpart *ɖu* have a more general meaning. First of all they can take nominals, which refer to festive occasions, as complements in order to express celebration. This is illustrated below:

(6) a. *Mi nyan wan bun krisneti*   Sranan
       1SG eat INDEF good Christmas
       'I had a nice Christmas.'
    b. *me-ɖu krismas le leiden*   Ewegbe
       1SG-eat Christmas LOC Leiden
       'I spent Christmas in Leiden.'

In all the languages considered here, words that express important occasions, like Independence Day, can occur as the complement of *nyan* and *ɖu*. However, the use of *nyan* to express celebration is more restricted for some speakers of Sranan. Thus, while some accept the expression *nyan vakansi*, literally 'eat holiday', for describing the spending of a holiday, others reject it. The equivalent of this expression, *ɖu mɔ́keke* in Ewegbe is perfectly acceptable. This suggests that the Gbe languages use the celebration sense more widely than Sranan does. For instance, all my Sranan consultants rejected *nyan fesa*, literally 'eat feast', to describe the celebration of a festival, yet the equivalent *ɖu azã* in Ewegbe and *ɖu xwe* in Fongbe are both acceptable.

One could say that the meaning of *nyan/ɖu* in the above instances is rather closer to 'to spend' and that it is the combination of this sense with the festival arguments that gives rise to the celebration interpretation. This position is supported by other uses of the verb: for instance, it can take the equivalent of money as its internal argument and give rise to a spend money interpretation. Most speakers of Sranan assume that when *nyan* takes the equivalent of money as its complement it necessarily means 'to embezzle'. This is certainly the default interpretation of *ɖu ga*, literally 'eat money', in Ewegbe. However, when the complement takes a possessive pronoun as its determiner, then the spend interpretation is the only one available. As (7b) shows, this is also the case in Sranan:

(7) a.   *me-ɖu nye ga ktã*   Ewegbe
          1SG-eat 1SG money all
          'I spent all my money.'
     b.   *mi nyan mi moni*   Sranan
          1SG eat 1SG money
          'I spent my money.'

These sentences show that spending someone else's money is not entailed in *ɖu ga* and *nyan moni* in Ewegbe and Sranan, respectively. One thing that is clear though is that the expressions suggest that one has spent all the money in question. This sense of "spending all", as it were, is also present in the combination of the EAT-verbs with time. Consider the examples below from Ewegbe and Sranan:

(8) a.   *N-a ɖu ga me n-m*   Ewegbe
          thing-DEF eat time containing.region give-1SG
          'The thing wasted (consumed) my time.'
     b.   *A sani nyan ten gi mi*   Sranan
          DEF thing eat time give 1SG
          'The thing wasted (consumed) my time.'

There is clearly a metonymic shift from spending to the result, which is wasting.

There is a use of the EAT-verb in Sranan and the Gbe languages that does not involve spending. Instead, it means 'to overcome'. The way of saying 'to defeat a person' in Ewegbe, which is ɖu ame dzi, literally 'eat person top', is slightly different from Fongbe where it is simply ɖu mɛ, 'literally eat person'. My Sranan consultants noted that one could say (9) below:

(9) Mi   nyan en[2]
     1SG eat   3SG
     'I defeated him/her.'

Related to the idea of defeating or overcoming a person is also the use of the EAT-verb to describe the casting of evil spell on a person. In Ewegbe, the way to say this is ɖu dzo ame, literally 'eat fire person'. While this expression does not exist in its literal form in Sranan, a consultant pointed out to me that the expression in (10) exists:

(10) Efu a   dagu beti en   dan   mi   e   nyan en
      If   DEF dog   bite 3SG then 1SG PROG eat   3SG
      'If a dog bites him/her then I am eating him/her.'

Since this form of "eating" is spiritual, it is doubtlessly related to Gbe uses where it refers to casting an evil spell.

Although I have stated that most of the expressions with the EAT-verb occur in other Kwa languages like Akan, not all of them do. For example, Akan does not use the verb to express casting evil spells. Instead, they talk of throwing medicine on the person. Another expression that does not exist in Akan but does in Sranan and the Gbe languages involves the effect of the sun, as shown by the sentences below:

(11) a.   ŋdɔ-   ɖu   ŋkú me   n-m
          sun-DEF eat face containing.region   for-1SG
          'The sun burned my face.'

---

2. An interesting comment made by the consultants who accepted this expression is that it is not "written Sranan" and, therefore, not "proper". It is supposed to be used only amongst friends. No doubt Dutch expressions are replacing these ones, leading people to treat the latter as non-standard. This might account for the fewer instances of use when compared to the Gbe languages.

b. *A   zon   nyan mi   fesi*
    DEF sun   eat   1SG face
    'The sun burned my face.'

The sentences show that both languages use the EAT-verb to indicate the effect of the sun on the skin. By contrast, Akan uses the verb *keka*, which is a reduplication of *ka* 'bite'. Examples such as these therefore suggest influence of the Gbe languages in the creation of the EAT-expressions.

Despite the parallels noted above, there are uses of the EAT-verb in Sranan and the Gbe languages that are not the same. For example the Gbe languages use it to describe the entry into a profession (e.g. *ɖu sɔ́fo*, literally 'eat pastor', which means to become a pastor). The popular expression below from Ewegbe is an illustration:

(12) *Ame   vɔ   kesé   ɖu   fia*
     person finish monkey chop chief
     'The lack of competent people has led to the incompetent becoming chiefs.'

The Gbe languages also use the expression to mean become ashamed (i.e. *ɖu ŋukpe* literally 'eat shame' in Ewegbe and *ɖu winya* in Fongbe and Ayizogbe). All these expressions do not exist in Sranan. By contrast, Sranan uses the EAT-verb to describe chatting with friends (*nyan tori* literally 'eat story') and forgetting to deliver a message (*nyan boskopu*, literally 'eat message'). Both expressions do not exist in any of the Gbe languages that I have investigated.

In this section, I have discussed one verb whose use in Sranan was doubtlessly influenced by uses in the Gbe languages. I noted that even though the verb is derived from the Pulaar word meaning food, the expressions that I discussed do not occur in that language. Furthermore, even though most of the expressions occur in other Kwa languages like Akan and would doubtlessly reinforce the use in Sranan, not all of them do. It is therefore possible to point out an expression or two that could have originated from the Gbe languages.

5. Summary

In this section I have described verbs from three semantic domains. The first are a class of change of state verbs discussed in the literature under the label of CUT and BREAK verbs. The second type comprises of basic deictic motion verbs, and the third is the verb that translates as 'to eat'. The discussion shows that Sranan has fewer verbs in all three instances and, therefore, makes fewer distinctions in the semantic domains than the Gbe languages. I noted that this difference *per se* does not pose a problem for the relexification theory because one could say that it is because Sranan relexifies more distinctions with fewer verbs. The bigger problem, as I have gone on to show, is that the BREAK-verb and COME and GO verbs have the semantics of their English etymons rather than those of the Gbe languages. They suggest that the creators of the creole did attempt to acquire these verbs. They must have simplified things in some cases, as shown by their use of *koti* for all kinds of barbering, and even the use of *broko* in several contexts where English has terms specific types of breaking events. However, the expressions containing these verbs in Sranan (e.g. *brokodey*) are English expressions. By contrast, the EAT- verb is not influenced by English at all but rather by the Gbe languages. We are all of a sudden confronted with expressions that exist in Sranan and the Gbe languages but not in English. It is tempting to attribute the influence of the Gbe languages in this domain to the fact that the word has an African origin. Note, however, that "African meaning" is also attributed to verbs with English etymon, such as the use of *dede* 'die' to describe a blunt instrument (cf. Huttar 2003, Huttar et al. 2007). Yet none of the verbs that I have encountered show such overwhelming parallels as the EAT-verb does. In describing the semantics of the EAT verb in Swahili, Sheikh and Wolff (1981) remark:

We may assume convergent diachronic development from "different usages" to "polysemy" across the continent, the motivations for which might be sought in common cultural practices.

It is well known that the African words retained in the creoles are those that are of cultural significance to the slaves. Huttar (2003) has also established in discussing color words, that transfer is most likely to occur in the domains where the cultures differ. In the next section I move away from the discussion of individual verbs to the argument structure of verbs in general.

6. Argument structure

A related, but separate issue is that of the argument structure of verbs in Sranan as compared with that of their counterparts in the Gbe languages. I use the term broadly, following Pinker who writes:

> Different subcategories of verbs make different demands on which of their arguments must be expressed, which can be optionally expressed, and how the expressed arguments are encoded grammatically – that is, as subjects, objects, or oblique objects (objects of prepositions or oblique cases). The properties of verbs in different subcategories are specified by their entries in the mental lexicon, in data structures called *argument structures*... (emphasis mine) (Pinker 1989:4)

My use of the term argument structure therefore includes not only the number of participants a verb can take but also the way in which they are realized (i.e. as direct or oblique arguments). Thus I discuss the kind of verbs that occur in intransitive, transitive and ditransitive constructions in Sranan and Gbe. Both languages express property concepts with verbs in a manner non-existent in English. However, I show that there is no one-to-one correspondence between the argument structure of all the verbs in the languages. For instance, the Gbe languages have obligatory complement verbs non-existent in Sranan. This makes the former appear to be a hypertransitive language when compared to languages like Sranan as well as English and Dutch.

6.1. Property concept predicates

Before looking at non-controversial verbs, I discuss some predicates that describe the arguments they are predicated of in Sranan and the Gbe languages. It is well known in the literature that property concepts, which occur mainly as adjectives in English, are expressed as verbs in African languages and the creoles. In the examples below, the concept 'to be bitter' is realized as a verb:

(13) a. *The medicine is bitter*   English
     b. *A dresi bita*   Sranan
     c. *atikea vé*   Ewegbe
     d. *amasin ɔ vɛ́*   Fongbe/Ayizogbe

It should be pointed out here that not everyone considers the forms above to be verbs. Some prefer to treat them as adjectives preceded by null copulas. The problem with such accounts is that the forms behave like "normal" verbs in the various languages. For instance, as the examples below show, the verbs, like their normal counterparts, occur with TMA elements:

(14) a. *Tɔ-a   le   si-sí-ḿ*   ("normal" verb in Ewegbe)
River-DEF PRES RED-flee-PROG
'The river is flowing.'
b. *Awu-a-wó   le   fu-fú-ḿ* (Ewegbe property concept verb)
Clothing-DEF-PL PRES RED-become.dry-PROG
'The clothes are drying'.
(15) a. *A   man   e   lon*   ("normal" verb in Sranan)
DEF man   IPFV run
'The man is running.'
b. *Den krosi   e   drey*   (Property-concept verb in Sranan)
DEF cloth   IPFV become.dry
'The clothes are drying'.

In Ewegbe, the progressive construction is formed with the be-located verb *le* (analyzed variously as an auxiliary or main verb), a reduplicated form of the verb, if intransitive, and an *-ḿ* suffix. The last two processes yield *sisíní* (*si-sí-ḿ*) from the non-controversial verb *sí* 'escape' (14a) and *fu-fú-ḿ* (*fu-fú-ḿ*) from the property-expressing predicate *fú* 'become dry' (15a). It is constructions like (14b) that make the proposal of null copula untenable. In Sranan too, both the normal one-place verb and property-describing predicate can occur with the progressive marker *e* suggesting that a null-copula analysis is based on considerations of translation equivalents from languages like English.

Table 5. Property expressing verbs

English	Sranan	Ewegbe	Fongbe	Ayizogbe
become cold	banauwtu	fá	fá	fá
become bent	beni	ŋlɔ́	fɛ	fɛ,
become bitter	bita	ve	vɛ	vɛ
become black	blaka	nyrɔ	wi	wi
become wide	bradi	keke	gblo	gblo
become difficult, confusing	dangra	flu	blu	blu
become dry	drey	fú	xú	xú
become far	fara	didi	de	dɛn

The list of property-expressing verbs include the ones given in Table 5. All the Sranan verbs in the above table participate in the causative/inchoative alternation where the transitive use of the verb has roughly the meaning 'cause to V-intransitivize' (cf. Levin and Rappaport 1995). By contrast, only two of the Gbe verbs (i.e. *keke/gblo* 'become wide' and *ŋlɔ́/fɛ̀* 'become bent') do. This means that the equivalent of *cause to become bitter* cannot be expressed with a transitive construction in the Gbe languages. The examples below illustrate the differences. Example (17c) shows that a periphrastic construction is required to make verbs like *to become bitter* causative:

(16) a.   ŋútsu-á   keke   mɔ́-á   Ewegbe
           man-DEF   become.wide   road-DEF
           'The man widened the path.'
     b.   A   man   bradi   a   pasi   Sranan
           DEF   man   become.wide   DEF   path
           'The man widened the path.'

(17) a.   Mi   bita   a   dresi   Sranan
           1SG   become.bitter   DEF   medicine
           'I make the medicine bitter (lit. I bittered the medicine).'
     b.   *Me vé   atíke-a   Ewegbe
           1SG   become.bitter   medicine-DEF
           'I make the medicine bitter (lit. I bittered the medicine).'
     c.   Me-wɔ   atíke-a   wò-vé   Ewegbe
           1SG-make   medicine-DEF   3SG-become.bitter
           'I made the medicine bitter.'

Sentences (16a and 16b) show that some property-concept verbs in the Gbe languages also participate in the causative/inchoative alternation, while (17b) shows that others do not. The periphrastic construction used to causativize *vé* 'become bitter' in (17c) is known as the overlapping construction (cf. Duthie 1996) and occurs in Ewegbe alone. Many of the Gbe variants (including Ewegbe) rather use a causative construction that contains a GIVE/MAKE verb, as the examples below illustrate:

(18)   Me-ná   atíke-á   vé   Gengbe
       1SG-make   medicine-DEF   become.bitter
       'I made the medicine bitter.'

What this shows is that although Sranan is like the Gbe languages in using verbs to describe property concepts, the argument structure of the verbs do not always correspond to that of the Gbe languages.

Sranan does have verbs that do not participate in the causative/inchoative alternation. As the examples below illustrate, such verbs also require the general periphrastic construction to make them causative as well:

(19) a. *A dresi tranga a boy
         DEF medicine become.strong DEF boy
         'The medicine made the boy strong'
     b. A dresi meki a boy tranga
         DEF medicine make DEF boy strong
         'The medicine made the boy strong.'

The Sranan and Gbe verbs, which do not participate in the causative/inchoative alternation include:

Table 6. One-place property concept verbs

English	Sranan	Ewegbe	Fongbe	Ayizogbe
become good	bun	nyo	nyɔ	nyɔ
become dead, die	dede	kú	kú	kú
become cooked	gari	bi	bí	bí
become low, insufficient	lagi	sue	hwe	hwe
be strong	tranga	sẽ́, sesẽ́	syɛn, syɛnsyɛn	syɛn

Levin and Rappaport (1995) suggest verbs that do not participate in the causative/inchoative alternation describe properties that are internally caused, i.e. states of affairs that are brought about by the inherent property of the argument. As such, they are outside the control of an external agent. While this is true for the verbs in Table 6, it is also undeniable that internal causation is a semantic feature. In other words, it is not the real world that determines whether a verb would or would not participate in the causative/inchoative alternation. What this suggests is that although Sranan and the Gbe languages use items belonging to the same lexical category to express property concepts, the semantics of the individual items are not exactly the same, hence the difference in their syntactic behavior. Clearly, the Gbe languages incorporate the internal-causation feature into a lot more property-expressing verbs than Sranan does. This means that Sranan ends up with a simplified lexicon, which in turn enables the use of the same verb to express in both spontaneous and caused change of state.

Some property concepts, which are expressed with intransitive verbs in Sranan, are rather expressed with inherent complement verbs (ICVs) in the Gbe languages. An ICV has been defined as a verb whose citation form is followed by a meaning-specifying complement (Nwachukwu 1987). Consider the examples below:

(20) a. *A man breni*   Sranan
         DEF man become.blind
     b. *Súnú ɔ́ tɔ́n nukn*   Fongbe/Ayizogbe
         Man DEF pierce eye
         'The man is blind
     c. *ŋtsu-a gba ŋk*   Ewegbe
         man-DEF break eye
         'The man is blind'.

In Section 1, I showed that the verb that expresses breaking in several parts in the Gbe languages can occur with the word meaning 'eye' to indicate that a person is blind. I stated that in Fongbe and Ayizogbe, the expression refers to the process of making someone blind. Sentence (20b) shows that these languages use *tɔ́n* which means 'to pierce' with the equivalent of 'eye' to describe someone who is actually blind. In other words, a blind person is considered to be someone who has pierced the eye. Note that while the verbs are not the same in the Gbe languages, the strategy of using a verb plus obligatory complement to express the concept of blindness is the same. Sranan, by contrast, uses an intransitive verb. Some property-expressing verbs that are rendered with ICVs are provided in Table 7.

To sum up, some property concepts are realized as verbs in the Gbe languages and Sranan. This is different from English and other Indo-European languages where they are realized as adjectives. Thus at a more general level, we can say that Sranan employs a strategy that is similar to that of the Gbe languages. However, as I have also shown, there is a big difference between the argument structure of the individual verbs: first of all, many verbs in Sranan lack the internally-caused feature and, therefore, can participate in causative/inchoative alternation. Furthermore, the Gbe languages express some of their properties with ICVs in contrast with Sranan. As I show in the following sections, the ICV phenomenon is rather pervasive is the Gbe languages. As a result, it makes the languages look more transitive when compared to Sranan.

Table 7. Property concepts expressed with ICVs in the Gbe languages

English	Sranan	Ewegbe	Fongbe	Ayizogbe
be happy	*breyti*	*kpɔ́ dzidzɔ* ('see happiness')	*hun xome* ('open stomach')	*hun xomɛ* ('open stomach')
be expensive	*diri*	*xɔ asi* ('receive price')	*vɛ axi* ('pain price'), *xɔ kwɛ* ('receive money')	*vɛ kwa* ('pain money')
be deaf	*dofu*	*kú tó* ('die ear')	*kú tó* ('die ear')	*ku to* ('die ear')
be stupid	*don*	*dzɔ movi*	*gu, lu, jɔ xlo*	*jɔ xlo*
be dirty	*doti*	*fo ɖi* ('hit dirt')	*egbo adun* ('cut dirt')	*gbo adun* ('cut dirt')
be shy	*ferleigi*	*kpe ŋu* ('heavy mouth')	*ku winyá* ('die shame')	*ku winyá* ('die shame')

6.2. "True" intransitive verbs in Sranan

In contrast to the verbs discussed in the previous section, there are single-argument predicates in both Gbe and Sranan that are considered to be "proper" intransitive verbs because their equivalents in English and other Indo-European languages are also intransitive verbs. An example is provided below:

(21) a. A   fowru frey   Sranan
        DEF   bird   fly
        'The bird flew.'
    b. Xeví-á   dzo   Ewegbe
    c. Xeví-ɔ́   zrɔ   Fongbe/Ayizogbe
        bird-DEF   fly
        'The bird flew.'

Examples of verbs, which occur as intransitives in all the languages, are provided in Table 8.

Table 8. True intransitive verbs

English	Sranan	Ewegbe	Fongbe	Ayizogbe
tremble	*beifi*	*fo*	*sisɔ*	*sisɔ*
breath	*bro*	*Gbɔ*	*gbɔ*	*gbɔ*
burn	*bron*	*fiá*	*fyɔ́*	*fyɔ́*
die	*dede*	*kú*	*kú*	*kú*
arrive	*doro*	*(vá) ɖó*	*wá (tlolo)*	*wá*
jump	*dyompo*	*dzo (kpo)*	*lɔn*	*lɔn*

Just like the property-expressing predicates discussed in the previous section, some concepts expressed by the intransitive verb in Sranan are rather expressed with the ICV in the Gbe languages. This is shown below:

(22) a. *A man dren esrede* Sranan
 b. *Súnú ɔ́ kˈ dlɔ́ sɔ* Fongbe
 c. *ŋútsu -a kˈ drɔ̃e etsɔ* Ewegbe
  man DEF ICV dream yesterday
  'The man dreamt yesterday.'

Some one-place verbs in Sranan, which are expressed with ICVs in the Gbe languages, are given in Table 9.

Table 9. Sranan intransitives vs. Gbe ICVs

English	Sranan	Ewegbe	Fongbe	Ayizogbe
think	denki	bu tame	lin (nu), lìn tamɛ	lin tamɛ
lie down	didon	mlɔ́ anyí	mlɔ́ ayĭ	mlɔ́ ayî
brag	dyaf	fo adegbe	flé nu, jla eḍéé	jla eḍéé
jump	dyompo	dzo (kpó)	lɔn (agbo)	??
fall down	fadon	dze anyí ('hit ground')	jɛ ayî ('hit ground')	jɛ ayî ('hit ground')

The discussion here, like the one in the previous section, shows that although both Sranan and the Gbe languages have equivalents of non-controversial intransitive verbs, the concepts expressed with some one-place predicates are rather expressed with a verb and an obligatory complement in the Gbe languages. In Essegbey (1999), I argue that obligatory complements are proper arguments and, therefore, that verbs like those in Table 9 have a different argument structure from their equivalents in Sranan.

6.3. Transitives

There are many verbs that occur as monotransitives in Sranan and the Gbe languages. However, the realization of the arguments differ in the sense that unspecified objects can be left unexpressed in Sranan but this is not the case in the Gbe languages. Instead, these objects are realized either as "generic complements", "cognate complements" or inherent complements (cf. Essegbey 1999). These are illustrated in the examples below:

(23) Generic complement
    a.   *Kofi nyan*   Sranan
    b.   *Kofi ɖu *(nú)*   Ewegbe
          Kofi eat thing
          'Kofi ate.'
    c.   *Kofi nyan bakba*   Sranan
    d.   *Kofi ɖu bladzo*   Ewegbe
          'Kofi ate plantains.'

(24) Cognate complement
    a.   *Kofi dansi*   Sranan
    b.   *Kofi ɖú *(ɣe)*   Ewegbe
          Kofi dance dance
          'Kofi danced.'
    c.   *Kofi dansi salsa*   Sranan
    d.   *Kofi ɖú salsa*   Ewegbe
          'Kofi danced salsa.'

(25) Inherent complement
    a.   *Kofi ferfi a oso esrede*   Sranan
          Kofi paint DEF house yesterday
          'Kofi painted the house yesterday.'
    b.   *Kofi si aŋɔ ná afé-a etsɔ*   Ewegbe
          Kofi smear oil DAT house-DEF yesterday
          'Kofi painted the house.'

In (23a), *nyan* occurs alone in an intransitive construction, and indicates that Kofi has eaten. The exact thing he has eaten is irrelevant so that the verb is able to occur without a complement. In the Ewegbe example (23b), an obligatory complement *nu* 'thing' occurs as the complement of the verb. A similar situation occurs with the sentences in (24). In Sranan, *dansi* 'dance' can occur alone if the particular dance is unspecified (cf. 24a). But as shown by (24b), the Ewegbe equivalent requires the complement *ɣe* 'dance', which is the semantic cognate. Finally, the Sranan verb *ferfi* in (24a) is expressed by the verb *si* 'smear' and complement *ami* 'oil'. In this case, the object of the painting activity is realized as the object of the preposition *ná*, unlike Sranan where it is realized as the direct object.

The use of inherent complements where Sranan uses monotransitives sometimes leads to the situation where the verbs in the Gbe languages have a ditransitive-type construction instead of the monotransitive of Sranan. This is illustrated below:

(26) a. *Kofi fasi a uma*   Sranan
     b. *Kofi dó alɔ nyɔ́nu ɔ́   wú*   Fongbe
     c. *Kofi kã́ así nyɔ́nu-a   ŋú*   Ewegbe
         Kofi ICV hand woman-DEF skin
         'Kofi touched the woman.'

The verb *dó* is followed by *alɔ* 'arm' and *nyɔ́nu wú* 'the woman's skin' in Fongbe while *kã́* is followed by *así* 'hand' and *nyɔ́nua ŋú* 'the woman's skin' in Ewegbe. Some of the monotransitive verbs in Sranan and their equivalent in the other languages are provided in Table 10.

Table 10. Transitive verbs

English	Sranan	Ewegbe	Fongbe	Ayizogbe
worship	ambegi	subɔ (Mawu)	sɛn (Mawu)	
buy	bai	fle (nu)	xɔ (nu)	xɔ (nu)
fry	baka	tɔ (nu)	sɔ (nu)	sɔ (nu)
bite	beti	ɖu, ká (aɖu)	hen (aɖu)	ɖu
dig	boro	ku do	kun (do)	kun
build	bow	tu xɔ	blo xɔ	gba (xɔ)
weave	brei	lɔ̃ (avɔ)	lɔn (avɔ)	lɔn (avɔ)

In sum, although Sranan and the Gbe languages have monotransitive verbs expressing the same concepts, their argument-realization properties are different: some of the transitive verbs in Sranan, unlike their equivalents in the Gbe languages, can occur without a complement when the internal argument is unspecified. In the Gbe languages, unspecified internal arguments of transitive verbs have to be expressed either as generic complements, cognate complements or inherent complements. Finally, some verbs take double complements in order to express a concept expressed with a verb and complement in Sranan.

6.4. Ditransitives

There are two types of ditransitive verbs in the Gbe languages: the position of the complements of the first type is interchangeable, as illustrated below:

(27) a. *Kofi ná ga Ami*
         Kofi give money Ami
         'Kofi gave Ami money.'

b. *Kofi ná Amí ga*
Kofi give Ami money
'Kofi gave Ami money.'

It can be observed from the translation of the verbs that they belong to the mainstream ditransitive verbs. Not surprisingly, their equivalents in Sranan are also ditransitive. However, the Sranan verbs have only one word order, as shown below:

(28) a. *Kofi gi Ami moni*
b. **Kofi gi moni Ami*

The ditransitive verbs that have interchangeable complement positions in the Gbe languages are:

Table 11. Ditransitive verbs

English	Sranan	Ewegbe	Fongbe	Ayizogbe
give	gi	ná	ná	ná
ask	aksi	bia	kan byɔ	byɔ
show	sori	fia	xlɛ	xlɛ
teach	leri	fia	kplɔn	kplɔn

Ewegbe is somewhat different from the other languages because it does not distinguish between the concepts of showing and teaching.

The second type of ditransitive verbs is mainly composed of ICVs. Unlike the "normal" ditransitive verbs, these ones have invariable word order, with only the complement which instantiates the theme argument occurring in immediate post-verbal position. *Do* and *ka* from Fongbe and Ewegbe respectively, discussed in (26b) and (26c), are examples of ditransitive ICVs. The example below with *da* shows that the complement has only one order of occurrence:

(29) a. *Kofi da tú Amí*   Ewegbe
Kofi ICV gun Ami
'Kofi shot at Ami.'
b. **Kofi da Amí tú*

As should be expected from the discussion in the previous sections, the concepts expressed by these verbs and their complements are mostly realized as monotransitive verbs in Sranan. For example, (29) is expressed in Sranan as (30):

(30) *Kofi sutu Ami*   Sranan

The table below summarizes the difference in the argument structure of ICV ditransitives when compared to Sranan and English:

Table 12. ICV ditransitives

English	Sranan	Ewegbe	Fongbe	Ayizogbe
touch Y	fasi Y	ká asî Y	dó alɔ Y	dó alɔ Y
shoot	sutu	da tú	da tú	da tú

Note that the two complements following the verbs in the Gbe languages are proper arguments of the verbs (cf. Essegbey 1999). Thus, the argument structure of these verbs too, like several verbs in the previous tables is different from that of Sranan.

There is, however, one instance where both Sranan and Ewegbe express a concept with an invariable ditransitive construction:

(31) a.   A   man   du   mi   sani   Sranan
      b.   ŋútsu-á   wɔ   náné-m   Ewegbe
            man-DEF   do   something-1SG
            'The man did something (bad) to me.'

The sentences can only mean that the person has done something negative. In order to express that something good was done, a dative SVC construction is used. Since *do* does not take three arguments in English, it is possible that this construction is due to substrate influence. However, it is not restricted to the Gbe languages; it also exists in Akan, another Kwa language spoken in Ghana, as the example below illustrates:

(32) *Papá nó á-yɛ   me   adéé á-ma   nó á-hye   me*
      man DEF PERF-do 1SG thing PERF-make 3SG PERF-burn 1SG
      'The man did something bad to me and it pained me.'

In contrast to what I have shown so far, there are ditransitive verbs in Sranan realized as monotransitive in the Gbe languages. Consider the examples below:

(33) a. *A man ferteri mi wan sani*   Sranan
     b. *ŋútsu-á gblɔ náné ná-m*   Ewegbe
         man-DEF say something DAT-1SG
         'The man told something to me.'
(34) a. *A man heisi mi wan buku*   Sranan
     b. *ŋútsu-á tsɔ́ agbalẽ yi dzi ná-m*   Ewegbe
         man-DEF take book go top DAT-1SG
         'The man raised a book for me.'

Note that while in the case of *ferteri* 'tell', we can say that Sranan took the argument structure of the verb directly from its Dutch equivalent (*vertellen*), the same cannot be said of *heisi*. Some of the verbs that show a mismatch between Sranan and Gbe are given in Table 13.

Table 13. Sranan - only ditransitives

English	Sranan	Ewegbe	Fongbe	Ayizogbe
beg X from Y	begi Y X	ɖe kúkú ná Y + that-clause	sà vò nú Y + that-clause	sà vò nú Y + that-clause
call X for Y	kari Y X	yɔ́ X (ná Y)	ylɔ X nú Y	ylɔX nú Y
to hand Y X	langa Y X	tsɔ́ X ná Y	sɔ X nú Y	sɔ X nú Y
lend Y X	leni Y X	dó/ yé X ná Y	nya X nú Y	nya X nú Y

Although *begi* 'beg' in Sranan occurs in the ditransitive in examples like *begi John wan sani* literally 'beg John a something', in the Gbe languages, one has to say 'appeal to John that he gives you something'. The table suggests that, just like the causative/inchoative alternation construction, Sranan uses the ditransitive construction more extensively. This is doubtless due to a generalization or simplification in the lexicon.

7. Conclusion

This chapter has investigated the semantics of verbs from three semantic domains in the Gbe languages and Sranan as well as the argument structure of verbs in general. It has been shown that verbs like the BREAK and PEEL verbs, and COME and GO verbs, in Sranan are very similar to their equivalents in English. Moreover, the argument structure of Gbe verbs, for the most part, differs from the counterpart in Sranan. This shows that the claim that the creators of Sranan used the properties of the Gbe lexicon, parametric values and semantic interpretation rules of Gbe grammar is untenable. It rather suggests that attempts were made to acquire the English spoken at the time and that the semantics of some verbs were indeed acquired. The influence of Gbe can be seen in the ditransitive construction containing a DO-verb and expressions containing the EAT-verb. However, I have shown that such expressions do not occur in the Gbe languages alone. In fact, the EAT verb not only occurs in Kwa languages but is widespread across African languages. If we may adopt Sheikh and Wolff's (1981) observation that common cultural practices account for the spread of expressions with this verb across languages, then it is likely that cultural factors play an important role in determining which verbs are acquired. This ties in with results of research that shows that African words, which are retained in Sranan, are those that have cultural significance. Further research into the semantics of all Sranan verbs and that of the major substrates may shed more light on the issue.

Morphology, cross-linguistic effects, and creole formation

Margot van den Berg

1. Introduction

Given the socio-historical circumstances in which the Surinamese creole languages have emerged it is no surprise that we find traces of West African languages in these creoles. Traces are found for example in the lexicon: Sranan Tongo *ase* 'witchcraft, sorcery' is clearly derived from the word *àzé* that is encountered in several Gbe languages. The Sranan form bears a close phonological resemblance to the Gbe form. It functions as a noun that denotes events and actions that can be subsumed under the label witchcraft or sorcery (with both negative and positive undertones) in Sranan Tongo as well as in the Gbe languages. The influence of the West African languages on the Surinamese creole languages is not restricted to the lexicon. However, the influence of the West African languages on the emergence of the grammatical system is a controversial matter. While a word such as *ase* is clearly of Gbe origin, different views have been proposed for the emergence of the grammatical system. For example, Migge (2006), Winford and Migge (2007) and Migge and Winford (2009) conclude that the TMA systems of the Surinamese creole s display many features that parallel those of the Gbe languages, while McWhorter (1999) maintains that the TMA systems of the Surinamese creoles are innovations as they dimly reflect patterns of the West African substrate languages. A solid methodology is needed to demonstrate cross-linguistic effects in the Surinamese creole languages (see van den Berg, Muysken, and Smith this vol.). Essential components are socio-historical and linguistic analyses. The socio-

---

Acknowledgements: The support and assistance of the University of Ghana (Legon) and the University of Lomé is hereby gratefully acknowledged. The Dutch Science Foundation (NWO) is acknowledged for the VENI grant to Margot van den Berg (275-89-005). Pieter Muysken, Norval Smith, Clement Appah, Evershed Amuzu, Komlan Essizewa, Felix Ameka, James Essegbey, Bettina Migge, Elvis Yevudey, Kamaïloudini Tagba and Solace Yankson are thanked for their comments on earlier drafts of this paper.

historical analysis should focus on the demographic development of the Surinamese population and its subgroups, the ethnolinguistic origin of the people, and the patters of interaction at the time when the language was formed, see also Arends (1995a) and Migge (2003a) among others. The linguistic analysis should not only include a comparison of creole features and their equivalents in the languages that contributed to their emergence, but also a way to show that the similarities that may be found between the creole and the contributing languages are cross-linguistic rather than random effects due to universals operating in first and second language acquisition and use.

The findings presented in this paper are based on historical rather than contemporary data in the case of Sranan Tongo. The Suriname Creole Archive holds a substantial collection of historical texts that form a window on language use in the 18th century (van den Berg & Bruyn 2008, Arends & Perl 1995). Cross-linguistic effects are identified on the basis of a comparison of 18th century Sranan Tongo features and their equivalents in varieties of the dominant European and African languages that contributed to the emergence of Sranan Tongo, that is English, Dutch, Akan languages and Gbe languages (Smith 1987, Arends 1995a). They are subsequently compared with their equivalents in contact languages that emerge out of contact between the same languages, but in different times, places and contact settings, such as those that are presently emerging from contact between English and the Akan and Gbe languages in urban areas in Ghana. A comparison of Early Sranan with other outcomes of contact between the Gbe and Akan languages and English provides a solid type of evidence of transfer of forms, features, functions, meanings or distributional properties from one language to another: If a specific feature occurs in 18th century Surinam as well as in 21st century Ghana, where the same languages are in contact, than it is a likely cross-linguistic effect of language contact rather than universals operating in first and/or second language acquisition and use.[1]

2. The Suriname Creole Archive

Sranan Tongo is one of the few creole languages for which a large body of historical texts is available documenting the language in earlier stages of development. The texts are stored in the Suriname Creole Archive (SUCA),

---

1. Furthermore, the feature should not be found in settings where these languages are not spoken.

a NWO funded computerized corpus of Early Sranan and Saramaccan texts that is under construction at the Radboud University Nijmegen in collaboration with the Max Planck Institute and the University of Amsterdam. It currently allows some quantitative analysis and search procedures facilitating automated extraction of data. The Sranan Tongo section of consists of several types of sources, ranging from language manuals, and court records to the Sranan version of the Saramaka Peace Treaty of 1762. The documents listed as language manuals include wordlists (Herlein 1718; Nepveu 1770; van Dyk c1765; Weygandt 1798); dialogues (Herlein 1718; Nepveu 1770; van Dyk v1765; Weygandt 1798); playlets (van Dyk c1765; Weygandt 1798) and a Sranan – German dictionary (Schumann 1783). They are outlined in table 1 below. The reader is referred to Arends (2002, 1989), Arends & Perl (1995), Bruyn (1995), Voorhoeve & Donicie (1963), Voorhoeve & Lichtveld (1975), van den Berg (2007) among others for more information on the authors and contents of the language manuals.

Table 1. Overview of types of Early Sranan documents

	SOURCES: LANGUAGE MANUALS			tokens
Early Sranan	Herlein (HL)	(1718)	w; dl	200
	Van Dyk (VD)	(c1765)	w; dl, p	14,000
	Nepveu (N)	(1770)	w; dl	700
	Schumann (SCHUM)	(1783)	dc	16,000
	Weygandt (WEY)	(1798)	w; dl, p	15,000
			Total	45,900
	OTHER			
	Court Records (CR)	(1707–1767)		500
	Sranan version of Saramaka Peace Treaty (SPT)			
			Total	1,900

(w = wordlist; dl = dialogue; p = playlet; dc = dictionary)

3. Languages in contact in 17th and 18th century Surinam

A number of studies are available that reconstruct in great detail the demographic developments of the Surinamese population in the long 18th century (Singler 1992, Arends 1995a, Dragtenstein 2002, Migge 2003a, van den Berg 2007). Socio-demographic data are drawn from a wide variety of historical sources, ranging from general census data, overviews of payments of head taxes, homestead and plantation counts by observant map-makers and other visitors, to plantation inventories in wills and registers of incoming slave ships and their cargo inventories. All in all, the data give a fairly good impression of the relative sizes of foreign-born and locally born populations of African and European descent in Surinam throughout the 18th century.[2] In short, Africans outnumbered Surinam-born Creoles on the plantations throughout the 18th century. Even in late 18th century Surinam, over a century after colonization, a large proportion of the plantation slaves had recently arrived from West Africa, because of the very high replacement rate of slaves. Only 30% of the slave population was locally born at that time (Arends 1995a: 269). The foreign-born planters, merchants, sailors and indentured servants came from all over Western Europe as well as the Caribbean and South America. The enslaved Africans were deported from various West African regions, sometimes via layovers on Caribbean islands.

Slaves of African descent were also brought to Surinam by relocation of planter families or through the Caribbean trade. For example, in a letter dated February 25, 1687, Willem Kerkninck from Curaçao seeks permission from the governor of Surinam, Cornelis van Aerssen van Sommelsdijck (1683–1688), to move to Surinam with his goods and slaves, "wegens den miserabelen toestand en gebrek op Curaçao" [because of the miserable situation and deficiency in Curaçao] (van den Berg 2000). In sum, 18th century Surinam was a multicultural and multilingual society due to immigration from Africa, Europe and the Caribbean. The demographic data facilitate a detailed reconstruction of the development of the population of Surinam in the formative period of the creole language and afterwards, showing not only an increasing numerical disparity between Europeans and Africans and a greater number of languages, but also an increasingly complex social structure of the colony with different social groups and social group identities emerging.

Much scholarly attention has been paid to the calculation of ratios of Africans to Europeans (and their descendants) as they present information on interaction patterns and access to European language models by Africans. However, while close contact and frequent interaction certainly are important factors in creole formation, factors such as social distance, atti-

---

2. The original Amerindian population of Surinam is not investigated in this paper. The influence of the Amerindian languages on the Surinamese Creoles in their formative period seems to be restricted to some names of local flora and fauna.

tude and the need or desire to mark a local and/or group identity via a new language, may be even more decisive. Rickford (1985) already remarks that attitude determines whether language input becomes language intake, which is subsequently reflected in the output. Roberts (2000) shows how social distancing gave impetus and accelerated the formation of Hawai'i Creole.[3] Thus we need to collect not only socio-demographic data on the demographic developments of the population but also on the patterns of interaction within the population to understand the processes that led to the emergence and subsequent development of the Surinamese creole languages, see also Arends (2001). Migge (2003a: 11) suggests that we look for data on the nature of the community settings as well as the official codes, loci, purpose and frequency of inter- and intra-group interaction in particular. It is not easy to find such data. It requires an integrated research methodology in which linguists, anthropologists, historians and even ethnobotanists work collectively, mining the archives for written material that can be used to reconstruct these patterns, in addition to the study of oral literature and contemporary linguistic and cultural practices that may complement the reconstruction of these patterns. In the remainder of this section I will discuss some socio-historical data on language use in 18th century Surinam. The functional differentiation of the languages spoken in Surinam in the late 17th and 18th century provides insight into the status and importance of these languages, and ultimately the attitudes towards these languages. Thus we advance our understanding of how the languages may have interacted at the societal and individual levels, in addition to how they contributed to the formation and subsequent development of the creole language.

18th Century Surinam was a highly segregated society. Numerous factors, ranging from place of birth (Surinam, Europe, Africa), societal status (free, Maroon, manumitted, enslaved, indentured, etc.), religion, gender, profession/function, duration of residence (early vs. late arrivals), place of residence (Paramaribo, old vs. new plantation, bush), economic success, and even skin color, contributed to one's position in society and how one was treated by the legislative powers as well as by individuals. At least, five types of speech communities can be discerned in general, each with

---

3. The impact of attitude is particular visible in situations of language growth, such as youth languages and the spread of English as a global language for example, as well as in situations of language decay, where the diminished status and importance of a language in a society results mostly from a change in attitude of its speakers under pressure of external (economical) factors.

their own subgroups. They are the enslaved Africans and their descendants, the freemen of African descent, the Europeans and their descendants, the Maroons, and the Amerindians.

The European languages Dutch, French, Portuguese, and German were particularly associated with the more formal domains of life of the European planters, merchants, indentured servants and their families, as is exemplified by numerous official documents in the archives that were written in these languages. Colloquial varieties of these languages must have also been used in less formal domains, where they may have been competing with the emerging contact language in the early days of the colony. Jan Reeps, a ship-wrecked sailor who stayed several months in Paramaribo in 1693, when there were at least 319 European freemen and 4756 slaves present in Surinam (van den Berg 2007), observed that the language of the former colonial power was used mostly by the slaves: "De Engelse hebben hier een colonie gemaeckt en wort die taal daer nog meest bij de slaven gesproken" [The English made a colony here and that language is mostly spoken by the slaves] (van Alphen 1963). However, Surinam-born descendants of European planters and merchants were often more proficient in the local creole language than in Dutch or another European language. This was one of the reasons for Claude Mourgues to petition in 1726 to open a school for the free white European population. In the proposal, he states that he will not permit any creole being spoken by the pupils during this two hour class (van Kempen 2002). Van Dyk (c1765) and Weygandt (1798) state that they intended their language instruction manuals to be read primarily by new arrivals, in particular Dutch merchants, plantation owners and directors, carpenters and masons who had to interact with slaves, and thus, had to be proficient in speaking the creole language. Weygandt (1798) further stipulates that the manual may also be useful for people living in Paramaribo, whose profession requires a good command of the Ccreole language. It was his experience that servants, shop owners, tailors and the like often expressed themselves "dikwils zich zeer gebrekkig en zomtyds onverstaanbaar uitdrukken" [often very poorly and sometimes even incoherently]. Weygandt was a member of one of the literary societies that emerged in Paramaribo in the late 18th century, and from his writings it is clear that it was not only his intention to facilitate interethnic communication, but also to show that the creole could be used for all sorts of purposes, including literary functions.

Because of the heterogeneous origin of the European population, other European languages in addition to informal varieties of Dutch, French and Portuguese as well as Dutch, French and Portuguese dialects may have been used in private as well as in public domains. Notwithstanding the debate between Norval Smith and Jacques Arends on the continuation of English influence in Surinam after most of the English planters left in the late 17th century, we regularly find instances of English being used in the public domain in the 18th century. For example, in 1759 Hermanus Leonard Brommet was interrogated in relation to an act of violence towards an Englishman. He had first battered a slave child of this Englishman for stealing a basket and for beating up his child who was in possession of the basket. The Englishman had come to his house for clarification, and it ended in a fight. Brommet reports that the Englishman addressed him in English, which he could only partly understand.[4]

In particular, when many Africans of the same ethnic group were living on a plantation, the African languages may have displayed a similar functional distribution as the European languages, ranging from formal to informal domains of life. Given the continuous influx of enslaved Africans, the anthropologist Richard Price suggests that "it would not be surprising, then, to find on the plantations in 1800 much purer 'Africanisms' in certain realms of life than existed in Saramaka at the same point in time" (1975: 471). Alternatively, the creole language may have been used in these domains, as shared ethnic identity did not always lead to the use of a shared African language as the main language of interaction and communication. One of the earliest creole text fragments, dating back to 1707, is a dialogue between the Africans Mingo and Waly. They most likely belonged to the same ethnic group, and they may have had one or more African languages in common, but they conversed in the creole rather than in a shared African language (van den Berg 2001). On the other hand, we also find examples such as the one presented by the African Coridon, who was interrogated in relation to a plantation raid on 2 April 1750. Coridon was born in Africa, but "[s]egt sijn land niet te kennen, also hij gevangene alhier heel klijn is gekoomen" [says he doesn't know his country as he was taken as a prisoner

---

4. The text in the original report reads as follows: "Waarop hij Engelsman antwoorde in t' Engelsch, voor soo ver als den ondergeschr_e daar uijt verstond, dat hem sulx niet raakte, dat dat mantje gestoolen was, en hij 't weerom wouw hebben of anders van des ondergesz_e Huijs zoude afhaalen; hem ondergesz_e daar op zeijde dan zoud gij doen als uw landslijde wel meer gewoon zijn te doen (...) uit de moorddaadige klauwen van dien Engelsman verlost hebben; dat den ondergeteekende die vervolgens ten zijne huijse gebragt wierd bevond verloren te hebben een paar schoenen die hij als sloffen aan had" (2 Juny 1759).

and brought here when he was very young].[5] When he was asked during the interrogation about his dealings with the plantation raiders and the language that they used for communication, as that may be a runaway group identifier, he answered that he did not speak to them in an African language, "maar wel in 't neger Engelsch" [but in the black English] (CR 1750). It may be the case that, since he was captured and deported to Surinam at a very young age, he was more proficient in the creole language than in the African languages that he spoke as a child. Alternatively, he may have opted for the creole rather than an African language, as it seemed the appropriate language to use given the situation and the interlocutors.

Not everybody was well versed in speaking the creole. Judicial records of interrogations of apprehended slaves and runaways of African descent mention regularly (in Dutch) that the interrogated person does not speak the creole language (van den Berg 2000). In some of those cases, another African, who had some command of both the creole and a common African language, acted as a translator, as in e.g. the case of Afrikaan, who lived on plantation Jagtlust, "sijnde een Cormantijn neeger die de neeger Engelsche Spraak niet magtig was en dies desselfs gedeclareerde door een neeger van die lande aart getranslateert sijnde heeft verclaert dat hij een nieuwe neeger was, doe de andere hem meede genoomen hebben en hij diens vervolgens van't gepasseerde niets weet" [being a Cormantin black who is incapable of speaking Sranan Tongo, and who declares, after translation by a black from the same area, that he is a new black, that at that time somebody else took him and that (therefore) he doesn't know anything about what has happened (in his absence)] (CR 1762).[6]

On other occasions Europeans acted as translators, as in the following case from 1773. When one of the plantations of Samuel Cohen Nassy was sold to the Coenen family in 1773, the 22 slaves of the plantation were not content with the new director, who was not of Jewish background similar to the former director. The new director was not willing to let the slaves have their time off for Sabbath and showed them little respect in general, referring to them as "smouse negers" [Jew blacks]. This caused the slaves of the plantation to revolt. The subsequent police investigation revealed that procedures concerning the transition in ownership of the plantation were not carried out correctly. When a plantation was sold, the slaves of the planta-

---

5. The reader is referred to Arends (1995) for more information on African children in Surinam.
6. The Dutch text is copied from the original document including all the original spelling inconsistencies, etc.

tion had to be asked if they were willing to serve under the new plantation director. If this procedure was not followed accurately, it could lead to an uprising on the plantation, and subsequently cause a nation-wide slave revolt, hence the concern of the government officials. The new director Coenen maintained that he informed the slaves of the change in ownership of the plantation, addressing them in the creole language, as it was his impression that they were proficient in the creole language. The slaves, however, maintained that they were kept ignorant of the change in ownership. They did not speak the creole; they were "nieuwe slaaven die de neeger engelsche taal niet verstonden en Cormantijns waaren" [new slaves who did not comprehend the creole language and were Cormantin] (CR 1773).[7] Their statements were supported by Europeans from neighboring plantations, as well as by director Reule from plantation Soeten who was well known for his skills as a "Cormantijns" translator. Reule had been asked to come down to the plantation to translate the information on the transition in ownership, but was overruled by Coenen, who persisted that the translation of the information about the change in ownership into "Cormantijns" was not necessary; he knew the plantation and its people, and it was his experience that most of them communicated in the creole. This example is interesting for a number of reasons, but is presented here as it underscores that both "Cormantijns", i.e. an Akan language, as well as the creole were to some extent "institutionalized".

From the mid-18th century onwards examples of formal uses of the creole are encountered more frequently. For example, the Saramaka Peace Treaty of 1762 was recorded in Sranan Tongo (Arends and van den Berg 2004) and Christian Grego and Johannes Alabi penned their letters on life as converted Christians in a variety of Saamaka that was used with non-Saamaka (van den Berg & Bruyn 2008, Arends 1995b). Even though Dutch was the dominant language in which the members of the literary societies of Paramaribo expressed themselves, Sranan Tongo was also part of their repertoire. The first instance of poetry in Sranan Tongo is the verse 'Een

---

7. It is interesting that the Africans referred to themselves as Cormantin slaves. They may have been accommodating towards the Europeans, who use the term 'Cormantijn(s)' (Dutch) and 'Coromantee' (English) and its spelling variants to refer to Africans, that is Akan or non-Akan, who came from the Gold Coast, where fort Kormantin was one of the major embarkation ports. On the other hand, Konadu (2010: 14) argues that the Akan themselves "were also very aware of who they were on the Gold Coast littoral and on the forest fringe, and they engaged the Americas through their foundational self-understandings".

huishoudelyke twist' by Hendrik Schouten that appeared in the second edition of Letterkundige Uitspanningen in 1783 (Voorhoeve & Lichtveld 1975). The play in Weygandt's (1798) instruction manual that was mentioned earlier is a Sranan Tongo adaptation of Paul F. Roos' verse titled 'Schets van het Plantaadjeleven' ('A sketch of plantation life'). By the end of the 18th century it is clear that the creole language was not only used as an innovative solution to the problem of interethnic communication, but that it was also established as the general local language, used in informal as well as formal domains alongside other European and African languages. The examples presented above show that, in the 18th century, as in contemporary Surinam, most people were multilingual to some extent, speaking more than one language, albeit at different levels of proficiency.

So far, I have only focused on speakers of the creole language of African and European descent living in the city and on the plantations. But throughout the 17th and 18th century slaves escaped from the plantations and formed societies in the interior. These Maroon societies differed sharply from the plantations in terms of demographic development. At the end of the 18th century, over a century after colonization, a large proportion of the plantation slaves had recently arrived from West Africa, because of the very high replacement rate of slaves in Surinam. Only 30% of the slave population was locally born at that time (Arends 1995a: 269). Even though precise figures on population growth of Maroon societies are lacking for the 17th and 18th century, Price estimates that by the late 18th century, "well over 99% of the Saramaka population would have been Surinam-born" (1975: 471). This is in sharp contrast with the Surinamese plantations. So while Africans outnumbered Surinam-born Creoles on the plantations throughout the 18th century, locally born Saramaccans soon formed the majority among the Saamaka population. For example, several (late) 17th century kinfolk of Alabi, a renowned chief of the Saamaka in the late 18th century, were already Surinam-born (Price 1990).[8] Furthermore, Saamaka society had been officially closed to newcomers since 1762, as this was one of the conditions stipulated in the peace treaty between the Saamaka and the Dutch colonial government (Arends & van den Berg 2004). Even though the Saamaka may have occasionally allowed new people into their midst, the newcomers would never have outnumbered the old-timers and locally born Saamaka. Given these socio-historical circumstances, it is

---

8. The Surinam-born forefathers of Alabi include Yáya (1684–1782), Dabí (1689–1765), Adjágbò (1705–1799), Abíni (1700–1767) and Akoomí (1700–1780) among others, see Price (1990: 10).

indeed more likely to find 'purer' Africanisms on the plantations rather than in Saramaka, as stated by Price (1975).

4. Cross-linguistic effects below word level

An emerging language requires a lexicon. Many words in Sranan Tongo can be traced back to English, Dutch, Portuguese, and less frequently, African and Amerindian languages, as shown by Smith (1987) and Koefoed and Tarenskeen (1996) on the basis of lexicostatistic analysis of a 200-word Swadesh list of basic vocabulary and a 3050 Sranan Tongo – Dutch – English word list (Woordenlijst Sranan – Nederlands – Engels 1980) respectively. Their findings on the sources of the lexical items on their lists are given in percentages in Table 2.

Table 2. Lexical sources of Sranan Tongo words

	Swadesh list of basic vocabulary (Smith 1987, 2001)	Sranan Tongo – Dutch - English word list (Koefoed & Tarenskeen 1996)
English	77.14%	18.00%
Dutch	17.58%	21.50%
English or Dutch	-	4.30%
Portuguese	3.70%	3.20%
African	1.59%	4.30%
innovations	-	36.00%
other	-	12.70%

Note that the 200-word Swadesh list and the 3050-word Woordenlijst Sranan – Engels (1980) are not comparable. While the Swadesh list focuses on basic vocabulary, the Woordenlijst Sranan – Engels (1980) is a list of frequently used words with a bias toward animal and plant names. It is therefore no surprise that we find a somewhat higher percentage of African sources in the Woordenlijst Sranan – Engels than in the Swadesh list, as animal and plant names belong to culturally significant domains like religion, food, crafts, health care etc., where African words are expected to be more numerous. The Sranan Tongo word *ase* 'witch, witchcraft' (< Gbe *àzɛ́*), which was mentioned in the introductory section of this chapter, falls into this category. Furthermore, Smith (1987, 2001b) focuses on the direct source of the phonological forms of the Sranan Tongo words, while Koefoed & Tarenskeen (1996) investigate the forms and the meanings and further, in the case of complex words, the internal structure. They find many self-made linguistic expressions in which (parts of) English, Dutch, and African forms are used in ways that differ from their source languages, with changed meanings and novel structures. Koefoed & Tarenskeen (1996) classify these expressions as innovations, even though (parts of) the forms can be traced back to other languages and other cross-linguistic effects can be observed. This is shown for some Early Sranan words for body parts in Table 3.

Table 3. Cross-linguistic effects in Early Sranan body part words

EARLY SRANAN	GBE		ENGLISH	DUTCH
Complex forms	Complex forms		Complex forms	
bóbbi-watra breast-fluid	*ànɔ́-sìn* breast-fluid	(Gun)	*mother's milk*	*moeder-melk*
hai-buba eye-skin	*nùkun-fló* eye-skin	(Fon)	*eyelid*	*ooglid*
Complex forms	Complex forms		Simplex forms	
bakka-futu back-foot	*àfɔ́- gódó* foot-back	(Gun)	*heel*	*hak*
kallabassi va heddi calabash of head	*tà-ká* head calabash	(Gun)	*skull*	*schedel*
Simplex forms	Simplex forms		Simplex forms	
billi 'belly; pregnancy' *belle* 'belly; pregnancy' *foeten* 'leg' *futu* 'leg; foot'	*xo* 'belly; pregnancy' *xoto* 'belly; pregnancy *affo* 'leg; foot' *àfɔ́* 'leg; foot'	(Old Gbe) (Gun) (Old Gbe) (Gun)	*belly* (*pregnancy*) *foot* (*leg*)	*buik* (*pregnancy*) *voet* (*leg*)

While a body part is denoted by a simplex lexeme in English (*heel*) or Dutch (*hak*), Early Sranan may have a complex word (such as *bakka-futu* [lit. back-foot] 'heel') resembling its Gbe equivalent. Furthermore, a body part word may be complex in English and Dutch, as well as Early Sranan, but the compound is not a retention of English. Although the word forms may be inherited from English, they appear to be combined in a Gbe way: The Sranan word for 'eyelid' is *hai-buba* (lit. eye-skin) as in the Gbe languages. Moreover, the range of meanings of the Sranan simplex forms corresponds frequently to the range of meanings of the Gbe lexemes, while there is less overlap with the English forms. While Sranan *futu* is obviously derived from English *foot*, it refers to both the foot and the leg – this is not the case in any 17th or 18th century varieties of English (Oxford English

Dictionary 1989; Wright 1898–1905). In the Grammaire Abrégée (1730), however, two different entries – foot and leg – are translated by the same word: *affo*. In the contemporary Gbe languages, this has not changed (Aboh and van den Berg 2002; Lefebvre and Brousseau 2002).

In the next section, the derivational processes of compounding and affixation are discussed in more detail. An overview of derivational morphemes that expand the lexicon in a productive manner is presented. Derivational morphemes are particularly interesting, as the word complexes in which they participate are generally regarded as tightly integrated closed structures. The degree of structural integration of a linguistic feature is an important linguistic factor in borrowing: derivational morphemes such as clitics and affixes are often regarded as difficult to identify in a source language and difficult to integrate into a recipient language; therefore they are not likely to be borrowed (Thomason 2001: 69). Furthermore, derivation is learned in a later acquisitional stage than compounding, which occurs relatively early in language acquisition. Various language acquisition studies have shown that L2 speakers tend to use compounding rather than derivation in the early stages of L2 acquisition. Compounding, in particular N-N compounding, can be used as a compensatory strategy, resulting in innovative compounds that are not encountered in the target language (see Broeder, Extra, van Hout 1996 among others). So in L2 varieties of English, we may find compounds such as shop-man, rather than derivations such as manager, among others.[9]

Derivational morphemes may not be borrowed, but they can be transferred. The following case reported in Broeder, Extra & van Hout (1996) presents an interesting example of transfer of features of a derivational L1 morpheme into an L2 item. Fatima, a Moroccan woman in the Netherlands learning Dutch, used the Dutch word *oma* 'grandmother', but from the discourse context it was clear that she was referring to her aunt, not her grandmother. The word *oma* in Fatima's speech actually consisted of the standard Dutch kinship term *oom* 'uncle' and the Arabic female suffix *-a*, resulting in the bilingual combination *oom-*a**, (i.e. 'uncle' + *-a*) 'aunt'. Fatima also used this strategy for reference to a female doctor in Dutch, producing *doktor-*a**, where dokter 'doctor' would have been sufficient in L1 Dutch (Broeder, Extra, van Hout 1996, see also Perdue 1993). These

---

9. Note that *shopman* was used in 19th century English, but in contemporary English it is rare (Oxford English Dictionary). It is unlikely that the L2 English speakers in the corpus of Broeder, Extra, van Hout (1996) had any knowledge of 19th century English.

examples show that L2 learners can (and will) combine derivational word formation strategies of different languages below word level, and further, that compounding of nominals is not the only productive lexical expansion strategy in earlier stages of L2 acquisition. Prerequisites for transfer are a) morphological awareness, that is, the ability to reflect upon and manipulate morphemes, and to use word formation rules to construct and understand morphologically complex words (Kuo and Anderson 2006), and b) perceived similarity in morphological structures of the languages involved (Pasquarella et al. 2011, Wang, Cheng, and Chen 2006). But note that even though Dutch has no female affix -a, Fatima only needed one Dutch word with female reference ending in a (oma 'grandmother') to set up an interlingual identification with the Arabic female affix -a and subsequently create productively derived nouns with female reference.

Urban vernaculars, and in particular highly hybrid juvenile sociolects such as Nouchi in Abidjan (Ivory Coast), Sheng in Nairobi (Kenya) and Camfranglais in Yaoundé and Douala (Cameroon) among others, display similar lexical manipulation on all linguistic levels, including morphology (Kießling and Mous 2004). Derivational crossing or morphological hybridization and dummy affixation are most common. In Camfranglais one finds for example hybridization by affixation of the Pidgin English agentive suffix –man to non-Pidgin English words: dɔ́nmàn 'easy going guy who is generous' (< French donner 'to give') and èlékémàn 'useless fool who is too strict with obeying rules unnecessarily' (Kießling 2005: 65).

4.1. Derivational morphemes in Early Sranan and Gbe and Akan languages

Lexical expansion strategies in Sranan Tongo have been studied by Bruyn (1989, 2002), van den Berg (2000, 2003, 2007), Braun (2001, 2009), and Plag and Braun (2003) among others. Migge (2003b) and Veenstra (2006) describe these strategies for Eastern Maroon Creole (Ndyuka, Pamaka) and Saamaka respectively. A major difference between Saamaka on the one hand, and Sranan and Eastern Maroon Creole (EMC) on the other, concerns the productivity of synthetic compounding. While synthetic compounds such as téi-mánu-ma (take-man-AFF) 'man eater' are plentiful in Saamaka, they are rare in Eastern Maroon Creole and Sranan.[10] Eastern Maroon Cre-

---

10. Unpublished field research by the author on word formation strategies in Paramaribo and several plantations in the Para district (Surinam) in 2003 suggests that synthetic compounding is not a productive lexical expansion strategy in

ole and Early Sranan further share a number of morphemes that are used to derive nouns, numerals and adverbs, see Table 4.

The categorical status of these morphemes has been debated. Some suggest they are lexemes, others claim some or all are derivational morphemes. While word complexes result from the combination of two lexemes in the former approach (compounding), they result from a morphological operation on a lexeme in the latter (derivation). Admittedly, most of these derivational morphemes share some semantic content with their free lexical sources, except for the numeral deriving morpheme -*tentin*.[11] However, derivations and compounds differ from each other with regard to productivity and regularity: the meaning of the derivational morpheme predicts the meaning of the productively derived word, while the meaning of the compound cannot always be deduced from its compositional meaning. Several relations are possible between two compounded morphemes. Moreover, it may be difficult to predict which lexemes may be compounded, but it is possible to predict the type of base a derivational morpheme will take (Lefebvre 1998, 2003; Lefebvre & Brousseau 2002; DeGraff 2001; see also Booij 2005). An overview of the most productive Early Sranan derivational morphemes, their bases and meanings is presented in Table 5.

The differences between the free forms and the bound morphemes -*man*, -*wan* and -*tron* indicate a loss of lexical autonomy of these forms suggesting that they may be regarded as true affixes, while this is less so in the case of the semi-affixes or affixoids -*somma*, -*sanni* and -*fasi*.[12] The latter

---

contemporary Sranan Tongo, though some synthetic compounds may be found in more acrolectal Sranan Tongo varieties of educated speakers in Paramaribo and the Netherlands, who also speak (Surinamese) Dutch. Synthetic compounds occur frequently in Dutch.

11. The suffix -*tentin* derives numerals ranging from twenty to ninety when it is attached to a numeral base denoting a numeral between two and nine. It has no homophonous free form in Early Sranan, contemporary Sranan or Eastern Maroon Creole; it is derived from the English construction in which *times* is preceded by a cardinal numeral and followed by *ten* or another numeral or expression of quantity to express the multiplication of the number, as in *thre tymes ten is thretty* (Oxford English Dictionary 1989; *four times fifty living men* (Oxford English Dictionary 1989) or *an animal of ten times my strength* (Oxford English Dictionary 1989), respectively.

12. The term semi-affix is applied to those morphemes that have an intermediate status between an affix and a free compounded morpheme. Semi-affixes are homophonous with simplex words, and their phonological, syntactic and semantic features display some overlap. In their complex morphological struc-

are less selective with regard to the category of their base, and they differ minimally with their simplex source etyma *somma* 'person, people, someone, who?', *sanni* 'thing, something, what?', and *fasi* 'manner, mode, nature, stature', in terms of phonology (van den Berg 2007).

Does the system of derivation in Early Sranan display cross-linguistic effects that can be traced back to the African languages that contributed to the formation and subsequent development of the creole language? Complex nouns, numerals, and adverbs are formed via a complex interplay of phonological and morphological processes in the Gbe and Akan languages. These include tonal changes, high tone suffixation, reduplication, permutation/object fronting, prefixation, suffixation, dropping of TMA and Polarity markers, as well as compounding, among others. Here, I focus primarily on postposed derivational morphemes, as they are the primary means of derivation in Early Sranan, but note that the overview of derivational morphology in the Gbe and Akan languages is relatively skewed as little attention is paid to derivation via prefixes and the other processes just mentioned.

Similar to Early Sranan, the Gbe and Akan languages have a limited set of morphemes that derive participant nouns (agent/patient/experiencer nouns), non-participant nouns (possessor nouns, nationality nouns, and identificational nouns),[13] diminutives, locative nouns, temporal nouns, manner expressions, and numerals. The overview in Tables 6 and 7 present a selection of postposed derivational morphemes in the Gbe and Akan languages, based on a number of scholarly works including Ameka (1991), Amuzu (2005), DaCruz (1998), Ofori (2006), Appah (2004, 2005), Agyekum (2008), Appah and Amfo (2011), among others, as well as my own observations during field work in Ghana in 2009, 2010, 2011 and 2012. It shows that even though the sets of derivational morphemes in the Gbe and Akan languages may be smaller than those of some of the world's languages, in particular the Gbe derivational system is more elaborate than it is sometimes made out to be in the creolist literature.

---

ture, however, they have a specialized function, which is usually more general and abstract than its simplex source. Semi-affixes are more productive and regular than compounds.

13. In line with Appah (2006) I speak of participant nouns and non-participant nouns. Participant nouns include agentive, patient, and experiencer nouns that are derived from verbs, as well as nouns that are derived from nouns that refer to participants in the event expressed by the nominal base. Non-participant nouns refer to location nouns as well as possessor nouns and nouns that typify referents by their qualities.

Table 4. Overview of productive Early Sranan and EMC derivational morphemes

EARLY SRANAN		1707–1767 CR	1718 HL	1762 SPT	c1765 VD	1770 N	1783 SCHUM	1798 WEY	EMC (NDYUKA)
Noun	-man	+	-	+	+	+	+	+	-man
Verb	-man	+	-	+	+	+	+	+	-man
Adjective	-man	+	-	+	+	+	+	+	-man
Adjective	-wan	-	-	+	+	-	+	+	-wan
Numeral	-tentin	-	-	-	+	-	+	+	-tenti
Numeral	-tron	-	-	-	+	+	+	+	-toon
Noun	-somma	-	-	+	-	-	+	+	-sama
Verb	-somma	-	+	+	+	-	+	+	-sama
Adjective; Quantifier	-somma	-	-	+	+	+	+	+	-sama
Noun	-sanni	-	-	-	-	-	+	+	-sani
Verb	-sanni	-	-	-	+	-	+	-	-sani
Adjective; Quantifier	-sanni	+	-	-	+	+	+	+	-sani
Noun	-fasi	-	-	-	-	-	+	+	-fasi
Verb	-fasi	-	-	-	-	-	+	+	-fasi
Adjective; Quantifier	-fasi	-	-	+	+	-	+	+	-fasi

Table 5. Derivation in Early Sranan

Derivational morpheme	Category of BASE	Word Category	Function
X-man	verb	noun	agent/experiencer of X (X is an activity)
X-man	noun	noun	agent/possessor of X
X-man	adjective	noun	animate referent has the quality of X
X-wan	adjective	noun	the referent can be identified by the quality of X
X-tentin	numeral	numeral	derives cardinal numerals 20–90 from numerals 2-9
X-tron	numeral	adverb	derives multiplicative numerals from cardinal numerals
X-somma	noun	noun	human referent is from a place denoted by X, or belongs to a group denoted by X
X-somma	adjective, quantifier	noun	specifying a human referent by the quality of X
X-sanni	noun	noun	non-human referent having the quality of X
X-sanni	adjective	noun	specifying a non-human referent by the quality of X
X-fasi	noun	adverb	in the manner of X
X-fasi	verb	adverb	in the manner of X
X-fasi	adjective	adverb	in an X manner
X-tem	noun	noun	time/season of X

Table 6. Functions of selected derivational morphemes in the Gbe languages[14]

Deriv. morph.	BASE Category	Word Category	Function	Source	Language
X-tɔ́	N, nominalized V, A	Noun	participant noun (agent of X, X is an activity)	tɔ́ 'father'	Ewe, Fon, Maxi, Gun, Aja, Gen, Waci, Xwela, Old Gbe
X-tɔ́	N, nominalized V, A	Noun	non-participant noun (possessor of possession/qualifying property X)	tɔ́ 'father'	Ewe, Gen, Waci, Xwela
X-tɔ́	N, nominalized V, A	Noun	non-participant noun (inhabitant/member of location/group X)	tɔ́ 'father'	Ewe, Aja, Gen, Waci, Xwela
X-tɔ́	Numeral	Numeral	ordinal of number X	tɔ́ 'father'	Gungbe
X-tɔ́	N, nominalized V, A	Noun	non-participant noun (referent can be identified by quality X)	tɔ́ 'father'	Ewe
X-nɔ̀	N, nominalized V, A	Noun	non-participant noun (possessor of possession/qualifying property X)	nɔ̀ 'mother'	Ewe, Fon, Maxi, Gun, Aja, Xwla, Gen
X-ɖě	N	Noun	Non-participant noun (referent is from place/group X).	ɖě 'person, someone'	Ewe (interior dialects)
X-si	N	Noun	Gender-specific non-participant noun (female referent is from place/group X)	si 'wife'	Ewe
X-lá	N, nominalized V	Noun	participant noun (agent of X, X is an activity)		Ewe
X-ví	N, nominalized V, A	Noun	diminutive of X	ví 'child'	Ewe, Gen, Gun, Fon, Xwla

14. Consulted works include Agyekum (2008), Ameka (1991), Appah (2004 2005, 2006), Appah and Amfo (2011), DaCruz (1998), Lefebvre (2002), Migge (2003), Ofori (2002), Osam (1993). Different forms are listed for different languages. Old Gbe refers to the language variety that is found in the historical sources *La Doctrina Christiana* (1658) and *La Grammaire Abregée* (1730), see Aboh (2000).

X-a	N, nominalized V, A	Noun	non-participant noun (referent can be identified by quality X)	Ewe
X-gbé	N	Noun	activity involving X	Ewe
X-nù	N, nominalized V, A	Noun	non-participant noun (inhabitant/member of location/group X)	Fon, Maxi, Gun
X-ɸé/ -fé/ -(k)pé	N, nominalized V, A	Noun	location where X takes place	aɸé 'house' Gen, Ewe, Waci, Fon
X-xu	N, nominalized V, A	Noun	location where X takes place	Aja
X-ten	N, nominalized V, A	Noun	location where X takes place	Maxi
X-mè	N, nominalized V, A	Noun	location that contains X	Ewe, Fon
X-tɔe	N, nominalized V, A	Adverb	in the manner of X, with X	Ewe
X-yi	nominalized V (+Obj)	Noun	time for X	Ewe
X-tɔli	N	Noun	season of X	Ewe
X-gbè	N, nominalized V, A	Noun	date of X	Ewe
X-gɔ́	Numeral	Numeral	ordinal of number X	Fon, Xwla
X-gɔ́n	Numeral	Numeral	ordinal of number X	Gen

Table 7. Functions of selected derivational morphemes in the Akan languages

Deriv. morph.	BASE Category	Word Category	Function	Source	Language
X-fo	N, nominalized V, A	Noun	participant noun (singular); agent/patient/experiencer of X		Fante, Akuapem
X-fo	N, nominalized V, A	Noun	participant noun (plural); agent/patient/experiencer of X	fo 'persons'	Fante, Akuapem
X-fo	N, nominalized V, A	Noun	non-participant noun (singular); nationality X, quality X		Fante, Akuapem
X-fo	N, nominalized V, A	Noun	non-participant noun (plural); nationality X, quality X	fo 'persons'	Fante, Akuapem
X-fɔ	N, nominalized V, A	Noun	participant noun (plural); agent/patient/experiencer of X	fo 'persons'	Asante
X-fɔ	N, nominalized V, A	Noun	non-participant noun (plural); nationality X, quality X	fo 'persons'	Asante
X-nyi	N, nominalized V, A	Noun	participant noun (singular); agent/patient/experiencer of X	o-nyi 'person'	Fante
X-nyi	N, nominalized V, A	Noun	non-participant noun (singular); nationality X, quality X	o-nyi 'person'	Fante
X-ni	N, nominalized V, A	Noun	participant noun (singular); agent/patient/experiencer of X	o-ni 'person'	Asante, Akuapem
X-ni	N, nominalized V, A	Noun	non-participant noun (singular); nationality X, quality X	o-ni 'person'	Asante, Akuapem
X-ba	N, nominalized V, A	Noun	diminutive of X	ɔ-ba 'child'	Fante, Akuapem Twi, Akuapem
X-wa	N, nominalized V, A	Noun	diminutive of X		[Akan]
X-e	Nominalized V	Noun	non-participant noun; result of X, quality of X identifies referent		[Akan]
X-e	nominalized V	Noun	location where X takes place		

Different views have been proposed with regard to the categorical status of some of the Gbe and Akan morphemes listed in the tables above. In particular the categorical status of the morphemes that may appear as free forms (Gbe tɔ́ 'father', nɔ́ 'mother', ví 'child'; Akan o-ni/o-nyi 'person', fo/foɔ 'person', ɔ-ba 'child') is under debate. Some view the derivational morphemes as compounded nouns, while others see them as suffixes. See Ameka (1991) and Appah (2004, 2005) for discussion.

4.1.1. Diminutives

Both the Gbe and the Akan languages derive diminutives via a derivational morpheme that can be traced back to the word for child, as is the case for a number of languages (Körtvélyessy and Stekauer 2011). Similarly, the diminutive is also derived from the word for child in Early Sranan, but the position of the Early Sranan form differs from that of the Gbe and Akan languages. In the Gbe and Akan languages, the derivational morpheme that forms a diminutive is postposed: *alḛ́-ví* sheep-DIM 'lamb' (Ewe, Ameka 1991: 209), *a-nomaa-ba* SG-bird-DIM, 'baby/small bird' (Fante, Appah and Amfo 2011: 88). However, the Early Sranan diminutive is usually formed via a nominal phrase in which the property item *pikin* 'small, child' modifies the head noun in pre-nominal position, as in (1a) and (1c). Contrary to the Gbe/Akan model, *pikin* precedes the noun it modifies; pikin in word-final position (inside a compound) refers to a child or the young of an animal as in (1b) and (1d).[15]

(1)   a. *pikin uman (Sch 1783: 135)*   b. *umanpikin (Sch 1783: 135)*
         small woman   woman child
         'girl, young woman'   'daughter'
   c. *pikin kau (Sch 1783: 135)*   d. *kaupikin (Sch 1783: 135)*
         small cow   cow child
         'young cow, small cow'   'calf'

---

15. Van Dyk (c1765:10, 37) was not aware of this distinction; he repeatedly translates *pikien homan*, lit. little woman as *dogter* (Dutch) 'daughter'; *homan pi(e)kien* or similar constructions with *pi(e)kien* in phrase final position are not encountered in the manual, the dialogues or the playlet.

If the Early Sranan diminutive expression was formed on the basis of a Gbe model or an Akan model or a Gbe/Akan model via transfer, it should follow the noun rather than precede it. As this is not the case, I conclude that no Gbe or Akan influence via transfer was involved in the emergence of the Early Sranan diminutive.

4.1.2. Location nouns

Location nouns are formed by means of a derivational morpheme that combines with a verbal base in the Gbe and Akan languages as well as Sranan Tongo. The morpheme *-e* derives locative nouns from nominalized verbs in the Akan languages. The Gbe languages have different forms that derive location nouns; some are listed in Table 4. In particular, the morpheme *-ɸé* (< Gbe *aɸé* 'house'), which is alternatively found as *-fé* and *-pé* in the literature,[16] is interesting as it bears some phonological resemblance to the morpheme *-pe* in Eastern Maroon Creole (Huttar & Huttar 1994, Migge 2003a). It is generally considered to be a more grammaticalized variant of *-peesi* (< English *place*). Both *-pe* and *-peesi* can be used to derive location nouns from verbal bases in Eastern Maroon Creole. On the basis of the close semantic and structural similarities between derived location nouns in Eastern Maroon Creole and the Gbe languages, Migge (2003a: 84) concludes that via interlingual association between the English and Gbe words for place/location, "the semantic and syntactic properties of the Gbe suffixes were projected onto (...) place in the original English compounds. Once reinterpreted, the newly emerged suffixes could be attached to other nouns and verbs to create new nominal concepts that would not have been part of the English input".

However, not all slaves in Surinam were Gbe speakers (Arends 1995a), and non-Gbe speakers may have done the same as the Gbe-speakers with a similar outcome. Compare for example Akan *ada-e* literally rest/sleep-place 'sleeping place' with Gengbe *edɔn-pe* literally rest/sleep-place 'sleeping place'. They are semantically and structurally similar; a nominalized verb, meaning to rest or to sleep, is combined with a derivational morpheme to form a location noun. Only a detailed comparison of a substantial number of Akan, Gbe and Eastern Maroon Creole location nouns can reveal

---

16. Note that *ɸé* and *-fé* are the same voiceless bilabial fricative represented by two different orthographic symbols; *-xwé* (a.k.a. *-χʷé*) is the Eastern Gbe cognate. According to Capo (1991), the Proto-Gbe form was /* χʷé/.

whether location nouns in Eastern Maroon Creole are modeled on Gbe, as claimed by Migge (2003a), or Akan, or that they are innovations. Even though socio-demographic evidence suggests that the majority of the slaves shipped to Surinam in the formative period of the Surinamese creole languagess were Gbe speakers (Arends 1995a), it is not unlikely that the Akan languages may have been the dominant ancestral languages of the Ndyuka. An alternate name for the Ndyuka, Okanisi, may have originated from Akan ɔkan-ni literally Akan-person 'Akan' (Konadu 2010).[17] If the majority of the Ndyuka had been Gbe, they would not have presented themselves as Akan.

Eastern Maroon Creole -pe not only derives location nouns from verbal bases, it is also involved in the formation of function words. In combination with the question particle o it forms a locative question word (o)pe 'where?'. With the singular definite article a 'the', it forms the deictic place adverb ape 'there', and with quantifiers such as ala 'all' it forms place adverbs, e.g. alape 'everywhere'.

Both the forms -pe(h) and -ple(si) are encountered in Early Sranan. Schumann (1783: 133) labels peh a "dictio enclitica", a clitic. Schumann further states that peh cannot occur as an independent lexeme.[18] Indeed, variants of peh are never encountered as free lexical items in the sources; they always co-occur with determiners, demonstratives, quantifiers or variants of the question particle hu, forming place adverbs and the question word meaning 'where?', respectively, as exemplified in (2). Note that the resulting construction may be split up by an infixed intensifier, as in (2c) and (2d), but this cannot be regarded as counterevidence to Schumann's claim concerning the status of -pe(h), as this type of expletive infixation can occur at the level of the syllable as well as the level of the word.

---

17. Thoden v. Velzen & Hoogbergen (2011:4) provide an alternate explanation of the term Okanisi. In their version, the name stems from the Auka plantation ca 90km south of Paramaribo on the Suriname river, people called several groups of Maroons (federations, in Thoden van Velzen and Hoogbergen's terms) from the area "vrije negers van Agter Auka" [free negroes from behind Auka]. These groups became known collectively as *Aukanners* (self denomination Okanisi), and later *Ndyuka,* which had previously been the name of one such federation.
18. "PEH macht für sich allein kein eigen Wort aus, sondern muss allemal an ein anderes hinten angehängt werden; als dann aber hat es die Bedeutung, einen "Art", "Plaz", "Stelle" anzuzeigen" [*peh* on its own is not a word, it can only occur in combination with another word and then it indicates manner, place or location] (Schumann 1783: 133).

Table 8. The bound morphemes -pe and -plesi in Early Sranan and Eastern Maroon Creole

	EARLY SRANAN							EMC
	1718 HL	1707–67 CR	1762 SPT	C1765 VD	1770 N	1783 SCHUM	1798 WEY	(NDYUKA)
function word -pe]$_{ADV/Q}$	ple	-	-	ply	-	peh	plee, pree + pré, prée	-pe]$_{ADV/Q}$
function word -plesi]$_{ADV/Q}$	plasje plesje plesse	-	plessie	plessi	pleisi	-	pleesie + plesie	-plesi]$_{ADV/Q}$
Verb-pe]$_N$	-	-	-	-	-	-	-	+ -pe]$_N$
Verb-plesi]$_N$	-	-	-	plessi	-	plesi	-	+ -plesi]$_N$

(2) a. *mi no sabi **hoe ple** alle santi kom oppo*
 1S NEG know Q place all thing come.out
 'I don't know where all (these) things came from.' (CR 1745)
 b. ***hoe ply** joe de hele de*
 Q place 2S COP all day
 ['waar heb je de heelen Dag geweest']
 'Where have you been all day?' (VD c1765: 71)
 c. ***no wan peh** mi de go,* ODER: ***no wan** reti **peh** mi de go*
 no one place 1S ASP go / NEG one right place 1S ASP go
 ['iche gehe nirgends hin, nach keinen eigentlichen, gewissen Ort']
 'I'm going nowhere in particular.' (Sch 1783: 134)
 d. *da srefi **peh** mi ben go tu*
 the same place 1S PAST go too
 ['eben dahin bin ich auch gegangen']
 'I have also been to that same place.' (Sch 1783: 134)

These findings suggest that *pe(h)* is a bound morpheme. However, it does not derive location nouns from verbs as its Eastern Maroon Creole equivalent. Complex words with a verbal base and (variants of) the form *peh* are not encountered in Schumann's dictionary, or in the other sources of Early Sranan.

Instead, location nouns can be formed by combining a verbal base with a variant of *plesi* 'place' (< English *place*): *zére plessi* literally sell-place 'market' (VD c1765: 9), *beriplesi* literally bury-place 'cemetery' (Sch 1783: 16), *lo-plesi* literally be.flat-place 'flat land' (Sch 1783: 102) etc. Thus, Early Sranan differs from Eastern Maroon Creole in the following: In Eastern Maroon Creole *-pe* as well as *-peesi* can be combined with a verbal base to form a location noun (Huttar & Huttar 1994, Migge 2003a), whereas only *-plesi* is combined with a verbal base in the sources of Early Sranan. Contemporary Sranan resembles Eastern Maroon Creole: *-pe* as well as *-plesi* can derive location nouns from verbal bases. Therefore I conclude that (a) at the time Eastern Maroon Creole and Early Sranan diverged, i.e. at the beginning of the 18th century, *-plesi* was the main form used to form function words as well as location nouns and that (b) the form *-pe(h)* emerged later as the result of grammaticalization in Early Sranan and in Eastern Maroon Creole independently, first in function words and later in location nouns. The findings are summarized in Table 8. It shows the distribution of types of constructions in the historical sources as well as spelling variants.

4.1.3. Participant and non-participant nouns

Participant nouns express agentive, patient, and experiencer meanings; they derive from nominalized verbs or nouns, that denote the activity or event in which the referent is participating. Non-participant nouns refer to locations or possessors, or they typify referents by their qualities. Participant and non-participant nouns can be formed via a number of ways in the Gbe and Akan languages, ranging from circumlocution to compounding and derivation, but the most productive strategy to derive participant nouns is by means of a derivational morpheme that is combined with a nominalized base, as illustrated for the Gbe languages in (3) from one of the oldest historical sources on the Gbe languages, the Grammaire Abregée (1730).

(3) Houcouton 'canotier' ('Old Gbe, Grammaire Abrègée 1730, see Aboh & van den Berg 2002)
hun-kún-tɔ́
boat-drive-AFF
'rower'

The derivational morpheme can be traced back to *tɔ́* 'father' in the Gbe languages, and to *o-ni/o-nyi* 'person' (singular) and *-fo/-fɔɔ* 'persons' (plural) in the Akan languages. While Gbe *tɔ́* 'father' and Akan *o-ni/o-nyi* 'person' can appear as free forms, *-fo/-fɔɔ* 'persons' has no equivalent free form in the contemporary Akan languages (Appah 2006). In Early Sranan, singular as well as plural participant and non-participant nouns are formed via the derivational morpheme *-man*. Note that man can further function as a free form meaning 'man' (< English/Dutch *man*). While the free form is gender-specific, referring exclusively to human males, the gender-neutral bound form can refer to human males and females as well as other animate beings (van den Berg 2003). In earlier work, I suggested on the basis of multiple similarities between word complexes ending in *-man* in Early Sranan and their equivalents in the Gbe languages that the Early Sranan strategy to derive participant and non-participant nouns may have been modeled on Gbe (van den Berg 2003, see also Migge 2003a), but I will show in the remainder of the chapter that an exclusive Gbe model may not tenable. I will present some preliminary findings on the basis of a comparison of 90 Early Sranan participant and non-participant nouns ending in -*man* with their historical and contemporary Akan and Gbe equivalents.[19] I looked for similarities in form and meaning, as well as in the internal structure of the base (if complex, i.e. consisting of more than one morpheme) and also categorical status of the base. The comparison brings out several similarities between the Akan and Gbe languages that make it difficult to maintain that the derivational morpheme -*man* was modeled on Gbe exclusively. In addition to words such as Early Sranan *aseh-man* 'witch, sorcerer' where the base can be traced back to a Gbe word, in this case *àzɛ́* 'witchcraft, sorcery', we also find Early Sranan words with a similar structure that have an Akan base. Compare for example Early Sranan *gongossa-man* 'liar, hypocrite, gossiper' with Akan (Twi) *ŋkoŋkonsá-ni* 'liar, hypocrite, gossiper'.

Table 9. Structural similarities of the base in Early Sranan and the Akan and Gbe languages

Early Sranan	Akan (Twi)	Gbe (Ewe)	Gloss
aseh-man	*ɔbayi-fo(ɔ)*	*àzɛ́-tɔ́*	'witch'
witchcraft-AFF	witchcraft-AFF	witchcraft-AFF	
begi-man	*ɔdesrɛ-fo(ɔ)*	*nubia-lá*	'beggar'
beg-AFF	beg-AFF	beg-AFF	
fredde-man	*ohu-fo(ɔ)*	*kle-nɔ*	'scared person'
fear-AFF	fear-AFF	fear-AFF	
potti-man	*oniha-fo(ɔ)*	*ahɛ-tɔ́*	'poor person'
poverty-AFF	poverty-AFF	poverty-AFF	
lau-man	*(ɔ)bɔdam-fo(ɔ)*	*tsukú-nɔ̀*	'mad person'
mad-AFF	madness-AFF	madness-AFF	
siki-man	*ɔyare-fo(ɔ)*	*dɔ-nɔ̀*	'sick person'
sick-AFF	sickness-AFF	sickness-AFF	
gudu-man	*osika-ni*	*hotsui-tɔ́*	'rich person'
good(s)-AFF	gold-AFF	cowry-AFF	
wroko-man	*odwumayɛ-fo*	*dɔ-wɔ-lá*	'worker'
work-AFF	work-do-AFF	work-do-AFF	

---

19. The Early Sranan forms come from various 18th century sources stored in the Suriname Creole Archive, whereas the Akan and Gbe words were retrieved from various dictionaries and language descriptions as well as translations by native speakers of the languages. At present the database includes the major Akan languages Twi, Akuapem and Fante as well as an Ewe variety of Ghana and Mina of Togo. Other Gbe languages (Fon, Adja) will be included as well as Gã-Dangme and further Kikongo in due time.

Early Sranan *adjabre-man* lies/falsehood-AFF 'liar' may also have an Akan base, as it bears some resemblance to Twi *ɔdabraba-fo* lies/falsehood-AFF 'liar'. Alternatively, it may be Gbe, as its Ewe equivalent is *adava-tɔ́* lies/falsehood-AFF 'liar'.

Further evidence against an exclusive Gbe model for the derivation of participant and non-participant nouns in Early Sranan is presented by examples such as the ones presented in Table 9. The categorical status of the base (prior to nominalization) is similar in the Akan and Gbe languages, so both the Akan languages and the Gbe languages could have provided the model for the Early Sranan noun. In addition, there are nouns ending in -*man* in Early Sranan that are more similar to their Akan equivalents than to their Gbe equivalents. While they are synthetic compounds in the Gbe languages, their Akan equivalents are not. Some examples are presented in Table 10.

Table 10. Structural similarities of the base in Early Sranan and the Akan languages, but not Gbe

Early Sranan	Akan (Twi)	Gbe (Ewe)	Gloss
baiman	*ɔtɔ –fo(ɔ)*	*nu-dzrà-lá*	'buyer'
buy-AFF	buy-AFF	thing-sell-AFF	
skrifiman	*ɔtwerɛ-foɔ*	*nu-ŋlɔ̃-lá*	'writer'
write-AFF	write-AFF	thing-write-AFF	
harkieman	*atie-fo(ɔ)*	*to-do-lá*	'listener'
hark-AFF	listen-AFF	ear-listen-AFF	
repieman	*ɔboa-fo(ɔ)*	*xɔ̀n-amè- tɔ́*	'helper'
help-AFF	help-AFF	help-person-AFF	
leiman	*ɔtoro-fo(ɔ)*	*aku-via- tɔ́*	'liar'
lie(s)-AFF	lies-AFF	neck-melt-AFF	
kruttuman	*ɔfutu-fo(ɔ)*	*nuxlɔ̃amena- lá*	'council'
council-AFF	*council*-AFF	*advice-give-*AFF	

Out of the sample of 90 words, of Early Sranan words ending in -*man* resemble their Ewe equivalents, while 31 cases are similar to the Akan languages. Thus, there is no evidence in this dataset that Sranan structure follows mainly Ewe structure and not Akan structure. In fact, these data suggest a higher Early Sranan-Akan similarity than Early Sranan-Ewe similarity (Z-test for comparing proportions 20 out of 90 versus 31 out of 90: Z = 1.8, p value = 0.069). These preliminary findings are in line with the hypothesis proposed by Konadu (2010), who suggests that, because of the their exceptional skills in to warfare, medicinal plant use and cultural and spiritual practice, the Akan people had a considerable influence on the newly emerging languages and cultures of the enslaved in settings such as Surinam, despite the fact that they never formed a majority among other Africans in the Americas. Further investigation is clearly needed.

English, Dutch, and the Akan and Gbe languages were not only in contact in the Caribbean and South America, but also in West Africa. Earlier, I illustrated morphological hybridization by affixation of the Cameroon Pidgin English agentive suffix *-man* to non-Pidgin English words. The agentive suffix *-man* also productively derives participant and non-participant nouns in Ghanaian English: Dako (2003) lists for example *afraid man* 'coward' (cf. Early Sranan freddeman), *booze man* 'drunkard', *force man* 'soldier', *parliaman* 'member of parliament' and *sufferman* 'person who has difficulties' among others in her glossary of Ghanaianisms. The glossary further contains words such as *wash(er)man* 'laundry man' among others, that are now obsolete in British English (Oxford English dictionary 1989), but that are also encountered in Early Sranan (*wassiman* 'washerman'). In addition, we find words such as *staffer* 'employed by the president' in the glossary. On the one hand they may be English retentions, as staffer is also encountered in American English. On the other hand, they might be innovations, as derivation through affixation of *-er* to a nominal base is not encountered frequently in the varieties of English as spoken in the United Kingdom or the United States; it is not a very productive process. It is a productive process, however, in both the Akan and the Gbe languages, as shown by examples such as ɔ*bayi-fo(ɔ)* witchcraft-AFF 'witch' and àzɛ́-tɔ́ witchcraft-AFF 'witch' respectively, that illustrate affixation of *-fo(ɔ)* and *-tɔ́* to a nominal base. Note that Akan and Gbe derivational morphemes can also be conjoined to non-Akan and non-Gbe bases. In 1985, a popular Ghanaian highlife number by Nana Ampadu was titled '*Driverfo*'; it was an ode to lorry (public transport) drivers (van der Geest 2009). The base of *driverfo* is the English derived noun *driver* that consists of a verbal base *drive* and the agentive affix *-er*. Even though the word is already marked for agentivity via *-er*, and awareness of the process of derivation via *-er* can be demonstrated for Ghanaian English, Akan *-fo* is added. Akan *-fo* is often regarded as a plural suffix, in particular in the Fante dialect of Akan, but it is also functions as a singular suffix marking identity in the Akan languages (Appah, 2006). Particularly in the case of the expression of occupational or professional identity, the participant noun is marked by the (singular) suffix *-fo(ɔ)*.[20] A similar but not identical example can be found

---

20. Appah (2006) shows that the distinction between the singular and the plural is marked by the prefix *o-* rather than the presumed plural suffix *-fo*.

in a Twi – German dictionary that was published in the late 19th century, almost a century earlier. In this dictionary, which was written by Johann Gottlieb Christaller in 1881, one finds the entry *kupafo* 'cooper'. *Kupafo* differs from *driverfo* in that the base *kupa* has no internal morphological structure. It is a nativized English borrowing, *cooper*, a derived noun with a verbal base *coop* that denotes the activity of hammering copper bands on wooden containers.[21] Interestingly, the same derived noun functions as a base in Early Sranan; Schumann lists *kupaman* in his Sranan Tongo – German dictionary (1783).

Nationality nouns are formed in a similar manner: the base denoting the nationality is borrowed, nativized, and combined with the derivational morpheme that expresses that the referent is form the located denoted by the base. Thus we find *frenkye-ni* French-AFF 'French' and *gyaman-ni* German-AFF 'German' in the Akan languages, and *frentsi-tó* French-AFF 'French' and *dzɛmã-tó* German-AFF 'German' in the case of Ewe(gbe).

The difference between *kupafo* (1881) and *driverfo* (1985) is particularly interesting as it underscores the intensification of contact between English and the African languages in Ghana from the late 19th century until the present day. While borrowing of words, which denote culture-specific items and concepts such as *kupa/cooper*, usually takes place in settings of moderate contact, the kind of morphological hybridization that is exemplified by *driverfo* is found in settings of intense contact. The latter is often encountered in multilingual societies with a majority of multilingual individuals. 19th Century Ghana differs from 20th century Ghana in that, nowadays, more and more people are proficient, albeit in different degrees of proficiency, in one or more African languages as well as English due to schooling.

5. Conclusion

In this chapter, I set up a comparison of Early Sranan complex words with their equivalents in the Akan and Gbe languages of Ghana in order to investigate cross-linguistic effects below word level in Early Sranan. Several types of cross-linguistic effects are encountered in the word formation processes of compounding and derivation, ranging from retention and bor-

---

21. A cooper is someone who makes containers such as barrels, wooden buckets and butter churns among others.

rowing of forms to various types of transfer of functions, meanings and distributional morphosyntactic properties.

While the forms of many compounded Early Sranan body part words mostly derive from English, influence from the Gbe languages is exhibited via the retention of the structure of the Gbe body part words in Early Sranan as well as the retention of Gbe meanings in some cases. Furthermore, influence from English as well as Dutch can be observed in addition to innovations that are typically Sranan Tongo.

Early Sranan as well as the Gbe and Akan languages (but not English) share a limited set of postposed derivational morphemes that can be characterized as semi-affixes or affixoids rather than true affixes. In general, there is little evidence of transfer of the Akan and Gbe sets of derivational morphemes. Nationality nouns and agentive, patient, and experiencer nouns are derived via different morphemes in the Gbe and Akan languages but not in the case of Early Sranan where they are all derived via the derivational morpheme *-man*. The Akan and Gbe diminutives are derived via postposed derivational morphemes that can be traced back to the words for 'child' in the Akan and Gbe languages, but the Early Sranan diminutive is formed via the attributive use of the property item YOUNG that can also function as a noun 'child, young' as well as verb 'being small/young/little'. In the case of the formation of location nouns, some convergence can be observed, triggered by the formal resemblance of Early Sranan *-peh*, Gbe *-ɸé/-pe/ -χʷé*, and, more distantly, Akan *-e*. However, Early Sranan *-peh* is not used to derive location nouns but rather location function words (*da-peh* 'there'). Location nouns are derived via *-plesi* (< English *place*) in Early Sranan and I have not found any examples that resemble their Akan or Gbe equivalents but not also their English equivalent.

While the findings present little support for the transfer of the set of Gbe and/or Akan derivational morphemes, cross-linguistic effects are observed in the formation of participant and non-participant nouns. Examples of participant and non-participant nouns are presented that illustrate similarities in form and meaning (retention), as well as similarities with regard to the internal structure and the categorical status of the base. Contrary to earlier claims that invoke a Gbe model for participant and non-participant nouns in the Surinamese creole languagess, the findings presented here suggest that Early Sranan is significantly more similar to the Akan languages than to Ewe. Further research is needed, in particular as substantial morphosyntactic differences between the Gbe languages have been observed (Capo 1991; Kluge 2006).

At the beginning of this chapter, I stated that a comparison of Early Sranan with other outcomes of contact between the Gbe and Akan languages and English provides a solid type of evidence of transfer of forms, features, functions, meanings or distributional properties from one language to another. In contemporary Ghana, the derivational morpheme -*man* productively derives innovative participant and non-participant nouns in Ghanaian English. Some of these Ghanaianisms are very similar to their Early Sranan equivalents, while differing from their British or American English equivalents (Early Sranan *freddeman* = Ghanaian English *afrai man* ≠ British English *coward*). Comparable examples of participant nouns with a non-Akan base and the Akan derivational morpheme -*fo* are also attested.

The qualitative and quantitative data presented in this chapter show that different types of cross-linguistic effects occur below word level in Early Sranan. Furthermore they show that only a detailed comparison of Early Sranan with the languages that contributed to its emergence can bring out the resourcefulness, linguistic creativity and innovativeness of the speakers of Early Sranan in 18th century Surinam.

Non-iconic reduplications in Eastern Gbe and Surinam

Enoch Aboh & Norval Smith

1. Introduction

The Surinam Creoles appear to have at least six types of non-ideophonic reduplication. Four of these – augmentative, iterative and diminutive verbal formation, and distributive plural noun formation – we will not discuss here, as their iconicity is so strong that they could not really ever be taken as "proof" of any direct substratal connection (cf. Kouwenberg and LaCharité 2003). Further, no definitive survey of iconic reduplicative (or repetitive) processes in the Eastern Gbe languages has been made. In this paper, then, we will restrict ourselves to an examination of two types of reduplication process occurring in the Surinam Creole languages, and address the question as to whether these are to be connected with reduplication processes occurring in Eastern Gbe languages. The two non-iconic reduplication processes dealt with hereunder are (non-productive) verbal noun formation, and adjective formation. Summary descriptive treatments of these exist for Sranan (Smith 1990; Adamson and Smith 2003), Saramaccan (Bakker 1987; Alleyne 1987), and Ndyuka (Huttar & Huttar 1997; Migge 2003).

The structure of this article will be as follows: first, we will take as our starting-point the existing analysis of Gun (Eastern Gbe) non-iconic reduplications by Aboh (2004a, 2005c, 2007a, 2007b). In this work, verbal and predicate reduplication is conditioned by syntactic configuration. Under the view taken by Aboh, "syntactic reduplications" appear to display a uniform structure. Only the surface syntactic structures are given below, as it is these that determine whether reduplication takes place. For a more detailed justification of these structures the reader should consult this work (sections 2, and 3). After discussing reduplication in Gungbe, we move onto similar structures in the Surinam Creoles to see to what extent they could be accounted for in terms of adstrate transfer (section 4).[1]

2. Syntax-driven verbal reduplication in Gun

It is a well-known fact that the Gbe languages (like most Kwa languages) display SVO/SOV alternations in finite clauses. However, the OV pattern is also found in non-finite contexts such as verbal nominalization. As we show in this paper, verbal or predicate reduplication is conditioned by the OV context. We start with VO/ OV in finite clauses.

2.1. Finite clauses

In finite clauses, the unmarked SVO word order is used with perfective verbal structures. In these structures, the verb always occurs in its bare form (see Aboh 2004a chapters 2 and 5)

(1) súrù **ɖà** núsɔ́nú ná mì   G
     Suru **cook** soup   for me
     'Suru **cooked** soup for me'

Under various aspectual conditions, however, SOV word order occurs. Example (2a) is a progressive sentence. Here the object precedes the verb, which precedes the beneficiary. These constructions also involve a sentence-final particle represented by a floating low tone in Gungbe. On the other hand, the prospective example in (2b) indicates that these constructions may involve an aspect marker that intervenes between the fronted object and the verb. This is evidence that object fronting does not serve case licensing. Observe, for instance that the preverbal position can also host certain adverbs (2c). Finally, the possibility of inserting the prospective marker between the fronted object (or phrase) indicates that there is, within the OV structure, an INFL-related position for marking aspect (see Aboh 2004a chapters 5 and 6, 2005c, 2007a for discussion).

---

1. Examples will be identified as to source by the following letter codes: G = Gun, F = Fon, Sa = Saramaccan, Sr = Sranan

(2) a. súrù tò núsɔ́nú ɖà ná mì ` G
Suru PROG soup cook for me PRTL[2]
'Suru is **cooking** soup for me'
b. súrù tò núsɔ́nú na ɖà ná mì ` G
Suru PROG soup PROS cook for me PRTL
'Suru is **about to cook** soup for me'
c. súrù tò dĕdè na zɔ̀n ` G
Suru PROG slowly PROS walk PRTL
'Suru is **about to start walking slowly**'

Starting with SVO, Aboh (2004a chapters 2, 5, and 6, 2005c, 2007a, 2007b) proposes that these OV structures result from object fronting to some position to the left of the prospective marker. The question therefore arises what the nature of this position is.

This question is related to the fact that, in these structures, reduplication has to take place if for, any reason, neither the object nor the prospective marker precede the verb. There are a number of such conditions. For instance, if an intransitive verb has no object in the progressive, reduplication is mandatory, as in (3).

(3) àvún to **gbí-gbò** ` G
dog PROG **bark.bark** PRTL
'A dog is **barking**'

A second condition is when the object is pronominal. In this case, the object clitic *follows* the verb, so that there is once again no pre-verbal object. Therefore the verb reduplicates, as in (4).

(4) súrù tò **ɖì-ɖà** è ná mì ` G
Suru PROG **cook-cook** 3SG for me PRTL
'Suru is **cooking** it for me'

A third condition is when the object is fronted under focus or questioning. Sentence (5) illustrates this.

(5) a. é-tɛ́ wè súrù tò ɖì-ɖà ná mì ` G
thing-Q FOC Suru PROG **cook.cook** for me PRTL
'What is Suru **cooking** for me?'

---

2. Under Aboh (2004, chapter 6) this particle is a nominalizer.

b. *núsónú   wè   súrù tò   ɖì-ɖà   ná mì* `   G
   soup   FOC   Suru PROG **cook.cook** for me PRTL
   'Suru is **cooking** SOUP for me.'

However, even if any of the above conditions applies reduplication still does not take place if the prospective marker *ná* is present. This is shown in (6) where the object is focused, but the sentence includes the prospective marker and reduplication is blocked.

(6) *núsónú   wέ   súrù tò   **ná   ɖà**   ná mì* `   G
    soup   FOC   Suru PROG PROS **cook** for me PRTL
    'Suru is just about to **cook** SOUP for me.'

It therefore appears from these data that there is a position to the left of the prospective marker *nà* that must be overtly realized by a phrase (e.g. the object, or an adverb). This produces the O-(*ná*)-V orders illustrated above. When no phrase can occur in this position, an INFL element (i.e. prospective *ná*) must immediately precede, leading to the order *ná*-V illustrated by example (6). However, the verb must reduplicate in the absence of *ná*. This produces the VV structures in (3), (4), and (5).

2.2. More on the structure of finite clauses

As argued in Aboh (2004a chapter 6, 2005c, 2007a), the interaction between the preverbal object position, the INFL *ná*, and the reduplicated verb is comparable to subject-verb relations in which an INFL element (e.g. an affix on the verb) licenses an unpronounced subject (e.g. in pro-drop languages). Under this description, the position left adjacent to the prospective marker *na* is a subject position, which when empty, requires verb reduplication.

The argumentation goes as follows: OV sequences involve the structure in (7) where an aspect verb (e.g. *tò*) selects for FP whose head F° encodes the sentence-final particle (e.g. the floating tone in (2)). F° selects for a small clause IP, where I°, sometimes realized by the prospective marker *ná*, takes a VP as its complement. The subject position of this small clause, [Spec IP], is subject to the EPP and must be overtly realized. In Gbe, this requirement is achieved by object fronting.

(7)   ...[$_{AspP}$ *tò* [$_{FP}$ [$_F$ ` [$_{IP}$ Object   [$_I$ *ná* [$_{VP}$...t$_{object}$...]]]]]]

When the object is missing, extracted, or cliticized, a null expletive (EXPL) is inserted in [Spec IP]. This expletive element is licensed under spec-head configuration either by the prospective marker under I°, which qualifies as a proper INFL element, or by the verb that raises to I° (in simple OV orders).

Recall that in Gungbe, and more generally in Gbe, the verb always occurs in its bare form, and the language does not tolerate subject pro-drop. This means that in situations where the subject position of the small clause is filled by an expletive, the language must find some way to license this empty element. Aboh (2004a, 2005c, 2007a) proposes that verb reduplication serves this purpose in the Gbe languages. This means that the reduplicated part of the verb functions as an inflectional morpheme that licenses the null expletive. A partial representation is given in (8).

(8)   ... tò [FP [F ` [IP   Expl [I VV   [VP   tv...to]]]]]

Under the partial representation in (8), the sentences illustrated above are assigned the structures in (9).

(9)   a. [= (2a)]   [AspP tò [FP [IP núsɔ́nú [I ɖà   G
      b. [= (3)]   [AspP tò [FP [IP ø   [I gbí-gbò   G
      c. [= (4)]   [AspP tò [FP [IP ø   [I ɖì-ɖà -ὲ   G
      d. [= (5a/b)] [AspP tò [FP [IP ø   [I ɖì-ɖà   G
      e. [= (6)]   [AspP tò [FP [IP ø   [I na [VP ɖà   G

We will not discuss these structures further, and the reader is referred to Aboh (2004a chapters 2, 5, and 6, 2005c, 2007a) where VO, OV, VV, and OVV structures are discussed in detail. Assuming that verbal (or predicate) reduplication is primarily determined by the factors described above, let us now look at instances of nominalizations in Gungbe where a reduplicated verb follows the object.

2.3. Nominalizations

A nominalized verbal structure shares some of the features observed in the previous section, but there are also differences, as pointed out in Aboh (2005c, 2007a). The presence of an object does not impede the occurrence of a reduplicated verb. However, the presence of a prospective marker does have this effect. Compare the sentences under (10).

(10) a. [àzɔ́n **wì-wà**] wè nɔ̀ jró súrù   G
    work do-do FOC HAB please Suru
    'Suru likes WORKING'
  b. súrù gbé [àzɔ́n **wì-wà**]   G
    Suru refuse work do-do
    'Suru refused to work.'
  c. [àzɔ́n **ná wà** dìn] má jró súrù   G
    work PROSP do now NEG please Suru
    'Working now does not please Suru.'

These nominalizations can appear in the same positions as DPs: in subject position (10a,c) and in object position (10b). Three additional facts are worth noting: (i) nominalization implies OV order, (ii) the verb reduplicates even though preceded by an object, (iii) reduplication does not appear in the presence of the prospective marker.

If it is true that verbal reduplication is conditioned by OV contexts as described above, one might wonder why the verb still reduplicates in (10a–b) leading to OVV sequences as opposed to the OV sequences described before. Yet, the blocking effect of the prospective marker in (10c) indicates that these OVV structures are parallel to cases of object fronting to the clausal periphery, as illustrated by the contrast between (5b) and (6). Taking this parallel seriously, Aboh (2005c, 2007a) explains OVV structures in terms of object fronting to a position different from the subject position of the small clause where it normally lands in simple OV structures. More specifically, it is argued that, unlike simple OV sentences where the object occurs in [Spec IP], OVV structures arise from object preposing to [spec FP]. As in the case of wh-extraction or focusing, this forces the insertion of a null expletive in [Spec IP] that must be licensed under spec-head by the reduplicated verb. As previously mentioned, insertion of the prospective marker blocks reduplication. Given this analysis, the sequences in (10) can be partially represented as in (11).

(11) a. [FP àzɔ́n [F [IP [I wì-wà wè nɔ̀ jró súrù   G
        work   do-do   ....
  b. súrù gbé [FP **àzɔ́n** [F [IP [I **wì-wà**]   G
        work   do-do
  c. [FP **àzɔ́n** [F [IP [I na wà dìn má jró súrù   G
        work   PROSP do

As argued for in Aboh (2005c), movement of the object to [spec FP] creates a theme-activity articulation comparable to a topic-comment structure. This is illustrated by the opposition between 'to do work' and 'working', which corresponds to the structures in (12a) and (12b) respectively.

(12) a. wà àzɔ́n   b. àzɔ́n **wì-wà**   G
         do   work   work do.do
         'to work'   Lit. 'work doing' (= 'working')

2.4. Summary

The discussion in these sections shows that while iconic reduplication could be analyzed as a mere morphological process that enables the language to enrich the lexicon, non-iconic reduplication may arise due to a requirement of syntax. In this respect, we have shown that verbal (or predicate) reduplication in Gbe serves to license an empty subject position. In this regard, the reduplicant behaves like an inflectional morphological element. With this description in mind, let us now turn to reduplicated adjectives.

3. Reduplicated adjectives

These only appear in attributive contexts. In Gungbe, they follow the noun, in contradistinction to the situation in the Surinam Creole languages (see section 6).

(13) a. àvún **kì-klò** lɔ́   G
         dog big-big DET
         'the big dog'
   b.   kpò-tín **xú-xú** lɔ́   G
        wood-stick dry-dry DET
        'the *dried* stick' [= 'the stick that has been dried'] [= end-state of process]
   c.   àzɔ́n **síɛ́n-síɛ́n**   G
         work difficult-difficult
         'a difficult work'

The reduplicated attributive adjectives in (13) clearly derive from verbs (or predicates). Indeed, in their predicate usage, these elements occur to the right of the DP, and are not reduplicated, as is illustrated in (14).

(14) a.   *kpò-tín   ló   (*xú-)xú*   G
          wood-stick DET   dry
          'the stick is dry' [= 'the stick is in a dry state']
    b.   *àzɔ́n   (*síɛ́n-)síɛ́n*   G
          work   difficult
          'work is difficult/work is generally difficult'

Note the relative positions of the property items and the determiner in (13b) and (14a). In (13b) the property item precedes the determiner, indicating that the whole construction is within the DP, while in (14a) the property item is external to the DP, and functions as the main verb.

Examples of non-reduplicated property items in (14) are clearly verbs in Gun. The verbal nature of these non-reduplicated predicates is also indicated by the fact that they combine with TMA markers (15a), they undergo predicate cleft (15b), and finally, they reduplicate when put in the progressive (15c). Again, such reduplication is blocked by an intervening prospective marker (15d).

(15) a.   *kpò-tín   ló   ná nɔ̀   **xú***   G
          wood-stick DET   FUT HAB   dry
          'the stick will often dry'
    b.   *xú kpò-tín   ló   xú*   G
          dry wood-stick DET   dry
          'the stick is DRY'
    c.   *kpò-tín   ló   tò   **xú-xú*** `   G
          wood-stick DET   PROG   dry.dry PRTL
          'the stick is drying up/ the stick is getting dry'
    d.   *kpò-tín   ló   tò   na   (*xú-)xú* `   G
          wood-stick DET   PROG   PROS   dry.dry   PRTL
          'the stick is starting to drying up'

These examples clearly confirm that Gungbe reduplicated attributive adjectives derive from verbs. In this regard, examples in (15c–d) are interesting because they indicate that reduplication of these verbs also occurs in OV contexts where no object (or phrase) can occur in the preverbal position, which we identified as a subject position of a small clause that has been selected by an aspect verb (see sections 2.2. and 2.3). In addition, though we use the term progressive to describe sequences like (15c), it is important to note from the interpretation that the intended meaning of this construction refers to a state, and is similar in that sense to a passive.

4. Adjectives structured

Given this last observation, it is reasonable to extend our analysis of verbal (or predicate) reduplication to reduplicated attributive adjectives. Aboh (2007a) adopts this reductionist hypothesis, and assumes that the structures underlying reduplicated adjectives in Gungbe are similar to those we have already noted previously.

Kanye (1994) and Aboh (2005b) have observed that clauses can be selected by determiners to form relative clauses. The latter proposes that the small clause which determines both OV and (O)VV structures in Gbe can be selected by a determiner to form a 'mini relative clause'. Under this approach the surface structure of the sequence in (13a), can be represented as in (16), where the modified noun phrase starts out as the only argument of the predicate adjective, but functions as the head of the 'mini relative clause' and raises to [spec FP]. As in the case of (O)VV structures, this forces the insertion of a null expletive in [Spec IP] that is licensed thanks to verbal reduplication.[3]

(16) [DP [FP àvún [F [I **kì-kló** [VP t$_{ki}$]] [D ló]]]   G
    dog   big-big   DET
    'the big dog'

It is worth noting that like the example in (15c), this sequence describes a state that is assigned to the modified noun, hence the attributive function.

If we grant the idea that the sequence FP can be selected by various elements including certain aspect verbs or auxiliaries and determiners, we observe the following parallels in structure.

(17) a.   (finite "OV" structure with Object)
         [AspP tò [FP [F ` [IP núsónú [I ɖà [VP   G
          Aspect   Object   Verb

---

3. See Aboh (2004, chapters 3, 4) for the syntax of DPs in Gungbe.

b. (finite "OV" structure with Prospective marker)
   [$_{AspP}$ tò [$_{FP}$ [$_F$ ` [$_{IP}$ Ø [$_I$ na [$_{VP}$ dà   G
       Aspect   ---   Aspect Verb
c. (finite "OV" structure with neither object fronting nor *na* insertion)
   [$_{AspP}$ tò [$_{FP}$ [$_F$ ` [$_{IP}$ Ø [$_I$ gbí-gbò [$_{VP}$ G
       Aspect   ---   Verb-Verb
d. (non-finite verbal noun structure)
   [$_{AspP}$ gbé [$_{FP}$ àzɔ́n [$_F$ [$_{IP}$ Ø [$_I$ wì-wà [$_{VP}$ G
       NP   ---   Verb-Verb
e. (attributive adjective structure)
   [$_{DP}$ [$_D$ [$_{FP}$ àvún [$_F$ [$_{IP}$ Ø [$_I$ **kì-klɔ́**]   G
       NP   ---   Verb-Verb

It is clear from this description that the common factor among the reduplicated cases is the presence of a null-element in [Spec IP] preceding the (inflected) verb. This makes the context of verbal (predicate) reduplication in Gbe quite specific and therefore possible to use as a test in the search for adstrate influence. We will now turn to the Surinam Creoles to find out whether the findings in Gbe extend to these languages as well.

5. The Surinam Creoles

We will first examine the case of reduplicated verbal nouns in the Surinam Creoles. Then we will turn to reduplicated adjective formation, from the point of view of Saramaccan. The three Surinam Creoles, Saramaccan, Ndyuka and Sranan, seem to differ little in their reduplications, so this seems to be a reasonable approach.

All three languages have two main types of non-iconic reduplication: a) a non-productive de-verbal nominalization process, and b) a fully productive adjectivalization process, largely based on verbs. The verbs that form the basis of both morphological processes cover a larger domain than in European languages, as most simple adjectival notions are represented in the Surinam Creoles by stative verbs. In this, they resemble Fongbe and Gungbe closely. In the Surinam Creoles there are also a very few non-reduplicated adjectives, as is the case in the Gbe languages.

5.1. Non-productive reduplicated verbal nouns

These forms were first examined in Smith (1990). The very non-productivity of these formations is indicated by their progressive phonological reduction over the years. The first element of the reduplication is now sometimes maximally reduced to the first part of a geminate consonant in Sranan.

(18)   Sranan reduplicated nouns
   a.   18th century   19th century   20th century   gloss
       baribari   babari   b(a)bári   tumult
       si(bi)sibi   sisibi   s(i)síbi   brush
       waiwai   wawai   w(a)wái   fan
   b.   kosikosi   koskosi   koskósi   curses
       krasikrasi   kras(i)krasi   kraskrási   rash
       gritgriti   gritigriti   gritgriti   grater

The list of such de-verbal nouns in Sranan and Saramaccan is fairly short. Table 1 is probably a fairly complete list. It is important to restrict this list to non-iconic cases. Some of the cases could in fact be interpreted as iterative. We have identified some possible iterative cases, and have marked these with asterisks. A number of these refer to implements whose use requires iterated movements.

The main types of verbs involved can be classified as in Table 2. The main types corresponding to one-, two-, and three-argument predicates are given in the fourth column. Less frequent types are put in brackets. The term "Result" corresponds most closely to the meaning of the verb itself, representing the end-state of the process represented in the verbal meaning. These are thus the forms that most closely resemble verbal nominalizations in Gbe. The reader will recall that these forms always involve reduplication. It is not entirely clear whether these nominalizations in the Gbe languages are solely (morpho)syntactic, or whether lexicalizations are involved in some cases.

However, it is equally clear that no morphosyntactic processes of reduplication are involved in the deverbal nominalizations that we see in the Surinam Creoles, whatever their relationship to some Gbe model might have been. A Gbe model involving deverbal nominalizing reduplication would, however, still seem to be the most likely source of these forms. This is supported by the fact that the 18th century form *maemaè*, unlike all other forms contained in the table, only occurs in a reduplicated form.

Table 1. Reduplicated de-verbal nouns in the Surinam Creoles

Sranan	Sr. base	Ndyuka	Saramaccan	gloss
b(a)bári	bári	babali, bali bali		tumult*
			bèbè < bè	yolk
bronbrón	brón	boonboon		burnt crust
djompodjómpo	djómpo			grasshopper*
dorodóro	dóro			sieve*
Fonfón	fón	fonfon	fumm fumm 18c.	blow, beating
Freyfréy	fréy	feefee		fly
gritgriti 19c.	gríti			grater*
		hei hei < hei		hill
Kankán	kán	kankan		comb
kap'kapoe 19c.	kápu			machete
kofukofu 19c.	kófu			cuff (blow)
Koskósi	kósi			curses
kosokóso	kóso	kosokoso		cough
kottikotti 18c.	kóti			slice
krabkrábu	krábu			scrapings*
krabbo-krabbo 18c.	krábu			rake*
kraskrási	krási	kaasikaasi	kasikaási 'sore'	rash
lauláu	láu	lawlaw 'crazy person' leilei 'herbal sedative' < lei		folly
			maemaè 18c.	grilling-frame
moimói	mói	moimoi 'gift'		finery
n(a)nái	nái	nanai(n)	nainai 18c.	needle
njanján	nján	nyanyan	njanjá(n)	food
			papiápapia	gossip
sakasáka	sáka	sakasaka 'crumbs'		dregs
sekséki	séki	sekeseke	shekisheki sp. seed 18c.	rattle*
s(i)síbi	síbi	sisibi		broom*
ta(i)tái	tái			bundle
titéi	tái	tetei < tei	tatái	rope
tjatjári	tjá(ri)	tyatya(l)i		headpad
w(a)wái	wái	wawai	wawái	fan*

The unreduplicated form corresponds to a Fon verb, *mè* 'grill, roast'. The reduplicated *mèmè*, would be a Fongbe nominalization, meaning 'grilling'. This clearly indicates that the change of meaning from that of a morphosyntactically forecastable nominalization to a lexicalized result noun must have taken place in the early history of the Surinam Creole languages.

Some differences among the various creole languages can also be identified in the table of forms. A distinction can be drawn between Sranan and Ndyuka on the one hand and Saramaccan on the other.

Table 2. The main types of reduplicated verbal noun

Verb	Internal Argument	External Argument	Verbal Noun
kóso 'cough' *láu* 'crazy' *fréy* 'fly'		Theme	Result, (Theme)
fón 'beat' *nján* 'eat' *tjári* 'carry'	Theme	Agent	Result, (Theme, Instrument)
gríti 'grate' *kán* 'comb' *nái* 'sew'	Theme, Instrument	Agent	Instrument, (Result)

Sranan and Ndyuka are closely related – Ndyuka derives from a form of Plantation Sranan spoken in the 18th century. Saramaccan can be assumed (see Smith (2002) for more on this point) to be the result of a mixture involving Sranan and some form(s) of Portuguese and/or Portuguese Creole spoken on Jewish plantations. This mixture was the language referred to as Djutongo ('Jewish language') in the colonial literature. It is of relevance for the history of these formations that where the base word in Sranan has been replaced in Saramaccan, the reduplicated form is lacking as well. Examples of this are given in Table 3.

Table 3. Sranan reduplications replaced in Saramaccan. N.B. Port. = Portuguese

Sranan base	Sranan redup.	Saramaccan verbal base	Saramaccan noun	Noun meaning
kán	*kankán*	*pénti* (Port.)	*pénti*	comb
brón	*bronbrón*	*tjumá* (Port.)	*tjumá-alísi*	burnt rice-crust
síbi	*s(i)síbi*	*baí* (Port.)	*basɔ́ɔ* (Port.)	brush

5.2. Adjectives in the Surinam Creoles

The reduplicated adjectives in the Surinam Creoles occur in a number of syntactic contexts. We will mention three main contexts. Additional types occur in complex morphological formations involving derivational and compound formations, which we will not discuss here. The first context we will illustrate is that of attributive adjectives.

(19)   Attributive adjectives in Saramaccan[4]
    a.   *dí laí-lái góni*
        DET load-load gun
        'the loaded gun' (Bakker 1987)
    b.   *dí deé-déé koósu*
        DET dry-dry cloth
        'the dry/dried cloth' (Bakker 1987)
    c.   *dí latjá-latja páu*
        DET split-split wood
        'the split wood' (Bakker 1987)
    d.   *dí síkí-síki wómi*
        DET sick-sick man
        'the sick man' (Alleyne 1987)
    e.   *dí lángá-lánga wómi*
        DET long-long man
        'the tall man' (Alleyne 1987)
    f.   *dí bígí-bígi wósu*
        DET big-big house
        'the big house' (Alleyne 1987)

Note the difference of semantic effect depending on whether the verbal base is a state verb, or a non-stative verb. In the latter case the reduplicative adjectives have a passive meaning. The precise nature of this is difficult to capture. Bakker (1987) qualifies it as "a kind of past participial meaning". Alleyne (1987) refers to it as a "stative adjective".

The passive sense is clearly evinced in examples (19a/c), which are derived from non-stative action verbs. Examples (19d–f) are derived from English quality items which are stative verbs in Saramaccan (though plain adjectives in English), and so cannot have passive meanings. Example

---

4. Note that we have not indicated tonal sandhi in the Saramaccan examples.

(15b) can be interpreted in either way, leading to a certain ambiguity between the meanings 'dry' and 'dried'.

The second type we will illustrate is that of predicative adjectives.

(20) Predicative adjectives
    a.   *dí ɓáta dɛ́*   **logo-logo**
        DET bottle LOC.CP round-round
        'the bottle is round' (Bakker 1987)
    b. *a   dɛ́*   **nákí-náki** *a   goón*
        3SG.NOM LOC.CP knock-knock LOC ground
        'he is lying beaten down to the ground' (Bakker 1987)
    c. *a   bi   dɛ́*   **tái-tái** *ku   búi*
        3SG.NOM PAST LOC,CP tie-tie INST string
        'he was tied with string' (Bakker 1987)
    d. *dí físi dɛ́*   **kúá-kúa**
        DET fish LOC.CP fresh-fresh
        'the fish is fresh' (Bakker 1987)
    e. *a   dɛ́*   **kándi-kándi** *n'-ɛn   ɓédi líɓa*
        3SG.NOM LOC.CP lie-lie LOC-3SG bed top
        'he is lying on bed' (De Groot 1977)

Once again, we observe the difference in sense between the stative and non-stative adjectives.

The third context that reduplicated adjectives occur in is in post-nominal position (21a–c), in which case they receive a resultative interpretation. Such adjectives can also be focussed by fronting (21 d/e).

(21) Resultative adjectives
    a. *dá mi dí   páu   latjá-latja*
        give 1SG DET wood split-split
        'give me the wood split' (Bakker 1987)
    b. *nɔ́ɔ i   sa njám-ɛn   kúá-kúa*
        and 2SG IRR eat-3SG.OBJ fresh-fresh
        'You'll eat it fresh'(De Groot 1977)
    c. *dí pikí wómi tá   njá dí gaán físi kúá-kúa*
        DET little man PROG eat DET big fish raw-raw
        'The little man is eating the big fish raw' (Haabo 2002)
    d. *kúá-kúa a tá   njá dí   gaán físi*
        raw-raw 3SG PROG eat DET big fish
        'he eats the big fish RAW' (Haabo 2002)

e. *síkí-síki mi kó féni hɛn*
sick-sick 1SG come find 3SG
'I found him SICK'

5.3. Saramaccan adjectives structured

Following previous discussion on verbal reduplication, we propose that attributive, predicative and resultative reduplication in Saramaccan derive from the same underlying structure as the one that triggers reduplication in Gungbe: FP. In addition, we suggest that predicative and resultative structures, which are comparable to OV structures in Gungbe (e.g. progressive and prospective), only differ in the overt versus covert realization of the aspectual verb (or locative copula) *dɛ̌*. We therefore represent those structures as in (22) and (23). Note that in each of these cases the reduplicated adjective is preceded by a null element in [Spec IP] just as in the Gbe languages.

(22) Predicative adjective
[$_{TP}$ dí fisi [$_{AspP}$ dɛ̌ [$_{FP}$ [$_F$ [$_{IP}$ Ø [$_I$ **kúá-kúa** [$_{VP}$ ....

(23) Resultative adjective
[$_{TP}$ dí fisi [$_{AspP}$ Ø$_{[dɛ̌]}$ [$_{FP}$ [$_F$ [$_{IP}$ Ø [$_I$ **kúá-kúa** [$_{VP}$ ....

With regard to attributive adjectives, however, we follow Aboh (2007b) in deriving them similarly to Gungbe (16): the bare NP moves to [Spec FP] leaving the subject position of the small clause unfilled. This forces the insertion of a null expletive, which must be licensed by reduplication of the predicative verb. This produces the intermediate stage in (24a), which is a headed 'mini' relative clause.

(24a) Attributive adjective
[$_{DP}$ [$_D$ dí [$_{FP}$ góni [$_{IP}$ Ø [$_I$ **láí-lái** [$_{VP}$ t$_{góni}$]]]]]

In order to obtain the right order in Saramaccan, however, we have to postulate an additional movement in terms of predicate inversion: the whole IP raises to a position to the left of the head of the 'mini relative clause', as illustrated in (24b). This is the final stage in Saramaccan.

(24b) Attributive adjective
[$_{DP}$ [$_D$ dí [$_{FP}$ [$_{IP}$ Ø [$_I$ **láí-lái** [$_{VP}$ t$_{góni}$] [$_{FP}$ góni [t$_{IP}$]]]]]

This movement results in prenominal adjective placement in Saramaccan and English as opposed to the Gbe languages, where adjectives are strictly postnominal.[5] Here we find influence from both the adstrate and superstrate. The context for reduplication is given by the same conditions as in Gbe, while the adjective-noun order comes from English.

6. The origin of predicative adjectives in the Surinam Creoles

The question has not been answered of what the model is for the predicative structures in the Surinam Creoles. Note these are either passive in meaning if the reduplicated verb is an action verb, or express a meaning similar to quality predicates if it is not.

(25) a. dí ɓáta dɛ̃ **logo-logo**
DET bottle LOC.CP round-round
'the bottle is round' (Bakker 1987)
b. a ɓi dɛ̃ **tái-tái** ku ɓúi
3SG.NOM PAST LOC.CP tie-tie INST string
'he was tied with string' (Bakker 1987)

Note also that this paradigm is parallel to aspects of the paradigm of non-reduplicated verbs.

(26) a. mi **síki** Sr
1SG sick
'I am sick'
b. a óso **férfi** Sr
DET house paint
'the house is painted'

The parallel lies herein, that each predicate has only one argument in these examples. In each of the paradigms, the second example is an action verb, which normally has an agent as its external argument, and a theme as its internal argument. This is illustrated in (27).

---

5. In this paper, we only consider deverbal prenominal adjectives in English (see also Kayne 1994).

(27) nórfu férfi a óso   Sr
     Norval paint DET house
     'Norval painted the house'

As soon as the agent is omitted, the path to a passive reading is opened. In this case, *oso* is inanimate so that no other reading would be possible. The theme gets raised to subject position. Kahrel (1987) claims that such one-argument structures become (derived) statives, thus changing the interpretation of the concomitant TMA markers to that applicable with underlying statives like *siki*.

Immediately the question arises of the meaning difference between the two types of structure.

(28) a. N_{theme} V
     b. N_{theme} LocCp VV

This is not always easy to determine. Alleyne (1987) gives a number of contrasts.

(29) a.   *a   dɛ̃dɛ*
          3SG dead
          'he is dead', 'he has died' (Alleyne 1987)[6]
     b.   *a   dɛ̃   dɛ̃dɛ-dɛ̃dɛ*
          3SG LOC.CP   dead-dead
          'he is dead' (i.e. having died some time ago) (Alleyne 1987)
(30) a.   *dí   boon jasa   kaa*
          DET   flour bake   already
          'the flour has already been baked' (Alleyne 1987)
     b.   *dí   boon dɛ̃   jasa-jasa   kaa*
          DET   flour LOC.CP bake-bake   already
          'the flour is already baked' (Alleyne 1987)

In (30) we can observe that the translations suggest the difference in English between the verbal participle and a de-verbal adjective.

Parallel to these usages it must be noted that we also have similar prenominal paradigms.

---

6. The third gloss given by Alleyne – 'he has been made dead' is actually an instantiation of the homophonous causative verb *dɛdɛ* 'to make dead'.

(31) a. dĩ dɛ̃dɛ wómi
         DET dead man
     b. dĩ dɛ̃dɛ-dɛ̃dɛ wómi
         DET dead-dead man
         'the dead man' (a/b) (Alleyne 1987)
(32) a. dĩ latjá páu
         DET chop wood
     b. dĩ latjá-latja páu
         DET chop-shop wood
         'the chopped wood' (a/b) (Alleyne 1987)

Alleyne could not get his informants to distinguish these pairs in meaning. Bakker (1987) did discover a temporal difference, which is possibly to be related to the distinction in (29).

To turn back to a possible Gbe model for these structures, let us look again at sentences (2a/3) repeated here as (33a/b).

(33) a. súrù tò   núsɔ́nú ɖà   ná mì `   G
         SuruPROG soup   cook for me PRTL[7]
         'Suru is **cooking** soup for me'
     b. àvún tò   **gbí-gbò** `   G
         dog PROG **bark.bark** PRTL
         'A dog is **barking**'

Note that (29a) is a two-argument verb. What happens if an action has its agent unexpressed. Note that this is often not possible in Gun, but that examples do occur.

(34) a. àvɔ̀ lɔ́ tò   bí-bɔ̀   `   tò àkpótín lɔ́ mɛ̀   G
         cloth DETPROG fold-fold PRTL LOC trunk DETin
         'the cloth is folded [i.e. in a folded state] in the trunk'
     b. míɔ́ngbán lɔ́ tò   tí-tá
         lamp   DETPROG light.light
         'the lamp is lit [i.e. in a lit state]'

Here we observe a number of things. In the absence of an agent the theme noun becomes the subject. The verb is no longer interpreted as an action verb, but as a state verb, as Kahrel (1987) claims for Saramaccan. And the

---

7. Under Aboh (2004, chapter 6) this particle is a nominalizer.

verb receives a passive interpretation, similarly to the reduplicated Saramaccan cases in (21b, 22b, 26b).

One lexical difference exists – in Gun *tò* is the progressive marker (homophonous with and of the same origin as *tò*, the locative copula), while in Saramaccan *dɛ́* is the locative copula (and the progressive marker is *tá*. However, in one of the antecedent components of Saramaccan, Sranan, the coastal plantation creole language, the verbal element used with the reduplicated forms is the locative copula *de*, which in earlier records of Sranan,s is indeed homophonous with the progressive marker *de*. This latter has since been reduced to *e*, in both Sranan and Ndyuka. Note that in Fon *ɖò* also has the same two functions. We are tempted to conclude that this difference – between progressive marker and locative Copula – was not relevant for earlier forms of the Surinam Creoles.

In any case, the parallels between structures like (30) in Gun, and (26b) etc. in Saramaccan and Sranan are very strong.

7. Conclusion

We conclude that both types of reduplication in the Surinam Creoles are derived from the Gbe adstrate. However, the basis for this statement is different in the two cases. In the first case, the unproductive verbal nouns, the most significant evidence is an isolated case of reduplication that descends from a Gbe (Fon) verbal noun.

In the case of reduplicated adjectives, these can be morphosyntactically derived. The reduplications are similarly explained to those in the Gbe languages, although the distribution of reduplication is different. The patterns have been significantly influenced by the superstrate language – English.

Substrate phonology, superstrate phonology and adstrate phonology in creole languages

Norval Smith

1. Introduction: stratal terminology

The study of the phonologies of creole languages is in most cases not very advanced, neither in synchronic nor diachronic terms. I have attempted in a number of recent papers (e.g. Smith 2008a, 2008b) to show that "creole phonology" is merely contact phonology, as far as the phonological effects themselves are concerned. The languages in contact are usually divided into two types: superstrate and substrate languages.

<u>Languages in contact</u>
– Superstrate language: a language spoken by a "dominant" social group
– Substrate language: a language spoken by a "dominated" social group

These terms have a long history in historical linguistics. For instance, various features of Romance languages were, correctly or incorrectly, attributed to the influence of the *substrate* Celtic languages spoken in the territories of the present France, Spain, Switzerland and Northern Italy before *superstrate* Latin was adopted there.

Clearly, these terms also have a close relation to the terms utilized by Ferguson (e.g. 1959) for describing situations of diglossia, H ("high") and L ("low"), which can refer both to two varieties of a single language and to two different languages. The replacement of one language by another, as in the example of the replacement of Gaulish (Celtic) by Latin, can/could take hundreds of years to achieve, and in the course of this process there would have been a state of diglossia in which the H language (Latin) would have replaced the L language (Gaulish) in an ever-increasing number of domains of use (and regions), until the L language eventually died out completely, probably in the 5th century A.D.

During this process there would have been various types of influence on both Latin and Gaulish due to the contact between them. One obvious illustration of this is the body of lexical items in French (and other Romance languages) of Gaulish origin, like *cheval* 'horse' from Gaulish *caballos* 'draught-horse', *char* 'chariot' from *carros* 'chariot', *chêne* 'oak' from *cassanos* 'alder', dialectal *verne/vergne* 'alder' from *werna* 'alder' (Delamarre 2003).

Later in history, parts of Northern France came under the control of the Salic Franks – this is why France is called France. The Salic Franks had a policy of equality between themselves and the native Gallo-Roman population. In such cases we cannot speak of H and L languages, rather of two H languages co-existing. In the event, (Salic) Frankish did not replace Gallo-Roman Latin, but was itself replaced by it. Similarly to Gaulish, however, Frankish has left traces in French in the form of numerous lexical items, such as *bleu* 'blue' from Frankish *blāo (Middle Dutch *blāu*) 'blue', *haie* 'hedge' from Frankish *hagja (Middle Dutch *hegge*) 'hedge', *gué* 'ford' from Frankish *wad (Old Dutch *wada*) 'ford', *garde* 'guard' from Frankish *warda 'guard', *guerre* 'war' from Frankish *werra 'disorder, quarrel' (Centre National de Ressources Textuelles et Lexicales 2012 *online*; Philippa et al. 2003-2009 *online*). For language contact phenomena in such a situation of social equality the term *adstrate* has been employed.

In the context of creole languages, the terms *substrate* and *superstrate* have been used in connection with the original languages of the slaves (African in the Caribbean) and the languages of the (European) colonial powers respectively. In connection with the present situation of (claimed) linguistic continua in a number of Caribbean territories where English-lexifier creoles are spoken, another set of terms is in use. These are *basilect*, or creole language that is least influenced by the local Standard English, *mesolect*, or creole that shows a significant amount of influence from Standard English, and finally, *acrolect*, referring to the local Standard English. Both the basilect and mesolect can be referred to as forms of creole language.[1] The mesolect would then show more adstratal influence from the colonial language.

So, the initial situation in which the colonial language (English) was the H language, and African languages the L languages, has usually been replaced by a situation in which the colonial language has remained the H language, but English-lexifier creoles have become the L languages, with a possible distinction between M (middle) languages, the mesolects, and L languages, the basilects.

---

1. Clearly the term *acrolectal creole*, which is sometimes used, is nonsensical. One form of a creole may be *more* acrolectal or *more* basilectal than another, but the acrolect itself is (a local form of) the colonial language.

1.1. New stratal definitions

For the purposes of the discussion of the contact phenomena giving rise to the creation of creole languages ("younger languages"), and other contact effects associated with creole languages, I would like to redefine the precise meanings of these terms.

I would like to reserve the terms substrate and superstrate languages for reference to the languages directly involved in the process of creolization itself. So the dominant language during creolization would be the superstrate language, while dominated languages that left a mark on the resultant creole language would be the substrate languages. African languages that were too little present to really influence things do not need to be referred to as substrate languages.

Once creolization is complete, in other words, once we have a language system that can be called a separate language, we have a different scenario. Now what we have is an ordinary language contact situation. Note that the H/dominant language is not necessarily the same language as the lexifier language of the creole; Surinam seems to be an obvious case of this. The combination of superstrate English and substrate Fongbe and Kikongo apparently gave us the English-lexifier creole language, Sranan. But things are not so simple as they seemed. The only external (short term) observer from the English period, Warren (1667), suggests that most of the slaves came from Guinea (i.e. West Africa), without going into any real detail. He suggests, however (see Smith, this volume, on the early history of Surinam), that there were several different linguistic groups present. I repeat his remarks here:

> They [the slaves, NS] are there a mixture of several nations, which are always clashing with one another, so that no conspiracy can be hatching, but it is presently detected by some party amongst themselves disaffected to the plot, because their enemies have a share in it... (Warren 1667: 19)

It might not be straining the interpretation of this remark to see in it a statement that a) three or more groups were represented, mostly West African, and b) that there was no dominant group. In addition, we have an internal (long-term) witness, Byam, who makes a statement quoted in Lack (2007b) concerning two ships arriving from Guinea in 1661.

To turn back to things we can be more certain of, among the slave ship voyages in the Voyages Database (2009), where voyages are recorded from 1664, we crucially find no voyages from West Central Africa until 1669, and no voyages stated explicitly to hail from the Slave Coast/Bight of Benin until 1677. In other words, no claim referring to either Kikongo or the Gbe languages as a substrate for the Surinam creoles can be substantiated. The slave populations in the earliest years of the colonization of Surinam can thus not be identified in terms of specific African sources.

It is undeniable, however, that Sranan came to stand as the L language in opposition to Dutch as the H language in the area of the coastal plantations. In the course of the last couple of centuries the Dutch spoken in Surinam has undergone a certain amount of influence from Sranan, while Sranan has in turn undergone influence from Dutch. Despite the disparity in power relations between these two languages I would like to refer to both kinds of relations as adstratal. In what follows, however, I will only be discussing influence from the dominant language on dominated languages.

New stratal definitions for creole languages
- Substrate influence: influence from the language of the initial "lower" social group involved in creolization
- Superstrate influence: influence from the language of the initial "higher" social group involved in creolization
- Adstrate influence: influence from the languages of non-creolizing social groups in contact

1.2. The coming sections

In subsequent sections, I will attempt to identify clear examples of adstrate and superstrate types of influence. I will draw these examples both from the creole languages of Surinam and those of Jamaica. Various aspects of the phonological adaptation of English words in the creole languages of Surinam will be examined in Section 2. In Section 3, I will look at the phonological influence of Fongbe and Kikongo, with a particular emphasis on the treatment of nasals. In Section 4, "Jamaican" creole languages will be treated. Under this term I include three languages: Jamaican Creole, Eastern (Windward) Maroon Creole (a.k.a. Maroon Spirit Language), and Western Maroon Creole, in its modern instantiation as Krio (see Smith, this volume, on Ingredient X). The results of my comparison of English, Sranan, Jamaican Creole, Eastern Maroon Creole and Krio will be treated in Section 5. In Section 6, I conclude that the exercise I have conducted in the course of this chapter brings us one step closer to revealing what I referred to in the chapter on Ingredient X as the Proto-Atlantic Slave Community Language

2. Substrate influence in Surinam? Some relevant phenomena

In order to examine a case of *apparent* substrate influence, let us look first at the developments of final English stressed syllables in Sranan, the coastal plantation creole language of Surinam. I utilize here the most relevant form of Standard English in comparison, the Early Modern English of the mid-17th century, based primarily on the exhaustive researches of Dobson (1957) and treated in Smith (1987).[2] I will initially use for my comparison modern Sranan, to introduce the subject in such a way as to enable me to make useful comparisons, and then return in section 2.2 with some remarks on the earlier developments in syllabic structure of Sranan and the other Surinam creoles.

2.1. The stressed syllables of English words in Sranan

I will kick off by examining a set of words with monosyllabic closed syllables illustrating various English vowels and their equivalents in Sranan. My main interest here is not the vowel equivalences, but the general shapes of resulting items in Sranan, which are all disyllabic.

Table 1. Non-final vocalic nuclei

English spelling	Sranan Tongo	EME	Current English
sleep	sribi	sliːp	sliːp
sick	siki	sɪk	sɪk
afraid	frede	əfreːd	əfreid
dead	dede	dɛd	dɛd
walk	waka	wɔːk	wɔːk
hot	ati	hɔt	hɔt, hɑt
hat	ati	hat	hæt
house	oso	həus > haus	haus
fight	feti	fəit > fait	fait

What can we observe from this table of equivalences, which is representative for the English vocabulary in Sranan? Two things. Firstly, no final con-

---

2. Available in digital form from the author.

sonants appear to be tolerated. Secondly, final syllables are required to be open. This open final syllable is achieved by adding an anaptyctic[3] vowel frequently of more or less forecastable quality. Details of this can be found in Smith (1977).

In Sranan, this last restriction does not apply to non-final syllables.[4] For some examples, see Table 2.

Table 2. Closed non-final syllables

English spelling	Sranan Tongo	EME	Current English
change	tyentye[5]	tʃeːndʒ	tʃeindʒ
remember	memre	rɪmembər	rɪmembə(r)
hark (*ask*)	arki, artyi	hɑrk	hɑːk
six	siksi	sɪks	sɪks

We can account for this phonotactic restriction with the help of Optimality Theory (OT), a theory in which various presumed universal phonological constraints are ranked differently in different languages (see McCarthy & Prince 1993, 1995). Two types of OT constraints are required for our typological comparison, Markedness constraints and Faithfulness constraints. Markedness constraints favour unmarked outputs from the phonology, while Faithfulness constraints try to preserve identity between the inputs and outputs of the phonology.

In more recent Sranan, this phonotactic restriction to open final syllables can be accounted for with the help of a more restricted version of the more general NOCODA constraint (no syllable may be closed, have a coda), which I will call NOWORDCODA. In other words, a version of NOCODA applies, but only at the word level – every word must end on in a vowel.[6] We can express the difference between English and Sranan with the help of two constraints, DEP(IO) and NOWORDCODA.[7]

---

3. I have adopted the term *anaptyctic* for this in preference to the rival terms *paragogic, supportive* and *epithetic*.
4. Earlier forms of Sranan, however, throw a different light on things. See Section 2.2.
5. In conformity with the general present spelling of Surinam creoles I will represent /tʃentʃe/ as /tyentye/. The three palatal phonemes of these languages will be transcribed as /dy, ty, ny/ corresponding phonetically to [dʒ, tʃ, ɲ/ respectively.
6. Note that in present-day Sranan the effects of phrasal phonology may cause the deletion of some word-final vowels. At the word-level, however, all items except unmodified recent Dutch loans have final vowels.
7. I will revise the term for NOWORDCODA later.

(1) a. [Faithfulness] DEP(IO): All phonological material in the output must be present in the input,[8] i.e. no inserted material is allowed.
b. [Markedness] NOWORDCODA: No word-final consonants are allowed.

Let us look first at an English tableau. The input/underlying/lexical form is in the top right cell in the tableau. Below possible output candidates are given. These candidates are generated by a mechanism called the Generator (GEN for short), which I will not discuss further here. The columns (2-*n*) give the constraints ranked in order of importance. The asterisks indicate violations of the constraint named in the first row of the column. The exclamation-mark is purely for the convenience of the reader. It indicates the constraint that leads to the non-selection of a candidate. The pointing finger indicates the successful candidate.

Tableau 1. DEP(IO) and NOWORDCODA in English

/hat/	DEP(IO)	NOWORDCODA
☞ hat		*
hati[9]	*!	

And now in Sranan:

Tableau 2. NOWORDCODA and DEP(IO) in Sranan

/hat/	NOWORDCODA	DEP(IO)
hat	*!	
☞ hati		*

NOWORDCODA is ranked higher than the relevant Faithfulness constraint, here DEP(IO), while the reverse ranking applies in English.

To express the relevant (factorial) typology I will employ a meta-tableau indicating which of the two constraints involved is ranked higher or lower in the two languages. What I refer to as a meta-tableau is a tableau comparing the relative ranking of more than one constraint in two different languages (cf. Tableau 3), or the relative ranking of one constraint to another (cf. Tableau 4). To refer to a single constraint, I will represent this in a more

---

8. In other words, the output segments are "dependent" on the input segments. This is the reason for the name DEP(IO) given to this constraint, which is short for DEPENDENT(INPUTOUTPUT).
9. 17-Sranan had /hati/ in this word. Initial /h/ was dropped later in Sranan.

compact fashion, just mentioning the relationship of the relevant Markedness constraint vis-à-vis the Faithfulness constraint <bracketed>:

Tableau 3. NoWordCoda in English and Sranan

Relative ranking Language	**Higher-ranked**	Lower-ranked
English	Dep(IO)	NoWordCoda
Sranan	NoWordCoda	Dep(IO)

Tableau 4. NoWordCoda in English and Sranan again

Constraint Language	NoWordCoda <Dep(IO)>	
English		Lower-ranked
Sranan	**Higher-ranked**	

2.2. Early Sranan syllabification

With respect to 17th century Sranan, we have a problem. Basically, our records only start in the early 1700s (van den Berg 2000). What can we deduce from these earlier sources that is relevant for our study of early Sranan phonology? I will briefly examine this under three headings:

– Word codas
– Consonant clusters
– Non-final and final vowel nuclei

These are the points affecting syllabification. I will treat them in a summary fashion here. As regards my methodology, all that requires to be said is that where Dutch words in 18th century Sranan suggest different phonotactics from English words, I assume that only the English words are informative as regards the phonotactics of 17th century Sranan. I will refer to this putative early stage of Sranan as 17-Sranan.

2.2.1. Word codas in 17-Sranan

The first comprehensive dictionary of Sranan (Schumann 1783) distinguishes between words with final /n/ and with final /m/. In modern Sranan, as in the other Surinam creoles, no such distinction is made, final *n* indicates that the vowel is nasalized, while final *m* does not occur in assimilated words. Phonetically a final velar nasal may appear, without any phonological significance. But there was apparently a contrast in the 18th century, as I will illustrate with the following examples.

(2) 18th century Sranan /n#/
    bronn   'burn'   < English *burn*
    penn   'pen'   < English *pen*
    tjen   'sugar-cane'   < English *cane*
    boon   'bone'   < English *bone*
    stoon   'stone'   < English *stone*
    mann   'man'   < English *man*
    sonn   'sun'   < English *sun*

(3) 18th Sranan /m#/
    drem   'dream'   < English *dream*
    drum   'drum'   < English *drum*
    shem   'shame"   < English *shame*
    tem   'time'   < English *time*
    komm   'come'   < English *come*
    nem   'name'   < English *name*
    fumm   'beat'   < Eastern Ijo *fom(u)*

The "wrong" nasal however sometimes occurs as in (4), all of which involve a reduced form of the intransitive preposition *down*:

(4)   *bukudumm*   'crouch down'   < English[10] (*buk-*) *down*
    fadomm   'fall (down)'   < English *fall down*
    liddom   'lie down'   < English *lie down*
    siddom   'sit'   < English *sit down*

What are we to make of this? Modern Saramaccan appears to offer an approach to the understanding of this problem. In the cases considered above, we have:

---

10. While the end of this word would appear to share the same English-derived terminal morph – it appears in modern Sranan as /bukun/ and /bukun-dun/, respectively 'stoop' and 'stoop down', the initial element appears to be from an older form of the Dutch verb *buk-* 'to stoop'. Older forms were *buku, boekoedóm*, where *oe* stands for [u].

(5) i. /n#/   ii. /m#/
         boónu < burn   ---
         péni   < pen   doón   < drum
         tyéni < cane   sén   < shame
         bónu   < bone   té(n) < time
         sitónu < stone   kó   < come
         mánu   < man   né   < name
         sónu   < sun   fón   < E.Ijo fom(u)

Corresponding to a final orthographic *n* in 18th century Sranan, modern Saramaccan has /n/ followed by an anaptyctic vowel, whereas corresponding to a final orthographic *m* in 18th century Sranan, modern Saramaccan has a final nasalized vowel (orthographically represented by a vowel followed by final *n*). This suggests that the final *n*, *m* in 18th century Sranan were phonologically distinct, although the nature of the distinction remains imprecise.[11]

How about the "wrong" nasal cases found in (4) above? What do we find here in Saramaccan?

(6) didón < lie down
     sindó < sit down

They seem to resemble the /m#/ cases in (5ii.). Note that the nasality of final vowels in Saramaccan appears to be less stable than in the other creole languages of Surinam. This however does not affect the issue we are concerned with here. One possible way of interpreting orthographic *m* in 18th century Sranan, that is suggested by (6), is that final *m* was an orthographical representation of a final nasalized vowel.

Attractive as this hypothesis might seem, there is a problem. Look at the following forms from Krio (Sierra Leone):

(7) i. /n#/   ii. /m#/
         bɔn   < burn   drim   < dream
         pɛn   < pen   drɔm   < drum
         ken   < cane   ʃem   < shame
         bon   < bone   tɛm   < time
         ston   < stone   kam   < come

---

11. Although the distribution of cases in Saramaccan is less clear-cut than I suggest here, the majority of cases derived from English originals behave in this way.

man	< *man*	nɛm	< *name*
san	< *sun*	---	

(8) fɔdɔ́m < *fall down*
 ledɔ́m < *lie down*
 sidɔ́m < *sit down*

In Sierra Leone Krio, final nasals are phonemically /n, m/, including those in the forms in (8). Note that we find precisely the same distribution among the three types of form as we do in 18th century Sranan, and modern Saramaccan. What could a possible solution to this conundrum be?

At least a partial answer is to be found in the modern creole languages and dialects of Surinam. Firstly, in an article by Jan Voorhoeve (Voorhoeve 1982)[12] information on a feature of Sranan is described that is important for our study. A small number of verbs which would nowadays be described as ending on a nasalized vowel end instead in /m/ when this forms a syllable onset before vowel initial clitic object/possessive pronouns. I give the full list of 13 verbs Voorhoeve quotes, accompanied by a slightly revised list of etyma, and an illustratory sentence from Voorhoeve. To help the reader I indicate with bold type where the etymon has a labial nasal /m/. This is only so in 7 out of the 13 cases. I indicate the closer connection between the /m/ and the following vowel by only separating them with a double breve.

(9) Sranan verbs with "/m/-epenthesis"

form	source	illustration	translation
form	*source*	*illustration*	*translation*
lon	< *run*	a lom‿ a boy	'he chased the boy'
fon	< **fom**[13]	mi fom‿ a boy	'I hit the boy'
bron	< *burn*	mi brom‿ a foto	'I burnt down the town'
kron	< **krom**[14]	mi krom‿ a tiki	'I bent the stick'
ston	< *stone*	mi stom‿ i dagu	'I threw stones at your dog'
kan	< **kam**[15]	mi kam‿ en wwiri	'I combed her hair'
lan	< **lam**[16]	mi lam‿ a boy	'I crippled the boy'
nyan	< **nyam**[17]	mi nyam‿ en	'I ate it'

---

12. Also Voorhoeve (1985).
13. < Eastern Ijo *fom(u)* 'to beat'.
14. < Dutch *krom* 'bent'.
15. < Dutch *kam* 'comb'.
16. < Dutch *lam* 'lame'.
17. < Wolof *nyam* 'eat', an Ingredient X word (see Smith, this volume, on Ingredient X).

span	< span[18]	mi spam‿ a uma	'I made the woman pregnant'
frstan	< verstaan[19]	mi frstam‿ en bun	'I understood him well'
kren	< climb	mi krem‿ a bon	'I climbed the tree'
swen	< swim	a swem‿ a liba	'I swam the river'
krin	< clean	mi krim‿ en yari	'I cleaned his garden'

Voorhoeve chooses to analyse this as the epenthesis of a transitive marker /m/. As Voorhoeve mentions, one could opt for an underlying distinction between final /m/ and /n/. This is not the choice he makes, although he doesn't actually tell us his reasons in so many words, apart from mentioning the exceptionality of the /m/ forms. I prefer to analyse this in terms of an underlying final /m/ in the stem. This immediately begs the question of what to do with the forms that do not have an underlying /m/.

Let us consider some of the forms that do not behave like those in (9). Once again I use examples from Voorhoeve (1982).

(10) Sranan verbs without "/m/-epenthesis"

form	source	illustration	translation
kon	< come	a ko a skoro	'he came to school'
swem	< swim	a swe a liba	'he swam in the river'
kon	< come	[kɔ̃ŋ!]	'come!'
nyam	< nyam	[ɲã̃ŋ!]	'eat!'
nyam	< nyam	[ɲã dẽ sani!]	'eat all things!
kon	< come	a kon tru [a kõ tru]	'it came true'[20]
ben	< been	mi be e go	'I was going'

Note that we have a mixture of /n/-final and /m/-final verbs in (10). The /n/-final verbs drop the /n/, and any sign of nasality before the clitics. The /m/-final verbs we saw in (9) do not occur in phonological contexts suitable for the underlying /m/ to be realised. They are in sentence-final position, or are not followed by vowel-initial object clitics. We can confidently say that there has been widespread confusion – many verbs that formerly had final /m/ no longer have any evidence of this, and a few verbs that formerly had final /n/ now have final /m/, but this is only visible only when vowel-initial clitic pronominal elements follow.

---

18. < Dutch *span-* 'to stretch'.
19. < Dutch *verstaan* 'to understand'.
20. This example was taken from the Sranan translation of the New Testament (Stichting Surinaams Bijbelgenootschap 2010).

All Surinam Creole dialects have traces of similar oppositions. The only case I want to mention here is that of Saramaccan, where the disappearance of final /m/ has progressed furthest. In Kouwenberg (1987) it is shown that the only two such surviving verbs are our old friends, the African-derived /fom/ and /nyam/. In Saramaccan /n/-final verbs retain their nasality: /fɛń/ 'tear' results in /fɛń ɛn/ [fɛ̃ɛ̃].

(11) Saramaccan contrasts
      form   source   illustration   translation
      fom   < fom   a bi ó fom ɛ̃ ɛ̃   'he would beat him'
      fɛn   < fɛn[21]   m fɛ̃ ɛ̃   'I tore it'

I will confine myself here to remarking that there is evidence for word-final nasal codas in 18th century Sranan, and therefore presumably in 17-Sranan.

Other word-coda types occur so rarely in Schumann (1783) that I will disregard them here.

There is a theoretical phonological problem here, which I will not attempt to address in this article. Syllable structure, in terms of Onset-Nucleus-Coda, tends to follow what has been called the Sonority Sequencing Principle (Clements 1990).

(12) The sonority sequencing principle
      Highest sonority: vowels (and semi-vowels)
                       liquids
                       nasals
                       fricatives
      Lowest sonority: stops (and affricates)

Syllable structure normally proceeds from the nucleus, usually a vowel, with the highest sonority to lesser degrees of sonority in the syllable margins. A good illustration of this principle would be the English word *trench*, beginning with a stop /t/, then a liquid /r/, and then a vowel /ɛ/. The vowel, the head or nucleus of the syllable, is then followed by a nasal /n/, and finally by a fricative /ʃ/. So the relative sonority of the segments rises from the first consonant of the onset to the nucleus, and then declines to the end of the syllable. If we look at the phononological structure of *words* in some languages, we find that at the beginning and end it is possible to have se-

---

21. This is Fongbe /fɛn/ 'split, tear off'. See Smith, this volume, on the Gbe lexical contribution to the Surinam Creoles.

quences that do not comply with the Sonority Sequencing Principle. There may also be other other restrictions.

These unprincipled segments are sometimes explained away with the assumption that they do not form part of the narrower syllabic structure. A simple example from English would be the word *stomp*, where the initial /s/ is more sonorous than the following /t/.

Turning to word-codas, we would expect to encounter five types of language, if this followed the guiding principle for syllable-codas:

(13) Expected typology of word-coda manners
    a.   Semivowel word-coda   + no coda
    b.   Liquid word-coda   + a.
    c.   Nasal word-coda   + b.
    d.   Fricative word-coda   + c.
    e.   Stop word-coda   + d.

This is not borne out by the evidence. Languages of the following types can easily be found.

(14) Expected types of word-coda
    13a. *Kwaza* (van der Voort 2000)
    13b. ......
    13c. *Fante* (Abakah 2005)
    13d. *Ancient Greek* /s, r, n, y/
    13e. *Dutch* (Booij 1995)

Many languages do not however admit word-final liquids:

(15) Unexpected liquid gaps
    13c. minus liquid *Akuapem* (Abakah 2005)
                              Laghuu (Edmondson & Ziwo 1999)
    13d. minus liquid ......
    13e. minus liquid *Shaoxing Chinese*[22] (Zhang 2006)
                              Chru (Thurgood 1999)

What can we deduce from this? Firstly, that there are few or no languages which only allow liquids and glides in codas. Secondly, it must be stated there are few (13d)-type languages like ancient Greek. If a language allows

---

22. This language also lacks final fricatives.

fricative codas, it generally also allows stop codas. Thirdly, there are numerous languages that allow nasal codas but not liquid ones. There are also languages that allow all manners of coda except liquids. Often these do not allow fricative codas either. In other words at the word-end liquids (and fricatives) seem to occur less than they should in terms of the Sonority Sequencing Principle.

In particular the implicational relationship between (13b) and (13c) seems to lack validity. While we do find languages of type (13c) like Fante (Abakan 2005) with nasal and liquid codas rather than languages with only liquid (and semivowel) codas, we find languages with nasal (and semivowel) codas but no liquid codas. This is what we find in 18-Sranan, and presumably 17-Sranan.

I will utilize a constraint, NoOBWDCD (NoOBSTRUENTWORDCODA), with the proviso that liquids are also excluded. In the modern creole languages of Surinam, my original NOWORDCODA will apply – there are no surface nasal *codas* at all except in unassimilated loans.

2.2.2. Consonant clusters in 17-Sranan

In 17-Sranan the situation with consonant clusters appears to have been very different from what it is now. Seen in terms of syllabicity, consonant clusters in present-day Sranan are of two types,[23] onset clusters like *bro* 'blow', *ibri* 'each' (< *every*), and intervocalic (non-nasal) coda-onset clusters like *arki* 'listen' (< *hark*), *aksi* 'ask'. It appears however that in older forms of the language these sequences were not in fact clusters. In Smith (2003b) I quote various examples from the Sranan version of the 1762 Saramaccan peace treaty between the Dutch and the Saramaccan maroons, as it is presented in Arends & van den Berg (2004).[24] Examples are given in (16).

---

23. I ignore initial /s/-clusters here. Even in Sranan these could appear with epenthetic vowels until comparatively recently, and this is still the norm in all Maroon Creoles. The problems presented by nasal clusters will be dealt with in Section 3.2.
24. The discrepancy in dates is explained by the fact that I worked from a preliminary version of their paper.

(16) Sranan clusters: modern and 18th century

English[25]	modern Sranan	Sranan 1762[26]	Saramaccan
broke	broko	**bor**oko	ɓoóko
court	krutu	**cour**outoe	kuútu
self	srefi	**ser**efie	seépi
ask	aksi	ha**kis**i	(h)ákísi
better	betre	be**ter**e	ɓétɛ
master	masra	ma**sar**a	mása
cover	kibri	ki**bir**ie	---

As we can see, many clusters of both types that exist in Modern Sranan are not clusters in earlier Sranan. In Smith (2003b) I quote "new" old data suggesting that originally all the creole languages of Surinam exhibited word-internal vowel epenthesis for all bar nasal clusters (Arends & van den Berg 2004; Hoogbergen & Polimé 2000). A table modified from that article is given here. Present-day Sranan has normally dropped the word-internal epenthetic vowels due to a wide-ranging application of syncope. The maroon creoles all retain the epenthetic vowels, but modern Ndyuka and Saramaccan have lost the post-epenthetic liquids in the meantime, while Aluku and Kwinti have retained them optionally (Bilby 1983). In Smith (2003a, b), I compared the breaking-up of English liquid clusters to a similar epenthesis phenomenon in the Gbe languages. I would now consider this to be an adstrate effect.

The only cluster-type that seems to have existed in the older Surinam creoles was the nasal cluster. What kind of cluster this was in terms of syllable-division is not completely clear as the various modern creoles differ in the possibilities they allow. To take word-initial nasal clusters first, these do not exist in Sranan.

In Saramaccan only /mb, nd, ndy[27]/ exist as complex onsets in all positions, with /ng/ not occurring initially but otherwise representing a possible onset.

---

25. Here I give the English word related to the Sranan one, which is not necessarily equivalent to the present-day Sranan meaning.
26. In fact the Sranan spellings vary considerably, for instance *self* is spelt as *serefie*, but also as *selfi* and *sreffie*. However, the fact that later forms of 19th century marronized plantation Sranan such as that spoken by the Aluku Maroons have variants such as /seléfi/ confirms the epenthesized nature of the clusters in earlier Sranan.
27. This is the current spelling for [ndʒ].

Table 3. Word-internal vowel epenthesis in non-nasal consonant clusters.[28]

EME	Sranan	Sranan 1762	Aluku	Kwinti	Ndyuka	Saramaccan
dry	drey		de(l)é	de(l)é	deé	dεέ
blow	bro		bo(l)ó	boló	boó	bɔɔ́
broke	broko	b(o)roko	bo(l)óko		boóko	boóko
ground	gron		go(l)ón	golón	goon	goon
grand	gran	g(a)ran-	ga(l)án		gaán	-
glass	grasi		gaáſi H	ga(l)ási	gaási	gaási
self	srefi	s(e)reffie	se(l)éfi		seéfi	seé(p)i
		selfi	seéi			
help	yepi/lepi	yerépi (1855)[31]	ye(l)épi		yeépi	heépi
	yrepi (1856)[29]	herépi (1855)				
	repi (1798)[30]	helpie				
hark	arki/artyi				haliki	haika
court	krutu	couroetoe courtoe	kuútu H		kuútu	kuútu
water	watra		wáta H	wáta	wátáa	wáta
better	betre	betere			bétée	bétε
master	masra	masara			másáa	mása
six	siksi		sigiſi	síkísi	sikisi/sigisi	sikísí
ask	aksi	hakisi			akísi	(h)ákísi

28. The Aluku data is from Bilby (1993), except words marked H, which are from Hurault (1983). The Kwinti data is from Huttar (1983) and Smith & Huttar (1984). The Ndyuka data is from Huttar (1972) and Huttar & Huttar (1972, 1994). The Saramaccan data is from Donicie & Voorhoeve (1963), Huttar (1972), and De Groot (1977).

29. 1856 = Wullschlägel (1856)

30. 1798 = Weygandt (1798). Here we find the first attempt at simplification of the awkward cluster *yr*-.

31. 1855 = Focke (1855). I give these examples here because they illustrate epenthesized clusters, and represent the same pattern illustrated in the 1762 treaty.

Other nasal clusters are described differently. Either a nasal coda, homorganic with the following (onset) consonant, is postulated (Rountree 1972), or as in Voorhoeve (1959) and McWhorter & Good (2012), a nasalized vowel preceding the same onset consonant. McWhorter & Good do not discuss the question of underlying and surface phonology, but they do allow for pronunciations such as [nt, mp, ŋk], with a syllable division between the two consonants, "when words are carefully articulated." Vinije (2011) often gives alternate pronunciations. I will assume an underlying cluster in such cases.

In Ndyuka nasals in initial "clusters" are always syllabic, so that the nasal forms a separate syllable nucleus (Huttar & Huttar 1994). Presumably as a consequence of this, the restrictions are fewer (Section 3.2).

In Sranan medial nasal clusters are always split up between syllables with the nasal as coda, and whatever follows as onset. In Ndyuka the pattern is the same word-internally (Huttar & Huttar 1972, 1984).

Summing up, the fact that both Kikongo and the Eastern Gbe langages only allow open syllables, and also the survival of a part of the onset nasal clusters in Saramaccan, suggested that the most likely situation in 17-Sranan was the same – only open syllables. However, as we have already seen in previous chapters I now regard this as less clear. It is quite possible that Saramaccan has come to display adstratal influence from Kikongo and Fongbe that did not have the same effect on Ndyuka, for instance. The Ndyuka treatment of the initial nasals in nasal clusters may well reflect a more successful strategy, in the sense that nasal clusters with voiceless obstruents could also be accommodated.

2.2.3. Non-final and final vowel nuclei

Yet another difference in terms of syllable structure between Standard English and 18th century Sranan, on the one hand, and our posited 17-Sranan is that the Sranan vowels developed from original closed syllable cases in *English* are all *monomoraic*[32]. I will avoid the complex problem of trying to describe the difference between tense and lax vowels in English by assuming that the difference is one between dimoraic and monomoraic vowels. This is probably the way the speakers of the main African substrate/adstrate languages perceived them anyway, so that this approach is fairly unprob-

---

32. Except for one exceptional case *aiti* 'eight'. I will ignore this case here.

lematic. For instance, this is the way they are generally reinterpreted in Jamaican Creole.

I will assume that vowel length is a marked phenomenon in the languages of the world. Many languages, such as Mandarin Chinese, lack a phonemic (underlying) length contrast in their vowel systems. I will translate this into the constraint NOLONGVOWEL, which is then applicable to Chinese, Spanish, and other languages, but not to Standard English nor to Jamaican. The relevant Faithfulness constraint is MAX-μ.

The definitions of the constraints are as follows:

(17) a. [Faithfulness] MAX-μ: "Maximize" the input morae[33] in the output. That is, any mora present in the input must also be present in the output. That is: if there are two morae in the input there should be two morae in the output.
b. [Markedness] NOLONGVOWEL: vowels with two identical morae are not allowed. A more formal definition would be $*\mu_i\mu_i$.

Let us look again at tableaux for the two languages:

First English:

Tableau 5. NOLONGVOWEL in English

/liiv/	MAX-μ	NOLONGVOWEL
☞ liiv		*
liv	*!	

And then 17-Sranan:

Tableau 6. NOLONGVOWEL in 17-Sranan

/liiv/	NOLONGVOWEL	MAX-μ
liibi	*!	
☞ libi		*

Once again, we can summarize these two tableaux as:

---

33. A mora is a length-unit applicable to vowels (sometimes including coda consonants). A short vowel can generally be equated with one mora, and a long vowel with two morae.

Tableau 7. NoLongVowel in English and 17-Sranan

Constraint Language	NoLongVowel < Max-μ >	
English		Lower-ranked
17-Sranan	**Higher-ranked**	

Let us now turn to a consideration of English diphthongs. We see from Table 3 that English diphthongs followed by coda consonants are consistently reduced or coalesced to single vowels in the records of Sranan.

Table 4. Diphthongs before English coda consonant

English spelling	Sranan	EME	Current English
house	oso	həus > haus	haus
fight	feti	fəit > fait	fait

Does this also apply when diphthongs are final? The answer is no. In this respect, English diphthongs differ from English final monophthongs, which are always realised short (i.e. monomoraically) in Sranan. Cf. *si* 'see', *go* 'go'.

Two pairs of final reflexes appear in Sranan for the dipthongs derived from Middle English /iː, uː/, /ai, ei/ and /au, ou/. /əi/ was in the process of lowering to /ai/ in the mid-17th century, as was /əu/ to /au/. The development paths [iː > əi > ai] and [uː > əu > au] seem to be obvious pathways phonetically. The English encountered by the slaves in Surinam was by no means uniform, and we can assume that insofar as some kind of koiné standard was spoken that this would also exhibit variation. I assume, with (Dobson 1957) that in the relevant period there was variation [əi ~ ai] and [əu ~ au], in Surinam just as there was in London at the time.

I assume a correspondence between /ai, au/ in Early Modern English and /ai, au/ in Sranan, and between /əi, əu/ in Early Modern English and /ei, ou/ in Sranan. This would seem to offer the simplest solution.

Table 5. Diphthongs in word-final position

English spelling	Sranan	EME	Current English
eye	ai	əi > **ai**[34]	ai
cry	krei	**krəi** > krai	krai
cow	kau	kəu > **kau**	kau
now	nou	**nəu** > nau	nau

---

34. The bold type indicates what I assume to have been the direct source for the Sranan reflex.

Here in the Early Modern English column the variant that probably gives rise to the Sranan form is indicated with bold type (see Smith 1987). A differential treatment of diphthongs according to position such as that we see here is of course not unheard of. Consider Latin alternations of the type:

(18) Latin diphthongal alternations
 plaud-ere 'to clap the hands' ex-plood-ere 'drive out by clapping'
 kaed-ere 'to cut' ex-kiid-ere 'to cut out'
 poen-a 'penalty' im-puun-itas 'impunity'

These alternations are explained in terms of the position of the main stress in Pre-Classical Latin, which, unlike Classical Latin, was assumed to have initial stress, and which preserved the diphthongal nature of the nucleus in the strongest syllable. In this case, however, the resulting monophthong was still dimoraic.

I will illustrate these various cases with tableaux for the three conditions: 1) the closed diphthong case; 2) the open diphthong case; and also, for completeness, 3) the open (long) vowel case. We will require some additional constraints to account for all three conditions. I will describe the new constraints that are required while recapping those previously mentioned.

(19) NOOBSTRUENTWORDCODA(NOOBWDCD) [Markedness constraint]
 No word-final obstruents (i.e. stops or fricatives) are allowed (in the output). This will not prevent semi-vowels appearing in coda-position, or (importantly) nasals. Liquids will be excluded, conceivably by a separate constraint.
 NOUNBALTROCHEE (NOUNBALT)[35] [Markedness constraint]
 This restricts trochaic feet to two morae in length. A mora is a weight element in a foot. A heavy syllable contains two morae, and a light syllable contains one mora.
 NOLONGVOWEL (NOLONGV) [Markedness constraint]
 No long vowels are allowed (in the output).

---

35. I will restrict myself here to stating that there is strong preference for *balanced trochees*, and unbalanced iambs in stress systems. This has been termed the *iambic-trochaic law* by Hayes (1985). Unbalanced trochees have a dimoraic accented syllable followed by a monomoraic unaccented syllable.

INTEGRITY (INT)   [Faithfulness constraint]
   No element of the input has multiple correspondents in the output (McCarthy & Prince 1995). No diphthongization of underlying monophthongs is allowed.
NODIPHTHONG (NODIPHTH)   [Markedness constraint]
   No diphthongs are allowed.
MAX-MORA (MAX-μ)   [Faithfulness constraint]
   "Maximize" the mora-input in the output. All vocalic morae in the input must be present in the output.
UNIFORMITY   [Faithfulness constraint]
   No element of the output has multiple correspondents in the input (McCarthy & Prince 1995). So underlying diphthongal structures will not be monophthongized.
DEP(IO)   [Faithfulness constraint]
   The output is "dependent" on the input. All phonological material in the output must be present in the input, i.e. no deleted material is allowed. Here this refers to anaptyctic vowels.

In what follows I include several lower-ranked constraints which are apparently not here required for the selection of the best output (optimal candidates). However, in sections 4 and 5, where I deal with three other creole languages, and compare them to each other in an attempt to get closer to what I consider to be the original form of the ancestor of the Atlantic creole languages, it is useful to be able to compare the rankings of various pairs of constraints which would differ from English.

First, I look more closely at the closed diphthong case. The brackets on the candidates in the tableau given above indicate their foot-structure. Syllables and feet are assigned by GEN to the output. I indicate a possible difference in syllabification with the notations /ai/ and /ay/. I will adopt the convention that /ai/ indicates a true diphthong, where GEN has assigned both vocalic segments to the nucleus. /ay/ indicates a non-diphthong, where GEN has put the /a/ in the nucleus, and the other vocalic segment in the coda, giving a so-called semi-vowel /y/. In other words:

(20)   /ai, au, oi, ei, ou/ etc.
       – are dipthongs
       – form a dimoraic nucleus
       /ay, aw, oy, ey, ow/ etc.
       – are vowel-semivowel sequences
       – have a monomoraic nucleus + semivowel coda

Tableau 8. Word-final closed diphthong (English > 17-Sranan)

/fait/	NoObWdCd	NoUnBalt	Integrity, NoLongV	NoDiphth	Max-μ	Uniformity	Dep(IO)
(fait)	*!			*			
(faiti)		*!		*!			*
☞ (feti)					*	*	*
(feeti)		*!	*			*	*
(fet)	*!				*	*	
(fayti)		*!					
(fayt)	*!						

While this turns out not to make a difference in the forms considered in Tableau 8, as all the forms with /ai/ or /ay/ are dispreferred, it does make a difference in Tableau 9.

The asterisks in the tableaux mark violations of constraints as we have seen above. The crucial violations, those that actually disqualify potential candidates, are indicated with an exclamation mark. These are referred to as *fatal violations* in Optimality Theory practice. Where I have put two constraints in the same column – indicating that they are not crucially ranked the same – I indicate violations with the initial letter of the relevant constraint. At the same time it must be said that I do not assume that all adjacent pairs of constraints necessarily represent crucial rankings. Tableau 8 is a compromise between readability and comprehensibility.

In the tableau, the highest-ranked constraint is indicated at the top of the second column, and the lower-ranked constraints are situated in order of importance to the right. The first, and thus most important constraint here, is the NoObstruentWordCoda constraint. This gets rid of the first, fifth and last candidate outputs.

The second constraint, NoUnbalancedTrochee, restricts (moraic) trochees to two morae in length. The second, fourth and sixth candidates contain three morae.

Now there is only one candidate left. This is the optimal (best) output. The remaining constraint-columns in the tableau are greyed, to indicate that any constraint violations indicated in these columns are irrelevant, as the choice of optimal output has already been made. Some of these constraint-columns may however be relevant in other cases. See the cases dealt with in Tableaux 9 and 10. And, as I have said above, some of these constraints become relevant, when they are more highly ranked in another language, such as English in our case, enabling them to play a crucial contrasting role in terms of typological comparisons. Note also that the best output may in fact have more constraint violations than failed outputs. This is because more important aspects of the phonology are represented by higher-ranked constraints. Lower-ranked constraints do not necessarily play any role at all in the choice of the optimal output.

The next constraint down, NoLongVowel, removes any candidate with a long (dimoraic) vowel. This disqualifies the fourth candidate output, which has a long vowel instead of the underlying dipthong. I have not here considered yet another possible output /*feet/, which would be disqualified by the same constraint.

Ranked the same as NoLongVowel is another constraint, Integrity, which forbids any element of the input from having multiple correspondents in the output, i.e. forbids diphthongization. This is not relevant here, but as we will see below, it will be required in another tableau.

The fifth constraint is NODIPHTHONG, which speaks for itself. This disqualifies the first two candidates.

The sixth constraint, MAX-MORA (MAX-μ), as we have already seen, demands the retention of all underlying morae of a lexical entry. The forms that violate this constraint (without crucial effect), the third and fifth candidate outputs, have one less mora than the input.

The next constraint down is UNIFORMITY, which forbids any single element of the output from having multiple corresponding elements in the input.

The last constraint is DEP(IO), which forbids the addition/insertion of material not present in the input. Any candidate with an anaptyctic vowel violates this constraint. Although of course, the high ranking of NOCONSONANTALWORDCODA *requires* the presence of an anaptyctic vowel in an optimal candidate.

Note the top-to-bottom order (on the left-hand side) in which the candidates are presented in the tableau is irrelevant.

Turning now to the "open diphthong" case illustrated by the Sranan form /kau/ in Tableau 9, it turns out that a form with /a/ as the nucleus and /w/ as the coda is preferred over the output candidate with the segmentally identical but syllabically different /au/ nucleus.

NOLONGVOWEL operates here to block the second candidate because of its long vowel. The NODIPHTHONG constraint blocks the choice of the true diphthong in the fourth candidate. The failure to realise (maximize) both morae of the input is fatal for the third candidate. The first candidate with a single /a/ in the nucleus, and the semi-vowel /w/ in the coda, therefore wins the day.

Finally, in the light of this last example, I have to look at the case involving the incorporation of EModE open (long) vowels in 17-Sranan. Here the vowel *is* shortened, in accordance with NOLONGVOWEL, as we see in Tableau 10.

The discussion of the first two candidates is simple. Although the second candidate has undergone no changes between input and output, it violates the highly-ranked constraint against long vowels. The first, and preferred, candidate only violates the lower-ranked MAX-μ.

Tableau 9. Word-final open diphthong (17-Sranan)

/kau/	NoOBWdCd	NoUnBalt	Integrity, NoLongV	NoDiphth	Max-μ	Uniformity	Dep(IO)
☞ (kaɷ)							
(koo)			L!			*	
(ko)					*!	**	
(kau)				*!			

Tableau 10. Word-final long vowel (17-Sranan)

/goo/	NoOBWdCd	NoUnBalt	Integrity,[36] NoLongV	NoDiphth	Max-μ	Uniformity	Dep(IO)
☞ (go)					*		
(goo)			L!				
(gau)			I!	*			
(gaw)			I!				

36. The capital letters here indicate which of the equally ranked candidates is violated.

With respect to the third candidate, [gau]³⁷, here there has been no internal assimilation or coalescence of a diphthong, rather the opposite. Here INTEGRITY blocks the fission of a monophthong. This is also applicable to the fourth candidate.

In the next section, I will discuss various types of apparent clusters, which might seem to pose a problem for our picture of early Sranan. In fact, it seems probable that the only clusters were onset clusters involving nasals, as I will tentatively conclude.

I will now examine the influence of the two main African languages in Surinam, Fongbe and Kikongo.³⁸ In previous work, I had assumed these to be substrate languages for the Surinam creoles. In preceding chapters, I have stated a different opinion: that the influence from these languages must be adstratal in nature, because of new data on the slave trade. I will continue to treat their influence as adstratal and return to the question of possible substrates at the end of the chapter.

3. Fongbe as the main African adstrate language in Surinam (and a wee bit of Kikongo).

That Fongbe is a language that has influenced the creole languages of Surinam is a position which seems to be supported by a lot of evidence. Although we can no longer assume that it is a substrate language for Surinam (see section 3.4), there are still extensive signs of influence from Fongbe (and/or other Eastern Gbe languages) in the Surinam Creoles. Kikongo has been of lesser importance, but has still also left some traces of influence.

Aboh (2006b) has demonstrated that specificity features in Sranan and Saramaccan noun phrases follow the patterns which pertain in the Gbe languages (including Fongbe); there are numerous lexical items from Fongbe in the Surinam Creoles, Saramaccan in particular, but also to a lesser extent in Sranan (see Smith, this volume, on Gbe lexical influence on the Surinam Creoles); phonological vowel epenthesis in liquid clusters (also formerly present in Sranan) has been related as I have stated (Smith 2003a, b) to a

---

37. The spelling *gaeu*, occurring in Herlein (1718) for "go", is probably modelled on the French spelling convention *eau* [o]. "Below" is also spelt *bie laeu*. Similarly we find *trou* for "true" [tru].
38. Schuchardt (1914) gives a dozen etymologies, or possible etymologies from Kikongo, and half a dozen from Ewe (Gbe). As far as West Africa was concerned he apparently had more access to sources on Twi/Akan, less prominent in the Surinam Creole lexica.

similar (phonetic) process in the Gbe languages; and non-iconic reduplication is used in both to form adjectives, to name but four cases (Adamson & Smith 2003; Aboh & Smith 2012, this volume on Non-iconic reduplications).

Let us turn now to a consideration of Fongbe vocalic structures. Most morphemes in Fongbe have short vowels; none have codas.[39] Examples of such morphemes would be the following:

(21) Typical Fongbe morphemes
 dɛ̀ 'saliva'   dɛn 'sweat'[dɛ̃]

Most morphemes are either monosyllabic, like the above two, or, and this applies only to some classes of nouns, have a vowel-prefix. Although this is presumably a remnant of the Niger-Congo noun-class system, it does not display the usual differences of prefix for singulars and plurals frequently found in that family. There are between 2 and 4 classes in different Gbe languages. Examples of such prefixed nouns include the following two:

(22) Fongbe nouns with "class" prefixes
 à-ɖí 'soap'   à-ɖì 'truth'

The initial vowels can still be assigned a marginal morphemic (but meaningless) status in Fongbe, in that they can be omitted under certain grammatical circumstances, such as in compounding.

Rare morphemes have a long vowel. These are truly exceptional, and the vowel is always (morpheme-)final, as in (23).

(23) Fongbe words with long vowels
 dàá 'father'   à-tɔ́ɔ́n 'five'   [atɔ̃́ɔ̃́]

In Fongbe, dimorphemic long vowels and diphthongs may be created by combining lexical stems with suffixes or post-clitics consisting of a single vowel, as in (24).

---

39. I will use the standard orthography for Gbe language segmental phonology. Vowel nasality is represented by writing the latter *n* after a vowel in what appears to be a "coda" position. Similar spelling conventions are used in the orthographies of the Surinam Creoles.

(24) Derived long vowels and diphthongs in Fongbe
   kɛ̀ + è > kɛ̀ɛ̀   'open it'
   tò + è > tòè   'arrange it'

Although, as observed above, morphemes are generally monosyllabic in Fongbe, words are often polysyllabic due to the frequent use of compounding. Due to the extreme rarity of long vowels in monomorphemic structures, very few long vowels occur in compound structures. And since suffixes and postclitics are word-final, most long vowels and diphthongs resulting from morpheme-concatenation will be surface word-final.

A comparison of these Fongbe patterns with what we have seen in Sranan words of older (i.e. English) origin so far reveals that there is a great deal of agreement in the patterns observed. The exception concerns the rare long vowels in Fongbe, found particularly in final position. A preliminary comparison of Sranan and Fongbe morphological structures reveals that the most useful comparison is between the shapes of Sranan *morphemes*[40] and Fongbe *words*. There is a difference in morphological structure, then, but the phonology is very similar.

3.1. Interactions of Fongbe and Kikongo speakers

After the early 1680s the dominant linguistic element in the slave population of Surinam was apparently Fongbe (or closely related languages).[41] This situation lasted until the mid-1720s, and tailed off during the 1730s. But we must also ask the question how most of the other half of the imported post-1670 slave population in Surinam, that was not of Fongbe origin, but consisted largely of Kikongo-speakers from Central Africa (untill about 1700), would have interpreted Fongbe phonological structures. We must assume at least some superficial knowledge of each other's languages on the part of both major groups of slaves.[42] In particular, some familiarity with the surface sound-structures – to take the most superficial linguistic

---

40. Although in both Sranan and Saramaccan phonological words with phonetically long final vowels can occur due to the concatenation of final vowels and postclitics – in a similar fashion to Fongbe.
41. I am assuming that the majority of slaves hailing from a particular region represent ethnic groups closer to the slave-ports rather than those at greater distances from them. It is known that the slave trade spread its tentacles far afield, but I believe this is a fairly safe assumption.
42. At least in terms of general phonetic shapes.

aspect, as these differed in quite a striking fashion. For instance the usual structures for nouns differ drastically, and the speakers of the two main language(-block)s could not but be aware of this:

(25) Prototypical shapes of nouns in Fongbe and Kikongo
Fongbe: (V)-CV(~)   (~) = vowels can be nasal
Kikongo: CV/N-CV(V)(N)CV

The exceptional and minority patterns in Fongbe would tend to escape the notice of non-Fongbe speakers. Major differences exist between final and non-final syllables in the two languages – I only consider non-analysable words here:

(26) Some general aspects of simple Fongbe and Kikongo words
Fongbe-final   Fongbe-non-final   Kikongo-final   Kikongo-non-final
± nasalization   no nasal vowel   no nasal rhyme   ± nasal cluster
± long vowel[43] short vowel   short vowel   ± long vowel

We can already see from these phonological aspects, that to a large extent, the Fongbe and Kikongo aspects of nasality are in complementary distribution. The final possibilities of Fongbe are equivalent in some sense to the non-final possibilities of Kikongo, and vice versa.

3.2. Nasality patterns in the Surinam Creole African adstrate languages

In support of this statement of prevalent patterns of nasal demarcation, I will mention here some Fongbe and Kikongo lexical items containing various nasal aspects that have shifted this nasality backwards or forwards in the word, becoming as it were, more typical of the other African adstrate.

For example, consider the word 'elephant', which occurs in all three creole languages in Surinam, Sranan, Saramaccan, and Ndyuka. This is a Bantu word, Kikongo /nzawu/. In Ndyuka, where initial sequences of syllabic nasal and fricative are allowed, we find /n.saw ~ n.zaw/.[44] In the other two languages this is a forbidden structure – in Sranan the corresponding word is /a.saw/.[45] More interesting is Saramaccan, which doesn't allow na-

---

43. Including final suffixes and post-clitics.
44. The dot indicates a syllable boundary.
45. There are parallels for the reinterpretation of #nC- as #aC-.

sal-fricative sequences initially but attempts to preserve the nasality of the morpheme in the only way feasible, by shifting it to the right. The automatic result is a nasalized diphthong – /zaũ/.[46] So the preservation of nasality in Saramaccan has resulted in a change from a Kikongo-like structure to a Fongbe-like structure. The high ranking of a constraint forbidding nasal-fricative sequences (NONASFRIC) in Saramaccan will ensure that any way of preserving nasality – and there is only one possibility due to the monosyllabicity of the form[47] – will result in an optimal form.

We also have examples of rare *disyllabic* Fongbe nouns like /de.gɔ̃/ 'shrimp'. This is a type of structure that seems to be avoided in Saramaccan – a disyllabic word with a final nasalized vowel. Because it is disyllabic, the final nasality can be shifted to the left, to the syllable onset. The result is Saramaccan /a.di.ngɔ/,[48] a Kikongo-like structure, with a nasal cluster instead of a final nasalized vowel in a disyllabic word-form. Note that the nasality remains in the second syllable, because /ng/ can occur syllable-initially.

For a Sranan example, compare the Fongbe form /a.ʤi.ʤã/ 'hedgehog'. The Sranan form is /dyin.dya.ma.ká/ where /maká/ means 'thorn', and the whole word means 'porcupine' The syllable-division is between the elements of the nasal cluster. In Saramaccan, the word is /a.dyi.ndyá/, because once again /ndy/ is allowed as a complex onset in this language. Here we recognize a Kikongo-type structure again.

A Fongbe compound with two nasalized vowels in succession is /xɔ̃-tɔ̃/ 'friend'. In Saramaccan, this word appears in the form /hɔn.tɔ ~ hɔ̃.tɔ/ 'have a good relation with' (Donicie & Voorhoeve 1963). Here we have a nasal cluster in intervocalic position – reminiscent of Kikongo, although the syllabification is basically English. Because this word has moved out of the category of Fongbe words, it cannot have an underlying final nasal vowel, which is a Fongbe feature. The nasalization is dropped – because the first syllable has a nasal vowel already. Although they are possible in Kikongo, clusters of nasals + *voiceless* stops are (not previously?) forbidden in onsets in Saramaccan. The only possible route to salvation at present is then the English one, with an intervocalic coda-onset cluster (or a nasalized vowel). As I will discuss below, however, I hypothesize that the original Saramaccan structure might have been /hɔ.ntɔ/. I give a summary of these in (27).

---

46. Note that the disyllabic /awu/ is converted into a dipththong due to a restriction on sequences /wu/ in Saramaccan.
47. All three languages reduce the Kikongo post-fricative portion of this word to a monosyllable.
48. The *a-* is presumably a noun-prefix from another Gbe language in this case.

(27) Interchanges between Fongbe- and Kikongo-type structures

Fongbe	Kikongo	Sranan	Ndyuka	Saramaccan
-	nzawu	asaw	nzau K	zã ũ F
degɔ̃	-	-	-	adingo K
adʒidʒã	-	dyindya K	dyindya K	adyindyá K
xɔ̃tɔ̃	-	-	-	hɔntɔ K

It is possible to view such influences as joint adstrate features. There does appear to be a fairly strict demarcation line between the Kikongo-type "nasality" and Fongbe-type "nasality" here. These two languages contrast in what they allow in non-final position. Fongbe allows nasalized vowels in non-final morphemes, but not non-finally within *morphemes*, phonologically at least. This means that vowel-nasalization occurs proportionately less in non-final position than in final position. In Kikongo, pre-consonantal nasals occur frequently. These assimilate to the following consonant in the permitted biconsonantal onset clusters. These pre-consonantal nasals are non-syllabic, and belong to the same syllable as the following consonant. So Ndibu (Kikongo dialect) *mbúlu* 'hairless part on side of forehead' (Daeleman 1972) is syllabified *mbú.lu*. Ntandu[49] (Kikongo dialect) *mbuungi* 'mildew' is syllabified *mbuu.ngi*. According to Rountree (1972) Saramaccan displays the same patterns with nasal clusters /mb, nd, ndʒ/ initially and /mb, nd, ndʒ, ng/ word-internally, but not with other nasal clusters, which also only occur word-internally (see remarks above). Present-day Kikongo has, in addition to initial nasal clusters, syllabic (prefixial) nasals initially (like Ndyuka), but these are not relevant for the period (the 17th century) that concerns us, since at that time these syllabic nasals were represented by the prefixes *mu-* and *mi-*. In other words syllabic nasals did not yet occur in Kikongo.

In Sranan, the syllable division proceeds as in English (or Dutch), and there are no nasal clusters word-initially.

Another difference between Sranan and Saramaccan is that Voorhoeve describes word-final nasality as being realised in Sranan by a nasalized vowel followed by a brief velar nasal, [Ṽŋ], whereas Rountree (1972) describes final nasality in Saramaccan in terms of either a nasalized vowel [Ṽ], or a nasalized vowel followed by a brief velar nasal, [Ṽŋ]. This is not of phonological significance, however, and can be regarded as allophonic realisations of a final nasalized vowel. I will assume the possible relevance of

---

49. (Ki-)Ntandu is the Kikongo dialect that displays (so far) the greatest lexical resemblance to the Surinam Creoles, especially Saramaccan.

a constraint at the phonetic level similar to the nasal coda condition (NASCODACOND) proposed by Bakovic (2001). This is a condition against specifying place in nasal codas, resulting in place assimilation word-internally (in association with an assimilation-favouring AGREE[PLACE]), and compelling a debuccalized nasal "glide"[50] in final position. Taking the differences in syllabification into account, this would seem to be applicable also to Saramaccan and Sranan in general.

The nasality in word-final position should not really be regarded as a proper coda consonant. The common factor is the assimilatory relationship that non-final nasals have with their suppliers of place, and the nasal feature that is either assigned to final vowels, or appears as final nasal glide is one of dependency.[51] However, some further thinking is required on this issue.
Summing up on all four languages and comparing them with English we can identify the following aspects of *dependent* nasal behaviour (shading indicates similarities):

Table 6. Types of dependent nasality in early Surinam contact languages

Language	Nasal Word Coda	Dependent nasality in final rhyme	Dependent nasality preceeding final rhyme	
			voiceless stop	voiced stop
Fongbe	no	nasal vowel	no	no
Kikongo	no	no	onset cluster	onset cluster
Saramaccan	no (possible earlier?)	nasal vowel ($\pm$ ŋ)	coda nasal + stop ~ (nasal vowel + stop)	onset cluster
Sranan	no (possible earlier?)	nasal vowel ($\pm$ ŋ)	coda nasal + stop	coda nasal + stop
English	possible	no	coda nasal + stop	coda nasal + stop

I will briefly illustrate the kinds of dependent nasality I refer to here. I give first the model of syllable structure I assume here, basically following Levin (Blevins) (1987):

---

50. This can take various forms depending on the language, including a velar nasal or a nasalized velar semi-vowel.
51. In terms of Dependency Phonology segmental representations.

(28) An X-bar model of syllable structure

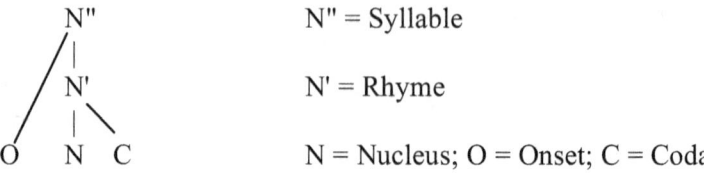

N" = Syllable

N' = Rhyme

N = Nucleus; O = Onset; C = Coda

This represents the headship relationships, and their dependencies, better than in the traditional Onset-Nucleus-Coda model. The two models are of course homomorphic.

I will first illustrate the three types of Dependent Nasality in the final rhyme listed in Table 6

(29) Dependent nasality in final rhyme

a. nasal vowel   b. nasal vowel + nasal glide

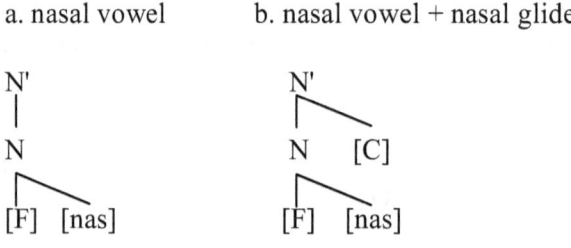

The Head and Dependency relationships are indicated by the vertical and slanted lines respectively.

Both types occur as surface reflexes (outputs) of a single underlying form in Saramaccan, e.g. the rhyme portion *an* of the word *fan* 'talk'. The square brackets around the coda [C] indicate that this element – a so-called "nasal glide" is purely a phonetic output entity – absent in the underlying form. The nasal feature ([nas] for the convenience of the reader) is dependent in each of the three cases. In (29a) it is a dependent feature of the V(owel). [F] stands for the Place features of the vowel which are in a Headship relation to the Dependent nasality. In (29b), to deal with the next simplest structure first, the nasal feature is a dependent of the rhyme (N') in coda position, which is "compelled" in Bakovic's words, as a debuccalized nasal "glide" in the output. Ndyuka is described as being largely the same as Sranan (Huttar & Huttar 1994: 548).

Now I turn to the Onset Cluster type of dependent nasality found in Saramaccan with word-internal post-nasal voiced, but not voiceless, stops.

Here the nasal is once again in a dependent situation. The place features are always the same as the following stop. In this, they exhibit the same place assimilation dependency as we see with the voiceless stop clusters I will deal with next. We can represent this as follows:

(30)   Dependent nasality in onset cluster

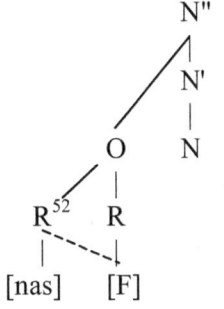

Note that the debate involving nasal clusters as against "prenasalized stops" in such cases becomes irrelevant if representations like those in (30) are employed. In fact we have both configurations at once. It is undeniably the case that sequencing of Roots (place-holders) is required in such cases, as post-nasalized onsets also exist – and give rise to the same debate as to cluster versus segment status. It would appear then that this type of representation is required in any case, as the claimed examples of languages exhibiting singleton pre-nasalized stops in contrast with nasal-stop clusters are hard to substantiate. The clear cases, like Kikongo, where initial nasals in such structures involve separate sequential morphemes, also become easier to represent in morphological terms. At any rate, the nasal acquires its place features from the following (sub-)root, and has to be regarded as dependent (in the cluster).

I now turn to the third type, where the nasal is in coda position and the following stop is in onset position. This has a more traditional representation, as I show in (31). Here the dependency is less obvious. However, it is clear that onsets have primacy over codas. This is made clear by the different status of the constraints governing the status of these two types – ONSET, requiring the presence of an onset, and NOCODA, requiring the absence of a coda. In addition the nasal once again derives its place features from the following stop.

---

52. The R here stands for Root, and is a means of representing complex Onsets, Nuclei, and Codas. It is no more than a place-holder.

(31) Dependent nasal codas

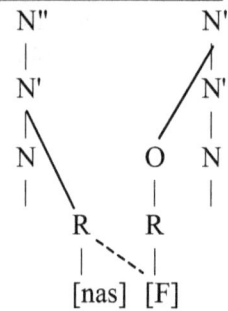

Note that while these two types, the voiced variant (30) and the voiceless variant (31), contrast in their syllabicity in present-day Saramaccan, there has been a historical drift occurring in the direction of voicing between the two types.

3.3. Drift towards Nasal Cluster Voicing (NCV)

Nasal Cluster Voicing has frequently, though by no means always, occurred in Saramaccan. It has also occurred in the other Surinam Creoles, though no two creoles exhibit identical application of the process. This has occurred apparently without ramifications for syllable structure outside of Saramaccan. However, it must be admitted that we have no way of knowing what the exact structure of syllables was like two or three hundred years ago. The only thing we can say with certainty is that /mb, nd, ndʒ, ng/ are syllable-initial in present Kikongo, as are all other nasal clusters in that language, and are also syllable-initial in present Saramaccan, to the exclusion of other nasal clusters. Thus it would seem not unreasonable to assume that this was also applicable to the intervening periods since the first language influenced the second more than 300 years ago. And that 17-Sranan, the earliest creole on Surinam soil, might also have had only onset nasal clusters.

I provide an overview below of cases where NCV has applied in one or more of the languages, based on the original colonial language forms. These represent more than half of the potential cases of NCV in words of English and Portuguese origin. Bold type indicates where NCV has applied, or the further phase of voiced stop deletion. The occurrence of grey cells in the Saramaccan columns indicates where we have Nasal Cluster Voicing within the available historical data for this language.

Table 7a. /mp/ > /mb/

English/ Portuguese	Saramaccan 1778	Saramaccan modern	Sranan 1783	Sranan 1855	Sranan modern	Ndyuka	Aluku
jump	djo**mb**o	dyó**mb**o[53]	djompo	djómpo / djó**mb**o	dyómpo	dyó**mb**o	dyómpo H
limpar	li**mb**a	li**mb**á	-	-	-	-	-
limpo	li**mb**o	li**mb**o	-	-	-	-	-
sempre	-	sémpe- sé**mb**e-	-	-	-	-	-

53. Note that in the orthographies current in Surinam, *ty, dy, ny* represent /tʃ, dʒ, ɲ/.

Table 7b. /nt/ > /nd/ (> /n/)

English/Portuguese	Saramaccan 1778	Saramaccan modern	Sranan 1783	Sranan 1855	Sranan modern	Ndyuka	Aluku
want	-	-	wanni	wánni	wáni	wáni	wáni H
hunt	hondi	hóndi	hondi	hónti	ónti	hónti	
paint	pindeh	pendé	penni / pendi	péni	péni	pénde	peni H
plant	-	paandí	planti	plánni	práni	paándi	paandi H
gentle	gendri	dyéndɛ	gendri	géndri	géndri	dyéndée	
country	contri	kɔ́ndɛ	kondre	kóndre	kóndri	kóndée	
cant (tilt)	kanti	kándi	kanti	kanti	kánti	kándi	kanti H
something	sondi	sondí	sanni	sanì	sáni	sáni	sani H
	sani	soní					
cantar	canta	kandá	-	-	-	-	-
conta	kónda	kónda	-	-	-	-	-
contar	condá	kondá	-	-	-	-	-
entrar	dindra	dendá	-	-	-	-	-
dentro	dindru	déndu	-	-	-	-	-
garganta	grangánda	(gangáa)	-	-	-	-	-
quente	kéndi	kéndi	-	-	-	-	-
quentar		kendé	-	-	-	-	-
mentir		mindí	-	-	-	-	-
juntar	sundà suntá	zuntá	-	-	-	-	-
junto	sundu suntu	zúntu	-	-	-	-	-

Table 7c. /ntʃ/ > /ndʒ/ (> /ɲ/) (and back formations /nk/ > /ng/ (> /ŋ/))

English/Portuguese	Saramaccan 1778	Saramaccan modern	Sranan 1783	Sranan 1855	Sranan modern	Ndyuka	Aluku
pinch[34]		píndya	pinji	piengie[55]	piñi	píngi	-
wench	wenje woenje	wɛ́ndyɛ	wendje	wéntje	wɛ́nke wɛ́ntye	piñi	-
bunch	bondji	bóngi	-	-	-	-	-
manchar		mandyá	-	-	-	-	-

54. "ch" represented /tʃ/ in in older forms of Standard English.
55. *ie* is Dutch orthography for [i].

Table 7d. /nk/ > /ng/ (> /ŋ/).

English/ Portuguese	Saramaccan			Sranan			Ndyuka	Aluku
	1778	1783	modern	1855	modern			
monkey	-	-	-	monki-mónki	monki-mónki		móngi	monki H
drink	dri**ng**i	dri**ng**i	dii**ng**i	drié**ng**i	driŋi		dií**ng**i	di(l)í**ng**i
drunk	dru**ng**u	dru**ng**u	dɔ́ɔ**ng**ɔ	dróe**ng**oe[56]	drúŋu		duú**ng**u	du(l)ú**ng**u
stink	ti**ng**i	ti**ng**i	tí**ng**i	tíe**ng**i	tíŋi		tí**ng**i	ti**ng**i H
sink	si**nk**i	-	sí**ng**i	-	-		-	-
sunk	-	su**ng**u	-	sóe**ng**oe	suŋu		sú**ng**u	sú**ng**u H
think	ti**ng**a	-	tí**ng**a	-	-		-	-
thankee	ta**ng**i	ta**ng**i	ta**ng**í	ta**ng**ì	taŋí		ta**ng**í	ta**ng**i H
hankercher[57]	ha**ng**isa	ha**ng**issa	háng**í**sa	ha**ng**ísa	aŋísa		a**ng**isa	-
fincar	fi**ng**a	-	fi**ng**á	-	-		-	-
roncar	lu**ng**à	-	lonká[58]	-	-		-	-

56. *oe* is the Dutch orthography for [u].
57. A dialect form of *handkerchief*.
58. This apparent reversal of post-nasal voicing must be interpreted as meaning that 18th century Saramaccan possessed both variants, and that apparently only the voiceless variant has survived.

Note that Sranan forms like *santje*,[59] *zanti, santi* 'something', *wantje*,[60] *wanti, wandi* 'want', *contreman, contriman* 'countryman', and *contre* 'country' occur in older documents up till the 1760s (Schuchardt 1914; Voorhoeve & Lichtveld 1975; Smith 1987; Arends & Perl 1995; van den Berg 2000).

At some point between then and the 20th century, /ng/ ([ŋg]) was simplified to /ŋ/. A parallel change affected /ndy/ (> /ɲ/) and many cases of /nd/ (> /n/).

What are we to make of these replacements of voiceless post-nasal stop clusters by voiced post-nasal clusters? A recent theoretical account of post-nasal voicing is Botma (2004: 172-178). Botma nowhere suggests that syllable structure is of relevance for post-nasal voicing. For instance in Japanese native words coda-onset structures are involved (Botma 2004: 175). He demonstrates that post-nasal voicing is caused by assimilation of a feature [L], which manifests itself as voicing in obstruents, and active nasality in sonorants.

This means that any post-nasal voicing is not determined by syllable structures, but that any voiced structure resulting from a change in voicing will be dealt with in the same way as already existing voiced structures. The question of whether the voicing of the stop element in the cluster has brought about a change in syllabification in Saramaccan cannot really be answered because of the aforementioned lack of knowledge as to syllabification processes at earlier stages.

Having regard to the fact that both the major African adstrates from the 1675–1680 onwards were consistently open-syllable languages, it might have been expected that 17-Sranan would also fall into this category. Our discussion of the facts of the distinction between final /m, n/ suggest otherwise.[61] 18-Sranan appears to have preserved this contrast. Apparently the surface phonemic opposition was lost in coda position shortly after the beginning of the 19th century.

An *underlying* distinction between word-final /m/ and /n/ has however endured until the present-day in some transitive verbs, when such a final /m/s are followed by vowel-initial clitic pronouns and therefore syllabified in *onset* position. Otherwise /m/ and /n/ both surface as basically nasalized

---

59. This must represent *santie*.
60. This must represent *wantie*.
61. Possibly the arrival of numerous slaves from the Gold Coast where languages are spoken like Akuapem that allow final /m, n/ was a factor.

vowels in final codas. In intransitive verbs the cues to the presence of this contrast are missing, so that there the neutralization has been complete.

There is one categorial exception to post-nasal voicing – the initial "nasal clusters" in Ndyuka. Here, as Huttar & Huttar (1994) describe them, we have syllabic nasals, agreeing in place with the following segment.

(32) Non-post-nasal voicing in initial nasal clusters in Ndyuka[62]

m̩boma	< m-boma (Kikongo)	'python'
m̩peto	< m-peto (Kikongo)	'trap'
n̩dika	< n-dika (Kikongo)	'fish trap'
n̩dyuka		'Ndyuka'
ŋgonini		'harpy eagle'
ŋkola	< ŋ-koola (W. Kikongo)	'snail'
n̩zau[63]	< n-zawu (Kikongo)	'elephant'
n̩sau[64]		as above

Here we do not encounter post-nasal voicing. Presumably the structural distance between a nasal in the syllable nucleus and the following onset is just too far for post-nasal voicing to operate, although nasal place assimilation works here as usual (although this *was* inherited from Kikongo). Note that this is the kind of *initial* nasal cluster that occurs both in Efik (Cook 1985), an important Cross River language, and in Twi-Akan (Welmers 1973).

3.4. What is the real substrate in Surinam?

The earliest slave voyages with a more precisely described source only date from 1664 (Voyages Database 2009). Earlier on we only find less precise references to "Guinea". From 1664 to about 1671 the majority of voyages recorded in the Voyages Database are from the Bight of Biafra. There are two main sources mentioned, Calabar and New Calabar. These are not geographically very close, as their names might somewhat erroneously suggest. Calabar is on the Calabar River, a tributary of the Cross River, and is not far from the border with Cameroon. New Calabar is on the New Calabar River in the Niger Delta, and is located about 200 km. west of Calabar.

---

62. /nt, nty/ appear to be absent in Ndyuka.
63. (Huttar & Huttar 1994: 546; De Groot 1984: 72).
64. The online Ndyuka dictionary gives this form (Languages of Suriname 2003)

Slaves exported from Calabar would no doubt reflect to a large degree reflect its linguistic surroundings. Calabar is located in an area largely peopled by speakers of Cross River languages. In a large area to the north-east, speakers of a Bantoid language, Ejagham, are found. In particular, many Cross River languages like Efik, Obolo and Ibibio allow consonant-final words (Connell 1994).

Slaves exported from New Calabar would reflect a greater diversity of linguistic backgrounds: Ijo languages from the Niger Delta area, Cross River languages from an area immediately to the north, Edoid languages to the north-west, and importantly Igbo and Igboid languages to the north-east. These languages tend to be more uniform in their phonological patterning, lacking word-final consonants. Some Ijo languages, however, do allow words in final /m/. The Cross River languages have many more final consonants, as I have just noted.

To sum up, we do not know enough yet to make any real statements about substrate phonological influence at all in Surinam. We can however talk about adstratal influence. The following section, concerned with creole languages spoken on, or originating from, Jamaica, may however give us food for thought.

4. Adstrate or substrate in Jamaica

In this section, I will attempt to establish aspects of the Proto-Jamaican Creole vowel system and syllable structure by comparing present-day Jamaican Creole with Krio and the Eastern Maroon Creole of Jamaica. My thesis is that all three are equally relevant for historical phonological work. My conclusion will be that the phonological shape of Jamaican Creole has been very significantly affected by its long cohabitation with English, and that Eastern Maroon Creole, insofar as it is recoverable from the incomplete data available, and Krio, when taken together, give us an insight into what Jamaican Creole itself may originally have looked like.

In Section 4.1, I examine the ways in which the stressed syllables – in particular the stressed rhymes – of Jamaican Creole differ from those of the Surinam Creoles. In Section 4.2, I perform a similar examination with respect to Eastern Maroon Creole. In 4.3, I do the same for Krio, which I regard primarily as the linear descendant of the Western Maroon Creole language of the expelled Trelawny Town Maroons.

4.1. Jamaican Creole

I will now turn to the best-known case of a Jamaican creole language, Jamaican Creole itself, in order to establish the conditions needed to illustrate a different kind of phonological adstrate effect. Consider the vowel system of Jamaican Creole (a.k.a. Patwa). This vowel system is similar to that of Standard English in a number of ways. It has a length contrast, generally paralleling the long/short or tense/lax contrast of English, although a number of frequently used monosyllabic words with open vowels have short reflexes. It also has diphthongs, once again generally parallelling the situation in English. In Table 8, I illustrate some of the equivalences.

Table 8. The English vowel length contrasts in Jamaican Creole.

English spelling	Jamaican phonemic	EME	Current English
sleep	sliip	sliːp	sliːp
sick	sik	sɪk	sɪk
afraid	fried ~ friad	freːd	freid
dead	ded	dɛd	dɛd
walk	waak	wɔːk	wɔːk
hot	hat	hɔt	hɔt, hat
hat	hat	hat	hæt
smoke	smuok ~ smuak	smoːk	smouk
bud	bod	bʌd	bʌd
wood	wud, hud, ud	wʊd	wʊd
root	ruut	ruːt	ruːt

Here I ignore the particular diphthongal nature of two Jamaican Creole reflexes of the two mid EME long vowels. These have been discussed in Smith & van der Vate (2006), and compared with Southwestern English dialect reflexes which are similarly diphthongal. The range of (phonetic) dialect realizations overlaps to a fair extent with the Jamaican Creole values of the vowels.

I consider that it is likely that a southwestern Standard English (i.e. Standard English with a southwestern accent) is reflected in the vowel qualities, which basically only differ in the dipthongization of the tense mid vowels, illustrated in Table 9.

Table 9. Southwest English dialect reflexes of Early Modern English tense mid vowels.

English spelling	East Devon Wright (1898-1905)	Somerset Wright (1898-1905)	West Dorset Wright (1898-1905)	Hilton, Dorset Widén (1949)
gate	giət, gæt	giət, geət, gjet	giət, gjet, gjæt	gⁱet
bake	beək	biək, beək	biək, beək	bⁱeːk, beːk
bacon		beəkən	beəkən	bⁱe(ː)kən
face		feəs	feəs	feːəs
gape		giəp, geəp, gæp	geəp	ga(ː)p
boat	bo̧ət, boːt	buət, bo̧ət	bwoət	bʷoət
goat	goət, goːt	go̧ət	gwoət	goːət
coat	ko̧ət,	kuət, ko̧ət, kwuət		kwo(ː)ət
board	boəd, boːd	buəd	bwoəd	boːərd
door	duːə(r)	duːə(r)		doːə(r)
cold		kuəld, kwoːld, koːld	kwoːld	kʷoːld

I consider that it is likely that a southwestern Standard English (i.e. Standard English with a southwestern accent) is reflected in the vowel qualities, which basically only differ in the dipthongization of the tense mid vowels, illustrated in Table 9.

Other than this Jamaican Creole has only the unrounding of low rounded vowels also found in many transatlantic forms of English including Standard American English and the Surinam creoles.

4.1.1. Comparison of Jamaican Creole and English constraint ranking

We saw in the previous section that, in general, Jamaican Creole has the same vowel quantities as Early Modern English. Short vowels where Early Modern English has them, tense/long high and low vowels where Early Modern English has them, and mid lowering diphthongs where Southwestern forms of English have them.

Ignoring the mid diphthongs for the moment – it is not certain whether these are actually the functional correspondents to the mid short vowels – we can conclude that the short vowels of Jamaican Creole correspond in general to the short vowels of EME and that the long vowels of Jamaican Creole correspond in general to the long vowels of EME. These relationships can be expressed in terms of the two constraints concerned with the maintenance or lack of maintenance of long vowels – MAX-μ and NOLONGVOWEL.

We express this in terms of the following constraint ranking, which corresponds to the historical antecedent and consequent pair EME and Jamaican Creole.

In Tableau 11, we see that the Faithfulness constraint MAX-μ (MAX-MORA) is ranked higher than the Markedness constraint NOLONGVOWEL.

Tableau 11. MAX-μ and NOLONGVOWEL in English and Jamaican Creole

Relative Ranking Language	**Higher-ranked**	Lower-ranked
English	MAX-μ	NOLONGVOWEL
Jamaican Creole	MAX-μ	NOLONGVOWEL

Similarly, when we examine the Early Modern English true diphthongs, we find similar diphthongs in Jamaican Creole (Table 9). The only real complication is to be found with /oi/. The modern English /oi/ has two historical sources, /oi/ and /ui/. These two were much confused, and basically fell together. According to Dobson (1957), three developments were around in the Early Modern English period. In the word *boil*, i. and ii. in Table 10 represented developments from older /ui/, and iii. the development from older /oi/. It is clear that Jamaican Creole represents i., and that Standard English represents iii.

Table 10. The English diphthongs in Jamaican Creole.

English spelling	Jamaican phonemic		EME	Current English
climb	klaim		kləim > klaim	klaim
house	hous		həus > haus	haus
boil	bwail	i.	bwəil > bwail	
		ii.	buil > bəil[65] > bail	
		iii.	bɔil	bɔil[66]

We are faced with a parallel result to the long vowel case. Jamaican Creole has diphthongs (in most cases) where Standard English has them. Diphthongs are a minority flavour in the languages of the world, and the Markedness constraint NODIPHTHONG has been proposed to account for this. A

---

65. The second development is still represented by Scots /bëil/.
66. The Jamaican and Current English forms of "boil" are derived from different variants.

Faithfulness constraint, UNIFORMITY, with an anti-monophthongization effect, has been proposed to counteract this markedness (or non-markedness) effect.

And again, if we rank the Faithfulness constraint above the Markedness constraint, we get the correct results for both English and Jamaican Creole.

Tableau 12. UNIFORMITY and NODIPHTHONG in English and Jamaican Creole

Relative Ranking Language	**Higher-ranked**	Lower-ranked
English	UNIFORMITY	NODIPHTHONG
Jamaican Creole	UNIFORMITY	NODIPHTHONG

I will not repeat the exercise here with regard to word codas. In general, barring a few isolated cases, Jamaican does not have anaptyxis.

We observe that Jamaican Creole does not differ significantly from English in the aspects studied. Usually the question is asked why and how creoles and their respective lexifier languages (the languages that supply the major/basic part of their lexicons) differ. The question should also arise in our minds why they do *not* differ in certain aspects. We have just seen two aspects, not necessarily related, in which English and Jamaican Creole do not differ. This question is then potentially as interesting as questions regarding their numerous differences.

I ascribe the greater influence of English on Jamaican Creole to *adstratal* influence from the lexifier language English. It is clear that both Sranan and Jamaican Creole have the same lexifier – English. The difference is that English was not only around in the formative period in Jamaican Creole, but was also continually present during the whole of its history. So I would explain things in these terms.

(33) Differences in stratal influence between Sranan and Jamaican Creole
　　　Sranan:　　　　　　　　Colonial Superstrate language:　　English
　　　　　　　　　　　　　　　Colonial Adstrate language:　　　Dutch
　　　　　　　　　　　　　　　African Adstrate language:　　　 Fongbe
　　　　　　　　　　　　　　　African Adstrate language:　　　 Kikongo
　　　Jamaican Creole:[67]　　Colonial Superstrate language:　　English
　　　　　　　　　　　　　　　Colonial Adstrate language:　　　English

---

67. I avoid the question of an African Adstrate/Substrate in Jamaican Creole here because I have not studied the situation sufficiently. Certainly the Eastern Maroon Creole examples seem to utilize frequent Twi-Akan word-forms to a greater degree.

Note that I have not regarded the mere presence of some lexical items from a particular language as being symptomatic of an adstratal influence.

At any rate, I regard (33) as providing a good start for an account of the very significant differences between Sranan and Jamaican Creole. In the next section, I will treat the former Eastern Maroon Creole (of Jamaica).

4.2. Another Case from Jamaica – Maroon Spirit Language/Eastern Maroon Creole (EMC)

The Maroon Spirit Language of Jamaica refers to a "language" whose use is at present very limited. It is only used to address the spirits of those ancestors of the Eastern Maroons of Jamaica who were born in Jamaica. Ancestors born in Africa are addressed in a vestigial African ritual language called Kramanti, based on Twi-Akan.

In fact, there is evidence that the Maroon Spirit Language was the former daily language of this Maroon group, which only ceased to be used as such around the beginning of the 20th century (Harris 1994). For this reason I will refer to it as Eastern Maroon Creole (EMC).[68] There are two groups of Maroons in Jamaica – the Western Maroons of the Cockpit Country, who at present, only speak Jamaican Creole, and the Eastern Maroons of the Blue Mountains. I will argue in the next section for the thesis that Krio also basically descends from a Maroon creole language (of Jamaica), that of the Western Maroons. I take my examples from Bilby (1983, 1992, 2005) and Harris (1994).

Of great interest is the EMC treatment of Early Modern English vowels, illustrated in Table 11. In this and the following tables, we cannot fail to be struck by the parallels with Sranan and the other Surinam creole languages. Bilby (1983, 1992) points to the occurrence of anaptyxis and the frequent monophthongization of English diphthongs, for instance.Now we observe a totally different picture from that presented in Jamaican Creole. The length contrasts of English are *not* preserved. The lexical forms are once again

---

68. Not to be confused with the term, Eastern Maroon Creole language of Surinam – Ndyuka-Aluku-Paramaccan-Kwinti. For the sake of clarity, I prefer to avoid the terms Leeward and Windward which are more normally used in the Caribbean, because of the general lack of extra-Caribbean knowledge about the direction of the prevailing winds in the Caribbean. So, here I refer to the Eastern Maroons of Jamaica (i.e. Windward Maroons) and the Western Maroons of Jamaica (i.e. Leeward Maroons).

based on English but the realization is as deviant in these items as that which we saw in Sranan.

Table 11. The English vowel length contrasts in Eastern Maroon Creole

English spelling	EMC	EME	Current English
weed	widi	wiːd	wiːd
stick	tiki	stɪk	stɪk
face	fesi	feːs	feis
dead	dede	dɛd	dɛd
black	blaka	blak	blæk
walk	waka	wɔːk	wɔːk
knock	naki	nɔk	nɔk, nɑ
broke	broko	broːk	brouk
wood	wudu, hudu, udu	wʊd	wʊd
tooth	tutu	tuːθ	tuːθ

So the reader will realise that by basically switching around the order of the same pair of Markedness and Faithfulness constraints utilized above, MAX-µ and NOLONGVOWEL, we get the rights results for vowel length, i.e. no contrastive vowel length. Here Eastern Maroon Creole agrees with Sranan.

Tableau 13. MAX-µ and NOLONGVOWEL in English and Eastern Maroon Creole

Relative Ranking Language	**Higher-ranked**	Lower-ranked
English	MAX-µ	NOLONGVOWEL
Eastern Maroon Creole	NOLONGVOWEL	MAX-µ

This can be reduced to:

Tableau 14. NOLONGVOWEL in English and Eastern Maroon Creole

Constraint Language	NOLONGVOWEL <MAX-µ>	
English		Lower-ranked
Eastern Maroon Creole	**Higher-ranked**	

Let us now turn to a consideration of EMC diphthongs in English closed syllables. These are illustrated Table 12.

Table 12. The English diphthongs in Eastern Maroon Creole.

English spelling	EMC	EME	Current English
climb	krem, klem	kləim > klaim	klaim
time	tem	təim > taim	taim
fight	fete	fəit > fait	fait
night	net	nəit > nait	nait
white	wete	wəit > wait	wait

For completeness' sake we need to examine the outcomes of these two types of vocal nucleus in open syllables.

Once again, we see that the result is quite different from that in Jamaican Creole. The two vowel qualities in the diphthong are merged or coalesced. In other words, we require a different ranking of the relevant Markedness and Faithfulness constraints, similar to what we have seen in Sranan.

However, before we look further at the question of constraints, we need to examine the treatment of open Early Modern English diphthongs in Eastern Maroon Creole. I will compare the results with those found in Sranan.

Table 13. Open English diphthongs in Eastern Maroon Creole.

English	Sranan	Jamaican	EMC	EME	Current English
fly	frei	flai	flei, frei	fləi > flai	flai
high	ei, hei	hai	hei	həi > hai	hai
cry	krei	krai	krei	krəi > krai	krai
tie(v)	tai	tai	titái	təi > tai	tai

When we compare the monophthongization that we find in both Sranan and EMC, and the open syllable "Non-monophthongization" that we once again find in both languages, we realise that a uniform account is required in the two languages in terms of constraint-ranking. The solution to this is then to conclude that the "diphthongs" in open syllables in Sranan and in EMC are not *nuclear* diphthongs at all, but combinations of the vowel /a/ and a semi-vowel coda. Support for this could be found in the freer combinations allowed in Sranan. /iy/ and /uw/ are disallowed, as they frequently are in different languages, because of their identity of place of articulation, but at least /ey, ay, oy, uy/ occur with a coda /y/, and /ew, aw, ow/ with a coda /w/.

This allows the NODIPHTHONG constraint to be ranked higher in these languages than in English. In English, /ai, au, oi/ are true diphthongs. This means that UNIFORMITY, which prevents underlying diphthongal structures from being monophthongized, must be ranked above NODIPHTHONG. This is another case where markedness takes priority over faithfulness.

Tableau 15. UNIFORMITY and NODIPHTHONG in English and EMC

Relative Ranking Language	**Higher-ranked**	Lower-ranked
English	UNIFORMITY	NODIPHTHONG
EMC	NODIPHTHONG	UNIFORMITY

or in simpler form:

Tableau 16. NODIPHTHONG in English and EMC

Constraint Language	NODIPHTHONG <UNIFORMITY>	
English		Lower-ranked
EMC	**Higher-ranked**	

Note that this ranking, like the previous one, does not mirror the English constraint ranking either.

Generally, in Eastern Maroon Creole, if a word ends in a consonant that is not a nasal, then an anaptyctic vowel is frequently added to the English stem. The reader has already seen this illustrated in Table 11 above. Bilby (1983: 64, fn. 13) discusses a personal communication from Ian Hancock, stating that some forms may be the result of a modern "deepening" by the addition of an anaptyctic vowel to an ordinary Jamaican Creole form rather than representing old retained forms. Bilby agrees and says that he has omitted nonce forms of this type. Some such forms may still be identified in his data from overuse of /i/ as anaptyctic vowel, the presence of long vowels, or an unexpected case of anaptyxis. For such examples see cases like those in Table 14.

Table 14. Doubtful EMC forms.[69]

English	Jamaican Creole	doubtful EMC form	expected EMC form
wood	ud, hud, wud	wudi	udu, hudu, wudu
weak	wiik	wiiki	wiki
eye	yai, hai	yaiye	*yai, *yei
round	roun	rouni	*ron

---

69. Only the starred forms do not occur. So in some cases, the expected forms do occur. The overall impression is then is that some informants render EMC forms more faithfully than others.

A test of a different kind that I have applied is given in Table 15: forms with the sequence /ai, au/ followed by an obstruent give /e, o/ in EMC. The degree to which an anaptyctic vowel occurs in such words tells us something, because the very vowel change is already sufficient to mark it as an EMC form.

Table 15. EMC forms with potential monophthongization *and* anaptyxis.

English	Jamaican Creole	EMC with anaptyxis	EMC without anaptyxis
fight	fait	fete	-
all right	aarait	arete	-
night	nait	-	net
ride	raid	rede	-
knife	naif	indepe (indufe /dufe)	-
house	house	-	os, "huss" (/hos/)

Here we find four out of six cases with double marking as EMC forms. This indicates that speakers more often than not seem to be not just aiming for *minimal* marking of forms as non-standard Jamaican Creole.

We have seen enough examples like those in Tables 11 and 15, to agree with Bilby's conclusion, that anaptyxis almost certainly formed part of the grammar of the former Eastern Maroon Creole of Jamaica. Once again we need to have recourse to the constraint NoObWordCoda. In English the output is constrained so as not to forbid codas, by ranking NoObWordCoda low, and the Faithfulness constraint (Dep(IO)) forbidding anaptyctic vowels high.

Tableau 17. NoConsonantalWordCoda in English and EMC.

Relative Ranking Language	**Higher-ranked**	Lower-ranked
English	Dep(IO)	NoObWordCoda
EMC	NoObWordCoda[70]	Dep(IO)

---

70. I leave the subject of final nasals open here. The situation is unclear. Sometimes anaptyctic vowels appear and sometimes they don't. But a similar situation exists in the Surinam Creoles, with differences within some varieties. A proper discussion would go far beyond the purposes of this article. One thing that there does seem to be agreement on is that anaptyctic vowels appear following obstruents and liquids.

Or summarizing again, as Tableau 18.

Tableau 18. NoCoda in English and EMC

Constraint Language	NoObWordCoda	<Dep(IO)>
English		Lower-ranked
EMC	**Higher-ranked**	

So, for a third time Eastern Maroon Creole phonology differs from English phonology. English allows coda consononants; EMC doesn't. I will ignore the exception for nasal codas here. In all three cases, it seems to agree with Sranan.

4.3. Krio

Krio is an English-lexifier creole spoken mainly, but not solely, in Sierra Leone. It has, however, many points of resemblance to English-lexifier creoles spoken in the Caribbean, including shared aspects of a pitch accent system (Devonish 2002). The origin of Krio – how it got to where it is now spoken – is controversial. I will not go into this question deeply here, as I have already addressed this topic in this volume (Ingredient X), but only briefly mention the two main contending theories. Both involve Nova Scotia in eastern Canada. Round about the end of the eighteenth century, two groups of slaves were transported from there to West Africa, one consisting of former slaves who had escaped from the American Southern States during the War of Independence in 1792, the other of a group of Western Maroons from Trelawny (a.k.a. Maroon Town), Jamaica in 1800, who had been cheated by the Governor, the Scot Alexander Lindsay, Earl of Balcarres, into leaving Jamaica in contravention of the articles of a truce agreement following the second Maroon War.

At about the same time, the United States moved some freed slaves to Liberia, where they still speak what can be regarded as a form of Black English. It is clear that Krio is not a form of Black English, as it does not resemble Liberian English at all, and we can most simply explain its many resemblances to Caribbean creole languages by assuming that it is to an important degree derived from a Western Maroon Creole language formerly spoken in Jamaica.

Let us now turn to an examination of the treatment of the English long vowel contrast in Krio.

Table 16. The English vowel length contrasts in Krio

English spelling	Krio	EME	Current English
weed	wid	wiːd	wiːd
stick	tɪk	stɪk	stɪk
face	fes	feːs	feis
bed	bed	bɛd	bɛd
cat	kyat	kat, kyat	kæt
call	kɔl	kɔːl	kɔːl
walk	[waka]⁷¹	wɔːk	wɔːk
hog	ɔg	hɔg	hɔg, hɑg
knock	[naki]	nɔk	nɔk, nɑk
root	rut	ruːt	ruːt
wood	wud	wʊd	wʊd

We see here that the English long/short contrast is not expressed, just as in the Surinam creoles, short vowels being used consistently.

Tableau 19. MAX-μ and NOLONGVOWEL in English and Krio.

Relative Ranking Language	Higher-ranked	Lower-ranked
English	MAX-μ	NOLONGVOWEL
Krio	NOLONGVOWEL	MAX-μ

or more simply:

Tableau 20. NOLONGVOWEL in English and Krio.

Constraint Language	NOLONGVOWEL <MAX-μ>	
English		Lower-ranked
Krio	**Higher-ranked**	

If we now turn to the Krio developments of English diphthongs, we get the following picture.

---

71. The forms given in square brackets display exceptional anaptyctic vowels. I will return to this point later on.

Table 17. The English diphthongs in Krio

English spelling	Krio	EME	Current English
climb	klɛm	kləim > klaim	klaim
time	tɛm	təim > taim	taim
fight	fɛt	fəit > fait	fait
night	nɛt	nəit > nait	nait
white	wɛt	wəit > wait	wait
boil	bwɛl	bwəil > bwail	bɔil

We observe the same coalescence of diphthongs as in Sranan. If we assume the relevance of the constraint NODIPHTHONG for the sake of convenience we get the following result.

Tableau 21. NODIPHTHONG in English and Krio

Constraint Language	NODIPHTHONG <MAX-μ>	
English		Lower-ranked
Krio	**Higher-ranked**	

Krio only has vowel anaptyxis in a few exceptional forms (see Table 5). Krio therefore has the same ranking of DEP(IO) and NOCWORDCODA as English does. In Krio, there are very many words with coda consonants.

Tableau 22. DEP(IO) and NOCWCODA in English and Krio

Relative Ranking Language	**Higher-ranked**	Lower-ranked
English	DEP(IO)	NOOBWORDCODA
Krio	DEP(IO)	NOOBWORDCODA

Or:

Tableau 23. NOCWCODA in English and Krio

Constraint Language	NOOBWORDCODA <DEP(IO)>	
English		Lower-ranked
Krio		Lower-ranked

Here Krio is distinguished from Sranan and Eastern Maroon Creole (Jamaica) in that it goes along with English.

5. English compared with the Surinam and Jamaican Creoles

Now we can compare all four creole languages with English. Let us briefly remind ourselves what the point of this exercise was. It was to compare a typical Caribbean (basilectal) English creole language, in this case Jamaican Creole, which had had adstratal contact with English for the whole of its history, with other creole languages with quite different historical relationships with English. Jamaican Creole is just one case among many. I could just as well have chosen Kittitian (St. Kitts Creole), or Creolese (Guyanese Creole), or Islander Creole (Providencia/San Andrés Creole), among others. These share either long-term political control by the United Kingdom, or else a long period of British political and linguistic domination.

The other three cases have quite varied histories, but they have one thing in common – a lack of prolonged adstratal contact with English. In the case of Sranan – the "eldest" Surinamese creole language – Surinam only remained an English colony for 16 years, and the English language probably was losing its significance by the period 1680-1690. For a more detailed examination of this see Smith (this volume on the early history of Surinam).

Some historical background to the formation of the Eastern (Windward) and Western (Leeward) Maroons of Jamaican is to be found in Smith (this volume on Ingredient X). The basis of the Eastern Maroons was supposedly formed during the English conquest of Jamaica from the Spanish in 1655. Many Spanish slaves chose marronage at this time. It is unclear when the linguistic change to an English-based creole took place. The formation of the Western Maroons can be more certainly established, as being the direct result of a slave insurrection in the Parish of Clarendon in 1690. Note that this was for practical purposes less than one generation after the beginning of the functioning of the English colony of Jamaica. In 1731, the First Maroon War broke out against both Eastern and Western Maroons, ending in humiliation for the English when they were forced to recognize the independent existence of, and sign separate treaties with, both the Western Maroons and Eastern Maroons in 1739. After 1739, no new escaped slaves were to join the maroons (Kopytoff 1976). In 1795, the Second Maroon War broke out with the Western Maroons of Trelawny Town, who in 1796 were tricked, as I have mentioned above, into deportation to Nova Scotia, in Canada.[72] In Jamaica (Bilby 1994), the difference between Maroon culture and general Jamaican culture has been slowly disappearing since the ending of slavery in 1838. And by the beginning of the 20th century, the Eastern

---

72. For more on this see Bilby (1984).

Maroon Creole language had ceased to be passed on as a fully functional language.

So the three groups, Sranan and the Surinamese Maroon Creoles – most notably Saramaccan and Ndyuka, Eastern Maroon Creole (Jamaica), and Krio (Western Maroon Creole) – share an important feature, the briefness of their exposure to Standard English. This is responsible for the ranking of specific pairs of Markedness constraints (vis-à-vis the Faithfulness constraints with which they crucially interact), illustrated in Tableau 24. The contrast with Jamaican Creole is particularly salient.

Tableau 24. Constraint typology of English vis-à-vis English-lexifier creole languages.

Con-straint[73] Language	NoObWordCoda <MrkC:Dep(IO)>	NoLongVowel <MrkC:Max-μ>	NoDiphthong <MrkC:Uniformity>
English	Lower-ranked	Lower-ranked	Lower-ranked
Jamaican Creole	Lower-ranked	Lower-ranked	Lower-ranked
Krio	Lower-ranked	**Higher-ranked**	**Higher-ranked**
EMC	**Higher-ranked**	**Higher-ranked**	**Higher-ranked**
17-Sranan	**Higher-ranked**	**Higher-ranked**	**Higher-ranked**

I assume that the common features of the two Jamaican Maroon varieties, Krio and Eastern Maroon Creole, are representative of all early Jamaican Creole. This would imply that the greater resemblances of Jamaican Creole to English are the result of changes that took place because of the greater and longer exposure to the English (and subsequently British) colonial power, and the English language, as compared to the Maroon varieties.

Note that Krio, as a descendant of Jamaican Western Maroon Creole, was as much removed from the influence of Standard English in the early days as Eastern Maroon Creole was. Both groups were subject to treaties made in 1739, and Krio only became subject to significant influence from Standard English much later on.

Both Krio and Jamaican Creole retain a few cases of vowel anaptyxis, and we have evidence for more cases of this type in archaic dialects of Krio (Hancock 1969; 1987), and older records of Jamaican Creole (Lalla 1986; D'Costa & Lalla 1989; Lalla & D'Costa 1990).

---

73. The ordering of the constraints in this comparative tableau has nothing to do with ranking. That information is contained in the various columns.

Table 18. Examples of sporadic anaptyxis in Krio and Jamaican Creole.

English	Sranan	Saramaccan	EMC	Krio	Pichí	Pichí 1938[74]	Jamaican
if	**efi, efu**	**éẽ**[75]	ef, if	ɛf, if	**ɛ̀fɛ**, ɛ̀f, if	*if*	ef
gentle	**gentri**	**dyɛnde**		**jentri**	**jentri**	**chentry**	**jentri**
like	**leki**	-	**laka**	**lɛke**, lɛk	**lɛke**, lɛk, làyk	*leke, lek*	**laka**, laik, laika
knock	**naki**	**náki**	**naki**	nak	nak	nak	nak
rat	**alata**	-	**rata**	**arata**	**arata**	**arata**	**rata**
stick	**tiki**	-	**tiki**	**tiki**, tik	tik, stik	*tik, stik*	tik
talk	**taki**	**táki**	**taki**, tak	tɔk	tɔk	*tok*	**taki**, tak, taak
walk	**waka**	**wáka**	**waka**	**waka**, wɔk	**waka**, wɔk	*uaca, uok*	waak
hear	**yere**	**yéi**		**yeri**	yer, hia	**yery**, *ia, yia*	**yeri**, yer, hier, hie

Table 19. Reverse anaptyxis

English	Sranan	Sranan 1855	Sranan 1783	Jamaican Cr.	Pichí	Krio
bury	beri	**béri**	beri	beri	**ber**	**ber**
carry	tyari, tya	tjári, tja', kjári	tjarri, tja, tjerri	**kyar**, kya, kyari, kye, kyeri	**ker**, keri, **kyer**, kyeri	**ker**, keri
crazy	-	-	-	kriezi	**kres**	**kres**
family	-	-	-	**fambl**, famb(i)li	**fambul**	**fambul**
softly	safri	**sáfri**	safri		**saful**	**saful**, safli
trouble	trobi	**tróbi**		trabl		**trɔb**,[76] trɔbul

---

74. Pichí 1938 is Mariano de Zarco (1938).
75. In this example, as also in /yéi/, the final consonant that caused anaptyxis has been lost since the 18th century.
76. This form is recorded as a verb by Hancock (1969). I have included it in this table as it conceivably might have been derived from a form resembling Sranan /trobi/, with subsequent reverse anaptyxis.

Can we conclude from this that Jamaican Creole and Krio used also to possess anaptyxis as a regular feature or not? The answer is not yet clear, and might not ever become so. There is an interesting piece of negative evidence, however, from Krio involving anaptyxis. This evidence consists of forms we might refer to as "reverse anaptyxis". Such forms are illustrated in Table 19, where I provide forms from different stages of Sranan first to illustrate a language that has compulsory anaptyxis, then Jamaican Creole as a language that typically does not. I follow that with five of the forms showing reverse anaptyxis in Krio (and its dialect Pichí).

What I have called reverse anaptyxis is not, as in anaptyxis, the addition of a supporting vowel after a consonant-final word but the removal of a final vowel, presumably because the speakers of the language were (erroneously) under the impression that the vowel concerned *was* an anaptyctic vowel (cf. Hancock 1969). This might be amenable to two explanations. Firstly, it might suggest that Krio had formerly had regular anaptyxis but at some stage lost it under a certain degree of influence from English. The influence would not have been strong enough to allow for a completely correct restoration, resulting in both overshoot, illustrated by the forms in Table 19, and undershoot, as in Table 18.

Another possibility might be that both Jamaican Maroon languages, EMC and Krio, formerly had variation in the presence or absence of anaptyxis, possibly determined by the syntactic envoirment, somewhat along the lines of the existing "de-anaptyxis" in the surface phonology of present-day Sranan. A flavour of this might be detectable in (Bilby 1983: 48) from EMC:

(34) "'tak na mi' ('talk to me' – in this context the final vowel of "taki" is usually deleted)"

6. Conclusion and speculation

In the context of creole languages, there is a significant difference in substratal and superstratal influence, and adstratal influences. The first two types are intimately involved in the formation of the creole language – creolization – while adstratal influence does not differ from any other kind of contact induced language change. In Ingredient X, I concluded that all the Atlantic Creole languages likely shared a common origin, or rather basis, in what I call there the Proto-Atlantic Slave Community Language (PASCL). There, I gave evidence from lexicon, syntax, and functional morphemes to support this thesis. Here, I make a start in drawing attention to parallels of a phonological nature.

What I had previously assumed to be substrate influence, partly due to lack of data, turns out not to be that, but rather adstrate influence. In a sense, although we now have earlier data for Surinam, suggesting the Bight of Biafra as the first-known source of slaves, this data still does not come from the very earliest period of the English colony.

Ultimately, assuming that the concept of a Proto-Atlantic Slave Community Language is correct, I think that I have demonstrated here that the original vowel system of the PASCL must have resembled that of the Surinam Creoles and the Jamaican Maroon Creoles – the short-vowel non-adstratal English creoles – rather than the long-vowel adstratal English creoles like Jamaican and Kittitian. Smith & van der Vate (2006) suggested that the lowering mid tense diphthongs in the latter type resulted from (adstratal) influence from S.W. English dialects in the 17th century.

Where did it all start? I think that we must proceed from the idea that there were both African and American sources for pidgins/creoles. Pidgins like Singler's Vernacular Liberian English (Singler 1997), and the pidgin evidenced in Hancock's early records of Sierra Leone (Hancock 1969: 13) do not seem to have crossed the Atlantic from the Americas. The Atlantic creoles must however have been created under the slave plantation system, which had its genesis in the Caribbean area. As candidates for the American source for the Atlantic Creole languages the only possible choices seem to be Baker's (1999) choice of St. Kitts, and van de Vate's choice of Barbados (van de Vate 2003), or probably both (Smith, this volume, on Ingredient X).

The possibility of Barbados is considered in Hancock (1969: 15–16) but rejected on the grounds that "the Barbadian Negroes probably had a better command of the English language than did slaves in other English-owned islands." However, the hypothesis adopted in Smith (2009a, this volume on Ingredient X) for Surinam, that an English-based creole could co-exist as a slave language with (koiné English) as a medium of inter-ethnic communication, makes this non-problematic. To quote Reeps' description of Surinam, made during a 7-month stay there in 1693 (van Alphen 1962/3): "De engelse hebben hier een colonie gemaeckt en wort die tael daer nog meest bij de slaven gesproken." [The English founded a colony here, and that language is still mostly spoken by the slaves.]

It would seem unlikely that van Alphen is referring to Sranan specifically with "that language", as that would mean that he had reason to identify Sranan with English. The Dutch he associated with during his stay, including the Governor, whose guest he was, would be well aware that Neger-

Engels ('Negro English'), as it was referred to in the 18th and 19th centuries, was not the same as English. That he would recognize this himself seems likely considering the non-intercomprehensability of the two languages, and the fact that he visited various plantations. He was himself very interested in the operation of plantations.

If, however, in line with what I hypothesize in Smith (2009a), English was only losing its importance in the period 1680-1690, it is possible that he was either referring to a still fairly widespread knowledge of koiné English, or the use of English combined with the use of Neger-Engels (a.k.a. Sranan).

It is certain that Sranan already existed, if for no other reason than that it formed one of the basic elements in the Saramaccan maroon creole language. The marronnage that led to the formation of the Saramaccan tribe can be dated to 1690 (Price 1983), and must have involved a pre-existing mixed English and Portuguese creole language, referred to by later Dutch observers as Dju-Tongo ('Jews' language') referring to the linguistic contribution of the Portuguese Jews.

To conclude with a question – What have I done in this article? I think I have shown, at some length, that three creole languages that have been less influenced by English/British colonial control exhibit similar developments of English vocalic nuclei, i.e. neutralization of English vowel length, and monophthongization of English diphthongs in closed syllables. The third phenomenon I examined, anaptyxis, showed a parallellism between the Surinam creole languages and in particular the Eastern Maroon Language of Jamaica. The third language, Krio, which I claim is basically derived from the Western Creole Language of Jamaica, displayed a small number of forms with anaptyctic vowels, although archaic forms of the language and older sources show more. That Krio formerly possessed anaptyxis seemed to be suggested by a phenomenon that I have referred to above as "reverse anaptyxis". Together, these three phenomena give us some idea of what the earliest forms of Caribbean creole English, uninfluenced for long periods by English as a dominant language, might have been like. Other older sources for other creole languages in the Caribbean area display scattered anaptyctic forms, and in the case of Jamaican Creole, even a couple of cases of reverse anaptyxis. It is not quite clear how these facts should be interpreted.

Except for these three cases, all the other English-lexifier creoles of the circum-Caribbean area reveal extensive phonological adstrate effects from English. The Surinam Creoles display, especially in their older recorded forms, a wide-ranging tendency to an open syllable structure. I would now interpret this as the effect of two or three generations of heavy slave imports from areas where Gbe languages and forms of Kikongo were spoken (with possible countervailing influence from Gold Coast languages) but regard this as representing phonological adstrate rather than substrate influence.

What the actual substrate language (or languages) was for the circum-Caribbean creole Englishes, is unfortunately beyond our ken at this moment.

The left periphery in the Surinamese creoles and Gbe: on the modularity of substrate transfer

Enoch Aboh

1. Introduction

This chapter investigates the left periphery in the clausal and nominal domains of the Gbe languages and the Surinamese creoles (Sranan, Saramaccan) and shows that substrate transfer is not a unitary syntactic phenomenon that could correspond to a strict one-to-one match between the relevant substrate languages and the creole. I show that substrate transfer can be selective and may target a set of features only, as well as the morphosyntax associated with it. In this case, the creoles and substrate languages manifest striking parallels with respect to the morphosyntax of only certain functional elements. Such parallels, I argue, cannot be attributed to independent development prompted by UG. For instance, the discussion in the first part shows that the Gbe languages and Saramaccan display a rich left periphery of the clause that provides room for discrete functional projections whose specifiers host distinct fronted elements (e.g. focus-phrases, wh-phrases, topic-phrases, questioned constituents, etc.) and whose heads host the C-type markers. These markers are the morphological realisations of the features [Force], [interrogative], [topic], [focus], [specific], [injunctive/deontic mood] that are associated with the left periphery, that is Comp. Assuming substrate influence, this would mean that Saramaccan exhibits a left periphery that is parallel to the Gbe left periphery in many respects. Accordingly, the distribution of *fu*, the presence of the focus marker *wɛ* (also realized as *wɛ̀~* in Gungbe and Fongbe), the properties of verb focusing, and the presence of a sentence-final question marker in Saramaccan are regarded as strong evidence for morphosyntactic inheritance. In the second part, I show that substrate transfer may consist of just a set of features. In such a situation, the morphosyntax, or the formal licensing conditions associated with that set of features, may be determined under the pressure of the superstrate language. For instance, the analysis of the determiner system indicates that the function of the determiners in Sranan is comparable to that of the determiners in the Gbe languages.[1] In all these languages, determiners express a specific versus non-specific opposition that distinguishes them from Germanic or Romance types of articles, which encode definite versus indefinite distinction. However, Sranan differs from Gungbe in that the specificity marker in this language exhibits syntactic properties that are found in Romance and Germanic languages, but not in the Gbe languages. This leads me to propose that the observed pragmatic/semantic parallels are due to substrate transfer where the appropriate features are retained but not their syntax. The latter is determined on the basis of the superstrate language (i.e. English). Following earlier works on Saramaccan and Gbe, I assume that Gbe and Saramaccan are of the type SVO.[2] Under Kayne (1994), this would mean that all structures are of the type spec-head-complement and contexts where the complement precedes the head must result from movement of the complement to a position higher than that targeted by the head (see Aboh 2004a, 2006a for discussion).

2. Complementation in Gbe and Saramaccan

Not much work has been done on the left periphery of the clause (or the complementizer system) in Saramaccan.[3] Under universalist approaches to creole genesis, it is often assumed that categories, such as complementizers, are lost during pidginization, but may be reconstructed in the course of creolization (Bickerton 1984, Byrne 1987). With this approach in mind, studies on complementation in Saramaccan often argue for an analysis in terms of verb serialization, assuming that Saramaccan does not have a proper complementizer. The so-called *verba sentiendi et declarandi* (e.g. say) are used to introduce a second verb (or a proposition). But as the language evolves, such verbs may grammaticalize into full complementizers that are first merged in Comp (Byrne 1987, Veenstra

---

1. In this paper, I use the term "determiner" as a cover term for article-like elements in Gungbe and the Suriname creoles which apparently correspond to English determiners such as "the" and "a". It is important, however, to keep in mind that the particles described here do not have the same distribution and semantic properties as their assumed English equivalents.
2. See Clements (1972), Capo (1991), Aboh (2004a), and references cited there for Gbe, and Byrne (1987), Sebba (1987), Veenstra (1996), Damonte (2002), and references cited there for Saramaccan.
3. In this chapter, I use the expressions left periphery of the clause and complementizer system interchangeably.

1996).⁴ A similar analysis has been made for complementation in Gbe (Kinyalolo 1993).

According to Smith (1987), Arends (1989), and much related work, the Gbe languages are potential substrate languages for Saramaccan. Building on this, one could argue for substrate transfer and suggest that complementation in Saramaccan develops from a Gbe substrate. This would mean that even though the diachronic analysis that implies a development from serial verb constructions to proper complementizers could be maintained for the Gbe languages, this need not be the case for Saramaccan. Such a view is compatible with Arends' (1999) analysis that complementizers are established in early Saramaccan. In this perspective, Aboh (2002, 2003a, 2005c, 2006a) shows that Saramaccan and Gungbe manifest striking parallels, for instance, the presence of distinct topic, focus, and question markers, which may have scope over a constituent inside the proposition or over the proposition as a whole. These markers, therefore, attract various constituents that are fronted to the sentence left periphery.

In this chapter, it is argued that such parallels are best understood in terms of substrate transfer.⁵ In this regard, Section 2.1 suggests that the so-called complementizer-like *fu* and the quasi-modal *fu* are the Saramaccan counterparts of the Gbe *ní*-type$_1$ and *ní*-type$_2$ complementizers that delimit the left periphery of the clause upward and downward, respectively (Aboh 2006a, 2007b). The discussion further suggests that the topic-focus articulation projects between these complementizers. Section 2.2 deals with striking parallels between Saramaccan and Gungbe with respect to verbal focusing. The conclusion reached there is that Saramaccan adopts the morphosyntax of the Gungbe-type languages. Similarly, section 2.3 indicates that, unlike topic and focus markers, which typically occur to the left edge, yes-no question markers in Gbe and Saramaccan surface to the right edge because they take scope over the proposition, which is displaced to the left. In this framework, the question marker encodes the head of a functional projection located within the left periphery and the fronted

---

4. Damonte (2002) analyzes the Saramaccan data in terms of the split-C hypothesis and further suggests that the development (or reconstruction) of the Saramaccan complementizer system could be attributed to a natural evolution that reflects the properties of UG.
5. The reader is referred to Rizzi (1997) for discussion on the complementizer system and to Aboh (2004a) for a comparative study of Gbe complementizer system.

proposition realises its specifier position (Aboh & Pfau 2010). Section 2.4 summarizes the proposed analysis.

2.1. *fu*-type$_1$/*fu*-type$_2$ versus *ní*-type$_1$/*ní*-type$_2$

The following examples indicate that, in Saramaccan and Gungbe, the left periphery of the sentence may host distinct elements. The sentences in (1) contain an embedded clause introduced by the complementizers *taa*/*ɖɔ̀* followed by a preposed topic, which in turn precedes the focus in a pre-subject position.[6]

(1) a. Mi sabi **taa** di pingo **de** hen **wɛ** Sema suti. Sar
1SG know that DET pig TOP 3SG-S FOC Sema shoot
'I know that, as for the pig, Sema shot it.'
b. Ùn sè **ɖɔ̀** dàn éhè ló **yà** éɔ̀ **wὲ** Kòfí hù. Gun
1SG hear that snake DEM DET TOP 3SG-S FOC Kofi kill
'I heard that, as for this snake, Kofi killed it.'

The data in (1) are empirical evidence that topic and focus occur in a space delimited to the left by the declarative complementizers and to the right by the subject. The topic-focus articulation manifests the fixed hierarchy topic > focus. The sentences in (2) further indicate that focus- and wh-phrases surface in the same position immediately to the left of the focus marker *wὲ*. Accordingly, I can attribute the sequencing in (2c) to the left periphery of the clause in Saramaccan and Gungbe (Aboh 2006a, 2007b).

---

6. Topic and focus constructions are common to Gbe even though the languages may vary with respect to whether the topic marker is overtly realized or not. For instance, while Gungbe and Gengbe/Ewegbe have overt topic markers *yà* and *la* respectively, Fongbe resorts to a pause between the topic phrase and the rest of the sentence. On the other hand all the Gbe languages involve a focus marker that occurs with focused phrases and wh-phrases (cf. Hazoumè, 1990). Similarly, it has been reported to me that Pamaka (another creole spoken in Surinam) involves the topic marker *dati* as shown in the following example. I thank B. Migge for providing these examples.
(i) *M'án bii, nefi dati án de ye.*
'I don't think so, as for this knife, it does not exist!'
Mi dati án de a ini.
'As for me, I am not part of it.'

(2) a. Andi wɛ Sema suti?   Sar
        what FOC Sema shoot
        'What did Sema shoot?'
    b. été wɛ̀ Kòfi hù?   Gun
        what FOC Kofi kill
        'What did Kofi kill?'
    c. [ɖɔ̀/taa] > Topic [yà/de] > Focus/Wh [wɛ̀]

In addition, Saramaccan displays two instances of *fu* (*fu*-type₁ and *fu*-type₂), which I assume to be the equivalents of the Gungbe forms *ní*-type₁ and *ní*-type₂ that delimit the complementizer system upward and downward (Aboh 2003a, 2006b). The sentences in (3) indicate that *fu*-type₁ may be selected by inceptive and desiderative verbs (3a), or introduce purpose clauses (3b).

(3) a. Amato ke fu/(*taa)Ayawa kisi di ogifoó a matu. Sar
        Amato want fu/ taa Ayawa catch DET owl LOC jungle
        'Amato wants Ayawa to catch the owl in the jungle.'
    b. Amato boi di gania fu nyan.   Sar
        Amato cook DET chicken fu eat
        'Amato cooked the chicken to eat.' (Prepositional comp)

According to Damonte (2002) verbs that select *fu*-type₁ (e.g. *da taanga* 'encourage', *duingi* 'force', *paamisi* 'promise', *da piimisi* 'give permission', *bigi* 'begin') require a complement with an irrealis meaning. This would mean that the complementizer *fu*-type₁ encodes the feature [irrealis] contrary to the declarative complementizer *taa*, which selects complements understood as realized.

On the other hand, the Gungbe *ní*-type₁ occurs in sentence-initial position, where it encodes conditional (4a), functions as time setting morpheme (4b), or introduces embedded yes-no questions (4c).

(4) a. Ní Kòfi sìgán wá fi é ná víví ná mì.   Gun
        ní-type₁ Kofi can come here 3SG FUT nice for mi
        'I will be happy if Kofi can come here.'
    b. Ní Kòfi wá mì yrɔ̀ è ná mì.   Gun
        when Kofi come you call 3SG for me
        'When Kofi comes, call him for me'
    c. Ùn kànbíɔ́ ní Kòfi sìgán wá fi?   Gun
        1SG ask ní-type₁ Kofi can come here
        'I asked if Kofi could come here.'

In both Saramaccan and Gungbe, *fu*-type₁ and *ní*-type₁ precede topic and focus phrases, suggesting that they merge under Force, in the functional projection ForceP.

(5) a. *Amato ke* **fu** *di ogifou de*
Amato want fu-type₁ DET owl TOP
Ayawa kisi en a matu. Sar
Ayawa catch 3SG LOC jungle
'As for the owl, Amato wants Ayawa to catch the it in the jungle.'
b. *Ùn kànbíɔ* **ní** *àkwékwè lɔ́ yà*
1sg ask ní-type1 banana DET TOP
Kòfí wè sìgán ɖù ì? Gun
Kofi FOC can eat 3SG
'I ask if, as for the banana, Kofi could eat it.'

In addition, the Gungbe example in (6) indicates that the declarative complementizer *ɖɔ̀* 'that' and *ní*-type₁ are in complementary distribution. Sentence (6a) shows that, like *ní*-type₁, the complementizer *ɖɔ̀* must precede topic phrases, as well as focus-, and wh-elements. The ungrammatical sentence (6b) indicates that *ní*-type₁ and the complementizer *ɖɔ̀* cannot co-occur.

(6) a. *Ùn kànbíɔ wè* **ɖɔ̀** *dáwè éhè yà*
1SG ask 2SG that man DEM TOP
ménù wè ná ɖì xɔ́ étɔ̀n? Gun
who FOC FUT believe word 3SG-POSS
'I asked you that, as for this man, who would believe him?'
b. **Ùn kànbíɔ wè* **ɖɔ̀ ní**
1sg ask 2sg that ní-type₁
Kòfí wè ɖì xɔ́ énɛ̌? Gun
Kofi FOC believe word that
'I asked if Kofi believed that?'

A possible interpretation of these facts is that the two complementizers *ɖɔ̀/taa* and *ní/fu*-type₁ compete for the same position (see Aboh 2004a, 2006a). This could be regarded as partial evidence for the common origin of *ní*-type₁ and *fu*-type₁. Despite the diverse functions that *ní*-type₁ and *fu*-type₁ play in the Gungbe and Saramaccan grammars, I conjecture that conditional is a sub-label of a class of syntactic features (e.g. future, prospective, counter-factual) that relate to irrealis modality. If this is the right characterization, we can further conclude that *fu*-type$_1$ developed from *ní*-type$_1$ under the pressure of substrate influence. Put more generally, the source of the Saramaccan *fu*-type$_1$ would be the Gbe *ní*-type$_1$.[7]

A piece of evidence supporting this view is that both Saramaccan and the Gbe languages display an homophonous element—referred to as *fu*-type$_2$ and *ní*-type$_2$—that encodes deontic mood (7a-b) or functions as a subjunctive complementizer (7c-d). Note from these examples that *fu*-type$_2$ and *ní*-type$_2$ occur to the right of the subject, where they precede tense and aspect markers.[8]

(7) a. *Amato fu ta boi di gania.*   Sar
        Amato fu-type$_2$ PROG cook DET chicken
        'Amato should/must be cooking the chicken.'
    b. *Kòfí ní nɔ̀ jì hàn.*   Gun
        Kofi ní-type$_2$ HAB sing song
        'Kofi should sing a song habitually.'
    c. *I taki taa fu a naki di dagu.*   Sar
        2SG say that fu-type$_2$ 3SG hit DET dog
        'You told him to hit the dog.' (Veenstra 1996:156)
    d. *À ɖɔ̀ ɖɔ̀ yɔkpɔ́ lɛ́ ní nyàn àvún lɔ́.*   Gun
        2SG say that child PL ní-type$_2$ chase dog DET
        'I said that the children should chase the dog.'

---

7. In most Gbe languages, this marker involves a nasal alveolar *n*– followed by a vowel. For instance, Fongbe displays *ní*, and Ewegbe *ne* (Kluge 2000, Aboh 2001b, 2004a).
    (ii) a. *Ní Kɔkú má ɖà àsɔ́n ɔ́ à é ná glé*   Fon
        ní-type$_1$ Koku NEG cook crab DET NEG 3SG FUT rotten
        'If Koku does not cook the crab, it will get rotten.'
      b. *Ne me-kpɔ Ama la m-a-yɔ-e*   Ewe
        ne-type$_1$ 1SG-see Ama TOP 1SG-POT-call-3SG
        'If I see Ami I will call her.'
8. Certain authors (e.g. Wijnen & Alleyne 1987, Damonte 2002) suggested that Saramaccan does not have a deontic mood marker. They proposed that the Saramaccan examples under (7) should be analyzed as instances of subordinate clauses, where *fu* is selected by a deontic (null) verb within the matrix clause. However, as Aboh (2006b, 2007) shows, such analysis is perfectly compatible with an approach where *fu*-type$_2$ is analyzed as a complementizer that merges under Fin.

In accounting for *fu*-type$_1$/*ní*-type$_1$ and *fu*-type$_2$/*ní*-type$_2$, I propose that these elements are components of the left periphery of the sentence. The irrealis complementizer *fu*-type$_1$/*ní*-type$_1$ merges in Force°, which heads the topmost projection (ForceP). *Fu*-type$_2$/*ní*-type$_2$, on the other hand, head Fin°, where they encode finiteness and mood features that match those of the proposition. This would mean that just like indicative, subjunctive or imperative clauses, the deontic (or injunctive) sentences described in (7) include mood specification in the left periphery and can be analyzed, on a par with imperative or subjunctive (Aboh 2004a, 2007b). Partial evidence for this analysis comes from Gungbe where the two *ní*-types may co-occur (8a). Note that *ní*-type$_1$ precedes the topic-focus articulation, while *ní*-type$_2$ follows in a post-subject position. Similarly, the example (8b) indicates that the declarative complementizer and the injunctive/subjunctive complementizer may co-occur.[9]

(8) a. *Ùn kànbíó **ní** òsó éhè yà ògán wè*
     1SG ask ní-type$_1$ horse DEM TOP chief FOC
     *mí **ní** zé è yì ná?* Gun
     1PL ní-type$_2$ take 3SG go give
     'I asked if, as for this horse, we should give it to the chief.'
   b. *É jè ḍɔ̀ jíkùn **ní** jà.* Gun
     3SG suit that rain ní-type$_2$ fall
     'It would be nice if it could rain.'

It appears from these examples that *ní*-type$_2$ always surfaces to the right of the element functioning as the subject of the proposition. On the assumption that *ní*-type$_2$ realises Fin°, I propose that such constructions require subject raising to [spec FinP]. This movement results from the fact that Fin° defines a predication within the complementizer system, where it connects the subject and the predicate. In Gungbe and Saramaccan, such predicative articulation requires a spec-head configuration that necessitates the subject of predicate be overtly realized, hence the movement of the canonical nominative subject to [spec FinP]. Under Chomsky's (1995) definition of the EPP, one could propose that Fin° has an EPP feature that must be checked before spell-out. This requirement is met by movement of

---

9. This means that the traditional hypothesis that mood markers are limited to the I-system like tense and aspect markers should be refined. See, for instance, Durrleman (2000, 2008), Aboh (2004a, 2006b, 2007) for discussion.

the subject of predicate to [spec FinP].[10] A crucial point that arises here is that [spec FinP] is not a case-related position. The following Gungbe example involving a sentence subject in pre- *ní*-type$_2$ position supports this hypothesis and further indicates that elements that occur in [spec FinP] must have their case checked elsewhere (Aboh, 2004a, 2006a, 2007b).

(9) [*Déxè yòkpó lέ tò hàn jì ɖó*] **ní**   *má*
     that child NUMPROG song sing like *ní*-type$_2$ NEG
     kpácá   dó wè blô   yé dó gán tàùn   Gun
     surprise at 2SG anymore 3PL plant force very
     'Don't you be surprised by the way the children are singing, they have been working hard!'

This leads me to conclude that, like its Gbe substrates, Saramaccan has two instances of *fu*. Deontic (or quasi-modal) *fu*-type$_2$ manifests Fin° where it encodes deontic mood like its Gbe *ní*-type$_2$ counterpart. However, complementizer-like *fu*-type$_1$, is a prepositional complementizer comparable to English *for*. Like *ní*-type$_1$, which expresses conditional, time or yes-no questions in Gbe, *fu*-type$_1$ merges under Force° where it encodes the feature irrealis (Damonte 2002, Aboh 2004a, 2006a, 2007b). In this regard, Saramaccan and Gbe manifest the complementizer system in (10) where TopP and FocP are distinct projections whose specifiers host the fronted topic- and focus-elements, while the heads encode the topic and focus features under Top° and Foc°, respectively. Following Cinque (1990), Rizzi (1997), and much related work, I propose that topic phrases move to [spec TopP] in order to check their topic features against the topic head, leaving a resumptive pronoun inside the inflectional domain. On the other hand, focus- and wh-phrases move to [spec FocP] to check their focus feature against the focus head, leaving a gap inside IP. Under this approach, the difference between focus and topic constructions with respect to the element inside the IP domain derives from the fact that focus constructions create a quantificational chain as opposed to topic constructions, which involve a non-quantificational chain. In addition, I assume that subject raising is determined by the EPP features under Fin° (10).

(10) [$_{ForceP}$ [$_{Force°}$ [*taa-fu/ɖɔ-ní*]$_{type1}$ [$_{TopP}$ *de/yà* [$_{FocP}$ *wὲ* [$_{FinP}$ Subject$_i$ [$_{Fin°}$ [*fu/ní*]$_{type2}$ ..t$_i$ ...]]]]]]

---

10. See also Cardinaletti (1997) for the discussion on two subject positions.

This representation accounts for the data under (1), repeated here as (11), in a straightforward manner. The topic-focus articulation projects between the two complementizer-types, Force and Fin, and the topic precedes the focus in both languages.

(11) a. *Mi sabi **taa** di pingo **de** hen **wɛ** Sema suti.* Sar
      1sg know that DET pig Top 3SG-S FOC Sema shoot
      'I know that, as for the pig, Sema shot it.'
   b. *Ùn sè ɖɔ̀ dàn éhè lɔ́ **yà** éɔ̀ **wɛ̀** Kòfí hù.* Gun
      1SG hear that snake DEM DET TOP 3SG-S FOC Kofi kill
      'I heard that, as for this snake, Kofi killed it.'

Under the proposed analysis, that Saramaccan includes a focus marker *wɛ* (Smith 1996), which is identical to the Fongbe and Gungbe focus markers, as well as two wh-words (i.e. *andi* 'what', *mbe* 'who') derived from the forms *àní* 'what' and *mɛ́* 'who' that are found in the Gbe languages of the Fon cluster (Capo 1991) can be regarded as a case of morphosyntax inheritance. The next section discusses verb focus constructions in Saramaccan and Gbe and shows that the properties shared by these languages are compatible with an analysis in terms of substrate influence.

2.2. V-focus in Gbe and Saramaccan

This section shows that even though there is cross-linguistic variation within Gbe as to how verb focus is realized and the type of structures that verb focus brings about across Gbe, there seems to be a strong parallel between verbal focus constructions in the Gungbe-type languages and Saramaccan.

2.2.1. V-focus in Gbe.

This section discusses verb focus in VO and OV constructions in Gbe, and shows that they involve different strategies that could be described as X-movement versus XP-movement. The examples in (12) illustrate the Gbe VO and OV constructions.[11] Most OV constructions involve a sentence-

---

11. See Awoyale (1997), Manfredi (1997), Aboh (2004a) for the discussion on the internal structure of OV constructions across Kwa.

final morpheme as *gbé* in (12b) or sometimes a sentence-final floating low toneme represented in (12c) by an additional stroke on the verb *xɔ̀*.

(12) a.   *Kòfí xɔ̀ wémà lɔ́*   Gun
          Kofi buy book DET
          'Kofi bought the book'
     b.   *Kòfí yì wémà lɔ́ xɔ̀ gbé*   Gun
          Kofi PROG book DET buy purpose
          'Kofi has gone to buy the book.'
     c.   *Kòfí tò wémà lɔ́ xɔ̀*   Gun
          Kofi PROG book DET buy-NR
          'Kofi is buying the book.'

In the VO sequences, the focused category could be either the verb, or a nominalised reduplicated verb. In both cases, a doublet of the verb occurs in the IP-internal position as schematised in (13a-b).

(13) a.   [FocP [Foc° V [IP ......V...]]]   Gun, Fon
     b.   [FocP [Nom-V-V] [Foc° [IP ....V...]]]   Ewe

In representation (13a) the fronted verb, which actually represents a root, is morphologically identical to the token in the IP-internal position. In (13b), however, the fronted verb is reduplicated contrary to the IP-internal token.

In the OV sequences, however, verb focus requires generalized pied-piping of the sequence containing the verb and its arguments. The preposed category leaves a gap in the IP-internal position, as shown in (14), where ΣP stands for the focused verbal sequence.

(14) [FocP [ΣP..[VP..]]$_i$ [Foc° [IP .....t$_i$.....]]]   Gun, Fon, Ewe

In this chapter, I discuss verb focus in VO sequences because only these constructions provide the relevant context for the analysis of language variations among Gbe on the one hand, and the parallels between Gbe and Saramaccan on the other. The discussion here will remain fairly descriptive and the reader is referred to Aboh (2003b, 2004a, 2006c), Aboh & Dyakonova (2009) and references cited there for a formal analysis of predicate fronting with doubling.

The representations (13a-b) indicate that verb focus in the VO sequences involves two strategies. This section further shows that these strategies correspond to two language-groups: the Gungbe-type languages versus the Ewegbe-type languages. This partition roughly corresponds to Kluge's (2000) Eastern versus Western Gbe groups.

In the Gungbe-type languages, verb focus requires fronting of the verb stem to sentence-initial position.[12] In these constructions, the IP-internal position must contain a doublet of the fronted verb and a gap is excluded, as illustrated by the contrast between the grammatical example (15a) and the ungrammatical sentence (15b). In the Gbe languages, these constructions express verb focus. I refer to the strategy described in (15a) as V-focus.

(15) a. [Gbá]$_i$ Séná [gbá]$_i$ xwé ló ná Kòfí.   Gun
build Sena build house DET for Kofi
b. *[Gbá]$_i$ Séná t$_i$ xwé ló ná Kòfí.   Gun
build Sena house DET for Kofi
'Sena BUILT the house for Kofi'

There is no lexical or semantic constraint on V-focus because verbs that can be focused include transitive and intransitive verbs (16a-b), double object construction verbs (16c), ergative verbs (16d) in the sense of Burzio (1986), and state verbs as in (16e).

(16) a. Ðù Séná ɖù blédì ló.   Gun
eat Sena eat bread DET
'Sena ate the bread.'
b. Fɔ́n yé fɔ́n bléblé.   Gun
stand 3PL stand quickly
'They stood up quickly.'
c. Ná Séná ná kwè ví lé   Gun
give Sena give money child NUM
'Sena gave the children some money.'
d. Wá yé wá.   Gun
arrive 3PL arrive
'They arrived.'
e. Bí Séná bí tàù.   Gun
intelligent Sena intelligent very
'Sena is very intelligent.'

In addition, the focused verb cannot move along with its arguments, a piece

---

12. This description also holds for Fongbe.

of evidence that V-focus involves the verb only (17). Put differently, V-focus is not an instance of VP-fronting.

(17) *[Gbá xwé lɔ́ ná Kòfi]ᵢ Sénà tᵢ.   Gun
    build house DET for Kofi Sena build
    'Sena built the house for Kofi.'

In their analysis of predicate fronting with doubling, Aboh and Dyakonova (2009) propose that the Gungbe construction involves head movement of the verb (V) to the focus head (Foc°). Some arguments in favor to this analysis include the fact that the verb cannot cyclically adjoin to the intervening tense and aspect markers on its way to Foc° (18a). Instead, sentence (18b) shows that the intervening I-type markers must remain in situ.

(18) a. *Ḍù-nɔ̀-ná Séná ḍù blédì lɔ́.   Gun
        eat-HAB-FUT Sena eat bread DET
    b. Ḍù Séná ná nɔ̀ ḍù blédì lɔ́.   Gun
        eat Sena FUT HAB eat bread DET
        'Sena will habitually eat the bread' (instead of selling it).

In addition, the sentences in (19) show that V-focus is clause-bound.

(19) a. *Ḍù ùn sè ḍɔ̀ Séná ná nɔ̀ ḍù blédì lɔ́   Gun
        eat 1SG hear that Sena FUT HAB eat bread DET
    b. Ùn sè ḍɔ̀ ḍù Séná ná nɔ̀ ḍù blédì lɔ́   Gun
        1SG hear that eat Sena FUT HAB eat bread DET
        'I heard that Sena will eat the bread habitually'

Finally, V-focus is sensitive to negation in that the fronted verb cannot cross a negation marker. In the following example, the sentence is ungrammatical under the reading in (a), but not (b).

(20) Ḍù Séná má ḍù blédì lɔ́   Gun
    eat Sena NEG eat bread DET
    a. *'Sena will not eat the bread' [i.e. she did not eat it, she sold it]
    b. 'Sena will not only eat the bread [i.e she will devour it]'

The reading in (20a), where the event of eating is denied, can only be obtained with the type of expletive construction in (21), where negation has scope over the whole proposition.

(21) *É   má   nyín   dù   Séná   dù   blédì   ló*   Gun
     3sg   NEG   be.COP eat   Sena   eat   bread   DET
     'It is not the case that Sena ate the bread'

Aboh & Dyakonova (2009) further propose that the second doublet inside the sentence derives from movement of the verb into an intermediate aspect position (i.e. V-to-Asp). Combined with the fronted verb that raises to Foc, this would mean that predicate focus with doubling is an instance of parallel chains as illustrated in (22), where only the copy common to both chains (i.e. the one inside the VP) is not pronounced (Chomsky 2005).

(22) [ForceP *dɔ́* [FocP [Foc° V [FinP…[AspP [Asp …V……… [VP……V̶……]]]]]]]

I will not enter the details of this analysis here and the reader is referred to the cited reference for further discussion. What matters for our description here is that V-focus in the Gungbe-type languages involves movement of the verb (i.e. the root) to the focus position (i.e. V-to-Foc movement).

In the Ewegbe-type languages, V-focus requires fronting of a nominalized reduplicated verb. The latter is combined with a non-reduplicated verb in IP-internal position. I refer to this process as VV-focus. Unlike V-focus, VV-focus is not clause-bound (23b).

(23) a. *Fo-fo-   é   wó   ɸo-   é.*   Ewe
        RED-hit FOC   3SG   hit   3SG
        'Beating s/he beat him/her.'
     b. *Fo-fo-   é   me   se   be   wo   fo   devi-a.*   Ewe
        RED-beat- FOC   1SG-   hear that 2SG- beat child-DET
        'I heard that beating the child he did.' (Ameka 1992: 12)

Abstracting away from verb movement to some aspect position (e.g. under habitual aspect) and object movement to a case licensing position, prior to verb focus (Aboh 2003b, 2004a), I suggest that the fronted VV-category is not a simple reduplicated lexical verb, but a maximal projection. Accordingly, V-focus involves V-to-Foc movement, while VV-focus requires movement of the nominalized remnant VP to [spec FocP].¹³ Put differently, VV-focus is a type of remnant VP-fronting where the fronted emptied VP is spelled out through reduplication.¹⁴ I therefore conclude that in VV-focus, the remnant VP moves to [spec FocP] to check its focus feature against Foc°. In both VV-focus and V-focus, the IP-internal verb moves to the aspect position as in (24).¹⁵

(24) [ForceP dɔ̀ [FocP Nom-VP [Foc° [FinP V O [VP t_verb t_object]]]]]

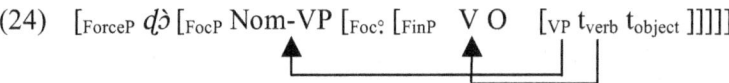

We now come to the characterization that the Gbe languages manifest two major strategies for verb focusing in VO sequences. In the Gungbe-type languages, the lexical verb checks its focus feature against Foc° by adjoining to it. In the Ewegbe-type language, however, the remnant VP moves to [spec FocP] where it checks its focus feature against Foc° and gets spelt out through reduplication.

2.2.2. *V-focus in Saramaccan.*

The analysis proposed here for the Gbe languages extends to Saramaccan in a straightforward manner. Like the Gungbe-type languages, Saramaccan has verb focus constructions where the lexical verb is moved to sentence initial position, while the IP-internal position contains a doublet.¹⁶

---

13. That the Ewegbe-type languages involve remnant VP-movement is further suggested by the fact that these languages show morphological reflex of V-to-Asp movement. For instance, the habitual aspect marker is an affix that cliticizes on to the verb in the Ewegbe-type languages, but it necessarily precedes the verb in the Gungbe-type languages where it is a free morpheme (see Aboh 2004a, Aboh & Dyakonova 2009 for discussion).
14. This suggests that reduplication is not due to nominalization (Aboh 2004a, 2005c).
15. Alternatively, one could assume that the reduplicated V is first merged in [spec FocP], leaving the lexical V in situ. This will also correctly explain why VV-focus manifests no sensitivity to clause-boundness. Choosing between those two analyses goes beyond the scope of the present chapter and I leave the matter for future research.
16. Byrne (1987) also reported that Saramaccan V-focus strategy extends to predicate adjectives, a difference compared to the Gbe languages, where no

(25) a. *Sì Kòfisì dì mujée bi tà woòkòa di kéiki.* Sar
see Kofi see DET woman PAST PROG work LOC DET church
'Kofi SAW the woman working at the church.'
b. *Lùku a tà lùku dì mìi tà kò a lio.* Sar
watch 3SG PROG watch DET child PROG come LOC river
'He is watching the child coming from the river.'
(Byrne 1987:58)

Just as in the Gbe languages, there seems to be no lexical or semantic constraint on the Saramaccan verbs that can be focused. For instance, the sentences under (26) indicate that verbal focusing may include unaccusative verbs as well as state verbs.[17]

(26) a. *Go Amato bi go na wooyo.* Sar
go Amato PAST go LOC market
'Amato went to the market.'
b. *Lùsu dì bànti lùsu.* Sar
loose the belt loose
'The belt is loose.' (Byrne 1987:59)

The examples (25-26) suggest that V-focus in Saramaccan is very similar to that in the Gungbe-type languages. Under substrate influence, I propose that Saramaccan replicates the morphosyntax of these languages. A fact supporting this hypothesis is that V-focus is clause-bound in both Saramaccan and the Gungbe-type languages (cf. the ungrammatical sentences under 27a-b). The Saramaccan focused verb cannot be extracted across the complementizer layer.[18] The same is true of the Gungbe ungrammatical example (19a) repeated here as (27c).

(27) a. **Boi dì mujée ke faa boi dì gbamba.* Sar
cook DET woman want fu-type$_1$ cook DET meat
'The woman wants to cook the meat.'

---

such construction exists. However, such asymmetry disappears if the so-called predicate adjectives are lexical verbs, as correctly suggested in the literature (e.g. Byrne 1987).

17. See Veenstra (1996) for the discussion on unaccusativity in Saramaccan.
18. According to Byrne (1987) certain speakers do accept such constructions, but my informants did not.

b. *Lùku a méni tàà dì wòmi mìi lùku dì wòsu. Sar
   look 3SG think that DET man child look DET house
   'He thinks that the little boy LOOKED at the house.'
   (Byrne 1987:59-60)
c. *Ɖù ùn sè ɖɔ̀ Séná ná nɔ̀ ɖù blɛ́ɖì lɔ́   Gun
   eat 1SG hear that Sena FUT HAB eat bread DET

In this regard, verb focus in Saramaccan and Gungbe differs from non-verbal constituent focusing because the former is clause-bound but not the latter. Accordingly, a focused embedded verb must occur within the left periphery of the embedded clause. This restriction does not hold on non-verbal constituent focusing where a focused phrase can occur either in the embedded or matrix clause. Consider, again the Saramaccan verbal focus sentence (28a), as opposed to the focus sentence (28b), where the subject of the embedded clause is focused to the matrix clause.

(28) a. A ke fu njàn dì mìi njàn dì muungà   Sar
        3SG want COMP eat DET child eat DET porridge
        'He wants the child to EAT the porridge.'(Byrne 1987:60)
     b. Dì mìi a ke fu njàn dì kuku.   Sar
        DET child 3SG want COMP eat DET cookie
        'THE CHILD wants to eat the cookie.'(Byrne 1987:56)

Just as in Gungbe-type languages, the Saramaccan focused verb cannot be extracted along with its internal arguments (29). This is evidence that there is no VP fronting in Saramaccan, unlike in Ewegbe-type languages.

(29) *[Sùku en] a sùku   Sar
     search 3SG 3SG search (Byrne 1987:97)

I conclude from these facts that V-focus in the Gungbe-type languages and Saramaccan involves movement of the focused verb to the complementizer system, where it checks its focus features against the focus head Foc°. In this view, V-to-Foc° is coupled with a parallel movement of the verb to an intermediate aspect position as argued for in Aboh & Dyakonova (2009) and further illustrated in (30) for Gungbe-type languages and Saramaccan.

(30) [$_{ForceP}$ ɖɔ̀-ní-type$_1$/taa-fu-type$_1$ [$_{FocP}$[$_{Foc°}$ V [$_{FinP}$... [$_{AspP}$ [$_{Asp}$...V... [VP...V...]]]]]]]

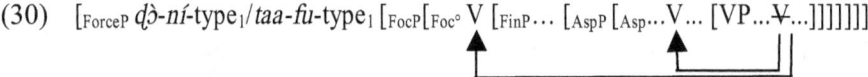

An objection to this analysis could be that verb focus (or predicate cleft) is found in almost all creoles, including those that might not have the Gungbe-type languages as potential substrate languages. Building on this, one could then suggest that V-to-Foc° movement is provided by UG as the unmarked option. For instance, this correctly explains the fact that typologically different languages, such as Russian, Yiddish, Portuguese, Spanish, Hebrew, etc display verb focusing or topicalization with doubling, (see Aboh 2006c, Aboh & Dyakonova 2009 and references cited there).

It is worth mentioning that I am not refuting the fact that V-to-Foc° movement results from a principle of UG, nor do I deny the fact that the architecture of the left periphery of the clause in general is primarily made available by UG. In the language contact situation where creoles were created, it seems reasonable to me to assume that the relevant morphosyntactic cues are provided by the languages in competition. I therefore propose that, in an emerging creole, some parameter settings as well as their associated morphosyntactic properties may be acquired under substrate influence. This would mean that verb focusing of the Gungbe-type provided additional morphosyntactic cues for the creators of Saramaccan to fix the parameters of the left periphery of the language the Gbe way.

The discussion in previous paragraphs shows that the Gungbe-type languages and Saramaccan share similar morphosyntactic properties with respect to verb focus. The following section discusses another morphosyntactic property of verb focus that lends further support to an analysis in terms of the Gungbe/Saramaccan-type languages versus other Gbe/creole-type partition.

In the Gungbe and Saramaccan examples discussed above, the fronted verb keeps its bare form as shown by the examples in (31). The conclusion reached there is that verb focus targets the verb inside VP.

(31) a. *Lùku a tà lùku dì mìi tà kò a lio.*   Sar
       watch 3SG PROG watch DET child PROG come LOC river
       'He is watching the child coming from the river.'
    b. [*Gbá*]$_i$ *Séná* [*gbá*]$_i$ *xwé ló ná Kòfí.*   Gun
       build Sena build house DET for Kofi
       'Sena built the house for Kofi.'

Yet, in most Creoles discussed in the literature, the focused verb seems to belong to a (nominalized) phrase. The following examples, taken from Seuren (1993:56), indicate that in Negerhollands, Haitian, Papiamentu,

Jamaican, Gullah, and Sranan (a sister creole to Saramaccan), the fronted verb is right adjacent to a copula-like element.

(32) a. *Da breek sender ka breek.*   Negerhollands
       is break they are-now broken
    b. *Se depale u ap depale.*   Haitian
       is stray you PRES stray
    c. *Ta kasa bo kier kasa*   Papiamentu
       is marry you want marry
    d. *A tiif Jan tiif di mango.*   Jamaican
       is steal John stole the mango
    e. *Da tiif I tiif mai buk.*   Gullah
       is steal he stole my book
    f. *Na bigi yu futu bigi.*   Sranan
       is big your feet big

In the framework adopted here, the contrast between Saramaccan and the creoles in (32) is straightforward. Saramaccan shares the left peripheral morphosyntactic features of the Gungbe-type languages. Instead, the other creoles seem to manifest the type of verbal focusing in which a nominalised verb phrase (ΣP) is fronted. This strategy, which is also found in OV contexts in Gbe, appears to be widespread in other Kwa languages (Manfredi 1993, Aboh 2003b, 2004a, 2005c, 2006c). This would mean that while the Gungbe-type languages might have played an important role in the development of the Saramaccan left periphery, other Gbe (or possibly Kwa) languages could have well influenced other portions of the Saramaccan grammar. In this respect, that the creoles in (32) manifest ΣP-focusing could be ascribed to substrate influence from other Gbe-type or Kwa languages. I am not claiming that Saramaccan is just the result of relexification of the Gungbe-type languages. Instead, the approach advocated for here is a multidimensional one that may involve different sources (Aboh 2006b, 2007b). This clearly suggests that only a precise comparative analysis of the type undertaken here can possibly tell to which extent a language-type played a decisive role in the emergence of a creole feature. The next section on sentence-final markers further establishes the link between the Gbe languages and Saramaccan.

2.3. On sentence final C-type markers in Gbe and Saramaccan

The discussion in the preceding sections shows that Gbe and Saramaccan display a rich structure involving distinct projections where the topic-, focus-, and wh-phrases are licensed. In Gbe and Saramaccan, the head of these projections are realized at PF by the topic and focus markers. As components of the C-domain, these markers occur in the left periphery, that is, between the complementizer and the subject, and one does not expect them to target other portions of the clause. Yet, a striking property of both Gbe and Saramaccan is that some supposedly left peripheral elements appear on the right edge. A case in point is the yes-no question marker that occurs sentence-finally.

2.3.1. The yes-no question markers in Gbe: on sentence final C-type markers

In Gbe languages, yes-no questions require a sentence-final question marker that encodes interrogative force. In Gungbe, the question marker surfaces as a sentence-final low tone that is represented here by an additional stroke ['] on the sentence-final syllable. Consider the following sentences.

(33) a. *Kòfí ḍù nú.*   Gun
     Kofi eat thing
     'Kofi ate.'
   b. *Kòfí ḍù nû?*   Gun
     Kofi eat thing-INTER
     'Did Kofi eat?'

Sentences (33a-b) form a minimal pair. On the surface level, the only difference between them is the intervention of the low tone in (33b) which triggers a question reading, as opposed to the statement in (33a). I propose that the low tone specific to Gungbe yes-no questions is the reflex of a question marker that encodes interrogative force. This toneme arguably originates from a morpheme that underwent partial deletion as the language evolved. Additional piece of evidence in favor of this analysis comes from Fongbe, which exhibits a sentence-final question marker *à* in yes-no questions (34).

(34) Kɔ̀kú yrɔ́ Kòfí à [Fon]
    Koku call Kofi INTER
    'Did Koku call Kofi?'

The above examples are clear evidence that the sentence-final question marker is typical of the Gbe languages, even though the languages vary as to whether the question marker is realized as a toneme or as a full morpheme. Under the hypothesis that interrogative force is a specification of Force°, that is, the topmost head of the complementizer system, one could think that the Gbe sentence-final question marker is evidence against the split-C hypothesis that integrates the yes-no marker in the left periphery. However, the Gbe data are consistent with an analysis in terms of movement of the IP (or the proposition) to the specifier position of the functional projection headed by the question marker (Rizzi 1997, Aboh 2004a, Aboh & Pfau 2010). In Gungbe, for example, the complementizer ɖɔ̀ 'that' and the question marker (i.e. the sentence-final low tone) can be realized simultaneously in the clause. Notice, in sentence (35), that the embedded yes-no question is introduced by the complementizer ɖɔ̀, which is merged in Force°. On the other hand, the question marker is realized sentence-finally, hence the additional low tone on lésì 'rice.'

(35) Ùn kànbíɔ́ ɖɔ̀ Kòfí ɖù lésì?   Gun
    1SG ask   that Kofi eat rice.INTER
    'I asked whether Kofi ate some rice?'

Pursuing the split-C hypothesis, I propose that the question marker encodes the interrogative force that is associated with a functional head Inter° that projects within the complementizer system and whose specifier hosts interrogative phrases. Given that the interrogative phrase (or sentence) is sandwiched between the complementizer and the question marker in (35), I further conclude that ForceP immediately dominates the functional interrogative projection, InterP.[19] This amounts to saying that Gungbe interrogative constructions necessarily involve leftward (snowballing) movement of the sentence to [spec InterP] to check the feature interrogative under Inter°.[20] As a result, the Gbe question marker must always surface in sentence-final position. This is not a trivial conclusion. We now suggest that another particularity of the Gbe languages is that they manifest right

---

19. See also Rizzi (2001) for a similar proposal for Italian.
20. See Aboh (2004a) for a detailed discussion of snowballing movement.

edge C-type markers because certain markers of the left periphery are licensed under a spec-head configuration where the complement moves to the specifier position of its head. The yes-no question in (35) is partially represented as in (36) (abstracting away from TopP and FocP).

(36) [ForceP [Force° ɖɔ̀ [InterP [Kòfí ɖù lésì]$_i$ [Inter° ∅ ... [FinP t$_i$]]]]]

In this regard, Aboh (2004a, b, c) shows that such movement also applies to the Gbe D-system where the noun complement must surface to the left of the specificity and number markers (see also the discussion part II of this chapter).

The same reasoning extends to the so-called clausal determiner in Gbe. Like the question marker, the clausal determiner occurs in sentence-final position and indicates that the information being conveyed is pre-established in discourse and/or specific. The sequence in (37a) includes the Gungbe specificity marker, while examples (37b) involves the clausal determiner. Observe that the specificity marker and the clausal determiner are homophonous.[21]

(37) a.   [[Mótò] ló]   Gun
           car   DET
           'the (aforementioned) car (e.g. the one we saw yesterday)'
      b.   [[Ðé Kòfí hɔ̀n] ló]   vé ná yé.   Gun
           as Kofi flee DET$_{CL}$ hurt for 3PL
           'The fact that Kofi fled (instead of waiting), hurt them.'

Under the proposed analysis, a natural account for the bracketed sequence in sentence (37b) is to assume that the Gungbe clausal determiner realizes the left periphery of the clause. Put differently, there is, within the complementizer system, a functional projection whose head is the locus of the clausal determiner and whose specifier hosts the whole sentence. This would mean that the Gbe clausal determiner and question marker occur sentence-finally because they have scope over the proposition. Following Aboh (2004a, b), I propose that this scope relation is established under specifier-head configuration as a consequence of which the proposition is fronted to the specifier position of the relevant (scope) marker located in the left periphery. We therefore conclude that a typical property of the Gbe languages is that they involve a series of left peripheral markers some of

---

21. See also Lefebvre (1992, 1998), Law & Lefebvre (1995).

which occur to the right edge as a result of movement of the complement of a head to some specifier position to the left. The necessity of this movement is determined by the fact that right-edge C-type markers take scope over the proposition. Building on this, I further propose that it is reasonable to consider the presence of such morphosyntactic feature in Saramaccan as a result of substrate influence. Notice that the universalist view fails to capture such facts because there is no, a priori, unmarked or default parameter setting that forces C-type markers to occur to the right.

2.3.3. The yes-no marker no in Saramaccan

In his discussion of question formation of Saramaccan, Byrne (1987:41) suggests that "Saramaccan follows the creole pattern with one exception. In yes-no questions, the interrogative particle *no* with the appropriate rising intonation may follow the S string". Put differently, Saramaccan yes-no questions involve a sentence-final question marker that encodes interrogative force. In this respect, sentence (38a) is a declarative (i.e. a statement), as opposed to sentence (38b), a yes-no question.

(38) a. *A   jei   taa manu   fu   en go a   foto.*   Sar
         3SG hear that husband for 3SG go LOC city
         'He heard that her husband went to the city.'
     b. *A   jei   taa manu   fu   en go a   foto *(no)?*   Sar
         3sg hear that husband for 3sg go LOC city
         'Did he hear that her husband went to the city?'

Byrne (1987) mentioned that the interpretative difference between the sentences (38a-b) reduces to the presence of the particle *no* (associated with the appropriate intonation) in (38b) but not in (38a). However, he reported that the apparent optional status of the particle *no* could indicate that it is a tag.

The analysis presented here differs from Byrne (1987) in that it suggests that the particle *no* is a question marker, not a tag. This hypothesis is motivated by the fact that none of the speakers I consulted allows yes-no questions of the type (38b) without the sentence-final question marker. In addition, Byrne's (1987) account cannot distinguish between the different question particles that occur sentence-finally in Saramaccan as discussed in (Habbo 2003). Finally, the Saramaccan focus and topic markers can occur sentence-finally as well, on a par with the question marker. This is indicated by the following dialogue from Rountree & Glock (1982:68).²²

(39) A: *Umfa   i   ta   sei di   bakuba?*   Sar
         how.much 2SG PROG sell DET banana
         'How much are you selling the banana?'

   B: *Wan   kwaliki wan maun*   Sar
        one   quarter DET hand
        '25cents   per   hand'

   C: *Di   baaka uwii **wɛ**?*   Sar
        DET black leave FOC
        'What about the greens?'

Similar examples are found in Gungbe.

(40) *Kòfí kò   dù   nú   kpó   wɛ̀?*   Gun
     Kofi already eat thing finish FOC-INTER
     'Has Kofi already finished eating?'

Putting all this together, I propose that Saramaccan displays a sentence-final question marker that has a morphosyntax similar to that of the Gbe yes-no question marker. Additional evidence that supports this analysis is that even though the focus marker occurs in the left periphery in Saramaccan and Gungbe, it may surface in sentence-final position under appropriate circumstances. In the Gungbe example (40), the focus marker takes scope over the proposition and surfaces in sentence-final position, similarly to the Saramaccan example (39C).

The presence of the focus marker *wɛ* in sentence-final position in these examples strongly suggests that in Gbe and Saramaccan, a left peripheral marker may surface on the right edge if it has scope over the proposition. Accordingly, I argue that, like its Gbe substrate, Saramaccan requires movement of the sentence to [spec InterP] in yes-no questions because the latter always takes scope over the proposition. Accordingly, both Saramaccan and Gbe involve right-edge C-type markers that encode interrogative force. I therefore conclude that the Saramaccan complementizer system involves a projection InterP whose head hosts the yes-no question marker *no*. This would mean that a sentence (38b) is derived as represented in (41).

---

22. See Aboh (2005a, b) for further discussion.

(41)   ...[InterP [FinP *A jei taa manu fu en go a Foto*]$_i$ [Inter° *no* [FinP t$_i$]]]

2.4. Summary

This section has shown that the Gbe languages and Saramaccan manifest a complementizer system that provides room for discrete functional projections, whose specifiers host distinct fronted elements (e.g. focus, wh-phrases, topic-phrases, etc.) and whose heads host distinct makers. These markers are considered the morphological realizations of the features [+interrogative], [+topic], [+focus], [+specific], [+injunctive], that are associated with the left periphery. The Gbe/Saramaccan left periphery is partially represented in (42), but see Aboh (2006a) for further discussion.

(42)   ForceP[$_{dɔ/taa;\ ní/fu\text{-type}1}$] > InterP[$_{á/no}$] > TopP[$_{yá/de}$] > FocP[$_{wɛ́/wɛ}$] > FinP[$_{ní/fu\text{-type}2}$]

Representation (42) supports the idea put forth in this chapter that Gbe and Saramaccan clauses manifest a similar morphosyntax in the case of their left periphery. With regard to the genesis of creoles, this would mean that the Saramaccan left periphery did not develop *ab ovo* or from English, but rather under the influence of Gbe. That there is a continuum between Gbe and Saramaccan is compatible with Arends' (1999) observation that complementizers were established in early Saramaccan.

The conclusion we reach here suggests that the idea that certain categories are lost in the course of pidginization and reconstructed later on in the course of creolization due to the bioprogram (or innate linguistic capacity) should be revised. While some language universals are needed to account for the existence of a split complementizer system, substrate influence is needed to account for (i) why Saramaccan has a complementizer system that is very much parallel to that of the Gungbe-type languages, but differs from that of English or Portuguese, and (ii) how such a complementizer system is transferred or acquired. In addition, by restricting itself to aspects of the complementizer domain, this chapter suggests that the sources of substrate influence might not be uniform. In this regard, the discussion in Section 3 indicates that substrate influence in the nominal domain has led to different results.

3. The nominal left periphery: the D-system in Gbe and Saramaccan

I consider now the left periphery of the nominal domain of the Gbe languages and the Surinamese creoles and show that substrate transfer is not a unitary syntactic phenomenon. I show that substrate transfer may target just a set of features, leaving the morphosyntax associated with it unfixed. This would mean that in such cases, substrate transfer doesn't seem to play an important role in setting the parameters that underlie the formal licensing conditions that apply to the set of features being transferred. Section 3.1 focuses on the D-system and shows that, while the function of the Sranan determiners is parallel to that of the Gbe languages in encoding specificity and number, their morphosyntax appears to be different from that of both the substrate and the superstrate languages. For example, I show that while Gungbe and Sranan fall into the same typological class with respect to the specific versus non-specific opposition, the morphosyntax of the specificity marker in these two languages is not exactly parallel. A possible solution could be that the parallels between Gungbe and Sranan are due to substrate transfer where the appropriate features are retained but not their syntax. In this regard, section 3.2 shows that, even though, the syntax of the Sranan determiner is different from that of Gungbe and English, the latter might have provided a favorable context for its development. Accordingly, both Gungbe and English feed into the emergence of the Sranan D-system. As the concluding remarks in section 3.3 show, what matters in the framework advocated here is not a particular choice, per se, but what may trigger that choice in a context of language contact. The proposed analysis extends to Saramaccan (Aboh 2003b), but I only refer to Sranan data for ease of discussion.[23]

3.1. The D-system in Gbe and Sranan

The following paragraphs discuss word order within the Sranan and Gungbe determiner phrase and show that these languages manifest bare noun phrases that are interpreted as (in)definite depending on the context. When the noun surfaces with the determiner, the resulting phrase (i.e. the DP) is necessarily understood as discourse specific.

---

23. The results presented here are further discussed in Aboh (2006a).

3.1.1. Bare nouns and the expression of definiteness

The following examples show that bare noun phrases have the same distribution in Gungbe and Sranan. In example (43), the bare noun '*banana*' is interpreted as generic or indefinite.

(43) a. *Kofi, go na wowoyo go bai bana tya kon gi mi* Sr
  Kofi go LOC market go buy banana carry come give 1SG
  'Kofi, go to the market to buy me banana(s)'
  b. *Kòfí, yì àxìmè bó   yì xɔ̀ àkwékwè wá ná mì.* Gun
  Kofi go market COORD go buy banana   come give 1SG
  'Kòfí go to the market to buy me banana(s).'

The Sranan example (44a) illustrates a context where the bare noun *bana* (in boldface) is interpreted as definite because it refers back to the banana that father brought, that is, the first instance of *bana* in the preceding relative clause. Similarly, the Gungbe headed relative clause in (44b) shows that the bare noun head is interpreted as definite.

(44) a. *Na a bana di ppa tya kon, dati a nyan.*
  FOC DET banana REL father carry come that 3SG eat
  *a   bere   hati, a nyan **bana*** Sr
  3SG stomach hurt 3SG eat banana
  'The banana that father brought that is what he ate. His stomach is aching because he ate the banana.'
  b. **Àkwékwè** [*ḑĕ pàpá hèn wá sɔ̀*] *wè é ḑù.* Gun
  banana   REL father hold come yesterday FOC 3SG eat
  'It is the banana that father brought yesterday that he ate.'

Building on example (44), I propose to define a definite noun phrase as having (pre)-identified referents where identification may be determined by some modifiers, or else from the context. Therefore, definiteness selects one object in the class of possible objects (Ihsane & Puskas 2001). Such definite referents occur as bare nouns in Sranan and Gungbe. In English, however, definiteness is necessarily encoded by the determiner *the*, and bare nouns of the Gungbe and Sranan type are excluded. For instance, the English counterpart of Gungbe (44b) is ungrammatical.

(44) c. **banana that daddy brought yesterday*

3.1.2. The expression of specificity

In this chapter, the term 'specificity' refers to nouns (or referents) previously established in discourse (i.e. old/known referents). For instance, a Sranan noun that occurs with the determiner (*n*)*a* is interpreted as specific definite (i.e. discourse anaphoric). In example (45), the first instance of *bana* in (45a), is interpreted as specific definite (i.e. the aforementioned banana) as opposed to (45b) where *bana* is (in)definite.

(45) a. *Kofi, teki a   bana tya gi mi.*   Sr
           Kofi take DET$_{[+spec, +def, -plur]}$ banana carry give 1SG
           'Kofi, give me the aforementioned banana [e.g. the one I brought yesterday].'
    b. *Kofi, teki bana   tya gi mi.*   Sr
           Kofi take banana carry give 1SG
           'Kofi, give me a/the banana.'

Note that the specific definite interpretation is also assigned to the first instance of *bana* in example (44a). On the other hand, a noun phrase preceded by the determiner *wan* is interpreted as specific indefinite (46a). Example (46b) shows that the two determiners cannot co-occur. Yet, the second interpretation assigned to (46b) suggests that the specific definite determiner *na* and the numeral *wan* can co-occur.

(46) a. *Kofi njan wan   (sortu) bana*   Sr
           Kofi eat DET$_{[+spec, -def, -plur]}$ sort   banana
           'Kofi ate a certain banana.'
    b. *Kofi, teki a   wan bana tya gi mi.* Sr
           FOC take DET$_{[+spec, +def, -plur]}$ one banana carry give 1SG
           '*Kofi, give me the certain banana [e.g. the one I brought yesterday].'
           'Kofi, give me the aforementioned one banana [i.e. the only one available].'

The situation in Sranan is reminiscent of that in Gungbe. Observe, for instance, that a noun phrase followed by the specificity markers *lɔ́* or *ɖé* is necessarily interpreted as specific definite and specific indefinite, respectively. In (47a), *távò cè* 'my table' is understood as non-specific definite, unlike the sequence *távò lɔ́*, which is interpreted as specific definite because it refers to a referent that has been pre-established in discourse. A similar contrast arises in example (47b), where the sequence *távò ɖé* is interpreted as indefinite specific, as opposed to the sequence *távò cè*. The ungrammatical example (47c) shows that the specificity markers *lɔ́* and *ɖé* compete for the same position.

(47) a. *Kɔ̀kú mɔ̀n **távò cè** bò ɖɔ̀*
Koku see table 1SG-POSS and say
*émì ná xɔ̀ **távò lɔ́**.* Gun
3SG FUT buy table DET[+spec, +def]
'Koku saw my table and said that he would buy that aforementioned table.'
b. *Kɔ̀kú mɔ̀n **távò cè** bò ɖɔ́ émì ná xɔ̀*
Koku see table 1SG-POSS and say 3SG FUT buy
távò ɖé. Gun
table DET[+spec -def]
'Koku saw my table and said that he would buy a certain table.'
c. **Kɔ̀kú mɔ̀n **távò lɔ́** **ɖé***
Koku see table DET[+spec, +def] DET[+spec, -def]

These examples indicate that the Gungbe and Sranan noun phrases are not determined for definiteness but for specificity. Put differently, while a noun phrase may be ambiguous with regard to definiteness (i.e. it may be interpreted as (in)definite or generic depending on the context), it is not with respect to specificity. Accordingly, these languages manifest a specific versus non-specific opposition. Assuming that definiteness applies to pre-identified noun phrases, while specificity includes D-linked noun phrases only, I conclude that a specific noun phrase is necessarily discourse-anaphoric, but a definite noun phrase may not be (Pesetsky 1987, Cinque 1990, Enç 1991, Campbell 1996, Ihsane & Puskás 2001). Aboh (2006b: 224) tentatively defines the combination of SPECIFICITY and DEFINITENESS in these languages as in (48):

(48) a. A specific definite noun phrase is strongly D(iscourse)-linked and represents a unique referent assumed to be known to both speaker and hearer, and to which the speaker intends to refer.
b. A specific indefinite noun phrase need not be D-linked. It represents an existing referent that the hearer may not know about, but one which the speaker has in mind and to which he/she intends to refer.

The description in (48) suggests that while these languages do not mark definiteness overtly, they systematically mark specificity, which in turn relates to: (i) the speaker's intent to refer, and (ii) whether the referent is assumed to be known to both speaker and hearer. Therefore, a specific definite noun phrase requires the marker *ló/na* as the morphological realization of the features [specific, definite], while a [specific indefinite] noun phrase must occur with *dé/wan* (*wan sortu*). Noun phrases that are interpreted as [non-specific, definite] or [non-specific, indefinite] occur as bare NPs.

Assuming that the features [±specific, ±definite] are properties of D°, I propose that Gungbe and Sranan bare noun phrases are full DPs where D° hosts a null morpheme that expresses the feature [-specific]. Under this approach, we expect bare noun phrases (i.e. non-specific noun phrases) and specific noun phrases to have the same distribution. This prediction is borne out as suggested by previous examples (see also Longobardi 1994, Aboh 2004b).

3.1.3. The expression of number

Gungbe and Sranan manifest determiners that encode plurality, but they differ as to the function and the distribution of these determiners.

While the Sranan determiners *na* and *wan* express the features [specific, definite, –plural] and [specific, indefinite, -plural], respectively, the features [specific, definite, +plural] are realized by the determiner *den* as shown in (49a). However, Sranan lacks an overt form that expresses the features [+specific, indefinite, +plural]. As example (49b) shows, some speakers use the form *wan tu* where plurality is expressed by a numeral (*tu*). Example (49c) shows that the singular specific definite marker *na* and its plural counterpart *den* are mutually exclusive.

(49) a. *Kofi, teki den bana tya gi mi.* Sr
Kofi take DET$_{[+spec, +def, +plur]}$ banana carry give 1SG
'Kofi, give me the aforementioned banana [e.g. the one I brought yesterday].'

b. *Kofi nyan wan tu bana* Sr
Kofi eat DET$_{[+spec, +def, -plur]}$ [PL] banana
'Kofi ate some bananas.'

c. **Kofi, teki na den*
Kofi take DET$_{[+spec, +def, -plur]}$ DET$_{[+spec, +def, +plur]}$

> *bana tya gi mi.*
> banana carry give 1SG

Gungbe differs from Sranan in that it has a number marker that encodes plurality and definiteness but may co-occur with the specificity markers, as shown in (50).

(50) a. *Kɔkú mɔ̀n **távò** lɛ́ tò àxìmɛ̀*   Gun
Koku see table NUMB at market
'Koku saw the tables at the market.'
b. *Kɔkú mɔ̀n **távò** lɔ́ lɛ́ tò àxìmɛ̀*   Gun
Koku see table DET[+spec, +def] NUMB at market
'Koku saw the specific tables at the market.'
c. *Kɔkú mɔ̀n **távò** ɖé lɛ́ tò àxìmɛ̀*   Gun
Koku see table DET[+spec, -def] NUMB at market
'Koku saw some specific tables at the market.'

The definite interpretation assigned to the noun phrase *távò lɛ́* 'the tables' in (50a) suggests that, in addition to the feature [+plural], the Gbe number marker may also encode definiteness as defined in (48b), that is, as pre-identified referents. The following examples in (51) support this hypothesis. In example (51a) the sequence *àkwékwè átɔ́n* 'five bananas' is interpreted as indefinite. Here the customer is asking for any five bananas (maybe out of a set of ten), because s/he is not interested in any particular set of five bananas. In example (51b), however, the definite sequence *àkwékwè átɔ́n lɛ́* refers to a pre-identified set of five bananas. In example (51c) the sequence *àkwékwè átɔ́n lɔ́ lɛ́* refers to a set of five bananas that has been previously established in discourse, hence the specific interpretation.

(51) a. *mì sà **àkwékwè átɔ́n** ná mì*   Gun
2PL sell banana five for 1SG
'Sell me five bananas.'
b. *mì sà **àkwékwè átɔ́n** lɛ́ ná mì*   Gun
2PL sell banana five NUMB for 1SG
'Sell me the five bananas.'
c. *mì sà **àkwékwè átɔ́n** lɔ lɛ́ ná mì*   Gun
2PL sell banana five DET[+spec, +def] NUMB for 1SG
'Sell me the aforementioned five bananas.'

Because the Gungbe number marker may encode definiteness in addition to the number feature, I conclude that it expresses some referential features.[24] These facts clearly suggest that the Gungbe determiner *ló* is primarily a specificity marker, not a definite determiner as often proposed in the literature (see, for example, Lefebvre 1998).

The above discussion may give the impression that the specificity marker and the number marker are completely independent. Yet, even though these markers can occur independently as in previous examples, a noun modified by a numeral encoding plurality (e.g. *àkwékwè átɔ́n* 'five bananas') cannot be marked as specific in the absence of the number marker. Compare the grammatical sentence (52a) to the ungrammatical example (52b) where the number marker is missing.

(52) a. mì sà **àkwékwè àtɔ́n ló**   lɛ́   ná mì Gun
         2PL sell banana   five DET[+spec, +def]   NUMB for 1SG
         'Sell me the aforementioned five bananas.'
    b. *mì sà **àkwékwè àtɔ́n ló**   --   ná mì Gun
         2PL sell banana   five DET[+spec, +def]   for 1SG
         'Sell me the specific five bananas.'

These data indicate that the number marker is required so as to establish concord (or agreement) between the plural expression in the nominal inflectional domain and the elements that are set off to the right edge, that is, the specificity and number markers. Following previous work on the parallels between the clausal and the nominal domains, I assume that the specificity and number markers are morphological expressions of the nominal left periphery DP and NumP, respectively (Abney 1987, Szabolcsi 1987, 1994, Longobardi 1994, Ritter 1995, Bernstein 1997, 2001, Aboh 2004a, b, 2006b). According to this view, the Gungbe nominal left periphery mimics the clausal left periphery in the sense that both systems manifest right edge markers, which have scope over the proposition or predicate, which is then fronted into their specifiers.

Compared to the Sranan data, however, it appears that, while Sranan manifests the opposition *na/wan* and *den* to encode the set of features [+specific, ±definite, ±plural], Gungbe manifest two types of determiners:

---

24. According to Essegbey (p.c.), the Ewegbe counterpart of the Gungbe (51a) has a generic meaning. In addition, Ewegbe excludes (51b), but allows (51c). These facts seem to confirm the definite nature of the plural marker in Gungbe, as opposed to Ewegbe, but I leave this matter for further study.

ló/dé express the features [+specific, ±definite] and *lέ* essentially manifests the feature [+plural].

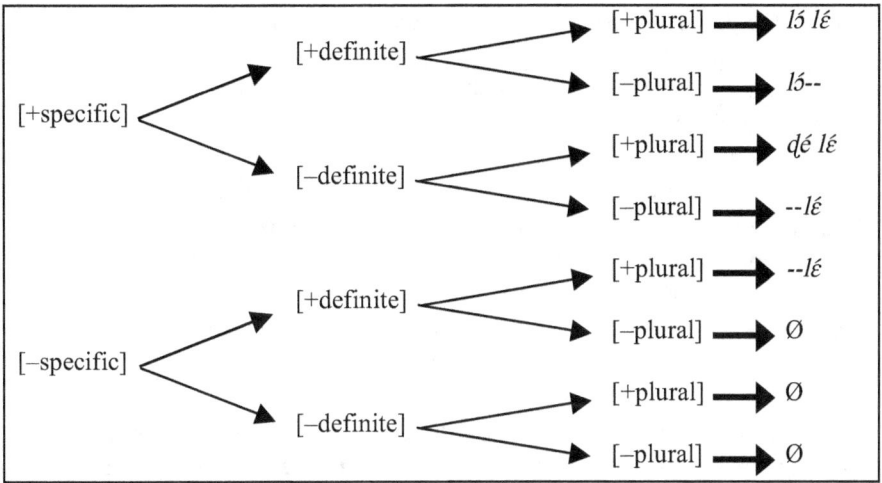

Figure 1. Gungbe

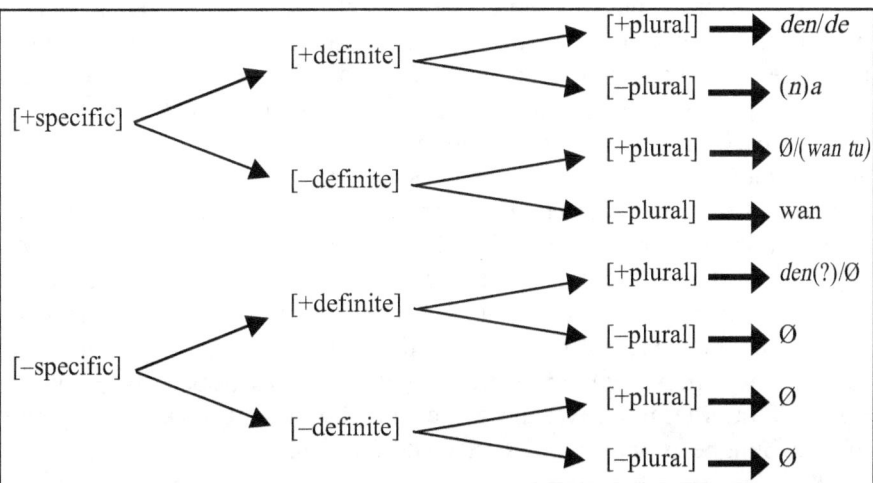

Figure 2. Sranan

Also notice that while the determiners *ló* and *na* are highly discourse-anaphoric, *dé* and *wan* appear to be less so. The former but not the latter always refer to a referent that has been established in previous discourse and that is known to both speaker and hearer.

The existence of the specific versus non-specific opposition in Gbe and Sranan in association with the expression of plurality and definiteness allows for the combinations indicated in Figures 1 and 2. The representations in these Figures are summarized in Table 1.

Table 1. The combinations of features expressed by the Gungbe and Sranan determiners

D-features	Gungbe	Sranan
[+spec, +def, +plur]	lɔ́ lɛ́	den
[+spec, +def, -plur]	lɔ́	na
[+spec, -def, +plur]	ɖé lɛ́	Ø (wan tu)
[+spec, -def, -plur]	ɖé	wan
[-spec, +def, +plur]	lɛ́	den(?)/Ø
[-spec, +def, -plur]	Ø [definite]	Ø [definite]
[-spec, -def, +plur]	Ø [generic]	Ø [generic]
[-spec, -def, -plur]	Ø [indefinite]	Ø [indefinite]

The last three rows of Table 1 show that Gungbe and Sranan are similar in allowing for bare noun phrases associated with the features [-spec, +def, -plur], [-spec, -def, +plur], and [-spec, -def, -plur] that are interpreted as definite, generic and indefinite, respectively. The two languages also pattern alike in allowing for distinct markers that encode discourse properties (i.e. specificity and number) in a way that English does not. Observe, however, that Sranan *na* and *den* express two different set of features each, unlike Gungbe specificity markers. In addition, the rows 3 and 5 show that the two languages do not manifest a one to one correspondence. In a sense, we reach a situation where the determiners serve similar semantic functions in these languages, but the forms they take appear to derive from different internal structures. The question then arises why are Sranan [+specific, -definite, +plural] noun phrases often realized as bare NPs or preceded by *wan tu*, while there seems to be no determiner (i.e. distinct from *den*) for expressing the features [-specific, +definite, +plural]? In order to answer these questions I will now consider the syntax of D in Gungbe as opposed to Sranan and English.

3.1.4. The derivation of determiners

In my account of the Gungbe facts, I propose that the specificity and number markers manifest distinct categories within the determiner system, DP-NumP, which I consider to belong to the nominal left periphery. Under the split-D hypothesis argued for in Aboh (2004a), D° heads the highest projection of this system that links the noun phrase (or the nominal predicate) to previous discourse. Num°, on the other hand, delimits the nominal left periphery downward as the interface between the nominal left periphery and the inflectional domain. Following Aboh (2004b: 7), I further assume that the specificity marker realises the head of a topic phrase (TopP) that projects between DP and NumP and expresses the features [±specific]. In Gungbe Top° is morphologically realized as *lɔ́*, the expression of the feature [+specific]. On the other hand, Num° encodes number (i.e. [±plural]) as well as nominal agreement (and definiteness) features that match those of the nominal inflectional domain. Building on Szabolcsi (1994), I argue that definiteness is determined within the nominal inflectional domain but is taken up again by Num° in the left periphery as the result of a concord process similar to that of number (53). In Gungbe, Num° is overtly realized by the marker *lɛ́*. Under this analysis therefore, the Gungbe determiner system can be illustrated as in (53), where it appears that D, comparable to Force on the clause level, is always non-overt in these languages.

(53) [DP [D [TopP [Top *lɔ́* [NumP [Num *lɛ́* [NP ......]]]]]]]

Building on representation (53), I suggest that the Gbe bare noun phrases can be seen as full DPs where Top° and Num° host null morphemes that express the feature [-specific], [-plural], or else do not project (Longobardi 1994, Aboh 2004a, b). Given that Top° and Num° are embedded within DP, whose head is always non-overt in these languages, the proposed description predicts that bare noun phrases (i.e. non-specific and singular noun phrases) will have the same distribution as specific and plural noun phrases (i.e. specific singular or plural noun phrases). As the data discussed here have shown this prediction is borne out.

With this analysis in mind, let us now consider the structure of pronouns. As already discussed in Aboh (2004a, chapter 4), Gungbe plural strong pronouns derive from a combination of a weak pronoun and the number marker as in (54a). Weak forms, on the contrary, exclude the number marker as shown in (54b). Accordingly, Gungbe weak pronouns involve a morphologically simple form that encodes both [person] and [number] specifications. On the other hand strong forms are morphologically complex and express [person] and [number] features separately.

(54) a. Mí-lέ / mì-lέ / yé-lέ   Gun
         1PL / 2PL / 3PL
         'We/you/they'
     b. Mí-(*lέ) / mì-(*lέ) / yé-(*lέ)   Gun
         1pl   / 2pl   / 3pl
         'We/you/they'

In order to account for these forms, I propose that weak pronouns involve a less articulated structure than full noun phrases in that they do not (always) project the DP-internal topic phrase. Under the assumption that D° and Num° express [person] and [number] respectively (Ritter 2005), I propose structure (54c) for deriving strong forms, while (54d) represents weak forms. In this analysis, the plural weak pronouns merge under Num° to encode number but must raise to D° to check the person feature.

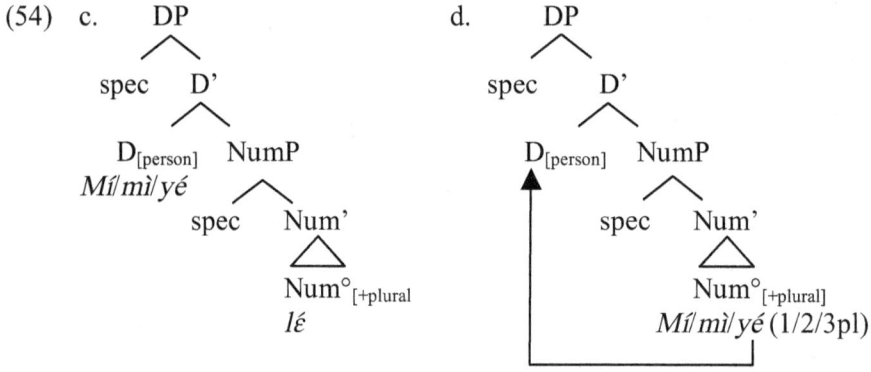

We can derive the structure of the determiners in Sranan on the basis of the representation in (54d) that accounts for the Gungbe weak pronouns. Put differently, I propose that the determiner merges under Num° to encode the features [±plural, ±definite] but must raise to D° as an expression of the features [±specific]. Accordingly, a single determiner expresses the set of features [±specific, ±definite, ±plural] as represented in (55).

This analysis is compatible with the fact that the determiners in Sranan and Saramaccan developed from pronominal forms (e.g. demonstrative, 3PL). That the Sranan determiner and the Gungbe weak pronouns manifest the same derivation shouldn't necessarily be seen as substrate transfer where the Sranan determiners are modelled on the Gungbe weak pronouns. Actually representation (54d) is also compatible with English determiners and weak pronouns. As I show in the following section, the more plausible analysis is therefore that English is the source of this structure in Sranan, with Gbe languages possibly acting as reinforcers. Accordingly, I assume that both Sranan and English realize the structure in (54d), where a single head encodes a set of features (i.e. specificity, number), while the same features are expressed by two distinct morphemes in Gungbe (54c-f).

(55)

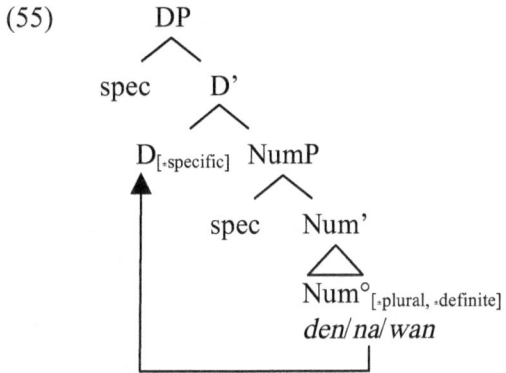

Building on this, I propose that the lack of distinct morphemes as the expression of D° and Num° is also responsible for the discrepancy in rows 3 and 5 of Table 1. *Wan* is a numeral that is inherently singular. Accordingly, when used as [specific indefinite] determiner, it cannot simultaneously encode plurality as a combination of the features [+spec, -def, +plur]. To circumvent this clash, some Sranan speakers resort to the form *wan tu* where we can reasonably assume that plurality is encoded by the numeral inside the nominal inflectional domain as represented in (56a). This derivation parallels with the usage of *wan sortu* to mark specific indefinite noun phrases in example (46a). Alternatively, one could propose that *wan tu* is a single morpheme that also encodes plurality. In this case, the derivation is parallel to (55). *Wan tu* merges under Num° but raises to D° as expression of the features [+spec, -def, +plur] (56a). Deciding between these two derivations is beyond the scope of this chapter and I leave the matter for further study.[25]

---

25. A third possibility would be to assume that the bimorphemic *wan tu* is parallel to Gungbe because *wan* expresses D° and *tu* encodes Num°. But such scenario would have to account for why the determiner *den*, the definite counterpart, is monomorphemic and does not involve the combination of say a demonstrative like *da*, and a numeral like *tu*. Cross-linguistically, the Sranan morpheme *wan*

(56) a.

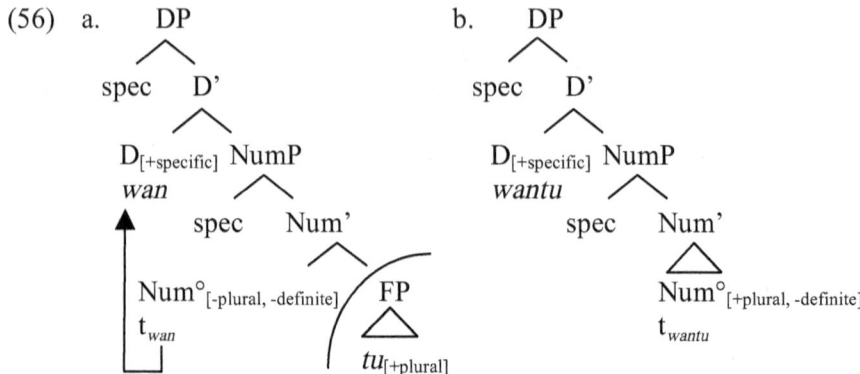

A similar clash arises with the combination of features [-spec, +definite, +plural]. The morpheme *den* is inherently plural and somehow referential (i.e. definite), being derived from a pronoun or a demonstrative (Bruyn 1995). As such, *den* merges under Num° but must raise to D° to encode the feature [+specific]. But the system doesn't seem to provide a way for licensing the feature [-specific] in this context (57). As a result, a noun phrase that is associated with the combination of features [-specific, +definite, +plural] surfaces as a bare noun (or for some speakers) preceded by *den*, which is therefore ambiguous with regard to the features [±specific, +definite, +plural].

(57)

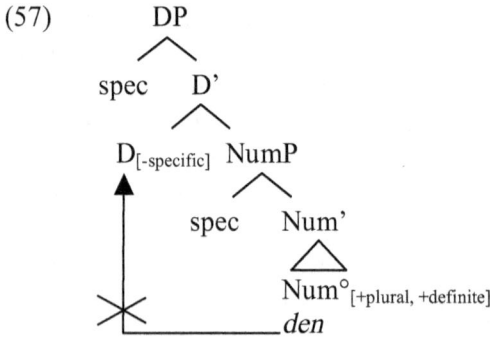

The conclusion here seems to be that Gungbe and Sranan pattern alike because they manifest a specific versus non-specific opposition and allow for definite, indefinite or generic bare noun phrases in a way that English

---

tu is comparable to the Spanish form *unos* where a determiner intrinsically singular is marked for plural.

does not. However, the determiners of both languages appear to manifest different morphosyntax. Put another way, the morphosyntax of the Sranan determiner is more like that of English. The question now is what triggers this asymmetry.

3.2. Same function, different syntax, why?

If we assume that the similarities between Sranan and Gungbe can be accounted for in terms of substrate influence, then the natural question to ask is what makes Sranan syntax deviate from the Gbe pattern. In what follows, I propose that English might have provided the impetus for this change, assuming that we take into account other differences between Gungbe and Sranan as opposed to English and Sranan.

A striking difference between Gungbe and Sranan is that while the determiner must follow the noun in Gungbe, it precedes it in Sranan (and English) as represented in (58).

(58) a. [NP ——] > ló/dé-lé
 b. na/wan-den > [NP ——]

With regard to (58a), I propose that specificity and number licensing in Gbe requires some type of predicate fronting whereby the predicate as a whole (that is, the extended projection of N represented by FP) moves to [spec NumP] and [spec TopP] as illustrated in (59).[26]

(59) [DP [D [TopP [Top ló [NumP [Num lé [NP......]]]]]]

The word order of the noun phrase in Sranan and English (58b) suggests that fronting does not occur in these languages, and specificity (and number) must be licensed otherwise. In this respect, Campbell (1996) proposes that in languages like English, the feature [specific] is checked by an operator in [spec DP]. The latter binds an empty category in the nominal domain. Building on this, we could assume that Sranan specific noun phrases are derived as represented in (60).

---

26. I refer the reader to Aboh (2004a, c) for the discussion on the structure of noun phrases in Gungbe.

(60)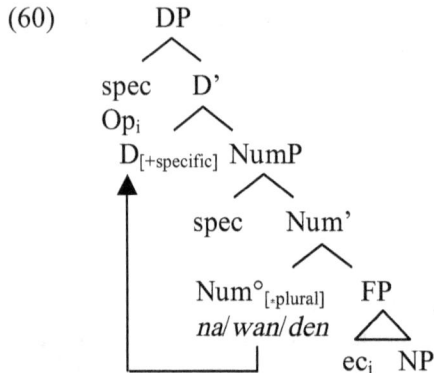

Compared to Sranan as described in (60), the representation of Gungbe in (59) suggests that the determiners will always follow the noun. Indeed, this word order also extends to all the nominal modifiers, which must follow the noun in the fixed order adjective > numeral > demonstrative, as shown in (61a). In a sense, except for the postposed demonstrative in Sranan, the sequence of the Gungbe nominal modifiers (i.e. adjective, numeral) is the mirror of that of the Sranan modifiers (61b).

(61) a. Kòfí wè xɔ̀ àvò [yù àwè **éhè/*fí**]
Kofi FOC buy cloth black two DEM/here
lɔ́ lɛ́   Gun
DET[+spec,+def] NUMB[+plur]
'Kofi bought these two black clothes.'

b. Kofi bai den [dri bigi]
Kofi buy DET[+spec, +def, +plur] three big
ipi-bana ***disi/ja***   Sr
heap_of_banana this/here
'Kofi bought these three big heaps of banana.'

Also notice from example (62) that while the relative clause is sandwiched between the specific head noun and the specificity and number determiners in Gungbe, it follows both the specificity and number determiner and the head noun in Sranan.

(62) a. *Kòfízé àvò [dĕ mí xɔ̀ sɔ̀] lɔ́ lé* Gun
Kofi take cloth REL 1PL buy yesterday DET$_{[+spec, +def]}$ NUMB$_{[+plur]}$
'Kofi took the clothes that we bought yesterday.'

b. *Den uma [di mi si na a*
DET$_{[+spec, +def, +plur]}$ woman REL 1SG se LOC DET$_{[+spec,+def,-plur]}$
wowoyo], den e kon Sr
market 3PL PROG come
'The women that I met at the market have come.'

The word orders in examples (61) and (62) suggest that Sranan and Gungbe nominal sequences differ in syntax. Sranan manifests a word order of the English-type. In this respect, the examples in (63) further show that Sranan and Gungbe differ because the Sranan postnominal demonstratives *disi/dati* (or the place adverb *ja/dape* 'here/there') can encode some type of emphasis, as in the English example *this heap here* versus *that heap there*. This construction is also found in Germanic and Romance languages (Bernstein 2001). In the literature, such examples are referred to as demonstrative reinforcement constructions. The following examples show that the Gbe languages lack such constructions, because the postnominal demonstrative determiner in these languages does not have an emphatic meaning.

(63) a. *This here guy* non-standard English
b. *Ce livre-ci* French
this book-here
'This book'
c. **dáwè éhè fí*[27] Gun
man DEM here

---

27. This sentence is perfectly grammatical if interpreted as 'the man is here.' An interesting fact that could suggest that the Gbe languages act as reinforcers is that, unlike other nominal modifiers, which must all precede the relative clause, the demonstrative may precede or follow the relative clause.
(iii) a. *dáwè éhè [dé wá fí]*
man DEM that come here
'This man that came here'
b. *dáwè [dé wá fí] éhè*
man that come here here
'This man here, that came here'
Interestingly, the interpretation of (iiib) suggests that this structure might involve focusing of the relative clause, a process similar to the demonstrative

In terms of the present discussion, the fact that English has such constructions supports the hypothesis that it provided the impetus for such development in Sranan. This suggests that the Gbe languages are not the primary source for post-nominal demonstrative in Sranan. If that were the case, one would wonder why such process, which systematically targets all noun modifiers in Gbe, only found its way through demonstratives in Sranan, without affecting the morphosyntax of adjectives, numerals, and relative clauses, which all appear prenominally in this language. The discussion on the clausal left periphery in the first part of this chapter suggests that such scenario is less likely. Similarly, one might ask what blocks demonstrative reinforcement constructions in Gungbe, but not in Sranan, even though both languages display postnominal demonstratives?

Again, it seems to me that the answer to this question lies in the underlying structure of the nominal sequence and the formal licensing conditions that it requires. Let us assume that Sranan and Gungbe display the (universal) hierarchy in (64).

(64) [$_{DP}$ [$_{D°}$ [$_{TopP}$ [$_{Top°}$ Specificity [$_{NumP}$ [$_{Num°}$ Number [$_{FP}$ Demonstrative [$_{FP}$ Numeral [$_{FP}$ Adjective [$_{NP}$ Head noun]]]]]]]]]]

However, the conditions on noun licensing differ in the two languages. In Gungbe, noun licensing requires two compulsory rules. The first consists of a systematic reversing rule that successively left-adjoins the noun to the preceding modifiers. This movement, referred to as snowballing in Aboh (2004a, b), is comparable to N-raising in some languages (e.g. Romance), where the noun raises past the modifiers to some inflectional position. This produces the order Noun-head>Adjective>Numeral>Demonstrative. As far as I can tell, there does not seem to be any semantic effect associated with this displacement, a fact that could explain the absence of the emphatic (or contrastive) force of postnominal demonstratives in this language.

The second obligatory rule as described in (59) appears a predicate fronting operation that forces movement of the constituent including the head noun and its modifiers (i.e. the nominal predicate) to [spec NumP] and [spec TopP/DP], as an instance of predicate fronting as proposed in (20). This fronting rule appears to have a semantic effect with regard to the interpretation of specificity or number. The combination of the two movements discussed here is described in (65).

---

reinforcement structures discussed above. The proper analysis of these structures goes beyond this chapter and I leave the matter for further research.

The left periphery in the Surinamese creoles and Gbe   365

(65) [DP [D° [TopP [Top° *ló* [NumP [Num° *lέ* [FP [FP *ɛ̀nɛ̀* [FP [FP *àwὲ* [FP [FP *ɖàxó* [NP xwé]]]]]]]]]]]

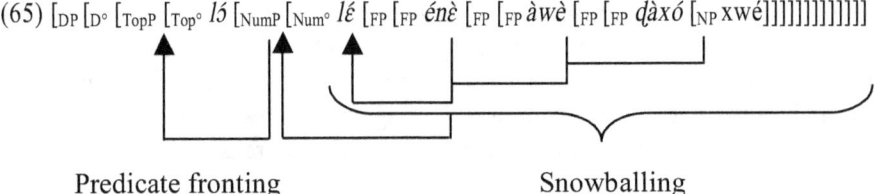

      Predicate fronting   Snowballing

It appears from this description that the combination of these two movement rules in Gbe exhausts all fronting possibilities that could give rise to demonstrative reinforcement. Put differently, the morphosyntax of the noun phrase in Gungbe (or in any other Gbe language) doesn't provide room for demonstrative reinforcement constructions to exist. This specific aspect of the grammar of these languages makes them different from the Suriname creoles. In Sranan, for instance, nominal modifiers precede the noun and specificity is licensed by an operator in the nominal left periphery (e.g. [spec DP]). Granting this, the grammar of Sranan makes room for a fronting rule that can optionally target the noun phrase (or some of its extended projection). This latter movement gives rise to demonstrative reinforcement, which may be related to emphasis. The Sranan situation is represented in (66).

(66) [DP Op [D° *den* [NumP [Num° t*den* [FP [FP *disi* [FP *dri* [FP *bigi* [NP *ipi banan*]]]]]]]]]

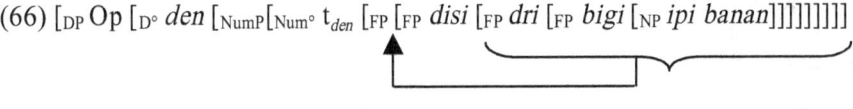

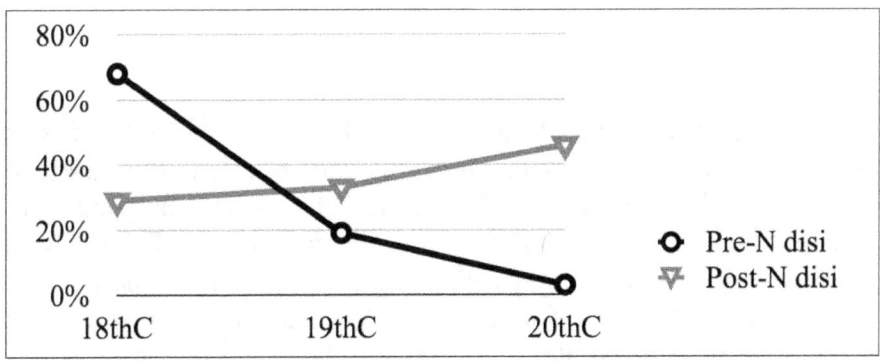

Figure 3. Bleaching of pragmatic effect (Adapted from Bruyn 1995)

A consequence of this analysis is that Sranan postnominal demonstrative constructions are analyzed as derived from a structure where the demonstrative is underlyingly prenominal. In this regard, it is worth mentioning that diachronic work by Bruyn (1995: 115) shows that the demonstratives *disi* and *dati* are used both prenominally and postnominally even though in different proportions. Figure 3 indicates that pre-N *disi* decreases in the course of time, while post-N *disi* increases.

3.2.1. Summary

Table 2 summarizes the discussion and shows that both Gungbe and English fed the morphosyntax of the nominal sequence in Sranan. While Gungbe provided the impetus for the development of discourse-related markers (i.e. the specific versus non-specific opposition) in Sranan, English has influenced its grammar. In this regard, a look at the second column shows that the grammar of Sranan appears to be different from both that of Gungbe and English. It is as if the creators of Sranan took advantage of both systems because the outcome appears to be more efficient than the grammar of Gungbe and English, respectively.

Table 2. Properties on the nominal sequence in Gungbe, Sranan, and English

	Gungbe	Sranan	English
Bare nouns	+	+	−
Spec vs. Non-spec	+	+	−
Modifier > noun	−	+	+
Noun > Modifier[intensifier]	−	+	(+)

4. Concluding remarks

The discussion in the preceding sections shows that substrate transfer is not a unitary phenomenon. The emergence of a feature in a given creole may be triggered different aspects of the languages in competition (see Aboh 2006b for further discussion). The analysis proposed here is compatible with situations where the function and the syntax of a set of features may be retained from either the substrate or the superstrate. In this regard, the discussion in Section 3 indicates that, even though the Gbe languages provide the appropriate context for the emergence of the specific versus non-specific opposition, as well as the use of bare nouns in Sranan and

Saramaccan, such feature transmission was not subject to morphosyntactic inheritance. On the other hand, the discussion in Section 2 suggests that Gungbe-like varieties have played a central role in the development of the Saramaccan clausal left periphery, as well as its morphosyntax. Accordingly, even though the two languages differ in many respects with regard to their TMA systems, Saramaccan manifests a subset of core morphosyntactic properties of the left periphery that are found in Gungbe, and cannot be easily attributed to language natural development or language universals.

Table 3 summarizes the properties of the Saramaccan and Gungbe left peripheries and shows that English manifests different structures from both Saramaccan and Gungbe.

Table 3. The left peripheries of Gungbe, Saramaccan, and English: an overview

Construction	Gungbe	Saramaccan	English
XP-focus	XP_i *wè* $[_{IP}$ — t_i —]	XP_i *wè* $[_{IP}$ — t_i —]	XP_i $[_{IP}$ — t_i —]
V-focus	V_i (*wè*) $[_{IP}$ — t_i —]	V_i *wè* $[_{IP}$ — V_i —]	VP_i $[_{IP}$ — t_i —]
XP-topic	XP_i *yà* $[_{IP}$ — pro_i —]	XP_i *de* $[_{IP}$ — pro_i —]	XP_i $[_{IP}$ — pro_i —]
Yes-no question	$[_{IP}$ ——] ` t_{IP} $[_{IP}$ ——] *à* t_{IP} (Fon)	$[_{IP}$ ——] *no* t_{IP}	Do-S-V-O

Relexification and clause-embedding predicates

Tonjes Veenstra

1. Introduction

This chapter presents an overview of sentence-embedding predicates and their associated syntax in Saramaccan, and the Gbe languages, especially Fon, and evaluates the different scenarios for creole genesis on the basis of that. In particular, I focus on the theory of Relexification (Muysken 1981, Lefebvre 1998).

Relexification is a theory about a process that takes place at the Lexicon-Syntax Interface. Thus, to find out whether a certain part of the grammar of a creole language is due to relexification (as opposed to processes of second language acquisition), it is important to look at those grammatical properties that are relevant to this interface. The influence of the lexicon on the syntax reveals itself most clearly in the case of clause-embedding predicates. It is clear that lexically specified differences exist between predicates with respect to selectional restrictions (*believe that* vs. **believe whether*), and possible control readings (*x promises y to come* → *x will come*; *x persuades y to come* → *y should come*) lead to different syntactic structures. If relexification does play an important role in the reconstitution of clause-embedding predicates, the predictions are very clear and straightforward.

(1) a. identical (or at least highly similar) selection patterns in the substrate language(s) and the creole
 b. high degree of stability of selection patterns in the creole

The leading question of this paper, therefore, is whether the syntax of clause-embedding predicates in Saramaccan strictly follows the patterns found in the substrate language Fon. Noonan (2007) presents a typology of embedding predicates and divides clause-embedding predicates in fourteen different classes, each class with its own set of characteristic semantic features. In finding an answer to this question, we restrict the discussion to two sets of clause-embedding predicates: (i) the semantically and syntactically less-integrated group of utterance, emotion, and propositional attitude predicates; (ii) the semantically and syntactically more-integrated group of phrasal predicates (i.e. aspectual verbs).

The paper is organized as follows. In Section 2, I sketch a model of creole genesis that incorporates processes of second language acquisition as well as the process of relexification. I argue that both processes are needed to account for the emergence of creole languages. In Section 3, I discuss the set of clause-embedding predicates consisting of utterance, emotion, and propositional attitude predicates in Fon and Saramaccan. Section 4 presents the case of aspectual verbs in the Gbe languages (and other West African languages in general) as compared to Saramaccan. I close off with some conclusions in Section 5.

2. Scenarios of creole genesis

All current theories of creolization regard second language acquisition as one of the determining factors in creole genesis, although the assumptions about its impact and the way it interacts with other contact phenomena, such as relexification, language shift, and language (re-)creation differ widely (cf. DeGraff 1999; Mufwene 1990, 2010; Muysken 1981, 2008; different contributions in Lefebvre, White & Jourdan 2006; Plag 2008a, 2008b, 2009a, 2009b; Kouwenberg 2009). Nevertheless, several authors have argued that processes of second language acquisition cannot solely account for the emergence of substrate-related grammatical properties of creole languages (Kouwenberg 2006; Siegel 2008). Although there is ample evidence of such grammatical properties of creoles (e.g. Kouwenberg 1994; Lefebvre 1998; Winford 2003, among many others), Siegel (2008) mentions three problems with transfer accounts of these properties: (i) scarcity of evidence of early transfer in interlanguage studies and in restricted pidgins, i.e. detailed descriptions of interlanguages of second language learners have not provided evidence of the process of transfer that is supposed to be the source of some creole features – especially those features that appear to be superstrate forms with substrate grammatical properties (see also Kouwenberg 2006); (ii) existence of transferred structures in expanded pidgins and creoles that seemingly had nowhere to transfer to, in particular transfer of word order in which there was no congruence between the word orders of the L1 and L2, and, as such, problematic for the Transfer-to-Somewhere Principle of Andersen (1983); (iii) creole features apparently from the substrate that were not found in the preceding pidgin (where textual evidence exists from both the creole and the preceding pidgin), e.g. the TMA system as well as for-complementation in Hawai'ian Creole English developed late and primarily within the population of locally-born speakers (Roberts 1998). This implies that adult learners cannot have been the sole contributors of grammatical properties (and structure) to creoles and that a scenario of creole genesis ought to involve multiple agents.[1] Becker & Veenstra (2003) reached a similar conclusion, and proposed that the process of creolization requires a three-generational scenario of language shift (cf. Bickerton 1977; Corne 1999; Roberts 2000). The main difference between creolization and other language-shift situations lies in a target shift in the case of creolization (see Baker 1990, 1996, for argumentation of this point). Such a scenario was first proposed in Corne (1994) for Tayo. Further evidence for this approach to creole genesis has been adduced by Jennings (1995) for Cayenne Creole and Becker & Veenstra (2003) for Mauritian Creole. The picture of the shift to creole is then as follows (from Becker & Veenstra 2003):

(2) Multi-generational scenario of creole genesis

G1 (foreign-born immigrants)	L1	ancestral language(s)
	L2	pidgin
G2 (first generation locally born)	L1	ancestral language(s)
	L1	pidgin/creole
G3 (second generation locally born)	L1	creole
	(L2	ancestral language(s))

In this scenario, the first generation (G1) consists of immigrants/slaves who pidginize the superstrate language. The next generation (G2) is that of the locally born children of G1. According to Corne (1994) this is the crucial generation. As he puts it (1994: 296), writing about the emergence of Tayo:

> Members of G2 retain their ancestral L1 ... but, like the children of immigrants everywhere, they have to acquire the language of the community as a whole. Their problem is that there is no community L1 apart from pidginized L2 French, and they must therefore acquire/create L1

---

1. Independent evidence comes from studies on computational modeling of creole genesis. In particular, Satterfield (2008) notes that her findings suggest that patterns of adult L2 acquisition presumed under standard L2 creole accounts are not sufficient to explain the emergence of these creoles.

competence on the basis of their exposure to (some subset of) the varieties of pidginized L2 French, variable over time and depending on personal circumstances ... It is they who participate in the creation of the nascent creole.

Members of the third generation (G3) are only indirectly exposed to their ancestral language(s), due to the presence of G1 and G2 speakers in their community; having largely lost their ancestral language(s), they can be considered the first monolingual speakers of the incipient creole.

Creolization is thus seen as a complex and multi-dimensional phenomenon, not one that can be accounted for by postulating a single mechanism but rather one that consists of at least two different processes, each with its own agents (Veenstra 1996: 195). The first process is that of untutored L2 acquisition, of which the first-generation adults (i.e. the different cohorts of slaves imported from West Africa) are the agents. This process is responsible for some of the SLA effects in the grammars of creole languages (Plag 2008a, 2008b, 2009a, 2009b). The second process is that of bilingual L1 acquisition, of which the children (i.e. the second generation, consisting of the creole population born in the colony) are the agents. In this process, we find, among other things, persistence of L1-related properties of grammar, and subsequent reinterpretation of superstrate material (Kouwenberg 2006, 2009).[2]

From this it follows that substrate influence in the case of creole languages is not a unified phenomenon, but rather we can speak of "Distributed Transfer" (Veenstra 2004):[3]

---

2. Satterfield (2005) even goes so far to claim that 'prototypical creole' structures emerge when a very small percentage of older bilingual children were present in the population.
3. Similar proposals can be found in the literature as early as Haugen's (1950) distinction between importation and calque, via Johanson's (1992) distinction between partial and global copying, Aboh's (2006b) pattern vs feature transmission, and Matras & Sakel's (2007) pattern vs matter replication, to Cabrera & Zubizarreta's (2004) observation that non-advanced learners focus on the L1 constructional properties of causatives, whereas advanced learners focus on L1 specific lexical properties of verb classes. Furthermore, Sanchez (2003, 2006) discusses the process of functional convergence, which typically takes place with bilingual speakers, and is akin to the process of relexification we know from creole studies (Lefebvre 1998) and contact linguistics in general (Muysken 1981).

(3) a. Substrate influence due to G1 (processes of SLA) is restricted to inheritance of general surface patterns but not specific grammatical properties.
   b. Substrate influence due to G2 (processes of bilingual acquisition) targets specific grammatical properties of the contributing source languages.

One of the leading research questions, therefore, is that when we find cross-linguistic influence whether these continuities from the substrate languages are due to processes of SLA or of bilingual acquisition.

One of the advantages of the multi-generational model in (2) is that it can incorporate the process of relexification in a natural way. Relexification is defined as the process of vocabulary substitution in which the only information adopted from the target language in the lexical entry is the phonological representation (Muysken 1981: 61). In the classic definition, the semantic representations of source and target language entries must partially overlap for relexification to occur; otherwise, the two entries would never be associated with each other:

(4) Relexification (Muysken 1981, 1988, Lefebvre 1998)

Original lexical entry
[phonology]$_i$
[semantic feature]$_k$
[syntactic feature]$_n$

Lexifier language
[phonetic string]$_j$ used in specific semantic and pragmatic contexts

\ /

New lexical entry
[phonology]$_j$ or [Ø]
[semantic feature]$_k$
[syntactic feature]$_n$

As argued extensively by Muysken (1981, 1997), Media Lengua is a prime example of a mixed language which arose through relexification, and cannot be considered to represent a stage in learning Spanish as a second language for the following two reasons: (i) many Media Lengua-speakers also speak fluent Spanish; (ii) Media Lengua is very different from Quechua-Spanish interlanguage. This is shown in the schematic contrast between Media Lengua and Spanish Interlanguage in central Ecuador (adapted from Muysken 2008) in Table 1.

In the creole context it is G2, the first-locally born generation, acquiring the emerging contact variety and their ancestral language(s) simultaneously that is responsible for the relexificational effects that have amply been documented for the Atlantic Creoles (see especially Lefebvre (1998) and Lumsden (1994, 1995, 1999) on Haitian Creole).[4]

Table 1. Systematic comparison of relexification and L2 learning in the Ecuadorian Andean context

	Media Lengua (relexification)	Interlanguage (L2 learning)
Structure	Complex	highly simplified
Degree of stabilization	rigid	highly variable
source	Quechua morpho-syntax and phonology with slight Spanish influence	Spanish morpho-syntax and phonology with Quechua influence
Function	in-group language	interethnic communication

In order to evaluate the role played by the different acquisition processes operative in creole genesis then, the rest of the chapter is focused on sentence-embedding predicates and their associated syntax in Saramaccan, and the Gbe languages, especially Fon. As noted in the introduction, the leading question of this paper is whether the syntax of clause-embedding predicates in Saramaccan strictly follows the patterns found in the substrate language Fon. To answer this question, we restrict the discussion to two sets of clause-embedding predicates. We discuss the semantically and syntactically less-integrated group of utterance, emotion, and propositional attitude predicates in Section 3. The semantically and syntactically more-integrated group of aspectual verbs is the topic of Section 4.

3. The syntax of clause-embedding predicates.

The relation between the matrix predicate and the embedded clause is expressed (or mediated) in the highest projection of that clause, namely ForceP (Rizzi 1997). According to him, only tensed complementizers can head ForceP. Such complementizers are then selected by particular classes of verbs that occur in the matrix clause. According to Lefebvre and

---

4. This conception of the notion of relexification diverges from the one argued for in Lefebvre (1998) along the following two parameters: (i) relexification does not occur with incipient adult SLA; (ii) the language pair in relexification is not superstrate -- substrate(s), but rather contact variety -- substrate. This is more in line with the original characterization, given in Muysken (1981, cf. also 2008).

Brousseau (2002), there are two tensed complementizers in Fon: ɖɔ and nú/ní. They argue that the first one is indicative and occurs with verbs from the SAY-class, whereas the second one is subjunctive and occurs with verbs from the WANT-class:

(5) a. Kɔkú ɖì ɖɔ Bàyí wá.
 Koku believe ɖɔ Bayi come
 'Koku believed that Bayi came.'
 b. È nyɔ Nú à ní yì.
 3SG good NU 2SG SUB leave.
 'It is good that you leave.'

If verbs select for an embedded question, ɖɔ is obligatorily present, suggesting that ɖɔ does not determine the typing of the clause.

(6) Ùn kán byɔ ɛ ɖɔ fitɛ yé nɔ nɔ àjí.
 1SG ask 3SG ɖɔ where 3PL usually live QP
 'I asked him/her where they live.'

The two complementizers are mutual exclusive.

(7) *Ùn jló ɖɔ ní à ní wá.
 1SG want ɖɔ NI 2SG SUB come
 'I want you to come.'

We take this to mean that they are base-generated in the same syntactic position.

(8) PRED [ForceP ɖɔ/ní [.....]]

The subjunctive marker is obligatory present in clauses introduced by nú (9). The complementizer ni can also appear as an irrealis mood marker in root clauses (10).

(9) *È nyɔ nú à yì.
 3SG good NU 2SG leave
(10) Bàyí ní ɖà wɔ.
 Bayi SUB prepare dough
 'Bayi should prepare dough.'

According to Kinyalolo (1993), there is a set of verbs in Fon, which is obligatorily followed by a ɖɔ-phrase (cf. Lefebvre & Brousseau 2002 for a caveat – see below). This is shown in Table 2.

Table 2. Fon verbs that take an ɖɔ complement

ɖɔ 'say, tell'	lin 'think'	kɛn 'bet'	kú drɔ 'dream'
kan by 'ask'	wɔn 'forget'	gbɛ 'refuse'	jlo 'want'
mɔn 'deny'	do akpa 'promise'	tùn 'know'	mɔ 'see'
flin 'remember'	se 'hear'	zɔn 'command'	ɖi 'believe'
yi gbe 'answer'	ɖo nukun 'hope'	xwlé 'swear'	gblɔn adan 'threaten'

The only exception is ɖɔ 'say' itself. Only if the verb is accompanied by a PP, is it obligatorily present, otherwise it is optional.

(11) É   ɖɔ   (ɖɔ)   Sìká   ná   wá.
     3SG say ɖɔ   Sika   IRR come
     'S/he said that Sika will come.'

(12) É   ɖɔ   nú   mí   *(ɖɔ)   Sìká   ná   wá.
     3SG say P   1SG ɖɔ   Sika   IRR come
     'S/he told me that Sika will come.'

Some of these verbs (obligatorily) select for a complement with a future tense-orientation, like *do akpa* 'promise', *gblɔn adan* 'threaten', whereas others don't seem to have similar temporal restrictions, e.g. *flin* 'remember'.

(13) a. Yè   gblɔn adan *(ɖɔ) émi   *(ná) hú   gbɔ   lɛ   bi.
         3PL   utter anger ɖɔ   LOG   IRR   kill goat PL   all
         'They threatened to kill all the goats.'
     b. Mi   flin   *(ɖɔ) Kɔkú hwlá   Asíbá sín gbɔ.
         1PL   remember   ɖɔ   Koku hide   Asiba GEN goat
         'We remember that Koku hid Asiba's goat.'

Lefebvre & Brousseau (2002) classify *jlo* 'want' differently. According to them, it selects either a tensed complement introduced by the complementizer *nú* (14a), an infinitival complement without an overt subject (14b), or an infinitival complement with an overt subject (14c) – the latter is a case of Exceptional Case Marking:

(14) a. É_i jló nú é_{i/j} *(ní) yì.
   3SG want NU 3SG SUBJ leave
   '(S)he wants to leave' OR '(S)he wants him/her to leave.'
 b. Kɔkú_i jló PRO_{i/*j} *(ná) gbà mɔtó ɔ.
   Koku want PRO DEF.FUT destroy car DEF
   'Koku wants to destroy the car.'
 c. É_i jló è_{*i/j} yì.
   3SG want 3SG leave
   '(S)he wants him/her to leave.'

I, therefore, leave out this verb out of the discussion.

What is of interest about the set of verbs from the list of Kinyalolo (1993) is that they do not form a homogenous class of clause-embedding predicates from a semantic point of view. If we adhere to the classification proposed by Rochette (1988),[5] we can observe that these predicates occur in every subclass in this system. In my view, this indicates that there are no particular strong restrictions in terms of the lexical argument structure of clause-embedding predicates operative on the selection of *ɖɔ* as the complementizer of the clause embedded under such verbs. The question, then, is how this set of verbs behaves syntactically in Saramaccan?[6] Do we

---

5. According to Rochette (1988), verbs are divided semantically as follows:

REFLECTIVE				EFFECTIVE
PROPOSITIONAL			EMOTIVE	
STATING	BELIEVING	KNOWING		

First, verbs divide into two major classes: effective and non-effective (or reflective) verbs. Effective predicates are verbs that describe a subject's relationship, whether causal, potential or other, to the performance of an action (examples: *to request, to see to*). Non-effective or reflective predicates are verbs which express a (human) subject's judgment concerning a proposition or event" (Rochette 1988: 21). Reflective predicates further divide into two classes: propositional and emotive verbs. Propositional verbs describe judgments of truth value (examples: *to assert, to negate, to say*) and emotive verbs describe judgements of personal relevance (examples: *to feel, to look, to be happy*). We will present the verbs under discussion in this paper according to this classification.

6. It is interesting to note that Papiamentu clearly shows that the distribution of the complementizers *ku* and *pa* is dependent on the indicative/subjunctive split, and, ultimately, related to the distinction between *propositional* and *emotive/effective* predicates (cf. Kouwenberg & Lefebvre 2007 for details).

find the same pattern, i.e. do all these verbs also select for one and the same complementizer? This will be one of the main topics for the remainder of this section. In addition, we will have a closer look at the left peripheral architecture of embedded clauses in Saramaccan, and compare it with the one found in the Gbe languages.

The equivalent of Fon *ɖɔ* is *táa* in Saramaccan. Like *ɖɔ*, *táa* can occur as a speech verb (derived from *táki*), and a serial verb/complementizer (in addition to a quotative marker, cf. Lefebvre & Loranger 2008). Unlike *ɖɔ*, however, speech verb *táa* cannot be followed by the serial verb/complementizer *táa*.

(15) *A   táa táa   a   ó   gó.
     3SG talk SAY 3SG M   go

Like *ɖɔ*, *táa* is not involved in clause-typing, i.e. it does not type the clause as *declarative*, since it can co-occur with embedded questions.

(16) De   bì tá kuútu táa   un-fa u   ó   dú dí sóni akí.
     3PL T   A   wonder SAY   how 1PL M do D   thing here
     'They were wondering how they would do this.'

There are two major patterns of sentential embedding in Saramaccan: sentences introduced by *táa* and/or *fu*. Damonte (2002) observes that they have the following distribution. As noted above, *táa* is a finite complementizer. As such, it cannot be used with a verb that requires an irrealis complement clause. The lexical item *fu*, on the other hand, is the so-called *subjunctive* complementizer, which is derived in (almost) every creole from the preposition meaning *for* in the relevant European lexifier language. It cannot be used with a verb like *know*, where a *realis* interpretation is usually assumed:

(17) a.   A   sabi táa/*fu di womi bi hondi di pingo.
          3SG know SAY   D man T hunt D pig
          'He knows that the man hunted the pig.' (Byrne 1987 148)

Allesaib & Veenstra (ms) show that the distribution of the complementizers *ki* and *pu* in Mauritian Creole is independent of any verb classification.

b. *A   ke   faa/*táa kisi   di ogifou a matu.*
    3SG want FOR=3SG catch D owl   P jungle
    'He wants him to catch the owl in the jungle.' (Byrne 1987: 138)

If the matrix verb is compatible with both a realised and an unrealised sentential complement, then both complementizers are possible.

(18) a. *A   taki táa   di mujee bi go a di keiki.*
         3SG say SAY   D   woman T   go P D   church
         'He said that the woman had gone to the church.'
     b. *A   bì táki f=én   kulé.*
         3SG T talk FOR=3SG run
         'He told him to run.' (warning)

The choice of the complementizer affects the interpretation of the embedded sentence According to Byrne (1987), the (main) difference in interpretation between *táa*-clauses and *fu*-clauses is that the event described by the clause introduced by *táa* is presupposed to have occurred or to occur in the near future, whereas the event described by the clause introduced by *fu* is not presupposed to have occurred nor to occur in the near future.

(19) a. *A   de fanoudu **fu** di womi bi wooko a di wosu.*
         3SG BE important FOR D   man T   work P D   house
         'It was important for the man to work in the house (but he probably didn't).'
     b. *A   de fanoudu **táa** di sembe bi go a matu.*
         3SG BE important SAY D   person T   go P jungle
         'It was important that the person had gone into the jungle (and he probably did).'

The two complementizers are not mutual exclusive (contra Aboh 2006b, Lefebvre & Loranger 2008 – cf. Wijnen & Alleyne 1987).

(20) *I   taki táa faa   naki di dagu.*
     2SG say SAY   FOR=3SG hit D   dog
     'You told him to hit the dog.' (Veenstra 1996: 156)

Lefebvre & Loranger (2008: 1173) commented on this example as follows: "There is one example, cited by Veenstra (1996a: 96), that appears to constitute a counter example to the expected mutual exclusion of the two forms." This is not an isolated example, however. In (21), five additional examples are given, of which the first two are taken from Wijnen & Alleyne (1987: 46). The other three examples appear in de Groot (1981):[7]

(21) a. *Mi paamisi táa u m bì ó gó ku hen.*
1SG promise SAY FOR 1SG T M go with 3SG
'I promised that I would go with him.' (Wijnen & Alleyne 1987: 46)

b. *Mi manda hen táa faa go.*
1SG send 3SG SAY FOR=3SG go
'I sent him away.' (Wijnen & Alleyne 1987: 46)

c. *A-n táki dá-én táa fu de kulé.*
3SG-NEG talk give-3SG SAY FOR 3PL run
'He didn't tell them that they should run away.'

d. *Di mi bì tá kó te tjiká a pási,*
then 1SG T A come till enough LOC way,
nóo a bì kái mi táa u mi tooná kó n=en.
then 3SG T call 1SG SAY FOR 1SG turn come LOC=3SG
'When I was already on my way, he called me to come back to him.'

e. *De tá sibá mi táa fu m=é féndi búnu woóko.*
3PL A curse 1SG SAY FOR 1SG=NEG find good work
'They put a spell on me, so that I didn't find a good job.'

These examples involve different matrix predicates (*paamisi, manda, táki, kái, sibá*, respectively), so it is not the case that the pattern is due to a particular lexical anomaly. The established fact that the two complementizers are not in complementary distribution, then, is a strong argument for an analysis in which the two complementizers are merged in two different structural positions, as in (25).

(22) PRED [$_{\text{ForceP}}$ *taa* .... [$_{\text{FinP}}$ *fu*]]

This is basically the analysis explicitly argued for in Damonte (2002). An additional argument for this type of analysis comes from the positions

---

7. Furthermore, Marleen van de Vate (p.c. May 2010) notes that the two complementizers are not in complementary distribution for the speakers she consulted in Pikin Slee during a recent fieldwork trip in 2009.

topics and foci relative to the complementizers in the CP-domain. The complementizer *fu* must follow both topics and focused elements, as in (23b).[8]

(23) a.   *A ke faa kisi di ogifou a matu.*
          3SG want FOR=3SG catch D owl P jungle
          'He wants him to catch the owl in the jungle.' (Damonte 2002)
    b.   *A ke a matu faa kisi di ogifou.*   TOP/FOC > *fu*
    c.   **A ke faa a matu kisi di ogifou.*   **fu* > TOP/FOC

The complementizer *táa*, on the other hand, has to precede both of them, as in (24c).

(24) a.   *A sabi táa di womi bi hondi di pingo.*
          3SG know SAY D man T hunt D pig
          'He knows that the man hunted the pig.' (Damonte 2002)
    b.   **A sabi di pingo táa di womi bi hondi.*   *TOP/FOC > *táa*
    c.   *A sabi táa di pingo di womi bi hondi.*   *táa* > TOP/FOC

The higher structure of the C-domain of Saramaccan contrasts with the one we encountered in Fon where the two complementizers are in complementary distribution (see above). The conclusion we draw is that the ordering of elements in the higher CP of Fon is not mirrored in Saramaccan, and that, therefore, the left peripheral architecture in Saramaccan has not been modelled after the one found in Fon.

Another difference between the two languages is to be found in so-called subjunctive clauses. In Saramaccan, modality markers are not possible in subordinate clauses introduced by *fu*, as shown in the next set of examples.

(25) a.   *Mi ké fu a dú dati.*
          1SG want FOR 3SG do that
          'I want him to do that.' (Wijnen & Alleyne 1987)
    b.   **A ke faa fu kisi di ogifou a matu.*
          3SG want FOR=3SG FOR catch D owl P jungle
          (Damonte 2002)

---

8. Unfortunately, we do not have data at hand in which topics and focussed elements co-occur with both complementizers.

c. *Miké fu a fu dú dati.
   1SG want FOR 3SG FOR do that (Kouwenberg & Lefebvre 2007)

As shown in (9), mood markers are obligatory present in embedded subjunctives in Fon. Thus, the syntax of *fu*-clauses in Saramaccan is not identical to the syntax of *nú*-clauses in Fon.

There seems to exist variation between speakers as to whether *fu* is able to occur in root clauses as a mood marker or not. Thus, some of the informants of Byrne (1987) accept the following type of examples:

(26) %Di womi bi fu wooko a di baaka wosu.
    D man T FOR work P D foreigner house
    'The man should have worked at the foreigner's house.'
    (Byrne 1987: 136)

Wijnen & Alleyne (1987), Veenstra (1996), Damonte (2002), McWhorter (2005), and van de Vate (2008) were not able to replicate the Byrne-results, however. We will assume that for the majority of Saramaccan speakers *fu* cannot be used as a mood marker in root contexts. Fon is also different in this respect: *ní* can function both as a subjunctive complementizer and as a mood marker occurring in independent (i.c. matrix) clauses. Note, in addition, that it is exactly for the group of speakers that do not have *fu* as a mood marker that the pattern with the co-occurring complementizers has been documented, explicitly in Veenstra (1996), Damonte (2002), and van de Vate (2009). This rules out an analysis, hinted at in Aboh (2006b), to treat the *fu* in (20–23) as instances of the Mood marker.

Summarizing, we can state that the syntactic architecture of the embedded clause in Fon and Saramaccan differ along the following two dimensions: (i) presence vs absence of co-occurring restrictions on complementizer combinations; (ii) absence vs presence of mood marking in embedded subjunctive clauses. The overall conclusion is, therefore, that the left peripheral architecture in Saramaccan has not been modelled after the one found in Fon, or the Gbe languages in general (cf. Aboh 2004a). This conclusion contradicts the claims made by Aboh (2006a) and Lefebvre & Lorranger (2008).

If we compare the Fon set of clause-embedding predicates with the set of verbs in Saramaccan, we get the following result. Whereas in Fon all the verbs, independent of the different verb classes they belong to, uniquely select for a *ɖɔ* -phrase (with the exception of *jlo* 'want', as noted above), we find a diffuse selectional pattern in Saramaccan. In total, four different patterns can be identified. The embedded clause is either introduced by the complementizer *táa*, the complementizer *fu*, a combination of both complementizers, or by no complementizer at all. Some verbs only select for one pattern, e.g. *piki* 'say, tell', *pidi* 'ask', *fia* 'deny', *sunja* 'dream', and *soi* 'swear' only take embedded clauses introduced by *táa*, whereas *niinga* 'refuse', *ke* 'hope' and *maa tongo* 'command, order' only select clauses headed by *fu*. Other verbs show variable behavior. The following combinations are found: *táa*/zero (e.g. *feekete* 'forget', *si* 'see'), and *táa/táa fu* (e.g. *taki* 'say, tell'). Absent is the combination *fu*/zero. The verb *paamisi* 'promise' seems to exhibit the full range of possibilities, as can be seen from (27).

(27) a. *táa fu*
 Mi paamisi táa u m bì ó gó ku hen.
 1SG promise SAY FOR1SGT M go with 3SG
 'I promised that I would go with him.'
 b. *táa*
 Mi paamísi dí míi táa mi ó kó heepi hén.
 1SG promise D child SAY 1SGM come help 3SG
 'I promised the child to help him.'
 c. *fu*, –SUBJECT
 Mi paamísi dí míi u kó heepi hén.
 1SG promise D child FOR come help 3SG
 'I promised the child to help him.'
 d. *fu*, +SUBJECT
 Mi paamísi dí míi fu mi kó heepi hén.
 1SG promise D child FOR1SG come help 3SG
 'I promised the child to help him.'
 e. ZERO
 Mi paamísi dí míi mi kó heepi hén.
 1SG promise D child 1SG come help 3SG
 'I promised the child to help him.'

The four patterns do not seem to correspond to any verb classification, as can be seen in Table 2.

We do not find, for instance, a similar split as in Papiamentu between propositional and emotive/effective predicates. The complementizer *táa* appears with verbs from all the different verb classes, the complementizer *fu* with verbs from all verb classes except a subclass of the propositional predicates containing verbs of knowing. The combination of the two complementizers is also not confined to one particular verb class.

Table 3. Classification in Saramaccan predicates and their complementizers

REFLECTIVE				EFFECTIVE
PROPOSITIONAL			EMOTIVE	
STATING	BELIEVING	KNOWING		
say táa/táa fu fu/ZERO swear táa see táa hear táa dream táa deny táa answer táa	think táa/fu believe táa	forget táa/ZERO know táa remember táa/ZERO	hope táa/fu want táa/fu/ZERO	promise táa/táa fu/ fu/ZERO command fu threaten táa refuse fu

This concludes Section 2, in which it was shown that the syntax of clause-embedding predicates in Saramaccan does not match up with that of Fon. In particular, the embedded C-domains in Saramaccan and the Gbe languages do not match. Whereas, in Fon, the two complementizers ɖɔ and ní/nú are in complementary distribution, the Saramaccan complementizers táa and fu can occur together. Furthermore, the variability in selection patterns encountered in this realm of grammar turns out to be highly problematic for a relexification scenario and seems to favour a scenario in terms of processes of second language acquisition instead.

4. The syntax of aspectual predicates

Turning now to aspectual verbs in the Gbe languages, they display a particular syntactic property. Whereas the Gbe languages generally display a strict VO-order, aspectual verbs trigger the so-called object verb construction (OVC, cf. Aboh 2009a), in which the object precede the lexical verb it is selected by. Examples from Gungbe (Aboh 2009a) are given in (28).

(28) a. *Àsíbá je lesì ḍù jí.* inceptive
 Asiba reach rice eat PRT
 'Asiba started eating rice.'
 b. *Àsíbá wá lesì ḍù gbé.* purpose
 Asiba come rice eat PRT
 'Asiba came in order to eat rice.'
 c. *Àsíbá tò lesì ḍù `.* progressive
 Asiba PROG rice eat PRT
 'Asiba is eating rice.'
 d. *Àsíbá gbɛ lesì ḍù.*
 Asiba refuse rice eat
 'Asiba refused to eat rice.'

In (28a–c), there is an overt sentence-final morpheme present (glossed here as PRT) that in conjunction with the preverbal aspectual verbs encodes mood/aspect specifications (inceptive, purpose, progressive, respectively), but example (28d) shows that such morpheme is not obligatory present.
Aboh (2004a, 2009a) convincingly shows that the object is not base-generated in the preverbal position, but is in a derived position via object shift. One argument is that the prospective aspect marker *ná* can intervene between the object and the lexical verb, as in (29).

(29) *Àsíbá wá lesì ná ḍù gbé.* Gungbe
 Asiba come rice PROSP eat PRT
 'Asiba came in order to eat rice [and she is about to do so].'
 (Aboh 2009a)

The most interesting property of this object shift, relevant to our discussion, is that it is lexically conditioned. Thus, it is not the case that the (total) class of aspectual verbs allows for object shift to take place in their complement. Manfredi (1997) contains a very detailed and informative discussion of non-finite OV-structures in Kwa (as well as Kru) languages. He basically distinguishes two constructions, free and bound, as shown in Figure 1. Only the latter, the bound construction, is of relevance for us. He shows that OV-structures do not surface across-the-board with aspectual verbs, but that the specific trigger for object shift underlies lexically conditioned variation.

Thus, there is variation between and within languages as to which aspectual verb allows for OV-structures in their complement, as shown in (30a) for mono-clausal constructions, and in (30b) for bi-clausal constructions.

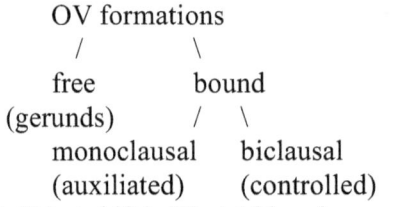

Figure 1. Object shift in West African langauges

(30) a.
Language	host for auxiliated OV
Ewe	progressive, prospective
Mina	progressive
Fon	progressive
Standard Yoruba	------
Òwórò Yoruba	perfective
Standard Ìgbo	------
Àvu-Ìgbo, Èchíè-Ìgbo	obligative
Nupé	resultative
Àkyé	imperfective
Àbe	------

b.
Language	host for controlled OV
Fon	start, stop, know
Standard Yoruba	learn, know, want
Standard Ìgbo	know
Àbe	begin, want, intend, like

The bottom line is that whether an aspectual verb allows for object shift in its complement has to be lexically specified in the lexical entry of that verb. Under the relexification hypothesis, it is therefore expected that this lexically-specified property, when present, would survive the creolization process, and show up in the relevant lexical entry of the creole.

In Fon, one of the major substrate languages of Saramaccan, object shift occurs in the progressive (30a) and with aspectual verbs *start/stop* (30b). Thus, the prediction is that in Saramaccan object shift will also occur in exactly these contexts. This claim is immediately falsified by the following data:

(31) a. PROGRESSIVE auxiliary constructions
Mé tá sumúku sigaléti.
1SG=NEG A smoke cigarette
'I am not smoking cigarettes.'
b. *Mé tá sigaléti sumúku.
1SG=NEG A cigarette smoke
(32) a. INCEPTIVE (*START*) control constructions
De séti tá sumúku sigaléti.
3PL start A smoke cigarette
'They started smoking cigarettes.'
b. *De séti sigaléti tá sumúku.
3PL start cigarette A smoke

In general, we can state that there is no context in Saramaccan in which the object is moved in front of the verb, i.e. Saramaccan exhibits no triggered object shift.

Van de Vate (2008) identified and discussed extensively the following set of aspectual (and modal) verbs in Saramaccan, listed in Table 11.4.

Table 4. Aspectual (and modal) verbs in Saramaccan (based on van de Vate 2008)

Aspectual		Modal	
Habitual	ló u	obligative	músu fu
Completive	kabá fu	epistemic	músu fu
Inceptive	bigí fu	obligative	ábi fu
		mental ability	sá u

Superficially, the presence of the complementizer *fu* seems to be optional, as in (33a). Note that object shift is ungrammatical, independently of the presence of *fu*, as can be seen in (33b):

(33) a. Mi kabá (u) féfi dí dóo.
1SG finish FU paint D door
'I finished painting the door.'
b. *Mi kabá (u) dí dóo féfi.
1SG finish FU D door paint

Nevertheless, we argue that we have to distinguish between the use of *kabá* as a main verb (merged in a lexical position followed by an embedded clause headed by *fu*) and as an aspectual verb (merged in a position in the functional domain of the clause, and not followed by an embedded clause).

The basic argument for the difference in categorial status comes from ideophone placement (Veenstra 2003).

Ideophones are words used to modulate more closely the lexical meanings of verbs and adjectives. They are partly onomatopoetic and are also sometimes referred to as 'phonaesthetic words'. They can be most closely identified with adverbs as a category, and are selected by particular verbs. They demarcate the right edge of the VP (cf. Rountree 1992; Veenstra 2003):

(34) a. *A wéti fáán/*njaa.*
   3SG white IDEOPHONE
   'It is snow-white.'
  b. *A náki/*kíi hen gbóó-gbóó.*
   3SG hit/kill 3SG IDEOPHONE
   'She hit him really hard.'

In (34a) it is shown that *wéti* 'white' can only be accompanied by *fáán*, and in (34b) shows that the ideophone *gbóó-gbóó* can only occur with the verb it is selected by (*náki* 'hit', but not *kíi* 'kill'). Ideophones can only be selected by full lexical verbs and not by aspectual verbs, as shown by the following contrast:

(35) a. *De kabá kéé u féfi di wósu.*
   3PL finish IDEOPHONE FU paint D house
   'They finished painting the house
  b. **De kabá kéé féfi di wósu.*
   3PL finish IDEOPHONE paint D house

In (35a) the lexical verb *kabá* selects for a complement introduced by the complementizer *fu*, and can be accompanied by an ideophone (*kéé*). If, on the other hand, the complementizer (*f*)*u* is absent, as in (35b), *kabá* has been reanalyzed as an aspectual verb, and, as such, is part of the INFL complex. Generated in this position, it cannot longer support its ideophone *kéé* anymore.

As Wijnen & Alleyne (1987: 49) observe, the presence or absence of *fu* also has an effect on the semantic interpretation, and leads to particular semantic shifts. Thus, in (36) we find a difference in modality, basically deontic *vs* epistemic. It is not clear, however, that the interpretational difference is necessarily (directly) related to the difference in categorical status.

(36) a. *I   sa   u   wooko!*
         2SG can/know FU   work
         'You can work!'(i.e. know how to)
   b. *I   sa   wooko   tide   no?*
       2SG can   work   today   Q
       'Can you work today?'

Summarizing, we can state that specific lexical information associated with particular aspectual verbs in the substrate language(s) did not survive the creolization process, and, as such, did not find its way into the emerging creole. As noted above, this is unexpected under a relexification scenario of creole genesis. Since the crucial operation in relexification is phonological relabelling, thereby leaving the syntactic and semantic features unchanged, the prediction would have been that this grammatical information would still be available, contrary to fact as shown above.

5. Conclusions

The goal of this chapter, as stated in the introduction, was to evaluate the role played by the different acquisition processes operative in creole genesis. We argued that there are (at least) two processes to be distinguished: (i) second language acquisition; (ii) relexification. The focus was on the theory of Relexification. The leading question of this paper, therefore, has been whether the syntax of clause-embedding predicates in Saramaccan strictly follows the patterns found in the substrate languages of the Gbe group, in particular Fon. To answer this question, we restricted the discussion to two sets of clause-embedding predicates: (i) the group of utterance, emotion and propositional attitude predicates (Section 2); (ii) the group of aspectual verbs (Section 3). The very precise predictions of the theory of Relexification were as follows (repeated from the introduction):

(40) a. identical (or at least highly similar) selection patterns in the substrate language(s) and the creole
   b. high degree of stability of selection patterns in the creole

We have shown that there is no overwhelming evidence for the process of relexification in the realm of the reconstitution of clause-embedding predicates in creole genesis. Quite to the contrary, in both cases the very precise predictions of the theory of Relexification have not been borne out in any detail at all. Thus, it was shown in Section 2 that in Fon there is an extensive class of clause-embedding predicates, distributed across the different predicate classes as defined by Rochette (1988), that solely select for complement clauses headed by the complementizer ɖɔ. The same set of verbs in Saramaccan, however, displays a very diffuse selectional pattern. We identified four different patterns. This is not expected under the theory of Relexification, because we expect not only identical (or highly similar) selectional patterns, but also the same variation in selectional patterns. Furthermore, it was shown that the syntactic architecture of the embedded clause in Fon and Saramaccan differs along the following two dimensions (i) presence vs absence of co-occurring restrictions on complementizer combinations; (ii) absence vs presence of mood marking in embedded subjunctive clauses. The overall conclusion, therefore, is that the left peripheral architecture of C-domain in Saramaccan has not been modeled after the one found in Fon, or the Gbe languages in general (cf. Aboh 2004a). Finally, we also showed that the theory of Relexification makes the wrong predictions in the realm of aspectual verbs. The patterns of lexically conditioned Object Shift with some of these predicates in Fon (in particular, expressing progressive, inceptive, or pausative aspect) have not been found in Saramaccan. Since the crucial operation in relexification is phonological (and only phonological) relabeling, thereby leaving the syntactic and semantic features unchanged, the prediction would have been that this grammatical information would still be available.

In conclusion, we can say that the process of relexification did not play a major role in the transformation and reconstitution of the linking mechanisms at the interface between the lexicon and the syntactic component that undoubtedly took place during the creolization process.

**Part III:
Wrapping up**

Conclusion: Feature distribution in the West Africa-Surinam Trans-Atlantic Sprachbund

Pieter Muysken

1. Introduction: The original hypotheses and further development of the analytical framework

This chapter presents some of the main lessons to be drawn from our overview in the previous chapters of this book. In Part I, *Setting the Scene*, we first provided some background to understand the historical settings of Surinam (Smith) and Benin (Aboh and Smith) and in particular the special relation between them, and the shared background of the English-lexifier Atlantic creoles (Smith). Subsequently, the notion of relexification is explored in more detail, in relation to other language contact scenarios in a chapter by Muysken.

In the Part II, *Language structures: a sprachbund?*, the members of our research team surveyed a number of elements and constructions, which had been identified previously as possibly shared between the languages of Benin and surrounding areas, and the creole languages of Surinam. In all cases, we had the initial expectation, before actually doing the comparative work, that there would be many similarities between patterns in the West African and the Surinam Creoles. The reasons for this are both derived from the general impressions in the creole studies literature (cf. e.g. Muysken 1994b), and from the specific historical considerations outlined in Smith's chapter on Surinam's history: short presence of the dominant lexifier, limited colonial control and early Maroon settlements, a limited set of African languages contributing in the formative period, and early transition to a sugar plantation economy. If African languages have played a major role anywhere in the genesis of Caribbean creoles, Suriname is the place to look.

In this sense our research started with a strong bias. Recall from the introduction and the chapter on relexification that we started this project with two major hypotheses:

This chapter owes a great deal to the input of all authors in this volume.

- Relexification plays a major role in the genesis of the Suriname creoles, and the features of the Suriname creoles.
- In the relexication process purely lexical properties are retained, while morpho-syntactic properties are not retained.

However, as the project progressed, it became transparent that an exclusive focus on relexification was not adequate; the data simply did not confirm these two hypotheses. In the chapter on relexification and contact, six language contact scenarios were discussed, including relexification, which may be grouped in terms of the stages in the process of genesis that they are most closely associated with:

- Those particularly relevant to the *earliest* stages of pidgin/creole genesis: relexification and second language (L2) learning;
- Those particularly relevant to *intermediate* stages: bilingual convergence and code-mixing
- Those particularly relevant to *late* stages in the process: borrowing and attrition.

In what follows, I will first briefly summarize the main findings from the chapters in the Part II. Then in Sections 3 and 4, I will evaluate the possible contributions of these processes to Surinam Creole genesis, in the light of these findings, and of factors which may be held responsible for the survival – or not – of a particular West African feature. Then in 5 and 6, I will try to shed new light on a more global question: to what extent do the Surinam Creoles resemble the languages of West Africa, and to what extent are they more like their European lexifiers? I will try to answer these questions using techniques from structural phylogenetics, techniques that help us map distances between languages graphically. Section 7 concludes this chapter.

2. Systematic overview of the grammatical findings

The different grammatical chapters yielded a number of remarkable findings, which will be presented one by one.

In the chapter *Trans-Atlantic patterns: the relexification of locative contructions in Sranan*, **Yakpo** and **Bruyn** propose that the copying of substrate patterns rather than individual items alone is responsible for the make-up of locative constructions in Sranan. A central part of the argument is that the corresponding Niger-Congo substrate patterns manifest a large degree of unity, and that this facilitated the relexification of morphosyntactic 'blue-prints' or 'skeletons' in Sranan. In some cases, the behavior of an individual item appears to result from what may be termed 'local relexification'. However, the existence of particular general patterns and constructions in the substrates turns out to be at least as relevant. At the same time, they show that Sranan does not necessarily replicate substrate patterns exactly: even if the Sranan structures covered here display a substrate bias in many aspects, other aspects reveal the intricate interplay of substrate, superstrate, and lexifier patterns, as well as internal development.

Essegbey, in *Verb Semantics and Argument Structure in the Gbe Languages and Sranan*, draws the conclusion that there is no relexification, in the strong sense, in argument structure and its expression in the Surinam Creoles. The verbs that he discusses are CUT & BREAK verbs, COME & GO verbs and the EAT verb. Essegbey shows that while the first two are very close to their equivalents in English, the EAT-verb is closer to its equivalent in the Gbe languages. He also shows that the overall argument structure of verbs in Sranan is different from that of the Gbe languages. This is mainly because of the phenomenon of obligatory object verbs in the Gbe languages. Essegbey does suggest, however, that the phenomenon of hypertransitivity might provide the basis for the Sranan cognate object construction.

The chapter by **van den Berg**, *Morphology, cross-linguistic effects, and creole formation,* begins with a description of the nominal derivational morphology of Early Sranan. The author concludes that the Early Sranan affixes and semi-affixes are largely innovative, with the exception of the suffix *-man* (and possibly *-peh/ -plessi*), which are likely to have a West African source. They cannot be straightforwardly accounted for, either in terms of the African substrate or the English superstrate. The second part of the paper deals with variation in the category of stative predicates in Early Sranan, and links this to the varying contribution of substrate and lexifier languages in creole genesis, on the basis of contemporary West African code-switching data gathered by the author and her team.[1]

---

1. Data collection and analysis in Ghana, Togo, and the Netherlands were a joint effort of dr. Margot van den Berg, dr. Evershed Kwasi Amuzu (University of Ghana, Legon), dr. Komlan Essizewa (University of Lomé) supported by student assistants Elvis Yevudey and Abena Kyere (University of Ghana, Legon), Kamailoudini Tagba and Tarno Akponi (University of Lomé) and Sophie Kirkels (Radboud University Nijmegen).

Aboh and **Smith,** in their *Non-iconic reduplications in Eastern Gbe and Surinam*, conclude that the reduplication of both verbal nouns and of adjectives in the Surinam Creoles is based on the Gbe substrate. However, for the unproductive verbal nouns, evidence comes from an isolated case of reduplication, while for reduplicated adjectives, the case can be made for direct morphosyntactic transfer. The patterns of distribution, however, show that there has also been significant English influence.

Smith's chapter, *Substrate phonology, superstrate phonology and adstrate phonology in creole languages,* concludes that Gbe language vocalic phonotactic patterns have played a very significant role in shaping the syllable structure of early forms of the Surinam Creoles. Patterns of nasality, however, show a striking demarcation effect whereby final syllables display Fongbe-type nasal properties, while non-final nasal syllables follow Kikongo patterns.

Aboh, in *The left periphery in the Surinamese creoles and Gbe: on the modularity of substrate transfer*, investigates the left periphery in the clausal and nominal domains of the Gbe languages and the Surinam Creoles. Aboh shows that substrate transfer is not a unitary syntactic phenomenon that could correspond to a strict one-to-one match between the relevant substrate languages and the creole. The discussion in the first part argues that both the Gbe languages and Saramaccan display a rich left periphery of the clause that provides room for discrete functional projections.

In the second part Aboh shows that substrate transfer may consist of just a set of features, rather than an actual pattern. The analysis of the determiner system indicates that the function of the determiners in Sranan is comparable to that of the determiners in the Gbe languages. However, Sranan differs from Gungbe in that the specificity marker in this language exhibits syntactic properties found in Romance and Germanic, but not in the Gbe languages. The observed pragmatic/semantic parallels are due to substrate transfer where the appropriate features are retained but not their syntax. A major morpho-syntactic difference is that the markers of these features precede the NP in Sranan, but follow in Gungbe. Aboh's conclusion is that Sranan exhibits syntax of the English lexifier here, but substrate discourse-related distinctions. A set of function words or clitics exhibits semantic but not formal parallels with the substrate languages.

Veenstra's chapter on *Relexification and clause-embedding predicates,* has its leading question whether the syntax of clause-embedding predicates in Saramaccan strictly follows the patterns found in the substrate language Fongbe. To find out whether a certain part of the grammar of a creole language is due to relexification or to SLA-processes, it is important to look at the relevant grammatical properties. The influence of the lexicon on the syntax reveals itself most clearly in the case of clause-embedding predicates. It is clear that there are differences between different predicates with respect to selection restrictions (*believe that* vs. *believe whether), and possible control readings (X *promises* Y *to come* → X *will come*; X *persuades* Y *to come* → Y *should come*), leading to different syntactic structures, but it is less evident whether the lexical properties of such predicates can also be influenced by syntactic properties of subordination structures. In finding an answer to this question, the paper restricts the discussion to two sets of clause-embedding predicates: (i) the semantically and syntactically relatively less integrated group of utterance, emotion, and propositional attitude predicates; (ii) the semantically and syntactically more integrated group of phasal predicates, aspectual verbs. The paper concludes that relexification cannot by itself predict the patterns found in Saramaccan.

On the basis of these case studies, it can be concluded that the structural affiliation of Surinam Creoles is a complex picture when considered across different language components. The results for the different chapters may be summarized as in Table 1.

Table 1. Contributions by the various authors to the chapters

Author(s)	Topic	General Conclusion
Yakpo and Bruyn	Locative constructions	Patterning on general Gbe models rather than individual items
Essegbey	Lexical semantics & Argument Structure	Not Gbe on the whole, except for a slight reflex of the hypertransitivity phenomenon
van den Berg	Morphology and word classes	Only partly modeled on Gbe patterns; Gbe morphological pattern limited to two affixes
Aboh and Smith	Reduplication	Gbe pattern productive only for resultative adjectives
Smith	Syllabic phonology	Gbe patterning in monosyllables; more complex (including Kikongo) patterning in polysyllables
Aboh	DP morpho-syntax and the Left periphery	Variable Gbe patterning
Veenstra	Complement selection	Only partly modeled on Gbe patterns

3. Interim conclusions

Before turning to specific explanations for the patterns found in Table 1, there are also some more general conclusions that can be drawn from these studies.

A first important conclusion in various studies was that the creators of the Suriname creoles did not form a homogeneous community. Rather, there was considerable **variation** from the very beginning, as is clear from the chapters by Yakpo and Bruyn, and van den Berg. Different structural and lexical options were present in the early creole. Clearly transfer of African features was sometimes tentative rather than definitive and pervasive.

A second conclusion is that the data suggest the central role of **advanced second language learning** and **bilingual usage**, again in the chapter by van den Berg, but also in Veenstra's chapter. These chapters suggest that a scenario with relexification as very early language learning is unlikely for the Surinam Creoles. Knowledge of rather complex patterns of the target second language is required to explain the patterns of interaction found between the substrate and the target. However, this does not mean that the main features of the Surinam Creole languages only emerged in the 18th century. Saramaccan, which split off in the late 17th century, has many of the relevant features as well. In addition, it is not clear how long the African languages retained their original features in a bilingual setting. To give just one example, while Helms-Park (2003) argues that the serial verb patterns of Vietnamese second language learners did not transfer into in their English speech, Moro (2014) shows that heritage Ambon Malay speakers in the Netherlands lose their serial patterns rather quickly in a bilingual setting. Very specific West African patterns may have disappeared quickly in the transplanted context.

Third, the chapters by Smith on syllable structure and Essegbey on reflexes of hypertransitivity stress the creative dimension of the process of creole genesis. **Language creation** processes must have played an important role, since otherwise it would be difficult to explain the newly created patterns found. In addition, several authors stress that, in order to explain the features of the Surinam Creoles, it is necessary to assume that early speakers, creators of the creole, strongly generalized from properties of individual lexical **items** to more general **patterns**. Smith shows that syllable structures were drawn upon, as abstract patterns, from two sources, Gbe and Kikongo, and Yakpo with Bruyn show that it is not possible to always base oneself on individual West African etyma to explain African influence: whole patterns or constructions need to be taken into consideration.

A fourth important conclusion is that processes of **simplification** and **selection** were frequently operative. Essegbey shows that the various meaning distinctions for different verb classes in the Gbe languages do not carry over to Sranan. Van den Berg argues that only a small portion of the nominalization possibilities that exist in Fongbe can be found in Early Sranan, and Aboh and Smith argue the same thing for reduplication. Aboh, finally, argues for the selection of properties from various sources to explain the particular combination of semantic properties from the languages of Benin combined with English word order in the noun phrase of the Surinam Creoles.

4. Possible explanations for the findings: factors involved

Why were some features of the languages of Benin retained in the process of genesis of the Surinam Creoles, and not others? To answer this question, I will explore various factors contributing to the survival of specific West African features here, and present these in the light of the different contact scenarios. As mentioned, relexification and second language (L2) learning were particularly relevant to the *earliest* stages of pidgin/creole genesis, while we assume bilingual convergence and code-mixing to be particularly relevant to the *intermediate* stages. Finally, borrowing and attrition may be particularly relevant to *late* stages in the process.

The factors determining Gbe survivals, in relation to scenarios for substrate formation, constitute the possible explanations for the findings. A first potential factor is *lexicality*, having the status of a single coherent lexical entry. Recall that our original hypothesis was that in the relexification process purely lexical substrate properties are retained, while morphosyntactic properties are not retained. That conclusion has only limited support from the findings in our study. Thus the classical relexification scenario may be of much less use than we had originally imagined. Similarly, the survival of African lexical items in full is also limited.

What other possibilities are there? In the light of the scenario's discussed in Muysken's chapter on relexification and briefly listed above, we will discuss factors that may have played a role in the retention or loss of certain West African features. A useful point of departure is the attrition literature, since this literature takes retention and loss as its central focus;

this point of reference slants the discussion a bit, of course, towards later stage scenarios of genesis, and can only be relevant in part.

In the literature on language attrition and loss (compare in particular the useful summary in Lambert and Moore 1986: 180), a number of features of linguistic elements are listed that may contribute to their retention rather than loss in a situation of linguistic attrition. One is *recency* (of use). Features that have recently been used are most likely to be remembered. This factor is not particularly useful for us, since it requires contemporary usage data for proper testing.

The same holds for *contrast, linguistic distinctiveness*, and *saliency*; properties that are contrastive and contribute to distinctiveness are more likely to survive in attrition processes. However, contrast and distinctiveness are best seen as properties of the 'outer form' of the West African languages (lexical shapes, morphology, phonology, surface morphosyntax), properties that have rarely survived. It could well be that more salient aspects of the substrate are retained, while less salient ones are lost. However, this property also refers mostly to the form of the item in question in the substrate, and these forms have been mostly lost, except for the Fongbe focus marker analyzed by Aboh.

The other factors are more relevant, potentially, although not always easy to apply rigorously. One possibility is *frequency* of use. Possibly highly frequent properties, items, or structures from the substrate are retained, while infrequent items are not. Frequency is by itself an attractive explanatory factor, since it is plausible from studies of e.g. language loss that frequency of reinforcement plays a role (Lambert and Moore 1986: 180), and the same holds for studies of linguistic priming (Bock 1986, 1989). If users continue using a certain form due to its frequency, the chance that it is incorporated will be higher.

There is also *regularity*. More regular patterns are retained; more irregular ones tend to be lost (Holloway 1997: 197–198; Lambert and Moore 1986: 180). Allomorphy of different formal manifestations of a morphosyntactic category tends to be reduced as well.

A third possibility is *complexity*. More complex patterns or meanings are lost; more simple patterns are retained (Lambert and Moore 1986: 180). On the base of the loss of Brule Spanish in traditionally Hispanic speaking communities in Louisiana, Holloway (1997: 197–198) argues that analytical futures are used frequently but that there is reduction in the morphologically expressed TMA system. This may be seen as the result of loss of morphological complexity.

A fourth option is *locality*. Possibly patterns which are 'local' in the sense that they only require processing immediately sequential elements may be easier to transfer than patterns which involve long distance dependencies.

A fifth possibility is the prominent role in *discourse* that certain West African features may have had. It has been noted that the pragmatic load of an item contributes to its survival, and in many communities the morphological forms of discourse markers are retained as well (Matras 2000). This has been documented for Singapore English, for instance (Soon Lay 2005). The retention of the Fongbe focus marker in Saramaccan, along with its concomitant morphosyntax, could well be explained in this same way. Again, however, this is mostly relevant for patterns and items of which the forms have been retained as well.

Lefebvre (2011) appeals to *semantic weight*, functional load, as a factor stimulating retention. Similarly, Dorian (1981: 147) argues for the situation of E. Southerland Gaelic in Scotland that strong retention rates characterize nominal number, verbal tense and verbal voice. There is moderate retention for case, nominal gender, and verbal number. These results could be viewed in terms of the semantic weight of the items involved.

Retention may involve the retention of forms as well as functions. Only in the case of lexical items and discourse markers is there retention of forms and their functions. For all other factors, only retention of function is involved. This is schematized in Table 2:

Table 2. Potential contribution towards retention of various factors

	Form retained	**Function retained**
Lexicality	X	X
Recency of use	X	X
Contrast	X	X
Linguistic distinctiveness	X	X
Saliency	X	X
Frequency		X
Regularity		X
Complexity		X
Locality		X
Discourse	X	X
Semantic weight		X

The result of trying to apply the factors listed to the results in the various chapters is given in Table 3:

Table 3. The potential role of the factors of Frequency, Regularity, Complexity, Locality, Discourse, and Semantic weight for the different grammatical components studied

	Frequency	Regularity	Complexity	Locality	Semantic weight	Result
Locative constructions	±	±	±	+	+	Patterning on general Gbe models rather than individual items
Lexical semantics & Argument Structure	−	−	±	+	±	Not on the whole Gbe, except for a reflex of the hypertransitivity phenomenon
Word classes	+	−	±	±	−	Only partly modelled on Gbe patterns,
Morphology	±	±	−	+	−	Gbe morphological pattern limited to one or two affixes
Reduplication	±	±	−	+	+	Gbe pattern productive only for adjectives
Syllabic phonology	+	+	−	+	−	Gbe patterning in monosyllables, more complex (including Kikongo) patterning in polysyllables
DP morpho-syntax and the Left periphery	+	+	+	±	±	Variable Gbe patterning
Complement selection	−	−	+	±	−	Only partly modelled on Gbe patterns

We notice that the frequency of certain patterns, often in conjunction with their regularity, certainly plays a role; regular and frequent patterns tend to survive much more easily. Furthermore, semantic weight may well play an important role. It is hard to evaluate the independent contribution of locality and complexity on the basis of this data set since the factors mentioned often occur together. They may play a role, but their contribution often is linked to that of other positive factors.

I should also note that even a positive specification for many of the factors does not necessarily lead to wholesale retention. DP morpho-syntax and the Left periphery, for instance, is not fully retained, even though it is positively specified for many of the factors involved.

5. How 'African' or 'European' are the Surinam Creoles?

How 'African' or 'European' are the Surinam Creoles? Have the surviving African features led to a profound reshaping of the creoles away from their lexifiers, so that they are truly 'African languages under a European lexical guise'? Or are they primarily like their European lexifiers, with a few special African features? A third alternative, of course, is that they are different in their structures from both lexifiers and substrates. To answer this question, we need some way to measure distance between languages. In what sense are languages 'close' or 'distant'?

There are a number of methodological considerations in measuring distance between the Surinam Creole languages, the lexifiers, and the West-African substrate languages, which we will discuss one by one.

5.1. The language selection issue

First of all, which languages are we counting in, when we measure language distance?

On the European side, English is uncontroversial as the main lexifier language of the creole languages of Surinam. Dutch was a secondary lexifier in a prestige variant of Sranan from the 18th century onward, but its structural influence is less straightforward. For Portuguese, the situation is not clear either. It had a secondary role as a lexifier in Saramaccan, but contributed much core vocabulary, and hence may have played an important role. However, there could have been an anterior Portuguese-lexifier creole that contributed this vocabulary, and hence direct structural influence from Portuguese is potentially limited. Nonetheless, there is good reason to include these three lexifier languages and no others.

Ever since the 'cafeteria principle' was introduced by Dillard (1970) to bring the discussion about possible African influence on Caribbean creoles onto a methodologically sound footing, care needs to be taken to select the correct contributing substrate languages. For the Surinam Creoles, there is good lexical evidence, as shown in Smith's chapter on Kikongo lexical influence, that Kikongo functioned as a second substrate, next to the Gbe languages. The Gbe contribution documented in Smith's chapter on Gbe lexical influence, is uncontroversial, but how much internal variation should we allow in the Gbe sources, since this is a continuum of related varieties spreading from Ewegbe to Gungbe.

Finally, there is the internal differentiation of the creoles to be taken into account. Did different Surinam Creoles undergo separate influences from the languages of Benin? Here we will include the well-documented 18th century Sranan, contemporary Sranan, and contemporary Saramaccan.

5.2. Structural phylogenetics

In recent years, various researchers have applied techniques from phylogenetics to structural data, inspired by the seminal articles of Dunn, Terrill, Reesink, Foley & Levinson (2005) and Dunn, Levinson, Lindström, Reesink & Terrill (2008). In these techniques, structural features are coded (often in a binary manner) and representational and analytical techniques from bioinformatics are used to represent distances between languages and model genealogical developmental patterns.

However, theoretical and methodological questions remain. Lexical distance measures assume that (mostly content) lexemes have equivalent 'weight' in establishing relationships. This assumption is based on the idea that all words count the same for measuring distance between languages, although the lexicon may have a much more complex structure. If this is problematic already for the lexicon, how likely is that structural distance features have the same weight? Does a 'major' parameter like VO/OV word order have the same weight as a detail of a comparative construction? Also, can we measure distance across components, and if so, how? Which components of the grammar are relevant here and what is the weight of these components?

These questions will require much further study, on the basis of concrete examples, and the establishment of best practices, since it never will be possible to develop measures of language distance independent of features selected or external criteria. Even this may turn out to be a futile exercise in the end. For closely related languages, it will be possible to use panel judgments about similarity and mutual comprehensibility, but this will not work for more distant languages.

5.3. Feature dependence and selecting a feature set

A crucial issue, which has not been solve yet, is mutual independence of features. There are many types of feature dependence. *Logical dependence* derives from properties of the categories themselves, as in the following two features:

(1)   (F1) L_X has postpositions > (F2) L_X has adpositions

A second possibility is *Functional dependence*, as in:

(2)   (F1) L_X has rigid word order ~ (F2) L_X has no full case system

Here the dependence derives from the complementary functions, grosso modo, of word order and case marking as two ways of marking grammatical relations in the clause. Obviously, this cannot be an absolute form of dependency. Possibly, it is bidirectional.

A third possibility is *Typological dependence*, defined over a global language sample. An example would be:

(3)   (F1) L_X has verb final word order ~ (F2) L_X has postpositions

Again this is a non-absolute, possibly bidirectional dependency, established by examining word order patterns in a large, areally and genealogically diversified, language sample.

Finally, the dependency might hold for the overall *Data set* (the specific language sample studied) rather than for all languages in the world.

(4)   (F1) L_X has verb medial word order ~ (F2) L_X has prepositions

In this study, we have limited ourselves to the features that formed the basis of the discussion in this book, and certainly there may be dependencies among the features that we have not been able to weed out. So far 82 features are included in the feature set, from 10 languages. The features or characters are drawn from the different chapters, and belong to the categories listed in Table 4.

Arguably, there is an uneven distribution across the different grammatical categories here. However, we doubt that the picture will change radically if different weights are assigned to the different category sets, or slightly different numbers of features are chosen per category.

Table 4. Distribution of the features across the different topics studied in his book

Author(s)	Feature (F) Category	# of Fs
Yakpo	Location	28
Essegbey	Mono-transitive verbs	1
Essegbey, van den Berg	Property items	7
Essegbey	Cut & Break	1
Essegbey	Eat	4
Van de Berg	Word formation	2
Aboh & Smith	Reduplication	6
Aboh & Smith	Copula	1
Smith	Syllable structure	4
Aboh	Determiners	5
Aboh	Verb focus	1
	Noun class prefixes	2
Veenstra	Predicate complement relations	20

So far 10 languages have been coded; they are discussed above and are listed in Table 5.

Table 5. Languages in the sample for the phylogenetic analysis

Benin/Congo	*Suriname*	*European lexifier*
Kikongo	early Sranan	English
Ewegbe	contemporary Sranan	Dutch
Gungbe	contemporary Saramaccan	Portuguese
Fongbe		

6. Resulting distance measures in a standard NeighborNet analysis and discussion

Having coded these 82 features for the 10 languages, we obtain the following simple NeighborNet (Huson and Bryant 2006). The NeighborNet reveals three clusters: the Gbe languages on one side, the Surinam Creoles in the middle and the European lexifiers on the other side. The structural distance of the creoles from the substrates and the lexifiers is comparable. Special mention should be made of Kikongo. It clusters separately from the Gbe languages, and is somewhat closer to the European languages for the features chosen. This may support the idea that the features chosen tend to reflect specific properties of the Gbe languages, which is probably not far from the truth in any case.

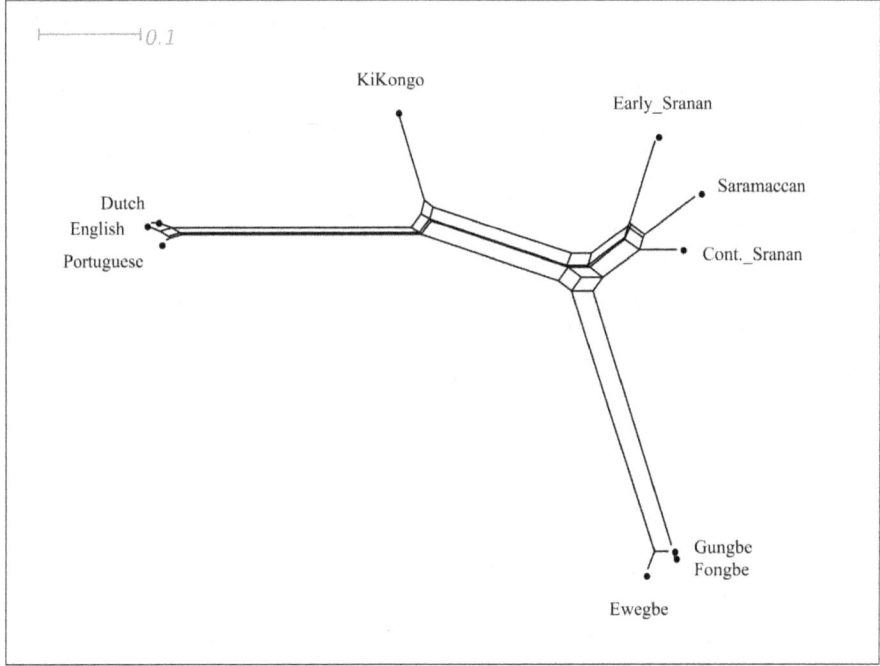

Figure 1. Simple NeighbourNet representing the distances between the languages in the sample surveyed

It should be kept in mind that the resulting distance measures in a NeighborNet analysis do not stand alone. Parallel to our own work reported on in this chapter, various other colleagues have applied structural phylogenetics to creole data, sometimes comparing them to non-creole data

Parkvall (2008) has compared the number and incidence of morphosyntactic distinctions made in creoles, as compared to other languages, on the basis of the WALS data (Haspelmath, Dryer, Gil & Comrie 2005) and his own coded data for creoles (WALS has no commonly recognized creoles in their language sample). He concludes that creoles as a group consistently make less morpho-syntactic distinctions than the other languages studied.

Bakker, Daval-Markussen, Parkvall & Plag (2011) study other features in creoles and non-creoles on the basis of the WALS data. They conclude that creoles form a separate cluster, when compared to other languages.

Finally, Daval-Markussen (2011) has taken the coded data from the Holm & Patrick (2007) comparative questionnaire on creoles and compared these to data coded by himself for the relevant lexifier and substrate languages. Again, the creoles are distant from the substrates as well as the superstrate languages.

These different papers differ in their results, but clearly show that a specific feature selection is crucial for determining the final outcome of a phylogenetic analysis. While there are many differences, all studies so far concur in the idea that, in structural terms, the creoles neither resemble their lexifiers nor their substrates very closely. What remains to be established is whether the creoles form a natural class in a linguistically interesting sense; for this, more detailed work comparing the Surinam Creoles to other creole languages in the Atlantic, Indian Ocean, and Pacific areas is needed. Furthermore, some independent way of characterizing a creole language needs to be found, to avoid circularity.

7. Conclusions and discussion

It is clear that the answer to the question of possible African structure survivals in the Surinam Creoles is a complex one. Some features have survived, others have not, and for the ones that have survived, they have often been profoundly transformed.

The most likely scenario is that the African languages played an important role in a stage after initial creolization, i.e. when the creole had already been formed as a nascent separate language. At the time, the African languages may have already been undergoing the processes of reduction and leveling characteristic of diaspora languages. The attrited form of the African languages may have primarily influenced the creole through processes of semantic and structural convergence, roughly as sketched in the work of Migge (2003), although the Saramaccan focus particle *wè*, retaining, as it does, the whole morphosyntax of the Fongbe/Gungbe focus particle *wɛ*, would require some special pleading.

Thus our work has arrived in a different place from where it started. We do not think that early stage contact scenarios were the primary source of the survival of African structural features in the Surinam Creoles, as in a relexification scenario. Furthermore, the creole languages are rather distinct, in structural terms, from their African roots, as they are from the European lexifiers.

Bibliography of work resulting from the Trans-Atlantic Sprachbund project

Norval Smith

The following is list of references to works, in addition to this volume, which arose directly or indirectly from the NWO Programme Project nr. 360-70-020: *A trans-Atlantic sprachbund? The structural relationships between the Gbe-languages of West Africa and the Surinamese creole language.*

Publications arising from the project

Aboh, Enoch Oladé
    2000 Object shift and verb movement in Gbe. In *Actes du 3e congrès mondial de linguistique africaine Lomé*, Kézié K. Lébikaza (ed.), 1–20. Kôln: Rüdiger Köppe Verlag.
    2001 The role of typology in language creation: a descriptive take. *Generative Grammar in Geneva* 2: 1–13.
    2001 Clitiques phonétiques ou clitiques tout court. In *Clitiques et cliticisation*, Claude Muller, Paulo de Carvalho, Laurence Labrune, Frédéric Lambert and Katja Ploog (eds.), 459–481. Paris: H. Champion.
    2002 Object shift and verb serialization: a cross-linguistic perspective. In *Incontro Di Grammatica Generativa Proceedings*, P. Bottari (ed.). Lecce, Italy: Congedo Editore.
    2002 La morphosyntaxe de la péripherie gauche nominale. In *La syntaxe de la définitude*, Anne Daladier and Anne Zribi-Hertz (eds.), 9–26. (Recherches Linguistiques De Vincennes 31) Saint Denis: Presses Universitaires de Vincennes.
    2003 Les constructions à objet préposé et les series verbales dans les lan-gues kwa. In *Typologie des langues d'afrique et universaux de la grammaire. Vol. 2: Benue-Kwa, Soninke, Wolof*, P. Sauzet and A. Zribi-Hertz (eds.), 15–40. Paris: L'Harmattan.
    2003 The category P in Gbe. In *Germania Et Alia. A Linguistic Webschrift for Hans Den Besten*, Jan Koster and Henk van Riemsdijk (eds.), online at http://www.let.rug.nl/~koster/DenBesten/Smith.pdf. Groningen: University of Groningen.

2004 Focus constructions across Kwa. In *KinyĩRa NjĩRa! Step Firmly on the Pathway*, Chege Githiora, Heather Littlefield, and Victor Manfredi (eds.), 7–22. (Trends in African Linguistics 6) Trenton, NJ: Africa World Press.

2004 Left or right? a view from the Kwa peripheral positions. In *Peripheries: Syntactic Edges and Their Effects*, David Adger, Cécile de Cat, and George Tsoulas (eds.), 165–190. (Studies in Natural Language and Linguistic Theory 59) Dordrecht: Kluwer Academic Publishers.

2004 Snowballing movement and generalized pied-piping. In *Trigger*, Anne Breitbath and Henk van Riemsdijk (eds.), 15–47. Berlin: Mouton.

2004 Toward a modular theory of creole genesis. Curaçao Creole Conference Papers. Electronic version FPI, Fudashon Pa Planifikason di Idioma, Jan Noorduynweg 32b, Curaçao, Neth. Antilles. (www.fpi.an).

2005 Object shift, verb movement, and verb reduplication. In *The Oxford Handbook of Comparative Syntax*, Guglielmo Cinque and Richard S. Kayne (eds.), 138–177. New York: Oxford University Press.

2005 The category P: The Kwa paradox. *Linguistic Analysis* 32: 615 – 646.

2006 Complementation in Saramaccan and Gungbe: the case of C-type modal particles. *Natural Language and Linguistic Theory* 24 (1): 1–55.

2006 The role of the syntax-semantics interface in language transfer. In *L2 Acquisition and Creole Genesis*, Claire Lefebvre, Lydia White, and Christine Jourdan (eds.), 221–252. Amsterdam: John Benjamins.

2007 La genèse de la périphérie gauche du saramaka: un cas d'influence du substrat? In *Grammaires Créoles Et Grammaire Comparative*, Karl Erland Gadell, and Anne Zribi-Hertz (eds.), 73–97. Saint-Denis: Presses Universitaires de Paris.

2009 Clause structure and verb series. *Linguistic Inquiry* 40: 1–33.

2010 The P-route. In *Mapping Spatial PPs*. In Guglielmo Cinque and Luigi Rizzi (eds.),*The Cartography of Syntactic Structures* Vol. 6. New York: Oxford University Press. 225–260.

Aboh, Enoch Oladé and Umberto Ansaldo
 2007 The role of typology in language creation: a descriptive take. In *Deconstructing Creole*, Umberto Ansaldo, Stephen Matthews and Lisa Lim (eds.), 39–66. (Typological Studies in Language 73) Amsterdam: John Benjamins.

Adamson, Lilian and Norval S.H. Smith
 2003 Productive derivational predicate reduplication in Sranan. In *Twice as Meaningful: Reduplication in Pidgins, Creoles, and Other Contact Languages*, Silvia Kouwenberg (ed.), 83–92. (Westminster Creolistics Series 8) London: Battlebridge.

Ameka, Felix
 2001 Ideophones and the nature of the adjective word class in Ewe. In *Ideophones*, F. Voeltz, K. Erhard, and Christa Kilian-Hatz (eds.), 25–48. (Typological Studies in Language 44) Amsterdam: John Benjamins.

2001 Ewe. In *Facts About the Major Languages of the World, Past and Present*, J. Gary and C. Rubino (eds.), 207–213. New York: New England Publishing Associates.
2002 The cultural scripting of body parts for emoticons: on jealousy and related concepts in Ewe. *Pragmatics and Cognition* 10: 25–47.
2002 Constituent order and grammatical relations in Ewe in typological perspective. In *The Nominative and Accusative and Their Counterparts*, Kiristin Davidse and Béatrice Lamiroy (eds.), 319–352. (Case and Grammatical Relations across Languages 4) Amsterdam: John Benjamins.
2002 The progressive aspect in Likpe: its implications for word order in Kwa. In *New Directions in Ghanaian Linguistics*, Felix Ameka and E. K. Osam (eds.), 85–111. Accra: Black Mask.
2003 Prepositions and postpositions in Ewe (Gbe): empirical and theoretical considerations. In *Typologie des langues d'afrique & universaux de la grammaire*, Anne Zribi-Hertz and Patrick Sauzet (eds.), 41–67. Paris: Harmattan.
2003 Today is far: situational anaphors in overlapping clause construc-tions in Ewe. In *Studies in the Languages of the Volta Basin I*, M. E Kropp Dakubu and E. K. Osam (eds.), 9–22. Legon: Department of Linguistics, University of Ghana.
2008 He died old dying to be dead right: transitivity and semantic shifts of die in Ewe. In *Crosslinguistic Perspectives on Argument Structure: Implications for Learnability*, Melissa Bowermann and Penelope Brown (eds.), 231–254. Mahwah, NJ: Erlbaum.

Ameka, Felix and James Essegbey
2006 Elements of Ewe grammar of space. In *Grammars of Space: Cognitive Explorations*, Stephen Levinson and David P. Wilkens (eds.), 359–399. Cambridge: Cambridge University Press.
2007 Cut and break verbs in Ewegbe and the causative/inchoative alternation construction. *Cognitive Linguistics* 18 (2): 241–250.

Arends, Jacques
2001 Social stratification and network relations in the formation of Sranan. In *Creolization and Contact*, Norval S.H. Smith and Tonjes Veenstra (eds.), 291–308. Amsterdam: John Benjamins.
2001 Simple grammars, complex languages. peer commentary to John Mcwhorter, 'the world's simplest grammars are creole grammars.' *Linguistic Typology* 5 (3/3): 180–182.
2002 The history of the Surinamese creoles I: a socio-historical survey. In *Atlas of the Languages of Suriname*, Ethne Carlin and Jacques Arends (eds.), 115–130. Leiden: KITLV Press.
2002 The historical study of creoles and the future of Creole Studies. In *Pidgin and Creole Linguistics in the 21st Century*, Glenn Gilbert (ed.), 49–68. New York: Peter Lang.

2002   Young languages, old texts: early documents in the Surinamese creoles. In *Atlas of the Languages of Suriname*, Ethne Carlin and Jacques Arends (eds.), 183–205. Leiden: KITLV Press.
2002   La 'déhistoricisation' de la créologenèse. In *la créolisation; a chacun sa vérité*, Albert Valdman (ed.), 143–156. (Études Créoles 25:1) Paris: L'Harmattan.
2005   Sranan. In *Encyclopedia of Linguistics*, Philipp Strazny (ed.), 1031. New York: Routledge.
2005   Saramaccan. In *Encyclopedia of Linguistics*, Philipp Strazny (ed.), 928. New York: Routledge.
2008   A demographic perspective on creole formation. In *Handbook of Pidgin and Creole Studies*, Silvia Kouwenberg and John Victor Singler (eds.), 309–331. Oxford: Blackwell Publishers.

Arends, Jacques and Margot van den Berg
2004   The Saramaka Peace Treaty in Sranan: an edition of the 1762 text (including a copy of the original manuscript). *Creolica*, available at http://www.creolica.net/Saramaka/saramakaPC.htm

Bruyn, Adrienne
2002   The structure of the Surinamese Creoles. In *Atlas of the Languages of Suriname*, Ethne Carlin and Jacques Arends (eds.), 153–182. Leiden: KITLV Press.
2003   Grammaticalization, réanalyse et influence substratique: quelques cas du sranan. In *grammaticalization et réanalyse: approches de la variation créole et française* Sibylle Kriegel (ed.), 25–47. Paris: CNRS Éditions.
2007   Bare nouns and articles in Sranan. In *Noun Phrases in Creole Languages. A Multi-Faceted Approach*, Marlyse Baptista and Jacqueline Guéron (eds.), 339–381. Amsterdam: John Benjamins.
2008   Grammaticalization in pidgins and creoles. In *Handbook of Pidgin and Creole Studies*, Silvia Kouwenberg and John Victor Singler (eds.), 385–410. Oxford: Blackwell Publishing.

Essegbey, James
2002   The syntax of inherent complement verbs in Ewe. In *New Directions in Ghanaian Linguistics*, Felix Ameka and E. K. Osam (eds.), 55–84. Accra: Black Mask.
2003   On definiteness asymmetry in double object constructions. In *Proceedings of the 3rd World Congress of African Linguisticsq*, K. Lebikaza (ed.), 127–141. Cologne: Rudiger Koeppe.
2004   Auxiliaries in serialising languages: on come and go verbs in Sranan and Ewegbe. *Lingua* 20 (114): 473–494.
2004   Demystifying inherent complement verbs in Ewe. In *typologie des langues d'afrique et universaux de la grammaire*, A. Zribi-Hetz and P. Souzet (eds.), 97–126. Paris: L'Harmattan.
2005   The basic locative construction in Gbe Languages and Surinamese creoles. *Journal of Pidgin and Creole Languages* 20 (2): 228–267.

2005   Ewe and Gbe Languages. In *Encyclopedia of Linguistics*, Philipp Strazny (ed.), 319. New York Routledge.
2006   Ewe. In *Encyclopedia of Languages and Linguistics*, Keith Brown (ed.), 369–370. Oxford: Elsevier.
2007   Cut and break verbs in Sranan. *Cognitive Linguistics* 18 (2): 231–240.
2007   Intransitive verbs in Ewe and the Unaccusativity Hypothesis. In *Cross-Linguistic Perspectives on Argument Structure: Implications for Learnability*, M.Bowerman and P. Brown (eds.), 213–230. New Jersey: Lawrence Erlbaum.

Essegbey, James and Felix Ameka
2007   'Cut' and 'break' verbs in Gbe and Suriname Creoles. *Journal of Pidgin and Creole Languages* 22 (1): 37–55.

Essegbey, James and S. Kita
2001   Pointing left in ghana: how a taboo on the use of the left hand influences gestural practices. *Gesture* 1 (1): 73–95.

Huttar, George L., James Essegbey, and Felix Ameka
2007   Gbe and Other West African sources of Suriname Creole semantic structures: implications for creole genesis. *Journal of Pidgin and Creole Languages* 22 (1): 57–72.

Kita, S. and James Essegbey
2003   Left-hand taboo on direction-indicating gestures in Ghana: when and why people still use left-hand gestures. In *Gestures. Meaning and Use*, M. Rector, I. Poggi and N. Trigo (eds.), 301–306. Porto: Gráficos Reunidos.

Migge, Bettina and Norval S.H. Smith
2007   Introduction: substrate influence in creole formation. *Journal of Pidgin and Creole Languages* 22 (1): 1–15.

Mous, Maarten
2001   Paralexification in language intertwining. In *Creolization and Contact*, Norval S.H.Smith and Tonjes Veenstra (eds.), 113–124. (Creole Language Library 23) Amsterdam: John Benjamins.

Mous, Maarten and Vinije Haabo
2002   P-Language In *Atlas of the Languages of Suriname*, Eithne Carlin and Jacques Arends (eds.), 163. Leiden: KITLV Press.

Muysken, Pieter
2001   The origin of creole languages: the perspective of second language learning. In *Creolization and Contact*, Norval S.H.Smith and Tonjes Veenstra (eds.), 157–174. (Creole Language Library 23) Amsterdam: John Benjamins.
2003   The Grammatical Elements in Negerhollands: Loss, Retention, Reconstitution. In *Germania Et Alia. A Linguistic Webschrift for Hans Den Besten*, Jan Koster and Henk van Riemsdijk (eds.), PAGE#S. Groningen: University of Groningen.

Muysken, Pieter and Paul Law
   2001   Creole Studies: a theoretical linguist's field guide. *Glot International* 5 (2): 47–57.

Price, Richard
   2007   Some anthropological musings on creolization. *Journal of Pidgin and Creole Languages* 22: 17–36.

Smith, Norval S.H.
   2001   Voodoo chile: differential substrate effects in Saramaccan and Haitian. In *Creolization and Contact*, Norval S.H.Smith and Tonjes Veenstra (eds.), 42–80. (Creole Language Library 23) Amsterdam: John Benjamins.

   2002   The history of the Suriname Creoles II: origin and differentiation. In *Atlas of the Languages of Suriname*, Ethne Carlin and Jacques Arends (eds.), 131–151. Leiden: KITLV Press.

   2003   New evidence from the past: to epenthesize or not to epenthesize: that is the question. In *Phonology and Morphology of Creole Languages*, Ingo Plag (ed.), 91–108.) Tübingen: Niemeyer.

   2003   The proverbial word in Sranan. . In *Germania Et Alia. A Linguistic Webschrift for Hans Den Besten*, Jan Koster and Henk van Riemsdijk (eds.), online at http://www.let.rug.nl/~koster/DenBesten/Smith.pdf. Groningen: University of Groningen.

   2003   Evidence for recursive syllable structures in Aluku and Sranan. In *Recent Developments in Creole Studies*, Dany Adone (ed.), 31–52. Tübingen: Niemeyer Verlag.

   2005   Pidgins. In *The Greenwood Encyclopedia of African American Folklore*, Anand Prahlad (ed.), 975–977. Westpirt, CT: Greenwood Press.

   2006   Very rapid creolization in the framework of the restricted motivation hypothesis. In *L2 Acquisition and Creole Genesis: Dialogues*, Claire Lefebvre, Lydia White, and Christine Jourdan (eds.), 49–65. Amsterdam: John Benjamins.

   2008   Creole phonology. In *Handbook of Creole Linguistics*, Silvia Kouwenberg and John Victor Singler (eds.), 98–129. Oxford: Blackwell Publishers.

   2009   English speaking in Early Suriname. In *Gradual Creolization: Studies Celebrating Jacques Arends*, Rachel Selbach, Hugo Cardoso, and Margot van den Berg (eds.), 305–326. (Creole Language Library 34) Amsterdam: John Benjamins.

   2008   The Origin of the Portuguese Words in Saramaccan: Implications for Sociohistory. In Roots of Creole Structures: Weighing the Contribution of *Substrates and Superstrates.*, Susanne Michaelis (ed.), 153–168. Amsterdam: John Benjamins.

2009   Simplification of a complex part of grammar or not?: What happened to Kikongo nouns in Saramaccan?. In *Complex Precesses in New Languages*, Enoh Aboh and Norval Smith (eds.), 51–73. Amsterdam: John Benjamins

Smith, Norval S.H. and Lilian Adamson
  2006   Tonal phenomena in Sranan. *STUFSTUF – Sprachtypologie und Universalienforschung* 59: 211–218.

Smith, Norval S.H. and Hugo Cardoso
  2004   A new look at the Portuguese element in Saramaccan. *Journal of Portuguese Linguistics* 3: 115–147.

Smith, Norval S.H. and Vinije Haabo
  2004   Suriname Creoles: phonology. In *A Handbook of Varieties of English: A Multimedia Reference Tool, Vol. 1 Phonology*, Bernd Kortmann, Edgar W. Schneider, Kate Burridge, Rajend Mesthrie, and Clive Upton (eds.), 525–564. Berlin: Mouton de Gruyter.
  2007   The Saramaccan implosives: tools for linguistic archaeology? *Journal of Pidgin and Creole Languages* 22: 101–122.

Smith, Norval S.H. and Marleen van de Vate
  2006   Population movements, colonial control and vowel systems. In *The Structure of Creole Words: Segmental, Syllabic and Morphological Aspects*, Parth Bhatt and Ingo Plag (eds.), 59–82. Tübingen: Niemeyer.

van den Berg, Margot
  2001   'Mingo joù no man': Oud-Sranan in verhoren en verslagen van rechtzaken. *OSO Tijdschrift voor Surinamistiek* 20 (2): 241–253.
  2003   Early 18th century Sranan –man. In *Phonology and Morphology of Creole Languages*, Ingo Plag (ed.), 231–251. (Linguistische Arbeiten 478) Tübingen: Niemeyer.
  2007   *A Grammar of Early Sranan*. Zetten: Manta.

van den Berg, Margot and Jacques Arends
  2004   Court Records as a source of authentic Early Sranan. In *Creoles, Contact, and Langauge Change*, Genevieve Escure and Armin Schwegler (eds.), 21–34. Amsterdam: John Benjamins.

Winford, Donald and Bettina Migge
  2007   Substrate influence in the emergence of the tense and aspect systems in the Creoles of Suriname. *Journal of Pidgin and Creole Languages* 22 (1): 73–99.

A preliminary list of probable Kikongo (KiKoongo) lexical items in the Surinam Creoles

Norval Smith

1. Introduction

In this article, I will try to sum up the present state of our knowledge concerning the presence of vocabulary items of Kikongo origin in the creole languages of Surinam. The obvious reason for the presence of a comparatively large number of Kikongo lexical items in the Surinam Creoles is the early importation of a large number of slaves from West Central Africa.

1.1. Importation figures

Only in the final years of the English colonial power in Surinam do importation figures for slaves begin to appear. In my earlier chapter on the early history of Surinam, I give figures for the slave trade with West Central Africa, supplied by the Voyages Database (2009).

1.2. Sources

The list of circa 185 Kikongo words represents the largest number of words identified so far in the Surinam Creoles, from any single African language source. However, this is partly due to the fact that Daeleman, a student of Kikongo, made an early study of the Kikongo words he found, or suspected, in the Saramaccan language (Daeleman 1972). This list was augmented for Ndyuka by Huttar (1985, 1986).

As is the case with the other list given here (on the Gbe lexical contribution to the Surinam Creoles), the Kikongo list is preliminary. That it is incomplete is evident. There are a fair number of items (around 20) that look as if they might begin with Bantu noun-class prefixes, and thus correspond to the characteristic pattern of class prefixation that appears with most nouns in Bantu languages. In contrast to nouns, verbs appear either in their bare stem form, or occasionally with Kikongo derivational suffixes (known as verb extensions in Bantu linguistics). They are thus more difficult to identify.

I have drawn most of my cited data from the three above-mentioned sources. Daeleman (1972) compares Saramaccan items of putative Kikongo origin with the Kikongo dialect that he himself studied most intensely – Ntandu, providing other relevant dialect attributions from time to time. In fact, Ntandu is probably not the precise direct source, or even the only source, of the Kikongo words in Saramaccan. There is a fairly consistent difference in development as regards one particular phonological feature. This concerns Kikongo nouns in /-ia ~ya#/. In Ntandu these tend to end in /i#/. This feature does not appear in Saramaccan. The Ntandu development could of course post-date the period of the slave trade.

(1) | Nr | Saramaccan | Ntandu | Other Kikongo | gloss |
|---|---|---|---|---|
| 010 | *ɓandya* | *m-baánsi* | *m-báansya* | side |
| 094 | *mayaya* | (*ma-*)*dyaádi* | (*ma-*)*dyaadya* | sp. grass |

2. Nouns

Kikongo, as a Bantu language, has a partially semantically based noun-class prefix system, with (normally) pairs of singular and plural prefixes in each class. In the default case, nouns have been transferred into the Surinam Creole languages in the form prefix+noun. In Smith (2009), I discussed a potential model of transference for Saramaccan, which could be extended to all the Surinam Creoles.

These class prefix+noun stem forms "borrowed" into Saramaccan are now holistic stems, but there is some evidence to support a position that, during the formative period of Saramaccan language, such words were seen as dimorphemic and that this was the default pattern for the incorporation of Kikongo nouns. Certain singular class prefixes had been lost under certain circumstances. In these cases, then, the form with the corresponding plural prefix was normally adopted instead (cf. Smith 2009).

To illustrate the general class prefix idea, I give Daeleman's account of the Ntandu noun-class system in Table 1. Note that Ntandu does not realise the singular prefix of gender 5/6, unless it is followed by a nasal cluster. Similarly (although not illustrated here), in Laman's (1964) Central Kikongo (identified as Mazinga by Söderberg (1985)), the singular prefix of gender 7/8 is similarly largely unrealised (p.c. T. Schadeberg). Daeleman (1972) notes more generally that the class 5 marker normally does not appear before a single consonant initial in Ntandu, Ndibu or Yaka, while the same applies to the class 7 marker in Yombe and Ndibu

In Saramaccan, we see a similar pattern to that obtaining in Ntandu. Additionally, however, we also find cases illustrating the Mazinga pattern, although in this case there are exceptions. Without a fuller knowledge of the realisation of Kikongo noun class systems we cannot, for instance, say that the Ndibu dialect played a significant role in the Kikongo part of the ethnic backround of Saramaccan Maroons.

There is also one possible example of a singular prefix in Kwinti of a word of gender 5/6 that would have none in Ntandu. This is *isanga* 'work shed' (Van der Elst 1975: 17), where other lects have the form *masanga*, which clearly displays the Kikongo plural prefix for this gender.

Table 1. The Ntandu noun-class system

Class	Noun prefix	Number	Realization restrictions
1	*mu-*	singular	Ǹ- before C
2	*ba-*	plural of 1	
3	*mu-*	singular	Ǹ- before C
4	*mi-*	plural of 3	Ǹ- before C
5	*di-*	singular	*di-* only before NC
6	*ma-*	plural of 5, 14, 15	
7	*ki-*	singular	
8	*bi-*	plural of 7	
9	*N-*	singular	
10	*N-*	plural of 9, collective of 11	
11	*lu-*	singulative	
13	*tu-*	plural of 11	
14	*bu-*	abstract nouns	
15	*ku-*	infinitives	
16	*ga-*	locative (surface)	
17	*ku-*	locative (distance)	
18	*mu-*	locative (inside)	
19	*fi-*	diminutive	

3. Verbs

The verbs that have been borrowed into the Surinam Creoles are largely disyllabic, and less frequently trisyllabic or tetrasyllabic. Most of the verb forms end in a final /-a/. This corresponds to the default final inflectional verb ending of Bantu languages. Disyllabic verbs in /-a/ all correspond to a monosyllabic Kikongo stem plus this final vowel. Most trisyllabic forms in /-a/ correspond however to a monosyllabic Kikongo stem followed by a so-called verb-extension followed by the final vowel. In contrast to the situation with nouns and their class prefixes, there is no evidence for assuming that the verb extensions were ever analysed as discrete morphemes in the Surinam Creoles. In Table 3, there are only a couple of examples at most of each extension.

4. Relevant phonological aspects

In this section, I will only mention two aspects of phonology. Firstly, we have a form of Meinhof's Law forbidding sequences of nasal onset clusters. The rationale for mentioning this is that it does not appear to be in a form that has been reported from Africa. The second aspect concerns the so-called Kikongo Tone-groups.

4.1. Meinhof's Law

A phonological restriction exists in the Saramaccan language against two successive sequences of nasal onset clusters. This was first noted by Daeleman (1972). Such a restriction also exists in many Bantu languages, where it is generally known as Meinhof's Law. This generally appears to operate differently from the way it applies in Saramaccan, however. I first illustrate some Saramaccan cases in (3):

(2)	Nr	Ntandu	Saramaccan	gloss
	008	m-báambi	ɓámbi	a large lizard
	019	m-boóngo	ɓɔngɔ	descendants
	041	n-gáanda	gandá	village
	042	n-gáandu	gandú	cayman (taboo)

Johnson (1979) reports the following variants of Meinhof's Law:

(3) Attested Forms of Meinhof's Law[1]
- a. $NC_{vd} > NN / \_\_ V (V) N$
- b. $NC_{vd} > N / \_\_ V (V) N$
- c. $NC_{vd} > N / \_\_ V (V) NC$

As can be seen from (2), this differs from the Saramaccan treatment, shown schematically in (3d).

(3) d. $NC_{vd} > C_{vd} / \_\_ V (V) NC$

Yet another development can be found in the treatment of Kimbundu words in Angolar. This treatment is shown in (3e), and appears in a single case in Saramaccan.

(3) e. $NC_{vd} > C_{vl} / NC V (V) \_\_$

This resembles what happens in what Meinhof (1932) refers to as the Kuanyama Law (in contrast to Meinhof's Law, termed by him the Ganda Law),[2]

(3) f. $NCvd > Cvd / NC V (V) \_\_$

with the difference that the dissimilated cluster leaves a voiceless stop behind. Some examples from Maurer (1995):

(4)
Kimbundu	Angolar	gloss
ki-mbandji	*mbandji ~ mbatxi*	side of body
m-binda	*mbita*	calabash
n-danji	*ndatxi*	root
n-gandu (crocodile)	*ngandu ~ ngatu*	shark

---

1. I have modified Johnson's formulation slightly to reflect the fact that I consider the onsets here to be nasal clusters rather than prenasalized stops.
2. Quoted from Kim (1999).

Kikongo words in Angolar seem however to display the Ganda Law:

(5) Kikongo   Angolar   gloss
     m-bongo   *mbogo*   descendant
     n-gembu   *ngebu*   bat

The case represented schematically in (3e), displaying what we could call the Angolar law, is the following:

(6) Kikongo   Saramaccan/Matawai   gloss
     m-púungu *a(m)púku*   forest spirit

4.2. Tone in nouns

In Kintandu, the following distribution of groups of tone patterns with nouns occurs. These are termed Tone-groups by Daeleman & Pauwels (1983). Each Tone-group occurs in one of four Tone-cases. The four Tone-cases refer to various syntactic contexts on which we will not further elaborate as it is not of relevance here. What is relevant is to show the different tone patterns that occur in the different Tone-cases for each Tone-group.

Table 2. Ntandu Tone-groups and Tone-cases, adapted from Daeleman (n.d.)

stem		case	tone-groups			
syl.	mora		a	b	c	d
		I	L–L (L) L	L–(L) **H** L	L–L (L) **H**	L–L (L) **H**
2	2		*ma-lafu*	*lu-ngwéni*	*ma-tutí*	*ma-kukú*
2	3		*ma-biibi*	*ki-wíina*	*ki-tuutú*	*ǹ-tuutú*
3	3		*ki-menina*	*ma-kyeléka*	*ki-kalála*	*ki-kokilá*
		II	L–L **H** L	L–(**H**) **H** L	L–**H** (L/**H**) L	L–**H** (L) L
2	2		*ma-lăfu*	*lu-ngwéni*	*ma-túti*	*ma-kúku*
2	3		*ma-bíıbi*	*ki-wíina*	*ki-túutu*	*ǹ-túutu*
3	3		*ki-menína*	*ma-kyéléka*	*ki-kálála*	*ki-kókila*
		III	L–L (L) L	L–(L) L L	L–L (L) L	L–L (L) L
2	2		*ma-lafu*	*lu-ngweni*	*ma-tuti*	*ma-kuku*
2	3		*ma-biibi*	*ki-wiina*	*ki-tuutu*	*ǹ-tuutu*
3	3		*ki-menina*	*ma-kyeleka*	*ki-kalala*	*ki-kokila*
		IV	L–L **H** L	L–(**H**) **H** L	L–**H** (**H**) **H**	L–**H** (**H**) **H**
2	2		*ma-lăfu*	*lu-ngwéni*	*ma-tútí*	*ma-kúkú*
2	3		*ma-bíıbi*	*ki-wíina*	*ki-túútú*	*ǹ-túútú*
3	3		*ki-menína*	*ma-kyéléka*	*ki-kálálá*	*ki-kókílá*

In this paper, I have not attempted to identify a single Tone-case as being the source of the tone-patterns in Saramaccan and Ndyuka nouns (Sranan only has lexical tone distinctions in ideophones). It may not even be relevant to attempt to do so. Daeleman (1972) made an attempt to relate Kikongo and Saramaccan tone-patterns, but this needs to be reviewed in view of the following more accurate list. However, this would involve too extensive an exercise to usefully carry out here.

4.3. Tone in verbs

Verbs in Kikongo are divided into two types, H(igh-toned) bases and L(ow-toned) bases. The Kikongo verbs are given in their infinitive form, without the infinitival prefix *ku-*. The discussion of the part tones have to play in verb inflection goes beyond the scope of this article.

5. Abbreviations used in the list

The following abbreviations are utilized in the list:

– Tone marking and ideophones
    H, x́: high tone
    L, x, x̀: low tone
    a/b/c/d: Kikongo noun tone-groups
    ID: ideophone
– Kikongo dialects
    NK: Northern Kikongo (Laman 1964)
    WK: Western Kikongo (Laman 1964)
    Kish: Kishikongo (Bentley 1887)
    Be: Bembe (Jacquot 1981)
    Cb: Cabinda
    Nd: Ndibu
    Nt1: first Ntandu meaning
    Nt2: second Ntandu meaning
    Vi: Civili
    Yo: Yombe

- Other languages³
    - Kb: Kimbundu
    - Kit: Kituba
    - Ya: Yaka (H30)
- Surinam Creoles
    - Al: Aluku
    - Nd: Ndyuka
    - Ndg: Ndyuka (Guiane)
    - Kw: Kwinti
    - M: Matawai
    - Pr: Paramaccan
    - Sa: Saramaccan
    - Sr: Sranan
- Persons/Organisations/Sources
    - Enc: Encyclopaedie van Nederlandsch West-Indië (Benjamin & Snelleman 1914-1917)
    - DeG: De Groot 1977
    - Et: Joint State University of Leyden, Summer Institute of Linguistics & Surinam Ministry of Education Surinam Creole Etymological Dictionary Project [cardfile consulted with the permission of the late Professor Jan Voorhoeve]
    - H: Huttar
    - Lo: Lombé (village; Donicie and Voorhoeve 1963)
    - Li: Golío (village; Donicie and Voorhoeve 1963)
    - Prc1: Price 1975
    - Prc2: Price 1983
    - L: Laman (Kikongo dictionary)
    - SIL: Summer Institute of Linguistics (online dictionaries)
    - Sw: Swartenbroeckx (Kikongo dictionary)
    - V: Vinije Haabo (Saramaccan manuscript dictionary)
    - [1778]: Schumann 1778 (Saramaccan)
    - [1783]: Schumann 1783 (Sranan)

The list is ordered alphabetically by the Saramaccan entries, as that is the language for which we have most Kikongo vocabulary. Lacking a Saramaccan word, an Ndyuka word is utilized, and lacking both, a Sranan word is utilized. The item on which the order is based is given in bold type. Implosive and plain voiced are ordered together. Voiced stops whose exact status is not

---

3. Possibly, this refers to Yombe (abbreviated My in Laman (1964))

known are presented with underlining.

The Proto-Bantu forms represent a preliminary identification based on the online Bantu Lexical Reconstructions 3 (BLR3) database (Bastin et al. 2003). Daeleman (1972) sometimes gives Proto-Bantu forms that are not in BLR3. I have indicated these with [D].

Daeleman (1972) sometimes provides no separate gloss for Kikongo forms as compared to Saramaccan forms. In such cases, identity of or close approximation in meaning can be assumed. I have attempted to confirm this in these cases.

Items from Huttar (1985, 1986) and Daeleman (1972) are not separately referenced in order to avoid cluttering the table up further. In particular cases, items should be checked against these three publications to avoid false attributions to the present writer. I have also made grateful use of the index of vernacular plant names of Suriname (van 't Klooster, Linderman, and Jansen-Jacobs 2003).

Items identified as containing implosive [ɓ, ɗ] by Haabo (2009) have been adjusted in all modern citations.

6. The list

Table 3. Kikongo words in the Surinam Creoles

Nr	KiNtandu Daeleman sg/pl; (+Sw)	Other KiKoongo, Yaka, KiMbundu, etc.	gloss	Proto-Bantu: tone & noun class; BLR3 number; 'gloss'	Saramaccan, Matawai	gloss	Sranan, Ndyuka, Aluku, Kwinti, Paramaccan	gloss[4]
001	n-káta d (+Sw)	Yo: khata Nd: nkáta (Sw)	porter's pad	*-kata HL 9/10; 1728 'head-pad'	**akata** agatta [1778]	headpad for loads		
002	fiúnda nkáta, n-káta d	fiúnda nkáta (Sw) Yo: khata	sit tailor-fashion, lap		lólu **akata**	sit tailor-fashion		
003	ki-mbóolo a	ki-mbôlo (Sw)	faux-gavial crocodile		**ambolo**, amollò [1778]	sp. large lizard		
004	n-yóka d	Be: nyókò/ bá-nyókò 9/2	snake (general)	*-yoka HL 9/10; 3536 'snake'			Nd: **anyooká**[5]	Sibon nebulata, sp. snake

---

4. Repeating header rows will be abbreviated on the following pages.
5. The form of this word, compared with the Bembe form, suggests that the /a-/ here is the plural prefix. This might also be the raison d'être for the /a-/ in the previous word.

Kikongo lexical contribution to the Surinam Creoles   427

Nr	KiNtandu	other	gloss	Proto-Bantu	Saramaccan	gloss	Sranan	gloss
005	m-púungu d	m-púngu (Sw) Kish: m-pungu$_N$ am-pungu$_A$	powerful fetish, Kish: fetish-image Nt: All-highest		apúku, Ma ampuku (Prc1)	forest spirit	Sr: apuku, Nd, Al: am-pukú	forest spirit
006	ǹkúlu 1/2 d	ba-kúlu (Sw), a-kulu [1651] (pl) Yo: ba-kulu (pl.), mu-/ba-kulu (L)	ancestors, the dead	*-kudu [D] 'adult, senior'	ɓakúlu	lower god, dwarf ghost	bakrú Nd: bakuú	ghost Nd: evil spirit
007	lu-báamba 11/12 d, m-báamba 10 d		sp. rattan Bot. Eremospatha haullevilleana				Nd: bambá	vine for tying
008	m-báambi d	m-bámbi (Sw)	monitor lizard	*-bambe HL 9; 82 'monitor'	ɓámbi, bámbi [1778]	sp. large lizard		
009	báangúla	bàngúla (Sw)	force (open), break open, pull down, disclose	*-bang-ud H V; 106 'open up'	bangulá, bangula [1778]	reckless, to trick, cheat, ID walking drunkenly (SIL), sway.	Al: bangula (Bi)	trip, stumble

Nr	KiNtandu	other	gloss	Proto-Bantu	Saramaccan	gloss	Sranan	gloss
010	[lu-baánsi 11/10 m-baánsi pl. a]	m-bànzì/sì (Sw) lu-banzi/ m-banzi [1651] Nd: m-báansya Kb: m-banji;	rib, side	*-banja LL 11/10; 96 'rib, side of body' *-banjɪ LH 11/10; 98	ɓandya, **banja** [1778]	side, beside, ribs	Nd: bánsa Nd: bánsa bón Kw: bandya bón	Nd: side Nd, Kw: rib (lit. 'side bone')
011		m-bàzu (L); vémbe (L)	fire!		**bazu**	grand fire		
012		Kish: e-vembe Kb: m-bembe	purslane		**bembé**, bembe [1779]	purslane		
013	ki-lɔ̃ti a 7/8		Bot. Cyrtosperma Senegalense		ɓiloli	sp. moss, dirt, soil (SIL)		
014	bi-loóngo pl. 8 a [ñ loóngo a]	bi-lóngo pl (Sw) Vi: bi-loongu	remedies, medicines [remedy, spell, taboo]		ɓiíngɔ (Prc1)	ritual ingredients	Sr: bilongo Al: bilongo	sp. amulet; medicine

Kikongo lexical contribution to the Surinam Creoles 429

Nr	KiNtandu	other	gloss	Proto-Bantu	Saramaccan	gloss	Sranan	gloss
015		Yo: n-gúúngú WK: ki-n-gungu (L)		*-gungu LL 3/4; 9/10	**bingúngu** (SIL); bingúngú (V)	stink bug	Nd: gunguúngu	sp. insect
016	ki-sǎka a	ki-sàka (Sw)	wicker funnel Nt: rat-trap		**bisaka**, bisakka [1778]	reed fish-trap		
017	m-bǒma a	m-bòma (Sw), m-boma [1651]	python	*-boma LL 9/10; 261 'python'	**bóma**, **bóma**, abóma (V), boma [1778]	water boa	Sr: abóma, boma, abóma [1778] Nd: mbóma Al: mboma	anaconda, water boa
018				*-bUmbU 7/8; 4230 'pubes'	**bóbmba**	vagina	Sr: bómbo, bombo [1783] Al: bombo Al: bombo olo	vulva vaginal opening
019	m-boóngo a	m-bòngo (Sw), mbongo [1651]	seeds, fruits, food, offspring, descendants		**bɔŋgɔ**, bongo [1778]	plantation, plant material, seeds, offspring, descendants		
020	m-bóongo d		large wood lizard		**boongó**	cayman	Nd: bongó Al: bongo	sp. armadillo

Nr	KiNtandu	other	gloss	Proto-Bantu	Saramaccan	gloss	Sranan	gloss
021	wáasi c	bwási (Sw), wázi (Sw), bwazi (B)	leprosy Nt: a skin disease	*-badi HL (5/6); 47 'scar, leprosy'	**buási-ma**, boassi [1778]	leper, leprosy [1778]	Sr: bwási, gwasi, boassì [1783] Nd: bwási, gwási Al: bwasi	leprosy
022		m-bùubu (L), bùbù (Sw)	dread, sth. dreadful, darkness		**bubú**	jaguar	Sr: bubu, boebóe [1855] Nd: bubú	monster, bugbear [1855] Nd: jaguar
023	mbulukoóko	mbúlu-kóko (Sw)	plantain-eater		**bukɭɔ** (Lo), mukɭɔ (Li)	black ibis	Nd: mbukókó, mukokó, bukókó Pr, Al: bukókó	green ibis, flamingo
024		buuku (H)	mushroom				Nd: **bukú**	mould, mushroom
025	m-buúmba a		mystery, secret		**búmba** (Prc1)	an important deity	Sr: bumba (Prc1)	an important deity
026		bùnduka (H)	fall down (of tree), be uprooted	*-bund-uk-V; 4334 'be thrown down'			Nd: **bunduka**	lean over (e.g. of trees)

Kikongo lexical contribution to the Surinam Creoles

Nr	KiNtandu	other	gloss	Proto-Bantu	Saramaccan	gloss	Sranan	gloss
027	buúngi a	bùngi (Sw) Yo: (di-)bungi Vi: m̀buunji	fog (Sw + mildew)	*-bUngI LL 11; 4455	búngi	cloud, fog, grey	Nd: bu(w)íngi Al: bungi Kw: bungi somóko	mist, fog, dust
028	m̀buúngi a	m-bùngi (Sw) Vi: m-buunji	mildew (Sw + fog)	*-bUng- L V; 4451 'to decay'	búngi, búndji, bundji [1778]	mold, mildew, mouldy [1778]		
029	ki-búungu a	(ki-)búngu (Sw)	earthenware pot, calabash		búngu, bungu [1778]	earthenware pot	Nd: búngú Ndg: bunguu Al: bungu	earthenware jug
030		Yo: lu-buta-buta Kish: lu-butia-butia	nightjar				Sr: buta-buta, boetà-boetà [1855]	nightjar
031		mbwèbwe (H)	something undeveloped	*-bUece 9; 4726 'unripe pumpkin' [?]			Nd: buwebuwe, bwebwe Al: bwebwe	fontanelle
032		ndíndi (Sw)	clitoris				Kw: diindí	vagina

Nr	KiNtandu	other	gloss	Proto-Bantu	Saramaccan	gloss	Sranan	gloss
033	[m-vúumbi c]	Kb: n-zumbi, zúmbi (Sw) [m-vúmbi (Sw) Ya: m-vúúmbi]	Kb: dead body, ancestral spirit; talisman [deceased, dead body]				Sr: **dyumbi**, djombi, djoembi [1855]	spirit
034	-fíy-a	fí(y)a (Sw)	bet, win bet		**fiá**, fia [1778]	compete, contradict		
035				*-pIng-a L V; 2541 'interlace. plait'	**fingá**, finga [1778]	to thread, lace		
036	fóko c		fold				Al: **kífoko**	corner
037	m-fúbu d		mat of pandan frondlets		**fúbu**	sp. plant	Nd: fúbú	plant used to weave mats
038		Ya: fúkú-fúku	loose soil	*-puk- L V; 2680 'dig'	**fuku-fuku**	soft, loose (soil)	Sr: fugu-fúgu (SIL)	loose, soft or shifting (sand)
039	-fúla	fula [1651]	blow	*-pud-a V	**fulá**	spray with the mouth	Nd: fulá Al: fula Sr: fulá	spray water from mouth, blow
040		Yo: fúlu-fúlu	loose (soil)	*-pud- L V	**fulu-fulu**	soft, loose (soil)	Al: fulufulu	spoiled, putrid

Nr	KiNtandu	other	gloss	Proto-Bantu	Saramaccan	gloss	Sranan	gloss
041	n-gáanda c	n-gánda (Sw), n-ganda [1651], ku-n-gánda Yo: n-gánda	open place in a village, court Nt: outside	*-ganda LH 9/10; 1324 'house, village, chief's enclosure'	**gandá**	village, clearing	Nd: gandá	open public parts of village
042	n-gáandu c	n-gándu (Sw) Vi: n-gaandu Be: n-gáandû 9/2 Kb: n-gandu;	crocodile Vi: cayman	*-gandu LH 9/10; 1326 'crocodile'	**gandú**	cayman (taboo)		
043	ki-gáanga d		pile of wood		**gangá**	fencing for resting headloads on		
044	ngéngéngéé	Vi: n̂-ngénge; ngé-ngé (Sw)	ting-a-ling; ringing (Sw)	*-gengede LHH; 1365 'bell'	**gengé, djendjé,** ginging [1778]	bell	Sr: gengén, gingèh [1783] Nd: gengé	bell
045	ngíngígíí		firmness, steadiness		**gíngi**	substantial, strong		
046	n-gúba c, ki-ngúbá-ngúba c	ngúba (Sw) Be: ngúbu (L) Be: ngúbà	peanut, small peanut		**gobo-góbo,** gobbogobbo [1778]	large peanut	Sr: gobogóbo, gobbo gobbo [1783]	sp. large peanut

434 Norval Smith

Nr	KiNtandu	other	gloss	Proto-Bantu	Saramaccan	gloss	Sranan	gloss
047	ki-kodi-kódi a	kòdi-kòdi (Sw) Kish: kodiongo	Adam's apple	*-kodo LL; 1886 'throat, gullet'			Sr: goro-góro Nd: **golingo**, goligo Kw: goongóo	throat, Adam's apple
048	n-goongólo a	millipede		*-gongodo HLH 5/6 (9/10); 1453 'millipede'			Nd: **goóngóon**	millipede
049		kámba (Sw), ma-kámba (pl.)	scar		kanɓa, **kamamba**	scarification		
050	ki-káandu d	kàndu (Sw) Yo: bi-kandu (pl.)	sign defending against thieves		**kándu**, kandúú (V), kandu [1778]	spell against thieves	Sr, Nd: kandú Al: kandu	spell against thieves
051	n-kàtánga c	n-kàtánga (Sw) Yo: khatanga	cramp		**katangá**	cramp	Nd: katanga	cramp, foot asleep
052		WK: ǹkatu (L)	sp. tree		katu	sp. tree	Nd: nkatú	sp. large vine
053	kédéé		hit home		**kɛ́ɖɛ́ɛ́**; kɛ́ɖɛɛ (V)	precisely, exactly; ID carefulness		

Nr	KiNtandu	other	gloss	Proto-Bantu	Saramaccan	gloss	Sranan	gloss
054	ki-bóto c	Cb: *ki-bòto* (Sw)	sp. legume tree Nt: Millettia laurentii		**kimbotó**, *kombotto* [1778]	Bot. Sapotaceae pouteria sp. tree with edible yellow fruit, [similar leaves?]	Sr, Nd: *kimboto* Al, Ndg: *kimboto*	sp. tree with edible fruit, Bot. Sapotaceae pouteria Al, Ndg: Bot. S. pradosia
	m-bǎa a	*m-bòta* (Sw)	Nt: Millettia versicolor					
055		*kína* (Sw) Yo: *kiína* a	taboo, rash		**kína**, *tyína*, *kjina*, *tchina* [1778]	taboo, leprosy	Nd: *kína* Al: *kina*	taboo
056	*nkódya*[6], *(ma-)kódi* d	*nkódi(a)* (Sw) WK: *kóola* (L)	snail Nt2: helix shell	*-koda HH 9/10; (D) 'sp. snail'	**kola**, *kolla* [1778]	snail with shell, snail-shell [1778]	*nkólá*	snail
057	*ma-kóongo* d,	Nd: *ma-kóongo*	ancestors, all the charms together; origin, kingdom; language of BK; BaKoongo tribe		**kóngo**, *mamákóngo*	spell against thieves		
	kóongo d,							
	ki-kóoongo d, *ba-kóoongo*							

6. This is not in Daeleman (n.d.) although it is suggested that it is Ntandu in Daeleman (1972).

Nr	KiNtandu	other	gloss	Proto-Bantu	Saramaccan	gloss	Sranan	gloss
058	kósŭl-a	Kit: kòsula (Sw), kòso-kóso, kòsu-kósu (Sw)	cough	*-koc-Ud- H V; 1870 'to cough'			Sr: **koso** (V), kosokoso (N); kosô (N); kosô-kosò (N) [1855]; kossòkkossò [1783], Al: koso-koso	cough
059		Kb: ka-kɔhɔkɔhɔ (N)	cough		kɔƷkɔ́, kohokkohò [1778]	cough	Nd: kookóo, koho kóho	cough
060		kūku sama (L)	large termitary				Nd: kukusa	red mud
061		WK: kūukumya (L)	munch	*-kUnkUny-a V; 5044 'gnaw, chew'	**kukunyán-kukunyán**, kukunja [1778]	nibble, gnaw		
062	kula	-kula	to cast off, drive off Nt: chase	*-kUd-a L V; 1994 pull	**kulá**	to pole a boat	Nd: kulá	to pole a boat; boat pole

Kikongo lexical contribution to the Surinam Creoles   437

Nr	KiNtandu	other	gloss	Proto-Bantu	Saramaccan	gloss	Sranan	gloss
063		ǹ-kúlu	quantity, abundance				Nd: **kulú**	group, crowd
064	kulula	kùlu-kùlu (Sw) kùlúlu (Sw)	shave short,[7] scale; bald; bald, over-shaved; close-cropped hair	*-kUd- L V; 1995 'scrape' *-kUd-Ud- L V; 1996 'scrape'; 4669 'shave'	**kululu**	pluck empty, bare, eaten bare		
	ki-kulúka a							
065	ǹkúmba d, kúmba d	nkúmba (Sw)	navel, protruding navel				Nd, Al, Sr, Kw: **kumbá**, gumbà [1783] Kw: kúumba	navel
066	ǹkuúmbi a	Kish: nkumbi	high dance drum	*-kUmbI 9; 4313 'sp. drum'	**kumbí** (Prc1)	serrated wooden cylinder scraped with piece of wood [Nasí clan]		

---

7. In Daeleman (n.d.) gieven as 'lose'.

Nr	KiNtandu	other	gloss	Proto-Bantu	Saramaccan	gloss	Sranan	gloss
067		kúndu (Sw)	knot, nodule	*-kundo HL 5/6,7/8; 2130 'knot'			**kundú**, koendóe [1855]	swelling, lump
068	ń-lálu c, ń-lálú-ń-lálu c		okra, Bot. Crassocephalum sarcobasis		**lalu**, lalù [1778]	okra		
069		Luangu	place-name		**lángu** (Prc2), luángo (Prc1), loango- [1778]	clan name; sacred language; 1st cpd. element	Sr: loango- [1777]	Loango- (first element in compounds)
070	ki-láwu d (bu-)láwu d	Yo: di-láawu Kit: ki-lau láu (Sw)	mad madman madness, insanity,	*-dadU LH 7; 804 'madness', *-dadUk- LV; 794 'be mad'	**laú**, lau [1778]	mad, crazy	Sr: laú, láu, laǽ [1855], lau [1783] Nd: láu, lawláw	mad, insane, crazy foolish, folly
	láwúla	Kish: lau	madden					
071	lébé-lébé	leboka [1651]	long & thin		lɓɛ́ɛ́, lɓɛ́- lɓɛ́	tall & thin; thin		

Nr	KiNtandu	other	gloss	Proto-Bantu	Saramaccan	gloss	Sranan	gloss
072		lèbé-lèbé (Sw)	limp, tender, flabby, supple	*-debe LL 14; 7748 'paralysis' < *-debId L; 881 'be slack, hanging'			Sr: **lebelebe**	indolent
073	n-kóongolo d, n-kóngóló-nkongolo d	n-kòngólo (Sw)	circle, rainbow, circumference, round;	*-kongodo HHH 9; 6856 'rainbow'				
		lu-kòngolo (Sw)	circle, rainbow, halo, periphery		**lokóngro** [1778]	halo round sun or moon		
074	lu-léngi b	lu-lengi (H)	harmless green snake				Nd: **loléngi**	sp. snake: Oxybeks aeneus, O. argenteus
075	[l-óoti] c	lóta, lóte/ lótia (Sw) Kish: lotia Yo: lootyá, lóota	skin disease [squamous skin disease]		**lontá**, lotto [1778]	spots on skin	Sr: lotá, lotta [1778], lota [1777]	spots on skin, scorbutic spot

Nr	KiNtandu	other	gloss	Proto-Bantu	Saramaccan	gloss	Sranan	gloss
076	vwáangi c	Kish: e-vwangi, vwángi (Sw)	thicket, brushwood		**lukpángi** (Lo), ukpángi (Li), lukwándyi (V), lukwangi [1778]	twigs of fallen tree, branch without leaves; bushes [1778]		
077		NK: lu-kwèto	mortising axe	cf. *-kUadUdo L_L; 4914 'adze'	**lukpetu**	adze	Kw: lékwétu	adze
078	[mása] (Sw); [mása]	Nd: máza (Sw) Lu: madia [1887]	water	*-dia HH 6; 1006 'water'	**madjaweh**, madjawé (DeG)	Grote Saramaka River		
079	ma-dúngu d	Yo: (ma-)dúungu Kish: e-dungu	scrotal hernia, scrotocele		manungú, **madungu** [1778]	scrotal hernia	Sr: mandungú, dungu, madóengoe [1855], madungu [1783] Nd: manungú	scrotal hernia, enlarged testicle

Nr	KiNtandu	other	gloss	Proto-Bantu	Saramaccan	gloss	Sranan	gloss
080	m-fingí 9/10 c	Kish: m-fingí	rat Nt: smallest mouse	*-pingi; 5697 'mouse' [see also pindyi]	**mafengé** (Lo), masengé (Li), mafãndjé, masenge (SIL), mafingè [1778]	sp. mouse, small rat		
081	ma-káku c	Yo: ma-kaáku a WK: (ma-)ká(a)ku (L)	sp. Cercopithecus		**makáku** [+1778]	monkey		
082	(ma-)kŭbu a		thornfish		**makobó**, makoobón (Et)	sp. fish		
083	kóonko c	(ma-)kónko (L)	grasshopper				Nd: **makonkón**	grasshopper
084	(ma-)kwaansya[8] a, ma-kwaánsa a	Nd: kwànza (Sw) Kish: e-kwanza	pimpel, scabies	*-kUany- V L; 4925 'scratch, itch'	**makpánja**, makwanya, makɔnyɔ (V)	pimples, rash		

8. In Daeleman (1971) it is implied (i.e. by non-indication of dialect) that /ma-kwaansya/ is an Ntandu form. However, Daeleman (n.d.) states that the Ntandu form is /ma-kwaánsa/.

Nr	KiNtandu	other	gloss	Proto-Bantu	Saramaccan	gloss	Sranan	gloss
085	(ma-)kúku d	(ma-)kúku, (ma-)kúkwa (Sw) Kb: ma-kukwa	hearthstones (from termitary)		**makúku**, makúku [1778]	earthenware potstand		
086	ki-léembe d		pepper, Bot. Piper umbellatum (Bois d'anisette)		**malembé-lembe**, malembe toko	P. marginatum, P. arboreum	Nd Al: malembe-lembe	Bot. Piper marginatum liana/shrub, (Anesi wiwiri)
087		(ma-)pàpi 6 (Sw) Kish: e-papi	wing, Nt: to flap wings	*-papI L_5; 6436 'wing' *-pap- V L; 2407 'flap wings'	**mapápi** (DeG), mapaapí (SIL)	wing point (DeG); sp. rice that is easy to pound	Nd: mapaapi Al: mapápi (Hu)	wing of bird
088	pap-a	Kb: (ma-) dimbondo	sp. wasp				Sr: **marbonsu**, marabónsoe [1855], malebonsse [1718]	large brown wasp, Polistes (esp. Vespidae, O. Hymenoptera)

Kikongo lexical contribution to the Surinam Creoles   443

Nr	KiNtandu	other	Proto-Bantu	gloss	Saramaccan	gloss	Sranan	gloss
089	(ma-)síílá[9]				masenge [see mafengé] masiá, massila [1778]	aftercrop of rice or peanuts		
090	(ma-)susá c	Yo: (ma-)sisa		Nt: Bot. Renealmia Americana	masisá, massisà [1778]	sp. plant	Sr: masusá, masoesá [1855] Nd: masusá Al: masusa Ndg: masisa, gaan masusa	Sr: Wood-ginger, Renealmia alpinia Nd: Renealmia exaltata, etc.
091	(ma-)swá d	Kil: swá (Sw) Kish: e-swa, ma-swa	*cUa HH; 684 'grass'	netting, mesh	masuá, masuwá (SIL), masuáh [1779]	fishtrap with net	Sr: maswá, masoewá [1856], masóewa [1855], mansoa [1777] Nd: masúa Al: maswa	reed fishtrap [1855], palm-stems (Enc.)
092		My: ma-tunga nyundu (L)			matungá, madunga [1779]	sp. thorny leaf	Nd: matungá máka	plant with thorns on leaves

9. Daeleman (1972: 12) indicates this as equivalent without glossing it.

Nr	KiNtandu	other	gloss	Proto-Bantu	Saramaccan	gloss	Sranan	gloss
093	(ma-)tútu a	(ma-)tútu (Sw) Kish: e-tutu	mouse		**matutu**	sp. small rat		
094	(ma-)dyaadya a[10], [(ma-)dyaádi a]	diàdiá, diàriá (Sw), e/ma-riaria [1651] Kish: e-diàdia	elephant grass		**mayaya**	sp. grass; overgrown with weeds and bushes		
095		(ma-)yòmbé	Yombe people; rhythmic dance to drums				Nd: **mayombe** (Prc1)	cult
096	lu-báki c 11/10	nuni a m-báki	bird of prey Nt: sparrow-hawk				Nd: **mbaki** Al: *mbaki*	Nd: araçari Al: green kingfisher
097		m-bàlu Ya: mbalu	chips	*-bad-Ud- L V; 17 'split open'	**mbalu**	chips; enamel surface (V)	Nd: *mbalu*	wood splinter

10. Here is another case where the implied Ntandu form does not agree with that in Daeleman (n.d.). Here the explicitly Ntandu form is /dyaádi/.

Nr	KiNtandu	other	gloss	Proto-Bantu	Saramaccan	gloss	Sranan	gloss
098		m-bàluka (L)	disease causing peeling of the skin	*-bad-Uk- H V; 41 'be split'	**mbalukpá**, baluká, balukpá	skin disease, peeling of skin surface (SIL)	Al: mbaluka (Hu)	rain-cloud
099		Kish: m-beka	precipice, cliff		**mbeka** (Et)	steep place, difficult		
100	bǎva a	m-bowa	love-lies-bleeding Bot. Amaranthus viridis	*-boga LL 9/10; 256 'vegetable'	**mboa**, mbowa, boa [1778]	sp. vegetable	Al Ndg: mboya	Bot. Amaranthus spinosus
101		m-bulu [1651] Nd: m-bùlu d (Sw)	eyebrows, forehead		**mbulu**, bulû, nblu, nbulù [1778]	hairless corners of forehead		
102	-biinda, -biindika	bìnda, bindìka (Sw), minda (L)	knot together, bind	*-bInd- L V; 205 'plait' [variant of *pInd]	**mindi** Mat: mindi, mindi [1778]	knot together, add to what has been said; +link [1778]		
103	m-oóngo a	m-òngo (Sw) Vi: m-oongu	hill, mountain	*-dUngU HH 3, 4495 'mountain'			Nd: **móngo**, mungo Al: mongo	mountain

Nr	KiNtandu	other	gloss	Proto-Bantu	Saramaccan	gloss	Sranan	gloss
104	ǹsóni c	Kish: n-soyo	Nt: thatching grass, Bot. Imperata cylindrica	*-cono H; 6565 'sp. grass'			Sr: **mosonjo**, mosonjò [1855]; mússunja, sunja, mussungu [1783]	sp. grass [+ inquisitor's trick 1855] [= papa-tassi 1783]
105	m-péto d	m-péto, pheto	trap Nt: ring	*-pet- L V; 2482 'bend, fold' *-pete HH 9/10; 2485 'ring' *- peto LL 3; 8084 'circle, bow'			Nd: **mpetó**	part of fish trap
106	m-pǐya a	m-piya (H)	red-billed dove				Nd: **mpiye** Al: ampiye, mpiye Ndg: mpiya	toucan with red beak front or breast, Ramphastos vitellinus ariel, Ramphastos sulfuratus

Nr	KiNtandu	other	gloss	Proto-Bantu	Saramaccan	gloss	Sranan	gloss
107	ǹkwáanga c	n-kwánga (Sw)	sp. plant, rattle with loose seeds		**mukangá**, mokwango [1778]	sp. plant (seeds used for rattles)		
108	ǹkúkutu d	mu-kūkutu (H)	black ant Nt: large stinging ant				Nd: **mukukú**	sp. small ant
109	mw-álála c	mwalálá (H) Kish: mwala-la	centipede				Nd: **mulálá**	centipede
110	ki-lóomba b 7/8 [ǹlóomba b]		Bot. Myrsti-caceae fami-ly [sp. grass]				Pr: **mulomba**	Bot. Myrsti-caceae fami-ly
111	ǹlunga c	n-lúnga (Sw), mu-lunga [1651]	armband, bracelet, anklet		muungá, **mulungà** [1778]	armband; knuckledus-ter		
112	ǹsókó 3/4	mi-sóko (H)	Nt: young leaf, tender young leaves				Nd: **musokoó**	leaf charm at entrances; young palm leaves

Nr	KiNtandu	other	gloss	Proto-Bantu	Saramaccan	gloss	Sranan	gloss
113	(ma-)táma b		cheek	*-tama HL 5/6; 2744 'cheek'	**mutáma**, mattamma [1778]	cheek	Kw: mtamá Nd: mantámá	cheek
114	ǹtéende d 3/4, ki-téende d 3/4	n-téndé (Sw), mu-tende	pepperbush, Bot. Capsicum frutescens				Sr: **moetínde 11** [1855]	sp. tree
115	ǹtete a	Kil: n-tété (Sw), mu-tètè (Sw), mu-tete [1651]	carrier's palm frond basket		**mutete**	carrier's basket	Sr: mutéte, moetítte [1855] Nd, Al: muteté Kw: m̀téte	basket
116	n-kyáama c	n-kiáma (Sw), ǹ-kyáma (L) NK: mu-kyáma (L)	rainbow (serpent that climbs up the sky)		**mutyáma**, mutjamma [1778]	rainbow	Nd: mutyáma, muntyámá Al: montyáma (Hu)	
117	veénda 5/6 a	Nd: (ma-)véénda, vènda (Sw) Kish: e-vela	baldness		**muvénda**, mofénda (Et), lovenda [1778]	hairless corners of forehead, receding hairline, bald head		

11. In this source, orthographic *oe* refers to /u/.

Nr	KiNtandu	other	gloss	Proto-Bantu	Saramaccan	gloss	Sranan	gloss
118	mw-áaya c	mw-áya (Sw) Kil: mw-à (Sw)	gape, yawn; space left by lack of incisors	*-mUa LL 3			Nd: **mwá** Al: moá (Hu) Nd: muwaa ID	yawn;
119	-lama	nàma (Sw) Yo: -naama Kish: lama	to stick	*-dam L V; 827 'to stick' (tr./intr.)	**namá**, tam-mà [1778]	to stick, touch	Nd: namá	to stick to, press against
120	-lamika	nàmîka, làmîka Yo: -naamika Kish: lamina, lamika, laminina	to stick stick to cause to stick; stick well	*-damIk L V; 833 'to stick' (tr.)	**namii**, tamii	sticky		
121	ǹnéku d	nekwa [1651]	poison Nt: live bait		**ndéku**, neku [1778]	fish poison	Sr: néku, nekóe [1855] Nd: nekó Al: neko	poison from liana Bot. Lonchocarpus sp. Leguminosae fam. [Sr: also sp. wood; 1855 sp. wood]
122		n-dika (H)	trap, net				**ndiká**	fishtrap

Nr	KiNtandu	other	gloss	Proto-Bantu	Saramaccan	gloss	Sranan	gloss
123	*ndɔ́ki* a	*n-dòki* (Sw), *n-dòki* [1651]	(be)witch(er)	*-dògÍ LL 1; 7090 'witch'	**ndɔki**-*má*, *dɔ́kkiman* [1778]	black magician		
	ki-ndɔ́ki a		witchcraft	*-dògÍ LL 14; 1103 'witchcraft'				
124		Boma (B80): *n-dju* Fuumu (B70): *n-ju* (pl) Tyo (B70): *n-zu*	sp. peanut		**ndyu**, *ndyú* [SIL], *nju*, *dju* [1778]	sp. round peanut		
125	*nzàà*	Yo: *nóóngó*, *nongo* [1651] Nd: *nóngo* (Sw)	saying		**nɔngɔ́**	riddle, saying, parable	Nd: *nongó*	proverb, story
126			red ID		**nyaa**, *nyaan* [SIL], *njaê* [1778]	red, shining ID	Sr: *nya*, *njáh* [1855] Nd: *nyaan*	red, yellow, glowing ID
127	*m-paanda*	Ya: *m-paanda*	fork, bough, stay	*-panda* [D] fork	**panda**	lever		
128	*mpéemba* a	Kish: *m-pemba*, *m-pémba* (Sw)	pipeclay	*-pemba* HH 9 (11); 2443 'white clay, kaolin'	Mat: *pimba doti*	kaolin	Sr: **pémba**(-*doti*) Al: *pémba*	white clay, kaolin

Kikongo lexical contribution to the Surinam Creoles 451

Nr	KiNtandu	other	gloss	Proto-Bantu	Saramaccan	gloss	Sranan	gloss
129	ki-mpeníc mpéensa d	WK: mpêni (Sw), m-péne (Sw) Yo: phééné Kish: ki-mpene	naked Nt1: nudity Nt2: bareness		pɛ́nɛ́nɛ́, pɛ̃nɛ̃pene	naked		
130	pete-pete	pètè-pètè (Sw)	soft, flabby, slimy		pete, pɛ̀ɛ-pɛtɛ, pete-pete, petee	mushy ID, salve-like, mushy ID	Sr: pete-péte, pétepete [1855] Nd: pete-pete	wet ID, soaking wet ID Nd: softness of mud ID
131	píí	pî, píi (Sw), pi [1651] Kish: pi-i	stillness ID		píí, pî [1778]	still ID	Sr: píí Nd: píí Al: píí	stillness ID
132	pídíí	pídi (Sw), pidipidi (L)	ID profound silence		pílí	still, hushabye ID		
133		m-pínda (Sw) Yo: phíindá	peanut		pindá, pinda [1778]	peanut	Sr Al Nd: pindá Sr: piendà [1855], pinda [1783]	peanut

Nr	KiNtandu	other	gloss	Proto-Bantu	Saramaccan	gloss	Sranan	gloss
134	m-piindi	Kit: m-píndi	fetish		pindi	image, idol, picture		
135	m-pingí (Sw), m-píngi c	phingi (H)[12]	mouse, smallest mouse	*-pingi; 5697 'mouse'	pindji (Li)	mouse	Nd: pingí (H)	mouse
136		m-pongo-mpongo[13]	creeper Bot. Cissus rubiginosa				Nd: póngó	fruit of a vine
137	lu-mpukusu, lu-mpúlukusu d	(lu-)mpukúsu (Sw)	bat		pukusu	bat	Nd: púkúsu	bat
138	-pula	Ya: pulúlu	Nt: to blow	*-pud- H V; 2672 'blow (oral)', *-pud-id H V; 3955 'blow (oral)'	pulúlú	air-bubbles in water	puulú	air-bubbles in water
139		puulá (L)	eviscerate				puulú	small adze for hollowing out dugouts

12. In Yombe an aspirated stop is equivalent to a nasal stop cluster in other Kikongo dialects.
13. Tones unknown.

Kikongo lexical contribution to the Surinam Creoles

Nr	KiNtandu	other	gloss	Proto-Bantu	Saramaccan	gloss	Sranan	gloss
140	m-púumbu d	m-púmbu (Sw)	Malebo Pool, ref. to (Ba)Húmbu/ Wumbu people Nt: country of the Bawúumbu		**púmbu**	a ritual language of the Saramaccan (Prc1)		
141	mu-nsála d	nsala (H), ǹsála (L)	lobster, shrimp		saasáa	shrimp	Nd: saasáa Sr: sarasara, sarasára [1855]	lobster, shrimp
142		n-sàkála (Sw)	poverty (Sw)		sákáa, sakáa, sakla [1778]	rags		
143	n-saku-nsáku	Kish: n-sakusaku	Nt: lemon plant Kish: small round reed		**sakasaku** (Li), mamasakusaku (Lo), másakusáku (SIL)	sp. fragrant grass; sp. vine, Bot. Cayaponia jenmanii		
	lu-saku-sáku a		Nt: Bot. Cyperus articulatus (grass)					
144	saka, sakula	Nd: sakáta	Nt: comb out, weed	*-cak-at- L V [D] 'weed'	sakatá	scratch, turn over ground, toss and turn		

Nr	KiNtandu	other	gloss	Proto-Bantu	Saramaccan	gloss	Sranan	gloss
144	n-saku-nsáku lu-sáku-sáku a	Kish: n-sakusaku	Nt: lemon plant Kish: small round reed Nt: Bot. Cyperus articulatus (grass)		**sakasaku** (Li), mamasakusaku (Lo), másakusáku (SIL)	sp. fragrant grass; sp. vine, Bot. Cayaponia jenmanii		
145	ǹ-sakúsu a	n-sàkúsu (Sw), mu-sakasu [1651]	bellows		**sakusu**, sakusu [1778]	blow, bellows, spray		
146		WK: (ma-)sanga (Sw)	hut or shelter of greenery		**massanga** [1778] (noted as an Ndyuka word)	forest hut	Kw: isangá Sr: masanga, massánga [1855], massanga [1783] Nd: masanga	Kw: workshed, shelter Sr, Nd: forest hut
147	n-sátu d		(revenge) hunger		**sátu**	revenge		

Kikongo lexical contribution to the Surinam Creoles   455

Nr	KiNtandu	other	gloss	Proto-Bantu	Saramaccan	gloss	Sranan	gloss
148	ǹséengele d, ǹsèngélé m-béélé (ki-)sèngélé (Sw), ki-séengele d	Nd: n-sèngelé (Sw) Nd: (kí-)sèngélé	handleless blade, handleless knife, axe	*-cedenge H–; 7841 'handleless tool' *-beede LLH; 124 'knife' *-beedi LLH 9; 133 'knife'	sengɛ́ɛ́, sengbɛ̧	machete/knife without handle;	sengre-bére, singrebére [1855] Pr, Sr: sengenefi Nd: sengee how, sengee nefi	handleless knife Nd: handleless machete, handleless knife.
149		Vi: selingo	ant		seéngba, séringwa [1778]	army ant		
150		n-síba (Sw)	whistle one carries	*-cIba HH 11; 5726 'whistled signal'	sibá, siba [1778]	flute amulet, wooden whistle		
151	-síba	siba (Sw), siba [1651] Kish: xiba	invoke fetish Nt: curse		sibá, sibà [1778]	curse		

Nr	KiNtandu	other	gloss	Proto-Bantu	Saramaccan	gloss	Sranan	gloss
152	-sík-a	síka m-búdi (Sw), síka (Sw) Vi: síka m-budi WK: síka tsambi	play the trumpet, play instrument WK: play organ (praying mantis)		**sikámbuti**	sp. beetle		
153	[ǹ-sǐnga a]	Kish: n-xinga Kish: n-xinga	string, cord, liana, creeper, vine; fibre of palm stem, of elephant's tail; Nt: liana; fibre	*-cinga LL 3/4; 622 'string, bodyhair'	**sínga** síngá-ási, sínga-muungá[14]	Maripa-palm leaves as dish; sisal, sp. fibre; protective Maripa-string armband	Al: sínga ási Al: **sínga**	agave fibre snare
154	di-n-singa		palmleaf-rib, also used as slipknot	see above				
155	n-sóombi d	nsómbé ~ nsómbi (Sw) Kish: nsombe	palm weevil, grub, horned beetle		**sómbi**, sombi [1779]	palm worm		
156	n-sóngi c	Kish: nsonge	Kish: snipe fish		**songé**	sp. fish	Sr: songe	sp. fish

14. muungá (see above) 'armband'

Kikongo lexical contribution to the Surinam Creoles 457

Nr	KiNtandu	other	gloss	Proto-Bantu	Saramaccan	gloss	Sranan	gloss
157		Yo: tsúusa	footplay, sp. dance		susá	dance performed after burial	Sr: susá, soesà [1855] Nd: susá	sp. dance or song
158	n-súsu d	n-súsu (Sw), n-susu [1651] Be: n-súsù, bà-n 9/2	hen	*-cUcU HH 9/10 (9/6); 698 'bird, chicken'	súsu	taboo-name 'hen'		
159	téngú-téngu		hopping		tengú-tengú; tengè	hop; lame, limping		
160	ky-aáka a	kiàka (Sw)			tyaká, tschakka [1778]	rattle (v/n)		
161	ky-áadi d	kiádi (Sw), ki-ari [1651] Yo: kiadi	pity, compassion, sorrow	*-jadI 3; 9101 'tear'	tyalí	regret	Al: tyali (Hu) Nd: tyalí	regret
162		Cab: kí-anga (Sw), ki-anga [1651]		*-ganga LL 14; 1334 'medicine'	tyanga; tyangaa (SIL)	fenced-in ritual washing place		
163	-kéé	ké (Sw), Yo: -khéeke ukeke [1651]	too little, tiny, small		tyáyáyé (ε)	undersized		
164		Ya: tyólóló			tyólóló, tchoroló [1778]	thin (of liquid foods)		

Nr	KiNtandu	other	gloss	Proto-Bantu	Saramaccan	gloss	Sranan	gloss
165	*ki-méenga* d	*ki-bénga* (Sw) Ya: *ki-béenga, ki-menga* [1651]	Nt: frying-pan		**tyubéngɛ**, *kibenge* [1778]	iron plate for baking cassava		
166		*kiùbúka* (Sw) Kish: *kiubu, kiubuku*	Kish: ID swallowing; jump about in water				Sr: **tyubun**	ID splashing
167	*tófù-tófù, -tófúna*	*tòfúna, tòfúka* (Sw)	spoil, crack; be spoilt, cracked		**tófu** (Lo), *tfɔ* (Li), *toffo* [1778]	dried up, rotten, spongy		
168	*lù-ku/ tù-ku* c	*lù-ku/ tù-ku* (Sw), *lu-ku/ tu-ku* [1651]	Nt: cassava-root beaten > flour > bread		**tokú**	small cassava dumplings		
169		*tòla* (Sw) Yo: *tóóla*	be fat, big, grow		**tolá**	misshape		
170		Ya: *tumbi-túmbi*			**tombí-tombí** (Li), *tópi-tópi* (Lo)	balding skull with hair in pigtails		
171		*ntóoto* (H) Yo: *thoóto* Be: (*mà-*)*tótò* 5/6	ripe banana		**toto**; *totto, tuttu* [1778]	sp. banana	Nd: *tontón*	mashed bananas

Nr	KiNtandu	other	gloss	Proto-Bantu	Saramaccan	gloss	Sranan	gloss
172	[bu-tóonga c]	tónzo (Sw) Yo: tóonzo c Vi: bu-toonzu			tɔnzó, tɔɔnsń, tonso [1778]	brains	Kw: m-toonsó	brains
173		Nd: túmbi (Sw) Kish: e-tumbi Kimb: di-tumbu [-túumba]	enclosed plot hillock raised bed Nt: to pile	*-tUmbI 5; 4276 'heap'	túmbu	garden-bed		
174	tûutu d 5/6	tûtu (Sw), e-tutu [1651] Kish: e-tutu	Nt: bamboo, tube, pipe, flute		tutú, tutù [1778]	horn	Sr: tutú, toetóe [1855], tutu [1783]; tutu, tootoo [1777] Nd: tutú	
175	véné 6 (= mpéne) (Sw)	Yo: véénénéé	Nt: naked		vénénéé [see 129]	naked		
176	vélélé	Yo: vínínií	15		véné´nɛ́ɛ́	cleared off, nothing left		

15. Given by Daeleman (1972) as equivalent, but without giving the exact meaning.

Nr	KiNtandu	other	gloss	Proto-Bantu	Saramaccan	gloss	Sranan	gloss
177	m-vúla d	m-vúla (Sw), m-vula [1651] Be: m-vúla/má-m-vúla 9/6 Kb: m-vula	rain	*-buda HL 9 368 rain	vula[16]	rain		
178		mvúmvu (Sw)	wasp		vunvu; wumwu [1778]	bee-eater	Sr: wunwun, voenvóen [1855]	bee, bumble bee
179		wála-wála (Sw) Yo: di-walá-wála	with a wide opening; large opening		waaa, **wala**-**wala**; war-rawarrà [1778]	open, wide open		
180		My: mw-ándi Vi: mw-andi Punu (B.40): mw-andji	sp.wood		wándji	sp. wood (tall with sticky sap)		
181	wáandu c	wándu (Sw), lwandu, bwandu ~ ngandu Kish: wandu	Bot. Cajanus cajan				Sr: **wandu**, wandóe, wandóe-pési [1855] Al: wandu pesi	pigeon pea, Bot. Cajanus cajan

16. Noted as báka-mátu-tóngɔ (backwoods language).

Kikongo lexical contribution to the Surinam Creoles 461

Nr	KiNtandu	other	gloss	Proto-Bantu	Saramaccan	gloss	Sranan	gloss
182	-yaambula	Yo: *yáambū*	uncover, expose; open	?*-jambU/d-LV; 8379 'undress, despoil'	**yamboo**, hamboo [S]	ID wide open		
183	yaangá		mockery	*-jang-a [D] 'to hate'	**yangá**	mockery		
184	yáanga d	yánga (Sw)	ritual washing place Nt: pond, lake	*-janja LH 9/10; 3221 'lake'	**yangá**	fence for ritual ablutions		
185	ǹyúundu c	Be: (mà-) nyúundù 9/6;	otter	*-jundu LH 9; 4358 'otter'	**yundú**	otter	Nd: nyuundú; Al: yúndu	otter
186	n-zawu a	n-zàu (Sw), n-zau [1651], Be: n-jágù [njáwù], bà-n-jágù 9/2	elephant	*-jogu LL 9/10 (9/6); 1607 'elephant'	**zaun**	elephant	Nd: nsaw (SIL), nzaw (H) Sr: asáw, azáw [1855]; asaù, ísaù [1783], sauw [1780]	elephant

7. Concluding words

It should not be thought that the sole influence claimed to be present in the Surinam Creoles from Kikongo is lexical.

Two instances of phonological influence have been suggested. Firstly, Smith (this volume on creole phonology) has suggested that the differing types of morpheme shapes in Kikongo and Fongbe has enabled differential effects in the expression of nasality to survive to the present day, particularly in Saramaccan. Kramer (2007, 2009) has suggested that Saramaccan tone-spread rules of Kikongo origin, applying to universal and non-universal quantifiers, coexist with other tone-spread rules of Fongbe origin, applying to serial verb constructions.

What lexical influence and phonological influence share is the fact that they are both aspects of form.

A preliminary list of probable Gbe lexical items in the Surinam Creoles

Norval Smith

1. Introduction

In this chapter, I give a provisional list of probable Gbe-derived lexical items. It is highly likely, in my opinion, that there are considerably more, based on the number of items that resemble Gbe words in their phonological shape, and the fact that new "cognates" keep cropping up.

Little has been published on this topic with the exception of Huttar (1985), which is concerned with Africanisms in Ndyuka. I have taken account of this article here, marking items on whose Gbe provenance I am in agreement with him with an asterisk.

As such it should not be surprising that there are a considerable number of words of Gbe derivation in the Surinam Creoles. There are two main reasons for this, both of which are equally applicable to the list of Ki-Koongo lexical items. Firstly, the Slave Coast was an extremely important source of slaves for Surinam from about 1680 onwards. This can be seen from the figures quoted from the Voyages Database (2009) in Chapter 2.

This source of slaves had observable effects on the ground in various ways. For instance, one of the three apparently African-derived vestigial ritual languages is based on an Eastern Gbe language, presumably largely Fongbe. This is known by various names among the different Afro-American ethnic groups, such as *Papá* (e.g. Saramaccan and Aluku) and *Fodú* (e.g. Sranan).

The second main reason for the preservation of Gbe-derived lexicon is marronnage. So the earliest maroon groups preserve the largest number of Gbe words. In Saramaccan, the language of the Maroon tribe of the same name, we find, for instance, 115 of the total of 138 Gbe items listed here.

2. Abbreviations

– Western Gbe languages
   E: Ewegbe
   G: Gengbe
– Eastern Gbe languages
   F: Fongbe
   G: Gungbe
   M: Maxigbe
   Ay: Ayizogbe
   A-G: Ayizogbe of Glo
   Al: Fongbe of Alada
– Other African languages
   Y: Yoruba
– Surinam Creole
   Nd: Ndyuka
   Mat: Matawai
– ID: ideophone
– IN: interjection
–Transcription
   b̲, d̲: stops whose nature – implosive or plain voiced – is uncertain
–Sources
   [1778]: Schumann 1778
   [1783]: Schumann 1783
   [1805]: Wietz 1805
   [1855]: Focke 1855
   [D]: De Groot 1977
   [Ha]: Hancock 1969
   [Hersk.]: Herskovits & Herskovits 1934
   [SIL]: SIL online dictionary
   [V]: Vinije Haabo 2011 (Saramaccan manuscript dictionary)
–Others
   f.: feminine (if relevant)
   m.: masculine (if relevant)
   sp.: species of

N.B. Gbe items are ordered according to the first consonant of the word. Initial vowels are meaningless noun-prefixes, which vary among the various languages, or may be absent.

3. The list

Table 1. Gbe words in the Surinam Creoles

Nr	Western Gbe	Eastern Gbe	gloss	Saramaccan	gloss	Sranan	gloss
001		F: bà	look for	ɓa	collect, ladle		
002		F: bèsé	frog	ɓése	toad, frog		
003		F: abɔ̌	millet	abɔ̀ [1778]	millet	abò [1783]	millet
004a		F: bó; F: bo-jrέ	magic, charm; ?	bódjee, bódjere [1778]	hypocrisy, magic [1778]		
004b		F: bojrɛ́tó	magician (magick-er)	bódjeé-ma, bódjɛɛ-ma [SIL]	hypocrite, knave		
005	E: botso						
006	E: βla	F: vlâ	loosen	bɔsɔ	loosen	brabra	sudden
007	E: dádá	G: dadá	sudden(ly)			dáda	elder sister
008	E: adḭ	F: adḭ; G: àdḭ	aunt	adḭ(n)		adí	abscess
009		F: dan-gbé	abscess snake	dagbé	abscess large snake (god)	dagwé, daguwesneki Nd: dag(u)we	boa constrictor
010		F: den-kpὲ	dagger	dekpe, dekwe	dagger		
011	E: adḭ	F: adḭ; G: àdḭ	native soap E: lye			adi; adi-watra [1855]	dried banana-skin ash; lye
012		F: dègɑ̀n	shrimp	adingɔ	shrimp		
013		F: adíngbὲ	epilepsy			adubé, adube, adimbe [1783] Nd: dumbé éde	epilepsy

Nr	Western Gbe	Eastern Gbe	gloss	Saramaccan	gloss	Sranan	gloss
014	E: dɔ́, dáloŃ	F: dɔ̃	sleep sleep (n.)			dodó [1855]	sleep
015	E: dɔ̃n		dull (look)	dóón	intensive with look ID		
016	E: dugblɔ̃		weak	dg̀bɔ	weak		
017	E: dralā		long, stretched stare, unmoving gaze	dálálá	straight ID		
018	E: dūn			dúúún, duun [SIL]	looking dumb ID	dun	look ID
019a	E: ɖú	F: ɖùwè	dance			du	dance feast
019b		F: wèɖú-wèɖú	mosquito larva	weduwedu	weevil, woodlouse		
020	E: ɸán		clear, light	fáán	very white ID	fan	very white ID
021	E: fé	F: fɛ̃	split, tear off	fen, fe [1778]	tear off, break off		
022	E: fie(n)	F: fyɛ́	start boiling E: be boiling hot	fiɛ́	burn (e.g. pepper)		
023	E: ɸiō		whistling	fofío	whistle	Nd: fiofío ID, fiyo fiyo	whistling
024	E: dzikpɛ	F: jìkpò	mushroom	(a)dikpókpo	toadstool		
025	E: dzridzá	F: àjíjá	hedgehog	adyindyá	porcupine	agidyá, gindya-maká, dyindya-maká	sp. porcupine
026	E: dzobo		turn over	dyobó	turn up ground		

Gbe lexical contribution to the Surinam Creoles   467

Nr	Western Gbe	Eastern Gbe	gloss	Saramaccan	gloss	Sranan	gloss
027		F: gá	arrow			Nd*: gá	poisoned arrow
028	E: agámàn	F: àgamàn	chameleon	agama	chameleon	agáma	sp. lizard
029	E: agatsa	F: agàsá G: agása	land crab	agása	crab		
030	E: (ɸan) gē̃		(sudden) belch			ge Nd: gee	belch
031	E: adzidá	F: àgiɖá	E: drum F: drumstick	agida	big drum	Nd: agida	sp. drum
032	E: gidigidi	F: gidigidi	F: violently E: with a loud noise	gidigidi	making noise		
033	E: gli E: gigli	F: glĩ	F: crush, grind E: grind coarsely, grate	gii, gili	grate past		
034		F: aglũzà	pig	gunsá	wild pig		
035		F: gó	knot	agó	knot, swelling		
036	E: gǎ	F: gò	gourd, bottle			Nd: gǎ	gourd
037		F: gò-ví	small gourd, bottle			gobi, gobi [1855]	small calabash, mug
038	E: gobō		hollowed (in a round fashion)			gobo Nd: góbo	bowl Nd: hollowed stool
039	E: agɔgó	F: gàgó	buttock	gàgó	rump	gogó [+ Nd]	rump
040	E: gɔdɔn	F: gɔ̀ndɔ́ n	be twisted	gɔndɔ gɔndɔ [SIL]	bent, crooked, crooked ID		

Nr	Western Gbe	Eastern Gbe	gloss	Saramaccan	gloss	Sranan	gloss
041		F: àgu(n) Y: àgún	gruel	(h)angú	gruel	angú	gruel
042	E: agbadzá	F: àgbajá	cartridge pouch	agbadjá, abadjà [1778]	crab egg pouch, loincloth		
043	E: agbagbá		carry loose on the head	agbágba	carry on head without hands		
044	E: agbã̀	F: àgbã̀ G: àgbã̀	dish, pot	agbán	earthen pot		
045		F: gbàgbé-tín	Pterocarpus tree	gbegbé	Pterocarpus tree	bebe	Pterocarpus tree
046		F: gblángblán	pretty, weak, slender	gbéléngbelen	good, pretty, strong		
047	E: gbĩn		firm, tight	gbɔlɔ, bloblo [1778]	lukewarm		
048	E: gblɔ	F: gblɔ	lukewarm				
049	E: gbɔ, gbɔn		bitter shrub	agbó-páu	bitter plant	Nd: gbíngbín	hard
050	E: gbɔxi, gbɔxee	G: gbɔ̀xã̀n gbɔ̀xã̀ngbɔ̀xã̀n	breathe ID			bo-enbo-en, bohén [1855]	cough
051		F: àgbŏ	Agbomey	agbó-nágɛ-tatái	sp. plant (lit. Agbo negro vine)		
052		F: ʁɛ̃̀	very (red)	heei	very (red)		
053		F: ʁèèlú	alas	heelú, helú [SIL], hehlu [1778]	woe IN	éru, helu [1783]; Nd: heelu	woe IN; [Nd: + curse]

Gbe lexical contribution to the Surinam Creoles   469

Nr	Western Gbe	Eastern Gbe	gloss	Saramaccan	gloss	Sranan	gloss
054	E: ʁíʁa, ʁaʁa	F: ʁíʁán, ʁínʁán	yawn	hóha, wówa	yawn		
055	E: ʁlɔn		tribe	lɔ́	clan	lo Nd: ló	clan
056	E: aʁlã̀		slimy excretion	lɔ	slippery, slaver		
057		F: ʁlún, F: ʁùnlún	grumble, low, mutter	hun; mbéi hun	disdain ID; (make) sigh		
058	E: βlukuku		owl			owrukuku, wurukuku, hurukuku [1855]	owl
059a	E: ʁo	F: ʁɔ̀	uproot, grub up	hɔn, hò [1778]	uproot		
059b				ahɔ́ ahô [1778] hɔ́	hoe, adze	Nd: ho	hoe, adze
060		F: ʁóχò F: ʁóχò-ví	twin twin child	hoho [1778], hohobi [Hersk.]	twin	oó, hóho [1783]	twin
061	E: aʁun	F: àʁún	mist, dew	ahhà [1778], ahu [1805]	mist, cloud, dew		
062		F: aʁɔmɛ̀ M: aʁɔ	F: brains M:fontanelle	ahumɛ, ahomɛ̀h [1778]	fontanelle		

Nr	Western Gbe	Eastern Gbe	gloss	Saramaccan	gloss	Sranan	gloss
063		G: χʷlàkpǎkpɛ̀	cockroach	ahalakpákpa; ahaakpakpa [V], aherapápa (1778), ahallapapa (1805)	cockroach		
064	E: χlɔ̃ G: è-χlɔ̃			húlu	be intimate		
065	E: aχɔ̃́			ahún, ahhà [1778]	grass		
066		F: χɔ̃́tɛ̃̀n	friend	hɔ̃́ntɔ	be friendly		
067		F: kanboí	shirt			kabay	shirt
068		F: kádá	sp. snake	kádá	sp. snake	Nd: akada	sp. boa
069		F: káàgò	¼ litre bottle	kágo	large calabash		
070		F: kàn;	consult (oracle);	kangaa, kangra [1778]	magic to prove guilt/innocence		
		F: glá	(be) strong				
		F: gla-glá	strong				
071		F: kákɛ́(-tín)	sp. Mimosa			katye	sp. Mimosa
072		F: akasá G: akasán	porridge			akansa	maize porridge
073	E: ké	F: keé	oh!	ké, kééé	expression of joy	ke, tye Nd: kee	oh! oh, ah!
074	E: keké	F: kɛ̀kɛ́	hoop, spindle, bike	keké	top, spindle	keké Nd: keké	spindle Nd: wheel
075	E: kèse		monkey	késikési	sp. monkey	késkési Nd: kesikesi	sp. monkey

Gbe lexical contribution to the Surinam Creoles   471

Nr	Western Gbe	Eastern Gbe	gloss	Saramaccan	gloss	Sranan	gloss
076		F: *klébésé*	sickness	*krebessè* [1778], *krubessè* [1778]	severe sore/rash		
077	E: *klo*	G: *ò-klo*	tortoise			Nd: *kòò*	land turtle
078	E: *kondō, kondɔ̄*		bent	*kɔndɔ, kondoo*	crooked, to bend ID		
079	E: *kú-nu*		sth. that can cause death	*kúnu*	curse, avenging spirit to slice	*kúnu* Nd: *kunu*	curse, avenging spirit
080	E: *kpa, a-kpā* (n.)	F: *kpà*	peel, cut	*kpan*			
081		F: *kpéjelekún, kpéjerekún*	Xylopia			*pegrekú, pedreku, pejrekù, pegrekù* [1783]	Xylopia
082	E: *kpī*		dark			*píí*	dark ID
083	E: *kpo*		blunt object	*akpó*	blunt arrowhead		
084		F: *àlàká*	cheek			Nd: *aláká*	cheek
085		F: *lɛ̀gɛ̀dɛ̀*	informer	*lɛgɛdɛ, lɛgɛdɛ-má alikbo* [1778]	lie lier		
086	E: *ali*	M: *àlìn* F: *alìn-kpo-tín àlìn* (f.)	hip hipbone		hip		
087	G: *alìn* E: *àlì* E: *ayi-kú*	F: *alìn-ví àlìn* (m.) F: *àì*	kidney	*alíbí*	kidney		

Nr	Western Gbe	Eastern Gbe	gloss	Saramaccan	gloss	Sranan	gloss
088	see 087 G: a(y)i E: ayî	see 087 G: ayi-ví? F: a(y)i-kún		alibí aibí [1778]	bean		bean
089	E: li	F: li	millet			alîh [1783]	millet
090	E: alɔ	F: alɔ G: ɖɔ ; F: ɖɔ̀kɛ̀	hand; wrist	alikpáu alukwétu	arm [SIL] wrist joint [D]		
091		F: lògòzò	tortoise	logoso	turtle		
092		F: lògbózò	rheumatism	loboso	lame		
093	E: longɔ̄n		oval	logo, logologo logoo [SIL]	round round, plump		
094		F: lókò(-tín) G: lókò	Iroko tree	lóko	sp. tree	lóko	sp. tree
095	E: lun E: lunlun	F: lun F: lùlù	ooze, slaver seep, leak loosen let fall, slip off	lùlú	dissolve, fall apart, unravel	Nd: lùlú	crumble
096		F: amidàn	snake	amida			
097		F: mé	neat, clean	mɛ́ɛ ID mɛ̌ ' [SIL]	bare, cleared up, clean		
098	E: mé, mḗn		grind fine, pound fine	mɛ̌; mɛ̌mɛ́ , mɛ̂ [1778]	pound fine, thresh; pounded fine		

Gbe lexical contribution to the Surinam Creoles   473

Nr	Western Gbe	Eastern Gbe	gloss	Saramaccan	gloss	Sranan	gloss
099	E: me, men	F: mê	roast, scorch, grind	maemaè [1778] Mat: meme	frame for drying meat		
100	E: ame-ka	F: mé	who?	ambé	who?		
101	E: mɔn G: è-mɔ̀n		trap	mɔ; mo [1778]	trap		
102		F: aní	what?	andí	what?		
103		F: nyonkúsí	acne	nyɑ̃kúsu	pimple		
104	E: ɸoɸolín		navel	pɔpá	vagina	Nd: popoí	vagina
105	E: ɸù, à-ɸù G: (à-)pù	F: χù	lake, sea	pú	pool, swamp		
106		F: sɛ́	soul	she [1778]	soul	seį; she, sje [1783]	soul
107		F: sián àyí; àyí-siánsián	squat; (fact of) squatting	siá; siásiá; sjasja [1778]	squatting frog		
108	E: atá	F: ǎá (F: kplá) A-G: asankpana	thigh (pocket) leg	asákpáa asaprá [1778]	squatting thighbone		
109	E: tatí		pestle	tatí	pestle		
110	E: tí		jump	tí ID	jump		
111	E: tɔ́		attentively	tón ID	attentively		
112	E: tón		only	tɔ́ ID	only, alone		
113	E: tɔgbo	F: tɔgbó	ancestor	tɔ́gbo, tógbo	great-grandparent		

Nr	Western Gbe	Eastern Gbe	gloss	Saramaccan	gloss	Sranan	gloss
114		F: tɔ̀lĩnlĩn_N	swimming, lit. water-diving	tolí tólíí ID	dive under thoroughly sunk		
115	E: tɔ̀; G: è-̀ tɔ̀	F: tɔ̀	water, river	tɔ̀nɛ́	water spirit		
116	E: atǫ́ atæ̀n	F: tǎn	sp. rat	tɔɔn; tuwwo [1778]	sp. red rat		
117	E: trǎn; E: trǎnyɔyɔ		lesser god; calling god to witness truth of statement F: an immortal	tɔ́áyɔ; toónyɔn [SIL]	obia spirit, obia		
118		F: yɔ̀ G: vɛ̀, F: vɛ̀ Ay: vɛ̀	red	ɓɛ	red		
119		F: vlívlí	chiaroscuro	vilivili	hazy		
120		F: àvíti	trap	aviti	trap	abiti	trap
121	E: avɔ̃̌	F: àvɔ̀	cloth	avɔ			
122	E: vodṹ	F: vodún	voodoo god	vodũ	sp. snake	fodú Nd: fodu	snake god
123		F: àwà	arm, upper arm, wing	ahwá-máun, ahɔ́máun [SIL]; ahɔmáu	shoulder (maun = hand, arm)		
124		F: wɛ̀ G: wɛ̀	contrastive focus marker	wɛ̀	contrastive focus marker		
125		F: wlá	fling, hurl oneself on	waa	scramble		

Gbe lexical contribution to the Surinam Creoles   475

Nr	Western Gbe	Eastern Gbe	gloss	Saramaccan	gloss	Sranan	gloss
126		F: yɛ̀	shadow, spirit	yeeyé	shadow (man/animal)	yéye	spirit
				yeyé [SIL]	shadow, spirit		
127		F: yɔ́	smelt, melt	yɔ	smelt, melt [SIL]		
128	E: yovú, yevú	F: yòvó	white man			yobó [1855]	white man
129	E: adza	F: àzàn	highest point, leaf, twig	azan	palm shoot		
130		Al: àzàngàndán	leg	azanganá	shinbone		
131	E: adzé	F: àzě	black magic	azé	black magic	azé [1855]	black magic
132		F: zín	press	zín	press		
133	E: dzo G: èzò	F: zò	fire	zo [Ha]	fire		
134	E: dzo-kã	G: zo-ká F: zò-kán	charcoal (fire+charcoal)	zonká, sokka [1778]	charcoal		
135		F: zo-mán	nettle (fire+leaf)	azɔ́ [V], azó-uwíi	nettle (fire+leaf)		
136	E: dzo-ké (E: nyen)		sparks (maggot)	azokínjenje(n)	firefly		
137		F: zegé	beetle	zegé-wasi-wási		(a)sege, azegè [1855]	beetle
138	E: zú		yam	sú	sp. taro, yam	Nd: su	taro

References

Abakah, Emmanuel Nicholas
   1995   Phonologucal analysis of word-final consonants in Akan. *Africa and Asia* 547–64.

Abney, Steven Paul
   1987   The English noun phrase in its sentential aspect. Cambridge, MA: Dept. of Linguistics and Philosophy, Massachusetts Institute of Technology PhD dissertation.

Aboh, Enoch Oladé
   2000   Old Gbe: notes from La Doctrina Christiana (1658) and La Grammaire Abregé. Paper presented at the Trans-Atlantic Sprachbund meeting. Amsterdam, September.
   2002   Complementation in Gbe and Saramaccan. Paper presented at the annual meeting of the SPCL. San Fransisco, 3–6 January.
   2003a   D: on the modularity of substrate influence. Paper presented at the International Workshop on Substrate Influence. Netherlands Institute for Advanced Study in the Humanities and Social Sciences, 23–26 April.
   2003b   Focus constructions across Kwa. In *Trends in African Linguistics 5*, Githiora, Chege, Heather Littlefield and Victor Manfredi (eds), 7–22. Trenton, NJ: Africa World Press.
   2004a   *The Morphosyntax of Complement-Head Sequences: Clause Structure and Word Order Patterns in Kwa.* Oxford/New York: Oxford University Press.
   2004b   Topic and focus within D. *Linguistics in the Netherlands* 21 (1): 1–12.
   2005a   The category P: the Kwa paradox. *Linguistic Analysis* 32: 615–646.
   2005b   Deriving relative and factive constructions in Kwa. In *Contributions to the Thirtieth Incontro di grammatica generativa*, Brugè, Laura, Giuliana Giusti, Nicola Munaro, Walter Schweikert, and Giuseppina Turano (eds.), 265–285. Venice: Libreria Editrice Cafoscarina.
   2005c   Object shift, verb movement, and verb reduplication. In *The Oxford Handbook of Comparative Syntax*, Cinque, Guglielmo and Richard S. Kayne (eds.), 138–177. New York: Oxford University Press.
   2006a   Complementation in Saramaccan and Gungbe: the case of C-type modal particles. *Natural Language and Linguistic Theory* 24 (1): 1–55.
   2006b   The role of the syntax-semantics interface in language transfer. In *L2 Acquisition and Creole Genesis*, Lefebvre, Claire, Lydia White and Christine Jourdan (eds.), 221–252. Amsterdam: John Benjamins.
   2006c   When verbal predicates go fronting. In *Papers on Information Structure in African Languages*, Fiedler, Ines and Anne Schwarz (eds.), 21–48. Berlin: ZAS.

2007a La genèse de la périphérie gauche du saramaka: Un cas d'influence du substrat? In *Grammaires créoles et grammaire comparative*, Gadelli, Karl Erland and Anne Zribi-Hertz (eds.), 73–97. Saint-Denis: Presses Universitaires de Paris.
2007b A 'mini' relative clause analysis for reduplicated attributive adjectives. In *Linguistics in the Netherlands*, Los, Bettelou and Marjo van Koppen (eds.), 1–13. Amsterdam: John Benjamins.
2009a Clause structure and verb series. *Linguistic Inquiry* 40 (1): 1–33.
2009b Competition and selection: that's all! In *Complex Processes in New Languages*, Aboh, Enoch Oladé and Norval S.H. Smith (eds.), 317–344. Amsterdam: John Benjamins.
2010 The P-route. In *Mapping Spatial PP*, Cinque, Guglielmo and Luigi Rizzi (eds.), 225–260. New York: Oxford University Press.

Aboh, Enoch Oladé and Umberto Ansaldo
2006 The role of typology in language creation: a descriptive take. In *Deconstructing Creole* Ansaldo, Umberto, Stephen Matthews and Lisa Lim (eds.), 39–66. Amsterdam: John Benjamins.

Aboh, Enoch Oladé and Margot van den Berg
2002 The structure of word formation in 18th century Sranan, Gungbe and 'Old Gbe'. Paper presented at the Biennial conference of the Society of Caribbean Linguistics St. Augustine, Trinidad and Tobago, 14–17 August.

Aboh, Enoch Oladé and Marina Dyakonova
2009 Predicate doubling and parallel chains. *Lingua* 119 (7): 1035–1065.

Aboh, Enoch Oladé and Roland Pfau
2010 Whats a *wh*-word got to do with it? In *Mapping the Left Periphery*, Bernicà, Paola and Nicola Munaro (eds.), 91–124. Oxford: Oxford University Press.

Aboh, Enoch Oladé and Norval S.H. Smith
2012 The morphosyntax of non-iconic reduplications: a case study in Eastern Gbe and the Surinam Creoles. In *The Moprhosyntax of Reiteration in Creole and Non-Creole Languages*, Aboh, Enoch Oladé, Norval S.H. Smith and A. Zribi-Hertz (eds.), 27–75. Amsterdam: John Benjamins.

Adam, Lucien
1883 *Les idiomes afro-aryen et maléo-aryen: Essai d'hybridologie*. Paris: Maisonneuve.

Adamson, Lilian and Norval S.H. Smith
2003 Productive derivational predicate reduplication in Sranan. In *Twice as Meaningful: Reduplication in Pidgins, Creoles, and Other Contact Languages*, Kouwenberg, Silvia (ed.), 83–92. London: Battlebridge.

Agyekum, Kofi
2008 The pragmatics of Akan greetings. *Discourse Studies* 10 (4): 489–512.

Aikhenvald, Alexandra Y.
　2006　Serial verb constructions in typological perspective. In *Serial Verb Constructions*, Aikhenvald, Alexandra Y. (ed.), 1–68. Oxford: Oxford University Press.

Akindélé, A. and C. Aguessy
　1953　*Contribution a l'étude de l'histoire de l'ancien royaume de porto-novo*. Dakar: IFAN.

Allesaib, Mushina and Tonjes Veenstra
　Ms　Data set mauritian creole. database on clause-embedding predicates. Zas Berlin

Alleyne, Mervin C.M. (ed.)
　1981　*Comparative Afro-American*. Ann Arbor, MI: Karoma.

Alleyne, Mervin C.M.
　1987　Predicate structures in Saramaccan. In *Studies in Saramaccan Language Structure*, Alleyne, Mervin C.M. (ed.), 71–87. Amsterdam and Kingston: Instituut voor Algemene Taalwetenschap & Folklore Studies Project and University of the West Indies

van Alphen, G
　1962–1963　Suriname in een onbekend journaal van 1693. *New West Indian Guide / Nieuwe West-Indische Gids* 42: 303–313.

Ameka, Felix
　1991　Ewe: its grammatical constuctions and illocutionary devices. Canberra: Australian National University PhD dissertation.
　1995　The linguistic construction of space in Ewe. *Cognitive Linguistics* 6: 139–181.
　2003　Prepositions and postpositions in Ewe (Gbe): empirical and theoretical considerations. In *Typologie Des Langues D'afrique & Universaux De La Grammaire*, Zribi-Hertz, Anne and Patrick Sauzet (eds.), 41–67. Paris: Harmattan.

Ameka, Felix, Enoch Oladé Aboh and James Essegbey
　2007　Moving from verbs to prepositions in Gbe (West Africa). Ms.

Ameka, Felix and James Essegbey
　2001　The expression of complex translational motion events in three verb-serializing languages. In *Annual Report 2001*, Kelly, Ann and Alissa Melinger (eds.), 94–97. Nijmegen: Max-Planck Institute for Psycholinguistics.
　2006　Elements of Ewe grammar of space. In *Grammars of Space: Cognitive Explorations*, Levinson, Stephen and David P. Wilkens (eds.), 359–399. Cambridge: Cambridge University Press.
　2007　Cut and Break verbs in Ewegbe and the causative/inchoative alternation construction. *Cognitive Linguistics* 18 (2): 241–250.

Ameka, Felix and Stephen Levinson
　2007　The typology and semantics of locative predicates: posturals, positionals, and other beasts. *Linguistics* 45 (5/6): 847–871.

Amuzu, Evershed K.
   2005. Ewe-English codeswitching: a case of composite rather than classic codeswitching. Canberra: Australian National University PhD dissertation.

Andersen, Roger W.
   1983 Transfer to somewhere. In *Language Transfer in Language Learning*, Glass, Susan and Larry Selinker (eds.), 177–201. Rowley, MA: Newbury House.

Anonymous
   1964 *Leçons de kikongo par des bakongo*. Eegenhoven: Louvain.

Ansre, Gilbert
   1966 The verbid - a caveat to "serial verbs". *Journal of West African Languages* 3: 29–32.

Appah, Clement
   2004 Nominal derivation from noun phrases in Akan. In *Studies in the Languages of the Volta Basin: Proceedings of the Annual Colloquium of the Legon-Trondheim Linguistics Project. Vol. 2*, Kropp Dakubu, M. and E. K. Osam (eds.), 166–182.
   2005 Nominal derivation from noun phrases in Akan. In *Studies in the Languages of the Volta Basin: Proceedings of the Annual Colloquium of the Legon-Trondheim Linguistics Project*, Kropp Dakubu, M. and E. K. Osam (eds.), 132–142.
   2006 *The Function of -nyi/-ni (-fo/-fo) in Derived Nouns in Akan*. Legon: University of Ghana Ms.

Appah, Clement and Nana Amfo
   2011 The morphopragmatics of the diminuitive morpheme (-ba/-wa) in Akan. *Lexis* 6 (1): 88–103.
   Available at http://lexis.univ-lyon3.fr/IMG/pdf/Lexis_6.pdf

Arends, Jacques
   1989. Syntactic developments in Sranan: creolization as a gradual process. Nijmegen: University of Nijmegen PdD dissertation.
   1995a Demographic factors in the formation of sranan. In *The Early Stages of Creolization*, Arends, Jacques (ed.), 233–285. Amsterdam: John Benjamins.
   1995b Introduction to Part I. In *Early Suriname Creole Texts: A Collection of 18th-Century Sranan and Saramaccan Documents*, Arends, Jacques and Matthias Perl (eds.), 11–71. Frankfurt: Ververt.
   1999 The development of complementation in Saramaccan. In *Proceedings of the 11th International Congress of Linguistics*, Caron, B. (ed.). Oxford: Pergamon. CD-ROM.
   2001 Social stratification and network relations in the formation of Sranan. In *Creolization and Contact*, Smith, Norval S.H. and Tonjes Veenstra (eds.), 291–308. Amsterdam: John Benjamins.

2002 The history of the Surinamese creoles I: a socio-historical survey. In *Atlas of the Languages of Suriname*, Carlin, Eithne and Jacques Arends (eds.), 115–130. Leiden: KITLV Press.

Arends, Jacques and Margot van den Berg
2004 The Saramaka Peace Treaty in Sranan: an edition of the 1762 Text (Including a Copy of the Original Manuscript). *Creolica*. Available at http://www.creolica.net/Saramaka/saramakaPC.htm

Arends, Jacques, Silvia Kouwenberg and Norval S.H. Smith
1995 Theories focusing on the non-European input. In *Pidgins and Creoles: An Introduction*, Arends, Jacques, Pieter Muysken and Norval S.H. Smith (eds.), 99–110. Amsterdam: John Benjamins.

Arends, Jacques, Pieter Muysken and Norval S.H. Smith, (eds.)
1995 *Pidgins and Creoles: An Introduction*. Amsterdam: John Benjamins.

Arends, Jacques and Matthias Perl
1995 *Early Suriname Creole Texts: A Collection of 18th-Century Sranan and Saramaccan Documents*. Frankfurt: Ververt.

Atlas et etudes sociolinguistiques des états du conseil de l'entente. 1983. Abidjan: ILA d'Abidjan et ACCT.

Auer, Peter, Frans Hinskens and Paul Kerswill, (eds.)
2005 *Dialect Change: Convergence and Divergence in European Languages*. Cambridge: Cambridge University Press.

Awóyalé, Yíwolá
1997 Object positions in Yoruba. In *Object Positions in Benue-Kwa: Papers from a Workshop at Leiden University*, Déchaine, Rose-Marie and Victor Manfredi (eds.), 7–30. The Hague: The Holland Academic Graphics.

Ayafor, Miriam
2008 Cameroon Pidgin English (Kamtok): morphology and syntax. In *Varietis of English 4: Africa, South and Southeast Asia*, Mesthrie, Rajend (ed.), 428–450. Berlin: Mouton de Gruyter.

Baily, Beryl L.
1966 *Jamaican Creole Syntax: A Transformational Approach*. New York: Cambridge University Press.

Baker, Philip
1990 Off target? *Journal of Pidgin and Creole Languages* 5 (1): 107–119.
1996 Pidginization, creolization, and Français Approximatif: review article of Chaudenson 1996. *Journal of Pidgin and Creole Languages* 11 (1): 95–120.
1999 On the origin and diffusiont of shared features among the Atlantic English Creoles. In *St. Kitts and the Atlantic Creoles: The Texts of Samuel Methews in Perspective*, Baker, Philip and Adrienne Bruyn (eds.), 315–364. London: University of Westminster Press.

Bakker, Peter
   1987   Reduplications in Saramaccan. In *Studies in Saramaccan Langauge Structure*, Alleyne, Mervin C.M. (ed.), 17–40. Amsterdam and Kingston: Instituut voor Algemene Taalwetenschap and Folklore Studies Project, University of the West Indies.
   1996   Language intertwining and convergence: Typological Aspects of Genesis of Mixed Languages. *Sprachtypologie und Universalienforschung* 49: 9–20.
   1997   *A Language of Our Own: The Genesis of Michif, the Mixed Cree-French Language of the Canadian Metis*. Oxford: Oxford University Press.
Bakker, Peter, Aymeric Daval-Markussen, Mikael Parkvall and Ingo Plag
   2011   Creoles are typologically distinct from non-creoles. *Journal of Pidgin and Creole Languages* 26 (1): 5–42.
Bakovic, Eric
   2001   Nasal place neutralization in Spanish. *University of Pennsylvania Working Papers in Linguistics* 7 (1): 2–13.
Bally, Charles
   1932   *Linguistique générale et linguistique française*. Paris: Leroux
Bastin, Yvonne, Acnreé Coupez, Evariste Mumba and Thilo Schadeberg
   2003   *Bantu Lexical Reconstructions* (BLR3).
Becker, Angelica and Tonjes Veenstra
   2003   The survival of inflectional morphology in French-related creoles: the role of SLA processes. *Studies in Second Language Acquisition* 25 (2): 283–306.
Ben-Ur, Aviva and Rachel Frankel
   2009   *Remnant Stones: The Jewish Cemeteries of Suriname: Epitaphs*. Vol. 2. Detroit: Hebrew Union College Press.
Benjamins, Herman Daniël and Joh F. Snelleman, (eds.)
   1914–1917 *Encyclopaedie Van Nederlandsch West-Indië*. The Hague/Leiden: Martinus Nijhoff/E.J. Brill.
Bentley, WIliam Holman
   1887   *Dictionary and Grammar of the Kongo Langauge, as Spoken at San Salvador, the Ancient Capital of the Old Kongo Empire, West Africa*. London: London Baptist Missionary Society.
van den Berg, Margot
   2000. 'Mi no sal tron tongo' Early Sranan in court records, 1667–1767. Radboud University Nijmegen MA Thesis. Available at http://home.hum.uva.nl/oz/vandenbergm
   2001   'Mingo joù no man': Oud-Sranan in verhoren en verslagen van rechtzaken. *OSO Tijdschrift voor Surinamistiek* 20 (2): 241–253.
   2003   Early 18th Century Sranan –man. In *Phonology and Morphology of Creole Languages*, Plag, Ingo (ed.), 231–251. Tübingen: Niemeyer.
   2007   *A Grammar of Early Sranan*. Zetten: Manta.

van den Berg, Margot and Adrienne Bruyn
  2008   The Early Surinamese Creoles in the Suriname Creole Archive (Suca). In *Linguistics in the Netherlands*, van Koppen, Marjo and Bert Botma (eds.), 25–36. Amsterdam: John Benjamins.
Bernhard, Virginia
  1999   *Slaves and Slaveholders in Bermuda 1616–1782*. Columbia MO: University of Missouri Press.
Bernstein, Judy
  1997   Demonstratives and reinforcers in Romance and Germanic languages. *Lingua* 102: 87–113.
  2001   Focusing the 'right' way in Romance determiner phrases. *Probus* 13 (1): 1–29.
Berry, Jack
  1966   *A Dictionary of Sierra Leone Krio*. Evanston, IL: U.S. Office of Education.
den Besten, Hans
  1987   Die Niederlandischen Pidgins der Alten Kapkolonie. In *Beiträge Zum 3. Essener Kolloquium Uber Sprachwandel Und Seine Bestimmenden Faktoren*, Boretzky, Norbert, Werner Enningre and Thomas Stolz (eds.), 9–40. Bochum: Brockmeyer.
Bickerton, Derek
  1981   *The Roots of Language*. Ann Arbor: Karoma Publishers.
  1984   The Language Bioprogram Hypothesis. *Behavioral and Brain Sciences* 7: 173–221.
Bilby, Kenneth
  1983   How the "older heads" talk: a Jamaican Maroon Spirit Possession Language and its relationship to the creoles of Suriname and Sierra Leone. *New West Indian Guide / Nieuwe West-Indische Gids* 57: 37–88.
  1984   The treacherous feast: a Jamaican Maroon historical myth. *Bijdragen tot de Taal-, Land- en Volkenkund* 140: 1–31.
  1992. Further observations on the Jamaican Maroon Spirit Language. Paper presented at the Annual meeting of the Society for Pidgin and Creole Linguistics, Philadelphia.
  1993   Latent intervocalic liquids in Aluku: links to the phonological past of a Maroon Creole. In *Atlantic Meets Pacific: A Global View of Pidginization and Creolization*, Bryne, Francis and John A. Holm (eds.), 25–35. Amsterdam: John Benjamins.
  1994   Maroon culture as a distinct variant of Jamaican culture. In *Maroon Heritage: Archaeological, Ethnographic and Historical Perspectives*, Agorsah, Kofi (ed.), 72–85. Kingston: Canoe Press, University of the West Indies.
  1996   Dictionary of Aluku (Boni), with comparitive data from other Atlantic Creoles. Preliminary version, A–B

2005 *True-Born Maroons*. Gainsville FL: University of Florida Press.

Bilby, Kenneth, Bernard Delpech, Marie Fleury and Diane Vernon
 1989 *L'alimentation des noirs marrons du maroni: vocabulaire. pratiques, representations [Preliminary Version]*. Cayenne: Centre ORSTOM de Cayenne, Institut Francais de Recherche Scietifique pour le Developpement en Cooperation.

Blanker, J.C.M. and J. Dubbeldam
 2005 *Sranantongo-Nederlands, Nederlands-Sranantongo*. Utrecht: Prisma.

Bock, J. K.
 1986 Syntactic persistence in language production. *Cognitive Psychology* 18: 355–387.
 1989 Closed class immanence in sentence production. *Cognition* 31: 163–186.

Bohnemeyer, Jürgen, M. Bowerman and Penelope Brown
 2001 Cut and break clips. In *Manual for the Field Season 2001*, Levinson, Stephen and Nick Enfield (eds.), 90–96. Nijmegen: Max Planck Institute for Psycholinguistics.

Booij, Geert
 1995 *The Phonology of Dutch*. Oxford: Oxford University Press.
 2005 Compounding and derivation: evidence for construction morphology. In *Demarcation in Morphology*, Dressler, W. U. and D. Kastovsky (eds.), 109–132. Amsterdam: John Benjamins.

Borer, Hagit and Kenneth Wexler
 1987 The maturation in syntax. In *Parameter Seting*, Roeper, T. and E. Williams (eds.), 123–172. Dordrecht: Reidel.

Boretzky, Norbert
 1983 *Kreolsprachen, Substrate und Sprachwandel*. Wiesbaden: Otto Harrassowitz.
 1993 The concept of rule, rule borrowing, and substrate influence in creole languages. In *Africanisms in Afro-American Language Varieties*, Mufwene, Salikoko S. (ed.), 74–92. Athens: University of Georgia Press.

Borges, Robert
 2013 *The Life of Language: Dynamics of Language Contact in Suriname*. Utrecht: LOT.

Braun, Maria
 2001 Complex words in Early Sranan: an investigation into creole morphology. Siegen: Universität Siegen MA thesis.
 2009 *Word-Formation and Creolisation: The Case of Early Sranan*. Tübingen: Nimeyer.

Braun, Maria and Ingo Plag
 2003 How transparent is creole morphology? In *Yearbook of Morphology 2002*, Booij, Geert and Jaap van Maarle (eds.), 81–104. Dordrecht: Foris.

Broeder, Peter, Guus Extra and Roeland van Hout
  1996 Word-formation devices in adult language acquisition. In *Approaches to Second Language Acquisition*, Sajavaara, Kari and Courtney Fairweather (eds.). Jyväskylä: University of Jyväskylä.
Bruyn, Adrienne
  1989 De nominale constituent in het 18de-eeuws Sranan. een beschrijving van grammaticale elementen en morfosyntactische processen. Amsterdam: University of Amsterdam MA Thesis.
  1995 *Grammaticalization in Creoles: The Development of Determiners and Relative Clauses in Sranan*. Amsterdam: IFOTT.
  1996 On identifying instances of grammaticalization in creole languages. In *Changing Meanings, Changing Functions: Papers Related to Grammaticalization in Contact Languages*. Baker, Philip and Anand Syea (eds.), 29–46. London: University of Wesrminster Press.
  2002 The structure of the Surinamese Creoles. In *Atlas of the Languages of Suriname*, Carlin, Ethne and Jacques Arends (eds.), 153–182. Leiden: KITLV Press.
  2003 grammaticalization, réanalyse et influence substratique: quelques cas du sranan. In *Grammaticalization et réanalyse: approches de la variation créole et française*. Kriegel, Sibylle (ed.), 25–47. Paris: CNRS Éditions.
  2008 Grammaticalization in pidgins and creoles. In *Handbook of Creole Linguistics*, Singler, John Victor and Silvia Kouwenberg (eds.), 385–410. Oxford: Blackwell Publishing.
  2009 Grammaticalization in creoles: ordinary and not-so-ordinary cases. *Studies in Language* 33: 312–337.
Bryne, Francis
  1987 *Grammatical Relations in a Radical Creole*. Amsterdam: Benjamins.
Burzio, Luigi
  1986 *Italian Syntax: A Government and Binding Approach*. Dordrecht: Reidel.
Cabrera, Monica and Maria Liusa Zubizarreta
  2004 The role of the L1 in the overgeneralization of causatives in L2 English and L2 Spanish. In *Contemporary Approaches to Romance Linguistics*, Auger, Julie, Clancy J. Clements and Barbara Vance (eds.), 15–30. Amsterdam: John Benjamins.
Campbell, Richard
  1996 Specificity operators in SpecDP. *Studia Linguistica* 2: 161–188.
Capo, Hounkpati B.C.
  1991 *A Comparative Phonology of Gbe*. Berlin: Foris.
Cardinaletti, Anna
  1997 Subjects and clause structure. In *The New Comparative Syntax*, Haegeman, Liliane (ed.), 33–63. London: Longman.

Carlin, Eithne and Jacques Arends, (eds.)
    2002   *Atlas of the Languages of Suriname.* Leiden: KITLV Press.
Cassidy, Fredric G. and Robert B. LePage
    1967   *Dictionary of Jamaican English.* Cambridge: Cambridge University Press.
Charry, Eddy, Geert Koefoed and Pieter Muysken (eds.)
    1983   *De Talen van Suriname.* Muiderberg: Coutinho.
Chatelain, Heli
    1888   *Grammatica Elementar do Kimbundu.* Genebra: Charles Schudardt.
Chaudenson, Robert
    1992   *Des îles, des hommes, des langues: essais sur la créolisation linguistique et culturelle.* Paris: L'Harmattan.
Chomsky, Noam
    1986   *Knowledge of Language.* New York: Praeger
    2005   On phases. MIT: Ms.
Christaller, Johann Gottlieb
    1881 (1933) *Dictionary of the Asante and Fante Language Called Tshi (Twi).* Basel: Basel Evangelical Missionary Society.
Cinque, Guglielmo
    1990   *Types of a' Dependencies* Cambridge, MA: MIT Press.
Clements, Georges N.
    1972.   The verbal syntax of Ewe. London: University of London PhD Dissertation.
    1990   The role of the sonority cycle in core syllabification. In *Papers in Laboratory Phonology I: Between the Grammar and Physics of Speech*, Kingston, John and Mary Beckman (eds.), 283–233. Cambridge: Cambridge University Press.
Connel, Bruce
    1994   The Lower Cross Languages: a ptolegomena to the classification of the Cross River Languages. *Journal of West African Languages* 2: 43–46.
Cook, Tom
    1985   *An Integrated Phonology of Efik: Volume 1.* Leiden: Leiden University PhD Dissertation.
Corne, Chris
    1994   Relativization and thematization in Tayo and the implications for creole genesis. *Journal of Pidgin and Creole Languages* 9: 283–304.
    1999   *From French to Creole.* London: University of Westminster Press.
van de Craats, Ineke, Norbert Corver and Roeland van Hout
    2000   Conservation of grammatical knowledge: on the acquisition of possessive noun phrases. *Linguistics* 38: 221–314.
    2002   The acquisition of possessive have-clauses by Turkish and Moroccan learners of Dutch. *Bilingualism and Language Cognition* 5: 147–174.

Creissels, Denis
    2006   Encoding the distinctions between location, source, and destination: a tyological study. In *Space in Languages: Linguistic Systems and Cognitive Categories*, Hickmann, May and Stéphane Robert (eds.), 19–28. Amsterdam: John Benjamins.

D'Costa, Jean and Barbara Lalla
    1989   *Voices in Exile: Jamaican Texts of the 18th and 19th Centuries.* Tuscaloosa AL: The University of Alabama Press.

DaCruz, Maxim
    1998   La dérivation lexicale en gbe. *GbeGbo Studies. Scientific Review of Labo Gbe* 2: 153–175.

Daeleman, Jan
    1972   Kongo element in Saramacca Tongo. *Journal of African Languages* 11: 11–44.
    nd   Kikóongo wordlists classified according to their respective tones. Available at http://webh01.ua.ac.be/markvandevelde/Kikoongo%20wordlists%20Jan%20Daeleman_COMBINED.pdf]

Daeleman, Jan and L. Pauwels
    1983   notes d'ethnobotanique ntándu (kóongo). principales plantes de la région de kisaántu : noms ntándu et noms scientifiques. *Africana Linguistica* 9: 149–255.

Dako, Kari
    2003   *Ghanaianisms: A Glossary.* Accra: Ghana University Press.

Dallas, Robert C.
    1803   *The History of the Maroons: From Their Origin to the Establishment of Their Chief Tribe at Sierra Leone.* London: T.M. Longman and O. Rees.

Damonte, Frederico
    2002   The complementizer layer in Saramaccan. In *Current Issues in Generative Grammar. 10th Colloquium on Generative Grammar, Selected Papers,* Leonetti, M., O. Fernandez Soriano and V. Escandell Vidal (eds.), 31–30. Alcalá de Henares: Universidad Alcalá de Henares.

Daval-Markussen, Aymeric
    2011   Of networks and trees in contact linguistics: new light on the typology of creoles. Aarhus: Aarhus Universitet Institut for antropologi, arkæologi og lingvistik MA thesis.

Declerck, Renaat
    1988   *Studies on Copular Sentences, Clefts and Pseudo-Clefts.* Berlin: De Gruyter Mouton.

DeGraff, Michal
    1999   Creolization, language change and language acquisition: an epilogue. In *Language Change and Creation: Creolization, Diachrony and Development*, DeGraff, Michal (ed.), 473–554. Cambridge, MA: MIT Press.
    2001   Morphology in creole genesis: a prolegomenon. In *Ken Hale: A Life in Language*, Kenstowicz, Michael (ed.), 53–121. Cambridge MA: MIT Press.
Delamarre, Xavier
    2003   *Dictionnaire de la language gauloise: une approche linguistique du vieux-celtique continental.* Paris: Éditions errance.
van der Elst, Dirk H.
    1975   The Coppename Kwinti: notes on an Afro-American tribe in Suriname I. *New West Indian Guide / Nieuwe West-Indische Gids* 50: 7–17.
van der Geest, Sjaak
    2009   "Anyway!": lorry inscriptions in Ghana. In *The Speed of Change: Motor Vehicles and People in Africa*, Luning, Gewald S. and K. van Walraven (eds.), 253–293. Leiden: Brill.
van der Voort, Hein
    2000   A grammar of Kwaza: a description of an endangered and unclassified indigenous language of Southern Rhondonia. Leiden: Leiden University PhD Dissertation.
Dereau, Leon
    1955   *Cours de kikongo.* Namur: Wesmael-Charlier.
Devonish, Hubert
    2002   On the Sierra Leone-Caribbean connection: hot on the trail of the 'toneshifted' items in Anglo-West African varieties. In *Talking Rhythm Stressing Tone: The Role of Prominence in Anglo-West African Creole Languages*, Devonish, Hubert (ed.), 165–180. Kingston: Arawak Publications.
Dillard, Joey L.
    1970   Principles in the history of American English: paradox, virginity and cafeteria. *Florida Foreign Language Reporter* 8 (1–2): 32–33.
Dobson, E.J.
    1957   *English Pronunciation, 1500–1700.* Oxford: Oxford University Press.
Donicie, Anton and Jan Voorhoeve
    1963   *De Saramakaanse woordenschat.* Amsterdam: Bureau voor Taalonderzoek in Suriname van de Universiteit van Amsterdam.
Dorian, Nancy
    1981   *Language Death: The Life Cucle of a Scottish Gaellic Dialect.* Philadelphia: University of Pennsylvania Press.
Dragtenstein, Frank
    2002   *'De Ondraaglijke Stoutheid Der Wegloopers': Marronage En Koloniaalbeleid 1667–1768.* Utrecht: IBS.

Dulay, Heidi and Marina Burt
  1974   Natural sequences in child second language acquisition. *Language Learning* 24: 37–53.
Dunn, Michael, Stephen Levinson, Eva Lindstrom, Ger Reesingk and Angela Terrill
  2008   Structural phylogeny in historical linguistics: methodological explorations applied in Island Melanesia. *Language* 84 (4): 710–759.
Dunn, Michael, G Reesink, R. Foley and Stephen Levinson
  2005   Structural phylogenetics and the reconstruction of ancient language history. *Science* 309: 2072–2075.
Durrleman, Stephanie
  2000   The architecture of the clause in Jamaican Creole. *Generative Grammar in Geneva* 1: 189–240.
  2008   *The Syntax of Jamaican Creole: A Cartographic Perspective*. Amsterdam: John Benjamins.
Duthie, Alan S.
  1996   *Introducing Ewe Linguistic Patterns*. Accra: Ghana University Press.
van Dyk, Pieter
  ca. 1765 *Nieuwe en nooit bevoorens geziene onderwijzinge in het Bastert Engels, of Neeger Engels, zoo als hetzelve in de Hollandse colonien gebruikt wordt*. Amsterdam: De Erven de Weduwe Jacobus can Egmont.
Edmondson, Jerold A. and Lama Ziwo
  1999   Laghuu or Xá Phó: a new language of the Yi Group. *Linguistics of the Tibeto-Burman Area* 22 (1): 1–10.
Enç, Mürvet
  1991   The semantics of specificity. *Linguistic Inquiry* 22: 1–26.
Escure, Genevieve
  2008   Belize and other Central American varieties: morphology and syntax. In *Varieties of English 2: The Americas and the Caribbean*, Schneider, Edgar (ed.), 732–762. Berlin: Mouton de Gruyter.
Essegbey, James
  1999   Inherent complement verbs in Ewe: towards an understanding of argument structure in Ewe. Leiden: University of Leiden PhD Dissertation.
  2003   On definiteness asymmetry in double object constructions. In *Proceedings of the 3rd World Congress of African Linguistics*, Lebikaza, K. (ed.), 127–141. Cologne: Rudiger Koeppe.
  2004   Auxiliaries in serialising languages: on come and go verbs in Sranan and Ewegbe. *Lingua* 20 (114): 473–494.
  2005   The basic locative construction in Gbe languages and Surinamese creoles. *Journal of Pidgin and Creole Languages* 20 (2): 228–267.
  2006   Ewe. In *Encyclopedia of Languages and Linguistics*, Brown, Keith (ed.), 369–370. Oxford: Elsevier.

2007   Cut and break verbs in Sranan. *Cognitive Linguistics* 18 (2): 231–240.
Essegbey, James and Felix Ameka
    2001.   Serialising languages: satellite-framed, verb-framed or neither. Paper presented at the 32nd Annual Conference on African Linguistics, University of California, Berkeley
    2007   'Cut' and 'Break' verbs in Gbe and Suriname Creoles. *Journal of Pidgin and Creole Languages* 22 (1): 37–55.
Essegbey, James and Adrienne Bruyn
    2002.   Moving into an out of Sranan: multiple effects of contact. Paper presented at the International Conference on Adpositions of Movement, Catholic University of Leuven, Leuven, Belgium.
Faraclas, Nicholas G.
    1987   Creolization and the tense-aspect-modality system of Nigerian Pidgin. *Journal of African Languages and Linguistics* 3 (2): 77–97.
    1996   *Nigerian Pidgin.* London: Routledge.
Ferguson, Charles
    1959   Diglossia. *Word* 15 (2): 325–340.
Fillmore, Charles
    1983   How to know whether you're coming or going. In *Essays of Deixis*, Rauh, G. (ed.), 219–227. Tübingen: Narr.
Fishman, Joshua
    1985   The societal basis of the intergenerational continuity of additional languages. In *Scientific and Humanistic Dimensions of Language: Festschrift for Robert Lado on the Occasion of His 70th Birthday*, Jankowsky, Kurt (ed.), 551–557. Amsterdam: John Benjamins.
Focke, Hendrik C.
    1855   *Neger-Engelsch Woordenboek.* Leiden: van den Heuvel.
Fortin, Jeffrey
    2006   "Blackened beyond our native hue": removal, identity and the trelawney maroons on the margins of the Atlantic world, 1796–1800. *Citizenship Studies* 10: 5–34.
Fyfe, Christopher, (ed.)
    1991   *"Our Children Free and Happy": Letters from Black Settlers in Africa in the 1790s.* Edinburgh: Edinburgh University Press.
Gass, Susan
    1996   Second language acquisition and linguistic theory: the role of language transfer. In *Handbook of Second Language Acquisition*, Ritchie, William C. and Tej K. Bhatia (eds.), 317–345. San Diego: Academic Press.
Gilbert, Glenn G.
    1985   Hugo Schuchardt and the Atlantic Creoles: a newly discovered manuscript "on the Negro English of West Africa". *American Speech* 60 (1): 31–63.

Goddard, Cliff
 1997 The semantics of coming and going. *Pragmatics* 7 (2): 147–162.

Gómez Rendón, Jorge
 2008 *Una lengua mixta en los andes: génesis y estructura de la media lengua.* Quito: Abya Yala.

Goury, L.
 2003 *Le ndyuka: une langue créole du surinam et de guyane française.* Paris: L'Harmattan.

Greene, Laurie
 1999 *A Grammar of Belizean Creole: Compilations from Two Existing United States Dialects.* New York: Peter Lang.

de Groot, A.H.P.
 1977 *Woordregister Nederlands–Saramakaans.* Paramaribo: VACO.
 1981 *Woordregister Sramakkaans–Nederlands.* Paramaribo: VACO.
 1984 *Tweedelig Woordregister: Auka–Nederlands, Nederlands–Auka.* Paramaribo: VACO.

Guerssel, M., K. Hale, M. Laughren, B. Levin and J. White Eagle
 1985 A cross-linguistic study of transitivity alternations. In *Papers from the Parasession on Causatives and Agentivity at the Twenty-First Regional Meeting* Eilfort, W. H., P. D. Kroeber and L. Peterson (eds.), 48–63. Chicago, IL: Chicago Linguistic Society.

Haabo, Vinije
 2009 *Saamaka – Holansi.* Wageninen: Ms.
 2013 Saamaka Woutubuku. *Ms*

Hackert, Stephanie
 2004 *Urban Bahamian Creole: System and Variation.* Amsterdam: John Benjamins.

Hackert, Stephanie and Magnus Huber
 2007 Gullah in the diaspora: historical and linguistic evidence from the Bahamas. *Diachronica* 24: 279–325.

Hale, K. and S.J. Keyser
 1987 *A View from the Middle.* Cambridge MA: Center for Cognitive Science at MIT.

Hancock, Ian
 1969 A provisional comparison of the English-Based Atlantic Creoles. *African Language Review* 8: 7–72.
 1980 Gullah and Barbadian: origins and relationships. *American Speech* 55: 17–35.
 1987 A preliminary classification of the Anglophone Atlantic Creoles with syntactic data from thirty-three representative dialects. In *Pidgin and Creole Languages: Essays in Memory of John E. Reinecke*, Gilbert, Glenn G. (ed.), 264–333. Honolulu: University of Hawaii Press.

Harris, Col. C.L.G.
　1994　　The true traditions of my ancestors. In *Maroon Heritage: Archaeological, Ethnographic, and Historical Perspectives*, Agorsah, Kofi (ed.), 36–63. Kingston: Canoe Press.
　nd　　*The Maroons of Moore Town (a Colonel Speaks)*. Moore Town, Jamaica: Ms.

Hartsinck, J.J.
　1770　　*Beschryving van Guiana, of de Wilde Kust in Zuid-America*. Amsterdam: Gerrit Tielenburg.

Haspelmath, Martin, Matthew Dryer, David Gil and Bernard Comrie, (eds.)
　2005　　*The World Atlas of Linguistic Structures*. Oxford: Oxford University Press.

Haugen, Einar
　1950　　The analysis of linguistic borrowing. *Language* 26: 210–231.

Hayes, Bruce
　1985　　Iambic and trochaic rhythm in stress rules. In *Proceedings of the 11th Annual Meeting of the Berkeley Linguistics Society*, Niepokuj, Mary, Mary VanClay, Vassiliki Nikiforidou and Doeborah Feter (eds.), 429–446. Berkeley CA: Berkeley Linguistics Society.

Hazoumè, Marc Laurent
　1990　　*Essai de classification synchronique*. Ottowa, Canada: C.R.D.I.

Heath, Jeffrey
　1984　　Language contact and language change. *Annual Review of Anthropology* 13: 367–384.

Heine, Bernd, Ulrike Claudi and Friederike Hünnemeyer
　1991　　*Grammaticalization: A Conceptual Framework*. Chicago: University of Chicago Press.

Heine, Bernd and Tania Kuteva
　2003　　On Contact Induced Grammaticalization. *Studies in Language* 27: 529–572.
　2005　　*Language Contact and Grammatical Change*. Cambridge: Cambridge University Press.
　2010　　Contact and grammaticalization. In *The Handbook of Language Contact*, Hickey, Raymond (ed.), 86–105. Oxford: Wiley-Blackwell.

Helms-Park, Rena
　2003　　Transfer in SLA and creoles: the implications of causative serial verb constructions in the interlanguage of Vietnamese ESL learners. *Studies in Second Language Acquisition* 25 (2): 211–244.

Herlein, J.D.
　1718　　*Beschrijvinge van de volksplantinge Zuriname: vertonende de opkomst dier zelver Colonie, etc. mitsgaders een vertoog van de Boschgrond, etc. Verrijkt met een landkaart (daar de legginge der Plantagien worden aangewezen) en kopere platen*. Leeuwarden: Injema (2e druk). UB, Amsterdam. UBM: 1803 G 11.

Herskovits, Melville and Frances Herskovits
   1934   *Rebel Destiny: Among the Bush Negroes of Dutch Guiana.* New York: Whittlesey House.
   1936   *Surinam Folklore.* New York: Columbia University Press.
Höftmann, Hildegard
   1993   *Grammatik des fɔn.* Leipzig: Langenscheidt.
   2003   *Dictionnaire fon – français.* Köln: Rüdiger Koppe Verlag.
Holloway, Charles E.
   1997   *Dialect Death: The Case of Brule Spanish.* Amsterdam: John Benjamins.
Holm, John A.
   1988   *Pidgins and Creoles: Volume 1, Theory and Structures.* Cambridge: Cambridge University Press.
Holm, John A. and Peter Patrick
   2007   *Comparative Creole Syntax: Parallel Outlines of 18 Creole Grammars.* London: Battlebridge Press.
Holm, John A. and Alison W. Shilling
   1982   *Dictionary of Bahamian English.* Cold Spring, NY: Lexik House.
Houssou, Avit-Prosper
   1990   *étude comparative de la determination nominale en gun et en wemegbe.* Abomey-Calavi: D.E.L.T.O., Université Nationale du Benin.
Huber, Magnus
   1997   Dat Tree Be White Man Chop: On The Story Of Genesis in West African Pidgin English. *The Carrier Pidgin* 25 (3): 4–6, 38–43.
   1999a   *Ghanaian Pidgin English in Its West African Context: A Sociohistorical and Structural Analysis.* Amsterdam: John Benjamins.
   1999b   On the origin and diffusion of Atlantic English Creoles: first attestations from Krio. In *St Kitts and the Atlantic Creoles: The Texts of Samuel Mathews in Perspective*, Baker, Philip and Adrienne Bruyn (eds.), 365–378. London: University of Westminster Press.
   2004   The Nova Scotia-Sierra Leone connection: new evidence on an early variety of African American Vernacular English in the diaspora. In *Creoles, Contact, and Language Change: Linguistic and Social Implications*, Schwegler, Armin, and Geneviève Escure (eds.), 67–95. Amsterdam: John Benjamins.
Hurault, Jean
   1983   Eléments de vocabulaire de la langue boni (aluku tongo). *Amsterdam Creole Studies* 4: 1–41.
Huson, D. and D. Bryant
   2006   Application of phylogenetic networks in evolutionary studies. *Molecular Biology and Evolution* 23 (2): 254–267.

Hutchinson, Thomas J.
   1861   *Ten Years' Wanderings among the Ethiopians.* London: Hurst and Blackett.

Huttar, George L.
   1972   A comparative word list for Djuka. In *Languages of the Guianas*, Grimes, Joseph E. (ed.), 12–21. Norman, OK: Summer Institute of Linguistics, University of Oklahoma.
   1975   Sources of creole semantic structures. *Language* 51: 684–695.
   1981   Some Kwa-like features of Djuka syntax. *Studies in African Linguistics* 12: 291–323.
   1983   Kwinti liquids. extracts from Kwinti field notes. Ms.
   1985   Sources of Ndyuka African vocabulary. *New West Indian Guide / Nieuwe West-Indische Gids* 59: 45–71.
   1986   Kikongo, Saramaccan and Ndyuka. In *Language in Global Perspective: Papers in Honor of the 50th Anniversary of the Summer Institute of Linguistics, 1935–1985*, Elson, B.F. (ed.), 563–586. Dallas: Summer Institute of Linguistics.
   1988   Notes on Kwinti: a creole of central Suriname. *Society for Caribbean Linguistics Occasional Paper* 20.
   2003   Scales of basicness in semantic domains and their application to creolization. In *Language and Life: Essays in Memory of Kenneth L. Pike*, Wise, M.R., T.N. Headland and R.M. Brend (eds.), 119–137. Dallas: SIL and University of Texas at Arlington.

Huttar, George L., James Essegbey and Felix Ameka
   2007   Gbe and other West African sources of Suriname Creole semantic structures: implications for creole genesis. *Journal of Pidgin and Creole Languages* 22 (1): 57–72.

Huttar, George L. and Mary Huttar
   1972   Notes on Djuka phonology. In *Languages of the Guianas, Volume 1*, Grimes, Joseph E. (ed.), 12–21. Norman OK: Summer Institute of Linguistics of the University of Oklahoma.
   1994   *Ndyuka.* London: Routledge.
   1997   Reduplication in Ndyuka. In *The Structure and Status of Pidgins and Creoles*, Spears, Aurthur K. and Donald Winford (eds.), 395–414. Amsterdam: John Benjamins.

Ihsane, Tabea and Genoveva Puskás
   2001   Specific is not definite. *Generative Grammar in Geneva* 2: 39–54.

Jackendoff, Ray
   1975   Morphological and semantic regularities in the lexicon. *Language* 51: 639–671.

Jacquot, A.
   1981   *Études beembe (congo): esquisse linguistique; devinettes et proverbes.* Paris: O.R.S.T.O.M.

Jarvis, Scott
   2000   Methodological rigor in the study of transfer: identifying L1 influence in the interlanguage lexicon. *Language Learning* 50: 245–309.
   2010   Comparison-based and detection-based approaches to transfer research. In *EUROSLA Yearbook 10*, Roberts, M. Howard, M.O. Laoire, and D. Singleton (eds.), 169–192. Amsterdam John Benjamins.

Jennings, William
   1995   The first generations of a creole society: Cayenne 1660–1700. In *From Contact to Creole and Beyond*, Baker, Philip (ed.), 21–40. London: University of Westminster Press.

Johanson, Lars
   1992   *Strukturelle Faktoren in türkischen Sprachkontakten*. Frankfurt am Main: Steiner.

Johnson, Marion R.
   1979   The natural history of Meinhof's Law in Bantu. *Studies in African Linguistics* 10 (3): 261–271.

Joint State University of Leyden-Summer Institute of Linguistics-Surinam Ministry of Education Surinam Creole etymological dictionary project. cardfile consulted with the permission of the late professor Jan Voorhoeve.

Jourdan, Christine
   2008   The cultural in pidgin genesis. In *The Handbook of Pidgin and Creole Studies*, Kouwenberg, Silvia and John Victor Singler (eds.), 359–381. Oxford: Blackwell.

Kahrel, P.
   1987   Stative verb formation in Saramaccan. In *Studies in Saramaccan Langauge Structure*, Alleyne, Mervin C.M. (ed.), 53–70. Amsterdam and Kingston: Instituut voor Algemene Taalwetenschap and the Folklore Studies Project at the Univeristy of the West Indies.

Kanye, Richard S
   1994   *The Antisymmetry of Syntax*. Cambridge, MA: MIT Press.

Kautzsch, Alexander and Edgar Schneider
   2000   Differential creolization: some evidence from earlier African American Vernacular English in South Carolina. In *Degrees of Restructuring in Creole Languages*, Neumann-Holzschuh, Ingrid and Edgar Schneider (eds.), 247–274. Amsterdam John Benjamins.

Kellerman, Eric
   1979   Transfer and non-transfer: where are we now. *Studies in Second Language Acquisition* 2: 37–57.

van Kempen, Michiel
   2002   *Een Geschiedenis van de Surinaamse Literatuur. Deel 1 & 2*. Paramaribo: Uitgeverij Okopipi.

Kießling, Roland
    2005   Bàk Mwà Mè Dó -Camfranglais in Cameroon. *Lingua Posnaniensis* 47: 87–107.
Kießling, Roland and Maarten Mous
    2004   Urban youth languages in Africa. *Anthropological Linguistics* 46 (3): 303–341.
Kim, H. S.
    1999   Meinhof's Rule in Bantu Revisited. *Linguistics* 7183–204.
Kinyalolo, Kasangati K. W.
    1993   On some syntactic properties of dó in Fòn. *Lingua* 91: 201–233.
van 't Klooster, Charlotte I.E.A., Jan C. Linderman and Marion J. Jansen-Jacobs
    2003   *Index of Vernacular Plant Names of Suriname*. Leiden: Nationaal Herbarium Nederland.
Kluge, Angela
    2000.   The Gbe language varieties of West Africa: a quantitative analysis of lexical and grammatical features. Cardiff: University of Wales, College of Cardiff MA Thesis.
    2006   Quanlitative and quantitative analysis of grammatical features elicited among the Gbe language varieties in West Africa. *Journal of African Languages and Linguistics* 22 (1): 53–86.
    2007   The Gbe language continuum of West Africa: a synchronic typological approach to prioritizing in-depth sociolinguistic research on literature extensibility. *Language Documentation and Conservation* 1: 182–215.
Koefoed, Geert and Jacqueline Tarenskeen
    1996   The making of languages from a lexical point of view. In *Creole Languages and Language Acquisition*, Wekker, Hermen (ed.), 119–138. Berlin: Walter de Gruyter.
Konadu, Kwasi
    2011   *The Akan Diaspora in the Americas*. Oxford: Oxford University Press.
Kopytoff, Barbara
    1976   The development of Jamaican Maroon ethnicity. *Caribbean Quarterly* 22: 33–50.
Körtvélyessy, Lívia and Pavel Stekauer, (eds.)
    2011   *Diminutives and Argumentatives in the Languages of the World*. Available at http://lexis.univ-lyon3.fr
Kossouho, Françoise F.
    1999   *Une esquisse d'étude comparative de trios parlers gbe: l'ajla, le gun, le wéme*. Abomey-Calavi: D.S.L.C., Université Nationale du Benin.
Koudenoukpo, Fatiou
    1991   *Le nominal et le syntagme nominal en wémèngbè*. Abomey and Calavi: D.E.L.T.O. and Université Nationale du Benin.

Kouwenberg, Silvia
1987 Morphophonemic change in Saramaccan pronominal forms. In *Studies in Saramaccan Language Structure*, Alleyne, Mervin C.M. (ed.), 1–15. Amsterdam and Kingston: Instituut voor Algemene Taalwetenschap & Folklore Studies Project and University of the West Indies
1994 *A Grammar of Berbice Dutch*. Berlin: Mouton de Gruyter.
2006 L1 transfer and the cut-off point for L2 acquisition processes in creole for-mation. In *L2 Acquisition and Creole Genesis*, Lefebvre, Claire, Lydia White and Christine Jourdan (eds.), 205–219. Amsterdam: John Benjamins.
2008 The problem of multiple substrates: the case of Jamaican Creole. In *Roots of Creole Structures: Weighing the Contribution of Substrates and Superstrates*, Michaelis, Suzanne (ed.), 1–27. Amsterdam: John Benjamins.
2009 The invisible hand in creole genesis: reanalysis in the formation of Berbice Dutch. In *Complex Processes in New Languages*, Aboh, Enoch Oladé and Norval S.H. Smith (eds.), 115–158. Amsterdam: John Benjamins.

Kouwenberg, Silvia and D. LaCharité
2003 More of the same: iconicity in reduplication and the evidence for substrate transfer in the genesis of Caribbean creole languages. In *Twice as Meaningful: Reduplication in Pidgins, Creoles and Other Contact Languages*, Kouwenberg, Silvia (ed.), 7–18. London Battlebridge.

Kouwenberg, Silvia and Claire Lefebvre
2007 A new analysis of the Papiamentu clause structure. *Probus* 19: 37–73.

Kramer, Marvin
2007 Tone quantifiers as a transferred feature from Kikongo. In *Synchronic and Diachronic Perspectives on Contact Languages*, Huber, Magnus and V. Velupillai (eds.), 43–66. Amsterdam: John Benjamins.
2009 Gradualism in the transfer of tone spread rules in Saramaccan. In *Gradual Creolization: Studies Celebrating Jacques Arends*, Selbach, Rachel, Hugo Cardoso and Margot van den Berg (eds.), 189–217. Amsterdam: John Benjamins.

Kroll, Judith and Natascha Tokowicz
2001 The development of a conceptual representation for words in a second language. In *One Mind, Two Languages: Bilingual Language Processing*, Nicol, Janet L. (ed.), 49–71. Oxford: Blackwell.

Kuo, L. and R Anderson
2006 Morphological awareness and learning to read: a cross language perspective. *Educational Psychologist* 41: 161–180.

Labat, Jean-Baptiste
   1730   *Grammaire abrégée ou entretien en langue françoise et celles des négres de juda*. Paris: G. Saugrain.
Labouret, Henri and Paul Rivet, (eds.)
   1929   *doctrina christiana – y explicacion de sus misterios en nuestro idiom español, y en lengua arda*. Paris: Institut d'Ethnologie.
Labov, William
   2001   *Principles of Linguistic Change, Volume II: Social Factors*. Oxford: Blackwell.
Lack, Alastair
   2007a   *Lieut. General William Byam: An Exiled Royalist*. Lulu Press.
   2007b   *Surinam Justice: A Justification by Robert Sandford of His Actions in Surinam Following His Expulsion by Lieut. Col. William Byam*. Lulu Press.
Lalla, Barbara
   1986   Tracing elusive phonological features of Early Jamaican Creole In *Focus on the Caribbean*, Görlach, Manfred and John A. Holm (eds.), 117–132. Amsterdam: John Benjamins.
Lalla, Barbara and Jean D'Costa
   1990   *Language in Exile: Three Hundred Years of Jamaican Creole*. Tuscaloosa: University of Alabama Press.
Laman, K. E.
   1964   *Dictionnaire kikongo-français, avec une étude phonétique décrivant les dialectes le plus importants de la langue dite kikongo*. Ridgewood NJ: Gregg Press.
Lambert, Richard D. and Sarah J. Moore
   1986   Problem areas in the study of language attrition. In *Language Attrition in Progress*, Weltens, Bert, Kees de Bot and Theo van Els (eds.), 177–186. Dordrecht: Foris.
Lamur, Humphrey
   1987   *The Production of Sugar and the Reproduction of Slaves at Vossenberg (Suriname): 1705–1863*. Amsterdam: Amsterdam Centre for Caribbean Studies.
Law, P. and Claire Lefebvre
   1995   On the relationship between event and predicate cleft in the Kwa Languages: The Case of Fongbe. *Linguistique Africaine* 14: 7–47.
Law, Robin
   1997   *The Kingdom of Allada*. Leiden: Research School CNWS, School of Asian, African, and Amerindian Studies.
Lefebvre, Claire
   1992   AGR in languages without person and number agreement: the case of the clausal determiner in Hatian and Fòn. *The Canadain journal of Linguistics* 37: 137–156.

1993   The role of relexification and syntactic reanalysis in Haitian Creole: methodological aspects of a research program. In *Africanisms in Afro-American Language Varieties*, Mufwene, Salikoko S. (ed.), 254–279. Athens: University of Georgia Press.
1998   *Creole Genesis and the Acquisition of Grammar: The Case of Haitian Creole.* Cambridge: Cambridge University Press.
1999   Substrate semantics in the verbal lexicon of Haitian Creole. *Studies in Language* 73: 61–103.
2011   The problem of the typological classification of creoles. In *Creoles, Their Substrates, and Language Typology*, Lefebvre, Claire (ed.), 3–33. Amsterdam: John Benjamins.

Lefebvre, Claire and Anne-Marie Brousseau
2002   *A Grammar of Fongbe.* Berlin: Mouton de Gruyter.

Lefebvre, Claire and Virginie Loranger
2006   On the properties of Saramaccan *fu*: synchronic and diachronic perspectives. *Journal of Pidgin and Creole Languages* 21 (2): 275–337.
2008   A diachronic and synchronic account of the multifunctionality of Saramaccan *táa*. *Linguistics* 46 (6): 1167–1228.

Lefebvre, Claire, Lydia White and Christine Jourdan, (eds.)
2006   *L2 Acquisition and Creole Genesis.* Amsterdam: John Benjamins.

Levin, Beth and Stephen Pinker
1991   Introduction to special issue of cognition on lexical and conceptual semantics. *Cognition* 41: 1–7.

Levin, Beth and Malka Rappaport Hovav
1995   *Unaccusativity: At the Syntax-Lexical Semantics Interface.* Cambridge, MA: MIT Press.

Levinson, Stephen
1992   Primer for the field investigation of spatial description and conception. *Pragmatics* 2 (1): 5–47.

Linguistics, Summer Institute of
       The Languages of Suriname Online. Available at http://www-01.sil.org/americas/suriname/Index.html

Longobardi, Giuseppe
1994   Reference and propper names: a theory of n-movement in syntax and logical form. *Linguistic Inquiry* 25: 609–665.

Lumsden, John
1994   Possession: substratum semantics in Hatian Creole. *Journal of Pidgin and Creole Languages* 9: 25–50.
1995   Aspect and lexical semantics in Hatian Creole. *The Linguistic Review* 12: 123–142.
1999   The role of relexification in creole genesis. *Journal of Pidgin and Creole Languages* 14: 225–258.

Malt, Barbara and Steven Sloman
   2003   Linguistic diversity and object naming by non-native speakers of English. *Bilingualism and Language Cognition* 6: 47–68.

Manfredi, Victor
   1993   Verb focus in typology of Kwa/Kru and Hatian. In *Focus and Grammatical Relations in Creole Languages*, Byrne, Frank and Donald Winford (eds.), 3–52. Amsterdam: John Benjamins.
   1997   Aspectual licensing and object shift. In *Object Position in Benue-Kwa*, Déchaine, Rose-Marie and Victor Manfredi (eds.), 87–122. The Hague: Holland Academic Graphics.

Mariano de Zarco, C.M.F. R.P.
   1938   *Dialecto inglés-africano o broken-english de la colonia española del golfo de guinea.* Turnhout: H. Proost y Cía.

Matras, Yaron
   2000   Fusion and cognitive basis for bilingual discourse markers. *International Journal of bilingualism* 4: 505–528.
   2009   *Language Contact.* Cambridge: Cambridge University Press.

Matras, Yaron and Jeanette Sakel
   2007   Investigating the mechanisms of pattern replication in language convergence. *Studies in Language* 31 (4): 829–865.

Maurer, Philippe
   1995   *L'angolar: un créole afro-portugais parlé à são tomé; notes de grammaire, textes, vocabulaires.* Hamburg: Buske.

McCarthy, John and Alan Prince
   1993   Prosodic morphology i: constraint interaction and satisfaction. *Technical report #3, Rutgers University Center for Cognitive Science* Available at http://works.bepress.com/john_j_mccarthy/53
   1995   Faithfulness and reduplicative identity. In *Massachusetts Occasional Papers in Linguistics 18: Papers in Optimality Theory*, Beckman, Jill, Suzanne Urbanczyk and Laura Walsh Dickey (eds.), 249–384. Amherst, MA: GLSA, University of Massachusetts.

McWhorter, John H
   1995   Sisters under the skin: a case for genetic relationship between the Atlantic English-Based Creoles. *Journal of Pidgin and Creole Languages* 10: 289–333.
   1999   A creole by any other name: streamlining the terminology. In *Spreading the Word: The Issue of Diffusion among the Atlantic Creoles*, Huber, Magnus and Mikael Parkvall (eds.), 5–28. London: University of Westminster Press.
   2005   *Defining Creole.* Oxford: Oxford University Press.

McWhorter, John H and Jeff Good
   2012   *A Grammar of Saramaccan Creole.* Berlin: De Gruyter.

Meinhof, Carl
   1932   *Introduction to the Phonology of the Bantu Languages.* Berlin: Dietrich Reimer & Ernst Vohsen.
Michaelis, Susanne, Philippe Maurer, Martin Haspelmath and Magnus Huber, (eds.)
   2013   *The Atlas of Pidgin and Creole Language Structures.* Oxford: Oxford University Press.
Migge, Bettina
   1998a   *Substrate Influence in the Formation of the Surinamese Plantation Creole: A Consideration of Sociohistorical Data and Linguistic Data from Ndyuka and Gbe.* Columbus: Ohio State University PhD Dissertation.
   1998b   Substrate influence in creole formation: the origin of the *give*-type serial verb constructions in the Surinamese Plantation Creole. *Journal of Pidgin and Creole Languages* 13: 215–265.
   2003a   *Creole Formation as Language Contact: The Case of the Suriname Creoles.* Amsterdam: John Benjamins.
   2003b   The origin of predicate reduplication in Eastern Suriname Maroon Creole. In *Twice as Meaningful: Reduplication in Pidgins, Creoles and Other Contact Languages*, Kouwenberg, Silvia (ed.), 7–18. London: Battlebridge.
   2006   Tracing the origin of modality in the creoles of Suriname. In *Structure and Variation in Language Contact*, Deumert, Ana and Stephanie Durrleman (eds.), 29–60. Amsterdam: John Benjamins.
Migge, Bettina and Donald Winford
   2009   The origin and development of possibility in the creoles of Suriname. In *Gradual Creolization: Studies Celebrating Jacques Arends*, Selbach, Rachel, Hugo Cardoso and Margot van den Berg (eds.), 129–154. Amsterdam: John Benjamins.
Miller, George A. and Phillip Johnson-Laird
   1976   *Language and Perception.* Cambridge: Cambridge University Press.
Moro, Francesca
   2014.   From serialising to non-serializing in Heritage Ambon Malay: a case of convergence toward Dutch. Paper presented at the TiN-dag, Utrecht, 1 February.
Mous, Maarten
   1994   Ma'a or Mbungu. In *Mixed Languages: 15 Case Studies in Language Intertwining*, Bakker, Peter and Maarten Mous (eds.), 175–200. Amsterdam: IFOTT.
Mufwene, Salikoko S.
   1990   Transfer and the substrate hypothesis in creolistics. *Studies in Second Language Acquisition* 12: 1–23.
   2001   *The Ecology of Language Evolution.* Cambridge: Cambridge University Press.

2005 Language evolution: the population genetics way. In *Gene, Sprachen, Und Ihre Evolution*, Hauska, Günther (ed.), 30–52. Regensburg: Universitätsverlag Regensburg.
2010 Second language acquisition and the emergence of creoles. *Studies in Second Language Acquisition* 32: 1–42.

Muysken, Pieter
1980 Sources for the study of Amerindian contact vernaculars in ecuador. . *Amsterdam Creole Studies* 3: 66–82.
1981 Halfway between Quechua and Spanish: the case for relexification. In *Historicity and Variation in Creole Studies*, Highfeld, Arnold and Albert Valdman (eds.), 52–78. Ann Arbor: Karoma Publishers.
1987 Prepositions and postpositions in Saramaccan. In *Studies in Saramaccan Language Structure*, Alleyne, Mervin C.M. (ed.), 89–102. Amsterdam: Instituut voor Algemene Taalwetenschaft.
1988 Lexical restructuring and creole genesis. In *Beiträge Zum 4. Essener Kolloquium Über 'Sprachkontakt, Sprachwandel, Sprachwechsel, Sprachtod' Vom 9.10.–10.10.1987 an Der Universität Essen*, den Besten, Hans and Thomas Stolz (eds.), 193–210. Bochum: Brockmeyer.
1994a Media Lengua. In *Mixed Languages: 15 Case Studies in Language Intertwining*, Bakker, Peter and Maarten Mous (eds.), 201–205. Amsterdam: Instituut voor Functioneel Onderzoek van Taal en Taalgebruik.
1994b Saramaccan and Haitian: a comparison. *Journal of Pidgin and Creole Languages* 9: 305–314.
1997 Media Lengua. In *Contact Languages: A Wider Perspective*, Thomason, Sarah G. (ed.), 365–426. Amsterdam: John Benjamins.
2000 *Bilingual Speech: A Typology of Code-Mixing.* Cambridge: Cambridge University Press.
2007 Introduction: conceptual and methodological issues in areal linguistics. In *From Linguistic Areas to Areal Linguistics*, Muysken, Pieter (ed.), 1–24. Amsterdam: John Benjamins.
2008 Creole studies and multilingualism research. In *Handbook of Pidgins and Creoles*, Singler, John Victor and Silvia Kouwenberg (eds.), 287–308. Oxford: Wiley-Blackwell.
2013 Media Lengua. In *The Survey of Pidgin and Creole Languages Vol. 3: Contact Languages Based on Languages from Africa, Asia, Australia, and the Americas*, Michaelis, Susanne, Philippe Maurer, Martin Haspelmath and Magnus Huber (eds.), 143–148. Oxford: Oxford University Press.

Muysken, Pieter and Norval S.H. Smith, (eds.)
1986 *Substrata Versus Universals in Creole Genesis.* Amsterdam: John Benjamins.

Myers-Scotton, Carol
  1993 *Duelling Languages: Grammatical Structure in Codeswitching.* Oxford: Clarendon Press.
  2002 *Bilingual Encounters and Grammatical Outcomes.* Oxford: Oxford University Press.
de Najera, José
  1658 [1929] Doctrina christiana – y explicacion de sus misterios en nuestro idiom español, y en lengua arda. In *Le Royaume D'arda Et Son Évangélisation Au Xviie Siècle*, Labouret, Henri and Paul Rivet (eds.). Paris: Institut d'Ethnologie.
Narrog, Heiko
  2005 On identifying modality again. *Language Sciences* 27: 165–192.
Nassy, David Cohen
  1778 *Essai historique sur la colonie de surinam sa foundation, ses progress, depuis son origine jusqu'a nos jours.* Paramaribo.
Nepveu, Jean
  1770 Annotatien op de Surinamsche Beschrijvinge van a° 1718. Municipal Archives, Amsterdam, Marquette-archive, nr. 231, inv. nr. 298
Noonan, Michael
  2007 Complementation. In *Language Typology and Syntactic Description, Vol. II: Complex Constructions*, Shopen, Timothy (ed.), 52–150. Cambridge: Cambridge University Press.
Nwachukwu, P. A.
  1987 The argument structure of Igbo verbs. Lexicon Project Working Papers 18, MIT Center for Cognitive Science.
Nyaku, F. K.
  1982 *Modzakaḍegbalẽ Enelia.* Accra: Adwinsa Publications.
Obianim, S. J.
  1990 *Eʋe Kɔnuwo.* Accra: Sedco Publishing.
Odlin, Terrence
  1989 *Language Transfer.* Cambridge: Cambridge University Press.
Ofori, Set
  2006. *Topics in Akan Grammar.* Bloomington: Indiana University PhD Dissertation.
Otheguy, Ricardo, Ana Celia Zentella and David Livert
  2007 Language and dialect contact in Spanish in New York: towards the formation of a speech community. *Language* 83: 770–802.
Oxford English Dictionary. 1989. Oxford: Oxford University Press.
Parkvall, Mikael
  2000 *Out of Africa: African Influences in Atlantic Creoles.* London: Battlebridge Publications.
  2008 The simplicity of creoles in a cross-linguistic perspective. In *Language Complexity*, Miestamo, Matti, Kaius Sinnemäki and Fred Karlsson (eds.), 265–285. Amsterdam: John Benjamins.

Pasquarella, A., X. Chen, K. Lam, Y. C. Luo and G. Ramirez
    2011   Cross-language transfer of morphological awareness in Chinese-English bilinguals. *Journal of Research in Reading* 34: 23–42.

Pazzi, Robert
    1979   *Introduction à l'histoire de l'aire culturelle ajatado*. Lomé: Université de Bénin, Institut National des Sciences Humaines.

Peace Corps
    1985   *Krio Language Manual.* Prepared and Printed by Peace Corps, Sierra Leone.

Pennycook, Alastair
    2010   *Language as a Local Practice.* London: Routledge.

Perdue, Clive
    1993   *Adult Language Acquisition: Crosslinguistic Perspectives.* Cambridge: Cambridge University Press.

Pesetsky, David
    1987   Wh-in-situ: movement and unselective binding. In *The Representation of (in)Definiteness*, Reuland, Eric and Alice ter Meulen (eds.), 98–129. Cambridge, MA: MIT Press.

Pinker, Stephen
    1989   *Learnability and Cognition: The Acquisition of Argument Structure.* Cambridge, MA: MIT Press.

Plag, Ingo
    2008a   Creoles as interlanguages: syntactic structure. *Journal of Pidgin and Creole Languages* 23 (2): 307–328.
    2008b   Creoles as interlanguages: inflectional morphology. *Journal of Pidgin and Creole Languages* 23 (1): 109–130.
    2009a   Creoles as interlanguages: word-formation. *Journal of Pidgin and Creole Languages* 24 (2): 339–362.
    2009b   Creoles as interlanguages: phonology. *Journal of Pidgin and Creole Languages* 24 (1): 121–140.

du Plessis, Solomon
    1752   *Recueil van egte stukken en bewyzen, door Salomon Du Plessis, Geweeze Raad van Policie en Crimineele Justitie in De Colonie Van Suriname en door Anderen, tegens Mr. Jacob Mauricius, Gouverneur-Generaal over de Colonie van Suriname, rivieren en districten van Dien, Collonel over de Militie aldaar etc. etc. etc. alsmeede door de Societijt van Suriname en denselven Gouverneur Mauricius tegens den gemelden Du Plessis en anderen, van tijd tot tijd, zoo ter vergadering van H.H.M. De Heeren Staten-Generaal, als van de Societeit van Suriname ingedient en overgelevert met en beneffens de resolutien van H.H. Mogende en van de Societyt daartoe betrekkelijk.* Amsterdam: Ms.

Poplack, Shana and Marjory Meecham
: 1995 Patterns of bilingual mixture: nominal structure in Wolof-French and Fongbe-French bilingual discourse. In *One Speaker, Two Languages: Cross-Disciplinary Perspectives on Code-Mixing*, Milroy, Lesley and Pieter Muysken (eds.), 199–232. Cambridge: Cambridge University Press.

Postma, J.
: 1990 *The Dutch in the Atlantic Slave Trade, 1600–1815*. Cambridge: Cambridge University Press.

Price, Richard
: 1975 *Saramaka Social Structure: Analysis of a Maroon Society in Suriname*. Rio Piedras: Institure of Caribbean Studies of the University of Puerto Rico.
: 1983 *First Time: The Historical Vision of an Afro-American People*. Baltimore: John Hopkins University Press.
: 1990 *Alábi's World*. Baltimore: John Hopkins University Press.

Puttenham, George
: 1589 *The Arte of English Poesie*. London: Stationers' Hall. Available at http://mural.uv.es/acuenmon/Puttenham.htm

Pye, Clifton
: 1996 K'iche Maya verbs of breaking and cutting. *Kansas Working Papers in Linguistics* 21: 87–98.

Rens, L. L. E.
: 1953 *The Historical and Social Background of Surinam's Negro-English*. Amsterdam: North Holland Publishing Company.

van Rheeden, Hadewych
: 1994 Petjo: the mixed language of the Indos in Batavia. In *Mixed Languages: 15 Case Studies in Language Intertwining* Bakker, Peter and Maarten Mous (eds.), 223–237. Amsterdam: Instituut voor Functioneel Onderzoek van Taal en Taalgebruik.

Rickford, John R.
: 1977 The question of prior creolization. In *Pidgin and Creole Linguistics*, Valdman, Albert (ed.), 190–121. Bloomington: Indiana University Press.
: 1980 How does *Doz* appear? In *Issues in English Creoles: Papers from the 1975 Hawaii Conference*, Day, Richard R. (ed.), 77–96. Heidelberg: Groos.
: 1985 Ethnicity as a sociolinguistic boundary. *American Speech* 60 (2): 99–125.

Rickford, John R. and Jerome S. Handler
: 1994 Textual evidence on the nature of of Early Barbadian Speech, 1676–1835. *Journal of Pidgin and Creole Languages* 9: 221–255.

Ritter, Elizabeth
　1995　On the syntactic category of pronouns and agreement. *Natural Language and Linguistic Theory* 13: 405–443.
Rizzi, Luigi
　1997　The fine structure of the left periphery. In *Elements of Grammar*, Haegeman, Liliane (ed.), 281–338. Dordrecht: Kluwer Academic Publishers.
　2001　On the position "int(errogative)" in the left periphery of the clause. In *Current Studies in Italian Syntax: Essays Offered to Lorenzo Renzi*, Cinque, Guglielmo and Giampaolo Salvi (eds.), 287–296. New York: Elsevier.
Roberts, Sarah J.
　1998　The role of diffusion in the genesis of Hawaiian Creole. *Language* 74: 1–39.
　2000　Nativization in the genesis of Hawaiian Creole. In *Language Change and Language Contact in Pidgins and Creoles*, McWhorter, John H (ed.), 257–300. Amsterdam: John Benjamins.
Rochette, Anne
　1988.　*Semantic and Syntactic Aspects of Romance Sentential Complementation*. Cambridge MA: MIT PhD Dissertation.
Ross, Malcom
　1996　Contact-induced change and the comparative method. In *The Compartive Method Reviewed*, Durie, Mark and Malcom Ross (eds.), 180–217. Oxford: Oxford University Press.
　2001　Contact-induced change in Oceanic Languages in Nort-West Melanesia. In *Areal Diffusion and Genetic Inheritance: Problems in Comparative Linguistics*, Aikhenvald, Alexandra Y. and R.M.W. Dixon (eds.), 134–166. Oxford: Oxford University Press.
Rountree, S. C.
　1972　The phonological structure of stems in Saramaccan. In *Languages of the Guianas, Volume 1*, Grimes, Joseph E. (ed.), 22–27. Norman OK: Summer Institute of Linguistics of the University of Oklahoma.
　1992　*Saramaccan Grammar Sketch*. Paramaribo: Summer Institute of Linguistics.
Rountree, S. C. and N. Glock
　1982　*Saramaccan for Beginners*. Paramaribo: Summer Institute of Linguistics.
Sanchez, L.
　2003　*Quechua-Spanish Bilingualism*. Amsterdam: John Benjamins.
　2006　Bilingual grammars and creoles: similarities between functional convergence and morphological elaboration. In *L2 Acquisition and Creole Genesis*, Lefebvre, Claire, Lydia White and Christine Jourdan (eds.), 277–294. Amsterdam: John Benjamins.

Satterfield, Teresa
  2005   The bilingual program: evidence for child bilingualism in the formation of creoles. In *Isb4: Proceedings of the 4th International Symposium on Bilingualism*, Cohen, J., K. McAlister, K. Rolstad and J. MacSwan (eds.), 2075–2094. Somervillw, MA: Cascadilla Press.
  2008   Back to nature or nurture: using computer models in creole genesis. In *Variation, Selection, Development: Probing the Evolutionary Model of Language Change*, Eckhart, Regine, Gerharf Jaeger and Tonjes Veenstra (eds.), 143–178. Berlin: Mouton de Gruyter.

Schuchardt, Hugo
  ca.1892   *Kreolische X: ueber das Negerenglische von Westafrika*. Translated in Hugo Schuchardt and the Atlantic Creoles: A Newly Discovered Manuscript "on the Negro English of West Africa". *American Speech* 60(1): 31–63
  1914   *Die Sprache der Saramakkaneger in Surinam*. Amsterdam: John Miller.

Schumann, C. L.
  1778   *Saramaccan Deutches Wörter-Buch*. In Die Sprache der Saramakkaneger in Surinam. Verhandelingen der Koninklijke Akademie van Wetenschappen te Amsterdam: Afdeling Letterkunde, Nieuwe Reeks Deel XIV:6, Schuchardt, Hugo (ed.) 1914. Amsterdam: Johannes Müller
  1783   *Neger-Englishes Wörterbuch*. Moravian archives, Utrecht / Paramaribo; MS 648.

Schwartz, Bonnie and Richard Sprouse
  1996   L2 cognitive states and the full transfer/full access model. *Second Language Research* 12: 40–72.

Sebba, Mark
  1987   *The Syntax of Serial Verbs: An Investigation in Sranan and Other Languages*. Amsterdam: John Benjamins.

Segurola, Basilo and Jean Rassinoux
  2000   *Dictionnaire Fon-Française*. Cotonou: Maison Regionale SMA.

Selbach, Rachel
  2008   The superstrate is not always the lexifier: Lingua Franca in the Babary Coast 1530–1830. In *Roots of Creole Structures: Weighing the Contribution of Substrates and Superstrates*, Michaelis, Susanne (ed.), 29–58. Amsterdam: John Benjamins.

Seuren, Pieter A. M.
  1981   Tense and aspect in Srann. *Linguistics* 19: 1043–1076.
  1993   The question of predicate clefting in the Indian Ocean Creoles. In *Focus and Grammatical Relations in Creole Languages*, Byrne, Frank and Donald Winford (eds.), 53–64. Amsterdam: John Benjamins.

Shanks, Louis
- 2000 *A Buku Fu Okanisi Anga Ingiisi Wowtu: Aukan–English Dictionary and English–Aukan Index*. Paramaribo: Instituut voor Taalwetenschap (SIL). Available at http://www.sil.org/americas/suriname/Aukan/English/AukanEngDictIndex.html

Sheikh, Sauda and Ekkehard Wolff
- 1981 Towards a semantic analysis of the verb Kula in Kiswahili. In *Festschrift Zum 60. Geburtstag Von P Anton Vorbichler I Teil*, Hoffmann, I. (ed.), 133–153. Vienna: Afro-Pub.

Siegel, D.
- 1999 Transfer constraints and substrate influence in Melanesian Pidgin. *Journal of Pidgin and Creole Languages* 14: 1–44.

Siegel, Jeff
- 2008 Pidgins/creoles and second language acquisition. In *Handbook of Pidgin and Creole Studies*, Singler, John Victor and Silvia Kouwenberg (eds.), 189–218. London: Blackwell.

Silva-Corvalán, Carmen
- 1994 *Language Contact and Change: Spanish in Los Angeles*. Oxford: Clarendon.

Simons, R. D.
- 1941 *Het Neger-Englesch, Spraakkunst en Taaleigen*. Paramaribo: Gouvernement van Suriname

Singler, John Victor
- 1988 The homogeneity of the substrate as a factor in pidgin/creole genesis. *Language* 64: 27–51.
- 1992 Nativization and pidgin/creole genesis: a reply to Bickerton. *Journal of Pidgin and Creole Languages* 7: 319–333.
- 1997 The configuration of Liberia's Englishes. *World Englishes* 16: 205–231.

Smith, Norval S.H.
- 1977 Vowel epenthesis in the Surinam Creoles. *Amsterdam Creole Studies* 1: 1–30.
- 1983 Review of John Holm & Alison Shilling, Dictionary of Bahamian English. *Amsterdam Creole Studies* 5: 113–116.
- 1987. *The Genesis of the Creole Languages of Suriname*. Amsterdam: University of Amsterdam PhD Dissertation.
- 1990 Deverbal nominalization in Sranan: a search for regularities. In *Unity and Diversity: Papers Presented to Simon C. Dik on His 50th Birthday*, Pinkster, H. and I Genee (eds.), 265–277. Dordrecht: Foris.
- 1996 Focus-marking wɛ in Saramaccan: grammaticalization or substrate. In *Changing Meanings, Changing Features: Papers Relating to Grammaticalization in Contact Languages*, Baker, Philip and Anand Syea (eds.), 113–128. London: University of Westminster Press

1997 Ingredient X: The common core of african words in the Atlantic Creoles. Paper presented at the Society of Pidgin and Creole Linguistics Conference, University of Westminster, London.
1999a Pernambuco to Suriname 1654–1665? The Jewish slave controversy. In *Spreading the Word: The Issue of Diffusion among the Atlantic Creoles*, Huber, Magnus and Mikael Parkvall (eds.), 251–298. London: University of Westminster Press.
1999b A preliminary account of some aspects of Leurbost Gaelic syllable structure. In *The Syllable Views and Facts*, van der Hulst, Harry and Nancy Ritter (eds. Berlin: Mouton de Gruyter.
1999c The vowel system of 18th century St. Kitts Creole: evidence for the history of the English Creoles. In *St. Kitts and the Atlantic Creoles: The Texts of Samuel Mathews in Perspective*, Baker, Philip and Adrienne Bruyn (eds.), 145–172. London: University of Westminster Press.
2000 The linguistic effects of early marronnage. In *Society for Caribbean Linguistics 13th Biennial Conference Presentations*, 288–301. Mona: University of the West Indies.
2001a Reconstructing proto Caribbean Pidgin English. Paper presented at the Pidginfest, University of Westminster.
2001b Voodoo chile: differential substrate effects in Saramaccan and Haitian. In *Creolization and Contact*, Smith, Norval S.H. and Tonjes Veenstra (eds.), 42–80. Amsterdam: John Benjamins.
2002 The history of the Suriname Creoles II: origin and differentiation. In *Atlas of the Languages of Suriname*, Carlin, Ethne and Jacques Arends (eds.), 131–151. Leiden: KITLV Press.
2003a Evidence for recursive syllable structures in Aluku and Sranan. In *Recent Developments in Creole Studies*, Adone, Dany (ed.), 31–52. Tübingen: Niemeyer Verlag.
2003b New evidence from the past: to epenthesize or not to epenthesize: that is the question. In *Phonology and Morphology of Creole Languages*, Plag, Ingo (ed.), 91–108. Tübingen: Niemeyer.
2006 Very rapid creolization in the framework of the restricted motivation hypothesis. In *L2 Acquisition and Creole Genesis: Dialogues*, Lefebvre, Claire, Lydia White and Christine Jourdan (eds.), 49–65. Amsterdam: John Benjamins.
2008a Contact phonology in creole languages. In *NELS 37: Proceedings of the 37th Annual Meeting of the North East Linguistic Society, Volume 2* Elfner, E. & M. Walkow (eds.), 223–238. Amherst, MA: GLSA (Graduate Linguistic Student Association), Department of Linguistics, University of Massachusetts.
2008b Creole phonology. In *The handbook of pidgin and creole studies*, Kouwenberg, Silvia & John Victor Singler (eds.) Malden MA: Blackwell Publishing Ltd, 98–129.

2009a English-speaking in early Suriname? In *Gradual Creolization: Studies Celebrating Jacques Arends*, Selbach, Rachel, Hugo Cardoso and Margot van den Berg (eds.), 306–326. Amsterdam: John Benjamins.
2009b Simplification of a complex part of grammar or not? what happened to Kikoongo nouns in Saramaccan? In *Complex Processes in New Languages*, Aboh, Enoch Oladé and Norval S.H. Smith (eds.), 51–73. Amsterdam: John Benjamins.

Smith, Norval S.H. and Hugo Cardoso
2004 A new look at the Portuguese element in Saramaccan. *Journal of Portuguese Linguistics* 3: 115–147.

Smith, Norval S.H. and George L. Huttar
1984 The development of the liquids in Kwinti. *Amsterdam Creole Studies* 4: 421–29.

Smith, Norval S.H., Ian E. Robertson and Kay Williamson
1987 The Ijo element in Berbice Dutch. *Language and Society* 16: 49–90.

Smith, Norval S.H. and Marleen van de Vate
2006 Population movements, colonial control and vowel systems. In *The Structure of Creole Words: Segmental, Syllabic and Morphological Aspects*, Bhatt, Parth and Ingo Plag (eds.), 59–82. Tübingen: Niemeyer.

Söderberg, Bertil
1985 *Karl Edvard Laman: Missionär, Språkforskare, Etnograf.* Stockholm: Svenska missionsförbundet.

Söderberg, Bertil and Ranger Widman
1966 *Kikongo.* Stockholm: Svenska Bokförlaget, Bonniers.

Soon Lay, Vivian Ler
2005 *An in-Depth Study of Discourse Partivles in Singapore English.* Singapore: National University of Singapore PhD dissertation.

Soremikun, B. S.
1988 *Two Approaches to Aladagbe Phonology: Segmental and Autosegmental.* University of Ilọrin Master Thesis.

Sprouse, Rex A.
2006 Full transfer and relexification: second language acquisition and creole genesis. In *L2 Acquisition and Creole Genesis: Dialogues* Lefebvre, Claire, Lydia White and Christine Jourdan (eds.), 169–181. Amsterdam: John Benjamins.

Stichting Surinaams Bijbelgenootschap
2010 *Nyun Testamenti: Het Nieuwe Testament in Het Sranan Tongo.*

Swartenbroekx, Pierre
1973 *Dictionnaire Kikongo Et Kituba – FrancAis.* Bandunu: CEEBA.

Sylvain, Suzanne
1936 *Le créole haitien: morphologie et syntaxe.* Port-au-Prince, Wetteren: Imprimerie de Meester.

Szabolcsi, Anna
 1987 Functional categories in the noun phrase. In *Approaches to Hungarian*, Kenesei, István (ed.), 167–190. Szeged: JATE.
 1994 The noun phrase. In *Syntax and Semantics*, Kiefer, Ferenc and Katalin E. Kiss (eds.), 179–274. New York: Academic Press.
Talmy, Leonard
 1985 Lexicalization patterns: semantic structure in lexical forms. In *Language Typology and Semantic Description, Vol. 3: Grammatical Categories and the Lexicon*, Shopen, Timothy (ed.), 57–149. Cambridge: Cambridge University Press.
 2000 *Toward a Cognitive Semantics, Vol. 2: Typology and Process in Concept Structuring*. Cambridge, MA: MIT Press.
Tavares, José L.
 1915 *Gramárica da língua do Congo (Kikongo)*. Luanda: Imprensa Nacional de Angola.
The Islander Creole English Bible Translation Committee
 2010 *Di Fos Five Buk a Di Nyuu Testament*. San Andres Island, Columbia: The AMEN-SD Movement and Wycliffe Bible Translators. Available at http://www.scriptureearth.org/data/icr/PDF/00-PNTicr-web.pdf
Thomason, Sarah G.
 2001 *Language Contact: An Introduction*. Edinburgh: Edinburgh University Press.
 2003 Contact as a source of language change. In *A Handbook of Historical Linguistics*, Janda, Richard and Brian Joseph (eds.), 687–712. Oxford: Blackwell.
Thurgood, Graham
 1999 *From Ancient Cham to Modern Dialects: Two Thousand Years of Language Contact and Change*. Honolulu: University of Hawai'i Press.
Trubetzkoy, Nikolaj
 1930 Proposition 16. In *Actes du premier congres international des linguists à la Hayed u 10–15 avril 1928*, 17–18. Leiden: A. W. Sijthoff
Turner, Lorenzo Dow
 1949 *Africanisms in the Gullah Dialect*. South Carolina: University of South Carolina Press.
van de Vate, Marleen
 2003. *Afrogenese of Caribogenese: Een Zoektocht naar de Ontstaansplaats van de Atlantische Engelse Creooltalen*. Amsterdam: University of Amsterdam MA Thesis.
 2008 I músu fu woóko taánga: restructuring in Saamáka. In *Tromsoe Working Papers on Language & Linguistics: Nordlyd 35, Special Issue on Complex Predicates*, Svenonius, Peter (ed.), 189–212. Tromsoe: CASTLE.

Veenstra, Tonjes
- 1996 *Serial Verbs in Saramaccan: Predication and Creole Genesis.* Dordrecht: ICG Printing.
- 2003 Menage à trois: how promiscuous are objects in resultatives. In *Recent Developments in Creole Studies*, Adone, Dany (ed.), 223–232. Tübingen: Niemeyer.
- 2004. Distributed transfer. Paper presented at the Workshop on Linguistic Borrowing, John F. Kennedy Institute, FU Berlin.
- 2006 Modelling creole genesis. In *Structure and Variation in Language Contact*, Deumert, Ana and Stephanie Durrleman (eds.), 61–83. Amsterdam: John Benjamins.

Voorhoeve, Jan
- 1957 The verbal system of Sranan. *Lingua* 6: 374–396.
- 1959 An Orthography for Saramaccan. *Word* 15: 436–445.
- 1973 Historical and linguistic evidence in favor of the relexification theory in the formation of creoles. *Language in Society* 2: 133–145.
- 1982 A note on ethenthetic transitive /m/ in Sranan Tongo. *Amsterdam Creole Studies* 4: 44–47.
- 1985 A note on epenthetic /m/ in Sranan Tongo. In *Diversity and Development in English-Related Creoles*, Hancock, Ian (ed.), 89–93. Ann Arbor: Koroma Publishers Inc.

Voorhoeve, Jan and Anton Donicie
- 1963 *Bibliographie du négro-anglais du surinam. avec une appendice sur les langues creoles parlées è l'intérieur du pays.* 's-Gravenhage: Nijhoff.

Voorhoeve, Jan and Ursy M. Lichtveld
- 1975 *Creole Drum: An Anthology of Creole Literature in Suriname.* New Haven, CT: Yale University Press.

Voyages: The Trans-Atlantic Slave Trade Database. 2009. http://www.slavevoyages.org. Accessed 24 April 2014.

Wang, Min, Chenxi Cheng and Shi-Wei Chen
- 2006 Contribution of morphological awareness to Chinese-English biliteracy acquisition. *Journal of Educational Psychology* 98 (3): 542–553.

Warren, George
- 1667 *An Impartial Description of Suriname.* London: W. Godbid.

Welmers, William E.
- 1973 *African Language Structures.* Berkeley: University of California Press.

Wendelaar, Wendela and Geert Koefoed
- 1988 "Sa" en "o" in het Sranan. *OSO Tijdschrift voor Surinamistiek* 7 (1): 63–75.

Westermann, Diedrich
 1905–1906 *Wörterbuch der Ewe-Sprache.* Berlin: Dietriech Reimer.
 1973 [1928] *Ewefiala: Ewe-English Dictionary.* Nendeln: Kraus Thompson.
Weygandt, G. C.
 1798 *Gemeenzame Leerwijze, Om Het Basterd of Neger-Engelsch Op Een Gemakkelyke Wyze Te Leeren Verstaan En Spreeken.* Paramaribo: W. W. Beeldsyder.
Whinnom, Keith
 1956 *Spanish Contact Vernaculars in the Phillipine Islands.* Hong Kong: Hong Kong University Press.
Widén, Bertil
 1949 *Studies on the Dorset Dialect.* Lund: C.W.K. Gleerup.
Wietz Joh, Ludwig
 1805 Die Apostel-Geschichte in die Saramakka-Neger-Sprache. In *Die Sprache der Saramakkaneger in Surinam. Verhandelingen der Koninklijke Akademie van Wetenschappen te Amsterdam: Afdeling Letterkunde, Nieuwe Reeks Deel XIV:6*, Schuchardt, Hugo (ed.) 1914. Amsterdam: Johannes Müller
Wijnen, Beppy and Mervin C.M. Alleyne
 1987 A note on fu in Saramaccan. In *Studies in Saramaccan Language Structure*, Alleyne, Mervin C.M. (ed.), 41–51. Amsterdam and Kingston: University of Amsterdam and University of the West Indies.
Wilkins, David P. and Deborah Hill
 1995 When *go* means *come*: questioning the basicness of basic motion verbs. *Cognitive Linguistics* 6: 209–259.
Williams, Kemp
 1991 Radical structuring in the Hausa lexicon: a prototype analysis of Hausa 'eat' and 'drink'. *Lingua* 85: 321–340.
Wilner, John
 1994 *Wortubuku Fu Sranan Tongo.* Paramaribo: Summer Institute of Linguistics.
 2003 *Wortubuku Ini Sranan Tongo: Sranan Tongo – English Dictionary.* Paramaribo: Summer Institute of Linguistics.
 2007 *Wortubuku Fu Sranan Tongo.* Paramaribo: Summer Institute of Linguistics.
Winford, Donald
 2000 Tense and aspect in Sranan and the creole prototype. In *Language Change and Language Contact in Pidgins and Creoles*, McWhorter, John H (ed.), 383–342. Amsterdam: John Benjamins.
 2003 *An Introduction to Contact Linguistics.* Oxford: Blackwell Publishing.
Winford, Donald and Bettina Migge
 2007 Substrate influence in the emergence of the tense and aspect systems in the creoles of Suriname. *Journal of Pidgin and Creole Languages* 22 (1): 73–99.

Wright, Joseph
    1898–1905 *The English Dialect Dictionary: Being the Complete Vocabulary of All Dialect Words Still in Use, or Known to Have Been in Use During the Last 200 Years: Founded on the Publications of the English Dialect Society.* London, New York: Frowde, Putnam's Sons.

Wullschlägel, H. R.
    1856   *Deutsch-Negerenglisches Wörterbuch, Nebst Ein Anhang Negerenglische Sprüchwörter Enthaltend.* Lobau: T. U. Duroldt. Available at http://www.sil.org/americas/suriname/Wullschlaegel/National/WullschlagelGerDict.html

Yakpo, Kofi
    2009   *A Grammar of Pichi.* Berlin / Accra: Isimu Media.

Zhang, Jisheng
    2006   *The Phonology of Shaoxing Chinese.* Utrecht: LOT.

Author index

Abakah, E.N. 274, 477
Abney, S. 354, 477
Aboh, E.O. 1, 8, 11, 13, 36, 39–64, 77, 143, 145, 148–150, 154, 161, 219, 225, 233, 241–260, 287–288, 323–66, 372, 379, 382, 385, 390, 393, 396–400, 406, 409–410, 415, 478–479, 497, 510
Adam, L. 107–108, 478
Adamson, L. 164, 241, 288, 410, 415, 478
Aguessy, C. 479
Agyekum, K. 222, 225, 478
Aikhenvald, A. 152, 479, 506
Akindélé, A. 45, 479
Allesaib, M. 378, 479
Alleyne, M.C. 1, 9, 108–109, 165, 241, 254, 258–259, 329, 379–382, 388, 479, 482, 495–497, 502, 513
van Alphen, G. 33, 212, 320, 479
Ameka, F. 142, 145, 148–50, 175–178, 187, 207, 222, 225, 228, 336, 410–413, 479, 490, 494
Amfo, N. 222, 225, 228, 480
Amuzu, E. 207, 222, 395, 480
Andersen, R.W. 125, 370, 480
Anderson, R. 220, 497
Ansaldo, U. 77, 410, 478
Ansre, G. 145, 149, 480
Appah, C. 207, 222, 225, 228, 233, 236, 480
Arends, J. 1, 8, 17–8, 23–4, 31–34, 91, 135, 161, 208–216, 229–230, 275–276, 301, 325, 347, 411–415, 480–481, 485–486, 497, 501, 509–510
Auer, P. 3, 228, 481
Awóyalé, Y. 332, 481
Ayafor, M. 84, 481

Baker, Ph. 5, 73, 75–76, 79, 104, 320, 371, 481, 485, 493, 495, 508
Bakker, P. 5, 91, 116, 121, 123, 241, 254–257, 259, 407, 482, 501–502, 505
Bakovic, E. 293–294, 482
Bally, Ch. 1, 482
Bastin, Y, 428, 482
Becker, A. 371, 482
Benjamins, H.D. 411, 482
Bentley, W.H. 423, 482
Ben-Ur, A. 32, 482
van den Berg, M.C. 1–14, 36, 40, 80–84, 86, 129, 207–239, 268, 275–276, 301, 395–399, 412–415, 478, 481, 482–483, 497, 501, 510
Bernhard, V. 79, 483
Bernstein, J. 354, 363, 483
Berry, J. 70, 483
den Besten, H. 121, 409, 414, 483, 502
Bickerton, D. 2, 6, 7, 10, 12, 324, 371, 483, 508
Bilby, K. 23, 67, 89, 95–100, 276–277, 308, 311–312, 316, 319, 483–484
Blanker, G. 155, 484
Bock, K. 400, 484
Bohnemeyer, J. 176, 484
Booij, G. 221, 274, 485
Borer, H. 120, 484
Boretzky, N. 108–111, 128, 173, 485
Borges, R. 17–18, 51, 484
Bowerman, M. 171, 411, 413, 485
Braun, M. 220, 484
Broeder, P. 219, 485
Brousseau, A.-M. 219, 221, 375–376, 501
Brown, K. 413, 489
Brown, P. 176, 411, 413, 484

Bruyn, A. 11, 13, 40, 120, 125, 135–174, 187, 208–209, 215, 220, 360, 365–366, 394, 397–398, 412, 481, 483, 485, 490, 493, 509
Bryant, D. 405, 493
Burt, M. 127, 489
Burzio, L. 334, 485
Byrne, F. 1, 324, 337–339, 345, 378–379, 382, 500, 507

Cabrera, M. 372, 485
Campbell, R. 351, 361, 485
Capo, H. 43–44, 54, 229, 238, 324, 332, 485
Cardinaletti, A. 331, 485
Cardoso, H. 35, 414–415, 497, 501, 510
Carlin, E. 1, 411–414, 481, 485–486, 509
Cassidy, F. 70, 87–90, 486
Charry, E. 1, 486
Chatelain, H. 162, 486
Chaudenson, R. 10, 23–24, 482, 486
Chen, S.-W. 220, 504, 512
Cheng, Ch. 220, 512
Chomsky, N. 4, 330, 336, 486
Christaller, J.G. 70, 237, 486
Cinque, G. 332, 351, 410, 477–478, 486, 506
Claudi, U. 141, 184, 492
Clements, G.N. 273, 324, 486
Clements, J. 485
Comrie, B. 407, 492
Connel, B. 303, 486
Cook, T. 302, 486
Corne, Ch. 7, 371, 486
Corver, N. 126–127, 486
Coupez, B. 482
van de Craats, I. 126–127, 486
Creissels, D. 141, 163, 171, 487

DaCruz, M. 222, 225, 487
Daeleman, J. 292, 417–418, 420–426, 435, 437, 441–4, 459, 487

Dako, K. 236, 487
Dallas, R. 94–96, 487
Damonte, F. 1, 324–325, 327, 329, 331, 378, 380–382, 487
Daval-Markussen, A. 407–408, 482, 487
D'Costa, J. 105, 217, 317, 487, 498
Declerck, R, 99–100, 487
DeGraff, M. 4–7, 221, 370, 488
Delamarre, X. 262, 488
Delpech, B. 484
Dereau, L. 163, 488
Devonish, H. 313, 488
Dillard, J. 113, 403, 488
Dobson, E.J. 88, 265, 280, 306, 488
Donicie, A. 70, 83, 209, 277, 291, 488, 514
Dorian, N. 401, 488
Dragtenstein, F. 209, 488
Dryer, M. 407, 492
Dubbeldam, J. 155, 484
Dulay, H. 127, 489
Dunn, M. 112, 404, 489
Durrleman, S. 330, 489, 501, 512
Duthie, A. 195, 489
Dyakonova, M. 333–340, 478
van Dyk, P. 209, 212, 228, 489

Edmondson, J. 274, 489
van der Elst, D. 419, 488
Enç, M. 351, 489
Escure, G. 87, 415, 489, 493
Essegbey, J. 1, 8, 13, 40, 131, 140, 143–145, 148–150, 162, 175–205, 207, 354, 395–399, 406, 411–413, 479, 489–490, 494
Extra, G. 219, 485

Faraclas, N. 84, 165, 490
Ferguson, Ch. 261, 490
Fillmore, Ch. 186, 490
Fishman, J. 7, 490
Fleury, M. 484
Focke, H. 70, 277, 464, 490

Foley, R. 404, 489
Fortin, J. 96, 492
Frankel, R, 32, 483
Fyfe, C. 94, 492

Gass, S. 127, 490
van der Geest, S. 236, 488
Gil, D. 407, 492
Gilbert, G. 97, 403, 490–491
Glock, N. 346, 506
Goddard, C. 186, 491
Gómez Rendón, J. 116, 491
Good, J. 278, 500
Goury, L. 1, 491
Greene, L. 83, 491
de Groot, A.H.P. 83, 255, 277, 302, 380, 424, 464, 491
Guerssel, M. 175, 491

Haabo, V. 255, 413, 415, 424–425, 464, 491
Hackert, S. 80, 92, 491
Hale, K. 175, 491
Hancock, I. 68–70, 79, 88, 104, 311, 317–320, 464, 491, 512
Handler, J. 79, 105, 505
Harris, C.L.G. 89, 99, 308, 492
Hartsinck, J.J. 26, 34, 492
Haspelmath, M. 407, 492, 501–502
Haugen, E. 173, 372, 492
Hayes, B. 281, 492
Hazoumé, M.L. 326, 492
Heath, J. 173, 492
Heine, B. 141, 169–170, 173, 184, 492
Helms–Park, R. 398, 492
Herlein, J.D. 209, 287, 492
Herskovits, F. 9, 108, 464, 494
Herskovits, M.J. 9, 108, 464, 493
Hill, D. 184–186, 513
Hinskens, F. 3, 481
Höftmann, H. 36, 141–149, 156, 493
Holloway, C. E. 400, 493

Holm, J. 70, 82–83, 108, 408, 483, 493, 498, 508
Houssou, A.-P. 54, 493
van Hout, R. 126–127, 219, 485, 486
Huber, M. 84, 92–96, 103–104, 491, 493, 497, 500–502, 509
Hünnemeyer, F. 141, 184, 492
Hurault, J. 277, 493
Huson, 406, 493
Hutchinson, T. 103, 494
Huttar, G. 1, 9, 70, 83, 124, 135, 161, 175, 192, 229, 232, 241, 277–278, 294, 302, 413, 417, 424–425, 463, 494, 510

Ihsane, T. 349, 351, 496

Jackendoff, R. 117, 494
Jacquot, A. 423, 494
Jansen–Jacobs, M. 496
Jarvis, S. 3–4, 495
Jennings, W. 371, 495
Johanson, L. 372, 495
Johnson, M. 421, 495
Johnson-Laird, Ph. 184, 501
Jourdan, C. 81, 90–91, 370, 410, 414, 477, 495, 497, 499, 506, 509–510

Kahrel, P. 258–259, 495
Kautzsch, A, 94, 495
Kayne, R. 257, 324, 410, 477
Kellerman, E. 127, 495
van Kempen, M. 212, 495
Kerswill, P. 3, 481
Keyser, S.J. 175, 491
Kießling, R. 220, 496
Kim, H.S. 421, 496
Kinyalolo, K, 325, 376–377, 496
van 't Klooster, C. 425, 496
Kluge, A. 44, 54, 63, 238, 329, 334, 496
Koefoed, G. 1, 217–218, 486, 496, 512

Konadu, K. 215, 230, 235, 496
Kopytoff, B. 316, 496
Körtvélyessy, L. 228, 496
Kossouho, F. 54, 496
Koudenoukpo, F. 54, 496
Kouwenberg, S. 21, 121, 135, 161, 241, 273, 370, 372, 377, 382, 410, 412, 414, 478, 481, 485, 495, 497, 501–502, 508–509
Kramer, M. 462, 497
Kroll, J. 127, 497
Kuo, L. 220, 497
Kuteva, T. 169–170, 173, 494

Labat, J.-B. 54, 61, 498
Labouret, H. 48, 54, 61, 498, 503
Labov, W. 3, 498
LaCharité, D. 241, 497
Lack, A. 20 24, 28–30, 34, 263, 498
Lalla, B. 105, 317, 487, 498
Lam, K. 220, 504
Laman, E. 418, 423–424, 498, 510
Lambert, F. 400, 409, 500
Lambert, R. 400, 498
Lamur, H. 18, 498
Laughren, M. 491
Law, P. 244, 414, 498
Law, R. 45, 48, 52, 498
Lefebvre, C. 1, 5–9, 111–114, 117, 119–120, 123, 173, 175, 219, 221, 225, 344, 354, 369–379, 382, 401, 410, 414, 477, 497–499, 506, 509, 510
LePage, R. 70, 87–88, 90, 486
Levin, BG. 175, 195–196, 293, 491, 499
Levinson, S. 141–142, 404, 411, 479, 484, 489, 499
Lichtveld, U. 31, 209, 216, 301, 512
Linderman, J. 425, 496
Lindstrom, E. 404, 489
Livert, D. 3, 503
Longobardi, G. 352, 354, 357, 499
Loranger, V. 1, 378–379, 499

Lumsden, J. 173, 374, 499
Luo, Y.C. 504

Malt, B. 127, 500
Manfredi, V. 332, 341, 385, 410, 477, 481, 500
Mariano de Zarco, C.M.F. 318, 500
Matras, Y. 170, 173, 372, 401, 500
Maurer, Ph. 421, 500–502
McCarthy, J. 266, 282, 500
McWhorter, J. 1,7, 67, 85, 104–105, 207, 278, 382, 411, 500, 506, 513
Meecham, M. 129, 505
Meinhof, C. 420–421, 495, 501
Michaelis, S. 112, 415, 497, 501, 502, 507
Migge, B. 1–2, 9, 13, 109, 112, 125, 135, 173, 207–211, 220, 225, 229–233, 241, 326, 408, 413, 415, 501, 512
Miller, G.A. 184, 501
Moore, J. 400, 409, 498
Moro, F. 398, 501
Mous, M. 119, 220, 413, 496, 501, 502, 505
Mufwene, S. 77, 113, 370, 484, 499, 501–502
Mumba, E. 482
Muysken, P. 1–14, 36, 81, 90–91, 107–132, 135, 173, 207, 369–374, 393–408, 413–414, 481, 486, 502, 505
Myers–Scotton, C. 117, 119, 123, 129, 503

de Najera, J. 28, 225, 503
Narrog, H. 1, 503
Nassy, D. Cohen 37, 214, 503
Nepveu, J. 34, 209, 503
Noonan, M. 369, 503
Nwachukwu, P.A. 197, 503
Nyaku, F.K. 149, 159, 503

Obianim, S.J. 156, 159, 503

Odlin, T. 127, 503
Ofori, S. 222, 225, 503
Otheguy, R. 3, 503

Parkvall, M. 109–112, 137, 407, 482, 500, 503, 509
Pasquarella, A. 220, 504
Patrick, P. 408, 493
Pauwels, L. 422, 487
Pazzi, R. 45–46, 504
Peace Corps 99, 504
Pennycook, A. 6, 504
Perdue, C. 219, 504
Perl, M. 1, 208–209, 301, 480
Pesetsky, D. 351, 504
Pfau, R. 326, 343, 478
Pinker, S. 175, 193, 501, 504
Plag, I. 220, 270, 372, 407, 414–415, 482, 484, 504, 509
du Plessis, S. 33, 504
Ploog, K. 409
Poplack, S. 129, 505
Postma, J. 17–18, 505
Price, R. 18, 35, 37–39, 62, 80, 213, 216–217, 321, 414, 424, 505
Prince, A. 266, 282, 500
Puskás, G. 349, 351, 494
Puttenham, G. 82, 505
Pye, C. 175, 505

Ramirez, G. 504
Rappaport Hovav, M. 195–196, 499
Rassinoux, J. 159, 179–182, 186, 507
Reesink, G. 404, 489
Rens, L. 1, 32, 217, 505
van Rheeden, H. 121, 505
Rickford, J. 79, 91, 101, 105, 211, 505
Ritter, E. 354, 358, 506
Rivet, P. 48, 54, 61, 498, 503
Rizzi, L. 325, 331, 343, 374, 410, 478, 506
Roberts, S. 6, 7, 211, 371, 506

Robertson, I. 11, 121, 510
Rochette, A. 377, 390, 506
Ross, M. 173, 506
Rountree, C. 278, 292, 346, 388, 506

Sakel, J. 372, 500
Sanchez, L. 372, 506
Satterfield, T. 371–372, 507
Schadeberg, T. 418, 482
Schneider, E. 94, 415, 489, 495
Schuchardt, H. 9, 70, 84, 97, 103, 128, 287, 301, 490, 507, 513
Schumann, C.L. 70, 143, 155, 160, 209, 230, 232, 237, 268, 273, 424, 464, 507
Schwartz, B. 127, 507
Sebba, M. 1, 324, 507
Segurola, B. 159, 179–182, 186, 507
Selbach, R. 136, 414, 497, 501, 507, 510
Seuren, P. 1, 340, 507
Shanks, L. 83, 508
Sheikh, S. 188, 192, 205, 508
Shilling, A. 70, 82–83, 493, 508
Siegel, J. 5, 7, 125, 370, 508
Silva-Corvalán, C. 128, 508
Simons, R.D. 1, 508
Singler, J. 67, 114, 165, 209, 320, 412, 414, 485, 495, 502, 508, 509
Sloman, S. 127, 500
Smith, N. 1–106, 108, 114, 121, 135–136, 161, 164, 188, 207–208, 213, 217, 241–322, 325, 332, 393, 396–399, 403–406, 409–415, 417–475, 478, 480, 481, 497, 502, 508–510
Snelleman, F. 424, 482
Söderberg, B. 163, 418, 510
Soon Lay, V. 401, 510
Soremikun, B.S. 54, 510
Sprouse, R. 10, 127, 509, 510
Stekauer, P. 228, 496
Swartenbroekx, P. 424, 510
Sylvain, S. 9, 108, 510

Szabolcsi, A. 354, 357, 511
Talmy, L. 141, 172, 187, 511
Tarenskeen, J. 217–218, 496
Tavares, J.L. 162, 511
Terrill, A. 404, 489
Thomason, S.G. 3, 12, 117, 219, 502, 511
Thurgood, G. 274, 511
Tokowicz, N. 127, 497
Trubetzkoy, N. 12, 511
Turner, L. 70, 103–104, 108–109, 511

van de Vate, M. 68, 79, 320, 380, 382, 387, 412, 510, 511
Veenstra, T. 1, 13, 36, 128, 220, 324, 329, 338, 369–390, 396–398, 406, 411, 413–414, 479, 480, 482, 507, 509, 512
Vernon, D. 484
Voorhoeve, J. 1, 9, 31, 70, 83, 117, 120, 173, 209, 216, 271–272, 277–278, 291–292, 301, 424, 488, 512
van der Voort, H. 274, 488

Wang, M. 220, 506, 512
Warren, G. 20, 23–24, 30, 32, 40–41, 263, 512
Welmers, W. 143, 302, 512
Wendelaar, W. 1, 512

Westermann, D. 70, 179, 183, 186, 513
Wexler, K. 120, 484
Weygandt, G.C. 209, 212, 216, 277, 513
Whinnom, K. 117, 120, 513
White, L. 477, 497, 499, 506, 509, 510
White Eagle, J. 175, 491
Widén, B. 305, 513
Widman, R. 163, 510
Wijnen, B. 329, 379–382, 388, 513
Wilkins, D. 184–186, 513
Williams, E. 484
Williams, K. 484, 513
Williamson, K. 11, 31, 121, 512
Wilner, J. 70, 155, 180–181, 513
Winford, D. 1–2, 9, 125, 135, 207, 370, 415, 494, 500, 501, 507, 513
Wolff, E. 188, 192, 205, 510
Wright, J. 219, 305, 514
Wullschlägel, H.R. 277, 514

Yakpo, K. 13, 40, 83–84, 87, 91–100, 104, 120, 135–174, 394, 397–398, 406, 514

Zentella, A.C. 3, 503
Zhang, J. 274, 514
Ziwo, L. 274, 489
Zubizarreta, M.L. 372, 485

Language index

Àbe 386
Afro-American Vernacular English (AAVE) 96
Aja 39, 43–65, 137, 145–146, 148, 225–226
Ajra (Ajla, Ajala) 46, 55, 56
Akan 6, 8, 14, 41–42, 111, 188, 190–191, 203, 208, 215, 220, 222, 227–230, 233–239, 275, 287, 302, 307–308, 470
Aku 89
Akuapem 227, 234, 274, 301
Àkyé 386
Allada 39, 45–52, 55, 58–65
Aluku 88, 92, 276–277, 297–300, 308
Ambon Malay 398
Ancient Greek 274
Angolar 421–422
Anlo 182–183
Anlogbe, see Anlo
Antiguan 73
Arabic 219–220
Atlantic 111
Àvu-Ìgbo 386
Ayizo 46–47, 50–65, 179–187, 191–199, 201–204
Ayizogbe, see Ayizo

Bahamian 70–72, 83
Bajan 73, 79
Bamana 6
Bantu 8, 21, 74, 111, 135, 161–165, 169, 290, 417–418, 420, 425
Basters Hottentot 121
Bazar Malay 121
Belizean 83, 87

Berbice Dutch 11, 114, 121
Boni, see Aluku
Brule Spanish 400

Carib 33–35
Caribbean Creoles 7, 9, 11, 14, 67–68, 82, 105–109, 114, 121, 128–132, 165, 313, 321–322, 393, 403
Cayenne Creole (Guyanais) 371
Chinese 121, 274, 279
Chru 274
Covè 55–56, 65
Cree 5, 121
Cross River 20, 302–303,

Daxe 65
Delto-Benuic 111
Dju-tongo 34–35, 39, 80, 321
Dutch 12, 22–23, 34, 36, 38, 41–42, 92, 116, 120–122, 136–145, 151–161, 164–173, 190, 193, 204, 208, 212, 214–222, 228, 233, 236, 238, 262, 264, 266, 268–275, 292, 299–300, 307, 320, 403, 406

Early Modern English 88–9, 265, 280–281, 305–308, 310
Eastern (Windward) Maroon Creole, see Maroon Spirit Language
Eastern Gbe 13, 21, 36, 41–46, 48, 52–53, 56, 61–64, 229, 241–259, 278, 287, 396, 463–475
Eastern Ijo 269, 271
Eastern Maroon Creole (Jamaica) 23, 88, 264, 303, 307–308, 312, 315, 317
Eastern Maroon Creole (Surinam) 88,

112, 220–221, 229–232, 309–313
Èchíè–Ìgbo 386
Edo (Edoid) 20, 303
Efik 6, 70–72, 124, 302–3
English lexifier Atlantic Creoles 67, 393
Ewe 6. 9, 40, 56, 63, 70–71, 124, 135, 137, 145–150, 153–161, 173–204, 225–228, 232–238, 287, 326, 329, 333–339, 354, 386, 401, 404, 406, 464
Ewegbe, see Ewe

Fante 227–228, 234, 236, 274–275
Fon 5–6, 11, 17–18, 21, 35–39, 48, 50–56, 60–64, 70–71, 87, 109, 111, 114, 117, 119, 123, 129, 137, 140–149, 153, 156, 159, 176–202, 218, 225–226, 234, 242, 250, 252–253, 260, 263–264, 270–273, 278, 287–293, 307, 323, 326, 329, 332–4, 342–343, 367–370, 374–378, 381–384, 386, 389–390, 396, 399–401, 408, 432, 462–464, 469
Fongbe, see Fon
Frankish 262
French 5, 9, 27, 30–31, 77, 81, 111, 114, 117, 120–121, 129, 212, 220, 237, 261–262, 287, 363, 371–372
Fulfulde 111

Gã 71
Gaelic 82, 401
Gaulish 261–262
Gbekon 57, 63, 65
Gbesi 56, 65
Gbokpa 56, 65
Gen 56, 61, 137, 145, 148, 195, 225–226, 229, 264
Gengbe, see Gen

Germanic 82, 140–141, 168–169, 325, 363, 396
Ghanaian Pidgin 84
Gullah 69, 73, 80, 86–87, 92, 94, 103–104, 108–109, 341
Gun 8, 11, 36, 52–58, 64, 137, 153, 202, 218, 225–226, 241–242, 245–250, 254–256, 259–260, 323–367, 385, 396, 404, 406, 408, 427, 429, 464
Gungbe, see Gun
Guyanese 25, 69–72, 78, 87, 316

Haitian Creole 5, 9, 111, 117, 119, 374
Hausa 188
Hawaiian Creole 7

Ibibio 6, 303
Igbo (Igboid) 6, 20–21, 70, 72, 111, 137, 303, 386
Indian Ocean creoles 408
Indo-European 12, 139, 151, 165, 171–172, 188, 197–198
Islander 84–87, 316
Italian 343

Jamaican Creole 21–24, 36, 69, 88–89, 91, 96, 103, 264, 279, 303–312, 316–321
Jamaican Maroon Spirit Language, see Maroon Spirit Language, Eastern Maroon Creole (of Jamaica)

Kamtok (Cameroonian Creole) 84, 89, 100
Khoikhoin 121
Kikongo 6, 8–9, 12–14, 17, 36–42, 74, 77, 113, 135, 137, 161–168,

171–172, 234, 263–264, 278, 287–296, 302, 307, 322, 396–398, 402–406, 415
Kimbundu 74, 161–162, 165, 421, 424
Ki–Ntandu, see Ntandu
Kituba 424
Kotafon 64
Kpase 56, 60, 63–64
Krio (often used for Sierra Leone Krio)
Kwa 111, 176, 188, 190–191, 203, 205, 242, 332, 341, 385
Kwaza 274
Kwinti 1, 25, 78, 88, 92, 276–277, 308, 419, 424, 426
Laghuu 274
Latin 261–262, 281
Loango 38–41, 438

Malay 107, 121
Malinke 6
Maroon Spirit Language, Eastern Maroon Creole (of Jamaica) 264
Matawai 1, 35, 80, 88, 422, 424, 464
Mauritian Creole 371, 378
Maxi 50, 53, 55–56, 64–65, 141, 225–226, 464
Maxigbe, see Maxi
Mazinga 418–419
Media Lengua 5, 116–118, 121–126, 130, 373–374
Mende 71, 74
Michif 5, 121
Mina 386
Miskito Coast Creole 25, 78
Movolo 65

Nama 121
Ndibu 292, 419, 423

Ndyuka 1, 8, 23, 25, 35–36, 39, 69, 78, 80, 83, 88, 92, 101, 112, 124, 220, 223, 230, 241, 250–253, 260, 276–278, 290, 292, 294, 297–300, 302, 308, 317, 417, 423–424, 454, 463–464
Negerhollands 114, 340–341
Niger–Congo 12, 109, 136, 151, 161, 163, 171–172, 288, 394
Nigerian Pidgin 84, 100
Ntandu (Ki–Ntandu) 292, 418–461
Nupé 386

Òwórò Yoruba 386

Pacific creoles 108
Pamaka 1, 88, 220, 326
Papiamentu 340, 341, 377, 383
Petjoh 121
Pichi (Fernando Po Krio) 84, 87, 89, 99–100, 102, 318–319
Pijin 5
Portuguese 10, 12, 22, 32, 34–37, 42, 47, 73, 80, 212, 217, 253, 296–300, 321, 347, 403
Portuguese Creole 34, 77, 253, 321, 403
Portuguese Pidgin 111, 117
Proto–Atlantic Slave Community Language (PASCL) 7, 85, 104, 106, 319–320
Proto–Bantu 425–462
Pulaar (variety of Fulfulde) 188, 191

Quechua 5, 116–8, 121, 123, 126, 130, 373–374

Romance 261, 324, 63–64, 396
Saamaka, see Saramaccan
Saramaccan 1, 8, 11, 18, 23, 25, 35–

39, 41, 43, 53, 62–65, 69–72, 78, 80, 83–88, 89, 101, 120, 128, 209, 215–216, 220, 241–242, 250–260, 269–271, 273, 275–278, 287–301, 317–318, 321, 323–390, 396–398, 401, 403–404, 406, 408, 416–475
Saxwe 60, 65
Seto 65
Shaoxing Chinese 274
Sierra Leone Krio (Krio) 23, 68–71, 75–76, 84, 87, 89, 92, 94–105, 264, 270–271, 303, 308, 313–319, 321
Singapore English 401
Spanish 3, 5, 48, 80, 94–95, 98, 116–123, 126, 128, 130, 279, 316, 340, 373–374, 400
St. Kitts 26–27, 73, 77, 79–82, 95, 316, 320
St. Vincent 25, 73, 78

Tayo 371
Tofin 65
Toli 46, 50, 58–60, 65

Twi 124, 227, 234–237, 287, 302, 307–308

Vietnamese 398
Virginian Black English 92

Waci 56, 61, 225–226
Weme 45–46, 50, 64
Western Bantu 135
Western Maroon Creole (Jamaica) 96, 101, 264, 303, 313, 317
Western Maroon Creole (Surinam) 88
West–Flemish 114
Wolof 71, 74, 188, 271
Xwela 49, 53, 56–57, 60–65, 225
Xwla 39, 46–50, 53, 56–58, 63–65, 225–226

Yaka 419, 424, 426
Yombe 419, 423–424, 444, 452
Yoruba 6, 386, 464
Zealandic 114

Subject, place, and historical figure index

accommodation 6
adjective attributive 248–250, 254–256
adjective predicate, predicative, verbal adjective 86, 110, 249, 255–257, 338
adjective reduplicated 247–250, 254–256, 260, 396
adjective resultative 255–256, 397
adjective word order 81, 120, 257, 362, 364
adposition 110, 141, 158–159, 166, 405
adstrate, adstratal 2, 8–10, 13–14, 22, 24, 30, 36, 39–42, 68, 91–92, 105, 161, 168–169, 242, 250, 257, 260, 264, 277–279, 290, 301–307, 319–322, 396
adverb, adverbial 68, 105–106, 121, 124, 132, 153–159, 166–167, 172–173, 221–224, 226, 230, 242, 244, 363, 388
Africanism 8, 107, 128, 131, 213, 217, 463
Agasuvi 47–48, 52–64
Agbomey, Abomey 45, 48–49, 52, 55, 64, 468, 495, 498
agentive suffix 220, 236
Aja-Tado, Aja, Tado 39, 43–47, 70, 137, 145–148, 225–226
Allada, Alada 37–39, 41, 45–50, 52, 55, 58–60, 62, 64
anaptyctic, epithetic, paragogic 266, 270, 282, 285, 311–312, 314, 319, 321
areal feature 161

argument structure 13, 175–205, 258, 377, 395
aspect 148, 150, 242, 244, 249–250, 256, 336, 339, 370, 374, 384–390, 397
completive 173, 387
habitual 156–157, 173, 329, 335–337, 387
imperfective 85–87, 100–103, 106, 174, 386
inceptive 327, 385, 327, 385–387, 390
pausative 390
progressive 132, 390
prospective 132, 186, 194, 242–243, 248–249, 251, 256, 260, 385–387, 390

Banister 32, 33
Barbados 7, 20, 24–30, 35, 68, 77–80, 82, 95, 98, 105, 320
bare noun 116, 348–349, 352, 356–357, 360, 366
Benin 8–9, 12–13, 17, 44–47, 137, 393, 399, 404, 406
Bight of Benin (Slave Coast) 21–22, 39, 51, 264
Bight of Biafra 19–22, 39, 51, 302, 320
bilingual convergence 13, 107, 115, 128, 131–132, 394, 399
black-white population ratio 68
bleaching 365
body-part 135, 139–140, 218, 238
break-verb 175–176, 179, 181–186, 192, 395

Byam 24, 28–32, 263

Cafeteria Principle 113, 403
calquing 131, 170, 173
causative 123, 132, 195–197, 204, 258, 372
Cayenne 30–31, 34, 80
clan 35, 38, 47, 438, 469
    Abaísa 37–39
    Lángu 38
    Matjáu 35–39
    Nasí 38, 437, 123, 219, 230, 243, 245, 271–272, 301, 337, 396
    enclitic 121, 230
    post-clitic 288–290
    proclitic 101
coda 89, 266–268, 273–302, 307–317
code-mixing, code-switching 107–108, 115, 129, 132, 394–395, 399
collocation 154, 157, 159
colonial, colonization 90–98, 101, 104–106, 114, 128, 136, 210, 212, 216, 253, 262, 264, 296, 307, 317, 320–321, 393
comparative 124, 404
complementation 324–325, 371
complementizer 73, 110, 122, 173–174, 324–332, 338–339, 342–347, 374–384, 387–390
complexity 83, 104, 131, 169, 400–402
compound 54, 110, 218–222, 228–229, 233, 235, 237–238, 254, 288–289, 291, 438
congruent lexicalization 129
consonant (s)
    cluster 268, 275, 277
    geminate 251

contrastive focus 11, 36, 63–64, 98, 474
copula 73, 85–87, 142, 148, 341
    equative 68, 86
    existential 85–87, 102, 105, 118, 132, 142, 146, 148, 173
    identificational 86–87, 98–102, 222
    locative 68, 87, 100, 102, 105–106, 149, 166, 256, 260
    null 194
    specificational 99–102
core lexical element 130
creolization 9, 17, 23–27, 39, 41, 68, 80–81, 104, 105, 181, 184, 263–264, 319, 324, 347, 370–372, 386, 389–390
    gradual 81
    initial 408
    post-creolization 36, 91
    rapid 36, 67–68, 81, 104
Crijnssen 30
cross-linguistic effect 6–8, 207–239, 395
cultural predominance 113
cut-verb 175, 182–183
CV 109, 290
    NCV 290–296
    pattern 109
    proclitic 101

definite 106, 324, 348–361
    definite article, determiner 101–103, 173, 230, 350
    definite noun phrase 349–352
    definiteness 142, 349–357
    indefinite 324, 349–353, 356, 359–360
    indefinite article, determiner 116,

173
  indefinite noun phrase 351–352
deictic 85, 100, 109, 123, 185–187, 192, 230
demography, demographic, demographics 2, 8, 10, 17–21, 23, 29, 32, 41, 111–113, 208–211, 213, 216, 230
demonstrative 106, 122–123, 230, 358–366
desiderative 327
determiner 109, 116, 121, 189, 230, 248–249, 323–324, 348–363, 396
  clausal 344
dialect leveling 5, 6
dialect mixture 3
diminutive 222, 225, 227–229, 238, 241, 419
discourse 173, 219, 344, 348, 350–1, 353, 355–357, 366, 396, 401–402
Doctrina Christina 48
DP 173, 246, 248–252, 256, 348, 352–365, 397, 402–403

eat-verb 175, 188–192, 205, 395
effective 377, 383–384
E-language 4
emotive 377, 383–384
epenthesis 271–272, 276–277, 287
ethnic group, ethnicity 5, 39, 43, 53–56, 90, 114, 126, 212–213, 216, 289, 320, 374, 419, 463
expanded pidgin 5, 68, 104, 370

Faithfulness 266–268, 279, 282, 306–310, 312, 317
feature pool 77
focus marker 36, 39, 323, 325–326, 332, 342, 346, 400–401, 474

Force 323, 327–332, 336–339, 342–347, 374–375, 380
Founder Principle 113
français populaire 114
frequency 127, 143, 169, 400–402
fronting 109, 148, 365
  object 222, 242–426, 250
  VP 335, 337, 339
  predicate 333, 335, 361, 364–365
function word, functional element 11, 44, 63–64, 101, 115, 119–129, 131, 231–232, 319, 323, 325, 347, 387

generation 6, 41, 82
  multi-generational 371, 373
  three-generation 7, 321, 371–373
  two-generation 6
Gold Coast 14, 20, 22, 33, 39, 42, 49, 51, 68, 215, 301, 322
grammaticalization 124–125, 128–129, 146–147, 152, 166, 173, 232
Grand Popo 45

Hernnhut 42
highlighter 36–37, 86–87, 98–103

iamb 281
iambic–trochaic law 281
ideophone 388
I-language 4
imperative 68, 83, 104, 330
Ingredient X 5, 7, 23, 35, 69–106, 264, 271, 313, 316, 319–320
inherent complement verb (ICV) 197–203
intensifier 173, 230, 363
interlanguage 6, 10, 114, 126, 370, 373–374

interrogative 123, 323, 342–347
intertwined language 1, 121

Jamaica 20–25, 36, 68–73, 78–80, 86–106, 264, 279, 303–321, 341
Jeken 45, 48–52
Jew, Jewish, Portuguese Jew 22, 31–38, 80, 214, 253, 321
Jews Savannah 32

Karboeger 34, 80

L2 learning 91, 108, 115, 125–127, 132, 374, 394, 399
language attrition 115, 130–131, 394, 399–400
language contact scenario 107–131, 393–394
lateral 109
left periphery 13, 323–367, 396–397, 402–403
lexical borrowing 107, 113, 130
lexical learning hypothesis 120
lingua franca 114
linguistic area 8, 12
linguistic distinctiveness 400–401
linguistic input 13, 23
linguistic interference 9
liquid 92, 273–276, 281, 287, 312
Loangodorp 38, 41
locality 401–402
manner of motion 148, 187–188
markedness 2, 127, 266–268, 279, 281–282, 306–307, 309–310, 317
maroon, marronnage 8, 22–25, 33–35, 42, 80, 89–102, 105–106, 112, 211–212, 216, 230, 275–276, 303, 308, 313–319, 393, 419, 463

mixed creole 11
modality, mood 1, 148, 330, 382, 385, 390
   deontic 323, 329–331, 388
   directive 83–84, 104
   epistemic 387–388
   indicative 330, 375, 377
   injunctive 323, 330, 347
   irrealis 327, 329–331, 375, 378
   jussive 83, 106
   potential 174
   subjunctive 84, 174, 329–330, 375, 377–378, 381–382, 390
modularity 13, 323, 396
mora 98, 278–285, 306, 422
   dimoraic, bimoraic 89, 278, 281–282, 284
   monomoraic 89, 278–282
morphology 13, 74, 110, 121, 185–239, 395, 397, 400, 402
   agglutinative 121
   derivational 40, 74, 110, 219–239, 254, 395
   inflectional 245, 247, 331, 354, 357, 359, 364, 419
motion event 140, 144–151, 166, 168, 171–172
multilingual 5, 6, 13, 91, 210, 216, 237
nasal 40, 102, 264, 269–313, 329, 396, 418–421, 452, 462
   cluster 275–278, 290–292, 295–296, 301–302, 418, 421
   harmony 109
   prenasalized 295, 421
nativization 6, 39
negation 335–336
negative existential 118
NeighborNet 406–407

Nevis 25–27, 78–82
Nominalization 235, 242, 245–246, 250–251, 253, 337, 399
non-iconic reduplication 13, 40, 241–259, 288, 396
non-participant noun 222, 225–227, 233–235, 238–239
noun class prefix 44–45, 52–53, 56, 64, 110, 161–162, 173, 406, 417–418
noun phrase 106, 116, 121, 129, 249, 287, 348–353, 356–361, 365, 399
nucleus 273, 278, 281–282, 285, 294, 302, 310
number 44, 225–226, 344, 348, 352–359, 361–364, 419, 426
numeral 116, 221–226, 350, 352, 354, 359, 362, 364

obligatory object verb 175, 395
obstruent 275, 278, 281, 284, 301, 312
Offra 39, 45
onset 271, 273, 275–278, 287, 291–296, 301–302, 420–421
Optimality Theory (OT) 266, 284
Out of Africa theories 67
OV 242–250, 256, 332–333, 384–386, 404
OVV 245–246

Papa dorp 37–38, 41
paralexification 119
Paramaribo 30, 33, 38, 211–212, 215, 220–221, 230
parameter 2, 4, 340, 345, 348, 374, 404
Parliamentarian 26–28
participant noun 222, 225–227, 233–235, 238–239
passive interpretation 260
pattern replication 107, 128–129, 131–132, 173
phonetic shape 111, 117, 120, 123, 289
phonology, phonological 7, 8, 13, 17, 37, 40, 43, 73, 109, 119, 126, 170, 222, 261–322, 373–374, 396–397, 400, 402
  reduction 131, 251
  segmental 109, 288, 193
  supra-segmental 109
phonotactic restriction 266
plantation 5, 10, 18, 21–24, 27–37, 42, 77, 80–81, 90–92, 113–116, 125, 128–129, 210–217, 220, 230, 253, 260, 264–265, 276, 320–321, 393, 429
plural 68, 106, 109, 227, 233, 236, 241, 288, 352–362, 418–419, 426
possessive 106, 161–164, 166–169, 174, 189, 271
postposition 109, 135, 139–140, 143–145, 148, 174, 405
predicate 110, 112, 141, 193–194, 198–199
  clause-embedding 13, 369–390, 396–397
  cleft 99, 100,102, 109, 248, 340
  doubling, reduplication 241–249, 333, 335–336, 340
  stative 13, 395
prefix 44–45, 52–65, 110, 161–162, 173, 222, 236, 288, 291–292, 406, 416–420, 423, 426, 464
preposition 73, 101–103, 106, 116, 121–122, 137–174, 187, 193, 200, 269, 327, 331, 378, 405

general locative preposition 138–139, 142–150, 162–166, 169, 171–174
pronominal system 109
property concept, property item 13, 40, 193–199, 225, 228, 238, 248, 340, 342, 344, 406

question 230, 342, 345, 367
   marker 106, 323, 325, 342–346
   word 39, 63, 73, 98, 230
   yes-no 325, 327, 331, 342–346, 367
quotative 378

reanalysis 5–6, 152, 154, 160
recency 400–401
reduplication 13, 40, 110, 191, 222, 241–260, 288, 337, 396–299, 402, 406
reflexive 110, 116, 132
regularity 41, 221, 400–402
relexification 9–14, 80, 107–173, 181, 192, 341, 369–390, 393–399, 408
   local 135, 147–148, 153, 160, 171, 395
   pattern 135–136, 152, 169–173
restructuring 24, 112, 114, 122, 125, 128–129, 140
result noun 253
rhyme 290, 293–294, 303
Royalist 26–28

saliency 127, 400–401
second language acquisition 2, 5–6, 10, 115, 125–126, 208, 369–370, 384, 389
selectional feature, restriction 118, 177, 369, 382, 390
semantics 8, 13, 34, 40, 109, 129–130, 135, 142, 154, 158, 160, 172
   lexical 109, 129, 397, 402
   overextension 127
   verb 113, 40, 175–205, 395
   weight 401–402
serial verb 109, 112, 120, 124, 145, 148, 150, 174, 325, 378, 398, 462
simplification 181–184, 204, 399
slavery 49, 81, 95, 114–115, 316
small clause 244–249, 256
société d'habitation 23–24
Sonority Sequencing Principle 273–275
spatial relation 135–172
specificity 287, 324, 344–365, 396
Sprachbund 8, 12–13, 133, 136, 173, 393, 403, 409
St. Kitts 27, 73, 77–82, 95, 316, 320
structural correspondence 111
structural elaboration 6
structural phylogenetics 14, 394, 404, 407
Structure Conservation Hypothesis 126
subcategorization 118, 120
subjunctive complementizer 174, 329–330, 378, 382
substrate, substratal 1–13, 108–115
   African 2, 12, 107–109, 113–114, 207, 278, 395, 403
   Congo, Kikongo 105–106
   Gbe 135, 143, 156, 168, 325, 331, 346, 396
   homogeneous 114
sugar (plantation) 23–24, 30–33, 113, 269, 393
superstrate 2, 5, 7, 10–13, 17, 22, 36,

42, 114, 136, 142, 159, 161, 165–169, 171–172, 257, 260–264, 307, 323–324, 348, 366, 370–374, 395–396, 408
syllable, syllabification 54, 230, 265–268, 271–278, 281–282, 285, 288–304, 309–310, 321, 342, 396–398, 402, 419–420
   disyllabic 265, 291, 419
   mono-syllabic 265, 288–291, 304, 420
   polysyllabic 289
syncope 276
synthetic compound 220–221, 235

tense mood aspect (TMA) 1–2, 73, 157, 194, 207, 222, 248, 258, 367, 371, 400
tone 11, 36, 63, 87, 109, 136, 173, 207, 222, 242, 244, 333, 342–343, 420–426
topic 132, 148, 174, 247, 323, 325–332, 340, 342, 345, 347, 357–358, 367, 381
Torarica 30–32
transfer 2–5, 9, 13, 112, 118, 120, 125–127, 136–137, 161, 165–168, 171–173, 192, 208, 219–220, 229, 238–9, 323–325, 347–348, 358, 366, 370, 372, 396, 398, 401
transitive, transitivity 145, 160, 201, 272, 301, 334
   ditransitive 193, 200–205
   hypertransitive 395–398, 402
   intransitive 160, 193–200, 243, 269, 302, 334
   monotransitive 199–203
translator 214–215

trochee 281, 284

Uniformitarian Principle 113
universal 1, 2, 10–12, 101, 112, 114, 122, 185, 208, 266, 324, 345, 347, 364, 367

verb focus, V-focus 323, 332–334, 336–340, 406
verbal participle 258
verbal reduplication 242, 246, 249, 256
verbs of saying 110
voice 229, 278, 291, 293–6, 300–301, 401, 421, 424, 464
vowel
   doubling 88
   epenthetic 275–276
   harmony 109
   Jamaica–type / Type–B system 88, 92, 103–5, 304–307
   long 88, 98, 279, 281, 284–290, 304–306, 311, 313, 329
   short 279, 288, 290, 305, 314, 320
   Surinam–type / Type–A system 88, 90, 92, 98, 103, 105, 278–287, 308–312, 314–315, 317

West Africa 2, 8–9, 12–14, 17, 20, 47, 54, 67, 100, 107–109, 113, 117, 120, 124, 129–132, 135, 140, 173, 176, 207, 210, 216, 236, 263, 287, 313, 370, 372, 386, 393–395, 398–403, 409
West Central Africa 8, 18, 20–22, 40, 263, 417
wh-element 328
Whydah (Glexwe) 45, 48–52, 56,

61–65
Willoughby 24–28, 30, 32, 34
word order 119, 127, 202, 348, 370,
    404–405
  noun phrase 361–364, 399

SOV 242
SVO 242

Xogbonu (Porto Novo) 45, 48, 50

www.ingramcontent.com/pod-product-compliance
Lightning Source LLC
Chambersburg PA
CBHW070255240426
43661CB00057B/2558